Men and Women of Renown
The Companion Volume

Michele Doucette, M.Ed.

Men and Women of Renown: The Companion Volume

Copyright © 2013, 2018 by Michele Doucette, St. Clair Publications

All rights reserved. No part of this publication may be reproduced or transmitted in any form or by any means, electronic or mechanical, including photocopying, recording, or by any information storage and retrieval system, without written permission from the author.

ISBN 978-1-935786-42-9

Printed in the United States of America by

St. Clair Publications

PO Box 726

McMinnville, TN   37111-0726

stclairpublications.com

Send all emails to michele.doucette@nf.sympatico.ca

Inside Cover Image: King Clovis I (my connection to 400 AD)

http://en.wikipedia.org/wiki/File:Sculpture.Notre.Dame.de.Corbeil.png

Table of Contents

Acknowledgements 1

Author's Note 3

Life in Early Acadie 4

My Maternal DNA Ancestress 8

Mothers of Acadia mtDNA Project 19

A Little Controversy 25

A Little More Controversy 26

Aboriginal Ancestry 28

My Percheron Ancestors 44

Celebrity Relations 1 47

Celebrity Relations 2 52

Celebrity Relations 3 55

Celebrity Relations 4 62

Celebrity Relations 5 67

Celebrity Relations 6 73

Celebrity Relations 7 75

Celebrity Relations 8 77

Celebrity Relations 9 78

Celebrity Relations 10 79

Celebrity Relations 11 80

Celebrity Relations 12 81

Celebrity Relations 13 82

Celebrity Relations 14 83

Celebrity Relations 15 84

Celebrity Relations 16	85
Celebrity Relations 17	86
Blank Consanguinity Chart	87
Filles du Roi	89
Carnigan-Salières Regiment	100
Catherine de Baillon	104
Descent from Antiquity	235
Merovingian Ancestry	236
Carolingian Dynasty	254
Capetian Dynasty	256
Saxon Kings	260
Normans	273
House of Plantagenet	284
The Irish Kings of Dalriada	288
Celtic Kings of Scotland	291
House of Dunkeld	296
Counts of Holland	300
Earl of Huntingdon	303
Counts of Flanders	307
House of Savoy	311
Duchy of Burgundy	314
Marchesi of Ivrea	321
Marchesi of Friulia	330
Dukes of Spoleto	339
Descendants of Boso, Count of Arles	348
Duchy of Provence	357
Kings of Upper Burgundy	361
Counts of Blois	366

Duchy of Clèves	369
Grand Princes of Kiev	373
Kings of Sweden	377
Ottonian Dynasty	380
House of Billung	391
Counts of Leuven	397
ArdennesVerdun Dynasty	401
Counts of Boulogne	406
House of Poitiers	412
Léonese Monarchs	416
Counts of Castile	421
House of Montdidier	426
Grimaldi of Beuil	441
Grimaldi of Antibes	444
Jehanne d'Arc	447
Further Descent from Antiquity	455
Byzantium Empire 1	481
Byzantium Empire 2	489
The Magyars	493
The First Crusade	499
(Kings of Jerusalem) Counts of Rethel	505
Counts of Andechs	510
Book Bibliography	517
Website Bibliography	523
About the Author	619

Acknowledgements

As an individual, I have always been driven by both a love of history and genealogy. In truth, genealogy is but history come alive.

In the organizing of the data contained herein, there are several key individuals who need to be thanked for their time, their patience and their invaluable assistance, namely;

John P. DuLong, for permission to reproduce the Baillon arms (that he created through the use of the Armorial Gold Heraldry Clip Art program) featured in the chapter entitled Catherine de Baillon; likewise, his postings in the soc.genealogy.medieval Google Group have always been most enlightening.

Members of the completed *Baillon Research Project*, whose drive appears to mirror my own in wanting to denote the most correct and up-to-date source information.

Denis Beauregard, for his knowledgable postings in the soc.genealogy.medieval Google Group; likewise, his FrancoGene website is absolutely marvelous.

Timothy Carmain-Périllos, a dear friend, for his historical knowledge, genealogical direction, wisdom, friendship and trust.

Roger LeBlanc, for his thoughtful postings as shared with the soc.genealogy.medieval Google Group members; likewise, it was Roger who first brought the Gallica website to my attention.

Gerard Poissonnier, for his insightful postings as shared with the soc.genealogy.medieval Google Group members; likewise, it was Gerard who provided me with much needed guidance as I began to venture into realms unknown, courtesy of the Gallica website.

As with any project of this magnitude, I have done my utmost to ensure the validity of my research findings through the sourcing and cross-referencing of data. Further to this, any errors and/or omissions that result are, most assuredly, my own.

Royal descent implies the possession of distinguished historical personages as ancestors, men and woman whose achievements are recorded in the pages of history, not only emperors and kings, but statesmen and warriors who have made history. It is true that the quantity of these ancestors blood that flows in any descendant's veins must be infinitesimally small, but so is the blood of that distant paternal ancestor. Though we may have but little of their blood coursing in our veins, yet we are proud of being descended from them, for they are our lineal ancestors. Furthermore, probably we have as much of their blood as any other person now living.

Pride of ancestry is not to be confused with pride of birth. The former is an unselfish emotion, while the possessor of the latter is probably a snob. Nor is one's interest in one's forefathers restricted to those who reflect honor on their descendants, but rather it is a longing to know the history of those whose blood flows in our veins; to preserve humbly our links with the past in hopes that our children may perform the same act of filial love for us. Rarely does man build for himself alone. He struggles in the short span of years allotted to him to set up, or preserve, a code of honour, and perhaps to provide material comfort for those of his flesh and blood who are to follow him: he is a link in a chain uniting the past and the future. As a man lives in the persons of his ancestors, so does he wish to live in his children and his children's children.

~ Marcellus Donald R. von Redlich

These words, as prefaced in his book, <u>Pedigrees of Some of the Emperor Charlemagne's Descendants</u>, were written in 1941.

Author's Note

As is always the case with any genealogy project that has expanded its boundaries beyond a single volume, it quickly became evident that the birth of this companion tome was going to be a necessity.

In keeping with the Native American teachings of my ancestors, I do my utmost to abide by these sacred instructions (as given by the Creator to Native People at the Time of Creation) as shared on April 9, 2012, during a Sagittarius Moon, by Tara Greene.[1] With Sagittarius being the Sacred Law of Justice, let us take the time to live this higher law.

Treat the Earth and all that dwell thereon with respect.

Remain Close to the Great Spirit.[2]

Show great respect for your fellow beings.

Work together for the benefit of all Mankind.

Give assistance and kindness wherever needed.

Do what you know to be right.

Look after the well being of mind and body.

Dedicate a share of your efforts to the greater good.

Take full responsibility for your actions.

Be truthful and honest at all times.

---

[1] https://www.taratarot.com/
[2] https://en.wikipedia.org/wiki/Great_Spirit

Life in Early Acadie

The early Acadian settlers were mostly farmers. Farms were located along the banks of rivers that flowed into the Baie Française (Bay of Fundy).

Grand-Pré was the great agricultural area of the colony.

Rather than clear the uplands, the Acadians drained the marshes along bays and rivers by building dykes (large, tall mounds of earth covered with grass) and aboiteaux (drainage systems with trap doors that let water out but not back in) to keep sea water out.

Then they would wait two years for the sea salt to be washed out by snow and rain.

After this, they could plant their crops on this new, rich farmland.

In the spring, the men repaired the old dykes and built new ones to gain more land.

They planted their crops.

They tended and sheared their herds of sheep.

In late summer and early fall they harvested their crops.

Once the harvest was in, they killed some of their cattle, hogs and sheep. They salted meat for the winter and traded what they did not need with the New Englanders who came by ship to trade.

From the New Englanders, the Acadians would get household items, sugar, molasses, machinery and other things they needed.

Over the winter, the men and older boys cut firewood and timber in the woods, built new homes, hunted and trapped.

Men made the furniture for the household; using the wood at hand, they made simple tables, chairs, beds, cradles and sideboards. They also made the family's footwear, either wooden shoes, as they wore in France, or Aboriginal moccasins for the winter.

The women did household chores, cooked, preserved food, did the laundry, made the family's clothes, milked the cows, fed the chickens and tended the vegetable gardens.

Sheep were kept for their wool. The women would card, spin and weave the wool for clothes and blankets. They knit socks and stockings. They also grew hemp and flax, which they wove into linen for clothes.

Daily Life: Way of Life – Acadians © Library and Archives Canada [3]

Acadia: Lifestyles in the Days of Our Ancestors [4]

Archaeological Research Report: 17th century Acadian Sluice [5]

Dating the Grand Pré Aboiteau [6]

Early Acadia (website of the deceased Tim Hébert) 1632 to 1755 [7]

---

[3] www.collectionscanada.gc.ca/settlement/kids/021013-2000.9-e.html
[4] www.virtualmuseum.ca/Exhibitions/Acadie/exposition_e.html
[5] amis-de-grand-pre.ca/documents/dossiers/fowler/aboiteau2006.pdf
[6] www.madlabsk.ca/2008-03.pdf
[7] www.acadian-cajun.com/acadia.htm

Early Acadian Villages and Settlements [8]

Encyclopedia of Acadian Life (website of the deceased Tim Hébert) [9]

French Emigrants to Acadia: Daily Life [10]

Galerie des Aboiteaux [11]

Grand Pré National Historic Site: Educational Activities (on Site) [12]

Historical Narratives of Early Canada: Expulsion of the Acadians [13]

Nova Scotia Museum Info Sheets (Acadians and Mi'kmaq)

[1] The Acadians One: Settlement [14]

[2] The Acadians Two: Farming [15]

[3] The Acadians Three: The Home [16]

The word Mi'kmaq derives from *nikmaq*, a salutation that means *my kin friends*; later, through misunderstandings, errors in transcription, and English pronunciation, this became Micmac, and the tribal designation. Sometime during the 1500s the Mi'kmaq began to trade with European explorers and fishermen.

---

[8] www.acadian-home.org/Pre-Deport-Villages.html
[9] www.acadian-cajun.com/encycl.htm
[10] https://www.histoire-genealogie.com/article.php3?id_article=956&lang=fr
[11] 139.103.17.56/cea/axe1/editio2/page1/aboit.cfm
[12] https://www.pc.gc.ca/en/lhn-nhs/ns/grandpre/activ/progs
[13] www.uppercanadahistory.ca/finna/finna6a.html
[14] https://ojs.library.dal.ca/NSM/article/view/5858/5201
[15] https://ojs.library.dal.ca/NSM/article/view/5859/5202
[16] https://ojs.library.dal.ca/NSM/article/view/5860/5203

Mi'kmaq tools made of bone and stone were gradually replaced with tools made of metal. Contact with French missionaries in the early 1600s led to an acceptance of Catholicism. This, combined with a growing dependence on French goods, led to an alliance between the French and the Mi'kmaq which lasted for over a century.

The Acadians and the Creation of the Dykeland (1680-1755) [17]

---

[17] www.landscapeofgrandpre.ca/the-acadians-and-the-creation-of-the-dykeland-1680ndash1755.html

My Maternal DNA Ancestress

My most distant maternal mtDNA ancestress was Edmée Lejeune.

1. **Edmée Lejeune** and François Gautrot
2. **Marie Gautrot** and Claude Thériot
3. **Marguerite Thériot** and Claude Landry
4. **Jeanne Landry** and François (dit Manne) Boudrot
5. **Marie Josèphte Boudrot** and Jacques Haché dit Gallant
6. **Marie Haché dit Gallant** and Pierre Doucet
7. **Pélagie Doucet** and Raphaël Blanchard
8. **Marie Blanchard** and Jean Lanteigne
9. **Françoise Lanteigne** and Agapit Doiron
10. **Romaine Doiron** and Jacques (Jim) Mallet
11. **Marie Philomène Mallet** and André Breau
12. **Mary Catherine (Kay) Breau** and James Henry (Harry) Feeley
13. **Anne Elizabeth Feeley** and Albert Doucette
14. **Michele Anne Doucette**

It had been inferred, quite erroneously, for many years, that the LeJeune sisters, Edmée and Catherine were Native American, but there had never been any documented proof to this allegation.

There had also been much speculation surrounding a possible connection between these sisters and Pierre Lejeune dit Briard, spouse of ---------- Doucet (d/o Germain Doucet, Sieur de LaVerdure, and unknown).

When I first began researching my French Acadian lines, well over 20 years ago, I learned the importance of sourcing as well as validating. Some sources, it was later proven, were more reliable than others.

Not wanting to continue to perpetuate false information, I decided to concentrate solely on what was coming out of the CEA at the Université de Moncton, courtesy of Stephen White.

Matrilineality is a system in which one belongs to one's mother's lineage.

A matriline is a line of descent from a female ancestor to a descendant in which the individuals in all intervening generations are female. Such can be traced both maternally as well as paternally.

However, it is the uterine ancestry of an individual that is a person's pure female ancestry, meaning a matriline leading from a female ancestor to that individual (from mother to daughter to daughter to daughter to daughter). The fact that mitochondrial DNA (mtDNA) is maternally inherited enables matrilineal lines of individuals to be traced through genetic analysis.

On November 30, 2006, my Family Tree mtDNA results were released, directly affiliating me with the U6a haplogroup.

Information supplied regarding this U6a result states that "the mitochondrial super-haplogroup U encompasses haplogroups U1 to U7 and haplogroup K. Haplogroup U6 is among the oldest of the U haplogroups with an origin approximately 50,000 years ago. It is a rare, but ancient haplogroup, and individuals bearing this lineage out of the Near East may have encountered Neanderthals as they moved around what is now the southern Mediterranean basin. In modern populations, it is found at highest frequency in Berber-speaking populations of North Africa and the Canary Islands. Its presence in

Portugal and Spain is the result of recent admixture most likely related to the Moorish occupation of Iberia."[18]

Additional research led me directly to the work of Bryan Sykes, Professor of Human Genetics at Oxford University, one of the world's leading geneticists who has been involved in high-profile cases dealing with ancient DNA. He is also the author of The Seven Daughters of Eve.

Professor Sykes "identified 36 women, who lived thousands of years ago, from whom almost everyone on Earth is directly descended through the maternal line. He has named these women and been able to determine upon which continent they lived. The so-called *Seven Daughters of Eve* subgroup represents the seven-clan mothers from whom almost all native Europeans are descended."[19]

In addition, Africa is able to lay claim "to 13 of the maternal clans. Although these are easily the most ancient clans in the world, a reflection of Africa's status as the cradle of humankind, it is still possible to construct the genetic relationship between them. By doing this, it is possible to show there is one maternal ancestor for all of Africa, and therefore for the rest of the world. She is referred to as *Mitochondrial Eve*."[20]

This particular Eve has no connection to the biblical Eve; apparently, she was coined in such a way by popular media.

Also known as African Eve, she lived approximately 200,000 years ago.

---

[18] Information received courtesy of the Family Tree DNA after accessing personal mtDNA test results.
[19] http://www.tsakanikas.net/matclans.html
[20] Ibid.

Professor Sykes tells us that, while not the only woman alive at the time, it is only her maternal lineage that has been able to survive, unbroken, to the present day. One cannot help but be absolutely astounded by such a revelation.

According to Professor Sykes, "she lived about 45,000 years ago in what is now northern Greece. She was among the first arrivals of a new, modern human to set foot in Europe. She was slender and graceful, in marked contrast to the thickset Neanderthals with whom she and her clan shared the land for another 20,000 years. Her kind brought with them a new and more sophisticated type of stone tool with which to hunt and butcher the abundant game animals that soon appeared on the walls of limestone caves as the first expression of human art. They spread right across Europe, west across France and north as far as the British Isles. As the climate deteriorated 25,000 years ago, the clan began its long migration south; eventually reaching Spain and founding what became a refuge for all humans during the coldest millennia of the last Ice Age. As the climate warmed, the scattered clan led the march back to the North to reclaim the once frozen lands." [21]

In accordance with the company started by Bryan Sykes, called Oxford Ancestors, one that is based in England, "broadly speaking the following clans and clades are similar although not exactly the same: U1 - Una, U2 - Uta, U3 - Uma, U4 - Ulrike, U5 - Ursula, U6 - Ulla and U7 - Ulaana. Groups U1 to U7, along with K (Katrine) all share a common maternal ancestor." [22]

It appears, therefore, that I belong to the Ulla clan, being of the U6a haplogroup.

---

[21] www.oxfordancestors.com/
[22] www.brian-hamman.com/IntroductionClanUrsulaHaplogroupU5.htm

Eileen Krause (Anthrogenealogy Response Center with the Family Tree DNA) has stated the following description of Haplogroup U6a:

This is a very interesting lineage for several reasons. First, I'm positive this lineage is not Native American in origin. The haplogroup U6a is not found in Native American populations, and generally haplogroup U6 is understood to be an African haplogroup.

Out of curiosity, I checked our database, which is largely European so understand it is biased to show more European samples than African, for individuals who are in haplogroup U6. Of the people who reported a country of origin, it turns out the country of origin with the greatest number of individuals in our database is France.

When someone belongs to a haplogroup that is found in both Native American and non-Native American populations, we often look at the matches to determine which lineage this person is matching. In your case, your group members [meaning the French Heritage DNA Project] are an exact match for four out of five of the U6a samples from France. In addition, several of the participants in our database who are U6a, who are an exact match in the HVR1 region, and who did not report a country of origin, have distinctly French surnames.

While the surname isn't necessarily descriptive of the origin of the direct maternal line, when I combine this with the fact that France was the country with the most U6a individuals in our database, it is very interesting.

From this information, I would conclude that the direct maternal line of your participants is not a Native American line; perhaps there is a European ancestor along that line further than the paper trail is able to trace, or perhaps the Native American ancestor is a male or a different female on that side of the family.

At this point, we still have the interesting question of how did U6a, which research indicates is primarily an African lineage, make it to Europe? Despite U6a's African origins, <u>I'm certain these lineages came to Canada from France based on the matches</u>.

How, then, did they get to France from Africa, where this haplogroup branch is most commonly found?

There are a number of possibilities.

U6 may have originated in Europe and this lineage simply did not migrate to Africa. On the other hand, if it originated in Africa, a family could have simply migrated into Europe, but there are also some historical events that would have brought some African lineages into the area.

For example, the Moors who invaded Spain left some lineages behind, which could have easily migrated into France.

Romans brought African slaves with them and spent a significant amount of time and effort in Gaul.

Phoenicians and other traders around the Mediterranean also traded along the coast of Europe; they are known to have traded with Cornwall, so they would easily have traded with France as well.

In each of these examples, some lineages would have spread from Africa into Europe (and vice versa).

Finally, U6a is not the most common haplogroup branch. More research will probably shed more light on what population groups it can be found in (both within Africa and outside of Africa) and possibilities for how it migrated and spread to these different areas. [23]

Based on this response from Eileen Krause, my U6a haplogroup result clearly shows that the maternal ancestors of Catherine and Edmée were European. Given that we know naught who their father was, there will never be a way of testing the male Y-DNA line as a means of comparison and cross-checking.

It also needs to be shared, herein, that my U6a result (which also happened to be *the very first test result* for the Lejeune sisters, specifically Edmée), has since been corroborated by 18 additional mtDNA test results. [24]

In summation, then, the Lejeune sisters confirm maternal ancestry to a European female, of a rare and ancient haplogroup. This DNA fact simply cannot be ignored.

In the explanatory words of Debra Katz, an mtDNA sister ……

A haplogroup involves a significantly large group of people, all of whom have a key mutation that sets them apart from the other haplogroups that exist.

The little band who left Africa around 70,000 years ago were all L3 (the haplogroup of the woman). Some mutations among them led to groups M and N. As the years went by, some N descendants split into R. Later, R split into U. What needs to be remembered is that these splits (mutation offshoots) happened on the scale of tens of thousands of years ago.

---

[23] Response from Eileen Krause as shared on the mtDNA Origins page as maintained by Lucie LeBlanc Consentino at www.acadian-home.org/frames.html
[24] https://www.familytreedna.com/public/mothersofacadia/default.aspx?section=mtresults

Within haplogroups exist subclades (which continue to be discovered as more and more genetic research is done); to put it simply, these are further divisions, due to mutations, into groups of more closely matched people, with the time scale being typically 10,000 years ago or less.

As a result, U split into U1, U2, etc. In turn, the U6 group had some dividing mutations and that led to U6a, U6b, etc.

While U6a is of North African origin, it must be remembered that this specific origin is close to 70,000 years old.

While this U6a branch ended up back in North Africa, approximately 25,000 years ago, some migration from there went to the Middle East, and then to Europe.

What does European mean in the case of U6a?

If it means descended from people who migrated to Europe first (around 50,000 years ago), then no, U6a is not European; however, a person of this haplogroup could easily have had ancestry in Europe for several thousand years, and perhaps even as much as 20,000 years.

Being in the same haplogroup subclade (as in U6a) means that individuals share a common ancestor within the last 2,000 to 5,000 years or so.

Being of the U6a7 subset, means that individuals share a common ancestor within the last 1,000 to 2,000 years or so.

Having become even further affiliated with U6a7a, an even more recent subset, means that a shared common ancestor lived within the last 500 to 800 years or so.

In addition, there are a group of us who are either exactly the same or almost exactly the same.

However, if one should be of the same haplogroup subclade, while also sharing the same haplotype (a specific string of genetic markers that are either exactly the same or almost exactly the same), this means that an individual is much more closely related.

There are many different haplotypes within one haplogroup. Those with the same haplotype may share an ancestor anywhere within a 200 to 1,500 year time frame.

Upon further DNA testing (and specifically the Full Genomic Sequence, or FGS), the Acadian cluster, meaning the Lejeune sisters, has since been identified as subclade U6a7a1. In addition, it is the FGS that determines a person's true haplotype.

According to Family Tree DNA, there is a 50% probability that our most recent common ancestor (MRCA) with Debra Katz (also U6a7a1), <u>with whom we share both a haplogroup subclade as well as a haplotype</u>, lived no longer than 24 generations ago (i.e. about 600 years ago, presuming 4.5 generations per century), which gives us a time frame of about 1400 to 1500, around the time of the Spanish Inquisition, when many Jews converted to Catholicism (further presenting a definite possibility for the maternal ancestor of the Lejeune sisters, given how closely we match markers with Debra, whose line is east European Jewish).

Clearly, this gives one much to ponder.

In keeping, my mtDNA results (Kit 73923) are also posted within the mtDNA results segment of the Canadian Anusim Family Tree DNA Project. [25]

---

[25] https://www.familytreedna.com/public/canadiananusim/

According to history, Sephardic Jews were forced to leave Spain and Portugal during the Spanish Inquisition. Many made their way to France, especially the southern part of France, known as Bayonne and Bordeaux. It was during the early 1600's that some of the Anusim (Jews forced to convert to Catholicism) who fled to France, ended up immigrating to New France, now known as Québec, seeking a life without religious persecution.

The objective of the Canadian Anusim Family Tree DNA Project is to prove this theory through the use of genetic means, thereby linking themselves through Canadian Anusim surnames, places of origin and DNA, to other Anusim and Jewish families, thus, re-establishing family ties that were lost during the Jewish diaspora.

Thanks must hereby be extended to Debra Katz, without whose words, shared in this segment, I would not have been able to glean a better understanding of my own mtDNA results. In addition, Bernard Secher,[26] the administrator of the U6 mtDNA Family Tree DNA Project, does his best to keep everyone up-to-date with regards to the newest findings.

In summation, all of my mother's sisters and brothers have the same mtDNA, meaning U6a7a1.

It must be remembered, however, that females are the only individuals who can pass it on to their daughters.

My sisters and I have the same mtDNA; so, too, do my nieces, and my daughter, share the same.

---

[26] secher.bernard.free.fr/blog/

Likewise, it is also the same for the daughters and granddaughters of my mother's sisters.

An interesting side note, while unrelated to this maternal genealogy, is that my parents had the same mtDNA. My father, through his mother Beatrice Muise, went back to Catherine Lejeune, biological sister of Edmée.

Mothers of Acadia mtDNA Project

In accordance with the Mothers of Acadian mtDNA Project, [27] [28] all of these women figure into our maternal line, thereby painting a picture of wondrous mtDNA diversity amongst the French Acadian women. For the most part, unless otherwise noted, you will locate these women in the French Acadian section of Men and Women of Renown: My Maternal Ancestry).

Amerindian woman, 1st spouse of ---------- Rousseau, 2nd spouse of Gabriel Girard dit St-Jean, belonged to Haplogroup A2-C64T (formerly listed as A2i). [29] [30]

Jeanne Aucoin, spouse of François Girouard dit LaVaranne, belonged to Haplogroup H. [31]

Michelle Aucoin, sister to Jeanne, spouse of Michel Boudrot, belonged to Haplogroup H.

Barbe Bajolet, 1st spouse of Isaac Pesseley, 2nd spouse of Martin Lefebvre, 3rd spouse of Savinien de Courpon, belonged to Haplogroup X2b. [32] [33]

Rose Bayon, spouse of Pierre Comeau, belonged to Haplogroup J*. [34] [35]

---

[27] https://www.familytreedna.com/public/mothersofacadia/default.aspx?section=mtresults
[28] acadian-ancestral-home.blogspot.ca/2011/06/founding-mothers-of-acadia-mtdna.html
[29] https://en.wikipedia.org/wiki/Haplogroup_A_(mtDNA)
[30] https://www.youtube.com/watch?v=KeH0dnNa420
[31] https://en.wikipedia.org/wiki/Haplogroup_H_(mtDNA)
[32] https://www.familytreedna.com/public/x
[33] dienekes.blogspot.ca/2012/10/ancient-mtdna-haplogroup-x2-from.html
[34] https://en.wikipedia.org/wiki/Haplogroup_J_(mtDNA)
[35] https://www.familytreedna.com/public/J-mtDNA/

Anne Bernon, spouse of Pierre Lavergne, belonged to Haplogroup T2. [36] [37]

Perrine Bourg, 1st spouse of Simon Pelletret, 2nd spouse of René Landry dit l'aîné, belonged to Haplogroup H14. [38] [39]

Renée Breau, spouse of Vincent Brun, belonged to Haplogroup H13a1a. [40] [41]

Marie Anne Canol, spouse of Jean Doiron (Douaron), belonged to Haplogroup W3. [42] [43]

Marguerite Caplan, Métisse spouse of François Larocque (refer to the French Canadian section of Men and Women of Renown: My Maternal Ancestry), belonged to Haplogroup C1c. [44] [45]

Jeanne Chebrat, spouse of Jean Poirier, belonged to Haplogroup HV4a1a. [46] [47] [48] [49]

Françoise Corbineau, spouse of Guillaume Trahan, belonged to Haplogroup H. [50]

Marguerite Doucet, spouse of Abraham Dugas, belonged to Haplogroup T2b. [51] [52]

---

[36] https://en.wikipedia.org/wiki/Haplogroup_T_(mtDNA)
[37] https://www.familytreedna.com/public/T2
[38] https://www.ncbi.nlm.nih.gov/pmc/articles/PMC2588665/
[39] https://www.familytreedna.com/public/mtdna_h14/default.aspx?section=results
[40] https://en.wikipedia.org/wiki/Haplogroup_H_(mtDNA)
[41] https://www.familytreedna.com/public/mtdna_h13/default.aspx?section=mtresults
[42] www.thecid.com/w3.htm
[43] https://www.familytreedna.com/public/haplogroupw/
[44] mtdna.blogspot.ca/
[45] https://www.familytreedna.com/public/C_Haplogroup_mtDNA
[46] https://en.wikipedia.org/wiki/Haplogroup_HV_(mtDNA)
[47] dienekes.blogspot.ca/2012/03/mtdna-haplogroup-hv4a1a-from-franco.html
[48] eng.molgen.org/viewtopic.php?t=115&p=6134
[49] https://academic.oup.com/mbe/article/25/8/1651/1110631
[50] https://en.wikipedia.org/wiki/Haplogroup_H_(mtDNA)
[51] https://en.wikipedia.org/wiki/Haplogroup_T_(mtDNA)

Françoise Gaudet, spouse of Daniel LeBlanc, belonged to Haplogroup J1b2. [53] [54] [55]

Marie Gaudet, sister to Françoise, spouse of Étienne Hébert, belonged to Haplogroup J1b2.

Martine Gauthier, spouse of Denis Gaudet, belonged to Haplogroup J1b1. [56] [57]

Angélique Giraud dit St-Jean, spouse of Joseph Bouthillier, daughter of **Amerindian woman**, spouse of Gabriel Girard dit St-Jean, belonged to Haplogroup A2-C64T (formerly listed as A2i). [58] [59]

Andrée Guyon, spouse of ---------- Bernard, belonged to Haplogroup T2. [60] [61]

Madeleine Hélie, spouse of Philippe Mius d'Entremont, belonged to Haplogroup J*. [62] [63]

Radegonde Lambert, spouse of Jean (Joannis) Blanchard, belonged to Haplogroup X2b4. [64] [65]

Antoinette Landry, spouse of Antoine Bourg, belonged to Haplogroup H. [66]

---

[52] https://www.familytreedna.com/public/T2
[53] https://www.familytreedna.com/public/J-mtDNA/
[54] http://journals.plos.org/plosgenetics/article?id=10.1371/journal.pgen.1000474
[55] https://www.ncbi.nlm.nih.gov/pmc/articles/PMC2265662/
[56] https://www.familytreedna.com/public/J-mtDNA/
[57] www.kerchner.com/haplogroups-mtdna.htm
[58] https://en.wikipedia.org/wiki/Haplogroup_A_(mtDNA)
[59] https://www.youtube.com/watch?v=KeH0dnNa420
[60] https://en.wikipedia.org/wiki/Haplogroup_T_(mtDNA)
[61] https://www.familytreedna.com/public/T2
[62] https://en.wikipedia.org/wiki/Haplogroup_J_(mtDNA)
[63] https://www.familytreedna.com/public/J-mtDNA/
[64] https://www.familytreedna.com/public/x
[65] michaelmarcotte.com/radegonde.htm
[66] https://en.wikipedia.org/wiki/Haplogroup_H_(mtDNA)

Marguerite LeBreton, spouse of Iréné (dit René) Duguay, belonged to Haplogroup D. [67] [68]

Geneviève Lefranc, spouse of Antoine Hébert, belonged to Haplogroup W1. [69] [70]

Catherine Lejeune, spouse of François Savoie, belonged to Haplogroup U6a7a1. [71]

Edmée Lejeune, sister to Catherine, spouse of François Gautrot, belonged to Haplogroup U6a7a1. [72] [73] [74] [75] [76] As shared in the proceeding chapter, Edmée Lejeune is my mtDNA line ancestress.

Perrine Rau, spouse of Jean Thériot, belonged to Haplogroup H4a1. [77]

Françoise Rousseau, spouse of Pierre LeViciare, daughter of **Amerindian woman**, belonged to Haplogroup A2-C64T (formerly listed as A2i). [78] [79]

Catherine Vigneau, spouse of Pierre Martin, belonged to Haplogroup T*. [80]

---

[67] https://en.wikipedia.org/wiki/Haplogroup_D_(mtDNA)
[68] https://www.familytreedna.com/public/D/
[69] https://en.wikipedia.org/wiki/Haplogroup_W_(mtDNA)
[70] https://www.familytreedna.com/public/haplogroupw/default.aspx
[71] https://www.familytreedna.com/public/U6mtdna/default.aspx?section=results
[72] https://mathildasanthropologyblog.wordpress.com/2008/06/08/mt-dna-haplotype-u6-study/
[73] http://michaelmarcotte.com/CLejeune.htm
[74] acadian-home.org/SAW-CloserLookRecords.html
[75] https://bmcevolbiol.biomedcentral.com/articles/10.1186/1471-2148-10-390
[76] https://www.familytreedna.com/public/dominicansephardim/default.aspx?section=results
[77] https://www.familytreedna.com/public/mtdna_h4/default.aspx
[78] https://en.wikipedia.org/wiki/Haplogroup_A_(mtDNA)
[79] https://www.youtube.com/watch?v=KeH0dnNa420
[80] https://www.familytreedna.com/public/T_FGS/

As shared previously, matrilineality is a system in which one belongs to one's mother's lineage.

A matriline is a line of descent from a female ancestor to a descendant in which the individuals in all intervening generations are female. Such can be traced both maternally as well as paternally.

However, it is the uterine ancestry of an individual that is a person's pure female ancestry, meaning a matriline leading from a female ancestor to that individual (from mother to daughter to daughter to daughter).

The fact that mitochondrial DNA (mtDNA) is maternally inherited enables matrilineal lines of individuals to be traced through genetic analysis.

Analysis of Native American mtDNA has revealed that *most* fall into four major haplogroups (A, B, C and D), with each of these haplogroups encompassing a coherent lineage of Native American specific mtDNA haplotypes, which trace back to a founding haplotype that is also present in Asia. [81] [82] In addition, Haplogroup X2a has also been found to be Native American. [83]

Analysis of European mtDNA variation has revealed that 99% of European mtDNA falls into nine haplogroups (H, I, J, K, T, R1b, U, V, W and X). [84] In addition, Haplogroup X2b has been found to be European. [85]

The mtDNA Haplogroups L1, L2 and L3 are found in sub-Saharan African lineages. [86]

---

[81] www.acadian-home.org/Haplogroups.html#top
[82] www.madsci.org/posts/archives/jun2000/959811537.Ge.r.html
[83] https://www.ncbi.nlm.nih.gov/pmc/articles/PMC1180497/
[84] www.acadian-home.org/Haplogroups.html#top
[85] https://www.ncbi.nlm.nih.gov/pmc/articles/PMC1180497/

Haplogroups H, I, J, K, T, U, V, W and X are found in nearly all lineages from Europe, North African and Western Asian Caucasians. [87]

Haplogroups A, B, C, D, E, F, G and M are found in the majority of the Asian, Oceania and Native American lineages. [88]

Haplogroups M and N are believed to represent the initial migration by modern humans out of Africa, with Haplogroup N being the ancestral haplogroup to almost all European haplogroups as well as many Eurasian ones. [89]

The Genographic Project [90] seeks to chart new knowledge about the migratory history of the human species by using sophisticated laboratory and computer analysis of DNA contributed by hundreds of thousands of people from around the world.

In this unprecedented and real-time research effort, the Genographic Project is closing the gaps of what science knows today about humankind's ancient migration stories.

---

[86] www.acadian-home.org/Haplogroups.html#top
[87] www.acadian-home.org/Haplogroups.html#top
[88] Ibid.
[89] Ibid.
[90] https://genographic.nationalgeographic.com/

A Little Controversy

There has been talk, *with unproven allegations*, that François Virgine de Montbel, Count d'Entremont, the son of Beatrice de Coligny d'Entremont and Claude Antoine Bon, Baron de Meouillon de Montauban, might actually be Philippe Mius d'Entremont (as married to Madeleine Hélie). Feel free to explore on your own.

Actes du Colloque l'Admiral de Coligny et son Temps [91]

A Little Controversy [92]

Famille du Tillet [93]

François Virgine Bon, Comte d'Entremont et de Montbel [94]

Marcotte Genealogy: François Virgine Bon [95]

Marcotte Genealogy via Melançon [96]

The Nicolas Mius Story [97]

---

[91] michaelmarcotte.com/MiusdEntremont.htm
[92] www.museeacadien.ca/argyle/html/egenealogy5.htm
[93] racineshistoire.free.fr/LGN/PDF/du_Tillet.pdf (page 5)
[94] genealogie.quebec/testphp/info.php?no=193963
[95] michaelmarcotte.com/francoisebon.htm
[96] michaelmarcotte.com/melancon.htm
[97] doris_muise.tripod.com/muise2.htm

A Little More Controversy

There has been talk, *with unproven allegations*, that François Savoie (as married to Catherine Lejeune) might actually be the illegitimate son of Thomas François Savoie, Prince of Carignan. Feel free to explore on your own.

Carignan Regiment [98]

Lineage from Adam (Michael Marcotte) [99]

Maison de Savoie (House of Savoy) [100]

Marcotte Genealogy via Frechette [101]

Michael Marcotte's Genealogy re Savoy [102]

Savoie Genealogy [103]

Spanish Royal Lineage (Michael Marcotte) [104]

---

[98] www.acadian-home.org/carignan-regiment.html
[99] michaelmarcotte.com/Adam.htm
[100] https://fr.wikipedia.org/wiki/Maison_de_Savoie
[101] michaelmarcotte.com/frechette.html
[102] michaelmarcotte.com/savoy.htm
[103] savoiegenealogy.blogspot.ca/
[104] michaelmarcotte.com/spkings.htm

Thomas Francis, 1st Prince of Carignan [105] [106]

https://commons.wikimedia.org/wiki/File:Tomasso_Francisco_savoycarignano.jpg

---

[105] www.princeton.edu/~achaney/tmve/wiki100k/docs/Thomas_Francis,_1st_Prince_of_Carignano.html

[106] https://en.wikipedia.org/wiki/Thomas_Francis,_Prince_of_Carignano

Aboriginal Ancestry

In genetic genealogy, we are now working with three types of DNA.

[1] Y-DNA, which MEN have on the Y chromosome,

[2] mtDNA which MEN and WOMEN both get from their mothers, and

[3] atDNA which makes up the other 21 chromosomes.

Autosomal DNA is an inherited collection from all of your ancestors in both MEN and WOMEN.

As per above, Y-DNA is passed from father to son, in a line of unbroken descent, unless there has been an adoption (or an illegitmate birth) somewhere in the family. As a result, Y-DNA is significantly valuable in following a specific surname.

While mtDNA is passed from a mother to all of her children, including the sons, it is only passed on to the females (from mother to daughter). The only difficulty with mtDNA is that the surname changes every generation, making it more challenging, but not impossible, to track.

By comparison, atDNA, in any individual, is a random collection of some of the DNA of all your ancestors, inherited 50% from each parent. Autosomes contain such things as hair color, eye color, facial features, height, body structure, health issues, etc.

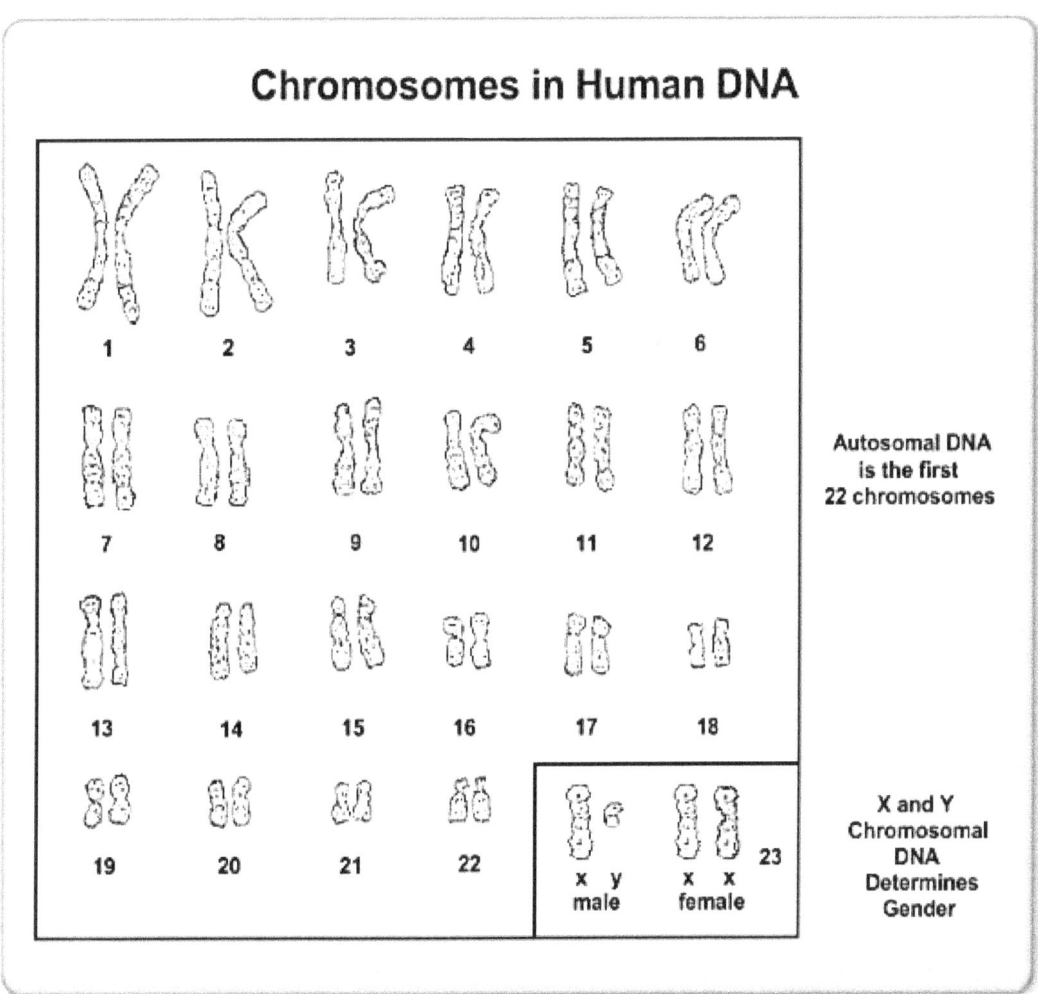

In humans, autosomes are the set of chromosomes pairs labelled 1 to 22. Chromosome 23 is the sex chromosome. Since autosomal DNA (atDNA) is made up of random combinations of genetic blocks of information, its uses in genealogy have been limited thus far.[107]

In truth, it is becoming clearer that genetic testing, for genealogical purposes, is currently the most powerful tool for genealogists.

---

[107] *atDNA in Depth* article, courtesy of the The Phillips DNA Project, accessed on July 23, 2011 at https://www.phillipsdnaproject.com/faq-sections/27-dna-questions-faqs/316-atdna-in-depth

MATERNAL 1A
Courtesy of mtDNA testing, the mother of Françoise Rousseau shows as belonging to HAPLOGROUP A2-C64T (formerly listed as A2i) [108] which is a native haplogroup.
1. ---------- Rousseau and <u>unidentified Amérindienne woman</u>
2. <u>Françoise Rousseau</u> and Pierre LeVicaire
3. <u>Anne LeVicaire</u> and Zacharie Amable Doiron
4. Jean Baptiste Doiron and Rose Bouthillier
5. Agapit Doiron and Françoise Lanteigne
6. Romaine Doiron and Jacques (Jim) Mallet
7. Marie Philomène Mallet and André Breau
8. Marie Catherine (Kay) Breau and James Henry (Harry) Feeley
9. Anne Elizabeth Feeley and Albert Doucette
10. Michele Anne Doucette

April 15, 2017 ADDENDUM

Victorin Mallet has researched and written two notable books; namely, <u>Métis acadiens de la Baie des Chaleurs</u> and <u>Évidences des communautés métisses autour de la Baie des Chaleurs</u>. It is in the second book that he proposes that Anne LeVicaire is *not* a sister to Marie LeVicaire (see Maternal 1B). While Pierre LeVicaire *is* the father of both Anne and Marie, it may be that the mother of Marie LeVicaire, a Mi'kmaq woman, was either [1] related to the Mi'kmaq wife of Gabriel Giraud dit St-Jean or [2] her daughter from a previous relationship.

---

[108] https://www.familytreedna.com/public/mothersofacadia/default.aspx?section=mtresults

MATERNAL 1B

Courtesy of mtDNA testing, the mother of Françoise Rousseau shows as belonging to HAPLOGROUP A2-C64T (formerly listed as A2i) [109] which is a native haplogroup.

1. ---------- Rousseau and <u>unidentified Amérindienne woman</u>

2. <u>Françoise Rousseau</u> and Pierre LeVicaire

3. <u>Marie LeVicaire</u> and François Gionet

4. <u>Geneviève Gionet</u> and Nicolas Chiasson

5. <u>Rosalie Chiasson</u> and Pierre Bonaventure Duguay

6. <u>Olive Duguay</u> and Dominique Mallet

7. Jacques (Jim) Mallet and Romaine Doiron

8. Marie Philomène Mallet and André Breau

9. Marie Catherine (Kay) Breau and James Henry (Harry) Feeley

10. Anne Elizabeth Feeley and Albert Doucette

11. Michele Anne Doucette

---

[109] https://www.familytreedna.com/public/mothersofacadia/default.aspx?section=mtresults

MATERNAL 2A

Courtesy of mtDNA testing, the mother of Angélique Giraud dit St-Jean shows as belonging to HAPLOGROUP A2-C64T (formerly listed as A2i) [110] which is a native haplogroup.

1. Gabriel Giraud dit St-Jean and <u>unidentified Amérindienne woman</u>

2. <u>Angélique Giraud dit St-Jean</u> and Joseph Bouthillier

3. <u>Geneviève Bouthillier</u> and Gabriel Albert

4. <u>Marie Albert</u> and Michel Parisé

5. <u>Marie Parisé</u> and Jean Lanteigne

6. Jean Lanteigne and Marie Blanchard

7. Françoise Lanteigne and Agapit Doiron

8. Romaine Doiron and Jacques (Jim) Mallet

9. Marie Philomène Mallet and André Breau

10. Marie Catherine (Kay) Breau and James Henry (Harry) Feeley

11. Anne Elizabeth Feeley and Albert Doucette

12. Michele Anne Doucette

---

[110] https://www.familytreedna.com/public/mothersofacadia/default.aspx?section=mtresults

MATERNAL 2A
Courtesy of mtDNA testing, the mother of Angélique Giraud dit St-Jean shows as belonging to HAPLOGROUP A2-C64T (formerly listed as A2i) [111] which is a native haplogroup.
1. Gabriel Giraud dit St-Jean and <u>unidentified Amérindienne woman</u>
2. <u>Angélique Giraud dit St-Jean</u> and Joseph Bouthillier
3. <u>Geneviève Bouthillier</u> and Gabriel Albert
4. Jean Baptiste Albert and Thérèse Lanteigne
5. Euphrosine Albert and Thomas Mallet
6. Dominique Mallet and Olive Duguay
7. Jacques (Jim) Mallet and Romaine Doiron
8. Marie Philomène Mallet and André Breau
9. Marie Catherine (Kay) Breau and James Henry (Harry) Feeley
10. Anne Elizabeth Feeley and Albert Doucette
11. Michele Anne Doucette

---

[111] https://www.familytreedna.com/public/mothersofacadia/default.aspx?section=mtresults

MATERNAL 2B

Courtesy of mtDNA testing, the mother of Angélique Giraud dit St-Jean shows as belonging to HAPLOGROUP A2-C64T (formerly listed as A2i) [112] which is a native haplogroup.

1. Gabriel Giraud dit St-Jean and <u>unidentified Amérindienne woman</u>

2. <u>Angélique Giraud dit St-Jean</u> and Joseph Bouthillier

3. <u>Agnès (Anne) Bouthillier</u> and Jean Canivet

4. <u>Thérèse Canivet</u> and Jean Baptiste Paulin

5. <u>Thérèse Paulin</u> and Julien Lanteigne

6. Jacques (Jimmie) Lanteigne and Marie Anne Hébert

7. Justine Lanteigne and Alexandre Landry

8. Marie Landry and Louis Breau

9. André Breau and Marie Philomène Mallet

10. Marie Catherine (Kay) Breau and James Henry (Harry) Feeley

11. Anne Elizabeth Feeley and Albert Doucette

12. Michele Anne Doucette

---

[112] https://www.familytreedna.com/public/mothersofacadia/default.aspx?section=mtresults

MATERNAL 2C

Courtesy of mtDNA testing, the mother of Angélique Giraud dit St-Jean shows as belonging to HAPLOGROUP A2-C64T (formerly listed as A2i) [113] which is a native haplogroup.

1. Gabriel Giraud dit St-Jean and <u>unidentified Amérindienne woman</u>
2. <u>Angélique Giraud dit St-Jean</u> and Joseph Bouthillier
3. René Bouthillier and Geneviève Chiasson
4. Rose Bouthillier and Jean Baptiste Doiron
5. Agapit Doiron and Françoise Lanteigne
6. Romaine Doiron and Jacques (Jim) Mallet
7. Marie Philomène Mallet and André Breau
8. Marie Catherine (Kay) Breau and James Henry (Harry) Feeley
9. Anne Elizabeth Feeley and Albert Doucette
10. Michele Anne Doucette

---

[113] https://www.familytreedna.com/public/mothersofacadia/default.aspx?section=mtresults

MATERNAL 3A

Courtesy of mtDNA testing, this unidentified spouse of Guillaume Caplan shows as belonging to HAPLOGROUP C1c [114] which is a native haplogroup thereby making Marguerite Caplan a Métisse.

1. Guillaume Caplan and <u>unidentified Amérindienne woman</u>
2. <u>Marguerite Caplan</u> and François Larocque
3. <u>Catherine Larocque</u> and Jean (Joannis) Chapadeau
4. <u>Madeleine Chapadeau</u> and François Duguay
5. <u>Marguerite Duguay</u> and Pierre Chiasson
6. <u>Anne (Nanette) Chiasson</u> and Joseph Hébert
7. <u>Marie Anne Hébert</u> and Jacques (Jimmie) Lanteigne
8. <u>Justine Lanteigne</u> and Alexandre Landry
9. <u>Marie Landry</u> and Louis Breau
10. André Breau and Marie Philomène Mallet
11. Marie Catherine (Kay) Breau and James Henry (Harry) Feeley
12. Anne Elizabeth Feeley and Albert Doucette
13. Michele Anne Doucette

---

[114] https://www.familytreedna.com/public/mothersofacadia/default.aspx?section=mtresults

MATERNAL 3A
Courtesy of mtDNA testing, this unidentified spouse of Guillaume Caplan shows as belonging to HAPLOGROUP C1c [115] which is a native haplogroup thereby making Marguerite Caplan a Métisse.
1. Guillaume Caplan and <u>unidentified Amérindienne woman</u>
2. <u>Marguerite Caplan</u> and François Larocque
3. <u>Catherine Larocque</u> and Jean (Joannis) Chapadeau
4. <u>Madeleine Chapadeau</u> and François Duguay
5. Pierre Bonaventure Duguay and Rosalie Chiasson
6. Olive Duguay and Dominique Mallet
7. Jacques (Jim) Mallet and Romaine Doiron
8. Marie Philomène Mallet and André Breau
9. Marie Catherine (Kay) Breau and James Henry (Harry) Feeley
10. Anne Elizabeth Feeley and Albert Doucette
11. Michele Anne Doucette

---

[115] https://www.familytreedna.com/public/mothersofacadia/default.aspx?section=mtresults

MATERNAL 3B

Courtesy of mtDNA testing, this unidentified spouse of Guillaume Caplan shows as belonging to HAPLOGROUP C1c [116] which is a native haplogroup thereby making Marguerite Caplan a Métisse.

1. Guillaume Caplan and <u>unidentified Amérindienne woman</u>
2. <u>Marguerite Caplan</u> and François Larocque
3. <u>Catherine Larocque</u> and Jean (Joannis) Chapadeau
4. <u>Marie Marguerite Chapadeau</u> and Louis Lanteigne
5. <u>Thérèse Lanteigne</u> and Jean Baptiste Albert
6. <u>Euphrosine Albert</u> and Thomas Mallet
7. Dominique Mallet and Olive Duguay
8. Jacques (Jim) Mallet and Romaine Doiron
9. Marie Philomène Mallet and André Breau
10. Marie Catherine (Kay) Breau and James Henry (Harry) Feeley
11. Anne Elizabeth Feeley and Albert Doucette
12. Michele Anne Doucette

---

[116] https://www.familytreedna.com/public/mothersofacadia/default.aspx?section=mtresults

MATERNAL 3B
Courtesy of mtDNA testing, this unidentified spouse of Guillaume Caplan shows as belonging to HAPLOGROUP C1c [117] which is a native haplogroup thereby making Marguerite Caplan a Métisse.
1. Guillaume Caplan and <u>unidentified Amérindienne woman</u> 2. <u>Marguerite Caplan</u> and François Larocque 3. <u>Catherine Larocque</u> and Jean (Joannis) Chapadeau 4. <u>Marie Marguerite Chapadeau</u> and Louis Lanteigne 5. Jean Lanteigne and Marie Parisé 6. Jean Lanteigne and Marie Blanchard 7. Françoise Lanteigne and Agapit Doiron 8. Romaine Doiron and Jacques (Jim) Mallet 9. Marie Philomène Mallet and André Breau 10. Marie Catherine (Kay) Breau and James Henry (Harry) Feeley 11. Anne Elizabeth Feeley and Albert Doucette 12. Michele Anne Doucette

---

[117] https://www.familytreedna.com/public/mothersofacadia/default.aspx?section=mtresults

MATERNAL 3B
Courtesy of mtDNA testing, this unidentified spouse of Guillaume Caplan shows as belonging to HAPLOGROUP C1c [118] which is a native haplogroup thereby making Marguerite Caplan a Métisse.
1. Guillaume Caplan and <u>unidentified Amérindienne woman</u>
2. <u>Marguerite Caplan</u> and François Larocque
3. <u>Catherine Larocque</u> and Jean (Joannis) Chapadeau
4. <u>Marie Marguerite Chapadeau</u> and Louis Lanteigne
5. Julien Lanteigne and Thérèse Paulin
6. Jacques (Jimmie) Lanteigne and Marie Anne Hébert
7. Justine Lanteigne and Alexandre Landry
8. Marie Landry and Louis Breau
9. André Breau and Marie Philomène Mallet
10. Marie Catherine (Kay) Breau and James Henry (Harry) Feeley
11. Anne Elizabeth Feeley and Albert Doucette
12. Michele Anne Doucette

---

[118] https://www.familytreedna.com/public/mothersofacadia/default.aspx?section=mtresults

MATERNAL 3C   **Courtesy of mtDNA testing, this unidentified spouse of Guillaume Caplan shows as belonging to HAPLOGROUP C1c [119] which is a native haplogroup thereby making Marguerite Caplan a Métisse.**
1. Guillaume Caplan and <u>unidentified Amérindienne woman</u>   2. <u>Marguerite Caplan</u> and François Larocque   3. <u>Marie Madeleine Larocque</u> and François Mallet   4. Jean Mallet and Marie Josèphe Duguay   5. Thomas Mallet and Euphrosine Albert   6. Dominique Mallet and Olive Duguay   7. Jacques (Jim) Mallet and Romaine Doiron   8. Marie Philomène Mallet and André Breau   9. Marie Catherine (Kay) Breau and James Henry (Harry) Feeley   10. Anne Elizabeth Feeley and Albert Doucette   11. Michele Anne Doucette

---

[119] https://www.familytreedna.com/public/mothersofacadia/default.aspx?section=mtresults

MATERNAL 4A

1. Pierre Larché and <u>Montagnais woman</u>

2. Michel Haché dit Gallant and Anne Cormier

3. Charles Haché dit Gallant and Geneviève Lavergne

4. Anne Haché dit Gallant and Joseph Chiasson

5. Geneviève Chiasson and René Bouthillier

6. Rose Bouthillier and Jean Baptiste Doiron

7. Agapit Doiron and Françoise Lanteigne

8. Romaine Doiron and Jacques (Jim) Mallet

9. Marie Philomène Mallet and André Breau

10. Marie Catherine (Kay) Breau and James Henry (Harry) Feeley

11. Anne Elizabeth Feeley and Albert Doucette

12. Michele Anne Doucette

Michel was baptized on April 24, 1668 in Trois Rivières, Québec. A copy of the document is displayed here.

MATERNAL 4B
1. Pierre Larché and <u>Montagnais woman</u>
2. Michel Haché dit Gallant and Anne Cormier
3. Jacques Haché dit Gallant and Marie Josèphe Boudrot
4. Marie Haché dit Gallant and Pierre Doucet
5. Pélagie Doucet and Raphäel Blanchard
6. Marie Blanchard and Jean Lanteigne
7. Françoise Lanteigne and Agapit Doiron
8. Romaine Doiron and Jacques (Jim) Mallet
9. Marie Philomène Mallet and André Breau
10. Marie Catherine (Kay) Breau and James Henry (Harry) Feeley
11. Anne Elizabeth Feeley and Albert Doucette
12. Michele Anne Doucette

Michel was baptized on April 24, 1668 in Trois Rivières, Québec. A copy of the document is displayed here.

My Percheron Ancestors

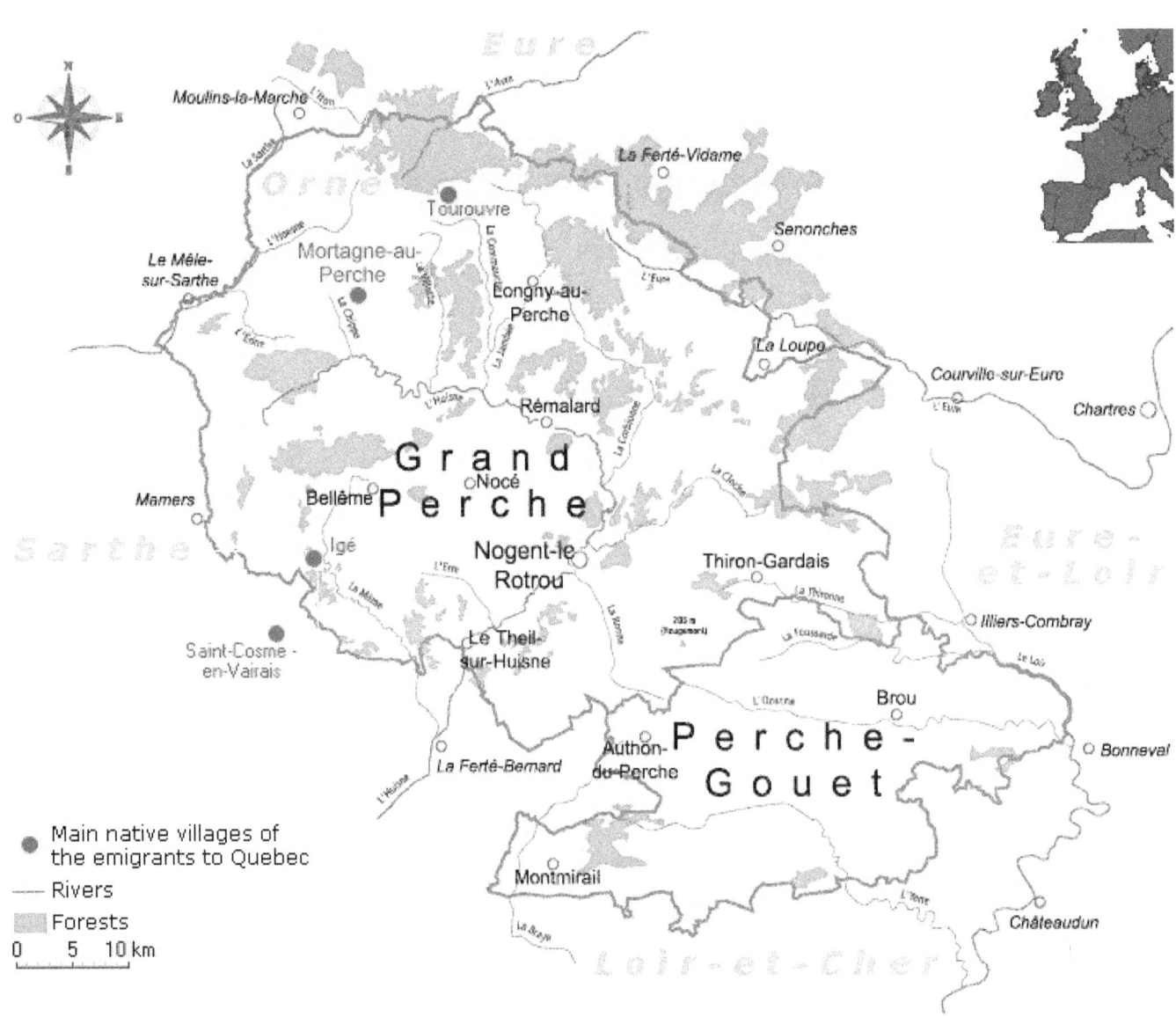

www.perche-quebec.com/files/perche/lieux/perche_en.htm

In the early 17th century, the Perche (France) was the point of departure for many French emigrants, and a number of major families in Quebec can trace their roots back to this particular region. [120]

If the contribution of the Perche to the settlement of Canada – approximately 5% of the French emigrants – can appear modest, it should be stressed that the Percheron emigration, the oldest one, is characterized by a remarkable prolificity ... wrote Françoise Montagne. [121]

The movement, launched in 1634, thanks to the capacity of conviction of Robert Giffard, [122] [123] represents a definitive originality in the French emigration to New France, one that was not due to misery, but rather to the spirit of adventure. [124]

Within the span of about thirty years, 146 adults who had various jobs, often related to construction (mason, carpenter, brick-maker, etc), and who represented 80 families, undertook the great voyage. [125] [126]

While some returned to live and work in their native country, the great majority, despite the Iroquois threat, chose to settle on the banks of the Saint Lawrence River in order to clear and thrive [within] the new territories. [127]

The Perche is located 100 miles west of Paris, and while not an official administrative subdivision of France, it remains a beautiful region with a rich history. [128]

---

[120] www.perche-quebec.com/files/perche/lieux/perche_en.htm
[121] Ibid.
[122] www.vt-fcgs.org/leperche.html
[123] www.apointinhistory.net/departure.php
[124] www.perche-quebec.com/files/perche/lieux/perche_en.htm
[125] www.apointinhistory.net/ganivet.php
[126] www.perche-quebec.com/files/perche/lieux/perche_en.htm
[127] Ibid.
[128] Ibid.

My Percheron ancestors include ……

[1] Marin Boucher [129] from Mortagne-au-Perche (see Celebrity Relations 2) is also an ancestor to Céline Dion, Angelina Jolie and Madonna. [130]

[2] Zacharie Cloutier [131] from Mortagne-au-Perche (see Celebrity Relations 3) is also an ancestor of Céline Dion, Madonna, [132] Camilla (Duchess of Cornwall), [133] Shania Twain, Angelina Jolie and Alanis Morissette. [134] [135]

[3] Pierre Gagné (Gasnier) from Igé (see Celebrity Relations 4) is also an ancestor to Céline Dion, Madonna, Hillary Rodham Clinton and Alanis Morisette. [136]

[4] Jean Guyon [137] from Tourouvre (see Celebrity Relations 5) is also an ancestor of Céline Dion, Madonna, Camilla (Duchess of Cornwall), Hillary Rodham Clinton, Shania Twain and Stéphane Dion. [138] [139]

---

[129] www.apointinhistory.net/boucher.php
[130] www.perche-quebec.com/files/perche/individus/marin_boucher.htm
[131] www.apointinhistory.net/cloutier.php
[132] https://www.nosorigines.qc.ca/GenealogieQuebec.aspx?genealogy=Ciccone_Madonna-Veronica-Louise&pid=623&lng=en
[133] https://www.nosorigines.qc.ca/GenealogieQuebec.aspx?genealogy=Shand_Camilla-Rosemary&pid=191271&lng=en
[134] www.perche-quebec.com/files/perche/individus/zacharie_cloutier_en.htm
[135] michaelmarcotte.com/morisset.html
[136] www.perche-quebec.com/files/perche/individus/pierre_gagne.htm
[137] www.apointinhistory.net/guyon.php
[138] www.perche-quebec.com/files/perche/individus/jean_guyon.htm
[139] michaelmarcotte.com/rodham.htm

Celebrity Relations 1

Many people of French-Canadian ancestry can claim descent from **Catherine de Baillon**. She was the daughter of Alphonse de Baillon and Louise de Marle, born about 1645, near Montfort-l'Amaury, Île-de-France, outside of Paris.

It has also been noted that her parents were members of minor French nobility.

Catherine de Baillon is my <u>first</u> French Canadian royal gateway ancestor, meaning that she presents a connection from New France to medieval nobility.

Jean Chrétien (19th Prime Minister of Canada) [140]

Céline Dion [141]

Angelina Jolie [142]

Roch Voisine [143]

---

[140] https://www.nosorigines.qc.ca/GenealogieQuebec.aspx?pid=5428

[141] https://www.nosorigines.qc.ca/GenealogieQuebec.aspx?genealogy=Dion_Celine&pid=760&lng=en

[142] https://www.nosorigines.qc.ca/GenealogieQuebec.aspx?genealogy=Jolie_Angelina&pid=191681&lng=en

[143] https://www.nosorigines.qc.ca/GenealogieQuebec.aspx?genealogy=Voisine_Rock&pid=1467&lng=en

Catherine de Baillon + Jacques Miville dit Deschênes	Catherine de Baillon + Jacques Miville dit Deschênes
Jean Miville dit Deschênes + Marie Madeleine Dubé	Charles Miville dit Deschênes + Marie Marthe Vallée
Angélique Miville dit Deschênes + Mathurin Bérubé	Catherine Miville + Jean Baptiste Duval
Joseph Bérubé + Angélique Thibault	Marie Josette (Josèphe) Duval + Jean Baptiste LeClerc
Pierre Bérubé + Catherine Hudon	Jean Baptiste LeClerc + Madeleine Thébault
Louis Bérubé + Marie Félicité Boucher	Madeleine LeClerc + Pascal Landry
Émérence Bérubé + Antoine Isabelle	Alexis dit Alexandre Landry + Justine Lanteigne
Philomène Isabelle + Jean Baptiste Barriault	Marie Landry + Louis Breau
Norbert Barriault + Alma Pelletier	André Breau + Marie Philomène Mallet
Ernestine Barriault + Charles Edouard Dion	Mary Catherine (Kay) Breau + James Henry (Harry) Feeley
Adhémar Dion + Thérèse Tanguay	Anne Elizabeth Feeley + Albert (Al) Doucette
Céline Dion	**Michele Anne Doucette**

I am a 10th cousin with Céline Dion.

Catherine de Baillon + Jacques Miville dit Deschênes	Catherine de Baillon + Jacques Miville dit Deschênes
Jean Miville dit Deschênes + Marie Madeleine Dubé	Charles Miville dit Deschênes + Marie Marthe Vallée
Marie Madeleine Miville dit Deschênes + Nicolas Lizotte	Catherine Miville + Jean Baptiste Duval
Nicolas Claude Lizotte + Marie Ursule Migneault dit Labrie	Marie Josette (Josèphe) Duval + Jean Baptiste LeClerc
Marie Anne Lizotte + François Bertrand	Jean Baptiste LeClerc + Madeleine Thébault
Joseph Marie Bertrand + Marie Judith Chaput	Madeleine LeClerc + Pascal Landry
Jean Baptiste Bertrand + Marie Marguerite Jetté	Alexis dit Alexandre Landry + Justine Lanteigne
Léon Bertrand + Marie Aglae Perreault	Marie Landry + Louis Breau
Louis J. Bertrand + Marie Virgine Adelphine Mayette	André Breau + Marie Philomène Mallet
Georges Bertrand + Angeline Leduc	Mary Catherine (Kay) Breau + James Henry (Harry) Feeley
Rolland Bertrand + Lois June Gouwens	Anne Elizabeth Feeley + Albert (Al) Doucette
Marcia Lynne (Marceline) Bertrand + Jonathan Voight	**Michele Anne Doucette**
Angelina Jolie	

I am a 10th cousin once removed with Angelina Jolie.

Catherine de Baillon + Jacques Miville dit Deschênes	Catherine de Baillon + Jacques Miville dit Deschênes
Jean Miville dit Deschênes + Marie Madeleine Dubé	Charles Miville dit Deschênes + Marie Marthe Vallée
Marie Madeleine Miville dit Deschênes + Nicolas Lizotte	Catherine Miville + Jean Baptiste Duval
Marie Josèphe Lizotte + Joseph Ouellet	Marie Josette (Josèphe) Duval + Jean Baptiste LeClerc
Brigette Josèphe Ouellet + Michel Saint-Pierre	Jean Baptiste LeClerc + Madeleine Thébault
Marie Josèphte Saint-Pierre + Joseph Jean Baptiste Blais	Madeleine LeClerc + Pascal Landry
Joseph Blais + Marie Boisvert	Alexis dit Alexandre Landry + Justine Lanteigne
Élisabeth Blais + François Chrétien	Marie Landry + Louis Breau
François Chrétien + Olivine Laforme	André Breau + Marie Philomène Mallet
Willie Chrétien + Marie Boisvert	Mary Catherine (Kay) Breau + James Henry (Harry) Feeley
Jean Chrétien, 19th Prime Minister of Canada	Anne Elizabeth Feeley + Albert (Al) Doucette
	Michele Anne Doucette

I am a 9th cousin once removed with Jean Chrétien.

Catherine de Baillon + Jacques Miville dit Deschênes	Catherine de Baillon + Jacques Miville dit Deschênes
Charles Miville dit Deschênes + Marie Marthe Vallée	Charles Miville dit Deschênes + Marie Marthe Vallée
Charles Miville dit Deschênes + Marie Madeleine Ouellet	Catherine Miville + Jean Baptiste Duval
Marie Angélique Miville + Antoine Michaud	Marie Josette (Josèphe) Duval + Jean Baptiste LeClerc
Marie Angélique Michaud + Étienne LeVasseur	Jean Baptiste LeClerc + Madeleine Thébault
Céleste LeVasseur + Hilaire Roy	Madeleine LeClerc + Pascal Landry
Étienne Roy dit Desjardins + Hélène Guéret	Alexis dit Alexandre Landry + Justine Lanteigne
Elzéar Roy dit Desjardins + Philomène Martin	Marie Landry + Louis Breau
Alfred Frédéric Voisine + Anna Soucy	André Breau + Marie Philomène Mallet
Maurille Voisine + Dorina Racine	Mary Catherine (Kay) Breau + James Henry (Harry) Feeley
Réal Voisine + Zélande Robichaud	Anne Elizabeth Feeley + Albert (Al) Doucette
Roch Voisine	**Michele Anne Doucette**

I am a 9th cousin with Roch Voisine.

Celebrity Relations 2

Marin Boucher + Perrine Mallet	Marin Boucher + Perrine Mallet
Jean Galeran Boucher + Marie LeClerc	Jean Galeran Boucher + Marie LeClerc
Marie Madeleine Boucher + Jean François Lavoie	Marie Anne Boucher + François Duval
Joseph Lavoie + Marie Geneviève Miville dit Deschênes	Jean Duval + Catherine Charlotte Miville dit Deschênes
Joseph Lavoie + Marie Madeleine Michaud	Marie Josèphe (Josette) Duval + Jean Baptiste LeClerc dit Francoeur
Josèphte Lavoie + Pierre Bernard Lévesque	Jean Baptiste LeClerc dit Francoeur + Madeleine Thébault
Geneviève Lévesque + Claude Létourneau	Madeleine LeClerc + Pascal Landry
Joseph Létourneau + Delina Paradis	Alexis dit Alexandre Landry + Justine Lanteigne
Marcelline Létourneau + Joseph Adélard Dion	Marie Landry + Louis Breau
Adélard Dion + Esther Levesque	André Breau + Marie Philomène Mallet
Charles Edouard Dion + Ernestine Barriault	Mary Catherine (Kay) Breau + James Henry (Harry) Feeley
Adhémar Dion + Thérèse Tanguay	Anne Elizabeth Feeley + Albert (Al) Doucette
Céline Dion	**Michele Anne Doucette**

I am a 10th cousin with Céline Dion.

Marin Boucher + Perrine Mallet	Marin Boucher + Perrine Mallet
Pierre Boucher + Marie Anne Saint Denis	Jean Galeran Boucher + Marie LeClerc
Marie Sainte Boucher + Jean Baptiste Migneault	Marie Anne Boucher + François Duval
Marie Ursule Migneault + Pierre Augustin Emond	Jean Duval + Catherine Charlotte Miville dit Deschênes
Marie Madeleine Emond + Antoine Gagnon	Marie Josèphe (Josette) Duval + Jean Baptiste LeClerc dit Francoeur
Marie Geneviève Gagnon + Henri Marie Gaudreau	Jean Baptiste LeClerc dit Francoeur + Madeleine Thébault
Marie Euphrosine Gaudreau + Augustin Fortin	Madeleine LeClerc + Pascal Landry
Narcisse Fortin + Félicité Rioux	Alexis dit Alexandre Landry + Justine Lanteigne
Narcisse Fortin + Rose Lajoie	Marie Landry + Louis Breau
Willard Fortin + Elsie Mae Fortin	André Breau + Marie Philomène Mallet
Madonna Louise Fortin + Silvio Anthony Ciccone	Mary Catherine (Kay) Breau + James Henry (Harry) Feeley
Madonna Veronica Louise Ciccone	Anne Elizabeth Feeley + Albert (Al) Doucette
	Michele Anne Doucette

I am a 10th cousin once removed with Madonna.

<u>Marin Boucher</u> + Perrine Mallet	<u>Marin Boucher</u> + Perrine Mallet
François Boucher + Florence Gorman	Jean Galeran Boucher + Marie LeClerc
Charles Boucher + Marguerite Agnès Marie Pelletier	Marie Anne Boucher + François Duval
Joseph Marie Boucher + Marie Madeleine Migneron	Jean Duval + Catherine Charlotte Miville dit Deschênes
Marie Geneviève Boucher + Pierre Durand	Marie Josèphe (Josette) Duval + Jean Baptiste LeClerc dit Francoeur
François Durand + Marie Geneviève Picard	Jean Baptiste LeClerc dit Francoeur + Madeleine Thébault
Julie Durand + Désiré Maillet	Madeleine LeClerc + Pascal Landry
Désiré Charles Mayette + Sophia Olivia Fortier	Alexis dit Alexandre Landry + Justine Lanteigne
Delina Adeline Mayette + Louis Bertrand	Marie Landry + Louis Breau
Georges Bertrand + Angeline Leduc	André Breau + Marie Philomène Mallet
Rolland Bertrand + Lois June Gouwens	Mary Catherine (Kay) Breau + James Henry (Harry) Feeley
Marcia Lynne (Marceline) Bertrand + Jonathan Voight	Anne Elizabeth Feeley + Albert (Al) Doucette
Angelina Jolie	**Michele Anne Doucette**

I am an 11th cousin with Angelina Jolie.

Celebrity Relations 3

In 1634, Zacharie Cloutier, a French carpenter, settled in New France, becoming one of the most influential pioneers of French Canada. By 1800, Cloutier's descendants numbered nearly 11,000.

Sketch of Zacharie Cloutier (the artist E. Senecal's version)

https://www.wikitree.com/wiki/Cloutier-202

Zacharie Cloutier + Sainte Dupont	Zacharie Cloutier + Sainte Dupont
Zacharie Cloutier + Madeleine Aymard	Zacharie Cloutier + Madeleine Aymard
Geneviève Cloutier + Joseph Guyon	René Cloutier + Marie LeBlanc
Joseph Guyon dit Lemoine + Elizabeth Guillet	Marie Catherine Cloutier + Alexis Gagné dit Béllavance, Sieur de La Fresnaye
Marie Josèphe Guyon dit Lemoine + Michel Coursolle	Marie Gagné dit Béllavance + Jean Baptiste Poulin
Marie Charlotte Coursolle + Ephraim Jones	Jean Baptiste Paulin + Thérèse Canivet
Sophia Jones + John Stuart	Thérèse Paulin + Julien Lanteigne
Mary Elizabeth Stuart + Sir Allan Napier MacNab, 1st Baronet, Premier of Canada West	Jacques (Jimmie) Lanteigne + Marie Anne Hébert
Sophia Mary MacNab + William Coutts Keppel, 7th Earl of Albermarle	Justine Lanteigne + Alexis dit Alexandre Landry
Colonel George Keppel of Albermarle + Alice Frederica Edmonstone	Marie Landry + Louis Breau
Sonia Rosemary Keppel + Roland Calvert Cubitt, 3rd Baron of Ashcombe	André Breau + Marie Philomène Mallet
Rosalind Maud Cubitt + Major Bruce Middleton Hope Shand	Mary Catherine (Kay) Breau + James Henry (Harry) Feeley
Camilla Rosemary Shand, Duchess of Cornwall	Anne Elizabeth Feeley + Albert (Al) Doucette
	Michele Anne Doucette

I am a 10th cousin once removed with Camilla Rosemary Shand, Duchess of Cornwall (second wife of Prince Charles).

Zacharie Cloutier + Sainte Dupont	Zacharie Cloutier + Sainte Dupont
Zacharie Cloutier + Madeleine Aymard	Zacharie Cloutier + Madeleine Aymard
Sainte Cloutier + Charles Fortin	René Cloutier + Marie LeBlanc
Louis Fortin + Anne Bosse	Marie Catherine Cloutier + Alexis Gagné dit Béllavance, Sieur de La Fresnaye
Claude Fortin + Marie Jeanne Methot	Marie Gagné dit Béllavance + Jean Baptiste Poulin
Joseph Romain Fortin + Marie Louise Delisle	Jean Baptiste Paulin + Thérèse Canivet
Joseph Fortin + Geneviève Fortin	Thérèse Paulin + Julien Lanteigne
François Fortin + Victoire Blier	Jacques (Jimmie) Lanteigne + Marie Anne Hébert
Henri Nazaire Fortin + Émilie Daniel	Justine Lanteigne + Alexis dit Alexandre Landry
Henri Guillaume Fortin + Marie Louise Demers	Marie Landry + Louis Breau
Elsie Louise Fortin + Willard Fortin	André Breau + Marie Philomène Mallet
Madonna Louise Fortin + Silvio Anthony Ciccone	Mary Catherine (Kay) Breau + James Henry (Harry) Feeley
Madonna Veronica Louise Ciccone	Anne Elizabeth Feeley + Albert (Al) Doucette
	Michele Anne Doucette

I am a 10th cousin once removed with Madonna.

<u>Zacharie Cloutier + Sainte Dupont</u>	<u>Zacharie Cloutier + Sainte Dupont</u>
Charles Cloutier + Louise Morin	Zacharie Cloutier + Madeleine Aymard
Elizabeth Ursule Cloutier + Nicolas Gamache	René Cloutier + Marie LeBlanc
Marie Gamache + Louis Guyon dit Dion	Marie Catherine Cloutier + Alexis Gagné dit Béllavance, Sieur de La Fresnaye
Joseph Joachim Dion + Marguerite Fournier	Marie Gagné dit Béllavance + Jean Baptiste Poulin
Joseph Dion SR + Yvonne Modeste Bernier	Jean Baptiste Paulin + Thérèse Canivet
Joseph Dion JR + Julie Chesnel	Thérèse Paulin + Julien Lanteigne
Joseph Adélard Dion + Marcelline Letourneau	Jacques (Jimmie) Lanteigne + Marie Anne Hébert
Adélard Dion + Esther Levesque	Justine Lanteigne + Alexis dit Alexandre Landry
Charles Edouard Dion + Ernestine Barriault	Marie Landry + Louis Breau
Adhémar Dion + Thérèse Tanguay	André Breau + Marie Philomène Mallet
Céline Dion	Mary Catherine (Kay) Breau + James Henry (Harry) Feeley
	Anne Elizabeth Feeley + Albert (Al) Doucette
	Michele Anne Doucette

I am a 10th cousin twice removed with Céline Dion.

Zacharie Cloutier + Sainte Dupont	Zacharie Cloutier + Sainte Dupont
<u>Zacharie Cloutier</u> + Madeleine Aymard	<u>Zacharie Cloutier</u> + Madeleine Aymard
Geneviève Cloutier + Joseph Guyon	René Cloutier + Marie LeBlanc
Marie Madeleine Guyon + Antoine Goulet	Marie Catherine Cloutier + Alexis Gagné dit Béllavance, Sieur de La Fresnaye
Marie Madeleine Goulet and François Sarrazin	Marie Gagné dit Béllavance + Jean Baptiste Poulin
François Sarrazin and Marguerite Benoit	Jean Baptiste Paulin + Thérèse Canivet
Marie Louise Sarrazin and François Charbonneau	Thérèse Paulin + Julien Lanteigne
François Charbonneau and Marie Pélagie Sylvestre	Jacques (Jimmie) Lanteigne + Marie Anne Hébert
Antoine Charbonneau and Marie Louise Lagarde dit St-Jean	Justine Lanteigne + Alexis dit Alexandre Landry
Zoé Charbonneau and Eusèbe Brisebois	Marie Landry + Louis Breau
Moïse Brisebois and Esther Anne Firmin	André Breau + Marie Philomène Mallet
Marie Eliza Brisebois and James Bertram Morrison	Mary Catherine (Kay) Breau + James Henry (Harry) Feeley
George Bertram Morrison and Eileen Pearce	Anne Elizabeth Feeley + Albert (Al) Doucette
Clarence Edwards and Sharron Morrison	**Michele Anne Doucette**
Eilleen Regina Edwards **aka Shania Twain**	

I am an 11th cousin once removed with Shania Twain.

<u>Zacharie Cloutier</u> + Sainte Dupont	<u>Zacharie Cloutier</u> + Sainte Dupont
Charles Cloutier + Marie Morin	Zacharie Cloutier + Madeleine Aymard
Élisabeth Ursule Cloutier + Nicolas Gamache	René Cloutier + Marie LeBlanc
Élisabeth Isabelle Gamache + Pierre Richard	Marie Catherine Cloutier + Alexis Gagné dit Béllavance, Sieur de La Fresnaye
Jean Baptiste Richard + Marie Angélique Boucher	Marie Gagné dit Béllavance + Jean Baptiste Poulin
Marie Anne Richard + Pierre Maillet	Jean Baptiste Paulin + Thérèse Canivet
Jean Baptiste Maillet + Ursule Maufette	Thérèse Paulin + Julien Lanteigne
Désiré Maillet + Julie Durand	Jacques (Jimmie) Lanteigne + Marie Anne Hébert
Désiré Charles Mayette + Sophia Olivia Fortier	Justine Lanteigne + Alexis dit Alexandre Landry
Delina Adeline Mayette + Louis Bertrand	Marie Landry + Louis Breau
Georges Bertrand + Angeline Leduc	André Breau + Marie Philomène Mallet
Rolland Bertrand + Lois June Gouwens	Mary Catherine (Kay) Breau + James Henry (Harry) Feeley
Marcia Lynne (Marceline) Bertrand + Jonathan Voight	Anne Elizabeth Feeley + Albert (Al) Doucette
Angelina Jolie	**Michele Anne Doucette**

I am a 12th cousin with Angelina Jolie.

<u>Zacharie Cloutier + Sainte Dupont</u>	<u>Zacharie Cloutier + Sainte Dupont</u>
Jean Cloutier + Marie Martin	Zacharie Cloutier + Madeleine Aymard
Jean Cloutier + Louise Bélanger	René Cloutier + Marie LeBlanc
Marie Anne Cloutier + Nicolas Morissette	Marie Catherine Cloutier + Alexis Gagné dit Béllavance, Sieur de La Fresnaye
Joseph Morissette + Marie Anne Guillemette	Marie Gagné dit Béllavance + Jean Baptiste Poulin
Joseph Marie Morissette + Catherine Blais	Jean Baptiste Paulin + Thérèse Canivet
Joseph Morissette + Marie Barbe Couture dit Lamonde	Thérèse Paulin + Julien Lanteigne
Édouard Morissette + Marine Boulé	Jacques (Jimmie) Lanteigne + Marie Anne Hébert
Joseph Hilaire Morissette + Noëlla McConnell	Justine Lanteigne + Alexis dit Alexandre Landry
Alan Joseph Morissette + Lucille Huneau	Marie Landry + Louis Breau
Alan Richard Morissette + Georgia Mary Ann Feuerstein	André Breau + Marie Philomène Mallet
Alanis Nadine Morissette (twin to Wade)	Mary Catherine (Kay) Breau + James Henry (Harry) Feeley
	Anne Elizabeth Feeley + Albert (Al) Doucette
	Michele Anne Doucette

I am a 10th cousin twice removed with Alanis Morissette.

Celebrity Relations 4

Pierre Gagné + Marguerite Rosée	Pierre Gagné + Marguerite Rosée
Louis Gagné dit Béllavance + Louise Picard	Louis Gagné dit Béllavance + Louise Picard
Marie Geneviève Gagné + Jean Baptiste Blanchet	Alexis Gagné dit Béllavance + Marie Catherine Cloutier
François Blanchet + Claire Fournier	Marie Gagné dit Béllavance + Jean Baptiste Poulin
Marie Françoise Blanchet + François Boulet	Jean Baptiste Paulin + Thérèse Canivet
Élisabeth Boulet + François Chesnel	Thérèse Paulin + Julien Lanteigne
Julie Chesnel + Joseph Dion JR	Jacques (Jimmie) Lanteigne + Marie Anne Hébert
Joseph Adélard Dion + Marcelline Letourneau	Justine Lanteigne + Alexis dit Alexandre Landry
Adélard Dion + Esther Levesque	Marie Landry + Louis Breau
Charles Edouard Dion + Ernestine Barriault	André Breau + Marie Philomène Mallet
Adhémar Dion + Thérèse Tanguay	Mary Catherine (Kay) Breau + James Henry (Harry) Feeley
Céline Dion	Anne Elizabeth Feeley + Albert (Al) Doucette
	Michele Anne Doucette

I am a 9th cousin once removed with Céline Dion.

Pierre Gagné + Marguerite Rosée	Pierre Gagné + Marguerite Rosée
<u>Louis Gagné dit Béllavance</u> + Louise Picard	<u>Louis Gagné dit Béllavance</u> + Louise Picard
Marie Anne Gagné + Pierre Guillaume Blanchet	Alexis Gagné dit Béllavance + Marie Catherine Cloutier
Françoise Blanchet + Louis Fortin	Marie Gagné dit Béllavance + Jean Baptiste Poulin
François Victor Fortin + Marie Louise Durand	Jean Baptiste Paulin + Thérèse Canivet
Geneviève Fortin + Joseph Fortin	Thérèse Paulin + Julien Lanteigne
François Fortin + Victoire Blier	Jacques (Jimmie) Lanteigne + Marie Anne Hébert
Henri Nazaire Fortin + Émilie Daniel	Justine Lanteigne + Alexis dit Alexandre Landry
Henri Guillaume Fortin + Marie Louise Demers	Marie Landry + Louis Breau
Elsie Mae Fortin + Willard Fortin	André Breau + Marie Philomène Mallet
Madonna Louise Fortin + Silvio Anthony Ciccone	Mary Catherine (Kay) Breau + James Henry (Harry) Feeley
Madonna Veronica Louise Ciccone	Anne Elizabeth Feeley + Albert (Al) Doucette
	Michele Anne Doucette

I am a 9th cousin once removed with Madonna.

Pierre Gagné + Marguerite Rosée	Pierre Gagné + Marguerite Rosée
Marie Marguerite Gagné + Pierre Lefebvre	Louis Gagné dit Béllavance + Louise Picard
Marguerite Lefebvre + Pierre Bourdeau	Alexis Gagné dit Béllavance + Marie Catherine Cloutier
Joseph Bourdeau + Marguerite Guérin	Marie Gagné dit Béllavance + Jean Baptiste Poulin
Catherine Véronique Bourdeau + Simon Campeau	Jean Baptiste Paulin + Thérèse Canivet
Archange Campeau + John Robert McDougall	Thérèse Paulin + Julien Lanteigne
James McDougall + Catherine Godet	Jacques (Jimmie) Lanteigne + Marie Anne Hébert
Mary Anne Frances McDougall + Antoine Martin	Justine Lanteigne + Alexis dit Alexandre Landry
Delia Martin + Daniel Murray	Marie Landry + Louis Breau
Della Murray + Edwin John Howell	André Breau + Marie Philomène Mallet
Dorothy Emma Howell + Hugh Ellsworth Rodham	Mary Catherine (Kay) Breau + James Henry (Harry) Feeley
Hillary Diane Rodham Clinton	Anne Elizabeth Feeley + Albert (Al) Doucette
	Michele Anne Doucette

I am a 10th cousin once removed with Hillary Rodham Clinton.

Pierre Gagné + Marguerite Rosée	Pierre Gagné + Marguerite Rosée
Louis Gagné dit Béllavance + Louise Picard	Louis Gagné dit Béllavance + Louise Picard
Pierre Gagné + Geneviève Fournier	Alexis Gagné dit Béllavance + Marie Catherine Cloutier
Pierre Gagné + Geneviève Letourneau	Marie Gagné dit Béllavance + Jean Baptiste Poulin
Jean Baptiste Gagné + Marie Anne Pellerin	Jean Baptiste Paulin + Thérèse Canivet
Jean Baptiste Gagné + Thérèse Roy	Thérèse Paulin + Julien Lanteigne
Vital Gagné + Marguerite Chamberland	Jacques (Jimmie) Lanteigne + Marie Anne Hébert
Hermine Gagné + Nazaire Mercier	Justine Lanteigne + Alexis dit Alexandre Landry
Marie Mercier + Joseph Morissette	Marie Landry + Louis Breau
Joseph Hilaire Morissette + Noëlla McConnell	André Breau + Marie Philomène Mallet
Alan Joseph Morissette + Lucille Huneau	Mary Catherine (Kay) Breau + James Henry (Harry) Feeley
Alan Richard Morissette + Georgia Mary Ann Feuerstein	Anne Elizabeth Feeley + Albert (Al) Doucette
Alanis Nadine Morissette (twin to Wade)	**Michele Anne Doucette**

I am a 10th cousin with Alanis Morissette.

Pierre Gagné + Marguerite Rosée	Pierre Gagné + Marguerite Rosée
Pierre Gagné dit Béllavance + Catherine Dobigeon	Louis Gagné dit Béllavance + Louise Picard
Louis Étienne Gagné + Anne Marie Tessier	Alexis Gagné dit Béllavance + Marie Catherine Cloutier
Pierre Gagné + Marie Catherine Longtin	Marie Gagné dit Béllavance + Jean Baptiste Poulin
René Amable Gagné + Marie Renée Hamelin	Jean Baptiste Paulin + Thérèse Canivet
Marguerite Gagné + Louis Trudeau	Thérèse Paulin + Julien Lanteigne
Louis Trudeau + Louise Dupuis	Jacques (Jimmie) Lanteigne + Marie Anne Hébert
Joseph Trudeau + Marie Malvina Cardinal	Justine Lanteigne + Alexis dit Alexandre Landry
Charles Émile Trudeau + Grace Elliott	Marie Landry + Louis Breau
Pierre Philippe Yves Elliott Trudeau + Margaret Sinclair	André Breau + Marie Philomène Mallet
Justin Pierre James Trudeau	Mary Catherine (Kay) Breau + James Henry (Harry) Feeley
	Anne Elizabeth Feeley + Albert (Al) Doucette
	Michele Anne Doucette

I am a 8th cousin three times removed with Pierre Philippe Yves Elliott Trudeau (15th Prime Minister of Canada).

I am a 9th cousin twice removed with Justin Pierre James Trudeau (23rd Prime Minister of Canada).

Celebrity Relations 5

Jean Guyon + Mathurine Robin	Jean Guyon + Mathurine Robin
Jean Guyon + Élisabeth Isabelle Couillard	Marie Guyon + François Bélanger
Pierre Guyon + Angélique Testu	Françoise Charlotte Bélanger + Jean Langlois dit Boisverdun
Louis Guyon + Marguerite Anne Gamache	Marie Madeleine Langlois dit Boisverdun + Jean LeClerc dit Francoeur
Joseph Joachim Dion + Marguerite Fournier	Joseph LeClerc dit Francoeur + Marguerite Françoise Durand
Joseph Dion SR + Yvonne Modeste Bernier	Jean Baptiste LeClerc dit Francoeur + Marie Josèphe (Josette) Duval
Joseph Dion JR + Julie Chesnel	Jean Baptiste LeClerc dit Francoeur + Madeleine Thébault
Joseph Adélard Dion + Marcelline Letourneau	Madeleine LeClerc + Pascal Landry
Adélard Dion + Esther Levesque	Alexis dit Alexandre Landry + Justine Lanteigne
Charles Edouard Dion + Ernestine Barriault	Marie Landry + Louis Breau
Adhémar Dion + Thérèse Tanguay	André Breau + Marie Philomène Mallet
Céline Dion	Mary Catherine (Kay) Breau + James Henry (Harry) Feeley
	Anne Elizabeth Feeley + Albert (Al) Doucette
	Michele Anne Doucette

I am a 10th cousin twice removed with Céline Dion.

Jean Guyon + Mathurine Robin	Jean Guyon + Mathurine Robin
François Guyon + Marie Madeleine Marsolet	Marie Guyon + François Bélanger
Geneviève Guyon + François de Chavigny	Françoise Charlotte Bélanger + Jean Langlois dit Boisverdun
Geneviève de Chavigny + Joseph Marie Hamelin	Marie Madeleine Langlois dit Boisverdun + Jean LeClerc dit Francoeur
Marguerite Euphrosine Hamelin + Daniel Daniel	Joseph LeClerc dit Francoeur + Marguerite Françoise Durand
Pierre Daniel + Rose Chavigny de La Chevrotière	Jean Baptiste LeClerc dit Francoeur + Marie Josèphe (Josette) Duval
Isodore Daniel + Marie Louise Orion	Jean Baptiste LeClerc dit Francoeur + Madeleine Thébault
Émilie Daniel + Henri Nazaire Fortin	Madeleine LeClerc + Pascal Landry
Henri Guillaume Fortin + Marie Louise Demers	Alexis dit Alexandre Landry + Justine Lanteigne
Elsie Mae Fortin + Willard Fortin	Marie Landry + Louis Breau
Madonna Louise Fortin + Silvio Anthony Ciccone	André Breau + Marie Philomène Mallet
Madonna Veronica Louise Ciccone	Mary Catherine (Kay) Breau + James Henry (Harry) Feeley
	Anne Elizabeth Feeley + Albert (Al) Doucette
	Michele Anne Doucette

I am a 10th cousin twice removed with Madonna.

Jean Guyon + Mathurine Robin	Jean Guyon + Mathurine Robin
Jean Guyon + Élisabeth Isabelle Couillard	Marie Guyon + François Bélanger
Joseph Guyon + Geneviève Cloutier	Françoise Charlotte Bélanger + Jean Langlois dit Boisverdun
Joseph Guyon + Marie Élisabeth Guillet	Marie Madeleine Langlois dit Boisverdun + Jean LeClerc dit Francoeur
Marie Josèphe Guyon + Michel Coursolle	Joseph LeClerc dit Francoeur + Marguerite Françoise Durand
Marie Charlotte Coursolle + Ephraim Jones	Jean Baptiste LeClerc dit Francoeur + Marie Josèphe (Josette) Duval
Sophia Jones + John Stuart	Jean Baptiste LeClerc dit Francoeur + Madeleine Thébault
Mary Elizabeth Stuart + Sir Allan Napier MacNab, 1st Baronet, Premier of Canada West	Madeleine LeClerc + Pascal Landry
Sophia Mary MacNab + William Coutts Keppel, 7th Earl of Albermarle	Alexis dit Alexandre Landry + Justine Lanteigne
Colonel George Keppel of Albermarle + Alice Frederica Edmonstone	Marie Landry + Louis Breau
Sonia Rosemary Keppel + Roland Calvert Cubitt, 3rd Baron of Ashcombe	André Breau + Marie Philomène Mallet
Rosalind Maud Cubitt + Major Bruce Middleton Hope Shand	Mary Catherine (Kay) Breau + James Henry (Harry) Feeley
Camilla Rosemary Shand, Duchess of Cornwall	Anne Elizabeth Feeley + Albert (Al) Doucette
	Michele Anne Doucette

I am an 11th cousin once removed with Camilla Rosemary Shand, Duchess of Cornwall (second wife of Prince Charles).

Jean Guyon + Mathurine Robin	Jean Guyon + Mathurine Robin
Jean Guyon + Élisabeth Isabelle Couillard	Marie Guyon + François Bélanger
Catherine Gertrude Guyon + Denis Belleperche	Françoise Charlotte Bélanger + Jean Langlois dit Boisverdun
Pierre Belleperche + Marie Anne Campeau	Marie Madeleine Langlois dit Boisverdun + Jean LeClerc dit Francoeur
Jeanne Belleperche + Joseph Pilet	Joseph LeClerc dit Francoeur + Marguerite Françoise Durand
Jeanne Marie Pilet + Joseph Charles Godet	Jean Baptiste LeClerc dit Francoeur + Marie Josèphe (Josette) Duval
Catherine Godet + James McDougall	Jean Baptiste LeClerc dit Francoeur + Madeleine Thébault
Mary Anne Frances McDougall + Antoine Martin	Madeleine LeClerc + Pascal Landry
Delia Martin + Daniel Murray	Alexis dit Alexandre Landry + Justine Lanteigne
Della Murray + Edwin John Howell	Marie Landry + Louis Breau
Dorothy Emma Howell + Hugh Ellsworth Rodham	André Breau + Marie Philomène Mallet
Hillary Diane Rodham Clinton	Mary Catherine (Kay) Breau + James Henry (Harry) Feeley
	Anne Elizabeth Feeley + Albert (Al) Doucette
	Michele Anne Doucette

I am a 10th cousin twice removed with Hillary Rodham Clinton.

Jean Guyon + Mathurine Robin	Jean Guyon + Mathurine Robin
Jean Guyon + Élisabeth Isabelle Couillard	Marie Guyon + François Bélanger
Marie Madeleine Guyon + Antoine Goulet	Françoise Charlotte Bélanger + Jean Langlois dit Boisverdun
Marie Madeleine Goulet + François Sarrazin	Marie Madeleine Langlois dit Boisverdun + Jean LeClerc dit Francoeur
François Sarrazin + Marie Marguerite Renaud Benoit	Joseph LeClerc dit Francoeur + Marguerite Françoise Durand
Marie Louise Sarrazin + François Charbonneau	Jean Baptiste LeClerc dit Francoeur + Marie Josèphe (Josette) Duval
François Charbonneau and Marie Pélagie Sylvestre	Jean Baptiste LeClerc dit Francoeur + Madeleine Thébault
Antoine Charbonneau and Marie Louise Lagarde dit St-Jean	Madeleine LeClerc + Pascal Landry
Zoé Charbonneau and Eusèbe Brisebois	Alexis dit Alexandre Landry + Justine Lanteigne
Moïse Brisebois and Esther Anne Firmin	Marie Landry + Louis Breau
Marie Eliza Brisebois and James Bertram Morrison	André Breau + Marie Philomène Mallet
George Bertram Morrison and Eileen Pearce	Mary Catherine (Kay) Breau + James Henry (Harry) Feeley
Clarence Edwards and Sharron Morrison	Anne Elizabeth Feeley + Albert (Al) Doucette
Eilleen Regina Edwards **aka Shania Twain**	**Michele Anne Doucette**

I am a 12th cousin with Shania Twain.

Jean Guyon + Mathurine Robin	Jean Guyon + Mathurine Robin
Claude Guyon + Catherine Colin	Marie Guyon + François Bélanger
Claude Guyon + Marie Catherine Blouin	Françoise Charlotte Bélanger + Jean Langlois dit Boisverdun
Joseph Guyon + Marie Brigitte Baucher	Marie Madeleine Langlois dit Boisverdun + Jean LeClerc dit Francoeur
Jean Baptiste Guyon + Marie Genevièe Morriset	Joseph LeClerc dit Francoeur + Marguerite Françoise Durand
Jean Baptiste Guyon + Françoise Lemieux	Jean Baptiste LeClerc dit Francoeur + Marie Josèphe (Josette) Duval
François Dion + Mathilde Bérubé	Jean Baptiste LeClerc dit Francoeur + Madeleine Thébault
Candide Dion + Louise Dubé	Madeleine LeClerc + Pascal Landry
Thomas Dion + Alice Dancause	Alexis dit Alexandre Landry + Justine Lanteigne
Léon Dion + Denyse Kormann	Marie Landry + Louis Breau
Stéphane Dion	André Breau + Marie Philomène Mallet
	Mary Catherine (Kay) Breau + James Henry (Harry) Feeley
	Anne Elizabeth Feeley + Albert (Al) Doucette
	Michele Anne Doucette

I am a 9th cousin three times removed with Stéphane Dion.

Celebrity Relations 6

Pierre Michaud + Marie Ancelin	Pierre Michaud + Marie Ancelin
Jean Baptiste Michaud + Marie Françoise Dupille	Pierre Michaud + Marie Madeleine Thibodeau dit Lalime
Jacques Michaud + Marie Josèphe Ouellet	Marie Angélique Michaud + Gilles Parisé
Marie Anne Michaud + Joseph Marie Roy dit Desjardins	Michel Ignace Parisé + Marie Albert
Hilaire Roy + Céleste LeVasseur	Marie Parisé + Jean Lanteigne
Étienne Roy dit Desjardins + Hélène Guéret	Jean Lanteigne + Marie Blanchard
Elzéar Roy dit Desjardins + Philomène Martin	Françoise Lanteigne + Agapit Doiron
Alfred Frédéric Voisine + Anna Soucy	Romaine Doiron + Jacques (James) Mallet
Maurille Voisine + Dorina Racine	Marie Philomène Mallet + André Breau
Réal Voisine + Zélande Robichaud	Mary Catherine (Kay) Breau + James Henry (Harry) Feeley
Roch Voisine	Anne Elizabeth Feeley + Albert (Al) Doucette
	Michele Anne Doucette

I am a 9th cousin once removed with Roch Voisine.

Pierre Michaud + Marie Ancelin	Pierre Michaud + Marie Ancelin
Jean Baptiste Michaud + Marie Françoise Dupille	Pierre Michaud + Marie Madeleine Thibodeau dit Lalime
Jacques Michaud + Marie Josèphe Ouellet	Marie Élisabeth Michaud + Pierre LeVasseur
Marie Anne Michaud + Joseph Marie Roy dit Desjardins	Joseph Clémont LeVasseur + Marie Madeleine Albert
Hilaire Roy + Céleste LeVasseur	Marie Josèphe LeVasseur + Charles Landry
Étienne Roy dit Desjardins + Hélène Guéret	Pascal Landry + Marie Véronique Guéret dit Dumont
Elzéar Roy dit Desjardins + Philomène Martin	Jean Pascal Landry + Madeleine LeClerc
Alfred Frédéric Voisine + Anna Soucy	Alexis dit Alexandre Landry + Justine Lanteigne
Maurille Voisine + Dorina Racine	Marie Landry + Louis Breau
Réal Voisine + Zélande Robichaud	André Breau + Marie Philomène Mallet
Roch Voisine	Mary Catherine (Kay) Breau + James Henry (Harry) Feeley
	Anne Elizabeth Feeley + Albert (Al) Doucette
	Michele Anne Doucette

I am a 9th cousin twice removed with Roch Voisine.

Celebrity Relations 7

Many people of French-Canadian ancestry can also claim descent from **Jacques Guéret dit Dumont**.

Jacques Guéret is my second French Canadian royal gateway ancestor, meaning that he presents a further connection from New France to medieval nobility.

Jean Gueret + Françoise de Méhérenc de Montmirel	Jean Gueret + Françoise de Méhérenc de Montmirel
René Guéret + Madeleine Vigoureaux	René Guéret + Madeleine Vigoureaux
<u>Jacques Guéret dit Dumont</u> + Anne Tardif	<u>Jacques Guéret dit Dumont</u> + Anne Tardif
Michel Guéret dit Dumont + Rose LeVasseur	Prisque Guéret dit Dumont + Marie Catherine Maupas dit Saint-Hilaire
Euphrosine Dumont + François Martin	Pierre Guéret dit Dumont + Marie Madeleine Véronique Morel dit La Durantaye
Michel Martin + Louise Thériault	Marie Véronique Guéret dit Dumont + Pascal Landry
Vital Martin + Suzanne Hébert	Jean Pascal Landry + Madeleine LeClerc
Philomène Martin + Elzéar Roy dit Desjardins	Alexis dit Alexandre Landry + Justine Lanteigne
Alfred Frédéric Voisine + Anna Soucy	Marie Landry + Louis Breau
Maurille Voisine + Dorina Racine	André Breau + Marie Philomène Mallet
Réal Voisine + Zélande Robichaud [144]	Mary Catherine (Kay) Breau + James Henry (Harry) Feeley
Roch Voisine	Anne Elizabeth Feeley + Albert (Al) Doucette
	Michele Anne Doucette

I am an 8th cousin once removed with Roch Voisine.

---

[144] https://www.nosorigines.qc.ca/GenealogieQuebec.aspx?genealogy=Voisine_Rock&pid=1467&lng=en

Celebrity Relations 8

Robert Caron + Marie Crevet	Robert Caron + Marie Crevet
Jean Baptiste Caron + Marguerite Gagnon	Marie Caron + Jean Picard
Marguerite Caron + Noël Paré	Louise Picard + Louis Gagné dit Béllavance
Louis Pierre Paré + Marie Josèphte Guay	Alexis Gagné dit Béllavance + Marie Catherine Cloutier
Marie Josèphte Paré + Marc François Carré	Marie Gagné dit Béllavance + Jean Baptiste Poulin
René François Carré + Marguerite Bigras	Jean Baptiste Paulin + Thérèse Canivet
François-Marie Amable Carré + Marie Louise Martin-Ladouceur	Thérèse Paulin + Julien Lanteigne
François Carré + Marie Joly	Jacques (Jimmie) Lanteigne + Marie Anne Hébert
François Carré + Emilie Labelle	Justine Lanteigne + Alexis dit Alexandre Landry
Pierre Carré + Melina Clémont	Marie Landry + Louis Breau
François Carré + Angeline Sauvé	André Breau + Marie Philomène Mallet
Percy Carrey + Katherine Oram	Mary Catherine (Kay) Breau + James Henry (Harry) Feeley
James Eugene Carrey	Anne Elizabeth Feeley + Albert (Al) Doucette
	Michele Anne Doucette

I am an 11th cousin once removed with Jim Carrey. [145]

---

[145] michaelmarcotte.com/carrey.htm

Celebrity Relations 9

Martin Aucoin + Barbe Minguet	Martin Aucoin + Barbe Minguet
Jeanne Aucoin + François Girouard dit LaVaranne	Jeanne Aucoin + François Girouard dit LaVaranne
<u>Marie Madeleine Girouard</u> + Thomas Cormier	<u>Marie Madeleine Girouard</u> + Thomas Cormier
Claire Cormier + Pierre Cyr	Alexis Cormier + Marie LeBlanc
Anne Cyr + Ambroise Martin dit Barnabe	Marguerite Cormier + Pierre Arseneau
Joseph Martin dit Barnabe + Marguerite Pitre	Marie Arseneau + Jean Victor (dit Menou) Breau
Joseph Martin + Marie Charpentier	Jean Magloire Breau + Marie Madeleine Bastarache dit Basque
Pierre Numa Martin + Marguerite Élodie Bossier	Simon Breau + Marie Brideau
Emile Paul Martin + Jennie Dixon (Dickson)	Louis Breau + Marie Landry
Ruth Elodie Martin + Elliott DeGeneres	André Breau + Marie Philomène Mallet
Elliott Everett DeGeneres + Elizabeth Pfeffer	Mary Catherine (Kay) Breau + James Henry (Harry) Feeley
Ellen DeGeneres	Anne Elizabeth Feeley + Albert (Al) Doucette
	Michele Anne Doucette

I am an 8th cousin once removed with Ellen DeGeneres.

Celebrity Relations 10

<u>Joseph Mathurin Meunier</u> + Françoise Fafard	<u>Joseph Mathurin Meunier</u> + Françoise Fafard
Elisabeth Meunier + Isaac Paquet dit Pasquier dit Lavallée	Jean Meunier + Marguerite Housseau
Charles Paquet dit Pasquier dit Lavallée + Jeanne Coulombe	Marguerite Meunier + François Michel dit La Ruine
Charles Paquet dit Lavallée + Marie Charlotte Allaire	Élisabeth (Isabelle) Michel + Jean Vincent dit Clémont
André Lavallée dit Paquet + Agathe Coitou dit St-Jean	Marie Josèphe Vincent + Joseph Hébert
Jean Baptiste Lavallée dit Paquet + Josette Dansereau	Joseph Hébert + Théotiste Doucet
Augustin Jean-Baptiste Lavallée dit Paquet + Charlotte Lalu dit Lamontagne	Joseph Hébert + Anne dite Nanette Chiasson
Augustin Jean-Baptiste Lavallée dit Paquet + Caroline Valentin dit Gregoire	Marie Anne Hébert + Jacques (Jimmie) Lanteigne
Calixa Lavallée	Justine Lanteinge + Alexis dit Alexandre Landry
	Marie Landry + Louis Breau
	André Breau + Marie Philomène Mallet
	Mary Catherine (Kay) Breau + James Henry (Harry) Feeley
	Anne Elizabeth Feeley + Albert (Al) Doucette
	Michele Anne Doucette

I am a 7th cousin five times removed with Calixa Lavallée, composer of the Canadian National Anthem. [146]

---

[146] michaelmarcotte.com/calixaL.htm

Celebrity Relations 11

Daniel LeBlanc + Françoise Gaudet	Daniel LeBlanc + Françoise Gaudet
<u>Jacques LeBlanc</u> + Catherine Hébert	<u>Jacques LeBlanc</u> + Catherine Hébert
François LeBlanc + Marguerite Boudrot	Marie LeBlanc + Alexis Cormier
Jacques LeBlanc + Nathalie Breau	Marguerite Cormier + Pierre Arseneau
Simon LeBlanc + Madeleine Richard	Marie Arseneau + Jean Victor (dit Menou) Breau
Sylvain LeBlanc + Marie Anne Cormier	Jean Magloire Breau + Marie Madeleine Bastarache dit Basque
Ferdinand LeBlanc + Marcelline Ouellet	Simon Breau + Marie Brideau
Ozime Ferdinand LeBlanc + Marie Marguerite Cormier	Louis Breau + Marie Landry
Henry J. LeBlanc + Genevieve Melanson	André Breau + Marie Philomène Mallet
Paul LeBlanc + Pat Grossman	Mary Catherine (Kay) Breau + James Henry (Harry) Feeley
Matt LeBlanc	Anne Elizabeth Feeley + Albert (Al) Doucette
	Michele Anne Doucette

I am an 8th cousin once removed with Matt LeBlanc (of the TV series, *Friends*). [147]

---

[147] michaelmarcotte.com/13blanc.html

Celebrity Relations 12

Thomas LeVasseur + Germaine Legris	Thomas LeVasseur + Germaine Legris
Jean LeVasseur + Marguerite Maheu	Jean LeVasseur + Marguerite Maheu
Laurent LeVasseur + Marie Marchand	Laurent LeVasseur + Marie Marchand
<u>Pierre LeVasseur</u> + Élisabeth Michaud	<u>Pierre LeVasseur</u> + Élisabeth Michaud
Jean Timothée LeVasseur + Claire Nadeau	Joseph Clémont LeVasseur + Marie Madeleine Albert
Étienne LeVasseur + Marie Angélique Michaud	Marie Josèphe LeVasseur + Charles Landry
Céleste LeVasseur + Hilaire Roy	Pascal Landry + Marie Véronique Guéret dit Dumont
Étienne Roy dit Desjardins + Hélène Guéret	Jean Pascal Landry + Madeleine LeClerc
Elzéar Roy dit Desjardins + Philomène Martin	Alexis dit Alexandre Landry + Justine Lanteigne
Alfred Frédéric Voisine + Anna Soucy	Marie Landry + Louis Breau
Maurille Voisine + Dorina Racine	André Breau + Marie Philomène Mallet
Réal Voisine + Zélande Robichaud	Mary Catherine (Kay) Breau + James Henry (Harry) Feeley
Roch Voisine	Anne Elizabeth Feeley + Albert (Al) Doucette
	Michele Anne Doucette

I am an 8th cousin once removed with Roch Voisine.

Celebrity Relations 13

Jean Blanchard + Radegonde Lambert	Jean Blanchard + Radegonde Lambert
Madeleine Blanchard + Michel Richard dit Sansoucy	Martin Blanchard + Françoise LeBlanc
Pierre Richard + Marguerite Landry	René Blanchard + Anne Landry
Anne Richard + Joseph Granger	René Blanchard + Marguerite Thériot
Rosalie Granger + Mathias Phaneuf	Olivier Blanchard + Catherine Amireau dit Mirau
Jean Félicien Phaneuf + Marguerite Bergeron	Raphaël Blanchard + Pélagie Doucet
Marcelline Phaneuf + Paul Paquin III	Marie Blanchard + Jean Lanteigne
Adélard Paquin + Marie Allaire	Françoise Lanteigne + Agapit Doiron
Albert Joseph Paquin + Agnes Jansen	Romaine Doiron + Jacques (Jim) Mallet
Brian Paquin + Marie Brophy	Marie Philomène Mallet + André Breau
Anna Paquin	Mary Catherine (Kay) Breau + James Henry (Harry) Feeley
	Anne Elizabeth Feeley + Albert (Al) Doucette
	Michele Anne Doucette

I am a 9th cousin twice removed with Anna Paquin.

Fly-Away Home (1996) was my first introduction to her as an actress.

She plays the mutant heroine Rogue in *X-Men* (2000), *X-Men 2* (2003), *X-Men: The Last Stand* (2006) and *X-Men: Days of Future Past* (2014).

Celebrity Relations 14

Jean Doiron + Marie Anne Canol	Jean Doiron + Marie Anne Canol
Charles Doiron + Françoise Gaudet	Charles Doiron + Françoise Gaudet
<u>Charles Doiron</u> + Anne Thériault	<u>Charles Doiron</u> + Anne Thériault
Honoré Doiron + Françoise Boudreau [148]	Charles Doiron + Marie Madeleine Thibodeau
Joseph Doiron + Anne Geneviève Hébert	Zacharie Amable Doiron + Anne LeVicaire
Jacques Santiago DeRouen + Marie Charlotte LeReux	Jean Baptiste Doiron + Rose Bouthillier
Jacques DeRouen + Adèle Bonin	Agapit Doiron + Françoise Lanteigne
Joseph Desiré DeRouen + Nathilde Bernard	Romaine Doiron + Jacques (James) Mallet
Gustave DeRouen + Marie Estelle Gary	Marie Philomène Mallet + André Breau
Eugène Gustave DeRouen + Odelia Broussard [149]	Mary Catherine (Kay) Breau + James Henry (Harry) Feeley
Agnès DeRouen + Lumis Albert Beyincé	Anne Elizabeth Feeley + Albert (Al) Doucette
Célestine Ann Beyincé + Matthew Knowles	**Michele Anne Doucette**
Beyoncé Giselle Knowles	

I am an 8th cousin once removed with Beyoncé Knowles.

---

[148] https://trees.ancestry.ca/tree/30695652/person/12545610348
[149] michaelmarcotte.com/beyonce.htm

Celebrity Relations 15

<u>Antoine Hébert</u> + Geneviève Lefranc	<u>Antoine Hébert</u> + Geneviève Lefranc
Jean Hébert + Marie Anne Doucet	Catherine Hébert + Jacques LeBlanc
Jacques Hébert + Jeanne Gautrot	Marie LeBlanc + Alexis Cormier
Jacques Hébert dit Boudiche + Anne Arseneau	Marguerite Cormier + Pierre Arseneau
Ambroise Hébert + Marie Poirier	Marie Arseneau + Jean Victor (dit Menou) Breau
Pierre Hébert + Julie St. Onge	Jean Magloire Breau + Marie Madeleine Bastarache dit Basque
François Hébert + Marguerite Roy	Simon Breau + Marie Brideau
Antoine Joseph Hébert + Rose Bernard	Louis Breau + Marie Landry
Louis Anthony Hébert + Gladys Marie LaMielle	André Breau + Marie Philomène Mallet
Claude (Clyde) Roger Hébert + Yolanda Picola	Mary Catherine (Kay) Breau + James Henry (Harry) Feeley
Marie Rose Hébert + Frank Lawrence Ruffalo	Anne Elizabeth Feeley + Albert (Al) Doucette
Mark Ruffalo	**Michele Anne Doucette**

I am a 10th cousin with Mark Ruffalo, American actor, humanitarian, social activist and film producer.

Celebrity Relations 16

Iréné (dit René) Duguay + Marguerite LeBreton [150]	Iréné (dit René) Duguay + Marguerite LeBreton
Jacques (Jacquot) Duguay + Véronique Chapados	François Duguay + Madeleine Chapadeau
Modeste Duguay + Julien Duguay	Pierre Bonaventure Duguay + Rosalie Chiasson
Adèle Duguay + Nazaire Lagacé	Olive Duguay + Dominique Mallet
Benjamin Meunier dit Lagacé + Elizabeth Smith	Jacques (Jim) Mallet + Romaine Doiron
Benjamin Meunier dit Lagacé + Sophie Adelaide Bélanger	Marie Philomène Mallet + André Breau
Lucille Lagacé + George Edward Trebek	Mary Catherine (Kay) Breau + James Henry (Harry) Feeley
George Alexander (Alex) Trebek	Anne Elizabeth Feeley + Albert (Al) Doucette
	Michele Anne Doucette

I am a 6th cousin once removed with George Alexander (Alex) Trebek, the host of the syndicated game show Jeopardy! since 1984.

---

[150] duguay.fafa-acadie.org/pdf/Reneduguayetsesenfants.pdf

Celebrity Relations 17

I have been attempting to investigate the genealogy of Canadian actor Yannick Bisson of *Murdoch Mysteries* fame; to no avail.

There is a possibility that he, too, may also connect with Gervais Bisson, husband of Marie Lereau. They were married in Saint-Cosme-de-Vair (also known as Saint-Cosme-en-Vairais), Sarthe, France, in 1635. [151] [152] [153]

---

[151] Tanguay, Mgr Cyprien. (1975) <u>Dictionnaire Généalogique des Familles Canadiennes</u>, Volume 1, page 54.
bibnum2.banq.qc.ca/bna/dicoGenealogie/src/0002/0022/0024/0026/3957-1-095.pdf
[152] www.francogene.com/genealogie-quebec-genealogy/195/195888.php
[153] www.francogene.com/genealogie-quebec-genealogy/002/002189.php

Blank Consanguinity Chart

A relationship by blood is also referred to as being related by consanguinity.

A relationship by marriage is sometimes referred to as being related by affinity.

A table or chart of consanguinity is helpful in identifying the degree of cousin relationship between two individuals using their most recent common ancestor as the reference point.

Cousinship between two individuals can then be specifically identified, in degrees and removals, by determining how close, generationally, the common ancestor is to each individual.

Consanguinity Chart [154]

Table of Consanguinity [155]

Feel free to send me an email (address located on the inside cover page) and I will send you a different consanguinity chart that can easily be used for plotting purposes.

---

[154] www.thegordondnaproject.com/Gordon_Consanguinity_Chart.html
[155] www.alanddavis.com/Chart.pdf

In order to ascertain the definitive relationship that exists between two people, begin by plotting the shared ancestor in the top left hand corner.

	Brother Sister	Aunt Uncle Nephew Niece	Great Aunt Uncle Nephew Niece	GG Aunt Uncle Nephew Niece	GGG Aunt Uncle Nephew Niece	GGGG Aunt Uncle Nephew Niece	GGGGG Aunt Uncle Nephew Niece
	Aunt Uncle Nephew Niece	FIRST Cousin	First Cousin Once Removed	First Cousin Twice Removed	First Cousin 3 Times Removed	First Cousin 4 Times Removed	First Cousin 5 Times Removed
	Great Aunt Uncle Nephew Niece	First Cousin Once Removed	SECOND Cousin	Second Cousin Once Removed	Second Cousin Twice Removed	Second Cousin 3 Times Removed	Second Cousin 4 Times Removed
	GG Aunt Uncle Nephew Niece	First Cousin Twice Removed	Second Cousin Once Removed	THIRD Cousin	Third Cousin Once Removed	Third Cousin Twice Removed	Third Cousin 3 Times Removed
	GGG Aunt Uncle Nephew Niece	First Cousin 3 Times Removed	Second Cousin Twice Removed	Third Cousin Once Removed	FOURTH Cousin	Fourth Cousin Once Removed	Fourth Cousin Twice Removed
	GGGG Aunt Uncle Nephew Niece	First Cousin 4 Times Removed	Second Cousin 3 Times Removed	Third Cousin Twice Removed	Fourth Cousin Once Removed	FIFTH Cousin	Fifth Cousin Once Removed
	GGGGG Aunt Uncle Nephew Niece	First Cousin 5 Times Removed	Second Cousin 4 Times Removed	Third Cousin 3 Times Removed	Fourth Cousin Twice Removed	Fifth Cousin Once Removed	SIXTH Cousin

Filles du Roi

The arrival of the French Filles du Roi at Québec (1667)

http://www.canadianheritage.org/reproductions/10100.htm

Filles du Roi was a term that meant daughters (wards) of the King.

These ladies, in large part, started the French Canadian population explosion that has, over 350 years, spread across North America. France was colonizing in North America and with fur traders, storekeepers, indentured servants, dockhands, clerics, farmers, settlers, and soldiers in New France, the population was mostly men.

King Louis XIV quickly came to realize that for this new colony to thrive there must be marriageable women; as a result, he offered 50 livres dowry in addition to whatever the lady brought with her and also sponsored her transportation.

There is a very specific timeframe that identifies these *Filles du Roi*.

They came between 1663 and 1673. Of the nearly 1000 women who undertook the journey, about 800 made it to Canada. These were not ladies of ill repute, some were from wealthy families, some were young widows with children, others were orphans.

As single women, all came to New France as potential marriage partners for the many men of New France. This very successful program helped to populate New France, making the settlement a viable one. Given their dowries, these women were able to choose *who* they wished to marry.

With all that is written about them, the details of *why* they chose to come to New France are, for the most part, lost to history.

One can only hope that at least one made the journey merely to experience the unknown and satisfy a pioneer spirit.

I descend from several *Filles du Roi*; namely,

[1] **Catherine (de) Baillon** (of minor French nobility) married Jacques Miville dit Deschênes on November 12, 1669, at Notre-Dame in Québec. [156] [157] [158] [159]

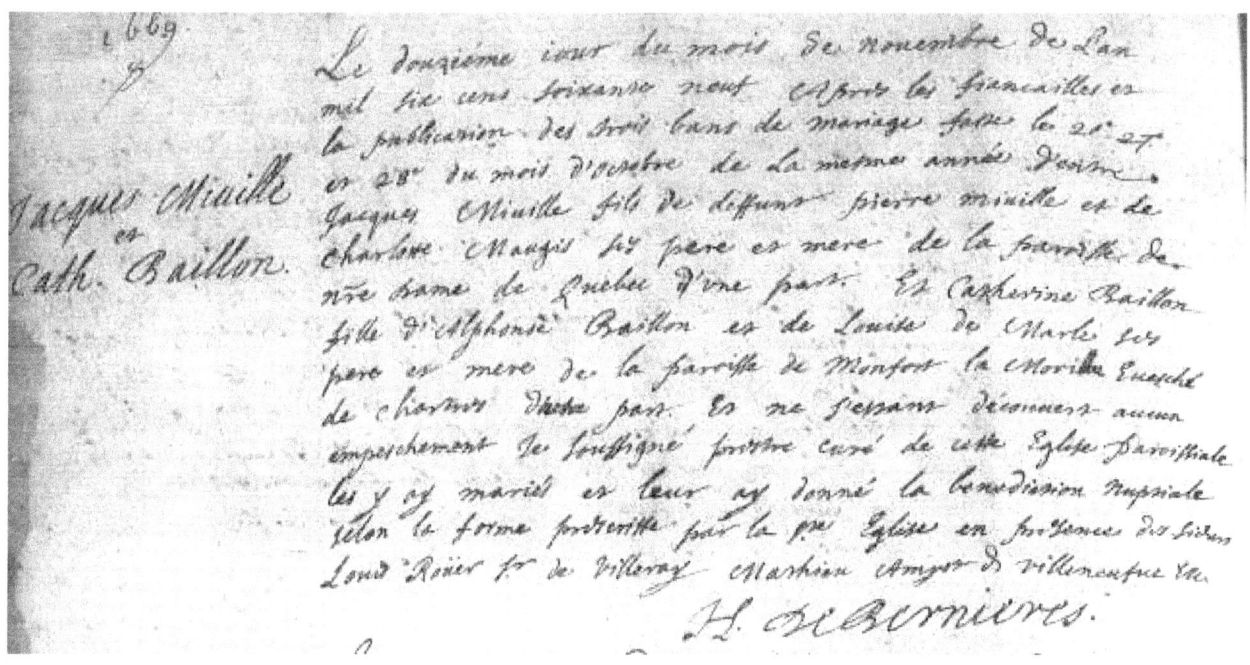

Marriage certificate of Jacques Miville dit Deschênes and Catherine de Baillon
Sources: Archives du Québec

---

[156] www.migrations.fr/ACTESFILLESDUROY/actesfillesduroy_B.htm
[157] https://www.ancestry.ca/interactive/1091/d13p_31410757
[158] https://www.wikitree.com/wiki/Baillon-1
[159] yamachiche.ca/toponymie/genealogie/section1.html

[2] **Marie Madeleine Boutet** (from the from the Île-de-France area) married Gervais Bisson on September 15, 1664 at Notre-Dame in Québec. [160] [161] [162] [163]

Marriage certificate of Gervais Bisson and Marie Madeleine Boutet

Sources: Archives du Québec

[3] **Marie Caillé** (from the Normandie area) married Pierre Paquet on August 26, 1668 at Île d'Orléans, Québec. [164] [165] [166] [167]

---

[160] https://www.ancestry.ca/interactive/1091/d13p_31410481
[161] Tanguay, Mgr Cyprien. (1975) Dictionnaire Généalogique des Familles Canadiennes, Volume 1, page 54.
bibnum2.banq.qc.ca/bna/dicoGenealogie/src/0002/0022/0024/0026/3957-1-095.pdf
[162] www.francogene.com/genealogie-quebec-genealogy/002/002189.php
[163] www.migrations.fr/ACTESFILLESDUROY/actesfillesduroy_B.htm

[4] **Marguerite Housseau** married Jean Meunier on October 5, 1670, at Sainte-Anne-de-Beaupré, Québec. [168] [169] [170] [171]

Marriage certificate of Jean Meunier and Marguerite Housseau

Sources: Archives du Québec

---

[164] Tanguay, Mgr Cyprien. (1975) <u>Dictionnaire Généalogique des Familles Canadiennes</u>, Volume 1, page 466.
bibnum2.banq.qc.ca/bna/dicoGenealogie/src/0002/0022/0052/0053/3957-1-506.pdf
[165] www.francogene.com/genealogie-quebec-genealogy/001/001110.php
[166] https://www.wikitree.com/wiki/Caillé-49
[167] yamachiche.ca/toponymie/genealogie/section4.html
[168] www.migrations.fr/ACTESFILLESDUROY/actesfillesduroy_H.htm
[169] https://www.ancestry.ca/interactive/1091/d13p_30981487
[170] https://www.wikitree.com/wiki/Housseau-3
[171] yamachiche.ca/toponymie/genealogie/section6.html

[5] **Jeanne LeCoq** (from the Île-de-France area) married Martin Moreau (her second husband), a soldier with the Carignan Salières Regiment, on January 18, 1672, at Notre-Dame in Québec. [172] [173] [174] She was first married to Guillaume duBost on September 8, 1670, at Notre-Dame in Québec. [175] [176]

Marriage certificate of Martin Moreau and Jeanne LeCoq

Sources: Archives du Québec

---

[172] https://www.ancestry.ca/interactive/1091/d13p_31410781
[173] https://www.wikitree.com/wiki/LeCocq-6
[174] yamachiche.ca/toponymie/genealogie/section3.html
[175] www.migrations.fr/ACTESFILLESDUROY/actesfillesduroy_L.htm
[176] https://www.wikitree.com/wiki/LeCocq-6

[6] **Marie Morin** married Noël Boissel on July 23, 1669 at Notre-Dame in Québec. [177] [178] [179] [180]

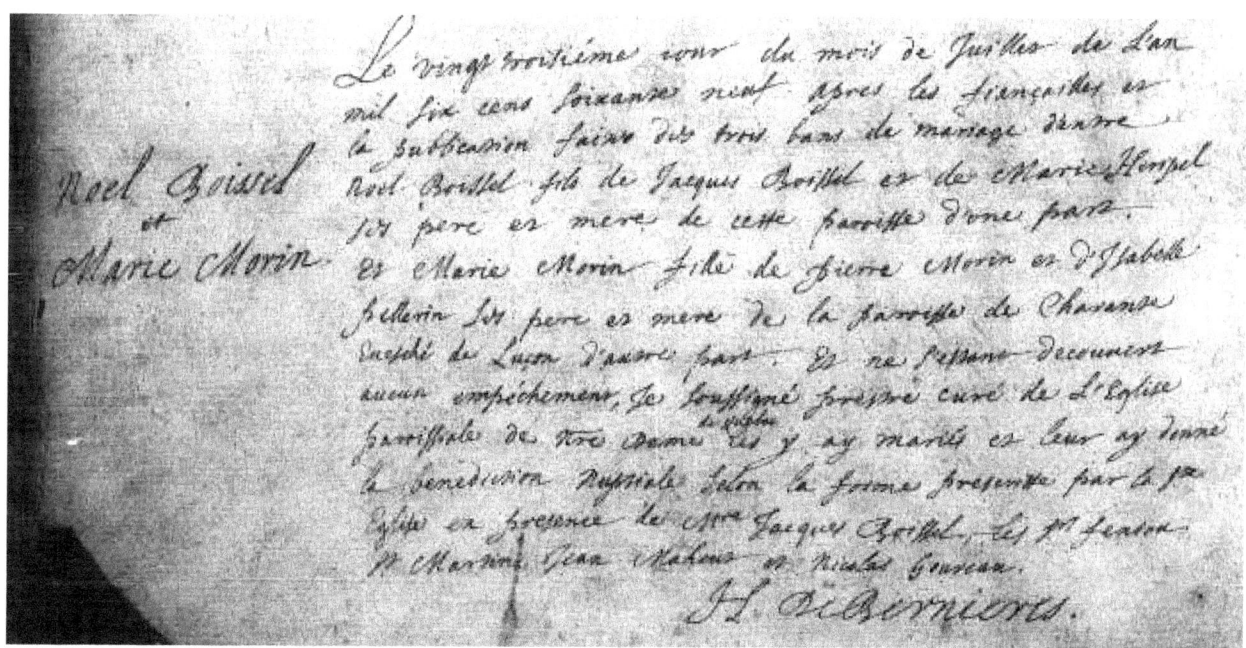

Marriage certificate of Noël Boissel and Marie Morin

Sources: Archives du Québec

---

[177] www.migrations.fr/ACTESFILLESDUROY/actesfillesduroy_M.htm
[178] https://www.ancestry.ca/interactive/1091/d13p_31410747
[179] https://www.wikitree.com/wiki/Morin-14
[180] yamachiche.ca/toponymie/genealogie/section6.html

[9] **Barbe d'Orange** married Jacques Tardif on October 6, 1669; it was their daughter, Anne, who married Jacques Guéret dit Dumont on April 19, 1694 in Beauport, Québec. [181] [182] [183] [184] [185]

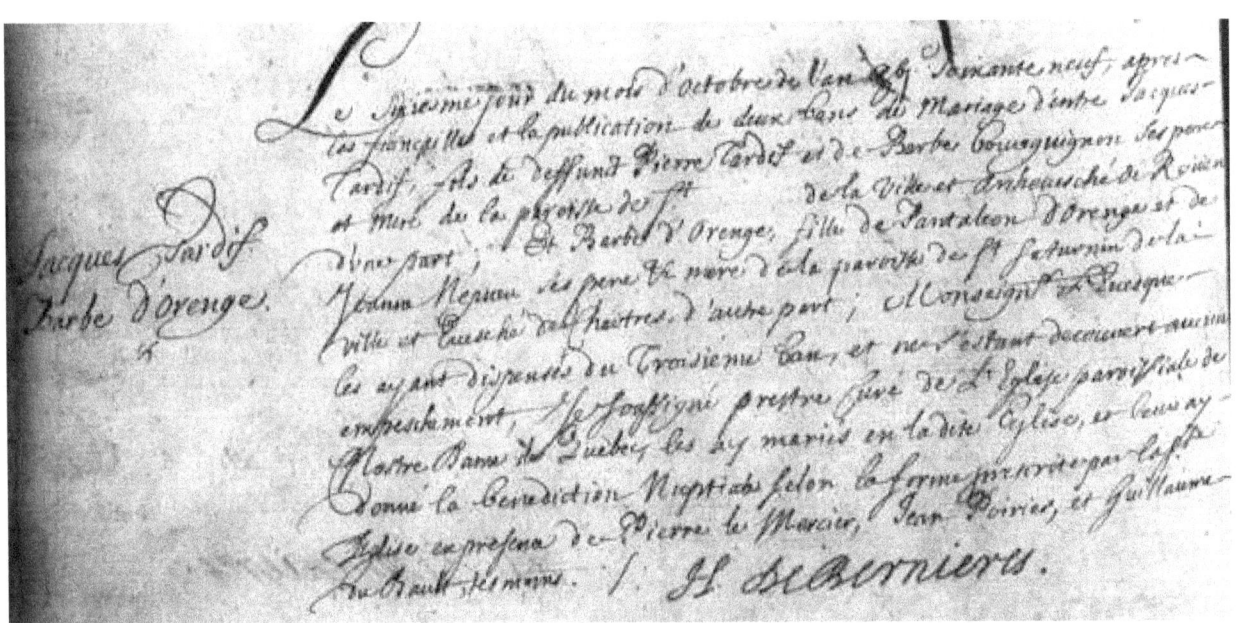

Marriage certificate of Jacques Tardif and Barbe d'Orange
Sources: Archives du Québec

---

[181] www.migrations.fr/ACTESFILLESDUROY/actesfillesduroy_D.htm
[182] https://www.ancestry.ca/interactive/1091/d13p_16021258
[183] https://www.ancestry.ca/interactive/1091/d13p_31410750
[184] https://www.wikitree.com/wiki/D'Orange-3
[185] yamachiche.ca/toponymie/genealogie/section6.html

[8] **Marie Roy** married Mathurin Thibodeau dit Lalime on July 11, 1667 at Notre-Dame in Québec. [186] [187] [188] [189]

Marriage certificate of Mathurin Thibodeau dit Lalime and Marie Roy

Sources: Archives du Québec

---

[186] https://www.ancestry.ca/interactive/1091/d13p_31410495
[187] www.migrations.fr/ACTESFILLESDUROY/actesfillesduroy_R.htm
[188] https://www.wikitree.com/wiki/Roy-964
[189] yamachiche.ca/toponymie/genealogie/section6.html

Actes de marriage des Filles du Roi [190]

Alphabetical Listing of the Filles du Roi [191]

Daughters of the King and Founders of a Nation: *Les Filles du Roi* in New France [192]

Filles du Roi [193]

Filles du Roi Project [194]

La Sociéte des Filles du Roi et Soldats du Carignan [195]

King's Daughters [196]

Les Filles du Roi [197] [198] [199] [200]

Les Filles du Roi (affiliated with high society) [201]

Les Filles du Roi (who canceled marriage contracts, thereby marrying other men) [202]

Les Filles du Roi (from the Île-de-France area) [203]

---

[190] www.migrations.fr/ACTESFILLESDUROY/actesfillesduroy_index.htm
[191] https://fillesduroi.org/cpage.php?pt=9
[192] https://digital.library.unt.edu/ark:/67531/metadc28470/m2/1/high_res_d/thesis.pdf
[193] http://www.lookbackward.com/perrault/filleroi/
[194] https://www.wikitree.com/wiki/Project:Filles_du_Roi#Our_Lists_of_Filles_du_Roi
[195] https://fillesduroi.org/
[196] www.francogene.com/gfna/gfna/998/fdr.htm
[197] www.acadian-home.org/kings-daughters-1.html
[198] www.mainewriter.com/articles/Filles-du-Roi.htm
[199] www.migrations.fr/700fillesroy.htm
[200] yamachiche.ca/toponymie/genealogie/chronique_19_filles_du_roy.html
[201] yamachiche.ca/toponymie/genealogie/section1.html
[202] yamachiche.ca/toponymie/genealogie/section2.html

Les Filles du Roi (from the Normandie area) [204]

Les Filles du Roi (from other parts of France) [205]

Les Filles du Roi (origin unknown) [206]

Program de Recherche en Démographie Historique (PRDH) list of the Filles du Roi [207]

Société d'histoire des Filles du Roy [208]

The Filles du Roi [209]

---

[203] yamachiche.ca/toponymie/genealogie/section3.html
[204] yamachiche.ca/toponymie/genealogie/section4.html
[205] yamachiche.ca/toponymie/genealogie/section6.html
[206] yamachiche.ca/toponymie/genealogie/section5.html
[207] https://www.prdh-igd.com/en/les-filles-du-roi
[208] lesfillesduroy-quebec.org/
[209] www.cbc.ca/history/EPCONTENTSE1EP2CH7PA5LE.html

Carnigan-Salières Regiment

The Carignan-Salières Regiment arrived in Quebec City in the summer of 1665, the first contingent arriving on June 18; this was the first expedition of royal troops to Canada.

The term Carignan-Salières regiment should be taken to include the 20 companies that formally made up the regiment plus the four companies (Berthier, La Brisandière, La Durantaye and Monteil) that arrived in Canada with the Marquis de Tracy. [210]

The reason is simple: while only the first 20 companies can truly be called members of the Carignan-Salières regiment, all 24 companies came over at the same time, with the same mission, under the same command structure and were all demobilized at the same time and given the same benefits and incentives to settle in Canada; as such, we can refer to them as one group, and the easiest way to refer to this group is by the name that identifies the majority. [211]

Each company was made up of three officers (a captain, a lieutenant and an ensign), two sergeants, three corporals, five anspessades and forty soldiers, including at least one drummer. [212]

Four other companies drawn from the regiments of Lignières, Chambellé, Poitou and Orléans coming from the West Indies also came to Quebec City with Marquis de Tracy, the new governor general. [213]

Considering that the colony had about 3200 inhabitants, the arrival of some 1200 soldiers and 80 officers had an extraordinary impact on its development. [214] A body of troops of this magnitude in Canada completely transformed what had until then been a precarious military situation for the colony. [215]

---

[210] www.vt-fcgs.org/Filles_and_Soldats_Program.html
[211] https://fillesduroi.org/cpage.php?pt=12
[212] www.vt-fcgs.org/Filles_and_Soldats_Program.html
[213] Ibid.
[214] Ibid.
[215] Ibid.

Finally, towns could be fitted out with suitable garrisons and new forts could be built to block the Richelieu River, the traditional route of the Iroquois. [216] In just a few weeks, the French went from the defensive stance that had been necessary for almost a quarter of a century to a new tactic: attacking the Iroquois on their own territory. [217]

I descend from several Carnigan-Salière Regiment soldiers; namely,

[1] **Martin Moreau** married Jeanne LeCoq (a Fille du Roi) on January 18, 1672, at Notre-Dame in Québec. [218] [219] Martin was a soldier with the Sorel Company. [220]

[2] **Olivier Morel de la Durantaye** married Françoise Duquet, widow of Jean Madry (surgeon), on September 14, 1670 in Québec. [221] [222] [223] [224] [225] [226] Captain of the Compagnie La Durantaye, they arrived in Québec on June 30, 1665. [227] [228] From 1670 to 1683, Olivier was attached to the Québec garrison, where he commanded one of the six companies of colonial regular troops. [229]

---

[216] www.vt-fcgs.org/Filles_and_Soldats_Program.html
[217] Ibid.
[218] https://www.wikitree.com/wiki/LeCocq-6
[219] https://www.ancestry.ca/interactive/1091/d13p_31410781
[220] www.migrations.fr/compagniescarignan/compagniedesorel.htm
[221] https://www.ancestry.ca/interactive/1091/d13p_31410764
[222] Tanguay, Mgr Cyprien. (1975) <u>Dictionnaire Généalogique des Familles Canadiennes</u>, Volume 1, page 443. bibnum2.banq.qc.ca/bna/dicoGenealogie/src/0002/0022/0047/0049/3957-1-483.pdf
[223] www.francogene.com/dossiers/noblesse-quebecoise.pdf (page 393 of 511)
[224] www.francogene.com/genealogie-quebec-genealogy/001/001633.php
[225] http://genealogie.quebec/testphp/info.php?no=51082
[226] www.migrations.fr/compagniescarignan/compagnieladurantaye.htm
[227] www.migrations.fr/compagniescarignan/compagnieladurantaye.htm
[228] http://www.biographi.ca/en/bio.php?id_nbr=1000
[229] Ibid.

Arrival of the Carnigan-Salière Regiment [230]

Carnigan-Salière Regiment [231]

Carnigan-Salières Regiment Companies [232]

Carnigan-Salières Regiment Lineage Chart (John P. DuLong) [233]

Carignan-Salières Regiment Officers and Soldiers (who married Filles du Roi) [234]

Carignan-Salières Regiment Officers and Soldiers (who settled in Canada) [235]

La Sociéte des Filles du Roi et Soldats du Carignan [236]

Notes on the Carnigan-Salière Regiment [237]

Regiment of Carignan [238]

Regiment Ships (arrived in New France in 1665) [239]

Thomas François de Savoie, Prince of Carignan [240]

---

[230] http://www.cbc.ca/history/EPCONTENTSE1EP2CH7PA3LE.html
[231] https://en.wikipedia.org/wiki/Carignan-Salieres_Regiment
[232] https://fillesduroi.org/cpage.php?pt=13
[233] www.habitant.org/carignan.htm
[234] https://fillesduroi.org/cpage.php?pt=15
[235] https://fillesduroi.org/cpage.php?pt=19
[236] https://fillesduroi.org/
[237] www.choquet-te.org/english/carign_e.html
[238] www.francogene.com/gfna/gfna/998/carignan.htm
[239] https://fillesduroi.org/cpage.php?pt=8
[240] https://en.wikipedia.org/wiki/Thomas_Francis,_Prince_of_Carignano

Catherine de Baillon

This segment of the book is the result of the dedicated diligence of many individuals in the area of medieval genealogy.

In the compilation of the data, I have done my best to avail of the most recent, noteworthy and credible sources available. Likewise, this segment will not be a written history on Catherine de Baillon. I leave that up to the experts, namely; Jean-René Côté, John P. DuLong, Roland Yves-Gagné, René Jetté (now deceased), Paul Leportier, Nicole Mauger, Gail F. Moreau, Raymond Ouimet, Anita Seni and Cyprien Tanguay.

Who would have thought that when I first began researching the Breau surname of my maternal ancestry that I would have ended up identifying Charlemagne as a long lost ancestor?

Many people of French-Canadian ancestry can claim descent from Catherine de Baillon.

Alphonse de Baillon, the father of Catherine, was Sieur de La Mascotterie. La Mascotterie was a hamlet of Layes, in a community of Essarts-le-Roi, canton and arrondissement of Rambouillet, Yvelines department.

The daughter of Alphonse de Baillon, squire, and Louise de Marle, seigneuress of the manor of Ragonant (Chevreuse Valley, Ile-de-France), Catherine was probably born at, or near, her father's farm at La Mascotterie, near Montfort-L'Amaury in the Chevreuse Valley, Île-de-France, in 1645. [241] A second marriage for both of her parents, they were members of minor French nobility.

While her parents were from old noble stock, at the time of Catherine's birth their financial situation was shaky. [242] To make matters worse, as the youngest of three, Catherine lost her father when she was but three years old. [243] Due to heavy debt, Louise had to relinquish most of her possessions. [244]

---

[241] Raymond Ouimet (raymond.ouimet@sympatico.ca) and Nicole Mauger (nicole.mauger@freesbee.fr), authors of <u>Catherine de Baillon: Enquête sur une fille du roi</u> https://www.septentrion.qc.ca/catalogue/catherine-de-baillon
www.genealogie.org/ancetres/gen0.htm
[242] Ibid.
[243] Ibid.
[244] Ibid.

Following the death of Alphonse, Louise donated all of his property to his son, Antoine; to her daughters, Louise and Marie Catherine, she promises each the sum of 600 pounds. [245]

The presence of Catherine de Baillon among the *Filles du Roi* is somewhat surprising for the following reasons: [1] although she had lost her father, she still had her mother, her guardians, and a brother with a good position at the Royal Court, [2] although she was not rich, she came with a dowry of 1000 pounds, [3] contemporary accounts suggest that she came to Canada against her will, probably after having been sequestered in the Salpêtrière Hospital in Paris, and [4] despite her dowry and her aristocratic origin, she was shunned by the twelve bachelors of noble birth in Quebec City, as rumors of ill repute may have preceded her to New France. [246]

The most *plausible* explanation was posited by Raymond Ouimet and Nicole Mauger in their book, Catherine de Baillon: Enquête sur une fille du roi.

Catherine's brother, Antoine, was equerry to Gaston Henry of Bourbon, Duke of Verneuil, Bishop of Metz, Viceroy of the Languedoc, and great uncle of Louis XIV. [247] It is quite probable that, after having met this great lord, Catherine became involved in a short affair with him. [248] In October 1668, however, the Duke of Verneuil married Charlotte Seguier, daughter of the Chancellor of France, Pierre Séguier. [249] [250]

---

[245] Raymond Ouimet (raymond.ouimet@sympatico.ca) and Nicole Mauger (nicole.mauger@freesbee.fr), authors of Catherine de Baillon: Enquête sur une fille du roi https://www.septentrion.qc.ca/catalogue/catherine-de-baillon
[246] Ibid.
[247] https://en.wikipedia.org/wiki/Henri,_Duke_of_Verneuil
[248] Raymond Ouimet (raymond.ouimet@sympatico.ca) and Nicole Mauger (nicole.mauger@freesbee.fr), authors of Catherine de Baillon: Enquête sur une fille du roi https://www.septentrion.qc.ca/catalogue/catherine-de-baillon
[249] Raymond Ouimet (raymond.ouimet@sympatico.ca) and Nicole Mauger (nicole.mauger@freesbee.fr), authors of Catherine de Baillon: Enquête sur une fille du roi

It may well be that Catherine lacked the proper discretion about her involvement with the Duke, and, to both protect his future at Court, as well as to avoid any embarrassment to his newly wed protector, Antoine may have arranged for his too talkative sister to be secluded in the Salpêtrière Hospital in Paris, where, we later see her emerging in order to emigrate to New France in 1669, bringing, with her, a dowry of 1000 pounds. [251]

Catherine came to New France in 1669, at the age of twenty-four, as a *Fille du Roi*. Translated, this means that she was a daughter (ward) of the Crown (King), an immigrant bride sent by royal officials to marry a settler of the colony.

The population, mostly men, consisting of fur traders, storekeepers, indentured servants, dockhands, clerics, farmers, settlers and soldiers, outnumbered females nearly two to one. King Louis XIV came to realize that in order for this new colony to thrive, economically as well as militarily, there must be marriageable woman.

In addition to sponsoring the transportation of these marriageable women, the King offered each 50 livres dowry to make the rigorous travel. Being from a family directly connected to nobility, Catherine carried an additional dowry of 950 livres.

There is a very specific time frame that identifies the Filles du Roi. They came between 1663 and 1673. With all that is written about them, the details of why they chose to come to New France are, for the most part, lost to history.

---

https://www.septentrion.qc.ca/catalogue/catherine-de-baillon
[250] https://en.wikipedia.org/wiki/Henri,_Duke_of_Verneuil
[251] Raymond Ouimet (raymond.ouimet@sympatico.ca) and Nicole Mauger (nicole.mauger@freesbee.fr), authors of Catherine de Baillon: Enquête sur une fille du roi
https://www.septentrion.qc.ca/catalogue/catherine-de-baillon

Catherine married Jacques Miville dit Deschênes on November 12, 1669 at Notre-Dame in Québec City.[252][253] The marriage contract was signed October 19th before notary Duquet.

They had six children …...[254][255]

[1] Marie Catherine (baptized September 3, 1670 at Notre-Dame in Québec)[256][257]

[2] Charles dit l'ainé (baptized September 8, 1671 at Notre-Dame in Québec)[258][259]

[3] Jean Bernard (baptized September 6, 1672 at Notre-Dame in Québec)[260][261]

[4] Marie Louise (baptized July 23, 1675 at Notre-Dame in Québec)[262][263]

[5] Charles dit lejeune (baptized September 1, 1677 at Notre-Dame in Québec)[264][265]

[6] Marie Claude (baptized November 30, 1681 in L'Islet-sur-Mer, Québec)[266]

---

[252] https://www.ancestry.ca/interactive/1091/d13p_31410757
[253] Tanguay, Mgr Cyprien. (1975) <u>Dictionnaire Généalogique des Familles Canadiennes</u>, Volume 1, page 219. bibnum2.banq.qc.ca/bna/dicoGenealogie/src/0002/0022/0047/0049/3957-1-476.pdf
[254] webhome.idirect.com/~letanu/baillon2/pafg01.htm#11114C
[255] www.miville.com/genealogy2.htm#anchor597337
[256] https://www.ancestry.ca/interactive/1091/d13p_31410608
[257] www.francogene.com/genealogie-quebec-genealogy/001/001079.php
[258] https://www.ancestry.ca/interactive/1091/d13p_31410622
[259] www.francogene.com/genealogie-quebec-genealogy/001/001079.php
[260] https://www.ancestry.ca/interactive/1091/d13p_31410635
[261] www.francogene.com/genealogie-quebec-genealogy/001/001079.php
[262] https://www.ancestry.ca/interactive/1091/d13p_31410675
[263] www.francogene.com/genealogie-quebec-genealogy/001/001079.php
[264] https://www.ancestry.ca/interactive/1091/d13p_31410702
[265] www.francogene.com/genealogie-quebec-genealogy/001/001079.php
[266] www.francogene.com/genealogie-quebec-genealogy/001/001079.php

In 1674, Catherine de Baillon and Jacques Miville settled in Grande-Anse (now L'Assomption), specifically the St. John River, where they spend considerable time and effort to clear the land and to make a business, for themselves, within the fur trade; unable to recover from the debt incurred several years prior, the couple is forced into bankruptcy. [267]

Life becomes so difficult that Jacques and Catherine eventually become farmers for the powerful businessman Charles Aubert de La Chesnaye. [268]

In faraway France, however, Catherine's brother, Antoine de Baillon, lived in Versailles where he served as Lieutenant of the Grand Dauphin, son of King Louis XIV. [269]

Appointed governor of the town of Pont de l'Arche, he married Marie Marthe Deruel de Beauregard, a wedding that, attended by many dignitaries of the court, took place at the Hotel Rambouillet in Paris. [270]

It can only be said that Catherine had clearly come so far, if only to experience the trials and tribulations of life in the New World.

There was an epidemic of *fièvres pourpres* which translates as "red fever" (possibly measles) at the end of 1687. [271]

---

[267] Raymond Ouimet (raymond.ouimet@sympatico.ca) and Nicole Mauger (nicole.mauger@freesbee.fr), authors of Catherine de Baillon: Enquête sur une fille du roi
https://www.septentrion.qc.ca/catalogue/catherine-de-baillon
www.genealogie.org/ancetres/gen0.htm
[268] Ibid.
[269] Ibid.
[270] Ibid.
[271]
https://groups.google.com/forum/?fromgroups#!searchin/soc.genealogy.french/catherine$20de$20baillon/soc.genealogy.french/pv0NW6k0vFQ/rvOW1qE_h7UJ%5B1-25%5D

Jacques died on January 27, 1688 and was buried on January 28, 1688, according to the parish records of Rivière-Ouelle, Québec.[272] Jacques was forty-nine years of age. Catherine, also buried on January 28, 1688 in Rivière-Ouelle, was about forty-three years of age.[273]

Signature of Catherine de Baillon [274]

This is a copy of her digitally enhanced signature from her 19 October 1669 marriage contract done before Pierre Duquet, notary (ANQ, reel no. 1710).

Signature of Jacques Miville dit Deschênes [275]

The Catherine Baillon Royal Connection Research Association [276] has been able to trace Catherine Baillon's ancestry back, with accurate documentation and citations, generation by generation, to Charlemagne,[277] the emperor of the western Holy Roman Empire, through the Le Bouteillier-Gavre gateway.

---

[272] hhttps://www.ancestry.ca/interactive/1091/d13p_31160734
[273] Ibid.
[274] habitant.org/baillon/index-original.htm
[275] www.miville.com/deschenes.htm
[276] habitant.org/baillon/
[277] habitant.org/baillon/figure2.htm

In addition, they were also able to trace Catherine Baillon's ancestry back, with accurate documentation and citations, generation by generation, to Theodoros II Dukas Lascaris, the emperor of the eastern Byzantine Empire, though the Chabot-Lascaris de Vintimille gateway.[278]

The web site continues to be maintained to act as a clearinghouse for information about Catherine Baillon and further research done to trace her ancestry.

John P. DuLong views a gateway ancestor as being *someone who comes to the New World from a noble or bourgeois background whose ancestors can be traced back in the Old World.*

He also thinks in terms of a *secondary type of gateway ancestor*, meaning *someone who comes from an important family linked to the higher nobility and leading back to royalty.*

In keeping, *the primary gateway ancestor is often from the lower nobility* whereas the *secondary gateway ancestor is usually the youngest son or daughter of a formerly prominent family marrying someone moving up the social ladder of success.*

Based on these definitions, Catherine de Baillon is a *primary gateway ancestor* for the simple reason that she can be *traced back to a number of minor noble and bourgeois families.*

In comparison, however, Catherine de Gavre, an ancestress of Catherine de Baillon, is a *secondary gateway ancestor because it is through her that it is easy to trace back to many major families of Northern France and Flanders.*

---

[278] habitant.org/baillon/lascaris.htm

The same holds true for Eudoxia Lascaris, another *second gateway ancestress* of Catherine de Baillon, primarily because she *leads back to Byzantium and many Eastern European families.* The challenge faced here, however, is that this lineage is not well documented.

Clearly, one usually has to go through many primary gateway ancestors, back several generations, before you manage to link up with a rare secondary gateway ancestor.

In the course of the Catherine Baillon research project, two key pieces of evidence to prove her royal ancestry were heraldic artifacts (that helped them prove connections between generations of noble families).

The **first** was the commemorative plaque created for Marguerite de Gavre d'Escornaix, youngest daughter of Arnould VI de Gavre, Baron d'Escornaix, and Isabelle de Ghistelles. As Abbéss of Ste-Gertrude, Nivelles, in modern-day Belgium, this plaque displays Marguerite's ancestral arms alongside the images of the Madonna and child, Ste-Marguerite, a crouching dragon, and a kneeling abbéss Marguerite in the middle. [279]

---

[279] habitant.org/baillon/armorial.htm

Commemorative Plaque created for Marguerite de Gavre d'Escornaix (1461) [280]

---

[280] Originally published in Jetté, René, DuLong, John P., Gagné, Roland-Yves, Moreau, Gail F. and Dubé, Joseph A. (2001) <u>Table d'ascendance de Catherine Baillon: 12 générations</u> (p 136). Montréal, Québec: Société Généalogique Canadienne Française.

The impaled arms at the top are those of Marguerite de Gavre d'Escornaix showing that she was the daughter of a Gavre d'Escornaix father and Ghistelles mother.

The arms of her grandparents appear to the right and the left.

On the top right are the arms of Gavre d'Escornaix her paternal grandfather and on the top left the arms of the de Roye her paternal grandmother. [281]

On the bottom right the arms of Ghistelles her maternal grandfather and the bottom left the arms of Dudzeele her maternal grandmother. [282]

In addition, the Ghistelles arms also display, in the upper right, the arms of Luxembourg.

This turned out to be a guidepost for the Baillon researchers that lead to the royal gateway via the Luxembourg family. [283]

The **second** important piece of heraldic evidence, used to prove Catherine de Baillon's ancestry, was the impaled seal of Catherine de Gavre d'Escornaix, the wife of Guy Le Bouteillier. [284]

The seal was used on several 1439 documents and bears the legend "S. Katherine le boutellier dame de la rochegniõ" while the arms on the right are those of her deceased husband Guy Le Bouteillier, seigneur of La Roche-Guyon, and the arms on the left are those of her father Arnould VI de Gavre, sire d'Escornaix. [285]

---

[281] Liedeke, Guy. (1957) *Histoire de la maison de Gavre et de Liedekerke* (pages 220 and 221). Bruxelles (Belgique): Tradition et Vie.
[282] Ibid.
[283] habitant.org/baillon/armorial.htm
[284] Ibid.
[285] Ibid.

Thus the seal proves that she was the wife of a Le Bouteillier, the daughter of a Gavre d'Escornaix, and the lady of La Roche-Guyon. [286]

Imprint of a plaster mold of the seal of Catherine de Gavre [287]

Archives Nationales de France

Salle de sigillographie et d'héraldique, *pieces originals*, n° 2018

---

[286] habitant.org/baillon/armorial.htm
[287] Originally published in Jetté, René, DuLong, John P., Gagné, Roland-Yves, Moreau, Gail F. and Dubé, Joseph A. (2001) <u>Table d'ascendance de Catherine Baillon: 12 générations</u> (p 106). Montréal, Québec: Société Généalogique Canadienne Française.

Catherine de Baillon Descending Lineage 1

[1] **Charles I (dit *Charlemagne*)**, King of the Franks and Emperor of the West, married Hildegard ---------- in 771.

[2] **Pépin I (originally born Carloman)**, King of Italy, married ---------- c. 795.

[3] **Bernard (illegitimate issue)**, King of Italy, married Cunégonde of Laon c. 815.

[4] **Pépin**, Count de Vermandois and ----------

[5] **Héribert I**, Count de Vermandois and ----------

[6] **Béatrice de Vermandois** married Robert I, King of France, c. 895.

[7] **Hugues *le Grand***, Duke of France, married thirdly Hedwige de Saxe between May 9 and September 14, 938 in either Mayence or Ingelheim.

[8] **Hugues *Capet***, King of France, married Adélaïde ---------- in the summer of 968.

[9] **Robert II**, King of France, married Constance de Provence between 1003 and 1005.

[10] **Henri I**, King of France, married Anne de Russie on May 19, 1051 in Reims.

[11] **Philippe I**, King of France, married Berthe de Holland between 1071 and 1073.

[12] **Louis VI**, King of France, married Adélaïde de Savoie in 1115.

[13] **Louis VII**, King of France, married Adèle de Blois et de Champagne on October 18, 1160.

[14] **Philippe II *Auguste***, King of France, married Agnès d'Andechs of Méranie in June 1196.

[15] **Princess Marie of France** married Henri I, Duke de Brabant, between April 8 and April 22, 1213, in Soissons. [288]

[16] **Élisabeth (also known as Ysabeau) de Brabant** married Count Dietrich (Thierry) de Clèves, Seigneur de Dinslaken, on March 19, 1233 in Louvain. [289] [290] With regards to French records, the name Élisabeth is often used, interchangeably, with that of Isabelle.

[17] **Mathilde de Clèves** married Gérard of Luxembourg, Seigneur de Durbury, in 1253.

[18] **Marguerite de Luxembourg** married Jean III de Ghistelles, Seigneur de Ghistelles, between 1284 and before June 1289.

[19] **Jean IV de Ghistelles**, seigneur de Ghistelles, married Marie de Heverskerke, Dame de Straten, shortly after June 1337.

[20] **Roger de Ghistelles**, ~~Seigneur de Dudzeele et de Straten~~, married Élisabeth ~~Marguerite~~, Dame de Dudzeele, in, or shortly before, 1357 (see page 182 for updated explanation).

[21] **Isabelle de Ghistelles** married Arnould VI de Gavre, Baron d'Escornaix, c. 1380-1390.

[22] **Catherine of Gavre d'Escornaix**, Dame de Vaux-sur-Orge et de La Boissière, married Guy I Le Bouteiller, Seigneur de La Bouteillerie et de La Roche-Guyon, after April 1419, about 1425.

[23] **Guy II Le Bouteillier**, Seigneur de La Bouteillerie et de La Roche-Guyon, married Isabeau Morhier, c. 1450.

---

[288] www.francogene.com/genealogie-quebec-genealogy/010/010372.php
[289] Jetté, René, DuLong, John P., Gagné, Roland-Yves, Moreau, Gail F. and Dubé, Joseph A. (2001) Table d'ascendance de Catherine Baillon: 12 générations (p 153). Montréal, Québec: Société Généalogique Canadienne Française.
[290] https://en.wikipedia.org/wiki/Henry_I,_Duke_of_Brabant

[24] **Jean Le Bouteillier**, Seigneur de La Bouteillerie, de Roquemont, de Vaux-sur-Orge et de La Boissière, married Marie de Venois between 1480-1490.

[25] **Bénigne Le Bouteillier**, Dame de La Boissière, married Jacques Maillard, Seigneur de Champagne, on April 16, 1516 in Montivilliers (Seine-Maritime).

[26] **Miles Maillard**, Seigneur du Breuil et de La Boissière, married Marie Morant on June 25, 1555.

[27] **Renée Maillard** married Adam de Baillon, Seigneur de Valence, c. 1580.

[28] **Alphonse de Baillon**, Sieur de La Mascotterie, married Louise de Marle c. 1630-1640, in the région de Chevreuse (Yvelines)

[29] **Catherine de Baillon** married Jacques Miville dit Deschênes on November 12, 1669 at Notre-Dame in Québec.

SOURCE

René Jetté, John P. Dulong, Roland-Yves Gagné, and Gail F. Moreau. 1997. "De Catherine Baillon à Charlemagne." Mémoies de la Société généalogique canadienne-français, Volume 48 (Autumn): 190-216. Figure 2, pp. 195-196. [291]

---

[291] habitant.org/baillon/figure2.htm

Catherine de Baillon Descending Lineage 2

[1] **Charles I (dit *Charlemagne*)**, King of the Franks and Emperor of the West, married Hildegard ---------- in 771.

[2] **Louis I (dit *le Pieux*)**, Louis the Pious, King of France, married Judith de Bavaria in December 842.

[3] **Charles II (dit *le Chauve*)**, Charles II (the Bald), King of France, married Irmentrude d'Orléans c. 875.

[4] **Louis II**, King of France, married Adélaïde

[5] **Charles III**, King of France, married Edgive d'Angleterre in 919.

[6] **Louis IV**, King of France, married Gerberge de Saxe in 939.

[7] **Charles**, Duke of Lower Lorraine, married Adélaïde ---------, in either 975 or 979.

[8] **Gerberge** de Basse-Lorraine, married Lambert I, Count of Louvain.

[9] **Lambert II**, Count de Louvain, married Oda de Basse-Lorraine.

[10] **Henri II**, Count de Louvain, married Adèle von der Betuwe.

[11] **Godefroy I**, Count de Brabant, Duke de Basse-Lorraine, married Ida de Chiny c. 1105.

[12] **Godefroy II**, Duke de Brabant, married Liutgarde de Sulzbach c. 1139.

[13] **Godefroy III**, Duke de Brabant, married Marguerite de Limbourg before 1155.

[14] **Henri I**, Duke de Brabant, married Princess Marie of France, between April 8 and April 22, 1213, in Soissons. [292]

[15] **Élisabeth (also known as Ysabeau) de Brabant** married Count Dietrich (Thierry) de Clèves, Seigneur de Dinslaken, on March 19, 1233 in Louvain. [293] [294] With regards to French records, the name Élisabeth is often used, interchangeably, with that of Isabelle.

[16] **Mathilde de Clèves** married Gérard de Luxembourg, Seigneur de Durbury, in 1253.

[17] **Marguerite de Luxembourg** married Jean III de Ghistelles, Seigneur de Ghistelles, between 1284 and before June 1289.

[18] **Jean IV de Ghistelles**, Seigneur de Ghistelles, married Marie de Heverskerke, Dame de Straten, shortly after June 1337.

[19] **Roger de Ghistelles**, ~~Seigneur de Dudzeele et de Straten~~, married Élisabeth ~~Marguerite~~, Dame de Dudzeele, in, or shortly before, 1357 (see page 182 for updated explanation).

[20] **Isabelle de Ghistelles** married Arnould VI de Gavre, Baron d'Escornaix, c. 1380-1390.

[21] **Catherine of Gavre d'Escornaix**, Dame de Vaux-sur-Orge et de La Boissière, married Guy I Le Bouteiller, Seigneur de La Bouteillerie et de La Roche-Guyon, after April 1419, about 1425.

[22] **Guy II Le Bouteillier**, Seigneur de La Bouteillerie et de La Roche-Guyon, married Isabeau Morhier, c. 1450.

---

[292] www.francogene.com/genealogie-quebec-genealogy/010/010372.php
[293] Jetté, René, DuLong, John P., Gagné, Roland-Yves, Moreau, Gail F. and Dubé, Joseph A. (2001) Table d'ascendance de Catherine Baillon: 12 générations (p 153). Montréal, Québec: Société Généalogique Canadienne-Française.
[294] https://en.wikipedia.org/wiki/Henry_I,_Duke_of_Brabant

[23] **Jean Le Bouteillier**, Seigneur de La Bouteillerie, de Roquemont, de Vaux-sur-Orge et de La Boissière, married Marie de Venois between 1480-1490.

[24] **Bénigne Le Bouteillier**, Dame de La Boissière, married Jacques Maillard, Seigneur de Champagne, on April 16, 1516 in Montivilliers (Seine-Maritime).

[25] **Miles Maillard**, Seigneur du Breuil et de La Boissière, married Marie Morant on June 25, 1555.

[26] **Renée Maillard** married Adam de Baillon, Seigneur de Valence, c. 1580.

[27] **Alphonse de Baillon**, Sieur de La Mascotterie, married Louise de Marle c. 1630-1640, in the région de Chevreuse (Yvelines)

[28] **Catherine de Baillon** married Jacques Miville dit Deschênes on November 12, 1669 at Notre-Dame in Québec.

SOURCE

René Jetté, John Patrick DuLong, Roland-Yves Gagné, Gail F. Moreau, and Joseph A. Dubé. Table d'ascendance de Catherine Baillon (12 générations). Montréal: Société Généalogique Canadienne-Française, 2001. Table 10, pp 20-21.

Catherine de Baillon Descending Lineage 3

[1] **Charles I (dit *Charlemagne*)**, King of the Franks and Emperor of the West, married Hildegard ---------- in 771.

[2] **Louis I (dit *le Pieux*)**, Louis the Pious, King of France, married Judith de Bavaria in December 842.

[3] **Charles II (dit *le Chauve*)**, Charles II (the Bald), King of France, married Irmentrude d'Orléans c. 875.

[4] **Princess Judith of France** married Baudouin I, Count de Flandres, in 862.

[5] **Baudouin II**, Count de Flandres married Elstrude d'Angleterre in 884.

[6] **Arnoul I**, Count de Flandres married Adèle de Vermandois in 934.

[7] **Baudouin III**, Count de Flandres married Mathilde de Saxe in 961.

[8] **Arnoul II**, Count de Flandres married Roselle (Suzanne) d'Italie c. 968.

[9] **Baudouin IV**, Count de Flandres married Ogive de Luxembourg c. 1012.

[10] **Baudouin V**, Count de Flandres married Princess Adélaïde de France in 1028.

[11] **Mathilde de Flandres** married Guillaume I *le Conquérant*, William the Conqueror, Duke de Normandie and King of England, in 1053.

[12] **Princess Adèle d'Angleterre** married Étienne II, Count de Blois et de Champagne, before 1085.

[13] **Thibault IV**, Count de Blois et de Champagne, married Mathilde de Carinthie in 1123.

[14] **Alix de Blois de Champagne** married Louis VII, King of France, on November 13, 1160.

[15] **Philippe II** *Auguste*, King of France, married <u>thirdly</u> Agnès d'Andechs de Méranie in June 1196.

[16] **Princess Marie of France** married Henri I, Duke de Brabant, between April 8 and April 22, 1213, in Soissons. [295]

[17] **Élisabeth (also known as Ysabeau) de Brabant** married Count Dietrich (Thierry) de Clèves, Seigneur de Dinslaken, on March 19, 1233 in Louvain. [296] [297] With regards to French records, the name Élisabeth is often used, interchangeably, with that of Isabelle.

[18] **Mathilde de Clèves** married Gérard de Luxembourg, Seigneur de Durbury, in 1253.

[19] **Marguerite de Luxembourg** married Jean III de Ghistelles, Seigneur de Ghistelles, between 1284 and before June 1289.

[20] **Jean IV, seigneur de Ghistelles**, married Marie de Heverskerke, Dame de Straten, shortly after June 1337.

[21] **Roger de Ghistelles**, ~~Seigneur de Dudzeele et de Straten~~, married Élisabeth ~~Marguerite~~, Dame de Dudzeele, in, or shortly before, 1357 (see page 182 for updated explanation).

[22] **Isabelle de Ghistelles** married Arnould VI de Gavre, Baron d'Escornaix, c. 1380-1390.

---

[295] www.francogene.com/genealogie-quebec-genealogy/010/010372.php
[296] Jetté, René, DuLong, John P., Gagné, Roland-Yves, Moreau, Gail F. and Dubé, Joseph A. (2001) <u>Table d'ascendance de Catherine Baillon: 12 générations</u> (p 153). Montréal, Québec: Société Généalogique Canadienne-Française.
[297] https://en.wikipedia.org/wiki/Henry_I,_Duke_of_Brabant

[23] **Catherine of Gavre d'Escornaix**, Dame de Vaux-sur-Orge et de La Boissière, married Guy I Le Bouteiller, Seigneur de La Bouteillerie et de La Roche-Guyon, after April 1419, about 1425.

[24] **Guy II Le Bouteillier**, Seigneur de La Bouteillerie et de La Roche-Guyon, married Isabeau Morhier, c. 1450.

[25] **Jean Le Bouteillier**, Seigneur de La Bouteillerie, de Roquemont, de Vaux-sur-Orge et de La Boissière, married Marie de Venois between 1480-1490.

[26] **Bénigne Le Bouteillier**, Dame de La Boissière, married Jacques Maillard, Seigneur de Champagne, on April 16, 1516 in Montivilliers (Seine-Maritime).

[27] **Miles Maillard**, Seigneur du Breuil et de La Boissière, married Marie Morant on June 25, 1555.

[28] **Renée Maillard** married Adam de Baillon, Seigneur de Valence, c. 1580.

[29] **Alphonse de Baillon**, Sieur de La Mascotterie, married Louise de Marle c. 1630-1640, in the région de Chevreuse (Yvelines)

[30] **Catherine de Baillon** married Jacques Miville dit Deschênes on November 12, 1669 at Notre-Dame in Québec.

SOURCE

René Jetté, John Patrick DuLong, Roland-Yves Gagné, Gail F. Moreau, and Joseph A. Dubé. <u>Table d'ascendance de Catherine Baillon</u> (12 générations). Montréal: Société Généalogique Canadienne-Française, 2001. Table 11, pp. 22-23.

Catherine de Baillon Descending Lineage 4

[1] **Charles I (dit *Charlemagne*)**, King of the Franks and Emperor of the West, [298] [299] [300] married secondly Hildegard [301] in 771.

[2] **Pépin I (originally born Carloman)**, King of Italy, [302] [303] married ---------- c. 795.

[3] **Bernard (illegitimate issue)**, King of Italy, [304] [305] married Cunégonde of Laon [306] c. 815.

[4] **Pépin**, Count de Vermandois [307] [308] married ----------.

[5] **Héribert I**, Count de Vermandois [309] [310] married ----------.

[6] **Béatrice de Vermandois** [311] [312] married Robert I, King of France, [313] [314] c. 895.

[7] **Hugues** *le Grand*, Duke of France, [315] married thirdly Hedwige de Saxe, [316] between May 9 and September 14, 938 in either Mayence or Ingelheim.

---

[298] fmg.ac/Projects/MedLands/CAROLINGIANS.htm#CharlemagneA
[299] fmg.ac/Projects/MedLands/CAROLINGIANS.htm#CharlemagneB
[300] www.stirnet.com/genie/data/ancient/fh/franks3.php
[301] fmg.ac/Projects/MedLands/SWABIAN%20NOBILITY.htm#Hildegardisdied783
[302] fmg.ac/Projects/MedLands/ITALY,%20Kings%20to%20962.htm#PepinIitalydied810A
[303] fmg.ac/Projects/MedLands/ITALY,%20Kings%20to%20962.htm#PepinIItalyB
[304] fmg.ac/Projects/MedLands/ITALY,%20Kings%20to%20962.htm#BernardItalyA
[305] fmg.ac/Projects/MedLands/ITALY,%20Kings%20to%20962.htm#BernardIitalyB
[306] fmg.ac/Projects/MedLands/FRANKISH%20NOBILITY.htm#Cunigundisdied835
[307] fmg.ac/Projects/MedLands/ITALY,%20Kings%20to%20962.htm#Pepindiedafter850A
[308] fmg.ac/Projects/MedLands/FRANKISH%20NOBILITY.htm#Pepindiedafter850B
[309] fmg.ac/Projects/MedLands/FRANKISH%20NOBILITY.htm#HeribertIdied900907A
[310] fmg.ac/Projects/MedLands/NORTHERN%20FRANCE.htm#HeribertIdied900907
[311] fmg.ac/Projects/MedLands/NORTHERN%20FRANCE.htm#Beatrixdied931
[312] racineshistoire.free.fr/LGN/PDF/Vermandois-Valois-Vexin.pdf (page 3)
[313] fmg.ac/Projects/MedLands/CAPET.htm#RobertIdied923B
[314] www.stirnet.com/genie/data/ancient/ae/capet01.php#link1

[8] **Hugues** *Capet*, King of France, [317] married Adélaïde de Poitou [318] in the summer of 968.

[9] **Robert II**, King of France, married Constance de Provence between 1003 and 1005. [319] [320] [321] [322] [323]

[10] **Henri I**, King of France, married Anne de Russie on May 19, 1051 in Reims. [324] [325] [326] [327] [328]

[11] **Philippe I** [329] [330] (King of France) married Berthe de Holland between 1071 and 1073. [331]

[12] **Louis VI** [332] [333] (King of France) married Adélaide de Savoie (of Savoy) de Maurienne in 1115. [334]

---

[315] fmg.ac/Projects/MedLands/CAPET.htm#Huguesdied956B
[316] fmg.ac/Projects/MedLands/GERMANY,%20Kings.htm#HedwigMHuguesRegentFrancedied956
[317] fmg.ac/Projects/MedLands/CAPET.htm#HuguesCapetdied996B
[318] fmg.ac/Projects/MedLands/AQUITAINE.htm#Adelaisdied1004
[319] https://en.wikipedia.org/wiki/Constance_of_Arles
[320] fmg.ac/Projects/MedLands/PROVENCE.htm#ConstanceArlesMRobertIIFrancedied1031
[321] https://en.wikipedia.org/wiki/Robert_II_of_France
[322] fmg.ac/Projects/MedLands/CAPET.htm#RobertIIdied1031B
[323] www.francogene.com/genealogie-quebec-genealogy/010/010405.php
[324] fmg.ac/Projects/MedLands/CAPET.htm#HenriIdied1060B
[325] www.francogene.com/genealogie-quebec-genealogy/010/010404.php
[326] https://en.wikipedia.org/wiki/Henry_I_of_France
[327] fmg.ac/Projects/MedLands/RUSSIA,%20Rurik.htm#AnnaIaroslavnadied1075
[328] https://en.wikipedia.org/wiki/Anne_of_Kiev
[329] fmg.ac/Projects/MedLands/CAPET.htm#PhilippeIdied1108B
[330] www.francogene.com/genealogie-quebec-genealogy/010/010403.php
[331] fmg.ac/Projects/MedLands/HOLLAND.htm#Berthadied1093
[332] fmg.ac/Projects/MedLands/CAPET.htm#LouisVIdied1137B
[333] www.francogene.com/genealogie-quebec-genealogy/010/010402.php
[334] fmg.ac/Projects/MedLands/SAVOY.htm#Adélaïdedied1154

[13] **Louis VII** [335] (King of France) married secondly Constance de Castile. [336]

[14] **Alix de France** [337] married Guillaume II (Talvas) de Ponthieu, Comte de Ponthieu. [338] [339]

[15] **Marie, Countess of Ponthieu**, [340] [341] married Simon de Dammartin, Comte de Ponthieu et de Montreuil [342]

[16] **Marie de Dammartin** [343] married Jean II de Pierrepont, Comte de Roucy. [344] [345]

[17] **Marie (Mathilde) de Roucy** [346] [347] married Jean de Garlande, Seigneur de Possesse. [348] [349]

---

[335] fmg.ac/Projects/MedLands/CAPET.htm#LouisVIIdied1180B
[336] fmg.ac/Projects/MedLands/CASTILE.htm#Constanzadied1160MLouisVIIFrance
[337] fmg.ac/Projects/MedLands/CAPET.htm#Alixdiedafter1200MGuillaumeIIIPonthieu
[338] fmg.ac/Projects/MedLands/NORTHERN%20FRANCE.htm#GuillaumeIIdied1221
[339] racineshistoire.free.fr/LGN/PDF/Ponthieu.pdf (page 8)
[340] fmg.ac/Projects/MedLands/NORTHERN%20FRANCE.htm#dauJeanIIRoucyMJeanGarlande
[341] racineshistoire.free.fr/LGN/PDF/Ponthieu.pdf (page 8)
[342] fmg.ac/Projects/MedLands/NORTHERN%20FRANCE.htm#SimonDammartinAumalePonthieud1239B
[343] fmg.ac/Projects/MedLands/NORTHERN%20FRANCE.htm#MarieDammartinMJeanIIRoucy
[344] fmg.ac/Projects/MedLands/NORTHERN%20FRANCE.htm#JeanPierrepontRoucydied125
[345] racineshistoire.free.fr/LGN/PDF/Roucy.pdf (page 6)
[346] fmg.ac/Projects/MedLands/NORTHERN%20FRANCE.htm#dauJeanIIRoucyMJeanGarlande
[347] racineshistoire.free.fr/LGN/PDF/Roucy.pdf (page 6)

[18] **Jean II de Garlande** married unknown.

[19] **Alix de Garlande** [350] married Dreux de Roye. [351]

[20] **Jeanne de Roye** married thirdly Arnould V de Gavre, Baron d'Escornaix. [352]

[21] **Isabelle de Ghistelles** married Arnould VI de Gavre, Baron d'Escornaix, c. 1380-1390.

[22] **Catherine of Gavre d'Escornaix**, Dame de Vaux-sur-Orge et de La Boissière, married Guy I Le Bouteiller, Seigneur de La Bouteillerie et de La Roche-Guyon, after April 1419, about 1425.

[23] **Guy II Le Bouteillier**, Seigneur de La Bouteillerie et de La Roche-Guyon, married Isabeau Morhier, c. 1450.

[24] **Jean Le Bouteillier**, Seigneur de La Bouteillerie, de Roquemont, de Vaux-sur-Orge et de La Boissière, married Marie de Venois between 1480-1490.

[25] **Bénigne Le Bouteillier**, Dame de La Boissière, married Jacques Maillard, Seigneur de Champagne, on April 16, 1516 in Montivilliers (Seine-Maritime).

[26] **Miles Maillard**, Seigneur du Breuil et de La Boissière, married Marie Morant on June 25, 1555.

[27] **Renée Maillard** married Adam de Baillon, Seigneur de Valence, c. 1580.

---

[348] fmg.ac/Projects/MedLands/PARIS%20REGION%20NOBILITY.htm#JeanGarlandePossessediedbefore1287
[349] racineshistoire.free.fr/LGN/PDF/Garlande.pdf (page 8)
[350] Ibid.
[351] racineshistoire.free.fr/LGN/PDF/Roye.pdf (page 5)
[352] racineshistoire.free.fr/LGN/PDF/Gavre.pdf (page 9)

[28] **Alphonse de Baillon**, Sieur de La Mascotterie, married Louise de Marle c. 1630-1640, in the région de Chevreuse (Yvelines)

[29] **Catherine de Baillon** married Jacques Miville dit Deschênes on November 12, 1669 at Notre-Dame in Québec.

SOURCE

DuLong, John P., and Jean Bunot. "Catherine de Baillon's de Roye Ancestry: Another Royal Gateway." Michigan's Habitant Heritage 30 (January 2009): 5-18.

PDF file located at habitant.org/baillon/De%20Roye%20Article.pdf

Catherine de Baillon Descending Lineage 5

At present, this is a *possible* lineage. If Guy Le Bouteiller, spouse of Catherine de Gavre d'Escornaix, is maternally descended from the Breaute and therefore the Léon family, as proposed by Jean Bunot, he has two royal lines of descent from the capetian houses of Dreux and Courtenay. The House of Courtenay is presented here.

[1] **Charles I (dit *Charlemagne*)**, King of the Franks and Emperor of the West, married Hildegard ---------- in 771.

[2] **Pépin I (originally born Carloman)**, King of Italy, married ---------- c. 795.

[3] **Bernard (illegitimate issue)**, King of Italy, married Cunégonde of Laon c. 815.

[4] **Pépin**, Count de Vermandois and ----------

[5] **Héribert I**, Count de Vermandois and ----------

[6] **Béatrice de Vermandois** married Robert I, King of France, c. 895.

[7] **Hugues *le Grand***, Duke of France, married thirdly Hedwige de Saxe between May 9 and September 14, 938 in either Mayence or Ingelheim.

[8] **Hugues *Capet***, King of France, married Adélaïde ---------- in the summer of 968.

[9] **Robert II**, King of France, married Constance de Provence between 1003 and 1005.

[10] **Henri I**, King of France, married Anne de Russie on May 19, 1051 in Reims.

[11] **Philippe I**, King of France, married Berthe de Holland between 1071 and 1073.

[12] **Louis VI** [353] [354] (King of France) married Adélaide de Savoie (of Savoy) de Maurienne in 1115. [355]

[13] **Pierre de France**, [356] seigneur de Courtenay, de Montargis, de Chateaurenard, de Champignelles, etc (1126-1183) m. 1150, Isabelle, dame de Courtenay et autres [357] [358]

[14] **Constance de Courtenay** [359] [360] (+ aft. 1231) m. 1188, Gasce de Poissy, seigneur de Chateaufort (+ 1189/90) [361] [362]

[15] **Mahaut (Mathilde) de Poissy**, [363] [364] dame de Chateaufort (1212/67) m. 1209, Bouchard I de Montmorency, seigneur de Marly, de Montreuil-Bonnin, de Saissac et de Londres (+ 1226) [365] [366]

---

[353] fmg.ac/Projects/MedLands/CAPET.htm#LouisVIdied1137B
[354] www.francogene.com/genealogie-quebec-genealogy/010/010402.php
[355] fmg.ac/Projects/MedLands/SAVOY.htm#Adélaïdedied1154
[356] fmg.ac/Projects/MedLands/CHAMPAGNE%20NOBILITY.htm#PierreCourtenaydied1183B
[357] fmg.ac/Projects/MedLands/CHAMPAGNE%20NOBILITY.htm#Elisabethdiedafter1205A
[358] racineshistoire.free.fr/LGN/PDF/Courtenay.pdf (page 3)
[359] fmg.ac/Projects/MedLands/CHAMPAGNE%20NOBILITY.htm#ConstanceCourtenaydiedafter1231
[360] racineshistoire.free.fr/LGN/PDF/Courtenay.pdf (page 4)
[361] fmg.ac/Projects/MedLands/PARIS%20REGION%20NOBILITY.htm#GascePoissyMConstanceCourtenay
[362] racineshistoire.free.fr/LGN/PDF/Poissy.pdf (page 7)
[363] fmg.ac/Projects/MedLands/PARIS%20REGION%20NOBILITY.htm#MathildePoissyMBouchardMarly
[364] racineshistoire.free.fr/LGN/PDF/Poissy.pdf (page 8)

[16] **Bouchard II de Montmorency**,[367][368][369] seigneur de Marly, de Montreuil-Bonnin, etc (+ 1250) m. 1233, Agnes de Beaumont-en-Gatinais (+ aft. 1260)[370][371]

[17] **Isabelle de Marly (Isabeau de Montmorency)**,[372][373] dame de Romanaville m. 1256, Robert de Poissy, seigneur de Radepont et Malvoisine (+ 1258 before his father)[374][375]

[18] **Mahaut de Poissy**, dame de Noyon-sur-Andelle, d'Hacqueville, de Radepont, de Pont-Saint-Pierre, de Fontaine-sous-Jouy, d'Acquigny, etc m. 1280, Hervé IV (V), des vicomtes de Léon, seigneur en partie de Chateauneuf-en-Thimerais et de Senonches (+ 1304)[376][377][378]

---

[365] fmg.ac/Projects/MedLands/PARIS%20REGION%20NOBILITY.htm#BouchardMarlydied1226
[366] racineshistoire.free.fr/LGN/PDF/Montmorency.pdf (page 15)
[367] fmg.ac/Projects/MedLands/PARIS%20REGION%20NOBILITY.htm#BouchardIIMarlydied1256
[368] racineshistoire.free.fr/LGN/PDF/Montmorency.pdf (page 15)
[369] racineshistoire.free.fr/LGN/PDF/Poissy.pdf (page 8)
[370] fmg.ac/Projects/MedLands/CENTRAL%20FRANCE.htm#AgnesBeaumontMBouchardMarly
[371] racineshistoire.free.fr/LGN/PDF/Beaumont-en-Gatinais.pdf (page 3)
[372] fmg.ac/Projects/MedLands/PARIS%20REGION%20NOBILITY.htm#IsabelleMarlyMGuyIIILevis
[373] racineshistoire.free.fr/LGN/PDF/Montmorency.pdf (page 15)
[374] fmg.ac/Projects/MedLands/PARIS%20REGION%20NOBILITY.htm#RobertPoissyMIsabelleMarly
[375] racineshistoire.free.fr/LGN/PDF/Poissy.pdf (page 11)
[376] racineshistoire.free.fr/LGN/PDF/Chateauneuf-en-Thymerais.pdf (page 6)
[377] www.tudchentil.org/IMG/pdf/Genealogie_des_Herve_de_Leon_vers_1180_-_1363_.pdf (page 5)
[378] https://fr.wikipedia.org/wiki/Hervé_IV_de_Léon_(seigneur_de_Léon)

[19] **Guillaume de Léon**, seigneur d'Hacqueville, de Fontaine-sous-Jouy, de Crestot, de Pont-Saint-Pierre, de La Franche Bouteillerie, etc m. c. 1315, Jeanne de Ferrieres [379]

[20] **Jean de Léon**, seigneur d'Hacqueville, de Fontaine-sous-Jouy, de Crestot, de Pont-Saint-Pierre, etc, capitaine de Chateau-Gaillard (1369) m. 1340, Jeanne de Varennes, dame de Menneval [380]

[21] **Jeanne de Léon**, dame de Menneval m. 1364, Roger II, seigneur de Breaute, de Neville, Drosay et de Houville [381]

[22] **Ne... de Breaute**, possibly heiress de La Franche Bouteillerie, sister of Roger III, seigneur de Breaute, de Neville et de Menneval, conseiller chambellan du duc de Bourgogne m. c. 1380/85 Jean Le Bouteiller, seigneur de La Bouteillerie (1382/1407) [382]

[23] **Guy I Le Bouteiller**, seigneur de La Vieuville, de La Bouteillerie et de La Roche-Guyon, conseiller chambellan du duc de Bourgogne, capitaine des villes et chateaux de Rouen et de Dieppe, bailli de Rouen, maitre d'hotel du duc de Bedford (+ 1438), himself ancestor of Catherine de Baillon (VIII degree), married Catherine of Gavre d'Escornaix, Dame de Vaux-sur-Orge et de La Boissière, after April 1419, about 1425.

[24] **Guy II Le Bouteillier**, Seigneur de La Bouteillerie et de La Roche-Guyon, married Isabeau Morhier, c. 1450.

[25] **Jean Le Bouteillier**, Seigneur de La Bouteillerie, de Roquemont, de Vaux-sur-Orge et de La Boissière, married Marie de Venois between 1480-1490.

---

[379] www.disnorge.no/slektsforum/viewtopic.php?t=11127
[380] Ibid.
[381] Ibid.
[382] Ibid.

[26] **Bénigne Le Bouteillier**, Dame de La Boissière, married Jacques Maillard, Seigneur de Champagne, on April 16, 1516 in Montivilliers (Seine-Maritime).

[27] **Miles Maillard**, Seigneur du Breuil et de La Boissière, married Marie Morant on June 25, 1555.

[28] **Renée Maillard** married Adam de Baillon, Seigneur de Valence, c. 1580.

[29] **Alphonse de Baillon**, Sieur de La Mascotterie, married Louise de Marle c. 1630-1640, in the région de Chevreuse (Yvelines)

[30] **Catherine de Baillon** married Jacques Miville dit Deschênes on November 12, 1669 at Notre-Dame in Québec.

SOURCES

[1] Rene Jette, John P. DuLong, Roland-Yves Gagne, Gail F. Moreau et Joseph A Dube. Table d'Ascendance de Catherine Baillon (2001), p.195-96, 110-12, 124, 141.

[2] Jean-Marc Roger. "Guy Le Bouteiller" in Actes du 101e Congres national des societes savantes.

[3] Lille, 1976 (1978); Various articles in French periodical Heraldique et Genealogie: de Léon (among others Patrice Birker), de Poissy (Patrice Birker, Edouard de Saint-Phalle), de Marly (Edouard de Saint-Phalle), de Breaute (Patrice Birker, Paul Leportier)

[4] Pere Anselme de Sainte-Marie; La Chesnaye-des Bois et Badier (article Breaute).

www.disnorge.no/slektsforum/viewtopic.php?t=11127

As per Jean Bunot ......

www.disnorge.no/slektsforum/viewtopic.php?t=11127

Whether or not any royal descent is ever proven for Guy Le Bouteiller, Catherine de Gavre did marry beneath her and she did it twice. Her second husband Simon Morhier, chevalier, seigneur de Villiers-le-Morhier was from a small knightly lignage from Gatinais. The marriage was probably made possible because her successive spouses were, at that time, proeminent political figures of the Anglo-Burgundian faction. Both had acquired extensive lands in occupied France through the generosity of english monarchs, making them a more attractive potential match. Guy Le Bouteiller was, for instance, granted the very important seigneurie of La Roche-Guyon, one of French Vexin's most impressive strongholds. Catherine de Gavre was the younger of ten children of the baron d'Escornaix, making her very unlikely to inherit anything. Therefore, without the perspective of an important dowry, maybe she was indead very content to have been married at all. In my opinio,n it is possible she was married for political reasons to a major Burgundian capitaine and chamberlain as a reward being a distant relative of the duke of Bourgogne through her Luxembourg Brabant ancestry. That remote connection may have been the real reason behind those essentially political unions.

Catherine de Baillon Descending Lineage 6

At present, this is a *possible* lineage. If Guy Le Bouteiller, spouse of Catherine de Gavre d'Escornaix, is maternally descended from the Breaute and therefore the Léon family, as proposed by Jean Bunot, he has two royal lines of descent from the capetian houses of Dreux and Courtenay. The House of Dreux is presented here.

[1] **Charles I (dit *Charlemagne*)**, King of the Franks and Emperor of the West, married Hildegard ---------- in 771.

[2] **Pépin I (originally born Carloman)**, King of Italy, married ---------- c. 795.

[3] **Bernard (illegitimate issue)**, King of Italy, married Cunégonde of Laon c. 815.

[4] **Pépin**, Count de Vermandois and ----------

[5] **Héribert I**, Count de Vermandois and ----------

[6] **Béatrice de Vermandois** married Robert I, King of France, c. 895.

[7] **Hugues *le Grand***, Duke of France, married <u>thirdly</u> Hedwige de Saxe between May 9 and September 14, 938 in either Mayence or Ingelheim.

[8] **Hugues *Capet***, King of France, married Adélaïde ---------- in the summer of 968.

[9] **Robert II**, King of France, married Constance de Provence between 1003 and 1005.

[10] **Henri I**, King of France, married Anne de Russie on May 19, 1051 in Reims.

[11] **Philippe I**, King of France, married Berthe de Holland between 1071 and 1073.

[12] **Louis VI** [383] [384] (King of France) married Adélaide de Savoie (of Savoy) de Maurienne in 1115. [385]

[13] **Robert Ier le Grand, comte de Dreux**, seigneur de Torcy, de Brie-Comte-Robert, de Chilly, de Longjumeau et de Savigny (1123-1188) [386] married 1152, Agnès, dame de Baudement, de Braine-sur-Vesle, de Fère-en-Tardenois, de Nesle-en-Tardenois, de Quincy, de Longueville et de Pontarcy (1130-1202/18) [387]

[14] **Robert II le Jeune, comte de Dreux** et de Braine, seigneur de Torcy, de Brie-Comte-Robert, de Chilly, de Longjumeau, de Nesle-en-Tardenois, de Fère-en-Tardenois, de Quincy, de Longueville et de Pontarcy (1154-1218) [388] [389] married 1184, Yolande de Coucy (+ 1222) [390] [391]

[15] **Éléonore de Dreux** (+ 1248) [392] [393] married 1212, Hugues III, seigneur de Châteauneuf-en-Thimerais (+ 1229) [394] [395]

---

[383] fmg.ac/Projects/MedLands/CAPET.htm#LouisVIdied1137B
[384] www.francogene.com/genealogie-quebec-genealogy/010/010402.php
[385] fmg.ac/Projects/MedLands/SAVOY.htm#Adélaïdedied1154
[386] fmg.ac/Projects/MedLands/PARIS%20REGION%20NOBILITY.htm#RobertIDreuxdied1188B
[387] fmg.ac/Projects/MedLands/PARIS%20REGION%20NOBILITY.htm#AgnesBrainedied1217
[388] fmg.ac/Projects/MedLands/PARIS%20REGION%20NOBILITY.htm#RobertIIDreuxdied1218B
[389] racineshistoire.free.fr/LGN/PDF/Dreux.pdf (page 2)
[390] fmg.ac/Projects/MedLands/CHAMPAGNE%20NOBILITY.htm#YolandeCoucydied1222
[391] http://racineshistoire.free.fr/LGN/PDF/Coucy.pdf (page 5)
[392] fmg.ac/Projects/MedLands/PARIS%20REGION%20NOBILITY.htm#ELéonoreDreuxdied1248

[16] **Marguerite de Châteauneuf**, dame en partie de Châteauneuf-en-Thimerais et de Senonches [396] married 1250/60, Hervé III, vicomte de Léon

[17] **Hervé IV (V), vicomtes de Léon**, seigneur en partie de Chateauneuf-en-Thimerais et de Senonches (+ 1304) [397] [398] [399] married 1280, Mahaut de Poissy, dame de Noyon-sur-Andelle, d'Hacqueville, de Radepont, de Pont-Saint-Pierre, de Fontaine-sous-Jouy, d'Acquigny, etc

[18] **Guillaume de Léon**, seigneur d'Hacqueville, de Fontaine-sous-Jouy, de Crestot, de Pont-Saint-Pierre, de La Franche Bouteillerie, etc m. c. 1315, Jeanne de Ferrieres [400]

[19] **Jean de Léon**, seigneur d'Hacqueville, de Fontaine-sous-Jouy, de Crestot, de Pont-Saint-Pierre, etc, capitaine de Chateau-Gaillard (1369) m. 1340, Jeanne de Varennes, dame de Menneval [401]

[20] **Jeanne de Léon**, dame de Menneval m. 1364, Roger II, seigneur de Breaute, de Neville, Drosay et de Houville [402]

---

[393] racineshistoire.free.fr/LGN/PDF/Dreux.pdf (Page 3)
[394] fmg.ac/Projects/MedLands/PARIS%20REGION%20NOBILITY.htm#HuguesChateauneufMELéonoreDreux
[395] racineshistoire.free.fr/LGN/PDF/Chateauneuf-en-Thymerais.pdf (pages 4 and 5)
[396] racineshistoire.free.fr/LGN/PDF/Chateauneuf-en-Thymerais.pdf (page 5)
[397] racineshistoire.free.fr/LGN/PDF/Chateauneuf-en-Thymerais.pdf (page 6)
[398] www.tudchentil.org/IMG/pdf/Genealogie_des_Herve_de_Leon_vers_1180_-_1363_.pdf (page 5)
[399] https://fr.wikipedia.org/wiki/Hervé_IV_de_Léon_(seigneur_de_Léon)
[400] www.disnorge.no/slektsforum/viewtopic.php?t=11127
[401] Ibid.
[402] Ibid.

[21] **Ne... de Breaute**, possibly heiress de La Franche Bouteillerie, sister of Roger III, seigneur de Breaute, de Neville et de Menneval, conseiller chambellan du duc de Bourgogne m. c. 1380/85 Jean Le Bouteiller, seigneur de La Bouteillerie (1382/1407) [403]

[22] **Guy I Le Bouteiller**, seigneur de La Vieuville, de La Bouteillerie et de La Roche-Guyon, conseiller chambellan du duc de Bourgogne, capitaine des villes et chateaux de Rouen et de Dieppe, bailli de Rouen, maitre d'hotel du duc de Bedford (+ 1438), himself ancestor of Catherine de Baillon (VIII degree), married Catherine of Gavre d'Escornaix, Dame de Vaux-sur-Orge et de La Boissière, after April 1419, about 1425.

[23] **Guy II Le Bouteillier**, Seigneur de La Bouteillerie et de La Roche-Guyon, married Isabeau Morhier, c. 1450.

[24] **Jean Le Bouteillier**, Seigneur de La Bouteillerie, de Roquemont, de Vaux-sur-Orge et de La Boissière, married Marie de Venois between 1480-1490.

[25] **Bénigne Le Bouteillier**, Dame de La Boissière, married Jacques Maillard, Seigneur de Champagne, on April 16, 1516 in Montivilliers (Seine-Maritime).

[26] **Miles Maillard**, Seigneur du Breuil et de La Boissière, married Marie Morant on June 25, 1555.

[27] **Renée Maillard** married Adam de Baillon, Seigneur de Valence, c. 1580.

[28] **Alphonse de Baillon**, Sieur de La Mascotterie, married Louise de Marle c. 1630-1640, in the région de Chevreuse (Yvelines)

---

[403] www.disnorge.no/slektsforum/viewtopic.php?t=11127

[19] **Catherine de Baillon** married Jacques Miville dit Deschênes on November 12, 1669 at Notre-Dame in Québec.

SOURCES

www.disnorge.no/slektsforum/viewtopic.php?t=11127

newsgroups.derkeiler.com/Archive/Soc/soc.genealogy.medieval/2005-09/msg01514.html

Michele Doucette Descending Lineage

Catherine de Baillon married Jacques Miville dit Deschênes on November 12, 1669 at Notre-Dame in Québec.

Charles Miville dit Deschênes married Marie Marthe Vallée on August 28, 1702 in Rivière-Ouelle, Québec.

Catherine Miville married Jean Baptiste Duval on February 6, 1736 in Ste-Anne-de-La-Pocatière, Québec.

Marie Josette (Josèphe) Duval married Jean Baptiste LeClerc on February 8, 1757 in L'Islet, Québec.

Jean Baptiste LeClerc married Madeleine Thébault on September 19, 1796 in Bathurst, New Brunswick.

Madeleine LeClerc married Pascal Landry on February 9, 1824 in Pointe Sapin, New Brunswick.

Alexis dit Alexandre Landry married Justine Lanteigne on May 1, 1854 in Caraquet, New Brunswick.

Marie Landry married Louis Breau on June 14, 1880 in Pokemouche, New Brunswick.

André Breau married Marie Philomène Mallet on October 17, 1906 in Chatham, New Brunswick.

Mary Catherine (Kay) Breau married James Henry (Harry) Feeley on September 1, 1930 in Amherst, Nova Scotia.

Anne Elizabeth Feeley married Albert (Al) Doucette on November 11, 1961 in Truro, Nova Scotia.

Michele Anne Doucette

Ahnentafel Luxembourg / Ghistelles (Baillon) [404]

Jean Bunot

Marguerite de Luxembourg, Dame de Ghistelles, is, in my opinion, the *main royal gateway* of Catherine de Baillon. She was the niece of the Count of Luxembourg, the Duke of Limbourg, and the Duchess of Lorraine, and a near relation to the Dukes of Brabant and the Counts of Hainaut-Hollande and Clèves. Her descendants are related, through her, to the French (Bonne de Luxembourg), English (Philippa de Hainaut) and German (Luxembourg-Bohemia) royals.

September 27, 2005

ADDENDUM

The Ahnentafel format is a genealogical numbering system for listing a person's direct ancestors in a fixed sequence of ascent. [405] [406] The key to reading an ahnentafel is to understand its numbering system.

Basically, you double any individual's number to get their father's number. You also double any individual's number and add one to get their mother's number. On your ahnentafel chart, for example, you would be number 1; your father would then be number 2 and your mother, number 3. Other than the starting person, males always have even numbers and women the odd numbers. In keeping with this system, (+ ----) simply refers to the year that they died.

---

[404] https://groups.google.com/forum/#!searchin/soc.genealogy.medieval/catherine$20de$20baillon/soc.genealogy.medieval/nkZ8c1HqFT0/PsKmi97HoAMJ%5B1-25%5D
[405] https://en.wikipedia.org/wiki/Ahnentafel
[406] https://www.familychronicle.com/Ahnentafel.html

1. Marguerite de Luxembourg-Durbuy (1293), m. 1284, Jean III, seigneur de Ghistelles, de Voormezele et de La Woestine, chambellan de Flandre (+ 1315)

2. Gerard de Luxembourg, seigneur de Durbuy, de Villance, de Marche-en-Famenne, de Nassogne, de Roussy, de Filsdorf et de Pailhe (par cession de son frere Henri V le Blond, comte de Luxembourg et d'Arlon, le 23 juin 1247), puis de Melin, de Sprimont et de Dalhem (en 1284, par cession du duc de Brabant en echange de ses droits sur le Limbourg), avoué de Villers-Sainte-Gertrude (en 1298, fief dependant de l'abbaye de Nivelles) (+ 1298/1303)

3. m. 1253, Mathilde de Clèves (+ 1304)

4. Walram IV, duc de Limbourg, comte d'Arlon, avoué de Rolduc et de Duisburg (1170-1226)

5. m. 1214, Ermesinde, comtesse de Luxembourg, de la Roche-en-Ardenne et de Durbuy 1186-1247)

6. Thierry de Clèves, dit l'Aine ou Primogenitus, seigneur de Dinslaken (1215-1245)

7. m. 1233, Isabelle de Brabant (1215-1273)

8. Henri III, duc de Limbourg, comte d'Arlon, avoué de Rolduc (1140-1226)

9. m. Sophie de Saarbrücken (+ 1214)

10. Henri IV l'Aveugle, comte de Luxembourg, de Namur, de La Roche-en-Ardenne, de Durbuy et de Longwy, avoué d'Echternach et de Saint-Maximin de Trèves (1113-1196)
11. m. 1168, Agnès de Gueldre (+ 1186)

12. Thierry VI Nust, comte de Clèves, avoué de Xanten, de Zyfflich, de Bedburg et de Saint-Willibrord de Wesel (1190-1260)
13. m. 1207, Mathilde, dame de Dinslaken (+ 1224)

14. Henri I le Guerroyeur, duc de Brabant, avoué de Nivelles, de Gembloux et d'Afflighem (+ 1235)
15. m. 1213, Marie de France (1198-1224)

16. Henri II, duc de Limbourg, comte d'Arlon, avoué de Saint-Trond (1110-1167)
17. m. 1136, Mathilde de Saffenberg, dame de l'avouérie de Rolduc (+ 1145)

18. Simon I, comte de Saarbrücken (1135/83)
19. m. Mechtilde (de Sponheim ?)

20. Godefroid I, comte de Namur, avoué de Saint-Aubain de Namur, de Floreffe et d'Andenne (+ 1139)
21. m. 1109, Ermesinde, comtesse de Luxembourg et de Longwy (+ 1141)

22. Henri, comte de Gueldre et de Zutphen, avoué de Roermond et d'Utrecht (1117-1182)
23. m. 1135, Agnès d'Arnstein (+ 1179)

24. Thierry V, comte de Clèves, avoué de Xanten, de Zyfflich et de Bedburg (1155-1193)
25. m. 1182, Marguerite de Hollande (+ 1203)

28. Godefroid III le Courageux, duc de Brabant, avoué de Nivelles, de Gembloux et d'Afflighem (+ 1190)
29. m. 1155, Marguerite de Limbourg, dame de la haute-avouérie de Saint-Trond (+ 1172)

30. Philippe II Auguste, roi de France (1165-1223)
31. m. 1196, Agnès d'Andechs-Méranie (1180-1201)

32. Walram III Paganus, comte de Limbourg et d'Arlon, avoué de Saint-Trond (+ 1139)
33. m. 1110, Judith de Gueldre, dame de Wassenberg (+ 1161)

34. Adolphe, comte de Saffenberg, de Norvenich et dans le pays de Cologne, avoué de Cologne, de Rolduc, de Marienthal et de Saint-Cassius de Bonn (+ 1158)
35. m. 1122, Marguerite de Schwarzenburg, nièce de Frederic I (de Schwarzenburg), archeveque de Cologne (+ 1122/34)

36. Frederic I, comte de Saarbrücken (+ 1135)
37. m. Gisèle

40. Albert III, comte de Namur et de La Roche-en-Ardenne, avoué de Stavelot-Malmedy, d'Andenne et de Saint-Aubain de Namur (+ 1107)
41. m. 1065, Ida de Saxe (+ 1102)

42. Conrad I, comte de Luxembourg et de Longwy, avoué de Stavelot-Malmedy, de Saint-Maximin de Treves et d'Echternach (+ 1086)
43. m. Clemence de Poitiers (1160-1129)

44. Gerard II le Long, comte de Gueldre, avoué de Roermond et d'Utrecht (+ 1131)
45. m. Irmengarde, comtesse de Zutphen (+ 1141/42)

46. Louis II, comte d'Arnstein (+ 1110/17)
47. m. Udelhilde d'Odenkirchen

48. Thierry IV, comte de Cleves, avoué de Xanten, de Zyfflich et de Bedburg (+ 1172)
49. m. 1155, Adélaïde de Sulzbach (+ 1189)

50. Florent III, comte de Hollande (+ Antioche 1190)
51. m. 1162, Ada d'Écosse (+ 1205)

56. Godefroid II le Jeune, duc de Brabant, avoué de Nivelles, de Gembloux et d'Afflighem (+ 1142)
57. m. Luitgarde de Sulzbach (+ 1162)

58. Henri II, duc de Limbourg, comte d'Arlon, avoué de Saint-Trond (+ 1167)
59. m. 1136, Mathilde de Saffenberg, dame de l'avouérie de Rolduc (+ 1145)

60. Louis VII le Jeune, roi de France (1120-1180)
61. m. 1160, Adèle de Blois-Champagne, regente de France (1140-1206)

62. Berthold VI, duc de Méranie et de Dalmatie, margrave d'Istrie, comte d'Andechs, de Plassenburg, de Wolfratshausen, de Neuburg et de Stein en Carniole, avoué de Benediktbeuern, de Tegernsee, de Brixen, de Formbach et de Langheim (+ 1204)
63. m. 1170, Agnès de Wettin (+ 1185)

64. Henri I, comte de Limbourg, duc de Basse-Lorraine, avoué de Saint-Trond (+ 1119)
65. m. Ne... (Adele ?), comtesse d'Arlon

66. Gerard I Flaminius, comte de Gueldre, seigneur de Wassenberg, avoué d'Utrecht, d'Erkelenz et de Roermund (+ 1138)
67. m. Sophie

68. Adalbert, comte de Saffenberg et de Norvenich, avoué de Rolduc/Klosterrath (+ 1109)
69. m. 1075, Mechtilde de Hollinde, dame de Rode-le-duc/Hertogenrath (+ 1110)

70. Engelbert, comte de Schwarzenburg et de Rotz (+ 1108/25)
71. m. Ne... de Mullemark

72. Sigebert I, comte en Saargau et de Saarbrücken (+ 1080/1105)

80. Albert II, comte de Namur, avoué d'Andenne et de Saint-Aubain de Namur (+ 1064)
81. m. Regelinde de Verdun (+ 1067)

82. Bernard II, duc de Saxe (995-1059)
83. m. 1020, Eilika de Schweinfurt (+ 1055)

84. Giselbert, comte de Luxembourg et de Salm, avoué d'Echternach et de Saint-Maximin de Treves (+ 1059)

86. Guillaume VI l'Aigret, comte de Poitiers, duc d'Aquitaine (+ 1058)
87. m. Ermesinde (+ 1059)

88. Gerard I Flamimius, comte de Gueldre, seigneur de Wassenberg, avoué d'Utrecht, d'Erkelenz et de Roermund (+ 1138)
89. m. Sophie

90. Othon II le Riche, comte de Zutphen et en Frise, avoué de Corvey (1059-1113)
91. m. Judith de Supplinburg, soeur de l'empereur Lothaire III de Supplinburg, duc de Saxe (+ 1118)

92. Louis I, comte d'Arnstein et d'Eimichgau (+ 1067/95)

96. Arnold, comte de Clèves, comte palatin de Tomburg, avoué de Xanten, de Zyfflich et de Bedburg (+ 1147/50)
97. m. 1125, Ida de Louvain (+ 1162)

98. Gebhard III, comte de Sulzbach, avoué de Kastl, de Niedernburg, de Regensburg, de Mondsee, de Niedermunster et de Berchtesgaden (+ 1188)
99. m. 1129, Mathilde de Bavière (+ 1183)

100. Thierry VI, comte de Hollande (+ 1157)
101. m. 1137, Sophie de Rheineck, comtesse de Bentheim (+ 1176)

102. Henri d'Écosse, comte de Northumberland et de Huntingdon (1115-1152)
103. m. 1139, Ada de Warenne-Surrey (+ 1178)

112. Godefroid I le Barbu, comte de Louvain, de Bruxelles et de Brabant, duc de Basse-Lorraine, avoué de Nivelles, de Gembloux et d'Afflighem (+ 1139)
113. m. 1105, Ida de Chiny (+ 1125)

114. Berenger II, comte de Sulzbach (+ 1125)
115. m. Adélaïde de Wolfratshausen-Diessen (+ 1125)

116. Walram III Paganus, comte de Limbourg et d'Arlon, avoué de Saint-Trond (+ 1139)
117. m. 1110, Judith de Gueldre, dame de Wassenberg (+ 1161)

118. Adolphe, comte de Saffenberg, de Norvenich et dans le pays de Cologne, avoué de Cologne, de Rolduc, de Marienthal et de Saint-Cassius de Bonn (+ 1158)
119. m. 1122, Marguerite de Schwarzenburg (+ 1122/34), niece de Frederic I (de Schwarzenburg), archeveque de Cologne

120. Louis VI le Gros, roi de France (1081-1137)
121. m. 1115, Adélaïde de Savoie (1092-1154)

122. Thibaut IV le Grand, comte de Blois, de Champagne et de Sancerre (+ 1152)
123. m. 1122, Mathilde de Carinthie (+ 1162)

124. Berthold V, duc de Méranie et de Dalmatie, margrave d'Istrie, comte d'Andechs, de Plassenburg, de Wolfratshausen, de Neuburg et de Stein en Carniole, avoué de Benediktbeuern, de Tegernsee, de Formbach et de Brixen (+ 1188)
125. m. 1152, Hedwige de Bavière, dame de Dachau (+ 1176)

126. Dedo V de Wettin, dit le Fort, comte de Groitzsch, de Rochlitz et d'Eilenburg, margrave de Basse-Lusace (+ 1190)
127. m. Mathilde de Heinsberg-Valkenburg, comtesse palatine de Saxe et de Sommerschenburg (+ 1189)

128. Udon, comte de Limbourg, avoué de Saint-Trond (+ 1061)
129. m. Judith/Jutta de Luxembourg-Basse-Lorraine

130. Walram II, comte d'Arlon (+ 1070)

136. Hermann IV, comte de Saffenberg et de Norvenich, avoué de Cornelimunster et du Grand-Saint-Martin de Cologne (1041-91)
137. m. Gepa

140. Berthold, comte de Schwarzenburg (+ 1090)
141. m. Richgarde de Sponheim (+ 1138)

160. Albert I, comte de Namur (+ 1011)
161. m. Adélaïde de Basse-Lorraine (+ 1012)

162. Gozelon, comte de Verdun, marquis d'Anvers, duc de Basse et de Haute-Lorraine (+ 1044)

164. Bernard I, duc de Saxe (+ 1011)
165. m. Hildegarde de Stade (+ 1011)

166. Henri, margrave de Schweinfurt et de Nordgau (+ 1017)
167. m. Gerberge de Gleiberg

172. Guillaume V le Grand, comte de Poitiers, duc d'Aquitaine et de Gascogne (+ 1030)
173. m. 1019, Agnes de Bourgogne (+ 1068)

180. Gottschalk, comte de Twenthe et de Hetter (+ 1080/4)
181. m. Adélaïde, comtesse de Zutphen et de Waldenburg, dame d'Alzey et des avouéries de Munster et de Borghorst

182. Gebhard, comte de Supplinburg (+ 1075)
183. m. Hedwig de Formbach (+ 1085/90)

194. Godefroid I le Barbu, comte de Louvain, de Bruxelles et de Brabant, duc de Basse-Lorraine, avoué de Nivelles, de Gembloux et d'Afflighem (+ 1139)
195. m. 1105, Ida de Chiny (+ 1125)

196. Berenger II, comte de Sulzbach (+ 1125)
197. m. Adélaïde de Wolfratshausen-Diessen (+ 1126)

198. Henri IX le Noir, duc de Bavière (1074-1126)
199. m. 1095, Ulfhilde de Saxe (+ 1126)

200. Florent II le Gros, comte de Hollande (+ 1121)
201. m. 1113, Gertrude ditre Petronille de Lorraine (+ 1144)

202. Othon I, comte de Rheineck et de Bentheim, comte palatin du Rhin, avoué de Rolandswerth (+ 1150)
203. m. 1115, Gertrude de Northeim, comtesse de Bentheim et de Rheineck (+ 1054/65)

204. David I le Saint, roi d'Écosse (1080-1153)
205. m. 1115, Mathilde, comtesse de Northumberland et de Huntingdon (+ 1131)

206. Guillaume II de Warenne, comte de Surrey et de Warenne, seigneur de Lewes, de Conisbrough, de Sandal, de Castle-Acre et autres lieux (+ 1138)
207. m. 1116, Isabelle de Vermandois (+ 1131)

224. Henri II, comte de de Louvain, avoué de Nivelles et de Gembloux (+ 1079)
225. m. Adele, comtesse de Betuwe et en Teisterbant (+ 1086)

226. Othon II, comte de Chiny, avoué d'Orval (+ 1125)
227. m. Alix de Namur (+ 1124)

228. Gebhard II, comte de Sulzbach (+ 1085)
229. m. 1079, Irmengarde de Rott-Vohburg (+ 1101)

230. Othon, comte de Diessen, de Wolfratshausen, de Thanning, d'Ambras et de Pustertal (+ 1129)
231. m. Justizia (d'Autriche ?)

232. Henri I, comte de Limbourg et d'Arlon, duc de Basse-Lorraine, avoué de Saint-Trond (+ 1119)
233. m. Adele, comtesse d'Arlon

234. Gerard I le Long ou Flaminius, comte de Gueldre, seigneur de Wassenberg, avoué d'Utrecht, d'Erkelenz et de Roermund (+ 1138)
235. m. Sophie

236. Adalbert, comte de Saffenberg et de Norvenich, avoué de Rolduc/Klosterrath (+ 1158)
237. m. Mechtilde de Hollinde, dame de Rode-le-duc/Hertogenrath (+ 1100)

238. Engelbert, comte de Schwarzenburg et de Rotz (1108/25)
239. m. Ne... de Mullemark

240. Philippe I, roi de France (1053-1108)
241. m. 1072, Berthe de Hollande (1055-1094)

242. Humbert II le Renforce, comte de Savoie (+ 1103)
243. m. 1090, Gisèle de Bourgogne (+ 1133)

244. Étienne I, comte de Blois, de Chartres, de Meaux et de Sancerre (1046-1102)
245. m. 1081, Adèle d'Angleterre, regente de Blois (1062-1138)

246. Engelbert II, duc de Carinthie, margrave d'Istrie (+ 1141)
247. m. 1105, Uta de Passau (+ 1137)

248. Berthold IV, comte d'Andechs et de Plassenburg, avoué de Benediktbeuern (+ 1151)
249. m. Sophie, margravine de Carniole, d'Istrie et de la marche des Wendes (+ 1132)

250. Othon IV, comte palatin de Bavière, de Wittelsbach et de Dachau, avoué de Freising et de Fischbachau (+ 1156)
251. m. Eilika, comtesse de Lengenfeld, de Pettendorf et de Feldheim (+ 1170)

252. Conrad le Grand, comte de Wettin, margrave de Misnie et de Lusace, comte de Groitzsch, de Rochlitz, de Brehna, de Camburg et d'Eilenburg, avoué de Chemnitz, de Naumburg, de Gerbstedt et de Petersberg (1098-1157)
253. m. Luitgarde de Ravenstein et Elschingen (+ 1145)

254. Gossuin II, seigneur de Heinsberg et de Valkenburg (+ 1167/69)
255. m. 1115, Aleidis, comtesse palatine de Saxe et de Sommerschenburg (+ 1170/80)

258. Frederic de Luxembourg, duc de Basse-Lorraine, comte de Limbourg, avoué de Stavelot-Malmedy et de Saint-Trond (+ 1065)
259. m. 1040, Gerberge de Boulogne (1055)

260. Walram I, comte d'Arlon (1032)
261. m. Adèle de Bar-Haute-Lorraine

272. Adolphe II, comte de Saffenberg, avoué de Deutz et de Werden (+ 1041)

280. Frederic I, avoué de Regensburg (+ apres 1075)

282. Engelbert I, comte de Sponheim, de Pustertal et de Kraichgau, avoué de Salzbourg (+ 1096)

283. m. Hadwig de Saxe (1091/1100)

320. Robert, comte de Namur (+ 981)

321. m. Ermengarde

322. Charles de France, dit de Laon, duc de Basse-Lorraine (953-991)

323. m. Adélaïde

324. Godefroid le Captif, comte de Verdun (+ 995)

325. m. Mathilde de Saxe (+ 1108)

328. Hermann Billung, margrave et duc de Saxe (+ 973)

329. m. Hildegarde

330. Henri I le Chauve, comte de Stade (+ 976)

331. m. Hildegarde de Reinhausen

332. Berthold, margrave de Nordgau (915-980)
333. m. Eilika de Walbeck (+ 1015)

336. Sigefroi, comte de Luxembourg et de la Moselle, abbé laique d'Echternach (+ 998)
337. m. Hedwige (+ 1020)

338. Heribert, comte de Gleiberg, de Kinziggau et de Wetterau (+ 992)
339. m. Irmintrude de Meingau et Avelgau

344. Guillaume IV Flebrace, comte de Poitiers, duc d'Aquitaine, abbé laique de Saint-Hilaire de Poitiers (+ 996)
345. m. 966, Emma de Blois (+ 1003)

346. Othon-Guillaume, comte de Bourgogne et de Nevers (958-1026)
347. m. 982, Ermentrude de Roucy (+ 1102)

360. Hermann, comte en Nifterlake

362, Liudolf, comte de Waldenburg, seigneur d'Alzey, avoué de Brauweiler, de Munster, de Borghorst et de Cologne (+ 1031)
363. m. Mathilde, comtesse de Zutphen

364. Bernard, comte de Supplinburg, de Harzgau, de Derlingau et de Nordthuringengau (+ 1069)
365. m. Ida de Querfurt

366. Frederic, comte de Formbach (+ 1065)
367. m. Gertrude de Handensleben (+ 1116)

388. Henri II, comte de Louvain, avoué de Nivelles et de Gembloux (+ 1079)
389. m. Adèle, comtesse de Betuwe et de Teisterbant (+ 1086)

390. Othon II, comte de Chiny (+ 1125)
391. m. Alix de Namur (+ 1124)

392. Gebhard II, comte de Sulzbach (+ 1085)
393. m. 1079, Irmengarde de Rott-Vohburg (+ 1101)

394. Othon, comte de Diessen, de Wolfratshausen, de Thanning, d'Ambras et de Pustertal (+ 1120/29)
395. m. Justizia (d'Autriche ?)

396. Welf I, duc de Bavière, comte d'Altdorf, de Lechrain et en Basse-Bavière (+ 1101)
397. m. 1070, Judith de Flandre (+ 1094)

398. Magnus I, duc de Saxe (+ 1106)
399. m. 1070, Sophie de Hongrie (+ 1095)

400. Thierry V, comte de Hollande (+ 1091)
401. m. 1083, Othelhildis

402. Thierry II le Vaillant, comte d'Alsace, duc de Haute-Lorraine, avoué de Remiremont, de Bouzonville, de Moyenmoutier de Saint-Evre de Toul, de Saint-Pierre, Saint-Martin et Saint-Arnoul de Metz, de Saint-Die et de Saint-Mihiel (+ 1115)
403. m. Hedwig de Formbach (1058-1090)

404. Hermann I, comte de Salm, roi de Germanie (+ 1088)
405. m. Sophie (+ 1059)

406. Henri le Gros, comte de Northeim, margrave de Frise, avoué de Helmarshausen et de Bursfelde (+ 1101)
407. m. 1086, Gertrude de Braunschweig (+ 1117)

408. Malcolm III Canmore, roi d'Écosse (1031-1093)
409. m. 1069/70, Sainte Marguerite d'Angleterre (1045-1093)

410. Waltheof II, comte de Northumberland, de Huntingdon et de Northampton (+ 1076)
411. m. 1070, Judith de Lens (+ apres 1076)

412. Guillaume I de Warenne, comte de Surrey et de Warenne, seigneur de Lewes, de Conisbrough, de Sandal, de Castle-Acre et autres lieux (+ 1089)
413. m. 1070, Gundrade, soeur de Gerbod de Saint-Bertin, comte de Chester (+ 1089)

414. Hugues de France, dit le Grand ou le Maisne, comte de Vermandois et de Valois, seigneur de Chaumont-en-Vexin (1056-1102)
415. m. 1067, Adélaïde, comtesse de Vermandois et de Valois (1065-1124)

448. Lambert II Balderic, dit le Ceinture, comte de Louvain, avoué de Nivelles et de Gembloux (+ 1062)
449. m. Oda de Verdun

450. Eberhard, comte en Betuwe et Teisterbant

452. Arnoul II, comte de Chiny, avoué d'Orval (+ 1106)

453. m. Adélaïde de Roucy (+ 1069)

454. Albert III, comte de Namur et de La Roche-en-Ardenne, avoué de Stavelot-Malmedy (+ 1102)

455. m. 1066, Ida de Saxe (+ 1102)

456. Gebhard I, comte de Sulzbach (+ 1071)

457. m. Ne... de Sulzbach

458. Kuno I, comte palatin de Rott et de Vohburg (+ 1086)

459. m. Uta de Diessen

460. Berthold II, comte de Diessen (1060)

461. m. Ne... de Hohenwart

464. Udo, comte de Limbourg, avoué de Saint-Trond (1061/1078)

465. m. Judith de Luxembourg-Basse-Lorraine

466. Walram II, comte d'Arlon (1070)

472. Hermann IV, comte de Saffenberg et de Norvenich, avoué de Cornelimunster et du Grand-Saint-Martin de Cologne (+ 1090)

473. m. Gepa

476. Berthold, comte de Schwarzenburg (+ 1090)

477. m. Richegarde de Sponheim

480. Henri I, roi de France (1008-1060)

481. m. 1051, Anne de Kiev (1036-1089)

482. Florent I, comte de Hollande (+ 1061)

483. m. 1050, Gertrude de Saxe (+ 1113)

484. Amedee II, comte de Savoie (+ 1080)

485. m. 1065, Jeanne de Genève

486. Guillaume I le Grand, comte de Bourgogne (+ 1087)

487. m. 1049/57, Étiennette de Bigorre (+ 1088)

488. Thibaut III, comte de Blois, de Chartres, de Tours, de Troyes, de Meaux et de Sancerre (+ 1089)
489. m. 1044/45, Gersende du Maine (1044/49)

490. Guillaume le Conquerant, duc de Normandie, roi d'Angleterre (1027-1087)
491. m. 1043, Mathilde de Flandre (1032-1083)

492. Engelbert I, comte de Sponheim, de Pustertal et de Kraichgau, avoué de Salzbourg (+ 1096)
493. m. Hadwig de Saxws (+ 1110)

494. Ulric, comte de Passau et de Pinningen (+ 1099)
495. m. Adélaïde de Lechsgemund-Frontenhausen (+ 1111)

496. Berthold III, comte d'Andechs, avoué de Benediktbeuern (+ après 1095)
497. m. Gisèle de Souabe

498. Poppo II, margrave de Carniole, d'Istrie et de la marche des Wendes (+ 1098/1103)
499. m. Richgardis de Sponheim

500. Othon II, comte de Scheyern et de Dachau, avoué de Freising et de Fischbachau (+ 1110)
501. m. Richarde d'Istrie-Carniole (+ 1107)

502. Frederic, comte de Pettendorf, de Lengenfeld et de Feldheim (+ 1137)

504. Thimo, comte de Wettin, de Kostritz et de Brehna, avoué de Naumburg et de Gerbstedt (+ 1091)
505. m. Ida de Northeim-Bavière

506. Adalbert, comte de Ravenstein
507. m. Berthe, dame d'Elschingen

508. Gossuin I, seigneur de Heinsberg et de Valkenburg (+ 1128)
509. m. 1085, Oda de Walbeck-Thuringe (+ 1152)

510. Frederic, comte palatin de Saxe et de Sommerschenburg (+ 1120)
511. m. 1091/945, Adélaïde de Laufen

516. Frederic, comte de Luxembourg et de la Moselle, avoué de Stavelot (+ 1019)
517. m. 985, Irmintrude de Gleiberg

518. Eustache à l'Oeil, comte de Boulogne (+ 1049)
519. m. Mathilde de Louvain

522. Thierry I, comte de Bar, duc de Haute-Lorraine, avoué de Saint-Mihiel, de Saint-Die et de MoyenmoutI (+ 1033)
523. m. Richilde de Bliesgau

544. Adolphe I, comte de Saffenberg, avoué de Deutz (1018/41)

564. Siegfried, comte de Sponheim et de la marche hongroise (+ 1065)
565. m. Richegarde, comtesse de Pustertal, de Norital, d'Inngau, dame de l'avouérie de Salzbourg

566. Bernard II, duc de Saxe (995-1059)
567. m. 1020, Eilika de Schweinfurt (1055)

640. Berenger, comte de Lommois (+ 947)

641. m. Symphorie de Hainaut

644. Louis IV d'Outremer, roi de France (920-954)

645. m. 939, Gerberge de Germanie, régente de France (913-984)

650. Hermann Billung, margrave et duc de Saxe (+ 973)

651. m. Hildegarde

660. Luder, comte de Stade

664. Arnoul, duc de Bavière (+ 937)

665. m. Judith de Franconie

666. Lorthaire, comte de Walbeck

672. Wigeric, comte d'Ardenne, palatin d'Aix-la-Chapelle (+ 919)

673. m. Cunegonde (+ 923)

678. Megingoz, comte d'Avelgau
679. m. Gerberge de Lorraine

688. Guillaume III Tete d'etoupe, comte de Poitiers, d'Auvergne et de Limoges, duc d'Aquitaine (+ 963)
689. m. 935, Gerloc dite Adèle de Normandie (+ 969)

690. Thibaut I le Tricheur, comte de Blois, de Chartres, de Dunois et de Tours, seigneur de Saumur, de Chinon et de Beaugency (+ 975)
691. m. 943, Ledgarde de Vermandois (+ 978)

692. Adalbert II, marquis d'Ivree, comte d'Aoste, roi d'Italie (936-971)
693. m. 956, Gerberge, comtesse de Mâcon, de Besançon et de Dole (+ 991)

694. Renaud, comte de Roucy, vicomte de reims (+ 947/65)
695. m. 945, Alberarde de Hainaut

724. Ezzo Erenfried, comte palatin de Basse-Lorraine, comte d'Auelgau et de Bonngau, avoué de Brauweiler (+ 1034)
725. m. 991, Mathilde de Germanie (+ 1025)

726. Othon I, comte de Zutphen (+ 1021) (= Othon de Hamerstein ?)

728. Liutger, comte de Harzgau et de Nordthuringengau (+ 1031)

730. Gebhard, comte de Querfurt (+ 1017)

731. m. Ne... de Hassegau

732. Tiemo/Dietrich, comte de Formbach et de Schweinachgau, avoué de Saint-Emmmeran, d'Altaich et de Formbach (+ 1049/55)

734. Conrad, comte de Handensleben (+ 1056)

776. Lambert II Balderic dit le Ceinture, comte de Louvain, avoué de Nivelles et de Gembloux (+ 1062)

777. m. Oda de Verdun

778. Eberhard, comte en Betuwe et Teisterbant

780. Arnoul II, comte de Chiny (+ 1106)
781. m. Adélaïde de Roucy (+ 1089)

782. Albert III, comte de Namur et de La Roche-en-Ardenne, avoué de Stavelot-Malmedy (+ 1102)
783. m. 1065, Ida de Saxe (+ 1102)

784. Gebhard I, comte de Sulzbach (+ 1071)
785. m. Ne... de Sulzbach

786. Kuno, comte palatin de Rott et de Vohburg (+ 1086)
787. m. Uta de Diessen

788. Berthold II, comte de Diessen (+ 1060)
789. m. Ne... de Hohenwart

792. Azzon II, marquis d'Este en en Ligurie orientale (+ 1097)
793. m. 1035, Cunegonde dite Kuniza Welf, comtesse de Basse-Bavière, de Lechrain et d'Altdorf (1020-1055)

794. Baudouin IV le Barbu, comte de Flandre (+ 1035)
795. m. 1030, Alienore de Normandie

796. Ordulf, duc de Saxe (+ 1063)
797. m. 1043, Ulfhilde de Norvege (+ 1071)

798. Bela I, roi de Hongrie (+ 1063)
799. m. 1039, Richeza de Pologne (1018-1059)

800. Florent I, comte de Hollande (+ 1061)
801. m. 1050, Gertrude de Saxe (+ 1113)

804. Gerard de Chatenois, comte d'Alsace et de Metz, duc de Haute-Lorraine, avoué de Remiremont, de Bouzonville, de Moyenmoutier, de Saint-Evre de Toul, de Saint-Pierre et Saint-Martin de Metz, de Saint-Die et de Saint-Mihiel (+ 1070)
805. m. Hadwide (+ 1067/80)

806. Frederic, comte de Formbach (1030-1059)
807. m. 1056, Getrude de Handensleben (+ 1116)

808. Giselbert, comte de Luxembourg et de Salm, avoué d'Echternach et de Saint-Maximin de Treves (+ 1059)

812. Othon I, comte de Northeim, duc de Bavière, avoué de Corvey (+ 1083)
813. m. 1050, Richenza de Lorraine-Souabe (+ 1083)

814. Egbert/Ekbert, comte de Braunschweig, margrave de Misnie et de Frise (+ 1068)
815. m. 1058/60, Irmingarde de Turin (+ 1078)

816. Duncan I le Gracieux, roi d'Écosse (1011-1040)
817. m. Suthen, parente/soeur de Siward, comte de Northumberland

818. Edouard l'Exile d'Angleterre (+ 1057)
819. m. Agathe

820. Siward le Danois, comte de Northumberland et de Huntingdon (+ 1021/55)
821. m. Aelfleda, comtesse de Northumberland

822. Lambert de Boulogne, comte de Lens (+ 1054)
823. m. 1053, Adélaïde de Normandie, comtesse d'Aumale (+ 1081)

824. Ranulf/Rodulf II, seigneur de Varennes
825. m. Emma

828. Henri I, roi de France (1008-1060)
829. m. 1051, Anne de Kiev (1036-1089)

830. Heribert IV, comte de Vermandois (1045/70)
831. m. 1065, Adèle, comtesse de Valois

896. Lambert I le Barbu, comte de Louvain, avoué de Nivelles et de Gembloux (+ 1015)
897. m. 985, Gerberge de Basse-Lorraine (975-1018)

898. Gozelon I, comte de Verdun, marquis d'Anvers, duc de Basse et de Haute-Lorraine (+ 1044)

900. Fretehard, comte en Teisterbant (+ 996)

904. Louis II, comte de Chiny (+ 1068)
905. m. Sophie de Verdun

906. Hulduin III, comte de Ramerupt et d'Arcis-sur-Aube (+ 1063)
907. m. Adele, comtesse de Roucy, vicomtesse de Reims (+ 1062)

908. Albert II, comte de Namur, avoué d'Andenne et de Saint-Aubain de Namur (+ 1064)
909. m. Regelinde de Verdun

910. Bernard II, duc de Saxe (995-1072)
911. m. 1020, Eilika de Schweinfurt (1055)

912. Hermann IV, duc de Souabe (+ 1038)
913. m. Adélaïde, marquise de Turin, comtesse de Suse et d'Auriate (+ 1090)

914. Berenger I, comte de Sulzbach et en Bavière

916. Poppo II, comte de Rott et de Vohburg (+ 1002/40)
917. m. Ne... Welf d'Altdorf

918. Frederic I, burgrave de Regensburg (+ apres 1075)

920. Frederic, comte de Diessen (+ 1003/30)

921. m. Cunegonde dite Kuniza de ohningen-Souabe (+ 1020)

922. Conrad, comte de Hohenwart (+ 1005)

930. Frederic de Luxembourg, duc de Basse-Lorraine, avoué de Stavelot-Malmedy et de Saint-Trond (+ 1065)

931. m. Gerberge de Boulogne (+ 1059)

932. Walram I, comte d'Arlon (1032)

933. m. Adèle de Bar-Haute-Lorraine

944. Adolphe II, comte de Saffenberg, avoué de Deutz et de Werden (1041)

952. Frederic I, avoué de Regensburg (+ apres 1075)

954. Engelbert I, comte de Sponheim. de Pustertal et de Kraichgau, avoué de Salzbourg (+ 1096)

955. m. Hadwig de Saxe (+ 1091/1100)

960. Robert II le Pieux, roi de France (972-1031)
961. m. 1003, Constance d'Arles (986-1032)

962. Iaroslav I le Sage, grand-prince de Kiev, prince de Novgorod (980-1054)
963. m. 1019, Ingegerd de Suede (+ 1050)

964. Thierry III le Hlosolymitain, comte de Frise et de Hollande (+ 1039)
965. m. Othelendis de Nordmark (+ 1044)

966. Bernard II, duc de Saxe (995-1059)
967. m. 1020, Eilika de Schweinfurt (+ 1055)

968. Odon, comte de Savoie (+ 1069)
969. m. 1046, Adélaïde, marquise de Turin, comtesse de Suse et d'Auriate (1015-1091)

970. Gerold, comte de Geneve, avoué de Saint-Victor de Geneve (1032/61)
971. m. Gisèle

972. Renaud I, comte de Bourgogne (990-1057)
973. m. 1016, Adélaïde dite Judith de Normandie (+ 1037)

974. Bernard II, comte de Bigorre (+ 1077)
975. m. Clemence de Barcelone (1062)

976. Eudes II, comte de Blois, de Chartres, de Dunois, de Tours, de Troyes, de Meaux et de Sancerre, seigneur de Chinon et de Saumur (+ 1037)
977. m. 1005, Ermengarde d'Auvergne (+ 1042)

978. Heribert eveillechien, comte du Maine (+ 1036)
979. m. Paule de Preuilly

980. Robert le Magnifique, duc de Normandie (+ 1035)
981. m. Herleve

982. Baudouin V de Lille, comte de Flandre, regent de France (1013-1067)
983. m. 1028, Adèle de France (+ 1079)

984. Siegfried, comte de Sponheim et de la marche hongroise (+ 1055)
985. m. Richgarde, comtesse de Pustertal, de Norital et d'Inngau, dame de l'avouérie de Salzbourg (+ 1040)

986. Bernard II, duc de Saxe (995-1072)
987. m. 1020, Eilika de Schweinfurt (1055)

990. Kuno de Harburg, comte de Lechsgemund et de Frontenhausen (+ 1092)
991. m. Mathilde d'Achalm

992. Berthold II, comte de Diessen (1025 - 1060)
993. m. Ne... de Hohenwart

994. Othon, margrave de Schweinfurt et de Nordgau, duc de Souabe (+ 1057)
995. m. 1036, Irmingarde de Turin (+ 1078)

996. Ulric II, margrave de Carniole et d'Istrie, comte de Weimar (+ 1070)
997. m. 1062, Sophie de Hongrie (+ 1095)

998. Engelbert I, comte de Sponheim, de Pustertal et de Kraichgau, avoué de Salzbourg (+ 1096)
999. m. Hadwig de Saxe (1091/1100)

1000. Othon I, comte de Scheyern, avoué de Freising (+ 1072)
1001. m. 1057, Haziga de Diessen (+ 1104)

1002. Ulric II, margrave de Carniole et d'Istrie, comte de Weimar (+ 1070)
1003. m. 1062, Sophie de Hongrie (+ 1095)

1004. Ruotger, comte de Feldheim
1005. m. Heilika, comtesse de Lengenfeld et de Pettendorf (+ 1117)

1008. Thierry II de Wettin, comte de Brehna et d'Eilenburg, margrave de Basse-Lusace (+ 1034)
1009. m. Mathilde de Misnie

1010. Othon I, comte de Northeim, duc de Bavière, avoué de Corvey (+ 1083)
1011. m. Richeza de Lorraine-Souabe (+ 1082)

1018. Siegfried II de Walbeck, comte en Thuringe septentrionale et en Delingau (1068/85)

1020. Adalbert, comte de Sommerschenburg et en Thuringe (1059)
1021. m. Oda de Merseburg, comtesse palatine de Saxe (+ 1088)

1022. Henri, comte de Laufen et en Lobdengau
1023. m. 1050, Ida de Werl

UPDATE RE MARGUERITE DE LUXEMBOURG LINEAGE

According to Jean Bunot, Marguerite de Luxembourg, Dame de Ghistelles, is, in his opinion, the *main royal gateway* of Catherine de Baillon.

Marguerite de Luxembourg married Jean III de Ghistelles, Seigneur de Ghistelles, between 1284 and before June 1289.

Jean IV de Ghistelles, seigneur de Ghistelles, married Marie de Heverskerke, Dame de Straten, shortly after June 1337.

Roger de Ghistelles, ~~Seigneur de Dudzeele et de Straten~~, married Élisabeth ~~Marguerite~~, Dame de Dudzeele, in, or shortly before, 1357.

habitant.org/baillon/Dudzeele%20Article%201.pdf

In addition to getting her name wrong, the authors of <u>Table d'ascendance de Catherine Baillon: 12 générations</u> also misunderstood the way the *seigneurie* of Straten came into the Ghistelles family. Several sources indicate that her given name was Isabeau, Isabelle or Élisabeth de Dudzeele.

With a sister named Marguerite as well as an aunt, also named Marguerite de Dudzeele, who is mentioned in a legal case of 1386-1387 associated with Roger de Ghistelles, it appears that <u>some historians confused these Marguerite's with Élisabeth</u>.

In accordance with a document found by Piot, she is clearly identified as Élisabeth.

In <u>Table d'ascendance de Catherine Baillon: 12 générations</u> it is suggested that Roger de Ghistelles was *seigneur* of Dudzeele through his marriage with Dame de Dudzeele, and that he was also the *seigneur* of Straten, through his mother, Marie de Haverskerke, and in turn through her mother, Marie de Straten. However, both the *seigneurie* of Straten and Dudzeele came to Roger through his wife Élisabeth (who was quite well off).

From her uncle Baudouin de Dudzeele, she inherited the fief of Westkapelle, the castle of Dudzeele with the sub-fief of Bonhem, and a second unnamed fief at Dudzeele as well as 80 *livres parisis* (a Parisian livre, a French monetary unit) of rent all within the *tonlieu* (a district in which one must pay a tax to transport or sell merchandise) of Bruges and within the land of the counts of Flanders.

in 1377-1378, in advance of her inheritence, she received 60 *arpents* (a French measurement of land close to an English acre in size) of land in a polder in the *seigneurie* of Straten in the parish of St-André from her mother.

She retro-ceded the *seigneurie* of Straten at St-André to her sister, but held on to the castle and *seigneurie* of Straten at Varsenare with the *ammanie* (an administrative district run by an *amman*) of Varsenare and the sub-fiefs situated at Stalhille and Jabbeke. At the death of her sister, Marguerite, who never married, Élisabeth regained the lands her sister had held.

In contrast, her husband, Roger de Ghistelles, was a younger son and appears to have been landless, so his match to Élisabeth was indeed fortunate for him.

Élisabeth de Dudzeele was a second cousin once removed of her husband, Roger de Ghistelles, both sharing a relationship back to Richard de Stanten III. Roger de Ghistelles became the seigneur of both Straten and Dudzeele through her rights of inheritance.

The Dudzeeles were a prominent Flemish family in the 13th and 14th centuries, but they died out in the male line and much of their history has been lost.

Armenian Connections for Catherine Baillon

Wives of Andrew II of Hungary

Roland-Yves Gagné

As I am the author of the article in the Mémoires, so please allow me to give some explanations concerning this question.

First, the Société généalogique canadienne-française published, in Summer 2001, the following article in its Mémoires, which is genealogical journal in French speaking countries with the highest amount of issues:

Roland Yves-Gagné and Paul Leportier. "L'ascendance de Michel d'Aigneaux d'Ouville." Mémoires de la Société généalogique canadienne-française 52:2 (Summer 2001): 95-104.

At the end, I explained how two settlers in New France, Michel d'Aigneaux d'Ouville and Catherine de Baillon, were descendants of an Armenian, Gabriel, governor of Melitene.

In a chart (Tableau 9, page 104), the lineage from Gabriel de Mélitène to Catherine de Baillon goes through André II of Hungary, whose daughter Marie of Hungary married Asèn II of Bulgaria.

So, the debate: who was the mother of Marie of Hungary? It could either have been Yolande de Courtenay (second spouse of Andrew II) or Gertrude von Meran (first spouse of Andrew II).

407

https://groups.google.com/forum/#!searchin/soc.genealogy.medieval/catherine$20de$20baillon/soc.genealogy.medieval/GP25rfFyaig/rM_BtwczEDMJ%5B1-25%5D

To draft the chart for <u>Mémoires</u>, I used a source: Philippe Struyf, Les comtes de Vintimille ou "des comtes de Vintimille aux Lascaris", Étude généalogique non terminée (the author died in 1996).

Struyf has a chart at 2.4 entitled "Eudoxie Lascaris et les Capétians", in which he states that Marie de Hongrie, x 1221 Jean Asèn II de Bulgarie, was the daghter of Yolande de Courtenay.

I had also put as a footnote Isenburg, which I just consulted at McGill University library (tafel 105, b. II). To the contrary, Isenburg states that Andreas II of Hungary married first before 1203 Gertrud von Meran, d. Bertold III von Meran, and they were the parents of Maria x 1221 Asan II king of Bulgaria.

This makes more sense indeed, and, at first glance, it seems that my source was wrong, and so was I. We see at the next generation how squeezed are the dates: Asan II's daughter Helene got married in 1235 with Theodore II Lascaris.

October 2, 2001

Ascendance de Guy I Le Bouteiller [408]

Seigneur de La Bouteillerie et de La Vieuville

Jean Bunot

Possible linkage from de Bréauté to the House of Dreux

The Ahnentafel format is a genealogical numbering system for listing a person's direct ancestors in a fixed sequence of ascent. [409] The key to reading an ahnentafel is to understand its numbering system.

Basically, you double any individual's number to get their father's number. You also double any individual's number and add one to get their mother's number. On your ahnentafel chart, for example, you would be number 1; your father would then be number 2 and your mother, number 3. Other than the starting person, males always have even numbers and women the odd numbers. In keeping with this system, (+ ----) simply refers to the year that they died.

1. Guy Ier Le Bouteiller, seigneur de La Bouteillerie et de La Vieuville, puis de La Roche-Guyon et de Bois-Guillaume, conseiller chambellan du duc de Bourgogne, capitaine de Dieppe et de Rouen, maître d'hôtel du duc de Bedford (+ 1438), ép. 1419/25, Catherine de Gavre-Escornaix, dame de La Boissière et de Vaux-sur-Orge (+ 1452/72)

---

[408] http://newsgroups.derkeiler.com/Archive/Soc/soc.genealogy.medieval/2005-09/msg01514.html
[409] https://en.wikipedia.org/wiki/Ahnentafel

2. Jean Le Bouteiller, seigneur de La Bouteillerie (+ après 1408)
3. ép. 1380/85, **Ne... de Bréauté**, dame de La Bouteillerie, soeur de Roger III, seigneur de Bréauté, de Néville et de Menneval, conseiller et chambellan du duc de Bourgogne, gouverneur de Normandie

4. Regnaut Le Bouteiller, chevalier (1382)

6. Roger II, seigneur de Bréauté, de Néville, de Drosay et de Houville
7. ép. 1364, **Jeanne de Léon**, dame de Menneval [410]

12. Guillaume II, seigneur de Bréauté, de Néville et de Drosay
13. ép. 1327, Catherine de Créquy (1332)

410

https://books.google.ca/books?id=ifVAAAAcAAJ&pg=PA398&lpg=PA398&dq=.+Jean+de+L%C3%A9on+%2B+Jeanne+de+Varennes&source=bl&ots=cFQVu838Ll&sig=8SIkVJw1Ih-WvwDNq5cjTIkagTU&hl=en&sa=X&ved=0ahUKEwj58Pqh8PDMAhVCVFIKHbm9B6QQ6AEIKTAE#v=onepage&q=.%20Jean%20de%20L%C3%A9on%20%2B%20Jeanne%20de%20Varennes&f=false

14. **Jean de Léon**, seigneur de Montaigu, puis de Hacqueville, de Fontaine-sous-Jouy, de Crestot, de Pont-Saint-Pierre et de La Franche-Bouteillerie, capitaine de Château-Gaillard (1369) [411]
15. ép. 1340, Jeanne de Varennes, dame de Menneval

24. Guillaume Ier, seigneur de Bréauté, vicomte de Montivilliers
25. ép. Jeanne, dame de Néville et de Drosay

26. Jean Ier l'Estandart, seigneur de Créquy, de Fressin et de Canaples (1289/1327)
27. ép. 1290/1300, Jeanne de Beauvais

28. **Guillaume Ier de Léon**, seigneur de Hacqueville, de Fontaine-sous-Jouy, de Pont-Saint-Pierre, de Crestot et de La Franche-Bouteillerie [412]
29. ép. 1315, Jeanne de Ferrières

---

[411] https://books.google.ca/books?id=ifVAAAAcAAJ&pg=PA398&lpg=PA398&dq=.+Jean+de+L%C3%A9on+%2B+Jeanne+de+Varennes&source=bl&ots=cFQVu838Ll&sig=8SIkVJw1Ih-WvwDNq5cjTIkagTU&hl=en&sa=X&ved=0ahUKEwj58Pqh8PDMAhVCVFIKHbm9B6QQ6AEIKTAE#v=onepage&q=.%20Jean%20de%20L%C3%A9on%20%2B%20Jeanne%20de%20Varennes&f=false

[412] https://fr.wikipedia.org/wiki/Hervé_V_de_Léon_(seigneur_de_Léon)

30. Mathieu de Varennes, seigneur de Menneval

48. Roger Ier, seigneur de Bréauté, de Brunes-en-Caux et de Foville
49. ép. Alix de Bournonville

52. Baudouin IV, seigneur de Créquy et de Fressin (1249/66)
53. ép. Marie d'Amiens, dame de Canaples (+ après 1338)

54. Guillaume II, châtelain de Beauvais, seigneur de Vascueil
55. ép. Éléonore Crespin, dame de Ferrières, de Ry et de Saint-Denis-le-Thiboust

56. **Hervé IV, vicomte de Léon**, seigneur en partie de Châteauneuf-en-Thimerais et de Senonches (+ 1304) [413]
57. ép. 1280, Mahaut de Poissy, dame de Noyon-sur-Andelle, de Hacqueville, de Radepont, de Pont-Saint-Pierre, de Fontaine-sous-Jouy, d'Acquigny et autres lieux

58. Jean, seigneur de Ferrières et de Grandcamp (1295/1342)
59. ép. 1290, Alix d'Harcourt, dame de Bougthéroulde

---

[413] racineshistoire.free.fr/LGN/PDF/Chateauneuf-en-Thymerais.pdf (page 6)

60. Florent de Varennes, seigneur de Menneval, amiral de France Durant la croisade de saint Louis (+ 1269)

104. Philippe, seigneur de Créquy et de Fressin (1238/55)

105. ép. 1224, Ide de Picquigny

106. Gilles d'Amiens, seigneur de Canaples et d'Outrebois (+ après 1284)

112. Hervé III, vicomte de Léon

113. ép. 1250/60, **Marguerite de Châteauneuf**, dame en partie de Châteauneuf-en-Thimerais et de Senonches [414]

114. Robert de Poissy, seigneur de Radepont et de Malvoisine (+ 1258)

115. ép. 1256, Isabelle de Marly, dame de Romanaville (+ 1292)

118. Jean Ier le Prud'homme, seigneur d'Harcourt, d'Elbeuf, de Brionne, de La Saussaye, de Néhou, d'Auvers, d'Aurilly et autres lieux, vicomte de Saint-Sauveur (+ 1280)

119. ép. 1240, Alix de Beaumont (+ 1275)

---

[414] racineshistoire.free.fr/LGN/PDF/Chateauneuf-en-Thymerais.pdf (page 5)

208. Baudouin III le Jeune, seigneur de Créquy et de Fressin
209. ép. 1200, Marguerite de Saint-Omer

210. Enguerrand, seigneur de Picquigny, vidame d'Amiens (+1211/24)
211. ép. Marguerite de Ponthieu (+ après 1209)

212. Pierre d'Amiens, seigneur de Canaples (+ après 1279)
213. ép. Hersende

224. Hervé II, vicomte de Léon (+ croisé 1218)
225. ép. 1210/15, Anne d'Hennebont, dame de Guéméné-Héboé

226. Hugues III, seigneur de Châteauneuf-en-Thimerais (+ 1229) [415] [416]
227. ép. 1212, **Éléonore de Dreux** (+ 1248) [417] [418]

---

[415] fmg.ac/Projects/MedLands/PARIS%20REGION%20NOBILITY.htm#HuguesChateauneufMELéonoreDreux

[416] racineshistoire.free.fr/LGN/PDF/Chateauneuf-en-Thymerais.pdf (pages 4 and 5)

[417] fmg.ac/Projects/MedLands/PARIS%20REGION%20NOBILITY.htm#ELéonoreDreuxdied1248

[418] racineshistoire.free.fr/LGN/PDF/Dreux.pdf (Page 3)

228. Guillaume de Poissy, seigneur de Noyon-sur-Andelle, de Radepont, de Hacqueville, de Pont-Saint-Pierre, de Fontaine-sous-Jouy, d'Acquigny et autres lieux (1270)
229. ép. avant 1243, Isabelle (? de Lévis)

230. Bouchard II, seigneur de Marly, de Montreuil-Bonnin en Poitou, de Saissac en Carcassès, de Picauville et de Londres (+ 1250)
231. ép. 1233, Agnès de Beaumont-en-Gâtinais (+ après 1260)

236. Richard, seigneur d'Harcourt, d'Elbeuf, de Brionne, de Beaumesnil, de La Saussaye, de Beauficel, de Cailleville et autres lieux (+ 1239/42)
237. ép. Jeanne Tesson de La Roche-Tesson, vicomtesse de Saint-Sauveur et du Cotentin, dame de Néhou, d'Auvers et d'Aurilly

238. Jean de Beaumont, seigneur de Villemomble, de Clignancourt et de Clichy-la-Garenne, grand chambrier de France (+ 1255/56)
239. ép. 1214, Alix, dame de Villemomble et de Clignancourt (+ avant 1233)

416. Baudouin II, seigneur de Créquy et de Fressin (1160/98)
417. ép. Clémence (1160)

418. Guillaume IV, châtelain de Saint-Omer
419. ép. 1171, Ide d'Avesnes

420. Guermond, seigneur de Picquigny, vidame d'Amiens (+ 1208)
421. ép. Flandrine (d'Amiens ?)

422. Jean Ier Talvas, comte de Ponthieu (+ Saint-Jean d'Acre 1191)
423. ép. 1175, Béatrix de Saint-Pol (+ 1204)

424. Thibaut d'Amiens, seigneur de Canaples
425. ép. Aélis

448. Hervé Ier, vicomte de Léon, seigneur de Landerneau, de Daoudour, de Coatméal, de Plougastel-Daoulas, de Crozon, de Penzé et de Bourgneuf-en-Poher (+ 1208)
449. ép. 1180, Marguerite de Rohan

452. Gervais, seigneur de Châteauneuf-en-Thimerais, de Bresolles, de Senonches et autres lieux
453. ép. Marguerite de Donzy

454. **Robert II le Jeune, comte de Dreux** et de Braine, seigneur de Torcy, de Brie-Comte-Robert, de Chilly, de Longjumeau, de Nesle-en-Tardenois, de Fère-en-Tardenois, de Quincy, de Longueville et de Pontarcy (1154-1218) [419] [420]
455. ép. 1184, Yolande de Coucy (+ 1222) [421] [422]

460. Bouchard Ier, seigneur de Marly, de Montreuil-Bonnin en Poitou, de Saissac en Carcassès, de Picauville et de Londres (+ 1226)
461. ép. 1209, Mahaut de Poissy, dame de Châteaufort (1212/67)

462. Guillaume de Beaumont, dit Pied-de-Rat, maréchal de France (1215/17)
463. ép. Jeanne

472. Robert II le Vaillant, seigneur d'Harcourt, de La Saussaye, de Beauficel et de Boessy-le-Châtel (1192/1212)
473. ép. 1179, Jeanne de Meulan, dame de Brionne, d'Elbeuf et de Beaumesnil

---

[419] fmg.ac/Projects/MedLands/PARIS%20REGION%20NOBILITY.htm#RobertIIDreuxdied1218B
[420] racineshistoire.free.fr/LGN/PDF/Dreux.pdf (page 2)
[421] fmg.ac/Projects/MedLands/CHAMPAGNE%20NOBILITY.htm#YolandeCoucydied1222
[422] racineshistoire.free.fr/LGN/PDF/Coucy.pdf (page 5)

474. Raoul V Tesson, seigneur de La Roche-Tesson, du Cinglais et de Trévières, baron de Thury, vicomte de Saint-Sauveur (+ 1213)
475. ép. Mathilde Patry de La Lande-Patry

832. Raoul, seigneur de Créquy (1160/+1181)

836. Guillaume III, châtelain de Saint-Omer
837. ép. Mathilde

838. Nicolas, seigneur d'Avesnes, de Condé, de Leuze et de Landrecies (+ 1169/71)
839. ép. 1150, Mathilde de La Roche-en-Ardenne

840. Guérand, seigneur de Picquigny, vidame d'Amiens (+ 1178)
841. ép. Mathilde

844. Guy II Talvas, comte de Ponthieu (+ Éphèse 1147)
845. ép. Ida

846. Anselme Ier, comte de Saint-Pol, seigneur d'Encre et de Lucheux
847. ép. Eustachie

848. Dreux, châtelain d'Amiens, seigneur de Flexicourt, de L'Étoile et de La Broye (+ 1195)
849. ép. Marguerite de Saint-Pol

896. Guyomarch VI l'Insensé, comte de Léon (+ 1179)
897. ép. 1150, Nobilis (du Faou, de Tréguier ?)

898. Alain III, vicomte de Rohan, seigneur de Guéméné (+ 1195)
899. ép. 1160, Constance de Bretagne, dame de Mur et de Corlay (+ 1184)

906. Hervé III, seigneur de Donzy, de Saint-Aignan-sur-Cher, de Gien, de Cosne-sur-Loir et autres lieux (1149/+1187)
907. ép. Mathilde du Perche-Gouët, dame de Montmirail, de Brou, de La Bazoche-Gouët, de La Chapelle-Guillaume, d'Authon-du-Perche, d'Arrou, d'Alluyes et de Dangeau

908. **Robert Ier le Grand, comte de Dreux**, seigneur de Torcy, de Brie-Comte-Robert, de Chilly, de Longjumeau et de Savigny (1123-1188) [423]
909. ép. 1152, Agnès, dame de Baudement, de Braine-sur-Vesle, de Fère-en-Tardenois, de Nesle-en-Tardenois, de Quincy, de Longueville et de Pontarcy (1130-1202/18) [424]

---

[423] fmg.ac/Projects/MedLands/PARIS%20REGION%20NOBILITY.htm#RobertIDreuxdied1188B

910. Raoul Ier, seigneur de Coucy, de Marle, de La Fère, de Vervins, de Crécy et autres lieux (+ 1191)
911. ép. 1164, Agnès la Boiteuse de Hainaut (+ 1168/73)

920. Mathieu de Montmorency, seigneur de Marly et de Verneuil (+ Constantinople 1204)
921. ép. Mahaut de Garlande (+ 1224)

922. Gasce de Poissy, seigneur de Châteaufort (+ 1189)
923. ép. 1188, Constance de Courtenay (+ après 1231)

924. Guillaume de Beaumont, chambellan du roi (+ 1191)

944. Guillaume, seigneur d'Harcourt, de Beauficel et de Boessy-le-Châtel (1124)
945. ép. Huë d'Amboise

424

fmg.ac/Projects/MedLands/PARIS%20REGION%20NOBILITY.htm#AgnesBrainedied1217

946. Robert III, comte de Beaumont-le-Roger et de Meulan, seigneur de Brionne, d'Elbeuf, de Beaumesnil, de Pont-Audemer, de Montfort-sur-Risle, de Préaux, de Vieilles et autres lieux (1163/99)
947. ép. Mathilde de Cornwall (1163/79)

948. Jourdain Tesson, seigneur de La Roche-Tesson, du Cinglais et de Trévières, baron de Thury (1170)
949. ép. Létice, vicomtesse de Saint-Sauveur et du Cotentin

950. Enguerrand Patry, seigneur de La Lande-Patry (+ 1195)
951. ép. Ne... de Creully

1664. Gérard, seigneur de Créquy et de Fressin (1096/1127)
1665. ép. Yolande

1672. Guillaume II, châtelain de Saint-Omer
1673. ép. Mélisende de Picquigny

1676. Gautier d'Oisy, seigneur d'Avesnes, de Condé, de Leuze et de Landrecies (+ 1147)
1677. ép. Ada de Mortagne-Tournai

1678. Henri de Namur, comte de La Roche-en-Ardenne, avoué de Stavelot-Malmédy (1102/38)
1679. ép. Mathilde de Limbourg (1148)

1680. Guermond, seigneur de Picquigny, vidame d'Amiens
1681. ép. Béatrix d'Aumâle

1688. Guillaume Ier Talvas, comte de Ponthieu, d'Alençon et de Bellême (+ 1171)
1689. ép. 1115, Hélie de Bourgogne (1080-1142)

1692. Hugues III, comte de Saint-Pol (+ 1141)
1693. ép. Béatrix

1696. Alléaume, châtelain d'Amiens (+ 1176)
1697. ép. Ade de Coucy

1698. Hugues III, comte de Saint-Pol (+ 1141)
1699. ép. Béatrix

1792. Hervé II le Grand, comte de Léon (+ 1169)

1796. Alain II, vicomte de Rohan, seigneur de Guéméné et de Guincamp (+ 1168)

1798. Alain II le Noir, comte de Richmond et de Guincamp (+ 1146)

1799. ép. 1137, Berthe, duchesse de Bretagne (+ 1158/64)

1812. Geoffroy III, seigneur de Donzy, de Saint-Aignan-sur-Cher et de Gien (+ 1157)

1813. ép. Garne, dame de Cosne-sur-Loir (1151)

1814. Guillaume IV Gouët, baron du Perche-Gouët, seigneur de Montmirail, de Brou, de La Bazoche-Gouët, de La Chapelle-Guillaume, d'Authon-du-Perche, d'Alluyes et de Dangeau (+ 1170)

1815. ép. 1150/55, Isabelle de Blois-Champagne, régente du Perche-Gouët (1130-après 1180)

1816. **Louis VI le Gros, roi de France** (1081-1137)

1817. ép. 1115, Adélaïde de Savoie (1092-1137)

1818. Guy, seigneur de Baudement, de Braine-sur-Vesle, de Quincy, de Longueville, de Nesle-en-Tardenois, de Fère-en-Tardenois et de Pontarcy

1819. ép. Alix

1820. Enguerrand II, seigneur de Coucy, de Marle, de La Fère, de Crécy, de Vervins et de Pinon (1131/47)
1821. ép. 1132, Agnès de Beaugency

1822. Baudouin IV le Bâtisseur, comte de Hainaut (1110-1171)
1823. ép. 1130, Alix de Namur (+ 1169)

1840. Mathieu Ier, seigneur de Montmorency, d'Écouen, de Marly, de Verneuil, de Conflans-Sainte-Honorine, d'Attichy et autres lieux (+ 1160)
1841. ép. 1126, Aline, bâtarde d'Angleterre et de Normandie

1842. Guillaume de Garlande, seigneur de Livry (1181/1204)
1843. ép. Idoine de Trie (1208)

1844. Gasce de Poissy, seigneur de Fresnes et de Maisons-sur-Seine (+ 1172)

1846. Pierre de France, seigneur de Courtenay, de Montargis, de Châteaurenard, de Tanlay, de Champignelles, de Charny et de Chantecoq (1126-1183)
1847. ép. 1150/55, Isabelle, dame de Courtenay et autres lieux

1888. Robert le Fort, seigneur d'Harcourt (1100)

1889. ép. Colette d'Argouges

1890. Hugues Ier, seigneur d'Amboise, de Chaumont-sur-Loire et de Montrichard (+ 1130)

1891. ép. 1103, Élisabeth, dame de Jaligny

1892. Waleran, comte de Beaumont-le-Roger et de Meulan, comte de Worcester, seigneur de Pont-Audemer, de Brionne, d'Elbeuf, de Beaumesnil, de Vieilles, de Préaux et autres lieux (+ 1166)

1893. ép. 1141, Agnès de Montfort, dame de Gournay

1894. Renaud/Reginald, bâtard d'Angleterre et de Normandie, seigneur de Dunstanville, comte de Cornwall (+ 1175)

1895. ép. 1140, Béatrice de Cardinham

1896. Raoul IV Tesson, seigneur de La Roche-Tesson et du Cinglais, baron de Thury

1897. ép. Adelize, dame de Trévières

1898. Néel V, vicomte de Saint-Sauveur (+ 1131)

1899. ép. Cécile, dame de Formigny

1900. Guillaume IV Patry, seigneur de La Lande-Patry (+ 1174)
1901. ép. Mathilde

1902. Richard, baron de Creully (+ 1184)
1903. ép. Mathilde, dame de Saint-Clair-sur-L'Elle et de Villiers-Fossard

Baillon Descent via Grimaldi Lineages

John P. Dulong, Ph.D.

There are some mistakes in Catherine Baillon's Grimaldi lineages found in the Table d'ascendance de Catherine Baillon (12 générations). Please see the following article for the correction of these mistakes.

habitant.org/baillon/Grimaldi%20Article.pdf

---

[425] https://boards.ancestry.ca/surnames.baillon/56/mb.ashx

Baillon Research Dead Ends [426]

John P. Dulong, Ph.D.

In another recent posting I promised to provide a list of Catherine de Baillon's ancestors who were dead ends for both my colleagues and I. Some of these ancestors will probably remain dead ends because there is no more data to be found, but it is my hope that eventually some of these problems will be solved.

Perhaps you are the person who has access to facts that we were unable to uncover that will lead to breakthroughs on these ancestors. Perhaps dead end is the wrong term to use; think of most of them as temporarily blocked.

The following list is for ancestors in generations IV through XI in our book, <u>Table d'ascendance de Catherine Baillon</u>. You really need to read our book to see where we left off and what clues, if any, we have about possible leads for these ancestors.

Our book only traces the first twelve generations of Catherine de Baillon's ancestry. Although there may be some dead ends in the XII generation, most of the ancestors we mention in this generation can be easily traced in standard French Medieval genealogy sources.

This list of dead end ancestors includes page number, ancestor number, name of the dead ancestor, name of his/her spouse and year of marriage.

I compiled this list rather quickly, so I may have overlooked some dead ends.

---

[426] https://groups.google.com/forum/#!searchin/soc.genealogy.medieval/catherine$20de$20baillon/soc.genealogy.medieval/busGBG5a--k/Ncj6xpLBO6UJ%5B1-25%5D

GENERATION IV

44:11 Marie Morant, wife of Miles Maillard, seigneur de Breuil et de La Boissière, m. 1555

45:14 Jean Bizet, seigneur de Paponville et de la Grandmaison, husband of Marguerite Chabot, m. 1580

GENERATION V

49:17 Philippe Vaultier, wife of Adam Baillon, sieur de Valance, m. ca. 1500/1510

GENERATION VI

63:49 Jacqueline Dupuis, wife of Waast de Marle, seigneur de Vaugien et de Villiers-St-Paul, m. ca. 1500

64:51 Louise Lemaistre, wife of Jean Lhuillier (or Luillier), seigneur de La Motte d'Égry et de Neufmoulin, m. between 1490 and 1520

GENERATION VII

75:66 Adam Le Seigneur, seigneur d'Épretot, no spouse identified

75:73 Perrette Le Chasseur, wife of Robert de La Saussaye, bourgeois de Beaugency, m. ca. 1450/1460

76:77 Catherine de Nézement, dame de Nézement et du Breuil, wife of Jacques de Morvillier, seigneur du Breuil et de Lignières, m. ca. 1450/1460.

77:80 Guillaume Maillard, seigneur de Champaigne (by right of his wife), husband of Isabeau de Hutenay, dame de Champaigne, m. ca. 1450/1460 (both of these ancestors are dead ends)

78:97 Sibylle Leblond, dame de Villiers-St-Paul, wife of Jean de Marle, seigneur de Villiers-St-Paul, m. ca. 1470/1480

80:104 Guillaume Le Sueur, seigneur de Bergy, conseiller du roi et général des monnaies, husband of Marguerite de Marle, m. after 1481 and probably before 1490

81:106 Samson Raoland (or Roland), bourgeois, élu de Meaux, et seigneur de Villers-les-Rigault, husband of Perrette Dumont, m. ca. 1490 (both are dead ends)

GENERATION VIII

93:144 Olivier de La Saussaye, bourgeois de Beaugency

93:152 Jean de Morvillier of Blois

93:156 Mathurin Gaillard, seigneur de Villemorand (or Villemourans), husband of Jean Calipeau(x), m. ca. 1420/1430 (both are dead ends)

102:211 Charlotte Cotin, wife of Germain de Marle, échevin de Paris, m. ca. 1460/1470

105:248 Honoré Lombart (or Lombard), lieutenant du bailli d'Antibes, 1523 (this is a Franco-Italian dead end)

GENERATION IX

111:317 Jeanne Louelle, dame de Villemancy-sur-Loire, wife of Alart de Beauvillier(s), seigneur du Plessis-Menart, m. ca. 1390/1400

114:341 Gauchère Le Vernier (or La Vernière), wife of Étienne Morhier, seigneur de Villiers-le-Morhier, m. ca. 1380/1389

114:342 Jean de Laigny (or Lagny), conseiller clerc du roi au Parlement de Paris, etc., husband of Jeanne de Marigny, m. ca 1405/1410 (both dead ends)

114:386 Jean de Thiembronne, seigneur de Mercq-St-Liévin et de Marles-les-Mines (good luck researching this chap, be sure you read all our notes about him)

118:420 Jean de Marle, bourgeois de Paris, husband of Marguerite Vivien, m. ca. 1430/1440 (both dead ends)

GENERATION X

123:633 Catherine de Courbenton, wife of Jean (or Jeannot called Gaucher) de Beauvillier(s), m. ca. 1360/1370

123:636 N ... Villebresme, husband of Gillette de Lespine, of the Lespine seigneurs de Claireau, m. ca. 1360/1370

124:672 Regnaut Le Bouteiller (or Le Bouteillier), chevalier, husband of N ... de St-Laurens (or Ste-Beuve), m. ca. 1350/1360 (both dead ends)

125:677 Jeanne (?) de Roye, wife of Arnould de Gavre, seigneur d'Escournaix (Schoorisse), de Croisilles, et de Staden, m. ca. 1350/1360 (note that this is a Flemish dead end)

NO LONGER A FLEMISH DEAD END (see page 207 for further information)

125:679 Marguerite de Dudzeele, dame de Dudzeele, wife of Roger de Ghistelles (or Gistel), seigneur de Dudzelle and de Straten (Straete), m. ca. 1357 (note that this is a Flemish dead end)

NO LONGER A FLEMISH DEAD END (see page 207 for further information)

125:680 Philippe Morhier, seigneur de Villiers-le-Morhier, husband of Tiphaine de Chavanne, m. ca. 1350/1360 (both dead ends)

126:686 Pierre de Marigny, lawyer in 1395

126:768 Guillaume de Marle, husband of Alix de Mailly, m. ca. 1350/1360

128:801 Marie Marcel, wife of Jean Lhuillier (or Luiller), conseiller du roi au Parlement de Paris, m. ca. 1350/1360

130:814 Guillaume Barbary, seigneur d'Esclimeu, husband of Catherine Alory (or Allory), m. ca. 1380/1390 (both dead ends)

133:973 Philippine de Castellane, wife of Pierre Liti, seigneur de Dosfrayres et de Bonson, m. ca. 1350/1360 (this is a Franco-Italian dead end)

133:977 Alaizette de Bagarris, wife of Laurent de Berre, m. ca. 1400/1410 (this is a Franco-Italian dead end)

GENERATION XI

141:1264 Adam de Beauvillier(s), seigneur de Morsant, husband of Perrette de St-Martin, dame de Cuigny, m. a little after 1344

141:1350 Jean de Léon, seigneur de Montagu, husband of Jeanne de Varennes (both dead ends)

143:1608 Philippe de Vitry, bourgeois de Paris

144:1618 Jean Gentien (or Gencian), bourgeois de Paris

144:1621 Alix de La Vigne, wife of Baudouin du Mont-St-Éloy

145:1624 Pierre des Landes, seigneur de Maigneville et de Beaurepaire, bourgeois de Paris, husband of Monfrine (or Manfrède) de Stancon, m. before 16 June 1344 (both dead ends)

148:1941 Catherine Doria, wife of Antoine Grimaldi, coseigneur de Monaco, etc., m. ca. 1320/1330 (this is a Franco-Italian dead end)

148:1944 Pisselino Liti, of Nice (this is a Franco-Italian dead end)

149:1953 Jean de Berre, seigneur de Berre, husband of Élisabeth de St-Sauveur, m. ca. 1370/1380 (this is a Franco-Italian dead end)

Frankly, I do not hold out much hope for those ancestors who are noted as being bourgeois. Given the period in which they lived, it is unlikely that anyone will be able to trace them back any further; nevertheless, I would like to be surprised.

Also, you have probably noticed that many of these dead ends are women.

A break though on any of these ladies might well lead to other important Medieval families.

Gee, with all these dead ends, it looks like we did not identify any ancestors at all.

However, I counted 196 ancestors in the first eleven generations. Out of that number only 52 are dead ends. That is about 27 percent. OK, we did our share; now let us see what you can do.

PS. My colleagues reviewed this posting before I released it. Fr. Dubé suggested I include the dead ends in generation XII. Perhaps I will in the future, but I just do not have the time to pull this information together right now. Besides, there is enough here to keep a team of genealogists busy for a few years. Nevertheless, Fr. Dubé specifically wanted me to mention 159:3879, Béatrice Féraud, wife of Guillaume Rostaing, Baron de Beuil, m. ca. 1268.

August 25, 2002

Catherine de Baillon's de Roye Ancestry: Another Royal Gateway

John P. Dulong, Ph.D. and Jean Bunot

PDF file located at habitant.org/baillon/De%20Roye%20Article.pdf

---

The Dudzeele and Straten Ancestry of Catherine de Baillon, Part 1
The Dudzeele and Straten Ancestry of Catherine de Baillon, Part 2

John P. Dulong, Ph.D.

DuLong, John P. "The Dudzeele and Straten Ancestry of Catherine de Baillon." Michigan's Habitant Heritage, Part 1: 32 (July 2011): 116-122. Part 2: 32 (October 2011): 156-166.

For a better copy of the map in Part 1 please see Map of the Seigneuries of the Dudzeeles and Straten Families, 1250-1400.

PDF file (Part 1) located at habitant.org/baillon/Dudzeele%20Article%201.pdf

PDF file (Part 2) located at habitant.org/baillon/Dudzeele%20Article%202.pdf

Possible Jewish Ancestor for Catherine Baillon

Jean P. Dulong, Ph.D.

Among the ancestors of Catherine de Baillon is Pisselino Liti. The Liti family was originally from San Remo in Italy, but migrated to the Nice area of what is now France, but was then part of Savoy, by the 1340s.

In the early 1400s Guillaume and Nicolas Liti were pawnbrokers. The latter was apparently associated in business with Symisson Levi, a Jew. E. Cais de Pierlas, in his ville de Nice pendant le premier siècle de la domination des princes de Savoie (de 1388 à la fin du XVe siècle) (Nice: Librairie Niçoise, [1898] 1976), pp. 243-244, and n. 2, after reporting these facts ask if the Liti could possibly have been Jewish? He notes that the word "judeii" appears in the registers when Nicolas Liti and Symisson [Levi] are mentioned together in relation to a pledge of 23 florins paid around 1409 on behalf of Georges de Drua, a judge and citizen of Nice. This judge has previously pawned several objects to Guillaume Liti.

Guillaume Liti was the seigneur of Dosfrayres, Bonson, and La Roquette du Var, a grandson of Pisselino Liti, and is in Catherine Baillon's ancestry. (See Jetté et al., Table d'ascendance de Catherine Baillon (2001), pp. 103, 120, 133, and 148).

If the Liti were of Jewish ancestry, then it appears they had been living as Catholics since at least Pisselino Liti's time as he was the owner of a galley named Ste. Marie. It would seem that a practicing Jew would be unlikely to honor the Virgin Mary by naming a ship after her. Of course, the Liti could have also remained Jewish in their private lives and only acted as Catholics in public.

---

[427]

https://groups.google.com/forum/?fromgroups#!searchin/soc.genealogy.french/catherine$20 de$20baillon/soc.genealogy.french/N3pMMGrOTBA/3N66BLlIAFgJ%5B1-25%5D

I assume there was a Jewish community in the fifteenth century in Nice, but how can I verify this and learn more about them?

Would it be typical for Jews at that time to be pawnbrokers?

Would non-Jews be pawnbrokers?

I seem to recall that the Medici arms with six red roundels became the symbol for pawnbrokers so they perhaps engaged in this occupation and they were not Jewish.

Has anyone done any research on the Liti family of Nice and San Remo?

Any clues or suggestions on how to pursue this possible Jewish ancestry further would be appreciated. It would be interesting to verify or deny this Jewish lineage. At this point, I would have to say the evidence is very weak for this Jewish ancestry.

January 2, 2004

ADDENDUM FROM AUTHOR

Refer to Pisselino Liti (Genealogy of French in North America), [428] the Patron of the galley Sainte-Marie, one of the thirty-two galleys that served the King of France under the orders of Charles Grimaldi, that left Nice, France, on May 6, 1349.

---

[428] www.francogene.com/genealogie-quebec-genealogy/196/196629.php

Eventual Update of Baillon Book [429]

John P. Dulong, Ph.D.

To all of you who are interested in the ancestry of Catherine de Baillon. I have now communicated with my colleagues, Gail F. Moreau-DesHarnais, Roland-Yves Gagné, and Joseph Dubé, and we all agree that eventually we would like to do an update on the Baillon book with additions and corrections. We would of course do this in honor of our friend and project leader the late René Jetté. However, it will be several years before we complete our current projects and are able to work together on an update.

Meanwhile, I have promised my colleagues to keep up the binder I have with additions and corrections to our Baillon research. I have about two inches of materials so far. Several of the additions and corrections have been gathered from postings on soc.genealogy.medieval. In addition, there were many new findings published by Côté and Sini, as well as Ouimet and Mauger, which will have to be incorporated into our update. We will of course give proper credit to the authors of these posts and articles.

My colleagues and I will continue to search for update materials. If you wish to send us any additions or corrections, then please contact me by email. Again, I want to make sure you all understand that the update is going to be several years in the future. When we start to work on it we will announce that the project has begun. Thank you for your continuing interest in our research.

December 14, 2005

---

[429] http://groups.google.com/group/soc.genealogy.medieval/browse_thread/thread/d5e0fc0c5b9fb3c7/d3be659a3938206e?lnk=st&q

Genealogical References - Catherine de Baillon

René Jetté, John P. DuLong, Roland Yves-Gagné and Gail F. Moreau. "From Catherine Baillon to Charlemagne." American-Canadian Genealogist 25:4 (Fall 1999): 170-200.

PDF file located at https://acgs.org/Download/ACGS_Baillon_1999.pdf

Jean-René Côté and Anita Seni. "La fortune de Catherine de Baillon." Mémoires de la Société généalogique canadienne-française 52:2 (Summer 2001): 123-144.

* This is an excellent, well researched, and very well documented article about Catherine Baillon's immediate family that explains the context of her decision to immigrate to New France.

Roland Yves-Gagné and Paul Leportier. "L'ascendance de Michel d'Aigneaux d'Ouville." Mémoires de la Société généalogique canadienne-française 52:2 (Summer 2001): 95-104.

* Catherine Baillon's Armenian ancestry is mentioned in this article.

René Jetté, John Patrick DuLong, Roland Yves-Gagné, Gail F. Moreau and Joseph A. Dubé. Table d'ascendance de Catherine Baillon (12 générations). Montréal: Société généalogique canadienne-française, 2001.

While this book is in French, there is an introductory chapter in English which explains the layout of the book and should help the reader navigate the material.

There are over 200 pages, hundreds of notes, several detailed proofs, illustrations, three maps and three appendices. This book is the result of ten+ years of work on the part of five genealogists.

Raymond Ouimet. "Catherine de Baillon et ses origines." Mémoires de la Société Généalogique Canadienne-Française 52:2 (Summer 2001): 105-106.

* In this short article Ouimet corrects a misconception that Catherine Baillon was born at Monfort-l'Amaury.

Nicole Mauger and Raymond Ouimet. Catherine de Baillon: enquête sur une fille du roi. Sillery, QC: Les éditions du Septentrion, 2001. [430]

* Mauger and Ouimet publish their findings on the social origins and family background of Catherine Baillon in this book.

Jean-René Côté and Anita Seni. "Champlain, les Chartier de Lotbinière et Catherine de Baillon ou l'avenir est en Nouvelle-France." Mémoires de la Société Généalogique Canadienne-Française 52:1 (Spring 2002): 11-37.

---

[430] https://www.septentrion.qc.ca/catalogue/Livre.asp?id=292

Raymond Ouimet and Nicole Mauger. "Catherine de Baillon: Une Exclue?" L'Ancêtre 29 (Autumn 2002): 23-30.

Ouimet and Mauger have a very different view of Catherine's life and motivations for coming to New France than do Côté and Seni. You must read over both sets of authors to understand their different views and to judge the evidence they submit.

Roland-Yves Gagné. "La Table d'ascendance de Catherine Baillon, cinq ans plus tard." Mémoires de la Société Généalogique Canadienne-Française 57:3 (Autumn 2006): 225-229.

Deals with Vaultier, Billebaut, Braque, de Marle, Le Sueur, Culdoe, des Landes, and Le Maistre ancestors of Catherine Baillon.

DuLong, John P. "Correction of Catherine Baillon's Grimaldi Ancestry." Michigan's Habitant Heritage 28 (April 2007): 53-63.

PDF file located at habitant.org/baillon/Grimaldi%20Article.pdf

DuLong, John P., and Jean Bunot. "Catherine de Baillon's de Roye Ancestry: Another Royal Gateway." Michigan's Habitant Heritage 30 (January 2009): 5-18.

PDF file located at habitant.org/baillon/De%20Roye%20Article.pdf

DuLong, John P. "The Dudzeele and Straten Ancestry of Catherine de Baillon." Michigan's Habitant Heritage, Part 1: 32 (July 2011): 116-122. Part 2: 32 (October 2011): 156-166.

For a better copy of the map in Part 1 please see Map of the Seigneuries of the Dudzeeles and Straten Families, 1250-1400.

PDF file (Part 1) located at habitant.org/baillon/Dudzeele%20Article%201.pdf

PDF file (Part 2) located at habitant.org/baillon/Dudzeele%20Article%202.pdf

Gail F. Moreau (translator) and John P. DuLong (editor). "Archange Godbout's Baillon, de Marle, and Le Sueur Families of France." Michigan's Habitant Heritage 13, no. 22 (April 1992): 40-51.

PDF file located at habitant.org/baillon/Godbout%20Translation.pdf

Roland-Yves Gagné. "Notule généalogique: Isabeau de Hutenay, fille de Thomas Whitney, ancêtre de Catherine de Baillon." Mémoires de la Société Généalogique Canadienne-Française 62:2 (Summer 2011): 119-120.

René Jetté. Dictionnaire Généalogique des Familles du Québec.

Tanguay, Cyprien. Dictionnaire Généalogique des Familles Canadiennes [431]

---

[431] bibnum2.banq.qc.ca/bna/dicoGenealogie/

Cited Genealogical Publications - Catherine de Baillon

[1] Socitété Généalogique Canadienne-Française [432]

Publisher of Mémoires de la Société généalogique canadienne-française

Publisher of Table d'ascendance de Catherine Baillon (12 générations)

3440, rue Davidson

Montréal, Québec

H1W 2Z5

info@sgcf.com

Due to the proliferation of viruses, ads, spam ... only emails with the word Genealogy in the Subject Line will be considered.

[2] American Canadian Genealogical Society [433]

Publisher of American-Canadian Genealogist

Treasurer

PO Box 6478

Manchester, NH

03108-6478

ACGS@acgs.org

---

[432] www.sgcf.com
[433] https://acgs.org

[3] Société de Généalogie de Québec [434]

Publisher of L'Ancêtre

CP 9066

Sainte-Foy, Québec

G1V 4A8

sgq@uniserve.com

---

[4] French Canadian Heritage Society [435]

Publisher of Michigan's Habitant Heritage

P.O. Box 1900

Royal Oak, MI

48068-1900

fchsmhelp@fchsm.org

---

[5] Septentrion website

Nicole Mauger and Raymond Ouimet. Catherine de Baillon: enquête sur une fille du roi. Sillery, QC: Les éditions du Septentrion, 2001. [436]

---

[434] https://www.sgq.qc.ca
[435] https://habitantheritage.org
[436] https://www.septentrion.qc.ca/catalogue/catherine-de-baillon

Website Information - Catherine de Baillon

A Century of New France: 1663 – 1763 [437]

Ancestral Armorial for Catherine Baillon [438]

Ancêtres de Catherine de Baillon [439]

Catherine de Baillon: Fille du Roi [440]

Catherine de Baillon's Royal Gateway Armorial to the Emperor of Byzantium [441]

Catherine de Baillon's Royal Gateway Armorial to the King of France [442]

Ascending Lineage from Catherine Baillon to Charlemagne [443]

Ascending Lineage from Catherine Baillon to Theodoros II Dukas Lascaris de Vintimille [444]

Baillon Armorial [445]

Catherine Baillon Royal Connection Research Association [446]

Catherine de Baillon, Fille du Roi en Amérique [447]

---

[437] http://168.144.16.165/books/canada3.htm
[438] habitant.org/baillon/armorial.htm
[439] webhome.idirect.com/~letanu/baillon1/pafg01.htm
[440] www.unicaen.fr/mrsh/prefen/notices/6607cb.pdf
[441] habitant.org/baillon/Baillon_Byzantine.pdf
[442] habitant.org/baillon/Baillon_France.pdf
[443] habitant.org/baillon/figure2.htm
[444] habitant.org/baillon/lascaris.htm
[445] habitant.org/baillon/armorial.htm
[446] habitant.org/baillon/

Dictionnaire Généalogique des Nos Origines (Miville, Baillon) [448]

Filles du Roi - King's Daughters [449]

Généalogie - Québec - Complement à Jetté [450]

Genealogy of French in North America (website belonging to Denis Beauregard) [451]

Jacques Francois Miville dit Deschênes [452]

Jacques Miville Sieur des Chesnes [453]

King's Daughters [454]

King's Daughters – Les Filles du Roi [455]

La Famille de Jacques Miville et Catherine de Baillon [456]

La Société des Filles du roi et soldats du Carignan, Inc. [457]

Les Filles du Roi de la Haute société [458]

---

[447] http://translate.google.com/translate?hl=en&sl=auto&tl=en&u=http%3A%2F%2Fwww.histoire-genealogie.com%2Fspip.php%3Farticle350
[448] www.francogene.com/dgo/dgo-miv.php
[449] http://www.lookbackward.com/perrault/filleroi/
[450] www.francogene.com/dgo/dgo.php
[451] www.francogene.com/gfna/gfna/998/index.htm
[452] https://www.geni.com/people/Jacques-Miville-dit-Desch%C3%AAnes-Sieur-des-Ch%C3%AAnes/6000000002129608063
[453] www.miville.com/genealogy2.htm
[454] https://en.wikipedia.org/wiki/Filles_du_roi
[455] www.acadian-home.org/kings-daughters-1.html
[456] www.francogene.com/genealogie-quebec-genealogy/001/001079.php
[457] https://fillesduroi.org/

Perre Miville dit Le Suisse [459]

SFDRSC: Filles du Roi [460]

The Filles du Roi [461]

Québec Royal Descends (website belonging to Denis Beauregard) [462]

soc.genealogy.french Google Group Posting: Les Sires de Créquy (Ancêtres de Catherine de Baillon) [463]

soc.genealogy.medieval Google Group Posting: Adam de Baillon: date of death/partage [464]

soc.genealogy.medieval Google Group Posting: Gavre-Schorisse [465]

soc.genealogy.medieval Google Group Posting: Joan of Arc and the Villebresme Family? [466]

soc.genealogy.medieval Google Group Posting: Le Bouteiller (Baillon) New Royal Gateway [467]

---

[458] www.leveillee.net/ancestry/fillesduroi1.htm
[459] https://www.geni.com/people/Pierre-Miville-dit-LeSuisse/6000000006414178343
[460] https://fillesduroi.org/cpage.php?pt=9
[461] www.whitepinepictures.com/seeds/i/12/sidebar.html
[462] www.francogene.com/gfna/gfna/998/qrd30.htm
[463] https://groups.google.com/forum/?fromgroups#!searchin/soc.genealogy.french/catherine$20de$20baillon/soc.genealogy.french/JXA6OrYIqUY/9_NWdA93u5gJ%5B1-25%5D
[464] https://groups.google.com/forum/#!searchin/soc.genealogy.medieval/catherine$20de$20baillon/soc.genealogy.medieval/WrT97Aq5mkc/6w0yo9j52wYJ%5B1-25%5D
[465] https://groups.google.com/forum/#!topic/soc.genealogy.medieval/Zat98rmU1sk
[466] https://groups.google.com/forum/#!topic/soc.genealogy.medieval/TnbKWNDCd0w
[467] https://groups.google.com/forum/#!searchin/soc.genealogy.medieval/Le$20Bouteiller$20(Ba

Final Words on Catherine Baillon

Michele Doucette, M.Ed.

Catherine (de) Baillon, is my first French Canadian royal gateway ancestor, meaning that she is my connection from New France to medieval nobility; as such, she is the 24th G granddaughter of Charlemagne. Having read the bestselling TDC by Dan Brown, otherwise known as The DaVinci Code, there is but a wee transition from the Carolingians to the Merovingians. Indeed, such a transition is made possible as a result of Charlemagne's great grandmother, Bertrade of Prüm, although there are conflicting accounts as to her parentage: she was either the daughter of Theodoric III of Neustria or the granddaughter of Dagobert I of Austrasia through her mother Irmina of Oeren. In either case, she is his primary direct Merovingian link.

Timothy Carmain-Périllos, a good friend of mine in Los Angeles, has shared that *if you can tie into a French, German or English noble family dating from the 14th century, which most people of western European descent can do easily, one can probably dig out a dozen or more documented lines back to Charlemagne. In keeping, his descendants were fairly well documented and, being royals and nobles, their descendants were as well.*

He goes further to say that *simple mathematics makes it a virtual certainty. Using a base figure of four generations per century (average) to get back to Charlemagne's time one goes back about 44 generations or so. That gives you 35,184,372,088,832 (thirty five trillion, one-hundred eighty-four billion, etc) 44th great-grandparents; the world's population in 800 AD was estimated to be at under half a billion.*

---

il-
lon)$20New$20Royal$20Gateway$20%7Csort:date/soc.genealogy.medieval/Ts6IoUhKVxc/Tt70tDgvMIgJ

In keeping, this means the likelihood is that, with the exception of very isolated aboriginal populations, everyone alive today descends from everyone alive and who reproduced in 800AD, including Charlemagne, many times over. The same can be said for both Confucius as well as the Prophet Mohammed. In fact, probably everyone living today descends from the Pharaohs of ancient Egypt as well.

Hence, whether or not we, as individuals, have the ability to trace specific lines, at some point the probabilities become certainties when you figure how many direct ancestors we would have had in comparison to the population of the world at that time.

Is there, in reality, a sacred bloodline?

Might we be the direct ancestors of such a bloodline?

Based on the genealogies published in Holy Blood, Holy Grail, many people on e-mail lists and websites, have continued to make bloodline claims which, according to Tim, *are fatally flawed and contain some pretty fanciful fabrications and "grafts" that never existed historically.*

Adding to this the attempts of other authors, who are not genealogists, weaving characters from literature and myth into the lines to create the illusion of cohesive connections that cannot be proven by conventional means, we end up with a classic catch 22, meaning that can neither be proven or disproven.

It then becomes a matter of what people choose to believe about themselves or others they promote as *bloodline*.

To make things even more interesting and intriguing, Steve Olson, author of <u>Mapping Human History: Genes, Race and Our Common Origins</u>, shares an article published online in <u>Slate Magazine</u>, [468] that states no matter how the court case between Dan Brown, author of <u>The Da Vinci Code</u>, and Michael Baigent, author of <u>The Holy Blood and The Holy Grail</u>, turns out, *both books are confused. If anyone living today is descended from Jesus, so are most of us on the planet.*

Going further, Steve shares that this *is an inevitable consequence of the strange and marvelous workings of human ancestry. In the resent past, each of us is descended from a small fraction of the people who were then alive. We're descended from our parents one generation ago, our grandparents two generations ago, our great-grandparents three generations ago, and so on.*

Steve continues to state that *assuming typical human mating patterns, your direct ancestors 20 generations ago consisted of somewhere between 600,000 and 1,000,000 different people.*

As further explained in <u>Modelling the recent common ancestry of all living humans</u>, [469] Douglas Rohde, Steve Olson and Joseph Chang have shared that in thinking about one's direct ancestors living 40 generations ago, in about the year AD 1000, this ancestral group *included many millions of people. Forty generations ago, almost everyone living today had ancestors in Europe, Asia and Africa, and many present day Asians, Europeans and Africans hadancestors in the Americas because of the continual exchange of mates across the Bering Strait.*

---

[468] www.slate.com/articles/health_and_science/science/2006/03/why_were_all_jesus_children.html

[469] https://www.nature.com/articles/nature02842

Mind you, it gets even stranger when Steve shares that if one were to go back 120 generations, to about the year 1000 BC, as explained in the above online article taken from Nature: International Weekly Journal of Science, *your ancestors then included everyone in the world who has descendants living today. And if you compared a list of your ancestors with a list of everyone else's ancestors, the names on the two lists would be identical.*

This means that *you and I are descended from all of the Africans, Australians, Native Americans and Europeans who were alive three millenniums ago, and still have descendants living today. That's also why so many people living today could be descended from Jesus.*

Steve goes further to say that if *Jesus had children and if those children had children so that Jesus' lineage survived, then Jesus is today the ancestor of almost everyone living on earth. True, Jesus lived two rather than three millenniums ago, but a person's descendants spread quickly from well-connected parts of the world like the Middle East.*

I like the way that he was able to draw this article to a close by writing that *people may like to think that they're descended from some ancient group while other people are not. But human ancestry doesn't work that way, since we all shared the same ancestors just a few millenniums ago. As that idea becomes more widely accepted, arguments over who's descended from Jesus won't result in lawsuits. And maybe, just maybe, people will have one less reason to feel animosity toward other branches of the human family.*

Never have truer words been spoken.

How different the landscape might look if more people realized that if there is such a bloodline, it includes all of us.

Monogram of Charlemagne from the subscription of a royal diploma

Signum (KAROLVS) Caroli gloriosissimi regis

A coin of Charlemagne with the inscription

KAROLVS IMP AVG (*Karolus imperator augustus*)

Author PHGCOM [470]

---

[470] https://en.wikipedia.org/wiki/File:Charlemagne_denier_Mayence_812_814.jpg

Charlemagne and his Scholars by Karl von Blaas

As located in *An Outline of Christianity: The Story of Our Civilization*, Vol. II

(New York: Bethlehem Publishers, Inc., 1926), p. 230.

Throne of Charlemagne (located inside Aachen Cathedral in Germany) circa 800 AD

December 3, 2010 © Gauis Caecilius [471]

---

[471] https://www.flickr.com/photos/gauiscaecilius/5596835007/in/set-72157626373329370

Gold Reliquary Bust of Charlemagne (14th century)

(contains the cranium of Charlemagne)

Located at Aachen Cathedral in Germany

Author Lokilech [472]

---

[472] https://en.wikipedia.org/wiki/File:Karl_der_gro%C3%9Fe.jpg

Sarcophagus of Charlemagne

Author Lokilech [473]

The Palatine Chapel was designed by Odo of Metz. He based it on the Byzantine church of San Vitale (completed 547 AD) in Ravenna, Italy. This accounts for the very eastern feel to the chapel, with its octagonal shape, striped arches, marble floor, golden mosaics, and ambulatory; it was consecrated in 805 AD to serve as the imperial church. [474]

When Charlemagne died in 814, he was buried in the chapel's choir. In 1000 AD, Emperor Otto III had Charlemagne's vault opened. It is said the body was found in a remarkable state of preservation, seated on a marble throne, dressed in imperial robes, with his crown on his head, the Gospels lying open in his lap, and his scepter in his hand. A large mural representing Otto and his nobles gazing on the dead Emperor was painted on the wall of the great room in the Town Hall. [475]

---

[473] https://en.wikipedia.org/wiki/File:AachenerDomSarg.jpg
[474] www.sacred-destinations.com/germany/aachen-cathedral
[475] Ibid.

In 1165, Emperor Frederick Barbarossa again opened the vault and placed the remains in a sculptured sarcophagus made of Parian marble, said to have been the one in which Augustus Caesar was buried. At Barbarossa's request, Charlemagne was canonized that same year.[476]

Thankfully Aachen Cathedral suffered very little damage in the World Wars. In 1978 it was one of the first 12 sites to make the entry into the UNESCO list of World Heritage Sites. The first German site and one of the first three European sites to be admitted, two decades of restoration work on the dome was completed in 2006.[477]

---

[476] www.sacred-destinations.com/germany/aachen-cathedral
[477] Ibid.

Descent from Antiquity

Like the British Royal Family, so, too, am I able to trace my genealogy back to the early Middle Ages, the period of European history lasting from the 5th century to approximately 1000 AD.

In retrospect, you could also refer to this project as a DFA (Descent from Antiquity) project of my own, meaning that it refers to establishing a well-researched, generation by generation descent of living persons from people living in antiquity.

The Merovingians established themselves in the former Roman provinces in Gaul, and Clovis I, following his victory over the Alemanni at the Battle of Tolbiac (496 AD) converted to Catholicism, laying the foundation of the Frankish Empire, the dominant state of medieval Western Christendom.

Starting with the Frankish realms at the beginning of the 9th century, Charlemagne united much of modern day France, western Germany and northern Italy into the Carolingian Empire. Scholarship and Classical learning flourished under Charlemagne leading to what 20th century historians called the Carolingian Renaissance.

Merovingian Ancestry

GENERATION 1 (49G grandfather)

Meroveus (Mérovée) [478]

There was evidently something very special about King Meroveus and his priestly successors, for not only were they accorded special veneration, but so, too, were they widely known for their esoteric knowledge and occult skills. This learned dynasty emerged in the ancient Nazarite tradition to become known as the long-haired Sorceror Kings.

Noted sorcerors in the manner of the Samaritan Magi, they firmly believed in the hidden powers of the honeycomb; the honeycomb was considered by philosophers to be the manifestation of divine harmony in nature because it is naturally made up of hexagonal prisms.

To the Merovingians, the bee was a most hallowed creature, having been a sacred emblem of Egyptian royalty. Likewise, they believed it to be a symbol of wisdom.

The Merovingians were not a line of created kings, but those of natural descent. Knowing their birthright, they based this natural selection and methods of ruling (by example and good works) upon King Solomon, their ancestor.

It is said that Mérovée was supposedly conceived when his mother, the wife of the king, encountered a Quinotaur (a sea monster that has the ability to change shape) while swimming.

---

[478] fmg.ac/Projects/MedLands/MEROVINGIANS.htm

I prefer to think along the lines of a foreign conqueror, coming from the sea, taking the dead king's wife (already pregnant) as his own (thereby impregnating her once again) in order to legitimize his claim.

GENERATION 2 (48G grandfather)

Childeric I [479] + Queen Basina of the Thuringians [480]

On May 27, 1653, a deaf-mute mason, named Adrien Quinquin, was working on a construction project near the church of Saint-Brice in Tournai, Belgium.

According to Abbé Cochet, he was down about 7 or 8 feet when a blow of the pick revealed a gold buckle and at least a hundred gold coins.

This surprise find caused him to throw down the tool and run about, waving his arms and trying to articulate sounds.

The first witnesses "who crowded around the trench saw some two hundred silver coins; human bones, including two skulls; a lot of rusted iron; a sword with a gold grip and a hilt ornamented in the gold-and-garnet cloisonné technique and sheathed in a cloisonné decorated scabbard; and numerous other gold items, among them, brooches, buckles, rings, an ornament in the form of a bull's head, and about three hundred gold cloisonné bees." [481] [482] [483]

---

[479] fmg.ac/Projects/MedLands/MEROVINGIANS.htm#Childericdied481
[480] fmg.ac/Projects/MedLands/THURINGIA.htm#Basinus
[481] content.yudu.com/Library/A18h8c/AncientEurope8000BCt/resources/496.htm
[482] https://www.encyclopedia.com/humanities/encyclopedias-almanacs-transcripts-and-maps/tomb-childeric
[483] https://gallica.bnf.fr/ark:/12148/btv1b7700172d

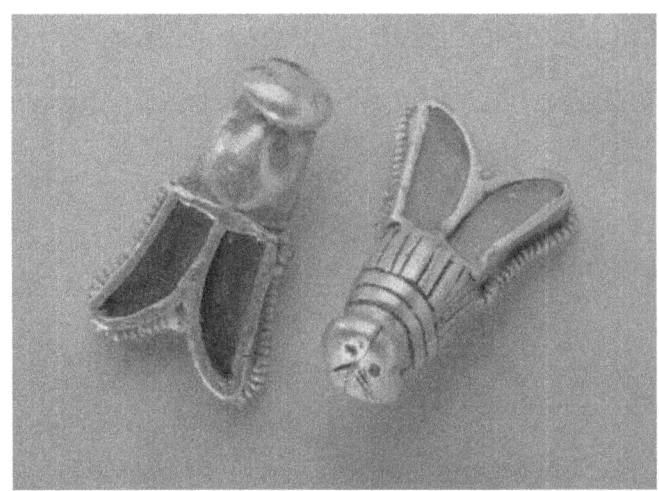

News of this treasure soon reached the archduke Leopold William, governor of the Austrian Netherlands, who had it sent to him in Brussels.

It was he who further ordered that a carefully written account of the find be made, confiding the collection for study to his personal physician, Jean-Jacques Chifflet, who was also a historian.

The outstanding find was a gold signet ring inscribed with the figure of an armed warrior and the name CHILDERICI REGIS.

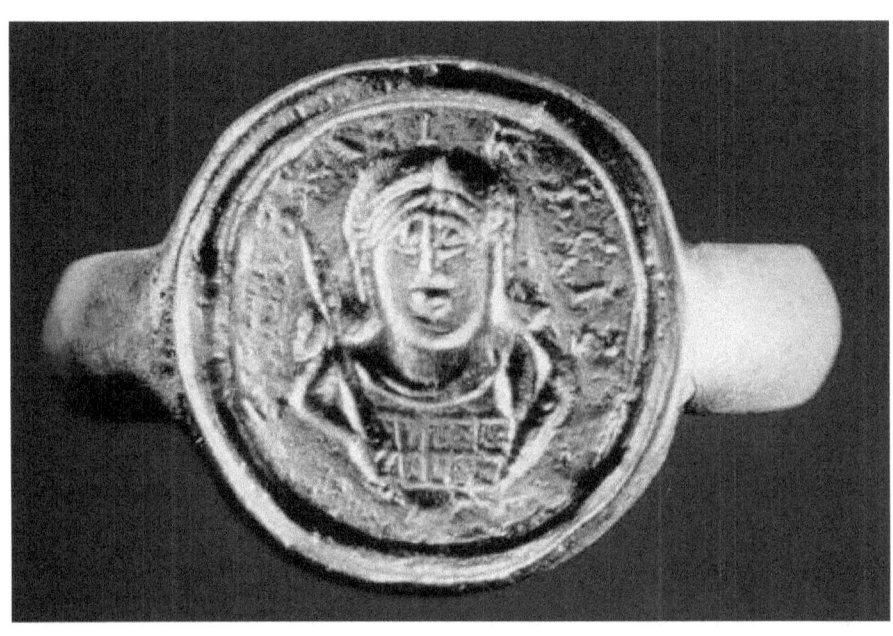

It was this ring that identified the tomb as belonging to Childeric, the father of Clovis I. [484]

It was in 1655 that Jean-Jacques Chifflet published a folio volume of 367 pages with 27 plates of engravings furnishing an excellent visual record of all the artifacts and a careful discussion and interpretative essay identifying the subject as the father of Clovis I, the great ancestor of the French monarchy. [485]

Truly, this discovery is the starting point of Merovingian archaeology, and Chifflet's study deserves to be considered the first truly scientific archaeological publication. [486]

This study "has proved all the greater a boon because most of the original artifacts have disappeared. The archduke took them home to Vienna when he retired. Upon his death in 1662, they came into the possession of Leopold I, emperor of Austria, who, in 1665, sent them to France as a diplomatic present to young King Louis XIV." [487]

The collection survived the French Revolution intact, but one night "in 1831 two thieves broke into the Bibliothèque Royal and stole the trove. By the time they were caught, most of the gold objects had been melted down, but a few artifacts, such as the gold cloisonné ornament of the sword, had been thrown into the Seine in leather sacks, and these were recovered." [488]

What do we honestly know about Childeric? The sixth-century ecclesiastic and historian Gregory of Tours tells us something of his life in Historia Francorum (The History of the Franks). [489]

---

[484] https://en.wikipedia.org/wiki/File:CHILDERICI_REGIS.jpg
[485] http://www.encyclopedia.com/article-1G2-3400400230/tomb-childeric.html
[486] Ibid.
[487] content.yudu.com/Library/A18h8c/AncientEurope8000BCt/resources/498.htm
[488] Ibid.
[489] www.fordham.edu/halsall/basis/gregory-hist.asp

While Childeric may have been the son of Merovech, he was considered a king so debauched that his own subjects drove him into exile for eight years among the Thuringians, at the court of King Basinus and Queen Basina. During this time the Roman general Aegidius ruled the Franks in his place. Upon his departure from court, Queen Basina followed him. They eventually married, and she gave birth to a son, Clovis.

Meanwhile Childeric fought a battle at Orléans against the Visigoths and another at Angers against the Goths and Saxons. When he died in about 481 AD, his son Clovis replaced him.

GENERATION 3 (47G grandfather)

Clovis I [490] + St. Clothilde de Burgundy [491]

King of the Salian Franks (481 to 486) as well as King of the Franks (486 to 511), by age 20 he was a powerful leader, destined to become the most influential figure in the West. He was the first King of the Franks to unite all the Frankish tribes under one ruler.

His wife, a Catholic, managed to convert him at a time when the entire Catholic Church was on the verge of collapse. Word of his conversion soon spread and everyone in his realm began converting.

Had it not been to please his wife, the entire course of history in Europe would have been dramatically different, and Catholics would probably have been relegated to some minor sect.

---

[490] fmg.ac/Projects/MedLands/MEROVINGIANS.htm#_Toc184188200

[491] fmg.ac/Projects/MedLands/BURGUNDY%20KINGS.htm#ChrotechildisOrClotildedied544

Instead, the Catholic bishops used this opportunity to maneuver the Merovingians strategically out of the picture. Clovis had unwittingly fallen victim to a conspiracy against the Messianic bloodline.

King Clovis died in Paris at the age of 45. His vast kingdom was divided among his four sons to rule, circa 511: Clotaire I in Soissons, Childebert I in Paris, Chlodomer in Orléans, and Theuderic I in Rheims.

GENERATION 4 (46G grandfather)

Clotaire I [492] + Aregund von Thuringia [493]

King of Soissons (511 to 558), King of Austrasia (555 to 558) and King of the Franks (558 to 561).

GENERATION 5 (45G grandfather)

Chilperic I [494] + Fredegund

King of Soissons (561 to 584) and King of the Franks (567 to 584).

GENERATION 6 (44G grandfather)

Clotaire II [495] + Haldetrude

King of Soissons (584 to 613) and King of the Franks (613 to 628).

---

[492] fmg.ac/Projects/MedLands/MEROVINGIANS.htm#ClotaireIdied561B
[493] fmg.ac/Projects/MedLands/THURINGIA.htm#Radegunddied587
[494] fmg.ac/Projects/MedLands/MEROVINGIANS.htm#ChilpericIdied584B
[495] fmg.ac/Projects/MedLands/MEROVINGIANS.htm#ClotaireIIdied629B

GENERATION 7 (43G grandfather)

Dagobert I [496] + Nantilde (Nanthilda)

King of the Soissons (622 to 628) and King of the Franks (628 to 639).

GENERATION 8 (42G grandfather)

Clovis II [497] + Bathilde (Batilde) de France

King of Nestria and Burgundy (639 to 655).

GENERATION 9 (41G grandfather)

Thierry (Theuderic) III [498] + Clotilde dite Doda

King of Nestria and Burgundy (675) and King of Austrasia (675 to 691).

GENERATION 10 (40G grandmother)

Bertrada of Prüm [499] [500] + unknown [501]

Bertrada founded Prüm Abbey, situated northwest of Trier, in 721 AD.

In 1975, another genealogy took into account three arguments that were proposed, all in keeping with Bertrada being the daughter of Thierry III and Clotilde dite Doda (meaning, that so, too, was she the sister of both Clovis IV and Clotaire IV).

---

[496] fmg.ac/Projects/MedLands/MEROVINGIANS.htm#DagobertIdied638B
[497] fmg.ac/Projects/MedLands/MEROVINGIANS.htm#ClovisIIdied657B
[498] fmg.ac/Projects/MedLands/MEROVINGIANS.htm#TheodericIIIdied691
[499] fmg.ac/Projects/MedLands/MEROVINGIANS.htm#TheodericIIIdied691
[500] fmg.ac/Projects/MedLands/FRANKSMaiordomi.htm#_Toc284006018
[501] Posited as possibly being Norbert d'Aquitaine, son of Hugobert d'Aquitaine and d'Irmine d'Oeren, courtesy of nobles-ancetres.pagesperso-orange.fr/Familles/Hugobert.pdf

This also presumes that Doda, herself, is the daughter of Ansegisel and Begga, as well as the granddaughter of St. Arnulf and St. Dode. [502]

- Fact 1: Bertrada's husband is anonymous, and related to the Hugobertides. [503]
- Fact 2: As the daughter of Thierry III, Bertrada is Merovingian.
- Fact 3: The properties of Rommersheim and Rumbach were shared between Pépin of Herstal (who transferred his shares to Charles Martel), and Doda (who transmitted her shares to Bertrada).

Christian Settipani argues, on the basis of onomastics and the inheritance of the villa of Rommersheim, that Bertrada of Prüm was daughter of Théodéric III, stating that … "King Theoderic III had a wife Doda. This Doda could have been a daughter of Ansegisel, son of another Doda. Ansegisel, presumably, shares Rommersheim between his son, Pippin of Herstal and his daughter Doda, king Theoderic's wife. Then Pippin's son, Charles Martel inherits Rommersheim, and likewise, Bertrada, Doda's daughter. This explains why King Clothar IV, son of Theoderic III, was called the cousin of Charles Martel in the Adémar of Chabannes chronicle" (November 16, 1999 posting on Gen-Medieval-L). [504] [505] [506]

In addition, Hans J.C. Schats supports this line as a likely possibility in "Voorouders van Karel de Grote." [507] When Bertrada donated land to the abbey of Prüm, the donation document was co-signed by her son Caribert and three witnesses, supposed to be her relatives, with the typical Merovingian names Bernier, Rolande and Thierry.

---

[502] Settipani, Christian. (1989) <u>Les ancêtres de Charlemagne</u>. Paris, France: Société atlantique d'impression.
[503] https://fr.wikipedia.org/wiki/Hugobertides
[504] https://groups.google.com/forum/?fromgroups#!topic/soc.genealogy.medieval/R393UJl9pds
[505] https://www.geni.com/people/Bertrade-de-Pr%C3%BCm/6000000001842551452
[506] https://en.wikipedia.org/wiki/The_Chronicon_of_Ademar_of_Chabannes
[507] www.kareldegrote.nl/

GENERATION 11 (39G grandfather)

Count Charibert de Laon [508] + unknown [509]

GENERATION 12 (first Frankish Carolingian ruler) (38G grandmother)

Bertrada de Laon [510] [511] + Pépin III (Duke of Brabant) The Short [512]

King of the Franks (751 to 768).

Pépin the Short, son of Charles Martel, in league with the Pope, was the first coronated king, deposing Childeric III, the next rightful successor of the Merovingian line. Thus began the line of Kings known as the Carolingians.

GENERATION 13 (37G grandfather)

Charlemagne [513] [514] (Charles I) + Hildegard [515]

GENERATION 14 (36G grandfather)

Carloman, renamed Pépin I [516] [517] (King of Italy) + unknown

---

[508] fmg.ac/Projects/MedLands/FRANKSMaiordomi.htm#_Toc284006018
[509] Posited as possibly being Bertrade de Cologne, daughter of Hugobert de Cologne et de Irmina d'Oeren, courtesy of nobles-ancetres.pagesperso-orange.fr/Familles/Hugobert.pdf
[510] fmg.ac/Projects/MedLands/FRANKSMaiordomi.htm#Bertradadied783
[511] nobles-ancetres.pagesperso-orange.fr/Familles/Hugobert.pdf
[512] fmg.ac/Projects/MedLands/CAROLINGIANS.htm#PepinleBrefFranksB
[513] fmg.ac/Projects/MedLands/CAROLINGIANS.htm#CharlemagneB
[514] www.francogene.com/genealogie-quebec-genealogy/010/010413.php
[515] fmg.ac/Projects/MedLands/SWABIAN%20NOBILITY.htm#Hildegardisdied783
[516] fmg.ac/Projects/MedLands/ITALY,%20Kings%20to%20962.htm#PepinIItalyB
[517] www.francogene.com/genealogie-quebec-genealogy/010/010412.php

GENERATION 15 (35G grandfather)

Bernard (illegitimate issue) [518] [519] (King of Italy) + Cunégonde of Laon

GENERATION 16 (34G grandfather)

Pépin II [520] [521] (Count of Vermandois) + unknown

GENERATION 17 (33G grandfather)

Héribert I [522] [523] (Count of Vermandois) + unknown

GENERATION 18 (32G grandmother)

Béatrice de Vermandois [524] [525] + Robert I (King of France) [526]

GENERATION 19 (31G grandfather)

Hughes le Grand [527] [528] (Duke of France) + Hedwige de Saxe (of Saxony) [529]

---

[518] fmg.ac/Projects/MedLands/ITALY,%20Kings%20to%20962.htm#BernardIitalyB
[519] www.francogene.com/genealogie-quebec-genealogy/010/010411.php
[520] fmg.ac/Projects/MedLands/FRANKISH%20NOBILITY.htm#Pepindiedafter850B
[521] www.francogene.com/genealogie-quebec-genealogy/010/010410.php
[522] fmg.ac/Projects/MedLands/NORTHERN%20FRANCE.htm#HeribertIdied900907
[523] www.francogene.com/genealogie-quebec-genealogy/010/010409.php
[524] fmg.ac/Projects/MedLands/NORTHERN%20FRANCE.htm#Beatrixdied931
[525] www.francogene.com/genealogie-quebec-genealogy/010/010408.php
[526] fmg.ac/Projects/MedLands/CAPET.htm#RobertIdied923B
[527] fmg.ac/Projects/MedLands/CAPET.htm#Huguesdied956B
[528] www.francogene.com/genealogie-quebec-genealogy/010/010407.php
[529] fmg.ac/Projects/MedLands/GERMANY,%20Kings.htm#HedwigMHuguesRegentFrancedied956

GENERATION 20 (30G grandfather)

Hughes Capet [530] [531] (first Capetian King of France) + Adélaide de Poitou [532]

GENERATION 21 (29G grandfather)

Robert II [533] [534] (King of France) + Constance de Provence [535]

GENERATION 22 (28G grandfather)

Henri I [536] [537] (King of France) + Anne de Kiev [538]

GENERATION 23 (27G grandfather)

Philippe I [539] [540] (King of France) + Berthe de Holland [541]

GENERATION 24 (26G grandfather)

Louis VI [542] [543] (King of France) + Adélaide de Savoie (of Savoy) de Maurienne [544]

---

[530] fmg.ac/Projects/MedLands/CAPET.htm#HuguesCapetdied996B
[531] www.francogene.com/genealogie-quebec-genealogy/010/010406.php
[532] fmg.ac/Projects/MedLands/AQUITAINE.htm#Adelaisdied1004
[533] fmg.ac/Projects/MedLands/CAPET.htm#RobertIIdied1031B
[534] www.francogene.com/genealogie-quebec-genealogy/010/010405.php
[535] fmg.ac/Projects/MedLands/PROVENCE.htm#ConstanceArlesMRobertIIFrancedied1031
[536] fmg.ac/Projects/MedLands/CAPET.htm#HenriIdied1060B
[537] www.francogene.com/genealogie-quebec-genealogy/010/010404.php
[538] fmg.ac/Projects/MedLands/RUSSIA,%20Rurik.htm#AnnaIaroslavnadied1075
[539] fmg.ac/Projects/MedLands/CAPET.htm#PhilippeIdied1108B
[540] www.francogene.com/genealogie-quebec-genealogy/010/010403.php
[541] fmg.ac/Projects/MedLands/HOLLAND.htm#Berthadied1093
[542] fmg.ac/Projects/MedLands/CAPET.htm#LouisVIdied1137B
[543] www.francogene.com/genealogie-quebec-genealogy/010/010402.php
[544] fmg.ac/Projects/MedLands/SAVOY.htm#Adélaïdedied1154

GENERATION 25 (25G grandfather)

Louis VII [545] [546] (King of France) + Adèle de Blois de Champagne [547]

GENERATION 26 (24G grandfather)

Philippe II Auguste [548] [549] (King of France) + Agnès d'Andechs de Méranie [550]

GENERATION 27 (23G grandmother)

Princess Marie de France [551] [552] [553] + Henri I (Duke of Brabant) [554]

GENERATION 28 (22G grandmother)

Élisabeth de Brabant [555] [556] [557] + Count Dietrich (Thierry) de Clèves [558]

---

[545] fmg.ac/Projects/MedLands/CAPET.htm#LouisVIIdied1180B
[546] www.francogene.com/genealogie-quebec-genealogy/010/010401.php
[547] fmg.ac/Projects/MedLands/CENTRAL%20FRANCE.htm#AdeleBloisdied1206
[548] fmg.ac/Projects/MedLands/CAPET.htm#PhilippeIIdied1223B
[549] www.francogene.com/genealogie-quebec-genealogy/010/010373.php
[550] fmg.ac/Projects/MedLands/CARINTHIA.htm#AgnesMeranodied1201
[551] fmg.ac/Projects/MedLands/CAPET.htm#Mariedied1238
[552] www.francogene.com/genealogie-quebec-genealogy/010/010372.php
[553] René Jetté, John P. DuLong, Roland-Yves Gagné and Gail F. Moreau; article entitled "From Catherine Baillon to Charlemagne" located in American Canadian Genealogist (pages 190, 191, 192). Issue 82, Volume 25, Number 4, 1999. Can be read online at https://acgs.org/Download/ACGS_Baillon_1999.pdf
[554] fmg.ac/Projects/MedLands/BRABANT,%20LOUVAIN.htm#HenriILotharingiaBrabantdied1235B
[555] fmg.ac/Projects/MedLands/BRABANT,%20LOUVAIN.htm#Elisabethdied1272
[556] www.francogene.com/genealogie-quebec-genealogy/010/010371.php
[557] René Jetté, John P. DuLong, Roland-Yves Gagné and Gail F. Moreau; article entitled "From Catherine Baillon to Charlemagne" located in American Canadian Genealogist

GENERATION 29 (21G grandmother)

Mathilde de Clèves [559] [560] [561] + Gérard de Luxembourg [562]

GENERATION 30 (20G grandmother)

Marguerite de Luxembourg [563] [564] [565] + Jean III de Ghistelles (who was a knight) [566]

GENERATION 31 (19G grandfather)

Jean VI de Ghistelles [567] [568] [569] + Marie de Haverskerke [570]

(page 190). Issue 82, Volume 25, Number 4, 1999. Can be read online at https://acgs.org/Download/ACGS_Baillon_1999.pdf

[558] fmg.ac/Projects/MedLands/FRANCONIA%20(LOWER%20RHINE).htm#Dietrichdied1245

[559] fmg.ac/Projects/MedLands/FRANCONIA%20(LOWER%20RHINE).htm#Mechtilddied1304

[560] www.francogene.com/genealogie-quebec-genealogy/010/010370.php

[561] René Jetté, John P. DuLong, Roland-Yves Gagné and Gail F. Moreau; article entitled "From Catherine Baillon to Charlemagne" located in American Canadian Genealogist (page 189). Issue 82, Volume 25, Number 4, 1999. Can be read online at https://acgs.org/Download/ACGS_Baillon_1999.pdf

[562] fmg.ac/Projects/MedLands/LIMBURG.htm#GerardDubuydied12981303

[563] Ibid.

[564] www.francogene.com/genealogie-quebec-genealogy/010/010369.php

[565] René Jetté, John P. DuLong, Roland-Yves Gagné and Gail F. Moreau; article entitled "From Catherine Baillon to Charlemagne" located in American Canadian Genealogist (pages 188, 189). Issue 82, Volume 25, Number 4, 1999. Can be read online at https://acgs.org/Download/ACGS_Baillon_1999.pdf

[566] racineshistoire.free.fr/LGN/PDF/Ghistelles.pdf (page 3)

[567] racineshistoire.free.fr/LGN/PDF/Ghistelles.pdf (page 4)

[568] www.francogene.com/genealogie-quebec-genealogy/010/010368.php

[569] René Jetté, John P. DuLong, Roland-Yves Gagné and Gail F. Moreau; article entitled "From Catherine Baillon to Charlemagne" located in American Canadian Genealogist

GENERATION 32 (18G grandfather)

Roger de Ghistelles [571] [572] [573] + ~~Marguerite~~ Élisabeth de Dudzeele (see page 182 for updated explanation)

GENERATION 33 (17G grandmother)

Isabelle de Ghistelles [574] [575] [576] + Arnould VI de Gavre [577]

GENERATION 34 (16G grandmother)

Catherine de Gavre d'Escornaix [578] [579] [580] + Guy I Le Bouteiller [581]

(page 188). Issue 82, Volume 25, Number 4, 1999. Can be read online at https://acgs.org/Download/ACGS_Baillon_1999.pdf

[570] racineshistoire.free.fr/LGN/PDF/Haverskerque.pdf (page 9)

[571] racineshistoire.free.fr/LGN/PDF/Ghistelles.pdf (page 8)

[572] www.francogene.com/genealogie-quebec-genealogy/010/010354.php

[573] René Jetté, John P. DuLong, Roland-Yves Gagné and Gail F. Moreau; article entitled "From Catherine Baillon to Charlemagne" located in <u>American Canadian Genealogist</u> (pages 185, 186, 187, 188). Issue 82, Volume 25, Number 4, 1999. Can be read online at https://acgs.org/Download/ACGS_Baillon_1999.pdf

[574] racineshistoire.free.fr/LGN/PDF/Ghistelles.pdf (page 8)

[575] www.francogene.com/genealogie-quebec-genealogy/010/010343.php

[576] René Jetté, John P. DuLong, Roland-Yves Gagné and Gail F. Moreau; article entitled "From Catherine Baillon to Charlemagne" located in <u>American Canadian Genealogist</u> (page 185). Issue 82, Volume 25, Number 4, 1999. Can be read online at https://acgs.org/Download/ACGS_Baillon_1999.pdf

[577] racineshistoire.free.fr/LGN/PDF/Gavre.pdf (page 9)

[578] racineshistoire.free.fr/LGN/PDF/Gavre.pdf (page 10)

[579] www.francogene.com/genealogie-quebec-genealogy/010/010336.php

[580] René Jetté, John P. DuLong, Roland-Yves Gagné and Gail F. Moreau; article entitled "From Catherine Baillon to Charlemagne" located in <u>American Canadian Genealogist</u> (pages 183, 184). Issue 82, Volume 25, Number 4, 1999. Can be read online at https://acgs.org/Download/ACGS_Baillon_1999.pdf

[581] http://racineshistoire.free.fr/LGN/PDF/Senlis.pdf (page 15)

Following the death of Guy I Le Bouteiller, Catherine married Simon Morhier (a knight) c. 1440. [582] [583]

GENERATION 35 (15G grandfather)

Guy II Le Bouteiller (a knight) [584] [585] [586] + Isabeau Morhier [587]

Isabeau was the daughter of Simon Morhier and Catherine de Gavre d'Escornaix. [588]

GENERATION 36 (14G grandfather)

Jean Le Bouteiller [589] [590] [591] + Marie de Venois

GENERATION 37 (13G grandmother)

Bénigne Le Bouteiller [592] [593] [594] + Jacques Maillard

---

[582] racineshistoire.free.fr/LGN/PDF/Gavre.pdf (page 10)
[583] René Jetté, John P. DuLong, Roland-Yves Gagné and Gail F. Moreau; article entitled "From Catherine Baillon to Charlemagne" located in <u>American Canadian Genealogist</u> (page 182). Issue 82, Volume 25, Number 4, 1999. Can be read online at https://acgs.org/Download/ACGS_Baillon_1999.pdf
[584] racineshistoire.free.fr/LGN/PDF/Senlis.pdf (page 15)
[585] www.francogene.com/genealogie-quebec-genealogy/010/010331.php
[586] René Jetté, John P. DuLong, Roland-Yves Gagné and Gail F. Moreau; article entitled "From Catherine Baillon to Charlemagne" located in <u>American Canadian Genealogist</u> (pages 182, 183). Issue 82, Volume 25, Number 4, 1999. Can be read online at https://acgs.org/Download/ACGS_Baillon_1999.pdf
[587] racineshistoire.free.fr/LGN/PDF/Morhier.pdf (page 4)
[588] Ibid.
[589] racineshistoire.free.fr/LGN/PDF/Senlis.pdf (page 15)
[590] www.francogene.com/genealogie-quebec-genealogy/010/010321.php
[591] René Jetté, John P. DuLong, Roland-Yves Gagné and Gail F. Moreau; article entitled "From Catherine Baillon to Charlemagne" located in <u>American Canadian Genealogist</u> (pages 179, 180, 181). Issue 82, Volume 25, Number 4, 1999. Can be read online at https://acgs.org/Download/ACGS_Baillon_1999.pdf

GENERATION 38 (12G grandfather)

Miles Maillard [595] [596] + Marie Morant

GENERATION 39 (11G grandmother)

Renée Maillard [597] [598] + Adam Baillon

GENERATION 40 (10G grandfather)

Alphonse Baillon [599] [600] + Louise de Marle

GENERATION 41 (9G grandmother)

Catherine Baillon [601] [602] + Jacques Miville dit Deschênes

---

[592] racineshistoire.free.fr/LGN/PDF/Senlis.pdf (page 15)
[593] www.francogene.com/genealogie-quebec-genealogy/010/010312.php
[594] René Jetté, John P. DuLong, Roland-Yves Gagné and Gail F. Moreau; article entitled "From Catherine Baillon to Charlemagne" located in American Canadian Genealogist (page 178). Issue 82, Volume 25, Number 4, 1999. Can be read online at https://acgs.org/Download/ACGS_Baillon_1999.pdf
[595] www.francogene.com/genealogie-quebec-genealogy/010/010307.php
[596] René Jetté, John P. DuLong, Roland-Yves Gagné and Gail F. Moreau; article entitled "From Catherine Baillon to Charlemagne" located in American Canadian Genealogist (pages 177, 178). Issue 82, Volume 25, Number 4, 1999. Can be read online at https://acgs.org/Download/ACGS_Baillon_1999.pdf
[597] www.francogene.com/genealogie-quebec-genealogy/010/010304.php
[598] René Jetté, John P. DuLong, Roland-Yves Gagné and Gail F. Moreau; article entitled "From Catherine Baillon to Charlemagne" located in American Canadian Genealogist (page 177). Issue 82, Volume 25, Number 4, 1999. Can be read online at https://acgs.org/Download/ACGS_Baillon_1999.pdf
[599] www.francogene.com/genealogie-quebec-genealogy/003/003676.php
[600] René Jetté, John P. DuLong, Roland-Yves Gagné and Gail F. Moreau; article entitled "From Catherine Baillon to Charlemagne" located in American Canadian Genealogist (pages 176, 177). Issue 82, Volume 25, Number 4, 1999. Can be read online at https://acgs.org/Download/ACGS_Baillon_1999.pdf

Catherine was a *Fille du Roi*. Accordingly, Catherine, being from a family directly connected to minor French nobility, carried a dowry of 950 livres plus 50 livres from the King of France.

GENERATION 42 (8G grandfather)

Charles Miville [603] + Marie Marthe Vallée

GENERATION 43 (7G grandmother)

Catherine Miville + Jean Duval dit Dupaulo

GENERATION 44 (6G grandmother)

Marie Josette Duval dit Dupaulo + Jean Baptiste LeClerc

GENERATION 45 (5G grandfather)

Jean Baptiste LeClerc + Madeleine Thébault

GENERATION 46 (4G grandmother)

Madeleine LeClerc + Pascal Landry

GENERATION 47 (3G grandfather)

Alexis dit Alexandre Landry + Justine Lanteigne

---

[601] www.francogene.com/genealogie-quebec-genealogy/001/001079.php
[602] René Jetté, John P. DuLong, Roland-Yves Gagné and Gail F. Moreau; article entitled "From Catherine Baillon to Charlemagne" located in <u>American Canadian Genealogist</u> (pages 175, 176). Issue 82, Volume 25, Number 4, 1999. Can be read online at https://acgs.org/Download/ACGS_Baillon_1999.pdf
[603] www.francogene.com/genealogie-quebec-genealogy/007/007848.php

GENERATION 48 (2G grandmother)

Marie Landry + Louis Breau

GENERATION 49 (1G grandfather)

André Breau + Marie Philomène Mallet

GENERATION 50 (maternal grandmother)

Mary Catherine (Kay) Breau + James Henry (Harry) Feeley

GENERATION 51 (my mother)

Anne Elizabeth Feeley and Albert Doucette were married on November 11, 1961 in Truro, Nova Scotia.

GENERATION 52 (me)

Michele Anne Doucette and Albert Joseph Stewart were married on August 24, 1985 in Truro, Nova Scotia.

Carolingian Dynasty

The Carolingian dynasty was a Frankish noble family with origins in both the Arnulfing and Pippinid clans of the 7th century AD. The term Carolingian was taken from the Latinised name of Charles Martel (*Carolus*), the grandfather of Charlemagne.

This family consolidated its power in the late 7th century, eventually making the offices of Mayor of the Palace hereditary, and, thereby, becoming the *de facto* rulers of the Franks as the real powers behind the throne.

Pépin III was not satisfied with being Mayor; he wanted more. In summation, he wanted to be king.

Coming to an arrangement with the Pope, by virtue of the spuriously forged document, none other than the <u>Donation of Constantine</u> (mysteriously discovered in 751 AD and supposedly written some 400 years earlier), he was proclaimed king, leading to the removal, and imprisonment, of the true Merovingian king, Childeric III. [604] [605] [606] [607] [608]

As a means of legitimizing a claim, as was generally the case with royalty, it must also be shared that the maternal great grandmother of Charlemagne was Bertrada of Prüm, a Merovingian princess.

Charlemagne is my 37th great grandfather, courtesy of the Catherine de Baillon link.

---

[604] https://en.wikipedia.org/wiki/Pepin_II_the_Middle
[605] https://en.wikipedia.org/wiki/Charles_Martel
[606] https://en.wikipedia.org/wiki/Pepin_the_Short
[607] doubleuoglobe.com/vol11/cn11-79.html
[608] https://en.wikipedia.org/wiki/Childeric_III

Pages 116 to 140 detail six descending lineages of Catherine de Baillon.

Pages 141 to 142 outline the descending lineage of the author.

The labyrinth is an ancient symbol that reveals wholeness as it combines with the picture of the spirals and circles into a meandering, yet purposeful, path; so, too, is this reflective of my genealogical endeavors.

Capetian Dynasty

As per HUGH THE GREAT [609] ...... It is important to realize that France as we know it today was not even close to being unified in the Medieval Age. It was broken up into a patchwork of duchies and counties, overseen by dukes and counts. They tirelessly competed with each other and the *kings* of "France." The Capetians actually ruled over what is called Lesser France. It is the area around Paris and Orleans, including the Ile-de-France or Isle of France. The Ile or Isle of France was not a standard island as we think of it today, but a surrounding land area to Paris. It was the base of the Capetians.

In reference to the Capetian dynasty, the largest and oldest European royal house, consisting of the descendants of Hugues Capet of France in the male line, and the Merovingian dynasty and the Carolingian dynasty in the female line, King Hugues is my 30th great grandfather.

■ Robert II, Count of Worms and Rheingau, Duke of Hesbaye

Robert of Hesbaye is the earliest known ancestor of the family known as the Robertians. He is also the earliest known male-line ancestor of the French royal family (including the Capetians, the Valois and the Bourbons, all of them his male-line descendents).

Robert of Hesbaye's father was *likely* the son of Thuringbert, Count of Worms and Rheingau, making him a grandson of Robert I, Duke of Neustria (c. 697–764). [610]

Robert of Hesbaye's mother was *possibly* Princess Chrotlind, daughter of Theuderic III, Merovingian king of Austrasia.

---

[609] https://liveasfreepeople.com/2017/11/01/hugh-the-great/
[610] www.stirnet.com/genie/data/ancient/ae/capet01.php#link1

It is also *possible* that Ingerman of Hesbaye (father of Ermengarde) and Cancor were brothers of Robert of Hesbaye.

Landrada, mother of Saint Chrodegang, Archbishop of Metz, is *likely* to have been his sister.

Ermengarde, wife of Emperor Louis the Pious was *most likely* his niece.

▪ Robert III, Count of Worms and Rheingau married Waldrada

▪ Robert IV the Strong, Duke of France and Count of Orléans married Adéläis (daughter of Hughes, Count of Tours) [611]

▪ King Robert I of France (922 to 923) married secondly Béatrice de Vermandois [612] [613] [614]

▪ Hugues the Great, Duke of France, married thirdly Hedwig de Saxe [615] [616] [617]

▪ King Hugues Capet of France (987 to 996) married Adélaïde d'Aquitaine [618] [619]

Hugues Capet was the founder of the French royal dynasty; a dynasty that has ruled France continuously until as late as 1848 (with a brief interregnum caused by the French Revolution). In addition, a junior line has held the Spanish Crown since 1700; the current monarch Juan Carlos I and his family being direct descendants.

---

[611] fmg.ac/Projects/MedLands/ALSACE.htm#Adelaisdiedafter866
[612] fmg.ac/Projects/MedLands/CAPET.htm#RobertIdied923B
[613] fmg.ac/Projects/MedLands/NORTHERN%20FRANCE.htm#Beatrixdied931
[614] www.stirnet.com/genie/data/ancient/fh/franks3.php#link1
[615] fmg.ac/Projects/MedLands/CAPET.htm#Huguesdied956B
[616] fmg.ac/Projects/MedLands/GERMANY,%20Kings.htm#HedwigMHuguesRegentFrancedied956
[617] www.stirnet.com/genie/data/ancient/fh/germany01.php#linklo
[618] fmg.ac/Projects/MedLands/CAPET.htm#HuguesCapetdied996B
[619] fmg.ac/Projects/MedLands/AQUITAINE.htm#Adelaisdied1004

- King Robert II of France (996 to 1031) married thirdly Constance d'Arles [620] [621]

- King Henri I of France (1031 to 1060) married Anne de Kiev [622] [623]

- King Philippe I of France (1060 to 1108) married Berthe de Holland [624] [625]

- King Louis VI of France (1108 to 1137) married Adélaïde de Maurienne [626] [627]

- King Louis VII of France (1137 to 1180) married Adèle de Champagne [628] [629]

- King Philippe II Auguste of France (1180 to 1223) married thirdly Agnès d'Andechs de Méranie [630] [631]

☐ Princess Marie of France married Henri I, Duke of Brabant [632] [633]

☐ Élisabeth de Brabant married Count Dietrich (Thierry) de Clèves [634] [635]

---

[620] fmg.ac/Projects/MedLands/CAPET.htm#RobertIIdied1031B
[621] fmg.ac/Projects/MedLands/PROVENCE.htm#ConstanceArlesMRobertIIFrancedied1031
[622] fmg.ac/Projects/MedLands/CAPET.htm#HenriIdied1060B
[623] fmg.ac/Projects/MedLands/RUSSIA,%20Rurik.htm#AnnaIaroslavnadied1075
[624] fmg.ac/Projects/MedLands/CAPET.htm#PhilippeIdied1108B
[625] fmg.ac/Projects/MedLands/HOLLAND.htm#Berthadied1093
[626] fmg.ac/Projects/MedLands/CAPET.htm#LouisVIdied1137B
[627] fmg.ac/Projects/MedLands/SAVOY.htm#Adélaïdedied1154
[628] fmg.ac/Projects/MedLands/CAPET.htm#LouisVIIdied1180B
[629] fmg.ac/Projects/MedLands/CENTRAL%20FRANCE.htm#AdeleBloisdied1206
[630] fmg.ac/Projects/MedLands/CAPET.htm#PhilippeIIdied1223B
[631] fmg.ac/Projects/MedLands/CARINTHIA.htm#AgnesMeranodied1201
[632] fmg.ac/Projects/MedLands/CAPET.htm#Mariedied1238
[633] fmg.ac/Projects/MedLands/BRABANT,%20LOUVAIN.htm#HenriILotharingiaBrabantdied1235B
[634] fmg.ac/Projects/MedLands/BRABANT,%20LOUVAIN.htm#Elisabethdied1272
[635] fmg.ac/Projects/MedLands/FRANCONIA%20(LOWER%20RHINE).htm#Dietrichdied1245

Élisabeth was also known as Ysabeau de Brabant; with regards to French records, the name Élisabeth is often used, interchangeably, with that of Isabelle. [636] [637]

☐ Mathildade Clèves married Gerard de Luxembourg

☐ Marguerite de Luxembourg married Jean III de Ghistelles

■ Jean IV de Ghistelles married Marie de Haverskerke

■ Roger de Ghistelles married Élisabeth ~~Marguerite~~ de Dudzeele (see page 182 for updated explanation)

☐ Isabelle (Ysabeau) de Ghistelles married Arnould VI de Gavre

☐ Catherine de Gavre d'Escornaix married Guy I Le Bouteiller

■ Guy II Le Bouteillier married Isabeau Morhier

■ Jean Le Bouteillier married Marie de Venois

☐ Bénigne Le Bouteillier married Jacques Maillard

■ Miles Maillard married Marie Morant

☐ Renée Maillard married Adam de Baillon

■ Alphonse de Baillon married Louise de Marle

☐ Catherine de Baillon

---

[636] Jetté, René, DuLong, John P., Gagné, Roland-Yves, Moreau, Gail F. and Dubé, Joseph A. (2001) Table d'ascendance de Catherine Baillon: 12 générations (p 153). Montréal, Québec: Société Généalogique Canadienne Française.
[637] https://en.wikipedia.org/wiki/Henry_I,_Duke_of_Brabant

Saxon Kings

In reference to the Saxon Kings of England, Wessex, and Kent, King Alfred, the Great, is my 35th great grandfather. This line began with Cerdic of the West Saxons, making him my 48th great grandfather.

- King Cerdic of the West Saxons (519 to 534) [638] [639] [640] [641]

- King Cynric of the West Saxons (534 to 560) [642] [643]

- King Ceawlin of the West Saxons (560 to 591) [644] [645]

- Cuthwine, who did not rule (died in battle in 584) [646]

- Cuthwulf, who did not rule [647]

- Ceolwald, who did not rule [648]

---

[638] fmg.ac/Projects/MedLands/ENGLAND,%20AngloSaxon%20&%20Danish%20Kings.htm#_Toc214769409
[639] www.stirnet.com/genie/data/ancient/ms/saxons02.php
[640] https://en.wikipedia.org/wiki/Cerdic_of_Wessex
[641] https://en.wikipedia.org/wiki/House_of_Wessex_family_tree
[642] fmg.ac/Projects/MedLands/ENGLAND,%20AngloSaxon%20&%20Danish%20Kings.htm#_Toc214769409
[643] https://en.wikipedia.org/wiki/Cynric_of_Wessex
[644] fmg.ac/Projects/MedLands/ENGLAND,%20AngloSaxon%20&%20Danish%20Kings.htm#_Toc214769409
[645] https://en.wikipedia.org/wiki/Ceawlin_of_Wessex
[646] https://en.wikipedia.org/wiki/Cuthwine
[647] https://en.wikipedia.org/wiki/Cutha_Cathwulf

- Cenred, who did not rule [649] [650]

- Ingild, who did not rule (died 718), brother of King Ine of Wessex [651] [652]

- Eoppa, who did not rule

- Eafa, who did not rule

- King Eahlmund of Kent (784 to 786) [653] [654]

- King Egbert of Wessex (802 to 827) and of all England (827 to 836) [655]

- King Aethelwulf of Wessex [656] (839-858) married Osburh, the daughter of Oslac of the Isle of Wight. [657]

Osburh's existence is known only from Asser's *Life of King Alfred*. [658] [659]

---

[648] https://en.wikipedia.org/wiki/Ceolwald_of_Wessex
[649] www.stirnet.com/genie/data/ancient/ms/saxons03.php#top
[650] https://en.wikipedia.org/wiki/Cenred_of_Wessex
[651] https://en.wikipedia.org/wiki/Ealhmund_of_Kent
[652] https://en.wikipedia.org/wiki/Ine_of_Wessex
[653] fmg.ac/Projects/MedLands/ENGLAND,%20AngloSaxon%20&%20Danish%20Kings.htm#EalhmundKentsucc784A
[654] www.stirnet.com/genie/data/ancient/ms/saxons05.php#link2
[655] fmg.ac/Projects/MedLands/ENGLAND,%20AngloSaxon%20&%20Danish%20Kings.htm#EcgberhtWessexB
[656] fmg.ac/Projects/MedLands/ENGLAND,%20AngloSaxon%20&%20Danish%20Kings.htm#AethelwulfWessexdied858B
[657] www.stirnet.com/genie/data/ancient/ms/saxons03.php#top
[658] https://en.wikipedia.org/wiki/Osburh
[659] https://en.wikipedia.org/wiki/Asser

She is best known for Asser's story about a book of Saxon songs which she showed to Alfred and his brothers, offering to give the book to whoever could first memorise it, a challenge which Alfred took up and won; a story that further exhibits the interest of high status ninth-century women in books, and their role in educating their children. [660]

Oslac, King Aethelwulf's *pincerna* (butler), was an important figure in the royal court and household. [661] He is further described as a descendant of King Cerdich's Jutish nephews, Stuf and Wihtgar, who conquered the Isle of Wight. [662]

■ King Alfred the Great of Wessex (871 to 899) married Ealhswith, daughter of a Mercian nobleman, Æthelred Mucil, Ealdorman of the Gaini, and his wife Eadburh [663 664 665 666 667]

■ King Edward (The Elder) of Wessex (899-924) married <u>thirdly</u> Eadgifu, daughter of Sigehelm, Ealdorman of Kent [668 669 670 671 672]

---

[660] https://en.wikipedia.org/wiki/Osburh
[661] Ibid.
[662] Ibid.
[663] fmg.ac/Projects/MedLands/ENGLAND,%20AngloSaxon%20&%20Danish%20Kings.htm#Alfreddied899B
[664] fmg.ac/Projects/MedLands/ENGLAND,%20AngloSaxon%20nobility.htm#Ealhswithdied904
[665] www.stirnet.com/genie/data/ancient/ms/saxons04.php#dau1
[666] https://en.wikipedia.org/wiki/Alfred_the_Great
[667] https://en.wikipedia.org/wiki/Ealhswith
[668] fmg.ac/Projects/MedLands/ENGLAND,%20AngloSaxon%20&%20Danish%20Kings.htm#Edwarddied924B
[669] fmg.ac/Projects/MedLands/ENGLAND,%20AngloSaxon%20nobility.htm#EadgifuM3EdwardWessex
[670] www.stirnet.com/genie/data/ancient/ms/saxons03.php#top

- King Edmund I of England (939-946) married Saint Ælfgifu of Shaftesbury [673] [674] [675]

- King Edgar (The Peaceful) of England (959-975) married Ælfthryth, the daughter of Ealdorman Ordgar of Devon (whilst her mother was a member of the royal family of Wessex) [676] [677] [678] [679]

- King Æthelred II (the Unready) of England (978-1013 and 1014-1016) married Ælfgifu of York, the daughter of Thored, Earl of southern Northumbria [680] [681] [682] [683]

- King Edmund II Ironside of England (23 April to 30 November 1016) married Ealdgyth, daughter of Edwin of Mercia. [684] [685] [686] [687]

---

[671] https://en.wikipedia.org/wiki/Edward_the_elder
[672] https://en.wikipedia.org/wiki/Eadgifu_of_Kent
[673] fmg.ac/Projects/MedLands/ENGLAND,%20AngloSaxon%20&%20Danish%20Kings.htm#Edmunddied921
[674] https://en.wikipedia.org/wiki/Edmund_I_of_England
[675] https://en.wikipedia.org/wiki/%C3%86lfgifu_of_Shaftesbury
[676] fmg.ac/Projects/MedLands/ENGLAND,%20AngloSaxon%20&%20Danish%20Kings.htm#Edgardied975B
[677] fmg.ac/Projects/MedLands/ENGLAND,%20AngloSaxon%20nobility.htm#AethelflaedMEdgar
[678] https://en.wikipedia.org/wiki/Edgar_the_Peaceful
[679] https://en.wikipedia.org/wiki/Ælfthryth,_Queen_of_England
[680] fmg.ac/Projects/MedLands/ENGLAND,%20AngloSaxon%20&%20Danish%20Kings.htm#AethelredIIdied1016B
[681] fmg.ac/Projects/MedLands/ENGLAND,%20AngloSaxon%20nobility.htm#AelfgivaMAethelredII
[682] https://en.wikipedia.org/wiki/Æthelred_the_Unready
[683] https://en.wikipedia.org/wiki/Ælfgifu_of_York

■ Prince Edward the Exile married Agatha, daughter of Stephen, King of Hungary. [688] [689] [690] [691]

☐ Saint Margaret of Scotland (also known as Margaret of Wessex) married King Malcolm III of Scotland [692] [693] [694] [695] [696]

■ King David I of Scotland married Matilda (Maud), Countess of Huntingdon (d/o Waltheof II, Earl of Northumbria and Judith of Lens; niece to King William I (of England) de St. Clair, 7th Duke of Normandy) [697] [698] [699] [700] [701]

---

[684] fmg.ac/Projects/MedLands/ENGLAND,%20AngloSaxon%20&%20Danish%20Kings.htm#Edmunddied1016B
[685] www.stirnet.com/genie/data/british/xyz/zzmisc03.php#link2
[686] https://en.wikipedia.org/wiki/Edmund_Ironside
[687] https://en.wikipedia.org/wiki/Ealdgyth_(floruit_1015%E2%80%931016)
[688] fmg.ac/Projects/MedLands/ENGLAND,%20AngloSaxon%20&%20Danish%20Kings.htm#Edmunddied1016B
[689] www.stirnet.com/genie/data/continent/hijk/hungary1.php#linkhi
[690] https://en.wikipedia.org/wiki/Edward_the_Exile
[691] https://en.wikipedia.org/wiki/Agatha,_wife_of_Edward_the_Exile
[692] fmg.ac/Projects/MedLands/ENGLAND,%20AngloSaxon%20&%20Danish%20Kings.htm#Margaretdied1093
[693] fmg.ac/Projects/MedLands/SCOTLAND.htm#MalcolmIIIdied1093B
[694] www.stirnet.com/genie/data/british/aa/atholl1.php#huntm
[695] https://en.wikipedia.org/wiki/Saint_Margaret_of_Scotland
[696] https://en.wikipedia.org/wiki/Malcolm_III_of_Scotland
[697] fmg.ac/Projects/MedLands/SCOTLAND.htm#DavidIdied1153B
[698] fmg.ac/Projects/MedLands/ENGLISH%20NOBILITY%20MEDIEVAL.htm#Matildadied1131
[699] www.stirnet.com/genie/data/british/zwrk/temp06.php#walf1
[700] https://en.wikipedia.org/wiki/David_I_of_Scotland
[701] https://en.wikipedia.org/wiki/Maud,_Countess_of_Huntingdon

- Prince Henry of Scotland, 3rd Earl of Huntingdon, married Ada de Warenne [702] [703] [704] [705] [706]

- Ada of Huntingdon married Count Floris III of Holland [707] [708] [709] [710] [711]

- Marguerite of Holland married Count Dietrich (Thierry) V de Clèves [712] [713]

- Count Dietrich (Thierry) VI de Clèves married Mathilde de Dinslaken [714]

- Count Dietrich (Thierry) de Clèves married Élisabeth de Brabant (d/o Henri I, Duke of Brabant, and Princess Marie of France) [715] [716]

Élisabeth was also known as Ysabeau de Brabant; with regards to French records, the name Élisabeth is often used, interchangeably, with that of Isabelle. [717] [718]

---

[702] fmg.ac/Projects/MedLands/SCOTLAND.htm#Henrydied1152
[703] fmg.ac/Projects/MedLands/ENGLISH%20NOBILITY%20MEDIEVAL.htm#Adadied1078
[704] www.stirnet.com/genie/data/british/ww/warren01.php#hunt
[705] https://en.wikipedia.org/wiki/Henry_of_Scotland
[706] https://en.wikipedia.org/wiki/Ada_de_Warenne
[707] mg.ac/Projects/MedLands/SCOTLAND.htm#Adadiedafter11Jan1205
[708] fmg.ac/Projects/MedLands/HOLLAND.htm#FlorisIIIdied1190
[709] www.stirnet.com/genie/data/continent/hijk/holland1.php#link2
[710] https://en.wikipedia.org/wiki/Ada_of_Huntingdon
[711] https://en.wikipedia.org/wiki/Floris_III,_Count_of_Holland
[712] fmg.ac/Projects/MedLands/HOLLAND.htm#Margaretadiedafter1203
[713] fmg.ac/Projects/MedLands/FRANCONIA%20(LOWER%20RHINE).htm#DietrichIIIdied12001203
[714] fmg.ac/Projects/MedLands/FRANCONIA%20(LOWER%20RHINE).htm#DietrichIVdied1260
[715] fmg.ac/Projects/MedLands/BRABANT,%20LOUVAIN.htm#Elisabethdied1272
[716] fmg.ac/Projects/MedLands/FRANCONIA%20(LOWER%20RHINE).htm#Dietrichdied1245

☐ Mathilda deClèves married Gerard de Luxembourg

☐ Marguerite de Luxembourg married Jean III de Ghistelles

■ Jean IV de Ghistelles married Marie de Haverskerke

■ Roger de Ghistelles married Élisabeth ~~Marguerite~~ de Dudzeele (see page 182 for updated explanation)

☐ Isabelle (Ysabeau) de Ghistelles married Arnould VI de Gavre

☐ Catherine de Gavre d'Escornaix married Guy I Le Bouteiller

■ Guy II Le Bouteillier married Isabeau Morhier

■ Jean Le Bouteillier married Marie de Venois

☐ Bénigne Le Bouteillier married Jacques Maillard

■ Miles Maillard married Marie Morant

☐ Renée Maillard married Adam de Baillon

■ Alphonse de Baillon married Louise de Marle

☐ Catherine de Baillon

---

[717] Jetté, René, DuLong, John P., Gagné, Roland-Yves, Moreau, Gail F. and Dubé, Joseph A. (2001) <u>Table d'ascendance de Catherine Baillon: 12 générations</u> (p 153). Montréal, Québec: Société Généalogique Canadienne Française.
[718] https://en.wikipedia.org/wiki/Henry_I,_Duke_of_Brabant

In keeping with the Saxon Kings of England, Wessex, and Kent, there exists a second line of descent.

- King Cerdic of the West Saxons (519 to 534) [719] [720] [721] [722]

- King Cynric of the West Saxons (534 to 560) [723] [724]

- King Ceawlin of the West Saxons (560 to 591) [725] [726]

- Cuthwine, who did not rule (died in battle in 584) [727]

- Cuthwulf, who did not rule [728]

- Ceolwald, who did not rule [729]

- Cenred, who did not rule [730] [731]

---

[719] fmg.ac/Projects/MedLands/ENGLAND,%20AngloSaxon%20&%20Danish%20Kings.htm#_Toc214769409
[720] /www.stirnet.com/genie/data/ancient/ms/saxons02.php
[721] https://en.wikipedia.org/wiki/Cerdic_of_Wessex
[722] https://en.wikipedia.org/wiki/House_of_Wessex_family_tree
[723] fmg.ac/Projects/MedLands/ENGLAND,%20AngloSaxon%20&%20Danish%20Kings.htm#_Toc214769409
[724] https://en.wikipedia.org/wiki/Cynric_of_Wessex
[725] fmg.ac/Projects/MedLands/ENGLAND,%20AngloSaxon%20&%20Danish%20Kings.htm#_Toc214769409
[726] https://en.wikipedia.org/wiki/Ceawlin_of_Wessex
[727] https://en.wikipedia.org/wiki/Cuthwine
[728] https://en.wikipedia.org/wiki/Cutha_Cathwulf
[729] https://en.wikipedia.org/wiki/Ceolwald_of_Wessex
[730] www.stirnet.com/genie/data/ancient/ms/saxons03.php#top
[731] https://en.wikipedia.org/wiki/Cenred_of_Wessex

- Ingild, who did not rule (died 718), brother of King Ine of Wessex [732] [733]

- Eoppa, who did not rule

- Eafa, who did not rule

- King Eahlmund of Kent (784 to 786) [734]

- King Egbert of Wessex (802 to 827) and of all England (827 to 836) [735]

- King Aethelwulf of Wessex [736] (839-858) married Osburh, the daughter of Oslac of the Isle of Wight. [737]

Osburh's existence is known only from Asser's *Life of King Alfred*. [738] [739] She is best known for Asser's story about a book of Saxon songs which she showed to Alfred and his brothers, offering to give the book to whoever could first memorise it, a challenge which Alfred took up and won; a story that further exhibits the interest of high status ninth-century women in books, and their role in educating their children. [740]

---

[732] https://en.wikipedia.org/wiki/Ealhmund_of_Kent
[733] https://en.wikipedia.org/wiki/Ine_of_Wessex
[734] fmg.ac/Projects/MedLands/ENGLAND,%20AngloSaxon%20&%20Danish%20Kings.htm#EalhmundKentsucc784A
[735] fmg.ac/Projects/MedLands/ENGLAND,%20AngloSaxon%20&%20Danish%20Kings.htm#EcgberhtWessexB
[736] fmg.ac/Projects/MedLands/ENGLAND,%20AngloSaxon%20&%20Danish%20Kings.htm#AethelwulfWessexdied858B
[737] www.stirnet.com/genie/data/ancient/ms/saxons03.php#top
[738] https://en.wikipedia.org/wiki/Osburh
[739] https://en.wikipedia.org/wiki/Asser
[740] https://en.wikipedia.org/wiki/Osburh

Oslac, King Aethelwulf's *pincerna* (butler), was an important figure in the royal court and household. [741] He is further described as a descendant of King Cerdich's Jutish nephews, Stuf and Wihtgar, who conquered the Isle of Wight. [742]

■ King Alfred the Great of Wessex (871 to 899) married Ealhswith, daughter of a Mercian nobleman, Æthelred Mucil, Ealdorman of the Gaini, and his wife Eadburh [743] [744] [745] [746] [747]

■ King Edward (The Elder) of Wessex (899-924) married thirdly Eadgifu, daughter of Sigehelm, Ealdorman of Kent [748] [749] [750] [751] [752]

☐ Edgiva (Edgifu) married King Charles III of France [753] [754] [755] [756] [757]

---

[741] https://en.wikipedia.org/wiki/Osburh
[742] Ibid.
[743] fmg.ac/Projects/MedLands/ENGLAND,%20AngloSaxon%20&%20Danish%20Kings.htm#Alfreddied899B
[744] fmg.ac/Projects/MedLands/ENGLAND,%20AngloSaxon%20nobility.htm#Ealhswithdied904
[745] www.stirnet.com/genie/data/ancient/ms/saxons04.php#dau1
[746] https://en.wikipedia.org/wiki/Alfred_the_Great
[747] https://en.wikipedia.org/wiki/Ealhswith
[748] fmg.ac/Projects/MedLands/ENGLAND,%20AngloSaxon%20&%20Danish%20Kings.htm#Edwarddied924B
[749] fmg.ac/Projects/MedLands/ENGLAND,%20AngloSaxon%20nobility.htm#EadgifuM3EdwardWessex
[750] www.stirnet.com/genie/data/ancient/ms/saxons03.php#top
[751] https://en.wikipedia.org/wiki/Edward_the_elder
[752] https://en.wikipedia.org/wiki/Eadgifu_of_Kent
[753] fmg.ac/Projects/MedLands/ENGLAND,%20AngloSaxon%20&%20Danish%20Kings.htm#Eadgifudiedafter951
[754] fmg.ac/Projects/MedLands/CAROLINGIANS.htm#CharlesIIIleSimpleFrancesB

- King Louis IV of France married Gerberga of Germany [758] [759] [760]

- Princess Matilda of France married King Conrad (The Peaceful) of Burgundy [761] [762] [763]

- Bertha of Burgundy married Count Odo(Eudes) I of Blois [764] [765] [766]

- Count Odo (Eudes) II of Blois married <u>secondly</u> Ermengarde d'Auvergne [767] [768]

- Count Theobald III of Blois married <u>secondly</u> Adela (Alix) of Valois. [769] [770]

- Count Étienne (Stephen) II of Blois married Adèle of Normandy [771] [772] [773]

---

[755] www.stirnet.com/genie/data/ancient/fh/franks3.php#chas
[756] https://en.wikipedia.org/wiki/Eadgifu_of_Wessex
[757] https://en.wikipedia.org/wiki/Charles_the_Simple
[758] fmg.ac/Projects/MedLands/CAROLINGIANS.htm#LouisIVFranceB
[759] fmg.ac/Projects/MedLands/GERMANY,%20Kings.htm#GerbergaM1GiselbertLorraineM2LouisIVFran
[760] www.stirnet.com/genie/data/ancient/fh/germany01.php#linklo
[761] fmg.ac/Projects/MedLands/CAROLINGIANS.htm#MathildeMConradIBurgundy
[762] fmg.ac/Projects/MedLands/BURGUNDY%20KINGS.htm#ConradIBurgundydied993B
[763] www.stirnet.com/genie/data/ancient/ae/burgundy1.php#top
[764] fmg.ac/Projects/MedLands/BURGUNDY%20KINGS.htm#BertheM1EudesIBloisM2RobertIIFrance
[765] fmg.ac/Projects/MedLands/CENTRAL%20FRANCE.htm#EudesIdied995
[766] www.stirnet.com/genie/data/continent/bb/blois1.php#top
[767] fmg.ac/Projects/MedLands/CENTRAL%20FRANCE.htm#EudesIIdied1037B
[768] fmg.ac/Projects/MedLands/AUVERGNE.htm#ErmengardeAuvergnediedafter1042
[769] fmg.ac/Projects/MedLands/CENTRAL%20FRANCE.htm#ThibautIIIdied1089B
[770] fmg.ac/Projects/MedLands/NORTHERN%20FRANCE.htm#AdélaïdeValoisMThibautIIIBlois
[771] fmg.ac/Projects/MedLands/CHAMPAGNE%20NOBILITY.htm#EtienneITroyesdied1048B
[772] www.stirnet.com/genie/data/continent/bb/blois1.php#link1

- Count Theobald IV of Blois married Matilda von Sponheim [774] [775]

☐ Adèle (Alix) of Champagne married King Louis VII of France [776] [777] [778] [779]

- King Philippe II Auguste of France (1180 to 1223) married <u>thirdly</u> Agnès d'Andechs de Méranie [780] [781]

☐ Princess Marie of France married Henri I, Duke of Brabant [782] [783] [784]

☐ Élisabeth de Brabant married Count Dietrich (Thierry) de Clèves [785] [786]

Élisabeth was also known as Ysabeau de Brabant; with regards to French records, the name Élisabeth is often used, interchangeably, with that of Isabelle. [787] [788]

☐ Mathilda deClèves married Gerard de Luxembourg

---

[773] www.stirnet.com/genie/data/continent/mn/normans2.php#linklo
[774] fmg.ac/Projects/MedLands/CENTRAL%20FRANCE.htm#ThibautIVdied1152B
[775] fmg.ac/Projects/MedLands/CARINTHIA.htm#Mathildedied1160
[776] fmg.ac/Projects/MedLands/CENTRAL%20FRANCE.htm#AdeleBloisdied1206
[777] fmg.ac/Projects/MedLands/CAPET.htm#LouisVIIdied1180B
[778] www.stirnet.com/genie/data/continent/cc/capet02.php#link2
[779] www.stirnet.com/genie/data/continent/bb/blois1.php#burge2
[780] fmg.ac/Projects/MedLands/CAPET.htm#PhilippeIIdied1223B
[781] fmg.ac/Projects/MedLands/CARINTHIA.htm#AgnesMeranodied1201
[782] fmg.ac/Projects/MedLands/CAPET.htm#Mariedied1238
[783] fmg.ac/Projects/MedLands/BRABANT,%20LOUVAIN.htm#HenriILotharingiaBrabantdied1235B
[784] www.stirnet.com/genie/data/continent/bb/brabant02.php#franm
[785] fmg.ac/Projects/MedLands/BRABANT,%20LOUVAIN.htm#Elisabethdied1272
[786] fmg.ac/Projects/MedLands/FRANCONIA%20(LOWER%20RHINE).htm#Dietrichdied1245
[787] Jetté, René, DuLong, John P., Gagné, Roland-Yves, Moreau, Gail F. and Dubé, Joseph A. (2001) <u>Table d'ascendance de Catherine Baillon: 12 générations</u> (p 153). Montréal, Québec: Société Généalogique Canadienne Française.
[788] https://en.wikipedia.org/wiki/Henry_I,_Duke_of_Brabant

☐ Marguerite de Luxembourg married Jean III de Ghistelles

■ Jean IV de Ghistelles married Marie de Haverskerke

■ Roger de Ghistelles married Élisabeth ~~Marguerite~~ de Dudzeele (see page 182 for updated explanation)

☐ Isabelle (Ysabeau) de Ghistelles married Arnould VI de Gavre

☐ Catherine de Gavre d'Escornaix married Guy I Le Bouteiller

■ Guy II Le Bouteillier married Isabeau Morhier

■ Jean Le Bouteillier married Marie de Venois

☐ Bénigne Le Bouteillier married Jacques Maillard

■ Miles Maillard married Marie Morant

☐ Renée Maillard married Adam de Baillon

■ Alphonse de Baillon married Louise de Marle

☐ Catherine de Baillon

Normans

King William I of England, 7th Duke of Normandy, has long been known throughout history as *William the Conqueror*. He is my 28th great grandfather.

- Hrólf the Ganger (Rollo) (1st Duke of Normandy) of Norway married Poppa [789] [790] [791]

- William I (Longsword) de St. Clair (2nd Duke of Normandy) and Sprota (a Breton captive and his concubine) [792] [793] [794]

- Richard I (The Fearless) de St. Clair (3rd Duke of Normandy) (illegitimate issue) married Gunnora [795] [796] [797] [798]

- Richard II (The Good) de St. Clair (4th Duke of Normandy) married Judith of Brittany [799] [800] [801] [802]

---

[789] fmg.ac/Projects/MedLands/NORMANDY.htm#RobertIdied928
[790] fmg.ac/Projects/MedLands/FRANKISH%20NOBILITY.htm#PoppaMRollo
[791] https://en.wikipedia.org/wiki/Rollo
[792] fmg.ac/Projects/MedLands/NORMANDY.htm#GuillaumeIdied905
[793] https://en.wikipedia.org/wiki/William_I,_Duke_of_Normandy
[794] https://en.wikipedia.org/wiki/Sprota
[795] fmg.ac/Projects/MedLands/NORMANDY.htm#RichardIdied996B
[796] fmg.ac/Projects/MedLands/NORMAN%20NOBILITY.htm#GunnoraMRichardINormandy
[797] https://en.wikipedia.org/wiki/Richard_I,_Duke_of_Normandy
[798] https://en.wikipedia.org/wiki/Gunnor
[799] fmg.ac/Projects/MedLands/NORMANDY.htm#RichardIIdied1026B
[800] fmg.ac/Projects/MedLands/BRITTANY.htm#JudithBretagnedied1017
[801] https://en.wikipedia.org/wiki/Richard_II,_Duke_of_Normandy
[802] https://en.wikipedia.org/wiki/Judith_of_Brittany

■ Robert (The Magnificent) de St. Clair (6th Duke of Normandy) and mistress Herleva de Falaise [803] [804] [805]

■ King William I (of England) de St. Clair (7th Duke of Normandy) (illegitimate issue) known throughout history as *William the Conqueror*, married Mathilda of Flanders [806] [807] [808]

☐ Adèle of Normandy married Count Stephen I of Blois [809] [810]

■ Count Theobald III (The Great) of Champagne (Theobald IV of Blois) married Matilda von Sponheim [811] [812]

☐ Adèle (Alix) of Champagne married King Louis VII of France [813] [814]

■ King Philippe II Auguste of France (1180 to 1223) married <u>thirdly</u> Agnès d'Andechs de Méranie [815] [816]

☐ Princess Marie of France married Henri I, Duke of Brabant [817] [818]

---

[803] fmg.ac/Projects/MedLands/NORMANDY.htm#RobertIIdied1035
[804] https://en.wikipedia.org/wiki/Robert_the_Magnificent
[805] https://en.wikipedia.org/wiki/Herleva
[806] fmg.ac/Projects/MedLands/ENGLAND,%20Kings%201066-1603.htm#WilliamIdied1087
[807] https://en.wikipedia.org/wiki/William_the_Conqueror
[808] fmg.ac/Projects/MedLands/FLANDERS,%20HAINAUT.htm#Mathildedied1083
[809] fmg.ac/Projects/MedLands/ENGLAND,%20Kings%201066-1603.htm#Adeladied1138
[810] fmg.ac/Projects/MedLands/CENTRAL%20FRANCE.htm#EtienneIdied1102B
[811] fmg.ac/Projects/MedLands/CENTRAL%20FRANCE.htm#ThibautIVdied1152B
[812] fmg.ac/Projects/MedLands/CARINTHIA.htm#Mathildedied1160
[813] fmg.ac/Projects/MedLands/CENTRAL%20FRANCE.htm#AdeleBloisdied1206
[814] fmg.ac/Projects/MedLands/CAPET.htm#LouisVIIdied1180B
[815] fmg.ac/Projects/MedLands/CAPET.htm#PhilippeIIdied1223B
[816] fmg.ac/Projects/MedLands/CARINTHIA.htm#AgnesMeranodied1201
[817] fmg.ac/Projects/MedLands/CAPET.htm#Mariedied1238

☐ Élisabeth de Brabant married Count Dietrich (Thierry) de Clèves [819] [820]

Élisabeth was also known as Ysabeau de Brabant; with regards to French records, the name Élisabeth is often used, interchangeably, with that of Isabelle. [821] [822]

☐ Mathilda de Clèves married Gerard de Luxembourg

☐ Marguerite de Luxembourg married Jean III de Ghistelles

■ Jean IV de Ghistelles married Marie de Haverskerke

■ Roger de Ghistelles married Élisabeth ~~Marguerite~~ de Dudzeele (see page 182 for updated explanation)

☐ Isabelle (Ysabeau) de Ghistelles married Arnould VI de Gavre

☐ Catherine de Gavre d'Escornaix married Guy I Le Bouteiller

■ Guy II Le Bouteillier married Isabeau Morhier

■ Jean Le Bouteillier married Marie de Venois

☐ Bénigne Le Bouteillier married Jacques Maillard

---

[818] fmg.ac/Projects/MedLands/BRABANT,%20LOUVAIN.htm#HenriILotharingiaBrabantdied1235B
[819] fmg.ac/Projects/MedLands/BRABANT,%20LOUVAIN.htm#Elisabethdied1272
[820] fmg.ac/Projects/MedLands/FRANCONIA%20(LOWER%20RHINE).htm#Dietrichdied1245
[821] Jetté, René, DuLong, John P., Gagné, Roland-Yves, Moreau, Gail F. and Dubé, Joseph A. (2001) Table d'ascendance de Catherine Baillon: 12 générations (p 153). Montréal, Québec: Société Généalogique Canadienne Française.
[822] https://en.wikipedia.org/wiki/Henry_I,_Duke_of_Brabant

- Miles Maillard married Marie Morant

- Renée Maillard married Adam de Baillon

- Alphonse de Baillon married Louise de Marle

- Catherine de Baillon

In keeping with the Normans, there exists a second line of descent.

- Hrólf the Ganger (Rollo) (1st Duke of Normandy) of Norway married Poppa [823] [824] [825]

- William I (Longsword) de St. Clair (2nd Duke of Normandy) and Sprota (a Breton captive and his concubine) [826] [827] [828]

- Richard I (The Fearless) de St. Clair (3rd Duke of Normandy) (illegitimate issue) married Gunnora [829] [830] [831] [832] [833]

- Richard II (The Good) de St. Clair (4th Duke of Normandy) married Judith of Brittany [834] [835] [836] [837]

- Robert (The Magnificent) de St. Clair (6th Duke of Normandy) and mistress Herleva de Falaise [838] [839] [840]

---

[823] fmg.ac/Projects/MedLands/NORMANDY.htm#RobertIdied928
[824] fmg.ac/Projects/MedLands/FRANKISH%20NOBILITY.htm#PoppaMRollo
[825] https://en.wikipedia.org/wiki/Rollo
[826] fmg.ac/Projects/MedLands/NORMANDY.htm#GuillaumeIdied905
[827] https://en.wikipedia.org/wiki/William_I,_Duke_of_Normandy
[828] https://en.wikipedia.org/wiki/Sprota
[829] fmg.ac/Projects/MedLands/NORMANDY.htm#RichardIdied996B
[830] fmg.ac/Projects/MedLands/NORMAN%20NOBILITY.htm#GunnoraMRichardINormandy
[831] fmg.ac/Projects/MedLands/NORMAN%20NOBILITY.htm#_Toc322790582
[832] https://en.wikipedia.org/wiki/Richard_I,_Duke_of_Normandy
[833] https://en.wikipedia.org/wiki/Gunnor
[834] fmg.ac/Projects/MedLands/NORMANDY.htm#RichardIIdied1026B
[835] fmg.ac/Projects/MedLands/BRITTANY.htm#JudithBretagnedied1017
[836] https://en.wikipedia.org/wiki/Richard_II,_Duke_of_Normandy
[837] https://en.wikipedia.org/wiki/Judith_of_Brittany
[838] fmg.ac/Projects/MedLands/NORMANDY.htm#RobertIIdied1035
[839] https://en.wikipedia.org/wiki/Robert_the_Magnificent
[840] https://en.wikipedia.org/wiki/Herleva

☐ Adéläide of Normandy (illegitimate issue) married Count Lambert II of Lens [841] [842]

☐ Judith of Lens married Waltheof II, Earl of Northumbria [843] [844]

☐ Countess Maud de Huntingdon married married King David I of Scotland (s/o King Malcolm III of Scotland and Saint Margaret of Scotland) [845] [846]

■ Prince Henry of Scotland, 3rd Earl of Huntingdon, married Ada de Warenne [847] [848] [849] [850]

☐ Ada of Huntingdon married Count Floris III of Holland [851] [852] [853] [854]

☐ Marguerite of Holland married Court Dietrich (Thierry) V de Clèves [855] [856]

---

[841] fmg.ac/Projects/MedLands/NORMANDY.htm#Adelaisdied1081
[842] fmg.ac/Projects/MedLands/NORTHERN%20FRANCE.htm#Lambertdied1054
[843] fmg.ac/Projects/MedLands/NORTHERN%20FRANCE.htm#Judithdiedafter1086MWaltheof
[844] fmg.ac/Projects/MedLands/ENGLISH%20NOBILITY%20MEDIEVAL.htm#Waltheofdied1076
[845] fmg.ac/Projects/MedLands/ENGLISH%20NOBILITY%20MEDIEVAL.htm#Matildadied1131
[846] fmg.ac/Projects/MedLands/SCOTLAND.htm#DavidIdied1153B
[847] fmg.ac/Projects/MedLands/SCOTLAND.htm#Henrydied1152
[848] fmg.ac/Projects/MedLands/ENGLISH%20NOBILITY%20MEDIEVAL.htm#Adadied1078
[849] https://en.wikipedia.org/wiki/Henry_of_Scotland
[850] https://en.wikipedia.org/wiki/Ada_de_Warenne
[851] fmg.ac/Projects/MedLands/SCOTLAND.htm#Adadiedafter11Jan1205
[852] fmg.ac/Projects/MedLands/HOLLAND.htm#FlorisIIIdied1190
[853] https://en.wikipedia.org/wiki/Ada_of_Huntingdon
[854] https://en.wikipedia.org/wiki/Floris_III,_Count_of_Holland
[855] fmg.ac/Projects/MedLands/HOLLAND.htm#Margaretadiedafter1203
[856] fmg.ac/Projects/MedLands/FRANCONIA%20(LOWER%20RHINE).htm#DietrichIIIdied12001203

- Count Dietrich (Thierry) VI de Clèves married Mathilde de Dinslaken [857]

- Count Dietrich (Thierry) de Clèves married Élisabeth de Brabant (d/o Henri I, Duke of Brabant, and Princess Marie of France) [858] [859]

Élisabeth was also known as Ysabeau de Brabant; with regards to French records, the name Élisabeth is often used, interchangeably, with that of Isabelle. [860] [861]

☐ Mathilda deClèves married Gerard de Luxembourg

☐ Marguerite de Luxembourg married Jean III de Ghistelles

- Jean IV de Ghistelles married Marie de Haverskerke

- Roger de Ghistelles married Élisabeth ~~Marguerite~~ de Dudzeele (see page 182 for updated explanation)

☐ Isabelle (Ysabeau) de Ghistelles married Arnould VI de Gavre

☐ Catherine de Gavre d'Escornaix married Guy I Le Bouteiller

- Guy II Le Bouteillier married Isabeau Morhier

- Jean Le Bouteillier married Marie de Venois

---

[857] fmg.ac/Projects/MedLands/FRANCONIA%20(LOWER%20RHINE).htm#DietrichIVdied1260

[858] fmg.ac/Projects/MedLands/BRABANT,%20LOUVAIN.htm#Elisabethdied1272

[859] fmg.ac/Projects/MedLands/FRANCONIA%20(LOWER%20RHINE).htm#Dietrichdied1245

[860] Jetté, René, DuLong, John P., Gagné, Roland-Yves, Moreau, Gail F. and Dubé, Joseph A. (2001) Table d'ascendance de Catherine Baillon: 12 générations (p 153). Montréal, Québec: Société Généalogique Canadienne Française.

[861] https://en.wikipedia.org/wiki/Henry_I,_Duke_of_Brabant

☐ Bénigne Le Bouteillier married Jacques Maillard

■ Miles Maillard married Marie Morant

☐ Renée Maillard married Adam de Baillon

■ Alphonse de Baillon married Louise de Marle

☐ Catherine de Baillon

In keeping with the Normans, there exists a third line of descent.

- Hrólf the Ganger (Rollo) (1st Duke of Normandy) of Norway married Poppa [862] [863] [864]

- Adela (Gerloc) of Normandy married Duke William III of Aquitaine [865] [866]

- Adéläide of Aquitaine married King Hugues Capet of France (987 to 996) [867] [868]

- King Robert II of France (996 to 1031) married Constance d'Arles [869] [870]

- King Henri I of France (1031 to 1060) married Anne de Kiev [871] [872]

- King Philippe I of France (1060 to 1108) married Berthe de Holland [873] [874]

- King Louis VI of France (1108 to 1137) married Adélaïde de Maurienne [875] [876]

- King Louis VII of France (1137 to 1180) married Adèle de Champagne [877] [878]

---

[862] fmg.ac/Projects/MedLands/NORMANDY.htm#RobertIdied928
[863] fmg.ac/Projects/MedLands/FRANKISH%20NOBILITY.htm#PoppaMRollo
[864] https://en.wikipedia.org/wiki/Rollo
[865] fmg.ac/Projects/MedLands/NORMANDY.htm#Gerlocdiedafter969
[866] fmg.ac/Projects/MedLands/AQUITAINE.htm#GuillaumeIPoitoudied963
[867] fmg.ac/Projects/MedLands/AQUITAINE.htm#Adelaisdied1004
[868] fmg.ac/Projects/MedLands/CAPET.htm#HuguesCapetdied996B
[869] fmg.ac/Projects/MedLands/CAPET.htm#RobertIIdied1031B
[870] fmg.ac/Projects/MedLands/PROVENCE.htm#ConstanceArlesMRobertIIFrancedied1031
[871] fmg.ac/Projects/MedLands/CAPET.htm#HenriIdied1060B
[872] fmg.ac/Projects/MedLands/RUSSIA,%20Rurik.htm#AnnaIaroslavnadied1075
[873] fmg.ac/Projects/MedLands/CAPET.htm#PhilippeIdied1108B
[874] fmg.ac/Projects/MedLands/HOLLAND.htm#Berthadied1093
[875] fmg.ac/Projects/MedLands/CAPET.htm#LouisVIdied1137B
[876] fmg.ac/Projects/MedLands/SAVOY.htm#Adélaïdedied1154
[877] fmg.ac/Projects/MedLands/CAPET.htm#LouisVIIdied1180B
[878] fmg.ac/Projects/MedLands/CENTRAL%20FRANCE.htm#AdeleBloisdied1206

- King Philippe II Auguste of France (1180 to 1223) married <u>thirdly</u> Agnès d'Andechs de Méranie [879] [880]

  - Princess Marie of France married Henri I, Duke of Brabant [881] [882]

  - Élisabeth de Brabant married Count Dietrich (Thierry) de Clèves [883] [884]

Élisabeth was also known as Ysabeau de Brabant; with regards to French records, the name Élisabeth is often used, interchangeably, with that of Isabelle. [885] [886]

  - Mathilda de Clèves married Gerard de Luxembourg

  - Marguerite de Luxembourg married Jean III de Ghistelles

- Jean IV de Ghistelles married Marie de Haverskerke

- Roger de Ghistelles married Élisabeth ~~Marguerite~~ de Dudzeele (see page 182 for updated explanation)

  - Isabelle (Ysabeau) de Ghistelles married Arnould VI de Gavre

  - Catherine de Gavre d'Escornaix married Guy I Le Bouteiller

---

[879] fmg.ac/Projects/MedLands/CAPET.htm#PhilippeIIdied1223B
[880] fmg.ac/Projects/MedLands/CARINTHIA.htm#AgnesMeranodied1201
[881] fmg.ac/Projects/MedLands/CAPET.htm#Mariedied1238
[882] fmg.ac/Projects/MedLands/BRABANT,%20LOUVAIN.htm#HenriILotharingiaBrabantdied1235B
[883] fmg.ac/Projects/MedLands/BRABANT,%20LOUVAIN.htm#Elisabethdied1272
[884] fmg.ac/Projects/MedLands/FRANCONIA%20(LOWER%20RHINE).htm#Dietrichdied1245
[885] Jetté, René, DuLong, John P., Gagné, Roland-Yves, Moreau, Gail F. and Dubé, Joseph A. (2001) <u>Table d'ascendance de Catherine Baillon: 12 générations</u> (p 153). Montréal, Québec: Société Généalogique Canadienne Française.
[886] https://en.wikipedia.org/wiki/Henry_I,_Duke_of_Brabant

- Guy II Le Bouteillier married Isabeau Morhier

- Jean Le Bouteillier married Marie de Venois

- Bénigne Le Bouteillier married Jacques Maillard

- Miles Maillard married Marie Morant

- Renée Maillard married Adam de Baillon

- Alphonse de Baillon married Louise de Marle

- Catherine de Baillon

House of Plantagenet

In reference to the House of Plantagenet, a branch of the Angevis (a royal house founded by Geoffrey V of Anjou, father of Henry II of England), [887] [888] [889] so, too, can we lay claim a few key ancestors in the beginning; namely …

- <u>Viscount Ingelger of Angers</u> married Adélaïde [890] [891]

- <u>Count Fulk I (The Red) of Anjou</u> married Roscille de Loches [892] [893]

- <u>Count Fulk II of Anjou</u> married Gerberge [894] [895]

- <u>Count Geoffrey I of Anjou</u> married Adèle de Meaux [896] [897]

- ☐ Ermengarde of Anjou married Count Conan I of Rennes, Duke of Brittany [898] [899]

- ☐ Judith of Brittany married Richard II (The Good) de St. Clair (4th Duke of Normany) [900] [901]

---

[887] https://en.wikipedia.org/wiki/House_of_Plantagenet
[888] https://en.wikipedia.org/wiki/Count_of_Anjou
[889] racineshistoire.free.fr/LGN/PDF/Plantagenets.pdf
[890] fmg.ac/Projects/MedLands/ANJOU,%20MAINE.htm#Ingelgerdied888
[891] fmg.ac/Projects/MedLands/FRANKISH%20NOBILITY.htm#AdelaisMIngelger
[892] fmg.ac/Projects/MedLands/ANJOU,%20MAINE.htm#FoulquesIdied941
[893] fmg.ac/Projects/MedLands/FRANKISH%20NOBILITY.htm#RoscilleMFoulquesIAnjou
[894] fmg.ac/Projects/MedLands/ANJOU,%20MAINE.htm#FoulquesIIdied958B
[895] fmg.ac/Projects/MedLands/CENTRAL%20FRANCE.htm#GerbergeMFoulquesIIAnjou
[896] fmg.ac/Projects/MedLands/ANJOU,%20MAINE.htm#GeoffroyIdied987B
[897] fmg.ac/Projects/MedLands/CHAMPAGNE%20NOBILITY.htm#Adeladied974
[898] fmg.ac/Projects/MedLands/ANJOU,%20MAINE.htm#ErmengardeMConanIBretagnedied992
[899] fmg.ac/Projects/MedLands/BRITTANY.htm#ConanIdied992

- Robert (The Magnificent) de St. Clair (6th Duke of Normandy) married Herleva de Falaise [902] [903] [904]

- King William I (of England) de St. Clair (7th Duke of Normandy), illegitimate son, [905] [906] known throughout history as *William the Conqueror* Mathilda of Flanders [907]

- ☐ Adèle of Normandy married Count Stephen I of Blois [908] [909]

- Count Theobald III (The Great) of Champagne (Theobald IV of Blois) married Matilda von Sponheim [910] [911]

- ☐ Adèle (Alix) of Champagne married King Louis VII of France [912] [913]

- King Philippe II Auguste of France (1180 to 1223) married <u>thirdly</u> Agnès d'Andechs de Méranie [914] [915]

- ☐ Princess Marie of France married Henri I, Duke of Brabant [916] [917]

---

[900] fmg.ac/Projects/MedLands/BRITTANY.htm#JudithBretagnedied1017
[901] fmg.ac/Projects/MedLands/NORMANDY.htm#RichardIIdied1026B
[902] fmg.ac/Projects/MedLands/NORMANDY.htm#RobertIIdied1035
[903] https://en.wikipedia.org/wiki/Robert_the_Magnificent
[904] https://en.wikipedia.org/wiki/Herleva
[905] fmg.ac/Projects/MedLands/ENGLAND,%20Kings%201066-1603.htm#WilliamIdied1087
[906] https://en.wikipedia.org/wiki/William_the_Conqueror
[907] fmg.ac/Projects/MedLands/FLANDERS,%20HAINAUT.htm#Mathildedied1083
[908] fmg.ac/Projects/MedLands/ENGLAND,%20Kings%201066-1603.htm#Adeladied1138
[909] fmg.ac/Projects/MedLands/CENTRAL%20FRANCE.htm#EtienneIdied1102B
[910] fmg.ac/Projects/MedLands/CENTRAL%20FRANCE.htm#ThibautIVdied1152B
[911] fmg.ac/Projects/MedLands/CARINTHIA.htm#Mathildedied1160
[912] fmg.ac/Projects/MedLands/CENTRAL%20FRANCE.htm#AdeleBloisdied1206
[913] fmg.ac/Projects/MedLands/CAPET.htm#LouisVIIdied1180B
[914] fmg.ac/Projects/MedLands/CAPET.htm#PhilippeIIdied1223B
[915] fmg.ac/Projects/MedLands/CARINTHIA.htm#AgnesMeranodied1201

☐ Élisabeth de Brabant married Count Dietrich (Thierry) de Clèves [918] [919]

Élisabeth was also known as Ysabeau de Brabant; with regards to French records, the name Élisabeth is often used, interchangeably, with that of Isabelle. [920] [921]

☐ Mathilda de Clèves married Gerard de Luxembourg

☐ Marguerite de Luxembourg married Jean III de Ghistelles

■ Jean IV de Ghistelles married Marie de Haverskerke

■ Roger de Ghistelles married Élisabeth ~~Marguerite~~ de Dudzeele (see page 182 for updated explanation)

☐ Isabelle (Ysabeau) de Ghistelles married Arnould VI de Gavre

☐ Catherine de Gavre d'Escornaix married Guy I Le Bouteiller

■ Guy II Le Bouteillier married Isabeau Morhier

■ Jean Le Bouteillier married Marie de Venois

☐ Bénigne Le Bouteillier married Jacques Maillard

---

[916] fmg.ac/Projects/MedLands/CAPET.htm#Mariedied1238
[917] fmg.ac/Projects/MedLands/BRABANT,%20LOUVAIN.htm#HenriILotharingiaBrabantdied1235B
[918] fmg.ac/Projects/MedLands/BRABANT,%20LOUVAIN.htm#Elisabethdied1272
[919] fmg.ac/Projects/MedLands/FRANCONIA%20(LOWER%20RHINE).htm#Dietrichdied1245
[920] Jetté, René, DuLong, John P., Gagné, Roland-Yves, Moreau, Gail F. and Dubé, Joseph A. (2001) Table d'ascendance de Catherine Baillon: 12 générations (p 153). Montréal, Québec: Société Généalogique Canadienne Française.
[921] https://en.wikipedia.org/wiki/Henry_I,_Duke_of_Brabant

- Miles Maillard married Marie Morant

- Renée Maillard married Adam de Baillon

- Alphonse de Baillon married Louise de Marle

- Catherine de Baillon

The Irish Kings of Dalriada

Fergus Mór mac Eirc (Fergus the Great) was a legendary king of Dál Riata. While this historicity may be debatable, his posthumous importance as the founder of Scotland in the national myth of Medieval and Renaissance Scotland is not in doubt. Rulers of Scotland from Kenneth I MacAlpin until the present time claim descent from Fergus Mór, [922] [923] my 47th great grandfather.

- King Eochaid Muinremuir of Dalriada

- King Erc MacEochaid of Dalriada [924] [925] [926]

- King Fergus Mór (The Great) of the Scots [927] [928] [929]

- King Domangart of the Scots [930] [931]

- King Gabráin of the Scots [932] [933]

---

[922] https://en.wikipedia.org/wiki/Fergus_Mór
[923] https://en.wikipedia.org/wiki/Kenneth_I_of_Scotland
[924] www.stirnet.com/genie/data/ancient/ms/scots1.php#link2
[925] www.stirnet.com/genie/data/ancient/ms/scots2.php#top
[926] https://en.wikipedia.org/wiki/Erc_of_Dalriada
[927] www.stirnet.com/genie/data/ancient/ms/scots2.php#top
[928] www.magma.ca/~mmackay/dalriada.html#dalriada
[929] https://en.wikipedia.org/wiki/Fergus_Mór
[930] www.stirnet.com/genie/data/ancient/ms/scots2.php#top
[931] https://en.wikipedia.org/wiki/Domangart_Réti
[932] www.stirnet.com/genie/data/ancient/ms/scots2.php#top
[933] https://en.wikipedia.org/wiki/Gabrán_mac_Domangairt

- King Áedán of the Scots [934] [935]

Arturius: A Quest for Camelot, [936] written by David F. Carroll, contains the irrefutable historical evidence of the existence of Arthur, who was none other than Arturius, son of Áedán mac Gabráin, King of the Dál Riata Scots (574 to 609 AD). [937] [938]

The kingdom of Dál Riata was situated in modern Argyll and Bute, Scotland, and parts of County Antrim, Ireland. [939] [940]

Should the legendary King Arthur of Camelot be proven to be the son of Áedán mac Gabráin, King of the Dál Riata Scots, as proposed by author David F. Carroll, then, so, too, would I be able to claim him as an ancestor (brother to King Eochaid I Buide of Scotland).

- King Eochaid I Buide of Scotland [941] [942]

- King Domnall Brecc of Scotland [943] [944]

- King Domangart of Scotland [945] [946]

---

[934] www.stirnet.com/genie/data/ancient/ms/scots2.php#top
[935] https://en.wikipedia.org/wiki/Áedán_mac_Gabráin
[936] https://www.electricscotland.com/history/Ascreen.pdf
[937] https://www.electricscotland.com/history/arturius.htm
[938] https://en.wikipedia.org/wiki/File:Dalriada.png
[939] https://en.wikipedia.org/wiki/Áedán_mac_Gabráin
[940] https://en.wikipedia.org/wiki/List_of_kings_of_Dál_Riata
[941] www.stirnet.com/genie/data/ancient/ms/scots2.php#top
[942] https://en.wikipedia.org/wiki/Eochaid_Buide
[943] www.stirnet.com/genie/data/ancient/ms/scots2.php#top
[944] https://en.wikipedia.org/wiki/Domnall_Brecc
[945] www.stirnet.com/genie/data/ancient/ms/scots2.php#top
[946] https://en.wikipedia.org/wiki/Domangart_mac_Domnaill

- King Eochaid II of Scotland [947] [948]

- King Eochaid mac Eochaid [949] [950]

- King Aed Find (Áed the White) or Áed mac Echdach of Scotland [951] [952]

- King Eochaid of Scotland [953] [954] [955]

- King Alpin of Scotland [956] [957] [958]

---

[947] www.stirnet.com/genie/data/ancient/ms/scots2.php#top
[948] https://en.wikipedia.org/wiki/Eochaid_mac_Domangairt
[949] www.stirnet.com/genie/data/ancient/ms/scots2.php#top
[950] https://en.wikipedia.org/wiki/Eochaid_mac_Echdach
[951] www.stirnet.com/genie/data/ancient/ms/scots2.php#top
[952] https://en.wikipedia.org/Áed_Find
[953] fmg.ac/Projects/MedLands/SCOTLAND.htm#_Toc389122935
[954] www.stirnet.com/genie/data/ancient/ms/scots2.php#top
[955] https://en.wikipedia.org/wiki/Eochaid_mac_Áeda_Find
[956] fmg.ac/Projects/MedLands/SCOTLAND.htm#_Toc389122935
[957] www.stirnet.com/genie/data/british/aa/alpin1.php
[958] https://en.wikipedia.org/wiki/Alpín_mac_Echdach

Celtic Kings of Scotland

In reference to the Celtic Kings of Scotland, King Kenneth I (MacAlpin of Scotland) is my 36th great grandfather.

- King Alpin of Scotland [959] [960] [961]

- King Kenneth I MacAlpin of Scotland (unsure when born, died February 13, 858) married ---------- [962] [963] [964] [965]

- King Constantine MacKenneth of Scotland (unsure when born, died 877) married ---------- [966] [967]

- King Donald II of Scotland (unsure when born, died 900) married ---------- [968] [969]

Donald II and his descendants represented the main line of the Kings of Alba and later Scotland.

- King Malcolm I of Scotland (unsure when born, died 954) married ---------- [970] [971] [972]

---

[959] fmg.ac/Projects/MedLands/SCOTLAND.htm#_Toc389122935
[960] www.stirnet.com/genie/data/british/aa/alpin1.php
[961] https://en.wikipedia.org/wiki/Alpín_mac_Echdach
[962] fmg.ac/Projects/MedLands/SCOTLAND.htm#_Toc389122935
[963] fmg.ac/Projects/MedLands/SCOTLAND.htm#KennethIA
[964] fmg.ac/Projects/MedLands/SCOTLAND.htm#KennethIB
[965] https://en.wikipedia.org/wiki/Kenneth_MacAlpin
[966] fmg.ac/Projects/MedLands/SCOTLAND.htm#KennethIB
[967] https://en.wikipedia.org/wiki/Causantín_mac_Cináeda
[968] fmg.ac/Projects/MedLands/SCOTLAND.htm#KennethIB
[969] https://en.wikipedia.org/wiki/Donald_II_of_Scotland
[970] fmg.ac/Projects/MedLands/SCOTLAND.htm#MalcolmIdied954A

- King Kenneth II of Scotland (unsure when born, died 995) married ---------- [973] [974]

- King Malcolm II of Scotland (born 954, died November 25, 1034 in Glamis Castle, Angus, Forfarshire, Scotland) married ---------- [975] [976]

- ☐ Bethóc married Crínán of Dunkeld (layabbot of the diocese of Dunkeld), Thane of Atholl [977] [978] [979] [980] [981] [982]

- King Duncan I of Scotland (born 1001, died 1040) married Suthen [983] [984]

- King Malcolm III of Scotland (unsure when born, died 1093) married Saint Margaret of Scotland (also known as Margaret of Wessex) [985] [986] [987] [988]

---

[971] fmg.ac/Projects/MedLands/SCOTLAND.htm#MalcolmIdied954B
[972] https://en.wikipedia.org/wiki/Malcolm_I_of_Scotland
[973] fmg.ac/Projects/MedLands/SCOTLAND.htm#MalcolmIdied954B
[974] https://en.wikipedia.org/wiki/Kenneth_II_of_Scotland
[975] fmg.ac/Projects/MedLands/SCOTLAND.htm#MalcolmIdied954B
[976] https://en.wikipedia.org/wiki/Malcolm_II_of_Scotland
[977] fmg.ac/Projects/MedLands/SCOTLAND.htm#BethocMCrinanMormaerdied1045
[978] https://en.wikipedia.org/wiki/Bethóc
[979] www.mathematical.com/bethoc.html
[980] fmg.ac/Projects/MedLands/SCOTLAND.htm#Crinandied1045
[981] https://en.wikipedia.org/wiki/Crínán_of_Dunkeld
[982] www.mathematical.com/mormaercrinande.html
[983] fmg.ac/Projects/MedLands/SCOTLAND.htm#DuncanIdied1040A
[984] fmg.ac/Projects/MedLands/SCOTLAND.htm#DuncanIdied1040B
[985] fmg.ac/Projects/MedLands/SCOTLAND.htm#MalcolmIIIdied1093B
[986] fmg.ac/Projects/MedLands/ENGLAND,%20AngloSaxon%20&%20Danish%20Kings.htm#Margaretdied1093
[987] https://en.wikipedia.org/wiki/Malcolm_III_of_Scotland
[988] https://en.wikipedia.org/wiki/Saint_Margaret_of_Scotland

- King David I of Scotland (born 1084, died 1153) married Maud, Countess of Huntingdon (d/o Waltheof II, Earl of Northumbria and Judith of Lens; niece to King William I (of England) de St. Clair, 7th Duke of Normandy) [989] [990] [991] [992]

- Prince Henry of Scotland, 3rd Earl of Huntingdon, married Ada de Warenne [993] [994] [995] [996]

  ☐ Ada of Huntingdon married Count Floris III of Holland [997] [998] [999] [1000]

  ☐ Marguerite of Holland married Count Dietrich (Thierry) V de Clèves [1001] [1002]

- Count Dietrich (Thierry) VI de Clèves married Mathilde de Dinslaken [1003]

- Count Dietrich (Thierry) de Clèves married Élisabeth de Brabant (d/o Henri I, Duke of Brabant, and Princess Marie of France) [1004] [1005]

---

[989] fmg.ac/Projects/MedLands/SCOTLAND.htm#DavidIdied1153B
[990] fmg.ac/Projects/MedLands/ENGLISH%20NOBILITY%20MEDIEVAL.htm#Matildadied1131
[991] https://en.wikipedia.org/wiki/David_I_of_Scotland
[992] https://en.wikipedia.org/wiki/Maud,_Countess_of_Huntingdon
[993] fmg.ac/Projects/MedLands/SCOTLAND.htm#Henrydied1152
[994] fmg.ac/Projects/MedLands/ENGLISH%20NOBILITY%20MEDIEVAL.htm#Adadied1078
[995] https://en.wikipedia.org/wiki/Henry_of_Scotland
[996] https://en.wikipedia.org/wiki/Ada_de_Warenne
[997] fmg.ac/Projects/MedLands/SCOTLAND.htm#Adadiedafter11Jan1205
[998] fmg.ac/Projects/MedLands/HOLLAND.htm#FlorisIIIdied1190
[999] https://en.wikipedia.org/wiki/Ada_of_Huntingdon
[1000] https://en.wikipedia.org/wiki/Floris_III,_Count_of_Holland
[1001] fmg.ac/Projects/MedLands/HOLLAND.htm#Margaretadiedafter1203
[1002] fmg.ac/Projects/MedLands/FRANCONIA%20(LOWER%20RHINE).htm#DietrichIIIdied12001203
[1003] fmg.ac/Projects/MedLands/FRANCONIA%20(LOWER%20RHINE).htm#DietrichIVdied1260

Élisabeth was also known as Ysabeau de Brabant; with regards to French records, the name Élisabeth is often used, interchangeably, with that of Isabelle. [1006] [1007]

☐ Mathilda deClèves married Gerard de Luxembourg

☐ Marguerite de Luxembourg married Jean III de Ghistelles

■ Jean IV de Ghistelles married Marie de Haverskerke

■ Roger de Ghistelles married Élisabeth ~~Marguerite~~ de Dudzeele (see page 182 for updated explanation)

☐ Isabelle (Ysabeau) de Ghistelles married Arnould VI de Gavre

☐ Catherine de Gavre d'Escornaix married Guy I Le Bouteiller

■ Guy II Le Bouteillier married Isabeau Morhier

■ Jean Le Bouteillier married Marie de Venois

☐ Bénigne Le Bouteillier married Jacques Maillard

■ Miles Maillard married Marie Morant

☐ Renée Maillard married Adam de Baillon

[1004] http://fmg.ac/Projects/MedLands/BRABANT,%20LOUVAIN.htm#Elisabethdied1272
[1005] http://fmg.ac/Projects/MedLands/FRANCONIA%20(LOWER%20RHINE).htm#Dietrichdied1245
[1006] Jetté, René, DuLong, John P., Gagné, Roland-Yves, Moreau, Gail F. and Dubé, Joseph A. (2001) Table d'ascendance de Catherine Baillon: 12 générations (p 153). Montréal, Québec: Société Généalogique Canadienne Française.
[1007] https://en.wikipedia.org/wiki/Henry_I,_Duke_of_Brabant

■ Alphonse de Baillon married Louise de Marle

☐ Catherine de Baillon

House of Dunkeld

As denoted on Wikipedia [1008]

Out of the House of Dunkeld grew a dynasty that would rule Scotland until the later 13th century. Crínán of Dunkeld (lay abbot of the diocese of Dunkeld) married Bethóc, daughter of King Malcolm II of Scotland (reigned 1005–1034). As Malcolm II had no son, the strongest hereditary claim to the Scottish throne descended through Bethóc, and Crínán's, eldest son Duncan I, who became King of Scots (reigned 1034–1040); some sources indicate that Malcolm II designated Duncan as his successor under the rules of tanistry because there were other possible claimants to the throne.

- Crínán of Dunkeld married Bethóc (d/o King Malcolm II of Scotland) [1009] [1010] [1011] [1012]

- King Duncan I of Scotland (born 1001, died 1040) married Suthen [1013]

- King Malcolm III of Scotland (unsure when born, died 1093) married Saint Margaret of Scotland (also known as Margaret of Wessex) married [1014] [1015] [1016] [1017] [1018] [1019]

[1008] https://en.wikipedia.org/wiki/Crínán_of_Dunkeld
[1009] fmg.ac/Projects/MedLands/SCOTLAND.htm#Crinandied1045
[1010] www.stirnet.com/genie/data/british/aa/atholl1.php#top
[1011] fmg.ac/Projects/MedLands/SCOTLAND.htm#BethocMCrinanMormaerdied1045
[1012] www.stirnet.com/genie/data/british/aa/alpin1.php#link1
[1013] fmg.ac/Projects/MedLands/SCOTLAND.htm#DuncanIdied1040B
[1014] fmg.ac/Projects/MedLands/SCOTLAND.htm#MalcolmIIIdied1093B
[1015] fmg.ac/Projects/MedLands/ENGLAND,%20AngloSaxon%20&%20Danish%20Kings.htm#Margaretdied1093
[1016] www.stirnet.com/genie/data/british/aa/atholl1.php#huntm
[1017] https://en.wikipedia.org/wiki/Malcolm_III_of_Scotland

- King David I of Scotland (born 1084, died 1153) married Maud, Countess of Huntingdon (d/o Waltheof II, Earl of Northumbria and Judith of Lens; niece to King William I (of England) de St. Clair, 7th Duke of Normandy) [1020] [1021] [1022] [1023] [1024] [1025]

- Prince Henry of Scotland, 3rd Earl of Huntingdon, married Ada de Warenne [1026] [1027] [1028] [1029]

  ☐ Ada of Huntingdon married Count Floris III of Holland [1030] [1031] [1032] [1033]

  ☐ Marguerite of Holland married Count Dietrich (Thierry) V de Clèves [1034] [1035]

- Count Dietrich (Thierry) VI de Clèves married Mathilde de Dinslaken [1036]

[1018] www.stirnet.com/genie/data/ancient/ms/saxons03.php#saint
[1019] https://en.wikipedia.org/wiki/Saint_Margaret_of_Scotland
[1020] fmg.ac/Projects/MedLands/SCOTLAND.htm#DavidIdied1153B
[1021] fmg.ac/Projects/MedLands/ENGLISH%20NOBILITY%20MEDIEVAL.htm#Matildadied1131
[1022] www.stirnet.com/genie/data/british/aa/atholl1.php#huntm
[1023] https://en.wikipedia.org/wiki/David_I_of_Scotland
[1024] www.stirnet.com/genie/data/british/zwrk/temp06.php#walf1
[1025] https://en.wikipedia.org/wiki/Maud,_Countess_of_Huntingdon
[1026] fmg.ac/Projects/MedLands/SCOTLAND.htm#Henrydied1152
[1027] fmg.ac/Projects/MedLands/ENGLISH%20NOBILITY%20MEDIEVAL.htm#Adadied1078
[1028] https://en.wikipedia.org/wiki/Henry_of_Scotland
[1029] https://en.wikipedia.org/wiki/Ada_de_Warenne
[1030] fmg.ac/Projects/MedLands/SCOTLAND.htm#Adadiedafter11Jan1205
[1031] fmg.ac/Projects/MedLands/HOLLAND.htm#FlorisIIIdied1190
[1032] https://en.wikipedia.org/wiki/Ada_of_Huntingdon
[1033] https://en.wikipedia.org/wiki/Floris_III,_Count_of_Holland
[1034] fmg.ac/Projects/MedLands/HOLLAND.htm#Margaretadiedafter1203
[1035] fmg.ac/Projects/MedLands/FRANCONIA%20(LOWER%20RHINE).htm#DietrichIIIdied12001203

- Count Dietrich (Thierry) de Clèves married Élisabeth de Brabant (d/o Henri I, Duke of Brabant, and Princess Marie of France) [1037] [1038]

Élisabeth was also known as Ysabeau de Brabant; with regards to French records, the name Élisabeth is often used, interchangeably, with that of Isabelle. [1039] [1040]

- ☐ Mathilda deClèves married Gerard de Luxembourg

- ☐ Marguerite de Luxembourg married Jean III de Ghistelles

- Jean IV de Ghistelles married Marie de Haverskerke

- Roger de Ghistelles married Élisabeth ~~Marguerite~~ de Dudzeele (see page 182 for updated explanation)

- ☐ Isabelle (Ysabeau) de Ghistelles married Arnould VI de Gavre

- ☐ Catherine de Gavre d'Escornaix married Guy I Le Bouteiller

- Guy II Le Bouteillier married Isabeau Morhier

- Jean Le Bouteillier married Marie de Venois

- ☐ Bénigne Le Bouteillier married Jacques Maillard

[1036] fmg.ac/Projects/MedLands/FRANCONIA%20(LOWER%20RHINE).htm#DietrichIVdied1260
[1037] fmg.ac/Projects/MedLands/BRABANT,%20LOUVAIN.htm#Elisabethdied1272
[1038] fmg.ac/Projects/MedLands/FRANCONIA%20(LOWER%20RHINE).htm#Dietrichdied1245
[1039] Jetté, René, DuLong, John P., Gagné, Roland-Yves, Moreau, Gail F. and Dubé, Joseph A. (2001) Table d'ascendance de Catherine Baillon: 12 générations (p 153). Montréal, Québec: Société Généalogique Canadienne Française.
[1040] httsp://en.wikipedia.org/wiki/Henry_I,_Duke_of_Brabant

- Miles Maillard married Marie Morant

☐ Renée Maillard married Adam de Baillon

- Alphonse de Baillon married Louise de Marle

☐ Catherine de Baillon

Counts of Holland

The Counts of Holland go back to the same time frame as King Alfred the Great of Wessex.

- Count Gerolf de Frisia married ---------- [1041]

- Count Dirk I de Frisia married Geva [1042]

- Count Dirk II de Frisia married Hildegard de Flandres [1043][1044][1045][1046]

- Count Arnulf de Frisia married Liutgard de Luxembourg [1047][1048]

- Count Dirk III de Frisia married Othelindis [1049][1050]

- Count Floris I de Frisia married Gertrude of Saxony [1051][1052]

- Count Dirk V de Frisia married Othelindis [1053]

[1041] fmg.ac/Projects/MedLands/HOLLAND.htm#_Toc181670219
[1042] fmg.ac/Projects/MedLands/HOLLAND.htm#_Toc181670221
[1043] www.stirnet.com/genie/data/continent/hijk/holland1.php#top
[1044] www.stirnet.com/genie/data/continent/defg/flanders1.php#linklo
[1045] fmg.ac/Projects/MedLands/HOLLAND.htm#DirkIIdied988
[1046] fmg.ac/Projects/MedLands/FLANDERS,%20HAINAUT.htm#Hildegarddied990
[1047] fmg.ac/Projects/MedLands/HOLLAND.htm#Arnulfdied993
[1048] fmg.ac/Projects/MedLands/LUXEMBOURG.htm#Liutgarddiedafter1005
[1049] fmg.ac/Projects/MedLands/HOLLAND.htm#DirkIIIdied1039B
[1050] fmg.ac/Projects/MedLands/BRANDENBURG,%20PRUSSIA.htm#OthelindisMDirkIIIHolland
[1051] fmg.ac/Projects/MedLands/HOLLAND.htm#FlorisIdied1061
[1052] fmg.ac/Projects/MedLands/SAXONY.htm#Gertruddied1113
[1053] fmg.ac/Projects/MedLands/HOLLAND.htm#_Toc181670222

- Count Floris II de Holland married Gertrude (Petronella) de Lorraine [1054] [1055]

- Count Dirk IV de Holland married Sophie von Rheineck [1056] [1057]

- Count Floris III de Holland married Ada of Huntingdon (d/o Henry of Scotland and Ada of Warenne) [1058] [1059] [1060] [1061] [1062]

- Marguerite of Holland married Count Dietrich (Thierry) V de Clèves [1063] [1064]

- Count Dietrich (Thierry) VI de Clèves married Mathilde de Dinslaken [1065]

- Count Dietrich (Thierry) de Clèves married Élisabeth de Brabant (d/o Henri I, Duke of Brabant, and Princess Marie of France) [1066] [1067]

Élisabeth was also known as Ysabeau de Brabant; with regards to French records, the name Élisabeth is often used, interchangeably, with that of Isabelle. [1068] [1069]

[1054] fmg.ac/Projects/MedLands/HOLLAND.htm#FlorisIIdied1121B
[1055] fmg.ac/Projects/MedLands/LORRAINE.htm#GertrudePetronilladied1144
[1056] fmg.ac/Projects/MedLands/HOLLAND.htm#DirkVIdied1157
[1057] fmg.ac/Projects/MedLands/FRANCONIA.htm#SophieRheineckdied1176
[1058] fmg.ac/Projects/MedLands/HOLLAND.htm#FlorisIIIdied1190
[1059] fmg.ac/Projects/MedLands/SCOTLAND.htm#Adadiedafter11Jan1205
[1060] https://en.wikipedia.org/wiki/Floris_III,_Count_of_Holland
[1061] https://en.wikipedia.org/wiki/Ada_of_Huntingdon
[1062] https://en.wikipedia.org/wiki/Counts_of_Holland
[1063] fmg.ac/Projects/MedLands/HOLLAND.htm#Margaretadiedafter1203
[1064] fmg.ac/Projects/MedLands/FRANCONIA%20(LOWER%20RHINE).htm#DietrichIIIdied12001203
[1065] fmg.ac/Projects/MedLands/FRANCONIA%20(LOWER%20RHINE).htm#DietrichIVdied1260
[1066] fmg.ac/Projects/MedLands/BRABANT,%20LOUVAIN.htm#Elisabethdied1272
[1067] fmg.ac/Projects/MedLands/FRANCONIA%20(LOWER%20RHINE).htm#Dietrichdied1245

☐ Mathilda deClèves married Gerard de Luxembourg

☐ Marguerite de Luxembourg married Jean III de Ghistelles

■ Jean IV de Ghistelles married Marie de Haverskerke

■ Roger de Ghistelles married Élisabeth ~~Marguerite~~ de Dudzeele (see page 182 for updated explanation)

☐ Isabelle (Ysabeau) de Ghistelles married Arnould VI de Gavre

☐ Catherine de Gavre d'Escornaix married Guy I Le Bouteiller

■ Guy II Le Bouteillier married Isabeau Morhier

■ Jean Le Bouteillier married Marie de Venois

☐ Bénigne Le Bouteillier married Jacques Maillard

■ Miles Maillard married Marie Morant

☐ Renée Maillard married Adam de Baillon

■ Alphonse de Baillon married Louise de Marle

☐ Catherine de Baillon

[1068] Jetté, René, DuLong, John P., Gagné, Roland-Yves, Moreau, Gail F. and Dubé, Joseph A. (2001) <u>Table d'ascendance de Catherine Baillon: 12 générations</u> (p 153). Montréal, Québec: Société Généalogique Canadienne Française.
[1069] https://en.wikipedia.org/wiki/Henry_I,_Duke_of_Brabant

Earl of Huntingdon

As denoted on Wikipedia [1070]

The Earl of Huntingdon is a title associated with the ruling house of Scotland, and latterly with the Hastings family. It is believed that if the legendary hero, Robin Hood, is to be taken as a true, historical character, he is most likely to have been the long forgotten Robert, Earl of Huntington, whose medieval tombstone can still be seen among the ruins of Kirklees Priory.

- Siward, Earl of Northumbria, married Ælfled of Northumbria [1071] [1072] [1073] [1074]

- Waltheof II, Earl of Northumbria, married Judith of Lens (d/o Adélaïde of Normandy and Lambert II, Count of Lens) who was niece to King William I (of England) de St. Clair (7th Duke of Normandy); the last of the major Anglo-Saxon earls to remain powerful after the Norman conquest of England in 1066. [1075] [1076] [1077]

[1070] https://en.wikipedia.org/wiki/Earl_of_Huntingdon

[1071] fmg.ac/Projects/MedLands/ENGLISH%20NOBILITY%20MEDIEVAL.htm#Waltheofdied1076

[1072] www.stirnet.com/genie/data/british/zwrk/temp06.php#walf1

[1073] www.stirnet.com/genie/data/british/ss4tz/swinton01.php#top

[1074] https://en.wikipedia.org/wiki/Siward,_Earl_of_Northumbria

[1075] fmg.ac/Projects/MedLands/ENGLISH%20NOBILITY%20MEDIEVAL.htm#Waltheofdied1076

[1076] fmg.ac/Projects/MedLands/NORTHERN%20FRANCE.htm#Judithdiedafter1086MWaltheof

[1077] https://en.wikipedia.org/wiki/Waltheof_II,_Earl_of_Northumbria

☐ Countess Maud de Huntingdon married married King David I of Scotland (s/o King Malcolm III of Scotland and Saint Margaret of Scotland) [1078] [1079] [1080]

■ Prince Henry of Scotland, 3rd Earl of Huntingdon, married Ada de Warenne [1081] [1082] [1083] [1084]

☐ Ada of Huntingdon married Count Floris III of Holland [1085] [1086] [1087] [1088]

☐ Marguerite of Holland married Count Dietrich (Thierry) V de Clèves [1089] [1090]

■ Count Dietrich (Thierry) VI de Clèves married Mathilde de Dinslaken [1091]

■ Count Dietrich (Thierry) de Clèves married Élisabeth de Brabant (d/o Henri I, Duke of Brabant, and Princess Marie of France) [1092] [1093]

[1078] fmg.ac/Projects/MedLands/ENGLISH%20NOBILITY%20MEDIEVAL.htm#Matildadied1131
[1079] fmg.ac/Projects/MedLands/SCOTLAND.htm#DavidIdied1153B
[1080] www.stirnet.com/genie/data/british/aa/atholl1.php#huntm
[1081] fmg.ac/Projects/MedLands/SCOTLAND.htm#Henrydied1152
[1082] fmg.ac/Projects/MedLands/ENGLISH%20NOBILITY%20MEDIEVAL.htm#Adadied1078
[1083] https://en.wikipedia.org/wiki/Henry_of_Scotland
[1084] https://en.wikipedia.org/wiki/Ada_de_Warenne
[1085] fmg.ac/Projects/MedLands/SCOTLAND.htm#Adadiedafter11Jan1205
[1086] fmg.ac/Projects/MedLands/HOLLAND.htm#FlorisIIIdied1190
[1087] https://en.wikipedia.org/wiki/Ada_of_Huntingdon
[1088] https://en.wikipedia.org/wiki/Floris_III,_Count_of_Holland
[1089] fmg.ac/Projects/MedLands/HOLLAND.htm#Margaretadiedafter1203
[1090] fmg.ac/Projects/MedLands/FRANCONIA%20(LOWER%20RHINE).htm#DietrichIIIdied12001203
[1091] fmg.ac/Projects/MedLands/FRANCONIA%20(LOWER%20RHINE).htm#DietrichIVdied1260

Élisabeth was also known as Ysabeau de Brabant; with regards to French records, the name Élisabeth is often used, interchangeably, with that of Isabelle. [1094] [1095]

☐ Mathilda deClèves married Gerard de Luxembourg

☐ Marguerite de Luxembourg married Jean III de Ghistelles

■ Jean IV de Ghistelles married Marie de Haverskerke

■ Roger de Ghistelles married Élisabeth ~~Marguerite~~ de Dudzeele (see page 182 for updated explanation)

☐ Isabelle (Ysabeau) de Ghistelles married Arnould VI de Gavre

☐ Catherine de Gavre d'Escornaix married Guy I Le Bouteiller

■ Guy II Le Bouteillier married Isabeau Morhier

■ Jean Le Bouteillier married Marie de Venois

☐ Bénigne Le Bouteillier married Jacques Maillard

■ Miles Maillard married Marie Morant

☐ Renée Maillard married Adam de Baillon

■ Alphonse de Baillon married Louise de Marle

[1092] fmg.ac/Projects/MedLands/BRABANT,%20LOUVAIN.htm#Elisabethdied1272

[1093] fmg.ac/Projects/MedLands/FRANCONIA%20(LOWER%20RHINE).htm#Dietrichdied1245

[1094] Jetté, René, DuLong, John P., Gagné, Roland-Yves, Moreau, Gail F. and Dubé, Joseph A. (2001) Table d'ascendance de Catherine Baillon: 12 générations (p 153). Montréal, Québec: Société Généalogique Canadienne Française.

[1095] https://en.wikipedia.org/wiki/Henry_I,_Duke_of_Brabant

☐ Catherine de Baillon

Counts of Flanders

The Count of Flanders was the ruler or sub-ruler of the County of Flanders from the 9th century until the abolition of the position by the French revolutionaries in 1790.

- Baldwin I, Count of Flanders, married Judith Martel (daughter of King Charles II of France) was granted lands and honours, which would evolve into the County of Flanders [1096] [1097]

- Baldwin II, Count of Flanders, married Ælfthryth of Wessex, daughter of King Alfred the Great [1098] [1099] [1100]

- Arnulf I, Count of Flanders, married Adela de Vermandois [1101] [1102] [1103]

- Baldwin III, Count of Flanders, married Mechtild of Saxony [1104] [1105] [1106]

- Arnulf II, Count of Flanders, married Rosala (Suzanne) d'Ivrea [1107] [1108] [1109]

[1096] fmg.ac/Projects/MedLands/FLANDERS,%20HAINAUT.htm#_Toc212185308
[1097] fmg.ac/Projects/MedLands/CAROLINGIANS.htm#JudithM1AethelwulfM2AethelbaldM3Baudouin
[1098] fmg.ac/Projects/MedLands/FLANDERS,%20HAINAUT.htm#BaudouinIIFlandersdied918
[1099] fmg.ac/Projects/MedLands/ENGLAND,%20AngloSaxon%20&%20Danish%20Kings.htm#Aelfthrythdied929MBaudouinIIFlanders
[1100] racineshistoire.free.fr/LGN/PDF/Flandres.pdf (page 2)
[1101] fmg.ac/Projects/MedLands/FLANDERS,%20HAINAUT.htm#ArnoulIdied964B
[1102] fmg.ac/Projects/MedLands/NORTHERN%20FRANCE.htm#Adeladied960
[1103] racineshistoire.free.fr/LGN/PDF/Flandres.pdf (page 3)
[1104] fmg.ac/Projects/MedLands/FLANDERS,%20HAINAUT.htm#BaudouinIIIdied962
[1105] fmg.ac/Projects/MedLands/SAXONY.htm#Mechtilddied1008
[1106] racineshistoire.free.fr/LGN/PDF/Flandres.pdf (page 3)

- Baldwin IV, Count of Flanders, married Ogive de Luxembourg [1110] [1111] [1112]

- Baldwin V, Count of Flanders, married Adela (Alix) Capet, daughter of King Robert II of France [1113] [1114] [1115]

☐ Matilda (Maud) of Flanders married King William I (of England) de St. Clair (7th Duke of Normandy) known throughout history as *William the Conqueror* [1116] [1117] [1118] [1119]

☐ Adèle of Normandy married Count Stephen I of Blois [1120] [1121]

- Count Theobald III (The Great) of Champagne (Theobald IV of Blois) married Matilda von Sponheim [1122] [1123]

☐ Adèle (Alix) of Champagne married King Louis VII of France [1124] [1125]

[1107] fmg.ac/Projects/MedLands/FLANDERS,%20HAINAUT.htm#ArnoulIdied987B
[1108] fmg.ac/Projects/MedLands/NORTHERN%20ITALY%20900-1100.htm#RozalaM1ArnoulIIFlandresM2RobertIIFrance
[1109] racineshistoire.free.fr/LGN/PDF/Flandres.pdf (page 3)
[1110] fmg.ac/Projects/MedLands/FLANDERS,%20HAINAUT.htm#BaudouinIVdied1035
[1111] fmg.ac/Projects/MedLands/LUXEMBOURG.htm#Ogivedied1030
[1112] racineshistoire.free.fr/LGN/PDF/Flandres.pdf (page 4)
[1113] fmg.ac/Projects/MedLands/FLANDERS,%20HAINAUT.htm#BaudouinVdied1067B
[1114] fmg.ac/Projects/MedLands/CAPET.htm#Adeladied1079
[1115] racineshistoire.free.fr/LGN/PDF/Flandres.pdf (page 4)
[1116] fmg.ac/Projects/MedLands/FLANDERS,%20HAINAUT.htm#Mathildedied1083
[1117] fmg.ac/Projects/MedLands/ENGLAND,%20Kings%201066-1603.htm#WilliamIdied1087
[1118] racineshistoire.free.fr/LGN/PDF/Flandres.pdf (page 4)
[1119] https://en.wikipedia.org/wiki/William_the_Conqueror
[1120] fmg.ac/Projects/MedLands/ENGLAND,%20Kings%201066-1603.htm#Adeladied1138
[1121] fmg.ac/Projects/MedLands/CENTRAL%20FRANCE.htm#EtienneIdied1102B
[1122] fmg.ac/Projects/MedLands/CENTRAL%20FRANCE.htm#ThibautIVdied1152B
[1123] fmg.ac/Projects/MedLands/CARINTHIA.htm#Mathildedied1160
[1124] fmg.ac/Projects/MedLands/CENTRAL%20FRANCE.htm#AdeleBloisdied1206
[1125] fmg.ac/Projects/MedLands/CAPET.htm#LouisVIIdied1180B

- King Philippe II Auguste of France (1180 to 1223) married <u>thirdly</u> Agnès d'Andechs de Méranie [1126] [1127]

□ Princess Marie of France married Henri I, Duke of Brabant[1128] [1129]

□ Élisabeth de Brabant married Count Dietrich (Thierry) de Clèves [1130] [1131]

Élisabeth was also known as Ysabeau de Brabant; with regards to French records, the name Élisabeth is often used, interchangeably, with that of Isabelle. [1132] [1133]

□ Mathilda de Clèves married Gerard de Luxembourg

□ Marguerite de Luxembourg married Jean III de Ghistelles

- Jean IV de Ghistelles married Marie de Haverskerke

- Roger de Ghistelles married Élisabeth ~~Marguerite~~ de Dudzeele (see page 182 for updated explanation)

□ Isabelle (Ysabeau) de Ghistelles married Arnould VI de Gavre

□ Catherine de Gavre d'Escornaix married Guy I Le Bouteiller

[1126] fmg.ac/Projects/MedLands/CAPET.htm#PhilippeIIdied1223B
[1127] fmg.ac/Projects/MedLands/CARINTHIA.htm#AgnesMeranodied1201
[1128] fmg.ac/Projects/MedLands/CAPET.htm#Mariedied1238
[1129] fmg.ac/Projects/MedLands/BRABANT,%20LOUVAIN.htm#HenriILotharingiaBrabantdied1235B
[1130] fmg.ac/Projects/MedLands/BRABANT,%20LOUVAIN.htm#Elisabethdied1272
[1131] fmg.ac/Projects/MedLands/FRANCONIA%20(LOWER%20RHINE).htm#Dietrichdied1245
[1132] Jetté, René, DuLong, John P., Gagné, Roland-Yves, Moreau, Gail F. and Dubé, Joseph A. (2001) <u>Table d'ascendance de Catherine Baillon: 12 générations</u> (p 153). Montréal, Québec: Société Généalogique Canadienne Française.
[1133] https://en.wikipedia.org/wiki/Henry_I,_Duke_of_Brabant

- Guy II Le Bouteillier married Isabeau Morhier

- Jean Le Bouteillier married Marie de Venois

- Bénigne Le Bouteillier married Jacques Maillard

- Miles Maillard married Marie Morant

- Renée Maillard married Adam de Baillon

- Alphonse de Baillon married Louise de Marle

- Catherine de Baillon

House of Savoy

The House of Savoy emerged in what is now called Switzerland. The name derives from the historical region of Savoy in what is now France and Italy. Over time, the house expanded from that region to rule almost all of the Italian Peninsula.

- Count Umberto (Humbert) I of Savoy married Auxilia [1134] [1135]

- Count Otto (Oddone) of Savoy married Adelaida di Susa [1136] [1137]

- Count Amadeus (Amedeo) II of Savoy married Jeanne de Genève [1138] [1139]

- Count Umberto (Humbert) II (The Fat) of Savoy married Gisèle de Bourgogne [1140] [1141]

- ☐ Adéläide of Savoy married King Louis VI of France [1142] [1143]

- King Louis VII of France (1137 to 1180) married Adèle (Alix) of Champagne [1144] [1145]

[1134] fmg.ac/Projects/MedLands/SAVOY.htm#HumbertIdied10471051
[1135] fmg.ac/Projects/MedLands/BURGUNDY%20Kingdom.htm#AuxiliaMHumbertISavoie
[1136] fmg.ac/Projects/MedLands/SAVOY.htm#Oddondied1060B
[1137] fmg.ac/Projects/MedLands/NORTHERN%20ITALY%20900-1100.htm#AdelaidaSusadied1091
[1138] fmg.ac/Projects/MedLands/SAVOY.htm#AmedeeIIdied1080
[1139] fmg.ac/Projects/MedLands/BURGUNDY%20Kingdom.htm#JeanneGenevaMAmedeeSavoie
[1140] fmg.ac/Projects/MedLands/SAVOY.htm#HumbertIIdied1103B
[1141] fmg.ac/Projects/MedLands/BURGUNDY%20Kingdom.htm#GiseleM1HumbertIIMaurienneM2RanieroMonfe
[1142] fmg.ac/Projects/MedLands/SAVOY.htm#Adéläidedied1154
[1143] fmg.ac/Projects/MedLands/CAPET.htm#LouisVIdied1137B

- King Philippe II Auguste of France (1180 to 1223) married <u>thirdly</u> Agnès d'Andechs de Méranie [1146] [1147]

  - Princess Marie of France married Henri I, Duke of Brabant [1148] [1149]

  - Élisabeth de Brabant marriedCount Dietrich (Thierry) de Clèves [1150] [1151]

Élisabeth was also known as Ysabeau de Brabant; with regards to French records, the name Élisabeth is often used, interchangeably, with that of Isabelle. [1152] [1153]

  - Mathilda deClèves married Gerard de Luxembourg

  - Marguerite de Luxembourg married Jean III de Ghistelles

- Jean IV de Ghistelles married Marie de Haverskerke

- Roger de Ghistelles married Élisabeth ~~Marguerite~~ de Dudzeele (see page 182 for updated explanation)

  - Isabelle (Ysabeau) de Ghistelles married Arnould VI de Gavre

---

[1144] fmg.ac/Projects/MedLands/CAPET.htm#LouisVIIdied1180B
[1145] fmg.ac/Projects/MedLands/CENTRAL%20FRANCE.htm#AdeleBloisdied1206
[1146] fmg.ac/Projects/MedLands/CAPET.htm#PhilippeIIdied1223B
[1147] fmg.ac/Projects/MedLands/CARINTHIA.htm#AgnesMeranodied1201
[1148] fmg.ac/Projects/MedLands/CAPET.htm#Mariedied1238
[1149] fmg.ac/Projects/MedLands/BRABANT,%20LOUVAIN.htm#HenriILotharingiaBrabantdied1235B
[1150] fmg.ac/Projects/MedLands/BRABANT,%20LOUVAIN.htm#Elisabethdied1272
[1151] fmg.ac/Projects/MedLands/FRANCONIA%20(LOWER%20RHINE).htm#Dietrichdied1245
[1152] Jetté, René, DuLong, John P., Gagné, Roland-Yves, Moreau, Gail F. and Dubé, Joseph A. (2001) <u>Table d'ascendance de Catherine Baillon: 12 générations</u> (p 153). Montréal, Québec: Société Généalogique Canadienne Française.
[1153] https://en.wikipedia.org/wiki/Henry_I,_Duke_of_Brabant

- ☐ Catherine de Gavre d'Escornaix married Guy I Le Bouteiller

- ■ Guy II Le Bouteillier married Isabeau Morhier

- ■ Jean Le Bouteillier married Marie de Venois

- ☐ Bérigne Le Bouteillier married Jacques Maillard

- ■ Miles Maillard married Marie Morant

- ☐ Renée Maillard married Adam de Baillon

- ■ Alphonse de Baillon married Louise de Marle

- ☐ Catherine de Baillon

Duchy of Burgundy

As denoted on Wikipedia [1154]

Otto-William (962 – 21 September 1026) was a son of Adalbert, King of Italy, and Gerberga of Mâcon. While his mother gave him what would be the Free County of Burgundy around Dôle in 982, he also inherited the Duchy of Burgundy, on the other side of the Saône, in 1002 from his stepfather, Eudes Henry the Great. At that time, the duchy corresponded to the diocese of Besançon in the Holy Roman Empire.

- Count Otto William of Burgundy married Ermentrude de Roucy [1155] [1156] [1157]

- Count Reginald I of Burgundy married to Alice of Normandy (daughter of Richard II (The Good) de St. Clair (4th Duke of Normandy) and Judith of Brittany) [1158] [1159]

- Count William I of Burgundy married Étiennette [1160] [1161]

- Raymond of Burgundy married Urraca, the reigning Queen of Léon and Castile (d/o King Alfonso VI of Léon and Castile and Constance of Burgundy) [1162] [1163] [1164] [1165]

[1154] https://en.wikipedia.org/wiki/Otto-William,_Count_of_Burgundy
[1155] fmg.ac/Projects/MedLands/BURGUNDIAN%20NOBILITY.htm#OthonIMacondied1026
[1156] fmg.ac/Projects/MedLands/NORTHERN%20FRANCE.htm#Ermentrudedied10021005
[1157] fmg.ac/Projects/MedLands/BURGUNDY%20Kingdom.htm#RenaudIComtedied1057B
[1158] fmg.ac/Projects/MedLands/BURGUNDY%20Kingdom.htm#_Toc310954253
[1159] fmg.ac/Projects/MedLands/NORMANDY.htm#Adelaisdiedafter1037
[1160] fmg.ac/Projects/MedLands/BURGUNDY%20Kingdom.htm#GuillaumeIdied1087B
[1161] https://en.wikipedia.org/wiki/William_I,_Count_of_Burgundy
[1162] fmg.ac/Projects/MedLands/BURGUNDY%20Kingdom.htm#RaimondAmousdied1107
[1163] fmg.ac/Projects/MedLands/CASTILE.htm#Urracadied1126B

- King Alfonso VII de Léon and Castile married Berenguela (Berengaria) de Barcelona [1166] [1167]

- Constance de Castile married King Louis VII of France [1168] [1169]

- Princess Alys de France, Countess of the Vexin, married William II, Count of Ponthieu and Montreuil, on August 20, 1195 [1170] [1171]

- Marie, Countess of Ponthieu and Countess of Montreuil, married Simon de Dammartin before September 1208 [1172] [1173]

- Marie de Dammartin married Jean II Count de Roucy, Seigneur de Pierrepont [1174] [1175] [1176]

[1164] https://en.wikipedia.org/wiki/Alfonso_VI_of_León_and_Castile
[1165] https://en.wikipedia.org/wiki/Constance_of_Burgundy
[1166] fmg.ac/Projects/MedLands/CASTILE.htm#_ALFONSO_VII_1112-1157,
[1167] fmg.ac/Projects/MedLands/CATALAN%20NOBILITY.htm#Berengueladied1149MAlfonsoVIICastile
[1168] fmg.ac/Projects/MedLands/CASTILE.htm#Constanzadied1160MLouisVIIFrance
[1169] fmg.ac/Projects/MedLands/CAPET.htm#LouisVIIdied1180B
[1170] fmg.ac/Projects/MedLands/CAPET.htm#Alixdiedafter1200MGuillaumeIIIPonthieu
[1171] fmg.ac/Projects/MedLands/NORTHERN%20FRANCE.htm#GuillaumeIIdied1221
[1172] fmg.ac/Projects/MedLands/NORTHERN%20FRANCE.htm#MariePonthieudied1250
[1173] fmg.ac/Projects/MedLands/NORTHERN%20FRANCE.htm#SimonDammartinAumalePonthieud1239B
[1174] fmg.ac/Projects/MedLands/NORTHERN%20FRANCE.htm#MarieDammartinMJeanIIRoucy
[1175] fmg.ac/Projects/MedLands/NORTHERN%20FRANCE.htm#JeanPierrepontRoucydied1251
[1176] DuLong, John. (2009) "Catherine de Baillon's de Roye Ancestry: Another Royal Gateway" (page 17). <u>Michigan's Habitant Heritage: Journal of the French-Canadian Heritage Society of Michigan</u>, Volume 30, Number 1, January 2009.

☐ Marie (Mathilde) de Roucy married Jean I de Garlande, Seigneur de Possesse[1177][1178][1179][1180]

■ Jean II de Garland, Seigneur de Possesse, married Agnès [1181][1182]

☐ Alix de Garlande dit de Possesse married Dreux de Roye, Seigneur de Germigny[1183][1184]

☐ Jeanne (Jacqueline) de Roye married Arnould V de Gavre[1185][1186][1187]

■ Arnould VI de Gavre, Baron d'Escornaix married Isabelle (Ysabeau) de Ghistelles [1188][1189]

[1177] fmg.ac/Projects/MedLands/NORTHERN%20FRANCE.htm#dauJeanIIRoucyMJeanGarlande

[1178] fmg.ac/Projects/MedLands/PARIS%20REGION%20NOBILITY.htm#JeanGarlandePossessediedbefore1287

[1179] DuLong, John. (2009) "Catherine de Baillon's de Roye Ancestry: Another Royal Gateway" (page 17). Michigan's Habitant Heritage: Journal of the French-Canadian Heritage Society of Michigan, Volume 30, Number 1, January 2009.

[1180] racineshistoire.free.fr/LGN/PDF/Garlande.pdf (page 8)

[1181] Ibid.

[1182] DuLong, John. (2009) "Catherine de Baillon's de Roye Ancestry: Another Royal Gateway" (page 17). Michigan's Habitant Heritage: Journal of the French-Canadian Heritage Society of Michigan, Volume 30, Number 1, January 2009.

[1183] Ibid, pages 14 and 15.

[1184] racineshistoire.free.fr/LGN/PDF/Roye.pdf (page 6)

[1185] Jetté, René, DuLong, John P., Gagné, Roland-Yves, Moreau, Gail F. and Dubé, Joseph A. (2001) Table d'ascendance de Catherine Baillon: 12 générations (pages 124 and 125). Montréal, Québec: Société Généalogique Canadienne Française.

[1186] DuLong, John. (2009) "Catherine de Baillon's de Roye Ancestry: Another Royal Gateway" (page 13). Michigan's Habitant Heritage: Journal of the French-Canadian Heritage Society of Michigan, Volume 30, Number 1, January 2009.

[1187] racineshistoire.free.fr/LGN/PDF/Gavre.pdf (page 9)

[1188] Jetté, René, DuLong, John P., Gagné, Roland-Yves, Moreau, Gail F. and Dubé, Joseph A. (2001) Table d'ascendance de Catherine Baillon: 12 générations (page 112). Montréal, Québec: Société Généalogique Canadienne Française.

☐ Catherine de Gavre d'Escornaix married Guy I Le Bouteiller [1190]

■ Guy II Le Bouteillier married Isabeau Morhier [1191]

■ Jean Le Bouteillier married Marie de Venois [1192]

☐ Bénigne Le Bouteillier married Jacques Maillard[1193]

■ Miles Maillard married Marie Morant

☐ Renée Maillard married Adam de Baillon

■ Alphonse de Baillon married Louise de Marle

☐ Catherine de Baillon

[1189] racineshistoire.free.fr/LGN/PDF/Gavre.pdf (page 9)
[1190] Ibid, page 10.
[1191] Ibid.
[1192] Ibid.
[1193] Ibid.

In keeping with the Duchy of Burgundy, there is a second line of descent.

■ Count Otto William of Burgundy married Ermentrude de Roucy [1194] [1195] [1196]

■ Count Reginald I of Burgundy married to Alice of Normandy (daughter of Richard II (The Good) de St. Clair (4th Duke of Normandy) and Judith of Brittany) [1197] [1198]

■ Count William I of Burgundy married Étiennette [1199] [1200]

☐ Gisela of Burgundy married Count Umberto(Humbert) II (The Fat) of Savoy [1201] [1202]

☐ Adéläide of Savoy married King Louis VI of France [1203] [1204]

■ King Louis VII of France (1137 to 1180) married Adèle de Champagne [1205] [1206]

■ King Philippe II Auguste of France (1180 to 1223) married thirdly Agnès d'Andechs de Méranie [1207] [1208]

[1194] fmg.ac/Projects/MedLands/BURGUNDIAN%20NOBILITY.htm#OthonIMacondied1026
[1195] fmg.ac/Projects/MedLands/NORTHERN%20FRANCE.htm#Ermentrudedied10021005
[1196] fmg.ac/Projects/MedLands/BURGUNDY%20Kingdom.htm#RenaudIComtedied1057B
[1197] fmg.ac/Projects/MedLands/BURGUNDY%20Kingdom.htm#_Toc310954253
[1198] fmg.ac/Projects/MedLands/NORMANDY.htm#Adelaisdiedafter1037
[1199] fmg.ac/Projects/MedLands/BURGUNDY%20Kingdom.htm#GuillaumeIdied1087B
[1200] https://en.wikipedia.org/wiki/William_I,_Count_of_Burgundy
[1201] fmg.ac/Projects/MedLands/BURGUNDY%20Kingdom.htm#GiseleM1HumbertIIMaurienneM2RanieroMonfe
[1202] fmg.ac/Projects/MedLands/SAVOY.htm#HumbertIIdied1103B
[1203] fmg.ac/Projects/MedLands/SAVOY.htm#Adéläidedied1154
[1204] fmg.ac/Projects/MedLands/CAPET.htm#LouisVIdied1137B
[1205] fmg.ac/Projects/MedLands/CAPET.htm#LouisVIIdied1180B
[1206] fmg.ac/Projects/MedLands/CENTRAL%20FRANCE.htm#AdeleBloisdied1206
[1207] fmg.ac/Projects/MedLands/CAPET.htm#PhilippeIIdied1223B

☐ Princess Marie of France married Henri I, Duke of Brabant[1209] [1210]

☐ Élisabeth de Brabant marriedCount Dietrich (Thierry) de Clèves [1211] [1212]

Élisabeth was also known as Ysabeau de Brabant; with regards to French records, the name Élisabeth is often used, interchangeably, with that of Isabelle. [1213] [1214]

☐ Mathilda deClèves married Gerard de Luxembourg

☐ Marguerite de Luxembourg married Jean III de Ghistelles

■ Jean IV de Ghistelles married Marie de Haverskerke

■ Roger de Ghistelles married Élisabeth ~~Marguerite~~ de Dudzeele (see page 182 for updated explanation)

☐ Isabelle (Ysabeau) de Ghistelles married Arnould VI de Gavre

☐ Catherine de Gavre d'Escornaix married Guy I Le Bouteiller

■ Guy II Le Bouteillier married Isabeau Morhier

■ Jean Le Bouteillier married Marie de Venois

[1208] fmg.ac/Projects/MedLands/CARINTHIA.htm#AgnesMeranodied1201
[1209] fmg.ac/Projects/MedLands/CAPET.htm#Mariedied1238
[1210] fmg.ac/Projects/MedLands/BRABANT,%20LOUVAIN.htm#HenriILotharingiaBrabantdied1235B
[1211] fmg.ac/Projects/MedLands/BRABANT,%20LOUVAIN.htm#Elisabethdied1272
[1212] fmg.ac/Projects/MedLands/FRANCONIA%20(LOWER%20RHINE).htm#Dietrichdied1245
[1213] Jetté, René, DuLong, John P., Gagné, Roland-Yves, Moreau, Gail F. and Dubé, Joseph A. (2001) <u>Table d'ascendance de Catherine Baillon: 12 générations</u> (p 153). Montréal, Québec: Société Généalogique Canadienne Française.
[1214] https://en.wikipedia.org/wiki/Henry_I,_Duke_of_Brabant

☐ Bénigne Le Bouteillier married Jacques Maillard

■ Miles Maillard married Marie Morant

☐ Renée Maillard married Adam de Baillon

■ Alphonse de Baillon married Louise de Marle

☐ Catherine de Baillon

Marchesi of Ivrea

The Anscarids or Anscarii or the House of Ivrea were a medieval Frankish dynasty of Burgundian origin which rose to prominence in Italy in the tenth century, even briefly holding the Italian throne. [1215]

- Margrave Anscar I of Ivrea married ---------- [1216] [1217] [1218]

Anscar was brother to the archbishop of Rheims, Fulk the Venerable. [1219]

- Margrave Adalbert I of Ivrea married Gisela of Friuli [1220] [1221] [1222]

- Margrave Berengar II of Ivrea, King of Italy, married Willa d'Arles [1223] [1224]

- Adalbert, King of Italy, married Gerberge [1225] [1226]

[1215] https://en.wikipedia.org/wiki/Anscarids
[1216] fmg.ac/Projects/MedLands/BURGUNDIAN%20NOBILITY.htm#AnscarioIivreadied898
[1217] fmg.ac/Projects/MedLands/NORTHERN%20ITALY%20900-1100.htm#_Toc285707738
[1218] https://en.wikipedia.org/wiki/Anscar_I_of_Ivrea
[1219] https://en.wikipedia.org/wiki/Fulk_(archbishop_of_Reims)
[1220] fmg.ac/Projects/MedLands/NORTHERN%20ITALY%20900-1100.htm#AdalbertoIivreaB
[1221] fmg.ac/Projects/MedLands/NORTHERN%20ITALY%20900-1100.htm#GiselaMAdalbertoIvreadied923
[1222] https://en.wikipedia.org/wiki/Adalbert_I_of_Ivrea
[1223] fmg.ac/Projects/MedLands/NORTHERN%20ITALY%20900-1100.htm#BerengarioIIitalydied966B
[1224] fmg.ac/Projects/MedLands/PROVENCE.htm#WillaMBerengarioIIivrea

- Count Otto William of Burgundy married widowed Ermentrude de Roucy [1227] [1228] [1229]

- Count Reginald I of Burgundy married to Alice of Normandy (daughter of Richard II (The Good) de St. Clair (4th Duke of Normandy) and Judith of Brittany) [1230] [1231]

- Count William I of Burgundy married Étiennette [1232] [1233]

- Raymond of Burgundy married Urraca, the reigning Queen of Léon and Castile (d/o King Alfonso VI of Léon and Castile and Constance of Burgundy) [1234] [1235] [1236] [1237]

- King Alfonso VII de Léon and Castile married Berenguela (Berengaria) de Barcelona [1238] [1239]

☐ Constance de Castile married King Louis VII of France [1240] [1241]

[1225] fmg.ac/Projects/MedLands/NORTHERN%20ITALY%20900-1100.htm#AdalbertoKingItalydied971
[1226] fmg.ac/Projects/MedLands/BURGUNDIAN%20NOBILITY.htm#GerbergeChalondied986
[1227] fmg.ac/Projects/MedLands/BURGUNDIAN%20NOBILITY.htm#OthonIMacondied1026
[1228] fmg.ac/Projects/MedLands/NORTHERN%20FRANCE.htm#Ermentrudedied10021005
[1229] fmg.ac/Projects/MedLands/BURGUNDY%20Kingdom.htm#RenaudIComtedied1057B
[1230] fmg.ac/Projects/MedLands/BURGUNDY%20Kingdom.htm#_Toc310954253
[1231] fmg.ac/Projects/MedLands/NORMANDY.htm#Adelaisdiedafter1037
[1232] fmg.ac/Projects/MedLands/BURGUNDY%20Kingdom.htm#GuillaumeIdied1087B
[1233] https://en.wikipedia.org/wiki/William_I,_Count_of_Burgundy
[1234] fmg.ac/Projects/MedLands/BURGUNDY%20Kingdom.htm#RaimondAmousdied1107
[1235] fmg.ac/Projects/MedLands/CASTILE.htm#Urracadied1126B
[1236] https://en.wikipedia.org/wiki/Alfonso_VI_of_León_and_Castile
[1237] https://en.wikipedia.org/wiki/Constance_of_Burgundy
[1238] fmg.ac/Projects/MedLands/CASTILE.htm#_ALFONSO_VII_1112-1157,
[1239] fmg.ac/Projects/MedLands/CATALAN%20NOBILITY.htm#Berengueladied1149MAlfonsoVIICastile
[1240] fmg.ac/Projects/MedLands/CASTILE.htm#Constanzadied1160MLouisVIIFrance

☐ Princess Alys de France, Countess of the Vexin, married William II, Count of Ponthieu and Montreuil, on August 20, 1195 [1242] [1243]

☐ Marie, Countess of Ponthieu and Countess of Montreuil, married Simon de Dammartin before September 1208 [1244] [1245]

☐ Marie de Dammartin married Jean II Count de Roucy, Seigneur de Pierrepont [1246] [1247] [1248]

☐ Marie (Mathilde) de Roucy married Jean I de Garlande, Seigneur de Possesse [1249] [1250] [1251] [1252]

[1241] fmg.ac/Projects/MedLands/CAPET.htm#LouisVIIdied1180B
[1242] fmg.ac/Projects/MedLands/CAPET.htm#Alixdiedafter1200MGuillaumeIIIPonthieu
[1243] fmg.ac/Projects/MedLands/NORTHERN%20FRANCE.htm#GuillaumeIIdied1221
[1244] fmg.ac/Projects/MedLands/NORTHERN%20FRANCE.htm#MariePonthieudied1250
[1245] fmg.ac/Projects/MedLands/NORTHERN%20FRANCE.htm#SimonDammartinAumalePonthieud1239B
[1246] fmg.ac/Projects/MedLands/NORTHERN%20FRANCE.htm#MarieDammartinMJeanIIRoucy
[1247] fmg.ac/Projects/MedLands/NORTHERN%20FRANCE.htm#JeanPierrepontRoucydied1251
[1248] DuLong, John. (2009) "Catherine de Baillon's de Roye Ancestry: Another Royal Gateway" (page 17). <u>Michigan's Habitant Heritage: Journal of the French-Canadian Heritage Society of Michigan</u>, Volume 30, Number 1, January 2009.
[1249] fmg.ac/Projects/MedLands/NORTHERN%20FRANCE.htm#dauJeanIIRoucyMJeanGarlande
[1250] fmg.ac/Projects/MedLands/PARIS%20REGION%20NOBILITY.htm#JeanGarlandePossessediedbefore1287
[1251] DuLong, John. (2009) "Catherine de Baillon's de Roye Ancestry: Another Royal Gateway" (page 17). <u>Michigan's Habitant Heritage: Journal of the French-Canadian Heritage Society of Michigan</u>, Volume 30, Number 1, January 2009.
[1252] racineshistoire.free.fr/LGN/PDF/Garlande.pdf (page 8)

- Jean II de Garland, Seigneur de Possesse, married Agnès [1253] [1254]

- Alix de Garlande dit de Possesse married Dreux de Roye, Seigneur de Germigny [1255] [1256]

- Jeanne (Jacqueline) de Roye married Arnould V de Gavre [1257] [1258] [1259]

- Arnould VI de Gavre, Baron d'Escornaix married Isabelle (Ysabeau) de Ghistelles [1260] [1261]

- Catherine de Gavre d'Escornaix married Guy I Le Bouteiller [1262]

- Guy II Le Bouteillier married Isabeau Morhier [1263]

- Jean Le Bouteillier married Marie de Venois [1264]

- Bénigne Le Bouteillier married Jacques Maillard [1265]

[1253] racineshistoire.free.fr/LGN/PDF/Garlande.pdf (page 8)
[1254] DuLong, John. (2009) "Catherine de Baillon's de Roye Ancestry: Another Royal Gateway" (page 17). Michigan's Habitant Heritage: Journal of the French-Canadian Heritage Society of Michigan, Volume 30, Number 1, January 2009.
[1255] Ibid, pages 14 and 15.
[1256] racineshistoire.free.fr/LGN/PDF/Roye.pdf (page 6)
[1257] Jetté, René, DuLong, John P., Gagné, Roland-Yves, Moreau, Gail F. and Dubé, Joseph A. (2001) Table d'ascendance de Catherine Baillon: 12 générations (pages 124 and 125). Montréal, Québec: Société Généalogique Canadienne Française.
[1258] DuLong, John. (2009) "Catherine de Baillon's de Roye Ancestry: Another Royal Gateway" (page 13). Michigan's Habitant Heritage: Journal of the French-Canadian Heritage Society of Michigan, Volume 30, Number 1, January 2009.
[1259] racineshistoire.free.fr/LGN/PDF/Gavre.pdf (page 9)
[1260] Jetté, René, DuLong, John P., Gagné, Roland-Yves, Moreau, Gail F. and Dubé, Joseph A. (2001) Table d'ascendance de Catherine Baillon: 12 générations (page 112). Montréal, Québec: Société Généalogique Canadienne Française.
[1261] racineshistoire.free.fr/LGN/PDF/Gavre.pdf (page 9)
[1262] Ibid, page 10.
[1263] Ibid.
[1264] Ibid.

- Miles Maillard married Marie Morant

- Renée Maillard married Adam de Baillon

- Alphonse de Baillon married Louise de Marle

- Catherine de Baillon

[1265] racineshistoire.free.fr/LGN/PDF/Gavre.pdf (page 10)

In keeping with the Marchesi of Ivrea, there is a second line of descent.

- Margrave Anscar I of Ivrea married ---------- [1266] [1267] [1268]

Anscar was brother to the archbishop of Rheims, Fulk the Venerable. [1269]

- Margrave Adalbert I of Ivrea married Gisela of Friuli [1270] [1271] [1272]

- Margrave Berengar II of Ivrea, King of Italy, married Willa d'Arles [1273] [1274]

- Adalbert, King of Italy, married Gerberge [1275] [1276]

- Count Otto William of Burgundy married widowed Ermentrude de Roucy [1277] [1278] [1279]

[1266] fmg.ac/Projects/MedLands/BURGUNDIAN%20NOBILITY.htm#AnscarioIivreadied898
[1267] fmg.ac/Projects/MedLands/NORTHERN%20ITALY%20900-1100.htm#_Toc285707738
[1268] https://en.wikipedia.org/wiki/Anscar_I_of_Ivrea
[1269] https://en.wikipedia.org/wiki/Fulk_(archbishop_of_Reims)
[1270] fmg.ac/Projects/MedLands/NORTHERN%20ITALY%20900-1100.htm#AdalbertoIivreaB
[1271] fmg.ac/Projects/MedLands/NORTHERN%20ITALY%20900-1100.htm#GiselaMAdalbertoIvreadied923
[1272] https://en.wikipedia.org/wiki/Adalbert_I_of_Ivrea
[1273] fmg.ac/Projects/MedLands/NORTHERN%20ITALY%20900-1100.htm#BerengarioIIitalydied966B
[1274] fmg.ac/Projects/MedLands/PROVENCE.htm#WillaMBerengarioIIivrea
[1275] fmg.ac/Projects/MedLands/NORTHERN%20ITALY%20900-1100.htm#AdalbertoKingItalydied971
[1276] fmg.ac/Projects/MedLands/BURGUNDIAN%20NOBILITY.htm#GerbergeChalondied986
[1277] fmg.ac/Projects/MedLands/BURGUNDIAN%20NOBILITY.htm#OthonIMacondied1026
[1278] fmg.ac/Projects/MedLands/NORTHERN%20FRANCE.htm#Ermentrudedied10021005
[1279] fmg.ac/Projects/MedLands/BURGUNDY%20Kingdom.htm#RenaudIComtedied1057B

- Count Reginald I of Burgundy married to Alice of Normandy (daughter of Richard II (The Good) de St. Clair (4th Duke of Normandy) and Judith of Brittany) [1280] [1281]

- Count William I of Burgundy married Étiennette [1282] [1283]

- Gisela of Burgundy married Count Umberto (Humbert) II (The Fat) of Savoy [1284] [1285]

- Adélaïde of Savoy married King Louis VI of France [1286] [1287]

- King Louis VII of France (1137 to 1180) married Adèle de Champagne [1288] [1289]

- King Philippe II Auguste of France (1180 to 1223) married thirdly Agnès d'Andechs de Méranie [1290] [1291]

- Princess Marie of France married Henri I, Duke of Brabant [1292] [1293]

- Élisabeth de Brabant married Count Dietrich (Thierry) de Clèves [1294] [1295]

[1280] fmg.ac/Projects/MedLands/BURGUNDY%20Kingdom.htm#_Toc310954253
[1281] fmg.ac/Projects/MedLands/NORMANDY.htm#Adelaisdiedafter1037
[1282] fmg.ac/Projects/MedLands/BURGUNDY%20Kingdom.htm#GuillaumeIdied1087B
[1283] https://en.wikipedia.org/wiki/William_I,_Count_of_Burgundy
[1284] fmg.ac/Projects/MedLands/BURGUNDY%20Kingdom.htm#GiseleM1HumbertIIMaurienneM2RanieroMonfe
[1285] fmg.ac/Projects/MedLands/SAVOY.htm#HumbertIIdied1103B
[1286] fmg.ac/Projects/MedLands/SAVOY.htm#Adélaïdedied1154
[1287] fmg.ac/Projects/MedLands/CAPET.htm#LouisVIdied1137B
[1288] fmg.ac/Projects/MedLands/CAPET.htm#LouisVIIdied1180B
[1289] fmg.ac/Projects/MedLands/CENTRAL%20FRANCE.htm#AdeleBloisdied1206
[1290] fmg.ac/Projects/MedLands/CAPET.htm#PhilippeIIdied1223B
[1291] fmg.ac/Projects/MedLands/CARINTHIA.htm#AgnesMeranodied1201
[1292] fmg.ac/Projects/MedLands/CAPET.htm#Mariedied1238
[1293] fmg.ac/Projects/MedLands/BRABANT,%20LOUVAIN.htm#HenriILotharingiaBrabantdied1235B

Élisabeth was also known as Ysabeau de Brabant; with regards to French records, the name Élisabeth is often used, interchangeably, with that of Isabelle. [1296] [1297]

☐ Mathilda de Clèves married Gerard de Luxembourg

☐ Marguerite de Luxembourg married Jean III de Ghistelles

■ Jean IV de Ghistelles married Marie de Haverskerke

■ Roger de Ghistelles married Élisabeth ~~Marguerite~~ de Dudzeele (see page 182 for updated explanation)

☐ Isabelle (Ysabeau) de Ghistelles married Arnould VI de Gavre

☐ Catherine de Gavre d'Escornaix married Guy I Le Bouteiller

■ Guy II Le Bouteillier married Isabeau Morhier

■ Jean Le Bouteillier married Marie de Venois

☐ Bénigne Le Bouteillier married Jacques Maillard

■ Miles Maillard married Marie Morant

☐ Renée Maillard married Adam de Baillon

■ Alphonse de Baillon married Louise de Marle

[1294] fmg.ac/Projects/MedLands/BRABANT,%20LOUVAIN.htm#Elisabethdied1272
[1295] fmg.ac/Projects/MedLands/FRANCONIA%20(LOWER%20RHINE).htm#Dietrichdied1245
[1296] Jetté, René, DuLong, John P., Gagné, Roland-Yves, Moreau, Gail F. and Dubé, Joseph A. (2001) Table d'ascendance de Catherine Baillon: 12 générations (p 153). Montréal, Québec: Société Généalogique Canadienne Française.
[1297] https://en.wikipedia.org/wiki/Henry_I,_Duke_of_Brabant

☐ Catherine de Baillon

Marchesi of Friulia

- Unruoch married Engletrude [1298]

- Eberhard, Duke of the March of Friulia, married Gisela (d/o Emperor Louis I and his second wife Judith) [1299] [1300] [1301]

- Berengar I, Marchese di Friulia, King of Italy, married Bertila de Spoleto [1302] [1303] [1304]

- ☐ Gisela of Friuli married Margrave Adalbert I of Ivrea [1305] [1306] [1307]

- Margrave Berengar II of Ivrea, King of Italy, married Willa d'Arles [1308] [1309]

- Adalbert, King of Italy, married Gerberge [1310] [1311]

[1298] fmg.ac/Projects/MedLands/FRANKISH%20NOBILITY.htm#_Toc371156058
[1299] fmg.ac/Projects/MedLands/FRANKISH%20NOBILITY.htm#EberhardDukeFriuliadied866A
[1300] fmg.ac/Projects/MedLands/NORTHERN%20ITALY%20900-1100.htm#EberhardDukeFriuliadied866
[1301] fmg.ac/Projects/MedLands/CAROLINGIANS.htm#GiselaMEberhardFriuliadied866
[1302] fmg.ac/Projects/MedLands/ITALY,%20Kings%20to%20962.htm#BerengarioIitalydied924B
[1303] fmg.ac/Projects/MedLands/NORTHERN%20ITALY%20900-1100.htm#BerengarioIitalydied924A
[1304] fmg.ac/Projects/MedLands/CENTRAL%20ITALY.htm#BertilaSpoletodied915
[1305] fmg.ac/Projects/MedLands/NORTHERN%20ITALY%20900-1100.htm#GiselaMAdalbertoIvreadied923
[1306] fmg.ac/Projects/MedLands/NORTHERN%20ITALY%20900-1100.htm#AdalbertoIivreaB
[1307] https://en.wikipedia.org/wiki/Adalbert_I_of_Ivrea
[1308] fmg.ac/Projects/MedLands/NORTHERN%20ITALY%20900-1100.htm#BerengarioIIitalydied966B
[1309] fmg.ac/Projects/MedLands/PROVENCE.htm#WillaMBerengarioIIivrea

- Count Otto William of Burgundy married widowed Ermentrude de Roucy [1312] [1313] [1314]

- Count Reginald I of Burgundy married to Alice of Normandy (daughter of Richard II (The Good) de St. Clair (4th Duke of Normandy) and Judith of Brittany) [1315] [1316]

- Count William I of Burgundy married Étiennette [1317] [1318]

- Raymond of Burgundy married Urraca, the reigning Queen of Léon and Castile (d/o King Alfonso VI of Léon and Castile and Constance of Burgundy) [1319] [1320] [1321] [1322]

- King Alfonso VII de Léon and Castile married Berenguela (Berengaria) de Barcelona [1323] [1324]

- ☐ Constance de Castile married King Louis VII of France [1325] [1326]

[1310] fmg.ac/Projects/MedLands/NORTHERN%20ITALY%20900-1100.htm#AdalbertoKingItalydied971

[1311] fmg.ac/Projects/MedLands/BURGUNDIAN%20NOBILITY.htm#GerbergeChalondied986

[1312] fmg.ac/Projects/MedLands/BURGUNDIAN%20NOBILITY.htm#OthonIMacondied1026

[1313] fmg.ac/Projects/MedLands/NORTHERN%20FRANCE.htm#Ermentrudedied10021005

[1314] fmg.ac/Projects/MedLands/BURGUNDY%20Kingdom.htm#RenaudIComtedied1057B

[1315] fmg.ac/Projects/MedLands/BURGUNDY%20Kingdom.htm#_Toc310954253

[1316] fmg.ac/Projects/MedLands/NORMANDY.htm#Adelaisdiedafter1037

[1317] fmg.ac/Projects/MedLands/BURGUNDY%20Kingdom.htm#GuillaumeIdied1087B

[1318] https://en.wikipedia.org/wiki/William_I,_Count_of_Burgundy

[1319] fmg.ac/Projects/MedLands/BURGUNDY%20Kingdom.htm#RaimondAmousdied1107

[1320] fmg.ac/Projects/MedLands/CASTILE.htm#Urracadied1126B

[1321] https://en.wikipedia.org/wiki/Alfonso_VI_of_León_and_Castile

[1322] https://en.wikipedia.org/wiki/Constance_of_Burgundy

[1323] fmg.ac/Projects/MedLands/CASTILE.htm#_ALFONSO_VII_1112-1157,

[1324] fmg.ac/Projects/MedLands/CATALAN%20NOBILITY.htm#Berengueladied1149MAlfonsoVIICastile

[1325] fmg.ac/Projects/MedLands/CASTILE.htm#Constanzadied1160MLouisVIIFrance

☐ Princess Alys de France, Countess of the Vexin, married William II, Count of Ponthieu and Montreuil, on August 20, 1195 [1327] [1328]

☐ Marie, Countess of Ponthieu and Countess of Montreuil, married Simon de Dammartin before September 1208 [1329] [1330]

☐ Marie deDammartin married Jean II Count de Roucy, Seigneur de Pierrepont [1331] [1332] [1333]

☐ Marie (Mathilde) de Roucy married Jean I de Garlande, Seigneur de Possesse [1334] [1335] [1336] [1337]

[1326] fmg.ac/Projects/MedLands/CAPET.htm#LouisVIIdied1180B
[1327] fmg.ac/Projects/MedLands/CAPET.htm#Alixdiedafter1200MGuillaumeIIIPonthieu
[1328] fmg.ac/Projects/MedLands/NORTHERN%20FRANCE.htm#GuillaumeIIdied1221
[1329] fmg.ac/Projects/MedLands/NORTHERN%20FRANCE.htm#MariePonthieudied1250
[1330] fmg.ac/Projects/MedLands/NORTHERN%20FRANCE.htm#SimonDammartinAumalePonthieud1239B
[1331] fmg.ac/Projects/MedLands/NORTHERN%20FRANCE.htm#MarieDammartinMJeanIIRoucy
[1332] fmg.ac/Projects/MedLands/NORTHERN%20FRANCE.htm#JeanPierrepontRoucydied1251
[1333] DuLong, John. (2009) "Catherine de Baillon's de Roye Ancestry: Another Royal Gateway" (page 17). <u>Michigan's Habitant Heritage: Journal of the French-Canadian Heritage Society of Michigan</u>, Volume 30, Number 1, January 2009.
[1334] fmg.ac/Projects/MedLands/NORTHERN%20FRANCE.htm#dauJeanIIRoucyMJeanGarlande
[1335] fmg.ac/Projects/MedLands/PARIS%20REGION%20NOBILITY.htm#JeanGarlandePossessediedbefore1287
[1336] DuLong, John. (2009) "Catherine de Baillon's de Roye Ancestry: Another Royal Gateway" (page 17). <u>Michigan's Habitant Heritage: Journal of the French-Canadian Heritage Society of Michigan</u>, Volume 30, Number 1, January 2009.
[1337] racineshistoire.free.fr/LGN/PDF/Garlande.pdf (page 8)

- Jean II de Garland, Seigneur de Possesse, married Agnès [1338] [1339]

- Alix de Garlande dit de Possesse married Dreux de Roye, Seigneur de Germigny [1340] [1341]

- Jeanne (Jacqueline) de Roye married Arnould V de Gavre [1342] [1343] [1344]

- Arnould VI de Gavre, Baron d'Escornaix married Isabelle (Ysabeau) de Ghistelles [1345] [1346]

- Catherine de Gavre d'Escornaix married Guy I Le Bouteiller [1347]

- Guy II Le Bouteillier married Isabeau Morhier [1348]

- Jean Le Bouteillier married Marie de Venois [1349]

- Bénigne Le Bouteillier married Jacques Maillard [1350]

[1338] racineshistoire.free.fr/LGN/PDF/Garlande.pdf (page 8)
[1339] DuLong, John. (2009) "Catherine de Baillon's de Roye Ancestry: Another Royal Gateway" (page 17). Michigan's Habitant Heritage: Journal of the French-Canadian Heritage Society of Michigan, Volume 30, Number 1, January 2009.
[1340] Ibid, pages 14 and 15.
[1341] racineshistoire.free.fr/LGN/PDF/Roye.pdf (page 6)
[1342] Jetté, René, DuLong, John P., Gagné, Roland-Yves, Moreau, Gail F. and Dubé, Joseph A. (2001) Table d'ascendance de Catherine Baillon: 12 générations (pages 124 and 125). Montréal, Québec: Société Généalogique Canadienne Française.
[1343] DuLong, John. (2009) "Catherine de Baillon's de Roye Ancestry: Another Royal Gateway" (page 13). Michigan's Habitant Heritage: Journal of the French-Canadian Heritage Society of Michigan, Volume 30, Number 1, January 2009.
[1344] racineshistoire.free.fr/LGN/PDF/Gavre.pdf (page 9)
[1345] Jetté, René, DuLong, John P., Gagné, Roland-Yves, Moreau, Gail F. and Dubé, Joseph A. (2001) Table d'ascendance de Catherine Baillon: 12 générations (page 112). Montréal, Québec: Société Généalogique Canadienne Française.
[1346] racineshistoire.free.fr/LGN/PDF/Gavre.pdf (page 9)
[1347] Ibid, page 10.
[1348] Ibid.
[1349] Ibid.

- Miles Maillard married Marie Morant

  ☐ Renée Maillard married Adam de Baillon

- Alphonse de Baillon married Louise de Marle

  ☐ Catherine de Baillon

[1350] racineshistoire.free.fr/LGN/PDF/Gavre.pdf (page 10)

In keeping with the Marchesi of Friulia, there is a second line of descent.

■ Unruoch married Engletrude [1351]

■ Eberhard, Duke of the March of Friulia, married Gisela (d/o Emperor Louis I and his second wife Judith) [1352] [1353] [1354]

■ Berengar I, Marchese di Friulia, King of Italy, married Bertila de Spoleto [1355] [1356] [1357]

☐ Gisela of Friuli married Margrave Adalbert I of Ivrea [1358] [1359] [1360]

■ Margrave Berengar II of Ivrea, King of Italy, married Willa d'Arles [1361] [1362]

■ Adalbert, King of Italy, married Gerberge [1363] [1364]

[1351] fmg.ac/Projects/MedLands/FRANKISH%20NOBILITY.htm#_Toc371156058

[1352] fmg.ac/Projects/MedLands/FRANKISH%20NOBILITY.htm#EberhardDukeFriuliadied866A

[1353] fmg.ac/Projects/MedLands/NORTHERN%20ITALY%20900-1100.htm#EberhardDukeFriuliadied866

[1354] fmg.ac/Projects/MedLands/CAROLINGIANS.htm#GiselaMEberhardFriuliadied866

[1355] fmg.ac/Projects/MedLands/ITALY,%20Kings%20to%20962.htm#BerengarioIitalydied924B

[1356] fmg.ac/Projects/MedLands/NORTHERN%20ITALY%20900-1100.htm#BerengarioIitalydied924A

[1357] fmg.ac/Projects/MedLands/CENTRAL%20ITALY.htm#BertilaSpoletodied915

[1358] fmg.ac/Projects/MedLands/NORTHERN%20ITALY%20900-1100.htm#GiselaMAdalbertoIvreadied923

[1359] fmg.ac/Projects/MedLands/NORTHERN%20ITALY%20900-1100.htm#AdalbertoIivreaB

[1360] https://en.wikipedia.org/wiki/Adalbert_I_of_Ivrea

[1361] fmg.ac/Projects/MedLands/NORTHERN%20ITALY%20900-1100.htm#BerengarioIIitalydied966B

[1362] fmg.ac/Projects/MedLands/PROVENCE.htm#WillaMBerengarioIIivrea

- Count Otto William of Burgundy married widowed Ermentrude de Roucy [1365] [1366] [1367]

- Count Reginald I of Burgundy married to Alice of Normandy (daughter of Richard II (The Good) de St. Clair (4th Duke of Normandy) and Judith of Brittany) [1368] [1369]

- Count William I of Burgundy married Étiennette [1370] [1371]

☐ Gisela of Burgundy married Count Umberto (Humbert) II (The Fat) of Savoy [1372] [1373]

☐ Adéläide of Savoy married King Louis VI of France [1374] [1375]

- King Louis VII of France (1137 to 1180) married Adèle de Champagne [1376] [1377]

- King Philippe II Auguste of France (1180 to 1223) married thirdly Agnès d'Andechs de Méranie [1378] [1379]

[1363] fmg.ac/Projects/MedLands/NORTHERN%20ITALY%20900-1100.htm#AdalbertoKingItalydied971
[1364] fmg.ac/Projects/MedLands/BURGUNDIAN%20NOBILITY.htm#GerbergeChalondied986
[1365] fmg.ac/Projects/MedLands/BURGUNDIAN%20NOBILITY.htm#OthonIMacondied1026
[1366] fmg.ac/Projects/MedLands/NORTHERN%20FRANCE.htm#Ermentrudedied10021005
[1367] fmg.ac/Projects/MedLands/BURGUNDY%20Kingdom.htm#RenaudIComtedied1057B
[1368] fmg.ac/Projects/MedLands/BURGUNDY%20Kingdom.htm#_Toc310954253
[1369] fmg.ac/Projects/MedLands/NORMANDY.htm#Adelaisdiedafter1037
[1370] fmg.ac/Projects/MedLands/BURGUNDY%20Kingdom.htm#GuillaumeIdied1087B
[1371] https://en.wikipedia.org/wiki/William_I,_Count_of_Burgundy
[1372] fmg.ac/Projects/MedLands/BURGUNDY%20Kingdom.htm#GiseleM1HumbertIIMaurienneM2RanieroMonfe
[1373] fmg.ac/Projects/MedLands/SAVOY.htm#HumbertIIdied1103B
[1374] fmg.ac/Projects/MedLands/SAVOY.htm#Adélaïdedied1154
[1375] fmg.ac/Projects/MedLands/CAPET.htm#LouisVIdied1137B
[1376] fmg.ac/Projects/MedLands/CAPET.htm#LouisVIIdied1180B
[1377] fmg.ac/Projects/MedLands/CENTRAL%20FRANCE.htm#AdeleBloisdied1206

☐ Princess Marie of France married Henri I, Duke of Brabant[1380][1381]

☐ Élisabeth de Brabant married Count Dietrich (Thierry) de Clèves[1382][1383]

Élisabeth was also known as Ysabeau de Brabant; with regards to French records, the name Élisabeth is often used, interchangeably, with that of Isabelle. [1384][1385]

☐ Mathilda de Clèves married Gerard de Luxembourg

☐ Marguerite de Luxembourg married Jean III de Ghistelles

■ Jean IV de Ghistelles married Marie de Haverskerke

■ Roger de Ghistelles married Élisabeth ~~Marguerite~~ de Dudzeele (see page 182 for updated explanation)

☐ Isabelle (Ysabeau) de Ghistelles married Arnould VI de Gavre

☐ Catherine de Gavre d'Escornaix married Guy I Le Bouteiller

■ Guy II Le Bouteillier married Isabeau Morhier

[1378] fmg.ac/Projects/MedLands/CAPET.htm#PhilippeIIdied1223B
[1379] fmg.ac/Projects/MedLands/CARINTHIA.htm#AgnesMeranodied1201
[1380] fmg.ac/Projects/MedLands/CAPET.htm#Mariedied1238
[1381] fmg.ac/Projects/MedLands/BRABANT,%20LOUVAIN.htm#HenriILotharingiaBrabantdied1235B
[1382] fmg.ac/Projects/MedLands/BRABANT,%20LOUVAIN.htm#Elisabethdied1272
[1383] fmg.ac/Projects/MedLands/FRANCONIA%20(LOWER%20RHINE).htm#Dietrichdied1245
[1384] Jetté, René, DuLong, John P., Gagné, Roland-Yves, Moreau, Gail F. and Dubé, Joseph A. (2001) Table d'ascendance de Catherine Baillon: 12 générations (p 153). Montréal, Québec: Société Généalogique Canadienne Française.
[1385] https://en.wikipedia.org/wiki/Henry_I,_Duke_of_Brabant

- Jean Le Bouteillier married Marie de Venois

- ☐ Bénigne Le Bouteillier married Jacques Maillard

- Miles Maillard married Marie Morant

- ☐ Renée Maillard married Adam de Baillon

- Alphonse de Baillon married Louise de Marle

- ☐ Catherine de Baillon

Dukes of Spoleto

- Suppo I, Duke of Spoleto, married ---------- [1386] [1387]

- Adelgis I, Duke of Spoleto, Count of Parma, married ---------- [1388]

- Suppo II, Duke of Spoleto, marruied ---------- [1389]

- Bertila de Spoleto married Berengar I, Marchese di Friulia, King of Italy [1390] [1391] [1392]

- Gisela of Friuli married Margrave Adalbert I of Ivrea [1393] [1394] [1395]

- Margrave Berengar II of Ivrea, King of Italy, married Willa d'Arles [1396] [1397]

- Adalbert, King of Italy, married Gerberge [1398] [1399]

[1386] fmg.ac/Projects/MedLands/FRANKISH%20NOBILITY.htm#SuppoIdied824
[1387] fmg.ac/Projects/MedLands/CENTRAL%20ITALY.htm#SuppoIdied824
[1388] Ibid.
[1389] Ibid.
[1390] fmg.ac/Projects/MedLands/CENTRAL%20ITALY.htm#BertilaSpoletodied915
[1391] fmg.ac/Projects/MedLands/ITALY,%20Kings%20to%20962.htm#BerengarioIitalydied924B
[1392] fmg.ac/Projects/MedLands/NORTHERN%20ITALY%20900-1100.htm#BerengarioIitalydied924A
[1393] fmg.ac/Projects/MedLands/NORTHERN%20ITALY%20900-1100.htm#GiselaMAdalbertoIvreadied923
[1394] fmg.ac/Projects/MedLands/NORTHERN%20ITALY%20900-1100.htm#AdalbertoIivreaB
[1395] https://en.wikipedia.org/wiki/Adalbert_I_of_Ivrea
[1396] fmg.ac/Projects/MedLands/NORTHERN%20ITALY%20900-1100.htm#BerengarioIIitalydied966B
[1397] fmg.ac/Projects/MedLands/PROVENCE.htm#WillaMBerengarioIIivrea

- Count Otto William of Burgundy married widowed Ermentrude de Roucy [1400] [1401] [1402]

- Count Reginald I of Burgundy married to Alice of Normandy (daughter of Richard II (The Good) de St. Clair (4th Duke of Normandy) and Judith of Brittany) [1403] [1404]

- Count William I of Burgundy married Étiennette [1405] [1406]

- Raymond of Burgundy married Urraca, the reigning Queen of Léon and Castile (d/o King Alfonso VI of Léon and Castile and Constance of Burgundy) [1407] [1408] [1409] [1410]

- King Alfonso VII de Léon and Castile married Berenguela (Berengaria) de Barcelona [1411] [1412]

☐ Constance de Castile married King Louis VII of France [1413] [1414]

[1398] fmg.ac/Projects/MedLands/NORTHERN%20ITALY%20900-1100.htm#AdalbertoKingItalydied971
[1399] fmg.ac/Projects/MedLands/BURGUNDIAN%20NOBILITY.htm#GerbergeChalondied986
[1400] fmg.ac/Projects/MedLands/BURGUNDIAN%20NOBILITY.htm#OthonIMacondied1026
[1401] fmg.ac/Projects/MedLands/NORTHERN%20FRANCE.htm#Ermentrudedied10021005
[1402] fmg.ac/Projects/MedLands/BURGUNDY%20Kingdom.htm#RenaudIComtedied1057B
[1403] fmg.ac/Projects/MedLands/BURGUNDY%20Kingdom.htm#_Toc310954253
[1404] fmg.ac/Projects/MedLands/NORMANDY.htm#Adelaisdiedafter1037
[1405] fmg.ac/Projects/MedLands/BURGUNDY%20Kingdom.htm#GuillaumeIdied1087B
[1406] https://en.wikipedia.org/wiki/William_I,_Count_of_Burgundy
[1407] fmg.ac/Projects/MedLands/BURGUNDY%20Kingdom.htm#RaimondAmousdied1107
[1408] fmg.ac/Projects/MedLands/CASTILE.htm#Urracadied1126B
[1409] https://en.wikipedia.org/wiki/Alfonso_VI_of_León_and_Castile
[1410] https://en.wikipedia.org/wiki/Constance_of_Burgundy
[1411] fmg.ac/Projects/MedLands/CASTILE.htm#_ALFONSO_VII_1112-1157,
[1412] fmg.ac/Projects/MedLands/CATALAN%20NOBILITY.htm#Berengueladied1149MAlfonsoVIICastile
[1413] fmg.ac/Projects/MedLands/CASTILE.htm#Constanzadied1160MLouisVIIFrance

☐ Princess Alys de France, Countess of the Vexin, married William II, Count of Ponthieu and Montreuil, on August 20, 1195 [1415] [1416]

☐ Marie, Countess of Ponthieu and Courtess of Montreuil, married Simon de Dammartin before September 1208 [1417] [1418]

☐ Marie de Dammartin married Jean II Count de Roucy, Seigneur de Pierrepont [1419] [1420] [1421]

☐ Marie (Mathilde) de Roucy married Jean I de Garlande, Seigneur de Possesse [1422] [1423] [1424] [1425]

[1414] fmg.ac/Projects/MedLands/CAPET.htm#LouisVIIdied1180B
[1415] fmg.ac/Projects/MedLands/CAPET.htm#Alixdiedafter1200MGuillaumeIIIPonthieu
[1416] fmg.ac/Projects/MedLands/NORTHERN%20FRANCE.htm#GuillaumeIIdied1221
[1417] fmg.ac/Projects/MedLands/NORTHERN%20FRANCE.htm#MariePonthieudied1250
[1418] fmg.ac/Projects/MedLands/NORTHERN%20FRANCE.htm#SimonDammartinAumalePonthieud1239B
[1419] fmg.ac/Projects/MedLands/NORTHERN%20FRANCE.htm#MarieDammartinMJeanIIRoucy
[1420] fmg.ac/Projects/MedLands/NORTHERN%20FRANCE.htm#JeanPierrepontRoucydied1251
[1421] DuLong, John. (2009) "Catherine de Baillon's de Roye Ancestry: Another Royal Gateway" (page 17). <u>Michigan's Habitant Heritage: Journal of the French-Canadian Heritage Society of Michigan</u>, Volume 30, Number 1, January 2009.
[1422] fmg.ac/Projects/MedLands/NORTHERN%20FRANCE.htm#dauJeanIIRoucyMJeanGarlande
[1423] fmg.ac/Projects/MedLands/PARIS%20REGION%20NOBILITY.htm#JeanGarlandePossessediedbefore1287
[1424] DuLong, John. (2009) "Catherine de Baillon's de Roye Ancestry: Another Royal Gateway" (page 17). <u>Michigan's Habitant Heritage: Journal of the French-Canadian Heritage Society of Michigan</u>, Volume 30, Number 1, January 2009.
[1425] racineshistoire.free.fr/LGN/PDF/Garlande.pdf (page 8)

- Jean II de Garland, Seigneur de Possesse, married Agnès [1426] [1427]

☐ Alix de Garlande dit de Possesse married Dreux de Roye, Seigneur de Germigny [1428] [1429]

☐ Jeanne (Jacqueline) de Roye married Arnould V de Gavre [1430] [1431] [1432]

- Arnould VI de Gavre, Baron d'Escornaix married Isabelle (Ysabeau) de Ghistelles [1433] [1434]

☐ Catherine de Gavre d'Escornaix married Guy I Le Bouteiller [1435]

- Guy II Le Bouteillier married Isabeau Morhier [1436]

- Jean Le Bouteillier married Marie de Venois [1437]

☐ Bénigne Le Bouteillier married Jacques Maillard [1438]

[1426] racineshistoire.free.fr/LGN/PDF/Garlande.pdf (page 8)
[1427] DuLong, John. (2009) "Catherine de Baillon's de Roye Ancestry: Another Royal Gateway" (page 17). Michigan's Habitant Heritage: Journal of the French-Canadian Heritage Society of Michigan, Volume 30, Number 1, January 2009.
[1428] Ibid, pages 14 and 15.
[1429] racineshistoire.free.fr/LGN/PDF/Roye.pdf (page 6)
[1430] Jetté, René, DuLong, John P., Gagné, Roland-Yves, Moreau, Gail F. and Dubé, Joseph A. (2001) Table d'ascendance de Catherine Baillon: 12 générations (pages 124 and 125). Montréal, Québec: Société Généalogique Canadienne Française.
[1431] DuLong, John. (2009) "Catherine de Baillon's de Roye Ancestry: Another Royal Gateway" (page 13). Michigan's Habitant Heritage: Journal of the French-Canadian Heritage Society of Michigan, Volume 30, Number 1, January 2009.
[1432] racineshistoire.free.fr/LGN/PDF/Gavre.pdf (page 9)
[1433] Jetté, René, DuLong, John P., Gagné, Roland-Yves, Moreau, Gail F. and Dubé, Joseph A. (2001) Table d'ascendance de Catherine Baillon: 12 générations (page 112). Montréal, Québec: Société Généalogique Canadienne Française.
[1434] racineshistoire.free.fr/LGN/PDF/Gavre.pdf (page 9)
[1435] Ibid, page 10.
[1436] Ibid.
[1437] Ibid.

■ Miles Maillard married Marie Morant

☐ Renée Maillard married Adam de Baillon

■ Alphonse de Baillon married Louise de Marle

☐ Catherine de Baillon

[1438] racineshistoire.free.fr/LGN/PDF/Gavre.pdf (page 10)

In keeping with the Dukes of Spoleto, there is a second line of descent.

- Suppo I, Duke of Spoleto, married ---------- [1439] [1440]

- Adelgis I, Duke of Spoleto, Count of Parma, married ---------- [1441]

- Suppo II, Duke of Spoleto, marruied ---------- [1442]

- ☐ Bertila de Spoleto married Berengar I, Marchese di Friulia, King of Italy [1443] [1444] [1445]

- ☐ Gisela of Friuli married Margrave Adalbert I of Ivrea [1446] [1447] [1448]

- Margrave Berengar II of Ivrea, King of Italy, married Willa d'Arles [1449] [1450]

- Adalbert, King of Italy, married Gerberge [1451] [1452]

[1439] fmg.ac/Projects/MedLands/FRANKISH%20NOBILITY.htm#SuppoIdied824
[1440] fmg.ac/Projects/MedLands/CENTRAL%20ITALY.htm#SuppoIdied824
[1441] Ibid.
[1442] Ibid.
[1443] fmg.ac/Projects/MedLands/CENTRAL%20ITALY.htm#BertilaSpoletodied915
[1444] fmg.ac/Projects/MedLands/ITALY,%20Kings%20to%20962.htm#BerengarioIitalydied924B
[1445] fmg.ac/Projects/MedLands/NORTHERN%20ITALY%20900-1100.htm#BerengarioIitalydied924A
[1446] fmg.ac/Projects/MedLands/NORTHERN%20ITALY%20900-1100.htm#GiselaMAdalbertoIvreadied923
[1447] fmg.ac/Projects/MedLands/NORTHERN%20ITALY%20900-1100.htm#AdalbertoIivreaB
[1448] https://en.wikipedia.org/wiki/Adalbert_I_of_Ivrea
[1449] fmg.ac/Projects/MedLands/NORTHERN%20ITALY%20900-1100.htm#BerengarioIIitalydied966B
[1450] fmg.ac/Projects/MedLands/PROVENCE.htm#WillaMBerengarioIIivrea
[1451] fmg.ac/Projects/MedLands/NORTHERN%20ITALY%20900-1100.htm#AdalbertoKingItalydied971

- Count Otto William of Burgundy married widowed Ermentrude de Roucy [1453] [1454] [1455]

- Count Reginald I of Burgundy married to Alice of Normandy (daughter of Richard II (The Good) de St. Clair (4th Duke of Normandy) and Judith of Brittany) [1456] [1457]

- Count William I of Burgundy married Étiennette [1458] [1459]

- Gisela of Burgundy married Count Umberto (Humbert) II (The Fat) of Savoy [1460] [1461]

- Adélaide of Savoy married King Louis VI of France [1462] [1463]

- King Louis VII of France (1137 to 1180) married Adèle de Champagne [1464] [1465]

- King Philippe II Auguste of France (1180 to 1223) married thirdly Agnès d'Andechs de Méranie [1466] [1467]

[1452] fmg.ac/Projects/MedLands/BURGUNDIAN%20NOBILITY.htm#GerbergeChalondied986
[1453] fmg.ac/Projects/MedLands/BURGUNDIAN%20NOBILITY.htm#OthonIMacondied1026
[1454] fmg.ac/Projects/MedLands/NORTHERN%20FRANCE.htm#Ermentrudedied10021005
[1455] fmg.ac/Projects/MedLands/BURGUNDY%20Kingdom.htm#RenaudIComtedied1057B
[1456] fmg.ac/Projects/MedLands/BURGUNDY%20Kingdom.htm#_Toc310954253
[1457] fmg.ac/Projects/MedLands/NORMANDY.htm#Adelaisdiedafter1037
[1458] fmg.ac/Projects/MedLands/BURGUNDY%20Kingdom.htm#GuillaumeIdied1087B
[1459] https://en.wikipedia.org/wiki/William_I,_Count_of_Burgundy
[1460] fmg.ac/Projects/MedLands/BURGUNDY%20Kingdom.htm#GiseleM1HumbertIIMaurienneM2RanieroMonfe
[1461] fmg.ac/Projects/MedLands/SAVOY.htm#HumbertIIdied1103B
[1462] fmg.ac/Projects/MedLands/SAVOY.htm#Adélaïdedied1154
[1463] fmg.ac/Projects/MedLands/CAPET.htm#LouisVIdied1137B
[1464] fmg.ac/Projects/MedLands/CAPET.htm#LouisVIIdied1180B
[1465] fmg.ac/Projects/MedLands/CENTRAL%20FRANCE.htm#AdeleBloisdied1206
[1466] fmg.ac/Projects/MedLands/CAPET.htm#PhilippeIIdied1223B
[1467] fmg.ac/Projects/MedLands/CARINTHIA.htm#AgnesMeranodied1201

☐ Princess Marie of France married Henri I, Duke of Brabant [1468] [1469]

☐ Élisabeth de Brabant married Count Dietrich (Thierry) de Clèves [1470] [1471]

Élisabeth was also known as Ysabeau de Brabant; with regards to French records, the name Élisabeth is often used, interchangeably, with that of Isabelle. [1472] [1473]

☐ Mathilda de Clèves married Gerard de Luxembourg

☐ Marguerite de Luxembourg married Jean III de Ghistelles

■ Jean IV de Ghistelles married Marie de Haverskerke

■ Roger de Ghistelles married Élisabeth ~~Marguerite~~ de Dudzeele (see page 182 for updated explanation)

☐ Isabelle (Ysabeau) de Ghistelles married Arnould VI de Gavre

☐ Catherine de Gavre d'Escornaix married Guy I Le Bouteiller

■ Guy II Le Bouteillier married Isabeau Morhier

■ Jean Le Bouteillier married Marie de Venois

[1468] fmg.ac/Projects/MedLands/CAPET.htm#Mariedied1238
[1469] fmg.ac/Projects/MedLands/BRABANT,%20LOUVAIN.htm#HenriILotharingiaBrabantdied1235B
[1470] fmg.ac/Projects/MedLands/BRABANT,%20LOUVAIN.htm#Elisabethdied1272
[1471] fmg.ac/Projects/MedLands/FRANCONIA%20(LOWER%20RHINE).htm#Dietrichdied1245
[1472] Jetté, René, DuLong, John P., Gagné, Roland-Yves, Moreau, Gail F. and Dubé, Joseph A. (2001) Table d'ascendance de Catherine Baillon: 12 générations (p 153). Montréal, Québec: Société Généalogique Canadienne Française.
[1473] https://en.wikipedia.org/wiki/Henry_I,_Duke_of_Brabant

- ☐ Bénigne Le Bouteillier married Jacques Maillard

- ■ Miles Maillard married Marie Morant

- ☐ Renée Maillard married Adam de Baillon

- ■ Alphonse de Baillon married Louise de Marle

- ☐ Catherine de Baillon

Descendants of Boso, Count of Arles

- Boso, Count of Arles, married ---------- [1474]

- Hubert, Count of Arles, married ---------- [1475]

- Theobald married Berta of Lotharingia (illegitimate daughter of Lothaire II, King of Lotharingia, and his mistress Waldrada) [1476] [1477]

- Boso, Count of Arles, married Willa (d/o Rudolf I, King of Upper Burgundy) [1478] [1479]

- ☐ Willa d'Arles married Margrave Berengar II of Ivrea, King of Italy [1480] [1481]

- Adalbert, King of Italy, married Gerberge [1482] [1483]

- Count Otto William of Burgundy married widowed Ermentrude de Roucy [1484] [1485] [1486]

[1474] fmg.ac/Projects/MedLands/PROVENCE.htm#_Toc371156099
[1475] fmg.ac/Projects/MedLands/PROVENCE.htm#Hugbertdied864B
[1476] fmg.ac/Projects/MedLands/PROVENCE.htm#Theotbalddied887895
[1477] fmg.ac/Projects/MedLands/LOTHARINGIA.htm#BertaM1ThibautArlesM2AdalbertIITuscany
[1478] fmg.ac/Projects/MedLands/PROVENCE.htm#BosoAvignonVaisindied936
[1479] fmg.ac/Projects/MedLands/BURGUNDY%20KINGS.htm#WillaMBosoVienne
[1480] fmg.ac/Projects/MedLands/PROVENCE.htm#WillaMBerengarioIIivrea
[1481] fmg.ac/Projects/MedLands/NORTHERN%20ITALY%20900-1100.htm#BerengarioIIitalydied966B
[1482] fmg.ac/Projects/MedLands/NORTHERN%20ITALY%20900-1100.htm#AdalbertoKingItalydied971
[1483] fmg.ac/Projects/MedLands/BURGUNDIAN%20NOBILITY.htm#GerbergeChalondied986

- Count Reginald I of Burgundy married to Alice of Normandy (daughter of Richard II (The Good) de St. Clair (4th Duke of Normandy) and Judith of Brittany) [1487] [1488]

- Count William I of Burgundy married Étiennette [1489] [1490]

- Raymond of Burgundy married Urraca, the reigning Queen of Léon and Castile (d/o King Alfonso VI of Léon and Castile and Constance of Burgundy) [1491] [1492] [1493] [1494]

- King Alfonso VII de Léon and Castile married Berenguela (Berengaria) de Barcelona [1495] [1496]

  ☐ Constance de Castile married King Louis VII of France [1497] [1498]

  ☐ Princess Alys de France, Countess of the Vexin, married William II, Count of Ponthieu and Montreuil, on August 20, 1195 [1499] [1500]

[1484] fmg.ac/Projects/MedLands/BURGUNDIAN%20NOBILITY.htm#OthonIMacondied1026
[1485] fmg.ac/Projects/MedLands/NORTHERN%20FRANCE.htm#Ermentrudedied10021005
[1486] fmg.ac/Projects/MedLands/BURGUNDY%20Kingdom.htm#RenaudIComtedied1057B
[1487] fmg.ac/Projects/MedLands/BURGUNDY%20Kingdom.htm#_Toc310954253
[1488] fmg.ac/Projects/MedLands/NORMANDY.htm#Adelaisdiedafter1037
[1489] fmg.ac/Projects/MedLands/BURGUNDY%20Kingdom.htm#GuillaumeIdied1087B
[1490] https://en.wikipedia.org/wiki/William_I,_Count_of_Burgundy
[1491] fmg.ac/Projects/MedLands/BURGUNDY%20Kingdom.htm#RaimondAmousdied1107
[1492] fmg.ac/Projects/MedLands/CASTILE.htm#Urracadied1126B
[1493] https://en.wikipedia.org/wiki/Alfonso_VI_of_León_and_Castile
[1494] https://en.wikipedia.org/wiki/Constance_of_Burgundy
[1495] fmg.ac/Projects/MedLands/CASTILE.htm#_ALFONSO_VII_1112-1157,
[1496] fmg.ac/Projects/MedLands/CATALAN%20NOBILITY.htm#Berengueladied1149MAlfonsoVIICastile
[1497] fmg.ac/Projects/MedLands/CASTILE.htm#Constanzadied1160MLouisVIIFrance
[1498] fmg.ac/Projects/MedLands/CAPET.htm#LouisVIIdied1180B
[1499] fmg.ac/Projects/MedLands/CAPET.htm#Alixdiedafter1200MGuillaumeIIIPonthieu

☐ Marie, Countess of Ponthieu and Countess of Montreuil, married Simon de Dammartin before September 1208 [1501] [1502]

☐ Marie de Dammartin married Jean II Count de Roucy, Seigneur de Pierrepont [1503] [1504] [1505]

☐ Marie (Mathilde) de Roucy married Jean I de Garlande, Seigneur de Possesse [1506] [1507] [1508] [1509]

■ Jean II de Garland, Seigneur de Possesse, married Agnès [1510] [1511]

[1500] fmg.ac/Projects/MedLands/NORTHERN%20FRANCE.htm#GuillaumeIIdied1221
[1501] fmg.ac/Projects/MedLands/NORTHERN%20FRANCE.htm#MariePonthieudied1250
[1502] fmg.ac/Projects/MedLands/NORTHERN%20FRANCE.htm#SimonDammartinAumalePonthieud1239B
[1503] fmg.ac/Projects/MedLands/NORTHERN%20FRANCE.htm#MarieDammartinMJeanIIRoucy
[1504] fmg.ac/Projects/MedLands/NORTHERN%20FRANCE.htm#JeanPierrepontRoucydied1251
[1505] DuLong, John. (2009) "Catherine de Baillon's de Roye Ancestry: Another Royal Gateway" (page 17). Michigan's Habitant Heritage: Journal of the French-Canadian Heritage Society of Michigan, Volume 30, Number 1, January 2009.
[1506] fmg.ac/Projects/MedLands/NORTHERN%20FRANCE.htm#dauJeanIIRoucyMJeanGarlande
[1507] fmg.ac/Projects/MedLands/PARIS%20REGION%20NOBILITY.htm#JeanGarlandePossessediedbefore1287
[1508] DuLong, John. (2009) "Catherine de Baillon's de Roye Ancestry: Another Royal Gateway" (page 17). Michigan's Habitant Heritage: Journal of the French-Canadian Heritage Society of Michigan, Volume 30, Number 1, January 2009.
[1509] racineshistoire.free.fr/LGN/PDF/Garlande.pdf (page 8)
[1510] Ibid.
[1511] DuLong, John. (2009) "Catherine de Baillon's de Roye Ancestry: Another Royal Gateway" (page 17). Michigan's Habitant Heritage: Journal of the French-Canadian Heritage Society of Michigan, Volume 30, Number 1, January 2009.

☐ Alix de Garlande dit de Possesse married Dreux de Roye, Seigneur de Germigny [1512] [1513]

☐ Jeanne (Jacqueline) de Roye married Arnould V de Gavre [1514] [1515] [1516]

■ Arnould VI de Gavre, Baron d'Escornaix married Isabelle (Ysabeau) de Ghistelles [1517] [1518]

☐ Catherine de Gavre d'Escornaix married Guy I Le Bouteiller [1519]

■ Guy II Le Bouteillier married Isabeau Morhier [1520]

■ Jean Le Bouteillier married Marie de Venois [1521]

☐ Bénigne Le Bouteillier married Jacques Maillard [1522]

■ Miles Maillard married Marie Morant

☐ Renée Maillard married Adam de Baillon

[1512] DuLong, John. (2009) "Catherine de Baillon's de Roye Ancestry: Another Royal Gateway" (pages 14 and 15). Michigan's Habitant Heritage: Journal of the French-Canadian Heritage Society of Michigan, Volume 30, Number 1, January 2009.
[1513] racineshistoire.free.fr/LGN/PDF/Roye.pdf (page 6)
[1514] Jetté, René, DuLong, John P., Gagné, Roland-Yves, Moreau, Gail F. and Dubé, Joseph A. (2001) Table d'ascendance de Catherine Baillon: 12 générations (pages 124 and 125). Montréal, Québec: Société Généalogique Canadienne Française.
[1515] DuLong, John. (2009) "Catherine de Baillon's de Roye Ancestry: Another Royal Gateway" (page 13). Michigan's Habitant Heritage: Journal of the French-Canadian Heritage Society of Michigan, Volume 30, Number 1, January 2009.
[1516] racineshistoire.free.fr/LGN/PDF/Gavre.pdf (page 9)
[1517] Jetté, René, DuLong, John P., Gagné, Roland-Yves, Moreau, Gail F. and Dubé, Joseph A. (2001) Table d'ascendance de Catherine Baillon: 12 générations (page 112). Montréal, Québec: Société Généalogique Canadienne Française.
[1518] racineshistoire.free.fr/LGN/PDF/Gavre.pdf (page 9)
[1519] Ibid, page 10.
[1520] Ibid.
[1521] Ibid.
[1522] Ibid.

■ Alphonse de Baillon married Louise de Marle

☐ Catherine de Baillon

In keeping with the Descendants of Boso, Count of Arles, there is a second line of descent.

- Boso, Count of Arles, married ---------- [1523]

- Hubert, Count of Arles, married ---------- [1524]

- Theobald married Berta of Lotharingia (illegitimate daughter of Lothaire II, King of Lotharingia, and his mistress Waldrada) [1525] [1526]

- Boso, Count of Arles, married Willa (d/o Rudolf I, King of Upper Burgundy) [1527] [1528]

- ☐ Willa d'Arles married Margrave Berengar II of Ivrea, King of Italy [1529] [1530]

- Adalbert, King of Italy, married Gerberge [1531] [1532]

- Count Otto William of Burgundy married widowed Ermentrude de Roucy [1533] [1534] [1535]

[1523] fmg.ac/Projects/MedLands/PROVENCE.htm#_Toc371156099
[1524] fmg.ac/Projects/MedLands/PROVENCE.htm#Hugbertdied864B
[1525] fmg.ac/Projects/MedLands/PROVENCE.htm#Theotbalddied887895
[1526] fmg.ac/Projects/MedLands/LOTHARINGIA.htm#BertaM1ThibautArlesM2AdalbertIITuscany
[1527] fmg.ac/Projects/MedLands/PROVENCE.htm#BosoAvignonVaisindied936
[1528] fmg.ac/Projects/MedLands/BURGUNDY%20KINGS.htm#WillaMBosoVienne
[1529] fmg.ac/Projects/MedLands/PROVENCE.htm#WillaMBerengarioIIivrea
[1530] fmg.ac/Projects/MedLands/NORTHERN%20ITALY%20900-1100.htm#BerengarioIIitalydied966B
[1531] fmg.ac/Projects/MedLands/NORTHERN%20ITALY%20900-1100.htm#AdalbertoKingItalydied971
[1532] fmg.ac/Projects/MedLands/BURGUNDIAN%20NOBILITY.htm#GerbergeChalondied986
[1533] fmg.ac/Projects/MedLands/BURGUNDIAN%20NOBILITY.htm#OthonIMacondied1026
[1534] fmg.ac/Projects/MedLands/NORTHERN%20FRANCE.htm#Ermentrudedied10021005
[1535] fmg.ac/Projects/MedLands/BURGUNDY%20Kingdom.htm#RenaudIComtedied1057B

- Count Reginald I of Burgundy married to Alice of Normandy (daughter of Richard II (The Good) de St. Clair (4th Duke of Normandy) and Judith of Brittany) [1536] [1537]

- Count William I of Burgundy married Étiennette [1538] [1539]

- Gisela of Burgundy married Count Umberto (Humbert) II (The Fat) of Savoy [1540] [1541]

- Adéläide of Savoy married King Louis VI of France [1542] [1543]

- King Louis VII of France (1137 to 1180) married Adèle de Champagne [1544] [1545]

- King Philippe II Auguste of France (1180 to 1223) married thirdly Agnès d'Andechs de Méranie [1546] [1547]

- Princess Marie of France married Henri I, Duke of Brabant [1548] [1549]

- Élisabeth de Brabant married Count Dietrich (Thierry) de Clèves [1550] [1551]

[1536] fmg.ac/Projects/MedLands/BURGUNDY%20Kingdom.htm#_Toc310954253
[1537] fmg.ac/Projects/MedLands/NORMANDY.htm#Adelaisdiedafter1037
[1538] fmg.ac/Projects/MedLands/BURGUNDY%20Kingdom.htm#GuillaumeIdied1087B
[1539] https://en.wikipedia.org/wiki/William_I,_Count_of_Burgundy
[1540] fmg.ac/Projects/MedLands/BURGUNDY%20Kingdom.htm#GiseleM1HumbertIIMaurienneM2RanieroMonfe
[1541] fmg.ac/Projects/MedLands/SAVOY.htm#HumbertIIdied1103B
[1542] fmg.ac/Projects/MedLands/SAVOY.htm#Adélaïdedied1154
[1543] fmg.ac/Projects/MedLands/CAPET.htm#LouisVIdied1137B
[1544] fmg.ac/Projects/MedLands/CAPET.htm#LouisVIIdied1180B
[1545] fmg.ac/Projects/MedLands/CENTRAL%20FRANCE.htm#AdeleBloisdied1206
[1546] fmg.ac/Projects/MedLands/CAPET.htm#PhilippeIIdied1223B
[1547] fmg.ac/Projects/MedLands/CARINTHIA.htm#AgnesMeranodied1201
[1548] fmg.ac/Projects/MedLands/CAPET.htm#Mariedied1238
[1549] fmg.ac/Projects/MedLands/BRABANT,%20LOUVAIN.htm#HenriILotharingiaBrabantdied1235B

Élisabeth was also known as Ysabeau de Brabant; with regards to French records, the name Élisabeth is often used, interchangeably, with that of Isabelle. [1552] [1553]

☐ Mathilda de Clèves married Gerard de Luxembourg

☐ Marguerite de Luxembourg married Jean III de Ghistelles

■ Jean IV de Ghistelles married Marie de Haverskerke

■ Roger de Ghistelles married Élisabeth ~~Marguerite~~ de Dudzeele (see page 182 for updated explanation)

☐ Isabelle (Ysabeau) de Ghistelles married Arnould VI de Gavre

☐ Catherine de Gavre d'Escornaix married Guy I Le Bouteiller

■ Guy II Le Bouteillier married Isabeau Morhier

■ Jean Le Bouteillier married Marie de Venois

☐ Bénigne Le Bouteillier married Jacques Maillard

■ Miles Maillard married Marie Morant

☐ Renée Maillard married Adam de Baillon

■ Alphonse de Baillon married Louise de Marle

[1550] fmg.ac/Projects/MedLands/BRABANT,%20LOUVAIN.htm#Elisabethdied1272
[1551] fmg.ac/Projects/MedLands/FRANCONIA%20(LOWER%20RHINE).htm#Dietrichdied1245
[1552] Jetté, René, DuLong, John P., Gagné, Roland-Yves, Moreau, Gail F. and Dubé, Joseph A. (2001) Table d'ascendance de Catherine Baillon: 12 générations (p 153). Montréal, Québec: Société Généalogique Canadienne Française.
[1553] https://en.wikipedia.org/wiki/Henry_I,_Duke_of_Brabant

☐ Catherine de Baillon

Duchy of Provence

After the division of the Carolingian Empire by the Treaty of Verdun (843), the first of the fraternal rulers of the three kingdoms to die was Holy Roman Emperor Lothair I, who divided his realm of the Middle Franks (Lotharingia), in accordance with the custom of the Franks, between his three sons. [1554]

Out of this division came the Kingdom of Provence, also known as Lower Burgundy, which was given to Lothair's youngest son, Charles, becoming became the Carolingian King of Provence. [1555]

It was in the aftermath of the death of Holy Roman Emperor Louis III that Provence began to be ruled by local counts placed under the authority of a margrave.

Hugh of Arles, brother-in-law to Louis, had served as duke and regent during his long blindness; hence, Louis' kingdom, upon his death, did not pass to his heirs.

In a treaty of 933, Hugh gave the Duchy of Provence to Rudolf II of Burgundy (as it ceased to be a separate kingdom). [1556] [1557] [1558]

Not recognized by the nobles of the country, Hugh of Arles (s/o Theobald, Count of Arles; a Frank from the Bosonid family, and Bertha, an illegitimate daughter of Lothair II, King of Lotharingia) was appointed Duke of Burgundy, its first margrave. [1559] [1560] [1561]

[1554] https://en.wikipedia.org/wiki/Count_of_Provence
[1555] Ibid.
[1556] Ibid.
[1557] https://en.wikipedia.org/wiki/Hugh_of_Italy
[1558] https://en.wikipedia.org/wiki/Bosonid

■ Count William I of Provence (called the Liberator) who was later installed as the Count of Arles, s/o Count Boso II of Arles (who was married to Constance of Viennois, daughter of Count Charles Constantine of Vienne, the s/o Holy Roman Emperor Louis III), <u>brother to Hugh of Arles</u>, King of Italy, married Adélaïs (Blance) d'Anjou [1562] [1563]

☐ Constance of Arles married King Robert II of France[1564] [1565]

■ King Henri I of France (1031 to 1060) married Anne de Kiev [1566] [1567]

■ King Philippe I of France (1060 to 1108) married Berthe de Holland [1568] [1569]

■ King Louis VI of France (1108 to 1137) married Adélaïde de Maurienne [1570] [1571]

■ King Louis VII of France (1137 to 1180) married Adèle de Champagne [1572] [1573]

■ King Philippe II Auguste of France (1180 to 1223) married <u>thirdly</u> Agnès d'Andechs de Méranie [1574] [1575]

[1559] https://en.wikipedia.org/wiki/Count_of_Provence
[1560] https://en.wikipedia.org/wiki/Hugh_of_Italy
[1561] https://en.wikipedia.org/wiki/Bosonid
[1562] fmg.ac/Projects/MedLands/PROVENCE.htm#GuillaumeIIArlesProvencedied993
[1563] fmg.ac/Projects/MedLands/ANJOU,%20MAINE.htm#AdelaisM1M2LouisVFranksdied987M3M4
[1564] fmg.ac/Projects/MedLands/PROVENCE.htm#ConstanceArlesMRobertIIFrancedied1031
[1565] fmg.ac/Projects/MedLands/CAPET.htm#RobertIIdied1031B
[1566] fmg.ac/Projects/MedLands/CAPET.htm#HenriIdied1060B
[1567] fmg.ac/Projects/MedLands/RUSSIA,%20Rurik.htm#AnnaIaroslavnadied1075
[1568] fmg.ac/Projects/MedLands/CAPET.htm#PhilippeIdied1108B
[1569] fmg.ac/Projects/MedLands/HOLLAND.htm#Berthadied1093
[1570] fmg.ac/Projects/MedLands/CAPET.htm#LouisVIdied1137B
[1571] fmg.ac/Projects/MedLands/SAVOY.htm#Adélaïdedied1154
[1572] fmg.ac/Projects/MedLands/CAPET.htm#LouisVIIdied1180B
[1573] fmg.ac/Projects/MedLands/CENTRAL%20FRANCE.htm#AdeleBloisdied1206

- Princess Marie of France married Henri I, Duke of Brabant[1576][1577]

- Élisabeth de Brabant marriedCount Dietrich (Thierry) de Clèves [1578][1579]

Élisabeth was also known as Ysabeau de Brabant; with regards to French records, the name Élisabeth is often used, interchangeably, with that of Isabelle. [1580][1581]

- Mathilda deClèves married Gerard de Luxembourg

- Marguerite de Luxembourg married Jean III de Ghistelles

■ Jean IV de Ghistelles married Marie de Haverskerke

■ Roger de Ghistelles married Élisabeth ~~Marguerite~~ de Dudzeele (see page 182 for updated explanation)

- Isabelle (Ysabeau) de Ghistelles married Arnould VI de Gavre

- Catherine de Gavre d'Escornaix married Guy I Le Bouteiller

■ Guy II Le Bouteillier married Isabeau Morhier

[1574] fmg.ac/Projects/MedLands/CAPET.htm#PhilippeIIdied1223B
[1575] fmg.ac/Projects/MedLands/CARINTHIA.htm#AgnesMeranodied1201
[1576] fmg.ac/Projects/MedLands/CAPET.htm#Mariedied1238
[1577] fmg.ac/Projects/MedLands/BRABANT,%20LOUVAIN.htm#HenriILotharingiaBrabantdied1235B
[1578] fmg.ac/Projects/MedLands/BRABANT,%20LOUVAIN.htm#Elisabethdied1272
[1579] fmg.ac/Projects/MedLands/FRANCONIA%20(LOWER%20RHINE).htm#Dietrichdied1245
[1580] Jetté, René, DuLong, John P., Gagné, Roland-Yves, Moreau, Gail F. and Dubé, Joseph A. (2001) Table d'ascendance de Catherine Baillon: 12 générations (p 153). Montréal, Québec: Société Généalogique Canadienne Française.
[1581] https://en.wikipedia.org/wiki/Henry_I,_Duke_of_Brabant

- Jean Le Bouteillier married Marie de Venois

- ☐ Bénigne Le Bouteillier married Jacques Maillard

- Miles Maillard married Marie Morant

- ☐ Renée Maillard married Adam de Baillon

- Alphonse de Baillon married Louise de Marle

- ☐ Catherine de Baillon

Kings of Upper Burgundy

The Kings of Upper Burgundy (present-day western Switzerland and the Franche-Comté) belong to the elder House of Welf, a dynasty of European rulers in the 9th through 11th centuries to 1055. [1582] Consisting of two groups, a Burgundian group and a Swabian group, the older of the two was the Burgundian group (my connection). [1583]

- Count Welf of Altorf (whose daughter Judith married Holy Roman Emperor Louis I) [1584]

- Count Conrad of Auxerre married Adélaïde of Tours [1585] [1586]

- Duke Conrad of Upper Burgundy married Waldrada [1587] [1588]

- King Rudolf I of Upper Burgundy married Willa [1589] [1590]

- King Rudolf II of Upper Burgundy married Berta of Swabia [1591] [1592]

Following his ascent to the throne in 912, Rudolf was asked by several Italian nobles to intervene in Italy on their behalf against Emperor Berengar in 922. [1593]

[1582] https://en.wikipedia.org/wiki/Elder_House_of_Welf
[1583] Ibid.
[1584] Ibid.
[1585] https://en.wikipedia.org/wiki/Conrad_I_of_Auxerre
[1586] https://en.wikipedia.org/wiki/Adélaïde_of_Tours
[1587] fmg.ac/Projects/MedLands/BURGUNDY%20KINGS.htm#ConradAuxerreMWaldrada
[1588] https://en.wikipedia.org/wiki/Conrad_II,_Duke_of_Transjurane_Burgundy
[1589] fmg.ac/Projects/MedLands/BURGUNDY%20KINGS.htm#RudolfIdied912B
[1590] fmg.ac/Projects/MedLands/PROVENCE.htm#WillaM1RudolfIUpperBurgundyM2HugoIArles
[1591] fmg.ac/Projects/MedLands/BURGUNDY%20KINGS.htm#RudolfIIdied937B
[1592] fmg.ac/Projects/MedLands/SWABIA.htm#Bertadied961

Having entered Italy, he was crowned King of the Lombards at Pavia.[1594] In 923, he defeated Berengar at Piacenza, wherein Berengar was murdered the following year, possibly at the instigation of Rudolf.[1595] The king then ruled Upper Burgundy and Italy together, residing alternately in both kingdoms.[1596]

In 926, however, the Italian nobility turned against him, requesting that Hugh of Arles, the effective ruler of Provence (or Lower Burgundy), rule them instead.[1597]

Rudolf returned to Upper Burgundy to protect himself, assuring Hugh's coronation as King of Italy in the process.[1598]

Interestingly enough, the Italians switched sides once again, declaring that they wished for Rudolf to reclaim the throne.[1599]

To prevent this, Hugh and Rudolf signed a treaty in 933, granting Rudolf rule of Lower Burgundy in exchange for his renunciation of all claims on the Italian throne, wherein Rudolf then married his daughter Adéläide to Hugh's son Lothar.[1600]

With the two Burgundian kingdoms successfully unified, Rudolf ruled until his death in 937; he was succeeded by Conrad.[1601]

- King Conrad (The Peaceful) of Burgundy married Matilda of France [1602] [1603]

[1593] https://en.wikipedia.org/wiki/Rudolph_II,_King_of_Burgundy
[1594] Ibid.
[1595] Ibid.
[1596] Ibid.
[1597] Ibid.
[1598] Ibid.
[1599] Ibid.
[1600] Ibid.
[1601] Ibid.

☐ Bertha of Burgundy married Count Odo (Eudes) I of Blois [1604] [1605]

■ Count Odo (Eudes) II of Blois married Ermengarde d'Auvergne [1606] [1607]

■ Count Thibaud III of Blois, Chartres, Châteaudun, Meaux, Sancerre and Troyes, [1608] [1609] [1610] married firstly Gersende of Maine. [1611]

■ Count Stephen I of Blois married Adèle of Normandy [1612] [1613]

■ Count Theobald III (The Great) of Champagne (Theobald IV of Blois) married Matilda von Sponheim [1614] [1615]

☐ Adèle (Alix) of Champagne married King Louis VII of France [1616] [1617]

■ King Philippe II Auguste of France (1180 to 1223) married thirdly Agnès d'Andechs de Méranie [1618] [1619]

[1602] fmg.ac/Projects/MedLands/BURGUNDY%20KINGS.htm#ConradIBurgundydied993B
[1603] fmg.ac/Projects/MedLands/CAROLINGIANS.htm#MathildeMConradIBurgundy
[1604] fmg.ac/Projects/MedLands/BURGUNDY%20KINGS.htm#BertheM1EudesIBloisM2RobertIIFrance
[1605] fmg.ac/Projects/MedLands/CENTRAL%20FRANCE.htm#EudesIdied995
[1606] fmg.ac/Projects/MedLands/CENTRAL%20FRANCE.htm#EudesIIdied1037B
[1607] fmg.ac/Projects/MedLands/AUVERGNE.htm#ErmengardeAuvergnediedafter1042
[1608] fmg.ac/Projects/MedLands/CENTRAL%20FRANCE.htm#ThibautIIIdied1089B
[1609] racineshistoire.free.fr/LGN/PDF/Sancerre.pdf (page 2)
[1610] racineshistoire.free.fr/LGN/PDF/Blois-Champagne.pdf (page 4)
[1611] fmg.ac/Projects/MedLands/MAINE.htm#GersendeM1ThibautIIIBloisM2AzzoIIEste
[1612] fmg.ac/Projects/MedLands/ENGLAND,%20Kings%201066-1603.htm#Adeladied1138
[1613] fmg.ac/Projects/MedLands/CENTRAL%20FRANCE.htm#EtienneIdied1102B
[1614] fmg.ac/Projects/MedLands/CENTRAL%20FRANCE.htm#ThibautIVdied1152B
[1615] fmg.ac/Projects/MedLands/CARINTHIA.htm#Mathildedied1160
[1616] fmg.ac/Projects/MedLands/CENTRAL%20FRANCE.htm#AdeleBloisdied1206
[1617] fmg.ac/Projects/MedLands/CAPET.htm#LouisVIIdied1180B

☐ Princess Marie of France married Henri I, Duke of Brabant[1620][1621]

☐ Élisabeth de Brabant marriedCount Dietrich (Thierry) de Clèves [1622][1623]

Élisabeth was also known as Ysabeau de Brabant; with regards to French records, the name Élisabeth is often used, interchangeably, with that of Isabelle. [1624][1625]

☐ Mathilda deClèves married Gerard de Luxembourg

☐ Marguerite de Luxembourg married Jean III de Ghistelles

■ Jean IV de Ghistelles married Marie de Haverskerke

■ Roger de Ghistelles married Élisabeth ~~Marguerite~~ de Dudzeele (see page 182 for updated explanation)

☐ Isabelle (Ysabeau) de Ghistelles married Arnould VI de Gavre

☐ Catherine de Gavre d'Escornaix married Guy I Le Bouteiller

■ Guy II Le Bouteillier married Isabeau Morhier

[1618] fmg.ac/Projects/MedLands/CAPET.htm#PhilippeIIdied1223B
[1619] fmg.ac/Projects/MedLands/CARINTHIA.htm#AgnesMeranodied1201
[1620] fmg.ac/Projects/MedLands/CAPET.htm#Mariedied1238
[1621] fmg.ac/Projects/MedLands/BRABANT,%20LOUVAIN.htm#HenriILotharingiaBrabantdied1235B
[1622] fmg.ac/Projects/MedLands/BRABANT,%20LOUVAIN.htm#Elisabethdied1272
[1623] fmg.ac/Projects/MedLands/FRANCONIA%20(LOWER%20RHINE).htm#Dietrichdied1245
[1624] Jetté, René, DuLong, John P., Gagné, Roland-Yves, Moreau, Gail F. and Dubé, Joseph A. (2001) Table d'ascendance de Catherine Baillon: 12 générations (p 153). Montréal, Québec: Société Généalogique Canadienne Française.
[1625] https://en.wikipedia.org/wiki/Henry_I,_Duke_of_Brabant

- Jean Le Bouteillier married Marie de Venois

- Bénigne Le Bouteillier married Jacques Maillard

- Miles Maillard married Marie Morant

- Renée Maillard married Adam de Baillon

- Alphonse de Baillon married Louise de Marle

- Catherine de Baillon

Counts of Blois

As denoted on Wikipedia [1626]

The County of Blois was originally centred in Blois, south of Paris, France. One of the chief cities, along with Blois itself, was Chartres. Associated with Champagne, Châtillon (the lords of which tended to reside in Blois), and later with the French royal family, to whom the county passed in 1391, Blois was later important during the Hundred Years' War. In addition, Joan of Arc (Jeanne d'Arc) based herself there.

- Count Theobald I of Blois married Luitgarde of Vermandois [1627] [1628]

- Count Odo (Eudes) I of Blois married Bertha of Burgundy [1629] [1630]

- Count Odo (Eudes) II of Blois married Ermengarde d'Auvergne [1631] [1632]

- Count Stephen I of Blois married Adèle of Normandy [1633] [1634]

- Count Theobald III (The Great) of Champagne (Theobald IV of Blois) married Matilda von Sponheim [1635] [1636]

[1626] https://en.wikipedia.org/wiki/Counts_of_blois
[1627] fmg.ac/Projects/MedLands/CENTRAL%20FRANCE.htm#ThibautIdied975
[1628] fmg.ac/Projects/MedLands/NORTHERN%20FRANCE.htm#Luitgarddiedafter977
[1629] fmg.ac/Projects/MedLands/BURGUNDY%20KINGS.htm#BertheM1EudesIBloisM2RobertIIFrance
[1630] fmg.ac/Projects/MedLands/CENTRAL%20FRANCE.htm#EudesIdied995
[1631] fmg.ac/Projects/MedLands/CENTRAL%20FRANCE.htm#EudesIIdied1037B
[1632] fmg.ac/Projects/MedLands/AUVERGNE.htm#ErmengardeAuvergnediedafter1042
[1633] fmg.ac/Projects/MedLands/ENGLAND,%20Kings%201066-1603.htm#Adeladied1138
[1634] fmg.ac/Projects/MedLands/CENTRAL%20FRANCE.htm#EtienneIdied1102B

☐ Adèle (Alix) of Champagne married King Louis VII of France [1637] [1638]

■ King Philippe II Auguste of France (1180 to 1223) married <u>thirdly</u> Agnès d'Andechs de Méranie [1639] [1640]

☐ Princess Marie of France married Henri I, Duke of Brabant [1641] [1642]

☐ Élisabeth de Brabant marriedCount Dietrich (Thierry) de Clèves [1643] [1644]

Élisabeth was also known as Ysabeau de Brabant; with regards to French records, the name Élisabeth is often used, interchangeably, with that of Isabelle. [1645] [1646]

☐ Mathilda deClèves married Gerard de Luxembourg

☐ Marguerite de Luxembourg married Jean III de Ghistelles

■ Jean IV de Ghistelles married Marie de Haverskerke

[1635] fmg.ac/Projects/MedLands/CENTRAL%20FRANCE.htm#ThibautIVdied1152B
[1636] fmg.ac/Projects/MedLands/CARINTHIA.htm#Mathildedied1160
[1637] fmg.ac/Projects/MedLands/CENTRAL%20FRANCE.htm#AdeleBloisdied1206
[1638] fmg.ac/Projects/MedLands/CAPET.htm#LouisVIIdied1180B
[1639] fmg.ac/Projects/MedLands/CAPET.htm#PhilippeIIdied1223B
[1640] fmg.ac/Projects/MedLands/CARINTHIA.htm#AgnesMeranodied1201
[1641] fmg.ac/Projects/MedLands/CAPET.htm#Mariedied1238
[1642] fmg.ac/Projects/MedLands/BRABANT,%20LOUVAIN.htm#HenriILotharingiaBrabantdied1235B
[1643] fmg.ac/Projects/MedLands/BRABANT,%20LOUVAIN.htm#Elisabethdied1272
[1644] fmg.ac/Projects/MedLands/FRANCONIA%20(LOWER%20RHINE).htm#Dietrichdied1245
[1645] Jetté, René, DuLong, John P., Gagné, Roland-Yves, Moreau, Gail F. and Dubé, Joseph A. (2001) <u>Table d'ascendance de Catherine Baillon: 12 générations</u> (p 153). Montréal, Québec: Société Généalogique Canadienne Française.
[1646] https://en.wikipedia.org/wiki/Henry_I,_Duke_of_Brabant

■ Roger de Ghistelles married Élisabeth ~~Marguerite~~ de Dudzeele (see page 182 for updated explanation)

☐ Isabelle (Ysabeau) de Ghistelles married Arnould VI de Gavre

☐ Catherine de Gavre d'Escornaix married Guy I Le Bouteiller

■ Guy II Le Bouteillier married Isabeau Morhier

■ Jean Le Bouteillier married Marie de Venois

☐ Bénigne Le Bouteillier married Jacques Maillard

■ Miles Maillard married Marie Morant

☐ Renée Maillard married Adam de Baillon

■ Alphonse de Baillon married Louise de Marle

☐ Catherine de Baillon

Duchy of Clèves

The Duchy of Clèves roughly covered the present-day German districts of the northern part of Clèves, Wesel and the city of Duisburg, as well as adjacents parts of the Limburg, North Brabant and Gelderland provinces in the Netherlands.

The old 11th century castle of Schwanenburg (Swan Castle), former residence of the Dukes of Clèves, founded on a steep hill, is located at the northern terminus of the Kermisdahl where it joins with the Spoykanal, which was previously an important transportation link to the Rhine. [1647]

The old castle has a massive tower (the *Schwanenturm*) which stands 180 feet (55 m) high, topped by a golden swan; one that is associated, in legend, with the Knight of the Swan, immortalized in Richard Wagner's *Lohengrin*. [1648]

The French legend of the Knight of the Swan is attached to the house of Bouillon, and although William of Tyre refers to it about 1170 as fable, it was incorporated without question by later annalists. [1649]

Forming part of the cycle of the chansons de geste, dealing with the Crusade, that relate how Helyas, Knight of the Swan, is guided by the swan to the help of the duchess of Bouillon and marries her daughter Ida or Beatrix in circumstances exactly parallel to the adventures of Lohengrin and Elsa of Brabant, and with the like result. [1650] [1651]

[1647] https://en.wikipedia.org/wiki/Kleve
[1648] Ibid.
[1649] encyclopedia.jrank.org/LOB_LUP/LOHENGRIN.html
[1650] Ibid.

Their daughter marries Eustache, Count of Boulogne, and has three sons, the eldest of whom, Godefroid (Godfrey), is the future king of Jerusalem. [1652] [1653] [1654]

In the French story, however, Helyas is not the son of Parzival, but of the king and queen of Lillefort, and the story of his birth, of himself, his five brothers and one sister is, with variations, that of *the seven swans* persecuted by the wicked grandmother, which figures in the pages of Grimm and Hans Andersen. [1655]

The house of Bouillon was not alone in claiming the Knight of the Swan as an ancestor, and the tradition probably originally belonged to the house of Clèves. [1656]

■ Count Dietrich (Thierry) I of Clèves married unknown. [1657]

■ Count Arnould I of Clèves married Ida of Louvain. [1658] [1659]

■ Count Dietrich (Thierry) II of Clèves married Adelaide, the daughter of Gebhard III of Sulzbach and Matilda of Bavaria. [1660] [1661]

[1651] https://books.google.ca/books?id=CzxbBT9VttwC&pg=PA75&lpg=PA75&dq=Helyas+%22The+Swan-Knight+of+lorraine&source=bl&ots=5FU_0GLFTm&sig=oTbGqlFXWktpyGng4C9pw9S_Lto&hl=en&sa=X&ei=uxuDUOexE4fh0wGN9YCADA&ved=0CDQQ6AEwBDge#v=onepage&q=Helyas%20%22The%20Swan-Knight%20of%20lorraine&f=false

[1652] http://www.1911encyclopedia.org/Lohengrin

[1653] https://rosamondpress.com/2012/05/17/royal-rosamond-had-an-accident/

[1654] https://www.britannica.com/topic/Lohengrin-German-legendary-figure

[1655] https://rosamondpress.com/2012/05/17/royal-rosamond-had-an-accident/

[1656] Ibid.

[1657] https://en.wikipedia.org/wiki/Dietrich_I,_Count_of_Cleves

[1658] fmg.ac/Projects/MedLands/FRANCONIA%20(LOWER%20RHINE).htm#ArnoldIdiedafter1146

[1659] fmg.ac/Projects/MedLands/BRABANT,%20LOUVAIN.htm#IdaLouvaindiedbefore1162

- Count Dietrich (Thierry) III of Clèves married Margaret of Holland [1662] [1663] [1664]

- Count Dietrich (Thierry) IV de Clèves married Mathilde de Dinslaken [1665]

- Count Dietrich (Thierry) de Clèves married Élisabeth de Brabant (d/o Henri I, Duke of Brabant, and Princess Marie of France) [1666] [1667]

Élisabeth was also known as Ysabeau de Brabant; with regards to French records, the name Élisabeth is often used, interchangeably, with that of Isabelle. [1668] [1669]

☐ Mathilda deClèves married Gerard de Luxembourg

☐ Marguerite de Luxembourg married Jean III de Ghistelles

- Jean IV de Ghistelles married Marie de Haverskerke

[1660] fmg.ac/Projects/MedLands/FRANCONIA%20(LOWER%20RHINE).htm#DietrichIIIdied12001203

[1661] fmg.ac/Projects/MedLands/BAVARIAN%20NOBILITY.htm#AdelheidSulzbachdied1189

[1662] fmg.ac/Projects/MedLands/FRANCONIA%20(LOWER%20RHINE).htm#DietrichIIIdied12001203

[1663] fmg.ac/Projects/MedLands/HOLLAND.htm#Margaretadiedafter1203

[1664] https://en.wikipedia.org/wiki/Ada_of_Huntingdon

[1665] fmg.ac/Projects/MedLands/FRANCONIA%20(LOWER%20RHINE).htm#DietrichIVdied1260

[1666] fmg.ac/Projects/MedLands/BRABANT,%20LOUVAIN.htm#Elisabethdied1272

[1667] fmg.ac/Projects/MedLands/FRANCONIA%20(LOWER%20RHINE).htm#Dietrichdied1245

[1668] Jetté, René, DuLong, John P., Gagné, Roland-Yves, Moreau, Gail F. and Dubé, Joseph A. (2001) Table d'ascendance de Catherine Baillon: 12 générations (p 153). Montréal, Québec: Société Généalogique Canadienne Française.

[1669] https://en.wikipedia.org/wiki/Henry_I,_Duke_of_Brabant

■ Roger de Ghistelles married Élisabeth ~~Marguerite~~ de Dudzeele (see page 182 for updated explanation)

☐ Isabelle (Ysabeau) de Ghistelles married Arnould VI de Gavre

☐ Catherine de Gavre d'Escornaix married Guy I Le Bouteiller

■ Guy II Le Bouteillier married Isabeau Morhier

■ Jean Le Bouteillier married Marie de Venois

☐ Bénigne Le Bouteillier married Jacques Maillard

■ Miles Maillard married Marie Morant

☐ Renée Maillard married Adam de Baillon

■ Alphonse de Baillon married Louise de Marle

☐ Catherine de Baillon

Grand Princes of Kiev

In reference to the Princes of Kiev, leading to the birth of the first Russian Empire, Grand Prince Rurik of Kiev is my 33rd great grandfather.

As taken from the webpage *Princes of Kiev* by Robert Sewell [1670]

Rurik, the Viking leader who is traditionally credited with founding the Russian state, was born in Friesland, a region in present-day Holland, which his father controlled. After leading raids in France, England, and Germany, Rurik gained control of a large tract of land in Jutland. Under pressure from the rival chieftains, however, he soon abandoned his claim.

In the 850's, Rurik and his brothers, Sineus and Truvor, led a band of Vikings into northwestern Russia where they established a settlement near Lake Ladoga in what is now northeastern Russia very near the border with Finland.

Rurik moved part of the settlement to nearby Novgorod, according to legend, at the invitation of the local Slavs. It was there he established the seat of his power, building a fortress from which he could rule the Russian lands.

His rule extended as far south as Kiev where his successors founded the powerful Kievan state, which lasted until the 1200's. From Rurik came the house of Rurikovitch which ruled Russia until the end of the 16th century.

- Grand Prince Rurik of Kiev married ---------- [1671]

- Grand Prince Igor of Kiev married ---------- [1672]

[1670] www.robertsewell.ca/kiev.html
[1671] fmg.ac/Projects/MedLands/RUSSIA,%20Rurik.htm#_Toc198014250

- Grand Prince Svyatoslav I of Kiev married ---------- of Hungary [1673] [1674]

- Grand Prince Vladimir I (The Great) of Kiev married Rogned of Polotsk [1675] [1676]

- Grand Prince Yaroslav I (The Wise) of Kiev married Ingigerd Olafsdottir of Sweden [1677] [1678]

- Princess Anna of Kiev married King Henri I of France [1679] [1680]

- King Philippe I of France (1060 to 1108) married Berthe de Holland [1681] [1682]

- King Louis VI of France (1108 to 1137) married Adélaïde de Maurienne [1683] [1684]

- King Louis VII of France (1137 to 1180) married Adèle de Champagne [1685] [1686]

- King Philippe II Auguste of France (1180 to 1223) married <u>thirdly</u> Agnès d'Andechs de Méranie [1687] [1688]

[1672] fmg.ac/Projects/MedLands/RUSSIA,%20Rurik.htm#_Toc198014250
[1673] fmg.ac/Projects/MedLands/RUSSIA,%20Rurik.htm#Sviatoslavdied972
[1674] fmg.ac/Projects/MedLands/HUNGARY.htm#PredslavaMSviatoslavIKiev
[1675] fmg.ac/Projects/MedLands/RUSSIA,%20Rurik.htm#VladimirIdied1015B
[1676] fmg.ac/Projects/MedLands/RUSSIA,%20Rurik.htm#Rognedadied1002
[1677] fmg.ac/Projects/MedLands/RUSSIA,%20Rurik.htm#IaroslavIdied1054B
[1678] fmg.ac/Projects/MedLands/SWEDEN.htm#IngigerdOlafsddied1050
[1679] fmg.ac/Projects/MedLands/RUSSIA,%20Rurik.htm#AnnaIaroslavnadied1075
[1680] fmg.ac/Projects/MedLands/CAPET.htm#HenriIdied1060B
[1681] fmg.ac/Projects/MedLands/CAPET.htm#PhilippeIdied1108B
[1682] fmg.ac/Projects/MedLands/HOLLAND.htm#Berthadied1093
[1683] fmg.ac/Projects/MedLands/CAPET.htm#LouisVIdied1137B
[1684] fmg.ac/Projects/MedLands/SAVOY.htm#Adélaïdedied1154
[1685] fmg.ac/Projects/MedLands/CAPET.htm#LouisVIIdied1180B
[1686] fmg.ac/Projects/MedLands/CENTRAL%20FRANCE.htm#AdeleBloisdied1206
[1687] fmg.ac/Projects/MedLands/CAPET.htm#PhilippeIIdied1223B
[1688] fmg.ac/Projects/MedLands/CARINTHIA.htm#AgnesMeranodied1201

- Princess Marie of France married Henri I, Duke of Brabant[1689] [1690]

- Élisabeth de Brabant marriedCount Dietrich (Thierry) de Clèves [1691] [1692]

Élisabeth was also known as Ysabeau de Brabant; with regards to French records, the name Élisabeth is often used, interchangeably, with that of Isabelle. [1693] [1694]

- Mathilda deClèves married Gerard de Luxembourg

- Marguerite de Luxembourg married Jean III de Ghistelles

- Jean IV de Ghistelles married Marie de Haverskerke

- Roger de Ghistelles married Élisabeth ~~Marguerite~~ de Dudzeele (see page 182 for updated explanation)

- Isabelle (Ysabeau) de Ghistelles married Arnould VI de Gavre

- Catherine de Gavre d'Escornaix married Guy I Le Bouteiller

- Guy II Le Bouteillier married Isabeau Morhier

- Jean Le Bouteillier married Marie de Venois

[1689] fmg.ac/Projects/MedLands/CAPET.htm#Mariedied1238

[1690] fmg.ac/Projects/MedLands/BRABANT,%20LOUVAIN.htm#HenriILotharingiaBrabantdied1235B

[1691] fmg.ac/Projects/MedLands/BRABANT,%20LOUVAIN.htm#Elisabethdied1272

[1692] fmg.ac/Projects/MedLands/FRANCONIA%20(LOWER%20RHINE).htm#Dietrichdied1245

[1693] Jetté, René, DuLong, John P., Gagné, Roland-Yves, Moreau, Gail F. and Dubé, Joseph A. (2001) Table d'ascendance de Catherine Baillon: 12 générations (p 153). Montréal, Québec: Société Généalogique Canadienne Française.

[1694] https://en.wikipedia.org/wiki/Henry_I,_Duke_of_Brabant

☐ Bénigne Le Bouteillier married Jacques Maillard

■ Miles Maillard married Marie Morant

☐ Renée Maillard married Adam de Baillon

■ Alphonse de Baillon married Louise de Marle

☐ Catherine de Baillon

Kings of Sweden

The Kings of Sweden also figure into my research, making King Eric VI my 31st great grandfather.

- King Eric VI (the Victorious) of Sweden married Sigrid [1695]

- King Olof Skötkonung of Sweden married Estred [1696]

- Ingegerd Olofsdotter of Sweden married GrandPrince Yaroslav I (The Wise) of Kiev [1697] [1698]

- Anna of Kiev married King Henri I of France [1699] [1700]

- King Philippe I of France (1060 to 1108) married Berthe de Holland [1701] [1702]

- King Louis VI of France (1108 to 1137) married Adélaïde de Maurienne [1703] [1704]

- King Louis VII of France (1137 to 1180) married Adèle de Champagne [1705] [1706]

[1695] fmg.ac/Projects/MedLands/SWEDEN.htm#_Toc190776896
[1696] fmg.ac/Projects/MedLands/SWEDEN.htm#_Toc190776897
[1697] fmg.ac/Projects/MedLands/SWEDEN.htm#IngigerdOlafsddied1050
[1698] fmg.ac/Projects/MedLands/RUSSIA,%20Rurik.htm#IaroslavIdied1054B
[1699] fmg.ac/Projects/MedLands/RUSSIA,%20Rurik.htm#AnnaIaroslavnadied1075
[1700] fmg.ac/Projects/MedLands/CAPET.htm#HenriIdied1060B
[1701] fmg.ac/Projects/MedLands/CAPET.htm#PhilippeIdied1108B
[1702] fmg.ac/Projects/MedLands/HOLLAND.htm#Berthadied1093
[1703] fmg.ac/Projects/MedLands/CAPET.htm#LouisVIdied1137B
[1704] fmg.ac/Projects/MedLands/SAVOY.htm#Adélaïdedied1154
[1705] fmg.ac/Projects/MedLands/CAPET.htm#LouisVIIdied1180B
[1706] fmg.ac/Projects/MedLands/CENTRAL%20FRANCE.htm#AdeleBloisdied1206

- King Philippe II Auguste of France (1180 to 1223) married <u>thirdly</u> Agnès d'Andechs de Méranie [1707] [1708]

▢ Princess Marie of France married Henri I, Duke of Brabant [1709] [1710]

▢ Élisabeth de Brabant married Count Dietrich (Thierry) de Clèves [1711] [1712]

Élisabeth was also known as Ysabeau de Brabant; with regards to French records, the name Élisabeth is often used, interchangeably, with that of Isabelle. [1713] [1714]

▢ Mathilda de Clèves married Gerard de Luxembourg

▢ Marguerite de Luxembourg married Jean III de Ghistelles

- Jean IV de Ghistelles married Marie de Haverskerke

- Roger de Ghistelles married Élisabeth ~~Marguerite~~ de Dudzeele (see page 182 for updated explanation)

▢ Isabelle (Ysabeau) de Ghistelles married Arnould VI de Gavre

▢ Catherine de Gavre d'Escornaix married Guy I Le Bouteiller

[1707] fmg.ac/Projects/MedLands/CAPET.htm#PhilippeIIdied1223B
[1708] fmg.ac/Projects/MedLands/CARINTHIA.htm#AgnesMeranodied1201
[1709] fmg.ac/Projects/MedLands/CAPET.htm#Mariedied1238
[1710] fmg.ac/Projects/MedLands/BRABANT,%20LOUVAIN.htm#HenriILotharingiaBrabantdied1235B
[1711] fmg.ac/Projects/MedLands/BRABANT,%20LOUVAIN.htm#Elisabethdied1272
[1712] fmg.ac/Projects/MedLands/FRANCONIA%20(LOWER%20RHINE).htm#Dietrichdied1245
[1713] Jetté, René, DuLong, John P., Gagné, Roland-Yves, Moreau, Gail F. and Dubé, Joseph A. (2001) <u>Table d'ascendance de Catherine Baillon: 12 générations</u> (p 153). Montréal, Québec: Société Généalogique Canadienne Française.
[1714] https://en.wikipedia.org/wiki/Henry_I,_Duke_of_Brabant

- Guy II Le Bouteillier married Isabeau Morhier

- Jean Le Bouteillier married Marie de Venois

- Bénigne Le Bouteillier married Jacques Maillard

- Miles Maillard married Marie Morant

- Renée Maillard married Adam de Baillon

- Alphonse de Baillon married Louise de Marle

- Catherine de Baillon

Ottonian Dynasty

As denoted on Wikipedia [1715]

The Ottonian dynasty was a dynasty of Germanic Kings (919-1024), named after its first emperor but also known as the Saxon dynasty after the family's origin. The family itself is also sometimes known as the Liudolfings, after its earliest known member Liudolf and one of its primary leading-names.

The Ottonian rulers are also regarded as the first dynasty of the Holy Roman Empire, as successors of the Frankish Carolingian dynasty and Charlemagne, who is commonly viewed as the founder of the Holy Roman Empire.

King Henry I (The Fowler) of Germany is my 32nd great grandfather.

- Duke Liudolf of Saxony married Oda [1716] [1717]

- Duke Otto I of Saxony married Hedwig [1718] [1719]

- King Henry I (The Fowler) of Germany married Mathilde [1720] [1721]

- Hedwige of Saxony married Hugues the Great, Duke of France [1722] [1723]

[1715] https://en.wikipedia.org/wiki/Ottonian_dynasty
[1716] fmg.ac/Projects/MedLands/SAXONY.htm#Liudolfdied866B
[1717] fmg.ac/Projects/MedLands/SAXONY.htm#Odadied913
[1718] fmg.ac/Projects/MedLands/SAXONY.htm#OttoErlauchtedied912
[1719] fmg.ac/Projects/MedLands/FRANCONIA.htm#Hedwigdied903
[1720] fmg.ac/Projects/MedLands/GERMANY,%20Kings.htm#HeinrichIGermanydied936B
[1721] fmg.ac/Projects/MedLands/SAXONY.htm#Mathildedied968

- King Hugues Capet of France (987 to 996) married Adélaïde d'Aquitaine [1724] [1725]

- King Robert II of France (996 to 1031) married Constance d'Arles [1726] [1727]

- King Henri I of France (1031 to 1060) married Anne de Kiev [1728] [1729]

- King Philippe I of France (1060 to 1108) married Berthe de Holland [1730] [1731]

- King Louis VI of France (1108 to 1137) married Adélaïde de Maurienne [1732] [1733]

- King Louis VII of France (1137 to 1180) married Adèle de Champagne [1734] [1735]

- King Philippe II Auguste of France (1180 to 1223) married <u>thirdly</u> Agnès d'Andechs de Méranie [1736] [1737]

    ☐ Princess Marie of Francemarried Henri I, Duke of Brabant [1738] [1739]

[1722] fmg.ac/Projects/MedLands/GERMANY,%20Kings.htm#HedwigMHuguesRegentFrancedied956
[1723] fmg.ac/Projects/MedLands/CAPET.htm#Huguesdied956B
[1724] fmg.ac/Projects/MedLands/CAPET.htm#HuguesCapetdied996B
[1725] fmg.ac/Projects/MedLands/AQUITAINE.htm#Adelaisdied1004
[1726] fmg.ac/Projects/MedLands/CAPET.htm#RobertIIdied1031B
[1727] fmg.ac/Projects/MedLands/PROVENCE.htm#ConstanceArlesMRobertIIFrancedied1031
[1728] fmg.ac/Projects/MedLands/CAPET.htm#HenriIdied1060B
[1729] fmg.ac/Projects/MedLands/RUSSIA,%20Rurik.htm#AnnaIaroslavnadied1075
[1730] fmg.ac/Projects/MedLands/CAPET.htm#PhilippeIdied1108B
[1731] fmg.ac/Projects/MedLands/HOLLAND.htm#Berthadied1093
[1732] fmg.ac/Projects/MedLands/CAPET.htm#LouisVIdied1137B
[1733] fmg.ac/Projects/MedLands/SAVOY.htm#Adélaïdedied1154
[1734] fmg.ac/Projects/MedLands/CAPET.htm#LouisVIIdied1180B
[1735] fmg.ac/Projects/MedLands/CENTRAL%20FRANCE.htm#AdeleBloisdied1206
[1736] fmg.ac/Projects/MedLands/CAPET.htm#PhilippeIIdied1223B
[1737] fmg.ac/Projects/MedLands/CARINTHIA.htm#AgnesMeranodied1201
[1738] fmg.ac/Projects/MedLands/CAPET.htm#Mariedied1238

☐ Élisabeth de Brabant married Count Dietrich (Thierry) de Clèves [1740] [1741]

Élisabeth was also known as Ysabeau de Brabant; with regards to French records, the name Élisabeth is often used, interchangeably, with that of Isabelle. [1742] [1743]

☐ Mathilda de Clèves married Gerard de Luxembourg

☐ Marguerite de Luxembourg married Jean III de Ghistelles

■ Jean IV de Ghistelles married Marie de Haverskerke

■ Roger de Ghistelles married Élisabeth ~~Marguerite~~ de Dudzeele (see page 182 for updated explanation)

☐ Isabelle (Ysabeau) de Ghistelles married Arnould VI de Gavre

☐ Catherine de Gavre d'Escornaix married Guy I Le Bouteiller

■ Guy II Le Bouteillier married Isabeau Morhier

■ Jean Le Bouteillier married Marie de Venois

☐ Bénigne Le Bouteilier married Jacques Maillard

[1739] fmg.ac/Projects/MedLands/BRABANT,%20LOUVAIN.htm#HenriILotharingiaBrabantdied1235B

[1740] fmg.ac/Projects/MedLands/BRABANT,%20LOUVAIN.htm#Elisabethdied1272

[1741] fmg.ac/Projects/MedLands/FRANCONIA%20(LOWER%20RHINE).htm#Dietrichdied1245

[1742] Jetté, René, DuLong, John P., Gagné, Roland-Yves, Moreau, Gail F. and Dubé, Joseph A. (2001) Table d'ascendance de Catherine Baillon: 12 générations (p 153). Montréal, Québec: Société Généalogique Canadienne Française.

[1743] https://en.wikipedia.org/wiki/Henry_I,_Duke_of_Brabant

- Miles Maillard married Marie Morant

  ☐ Renée Maillard married Adam de Baillon

- Alphonse de Baillon married Louise de Marle

  ☐ Catherine de Baillon

In keeping with the Ottonian dynasty, there exists a second line of descent.

- Duke Liudolf of Saxony married Oda [1744] [1745] [1746]

- Duke Otto I of Saxony married Hedwig [1747] [1748]

- King Henry I (The Fowler) of Germany married Mathilde [1749] [1750]

- ☐ Gerberga of Saxony married King Louis IV of France [1751] [1752]

- Prince Charles, Duke of Lower Lorraine, married Adélaïs de Troyes [1753] [1754]

- ☐ Gerberga of Lower Lorraine married Count Lambert I of Leuven [1755] [1756]

- Count Lambert II of Leuven married Uda de Lotharingia [1757] [1758]

[1744] fmg.ac/Projects/MedLands/SAXONY.htm#Liudolfdied866B
[1745] fmg.ac/Projects/MedLands/SAXONY.htm#Odadied913
[1746] https://en.wikipedia.org/wiki/Billung
[1747] fmg.ac/Projects/MedLands/SAXONY.htm#OttoErlauchtedied912
[1748] fmg.ac/Projects/MedLands/FRANCONIA.htm#Hedwigdied903
[1749] fmg.ac/Projects/MedLands/GERMANY,%20Kings.htm#HeinrichIGermanydied936B
[1750] fmg.ac/Projects/MedLands/SAXONY.htm#Mathildedied968
[1751] fmg.ac/Projects/MedLands/GERMANY,%20Kings.htm#GerbergaM1GiselbertLorraineM2LouisIVFran
[1752] fmg.ac/Projects/MedLands/CAROLINGIANS.htm#LouisIVFranceB
[1753] fmg.ac/Projects/MedLands/LOTHARINGIA.htm#CharlesdukeLowerLothringiadied991
[1754] fmg.ac/Projects/MedLands/CHAMPAGNE%20NOBILITY.htm#dauRobertM970CharlesFrance
[1755] fmg.ac/Projects/MedLands/LOTHARINGIA.htm#GerbergaMLambertILouvaindied1015
[1756] fmg.ac/Projects/MedLands/BRABANT,%20LOUVAIN.htm#LambertILouvaindied1015
[1757] fmg.ac/Projects/MedLands/BRABANT,%20LOUVAIN.htm#LambertIILouvaindiedafterSep1062B

- Count Henry II of Leuven married Adelheid [1759] [1760]

- Count Godfrey I of Leuven, Duke of Lower Lotharingia married Ida de Chiny [1761] [1762]

- Count Godfrey II of Leuven, Duke of Lower Lotharingia married Lutgardis von Sulzbach [1763] [1764]

- Count Godfrey III of Leuven, Duke of Lower Lotharingia married Margareta van Limburg [1765] [1766]

- Duke Henri I of Brabant married Princess Marie of France [1767] [1768]

- Élisabeth de Brabant married Count Dietrich (Thierry) de Clèves [1769] [1770]

[1758] fmg.ac/Projects/MedLands/LOTHARINGIA.htm#UdaMLambertIIILouvain
[1759] fmg.ac/Projects/MedLands/BRABANT,%20LOUVAIN.htm#HenriIIILouvaindied1078
[1760] fmg.ac/Projects/MedLands/HOLLAND.htm#AdelheidMHenriIILouvaindiedafter1086
[1761] fmg.ac/Projects/MedLands/BRABANT,%20LOUVAIN.htm#GodefroiILouvainVLowLothdied1139B
[1762] fmg.ac/Projects/MedLands/LOTHARINGIAN%20(UPPER)%20NOBILITY.htm#IdaChimaydiedbefore1125MGodefroiBrabant
[1763] fmg.ac/Projects/MedLands/BRABANT,%20LOUVAIN.htm#GodefroiVILowLothdied1142
[1764] fmg.ac/Projects/MedLands/BAVARIAN%20NOBILITY.htm#LutgardisSulzbachdiedafter1162
[1765] fmg.ac/Projects/MedLands/BRABANT,%20LOUVAIN.htm#GodefroiVIILowLothdied1190B
[1766] fmg.ac/Projects/MedLands/LIMBURG.htm#Margueritedied1172
[1767] fmg.ac/Projects/MedLands/BRABANT,%20LOUVAIN.htm#HenriILotharingiaBrabantdied1235B
[1768] fmg.ac/Projects/MedLands/CAPET.htm#Mariedied1238

Élisabeth was also known as Ysabeau de Brabant; with regards to French records, the name Élisabeth is often used, interchangeably, with that of Isabelle. [1771] [1772]

☐ Mathilda de Clèves married Gerard de Luxembourg

☐ Marguerite de Luxembourg married Jean III de Ghistelles

■ Jean IV de Ghistelles married Marie de Haverskerke

■ Roger de Ghistelles married Élisabeth ~~Marguerite~~ de Dudzeele (see page 182 for updated explanation)

☐ Isabelle (Ysabeau) de Ghistelles married Arnould VI de Gavre

☐ Catherine de Gavre d'Escornaix married Guy I Le Bouteiller

■ Guy II Le Bouteillier married Isabeau Morhier

■ Jean Le Bouteillier married Marie de Venois

☐ Bénigne Le Bouteillier married Jacques Maillard

■ Miles Maillard married Marie Morant

☐ Renée Maillard married Adam de Baillon

■ Alphonse de Baillon married Louise de Marle

[1769] fmg.ac/Projects/MedLands/BRABANT,%20LOUVAIN.htm#Elisabethdied1272
[1770] fmg.ac/Projects/MedLands/FRANCONIA%20(LOWER%20RHINE).htm#Dietrichdied1245
[1771] Jetté, René, Dulong, John P., Gagné, Roland-Yves, Moreau, Gail F. and Dubé, Joseph A. (2001) Table d'ascendance de Catherine Baillon: 12 générations (p 153). Montréal, Québec: Société Généalogique Canadienne Française.
[1772] https://en.wikipedia.org/wiki/Henry_I,_Duke_of_Brabant

☐ Catherine de Baillon

In keeping with the Ottonian dynasty, there exists a third line of descent.

- Duke Liudolf of Saxony married Oda [1773] [1774] [1775]

- Duke Otto I of Saxony married Hedwig [1776] [1777]

- King Henry I (The Fowler) of Germany married Mathilde [1778] [1779]

- ☐ Gerberga of Saxony married King Louis IV of France [1780] [1781]

- ☐ Princess Matilda of France married King Conrad (The Peaceful) of Burgundy [1782] [1783]

- ☐ Bertha of Burgundy married Count Odo (Eudes) I of Blois [1784] [1785]

- Count Odo (Eudes) II of Blois married Ermengarde d'Auvergne [1786] [1787]

- Count Stephen I of Blois married Adèle of Normandy [1788]

[1773] fmg.ac/Projects/MedLands/SAXONY.htm#Liudolfdied866B
[1774] fmg.ac/Projects/MedLands/SAXONY.htm#Odadied913
[1775] https://en.wikipedia.org/wiki/Billung
[1776] fmg.ac/Projects/MedLands/SAXONY.htm#OttoErlauchtedied912
[1777] fmg.ac/Projects/MedLands/FRANCONIA.htm#Hedwigdied903
[1778] fmg.ac/Projects/MedLands/GERMANY,%20Kings.htm#HeinrichIGermanydied936B
[1779] fmg.ac/Projects/MedLands/SAXONY.htm#Mathildedied968
[1780] fmg.ac/Projects/MedLands/GERMANY,%20Kings.htm#GerbergaM1GiselbertLorraineM2LouisIVFran
[1781] fmg.ac/Projects/MedLands/CAROLINGIANS.htm#LouisIVFranceB
[1782] fmg.ac/Projects/MedLands/CAROLINGIANS.htm#MathildeMConradIBurgundy
[1783] fmg.ac/Projects/MedLands/BURGUNDY%20KINGS.htm#ConradIBurgundydied993B
[1784] fmg.ac/Projects/MedLands/BURGUNDY%20KINGS.htm#BertheM1EudesIBloisM2RobertIIFrance
[1785] fmg.ac/Projects/MedLands/CENTRAL%20FRANCE.htm#EudesIdied995
[1786] fmg.ac/Projects/MedLands/CENTRAL%20FRANCE.htm#EudesIIdied1037B
[1787] fmg.ac/Projects/MedLands/AUVERGNE.htm#ErmengardeAuvergnediedafter1042

■ Count Theobald III (The Great) of Champagne (Theobald IV of Blois) married Matilda von Sponheim [1789] [1790]

☐ Adèle (Alix) of Champagne married King Louis VII of France [1791] [1792]

■ King Philippe II Auguste of France (1180 to 1223) married <u>thirdly</u> Agnès d'Andechs de Méranie [1793] [1794]

☐ Princess Marie of France married Henri I, Duke of Brabant [1795] [1796]

☐ Élisabeth de Brabant married Count Dietrich (Thierry) de Clèves [1797] [1798]

Élisabeth was also known as Ysabeau de Brabant; with regards to French records, the name Élisabeth is often used, interchangeably, with that of Isabelle. [1799] [1800]

☐ Mathilda de Clèves married Gerard de Luxembourg

[1788] fmg.ac/Projects/MedLands/CHAMPAGNE%20NOBILITY.htm#EtienneITroyesdied1048B
[1789] fmg.ac/Projects/MedLands/CENTRAL%20FRANCE.htm#ThibautIVdied1152B
[1790] fmg.ac/Projects/MedLands/CARINTHIA.htm#Mathildedied1160
[1791] fmg.ac/Projects/MedLands/CENTRAL%20FRANCE.htm#AdeleBloisdied1206
[1792] fmg.ac/Projects/MedLands/CAPET.htm#LouisVIIdied1180B
[1793] fmg.ac/Projects/MedLands/CAPET.htm#PhilippeIIdied1223B
[1794] fmg.ac/Projects/MedLands/CARINTHIA.htm#AgnesMeranodied1201
[1795] fmg.ac/Projects/MedLands/CAPET.htm#Mariedied1238
[1796] fmg.ac/Projects/MedLands/BRABANT,%20LOUVAIN.htm#HenriILotharingiaBrabantdied1235B
[1797] fmg.ac/Projects/MedLands/BRABANT,%20LOUVAIN.htm#Elisabethdied1272
[1798] fmg.ac/Projects/MedLands/FRANCONIA%20(LOWER%20RHINE).htm#Dietrichdied1245
[1799] Jetté, René, DuLong, John P., Gagné, Roland-Yves, Moreau, Gail F. and Dubé, Joseph A. (2001) <u>Table d'ascendance de Catherine Baillon: 12 générations</u> (p 153). Montréal, Québec: Société Généalogique Canadienne Française.
[1800] https://en.wikipedia.org/wiki/Henry_I,_Duke_of_Brabant

☐ Marguerite de Luxembourg married Jean III de Ghistelles

■ Jean IV de Ghistelles married Marie de Haverskerke

■ Roger de Ghistelles married Élisabeth ~~Marguerite~~ de Dudzeele (see page 182 for updated explanation)

☐ Isabelle (Ysabeau) de Ghistelles married Arnould VI de Gavre

☐ Catherine de Gavre d'Escornaix married Guy I Le Bouteiller

■ Guy II Le Bouteillier married Isabeau Morhier

■ Jean Le Bouteillier married Marie de Venois

☐ Bénigne Le Bouteillier married Jacques Maillard

■ Miles Maillard married Marie Morant

☐ Renée Maillard married Adam de Baillon

■ Alphonse de Baillon married Louise de Marle

☐ Catherine de Baillon

House of Billung

The House of Billung was a dynasty of Saxon noblemen in the 9th through 12th centuries, making Hermann Billung, Margrave of Saxony, my 32nd great grandfather.

- Billung von Stubenskorn (c. 860-967) [1801] [1802]

- Hermann Billung, Margrave of Saxony married Oda [1803]

- Duke Bernard I of Saxony married married Hildegard von Stade [1804] [1805]

- Duke Bernard II of Saxony married Eilika von Schweinfurt [1806] [1807]

- ☐ Gertrude of Saxony married Count Floris I de Frisia [1808] [1809]

- Count Dirk V de Frisia married Othelindis [1810]

- Count Floris II de Holland married Gertrude (Petronella) de Lorraine [1811] [1812]

- Count Dirk IV de Holland married Sophie von Rheineck [1813] [1814]

[1801] fmg.ac/Projects/MedLands/SAXONY.htm#_Toc155952301
[1802] https://en.wikipedia.org/wiki/Billung
[1803] fmg.ac/Projects/MedLands/SAXONY.htm#_Toc155952301
[1804] fmg.ac/Projects/MedLands/SAXONY.htm#BernhardIdied1011B
[1805] fmg.ac/Projects/MedLands/SAXON%20NOBILITY.htm#HildegardeStadedied1011
[1806] fmg.ac/Projects/MedLands/SAXONY.htm#BernhardIIdied1059
[1807] fmg.ac/Projects/MedLands/BAVARIAN%20NOBILITY.htm#EilikaSchweinfurtdied1055
[1808] fmg.ac/Projects/MedLands/SAXONY.htm#Gertruddied1113
[1809] fmg.ac/Projects/MedLands/HOLLAND.htm#FlorisIdied1061
[1810] fmg.ac/Projects/MedLands/HOLLAND.htm#_Toc181670222
[1811] fmg.ac/Projects/MedLands/HOLLAND.htm#FlorisIIdied1121B
[1812] fmg.ac/Projects/MedLands/LORRAINE.htm#GertrudePetronilladied1144

■ Count Floris III de Holland married Ada of Huntingdon (d/o Henry of Scotland and Ada of Warenne) [1815] [1816] [1817] [1818] [1819]

☐ Marguerite of Holland married Count Dietrich (Thierry) V de Clèves [1820] [1821]

■ Count Dietrich (Thierry) VI de Clèves married Mathilde de Dinslaken [1822]

■ Count Dietrich (Thierry) de Clèves married Élisabeth de Brabant (d/o Henri I, Duke of Brabant, and Princess Marie de France) [1823] [1824]

Élisabeth was also known as Ysabeau de Brabant; with regards to French records, the name Élisabeth is often used, interchangeably, with that of Isabelle. [1825] [1826]

☐ Mathilda deClèves married Gerard de Luxembourg

[1813] fmg.ac/Projects/MedLands/HOLLAND.htm#DirkVIdied1157
[1814] fmg.ac/Projects/MedLands/FRANCONIA.htm#SophieRheineckdied1176
[1815] fmg.ac/Projects/MedLands/HOLLAND.htm#FlorisIIIdied1190
[1816] fmg.ac/Projects/MedLands/SCOTLAND.htm#Adadiedafter11Jan1205
[1817] https://en.wikipedia.org/wiki/Floris_III,_Count_of_Holland
[1818] https://en.wikipedia.org/wiki/Ada_of_Huntingdon
[1819] https://en.wikipedia.org/wiki/Counts_of_Holland
[1820] fmg.ac/Projects/MedLands/HOLLAND.htm#Margaretadiedafter1203
[1821] fmg.ac/Projects/MedLands/FRANCONIA%20(LOWER%20RHINE).htm#DietrichIIIdied12001203
[1822] fmg.ac/Projects/MedLands/FRANCONIA%20(LOWER%20RHINE).htm#DietrichIVdied1260
[1823] fmg.ac/Projects/MedLands/BRABANT,%20LOUVAIN.htm#Elisabethdied1272
[1824] fmg.ac/Projects/MedLands/FRANCONIA%20(LOWER%20RHINE).htm#Dietrichdied1245
[1825] Jetté, René, DuLong, John P., Gagné, Roland-Yves, Moreau, Gail F. and Dubé, Joseph A. (2001) Table d'ascendance de Catherine Baillon: 12 générations (p 153). Montréal, Québec: Société Généalogique Canadienne Française.
[1826] https://en.wikipedia.org/wiki/Henry_I,_Duke_of_Brabant

☐ Marguerite de Luxembourg married Jean III de Ghistelles

■ Jean IV de Ghistelles married Marie de Haverskerke

■ Roger de Ghistelles married Élisabeth ~~Marguerite~~ de Dudzeele (see page 182 for updated explanation)

☐ Isabelle (Ysabeau) de Ghistelles married Arnould VI de Gavre

☐ Catherine de Gavre d'Escornaix married Guy I Le Bouteiller

■ Guy II Le Bouteillier married Isabeau Morhier

■ Jean Le Bouteillier married Marie de Venois

☐ Bénigne Le Bouteillier married Jacques Maillard

■ Miles Maillard married Marie Morant

☐ Renée Maillard married Adam de Baillon

■ Alphonse de Baillon married Louise de Marle

☐ Catherine de Baillon

In keeping with the House of Billung, there exists a second line of descent.

- Billung von Stubenskorn (c. 860-967) [1827] [1828]

- Hermann Billung, Margrave of Saxony married Oda [1829]

  ☐ Mathilda married Count Godrey I of Verdun [1830] [1831]

- Count Gozelon I, Duke of Upper Lotharingia married ---------- [1832]

  ☐ Uda of Lotharingia (sometimes called Oda of Verdun) married Count Lambert II of Leuven [1833] [1834]

- Count Henry II of Leuven married Adelheid [1835] [1836]

- Count Godfrey I of Leuven, Duke of Lower Lotharingia married Ida de Chiny [1837] [1838]

[1827] fmg.ac/Projects/MedLands/SAXONY.htm#_Toc155952301
[1828] https://en.wikipedia.org/wiki/Billung
[1829] fmg.ac/Projects/MedLands/SAXONY.htm#_Toc155952301
[1830] fmg.ac/Projects/MedLands/SAXONY.htm#Mechtilddied1008
[1831] fmg.ac/Projects/MedLands/LOTHARINGIAN%20(UPPER)%20NOBILITY.htm#Godefroidied995B
[1832] fmg.ac/Projects/MedLands/LOTHARINGIA.htm#Gozelondied1044A
[1833] fmg.ac/Projects/MedLands/LOTHARINGIA.htm#UdaMLambertIIILouvain
[1834] fmg.ac/Projects/MedLands/BRABANT,%20LOUVAIN.htm#LambertIIILouvaindiedafterSep1062B
[1835] fmg.ac/Projects/MedLands/BRABANT,%20LOUVAIN.htm#HenriIIILouvaindied1078
[1836] fmg.ac/Projects/MedLands/HOLLAND.htm#AdelheidMHenriIIILouvaindiedafter1086
[1837] fmg.ac/Projects/MedLands/BRABANT,%20LOUVAIN.htm#GodefroiILouvainVLowLothdied1139B

- Count Godfrey II of Leuven, Duke of Lower Lotharingia married Lutgardis von Sulzbach [1839] [1840]

- Count Godfrey III of Leuven, Duke of Lower Lotharingia married Margareta van Limburg [1841] [1842]

- Duke Henri I of Brabant married Princess Marie of France [1843] [1844]

☐ Élisabeth de Brabant married Count Dietrich (Thierry) de Clèves [1845] [1846]

Élisabeth was also known as Ysabeau de Brabant; with regards to French records, the name Élisabeth is often used, interchangeably, with that of Isabelle. [1847] [1848]

[1838] fmg.ac/Projects/MedLands/LOTHARINGIAN%20(UPPER)%20NOBILITY.htm#IdaChimaydiedbefore1125MGodefroiBrabant

[1839] fmg.ac/Projects/MedLands/BRABANT,%20LOUVAIN.htm#GodefroiVILowLothdied1142

[1840] fmg.ac/Projects/MedLands/BAVARIAN%20NOBILITY.htm#LutgardisSulzbachdiedafter1162

[1841] fmg.ac/Projects/MedLands/BRABANT,%20LOUVAIN.htm#GodefroiVIILowLothdied1190B

[1842] fmg.ac/Projects/MedLands/LIMBURG.htm#Margueritedied1172

[1843] fmg.ac/Projects/MedLands/BRABANT,%20LOUVAIN.htm#HenriILotharingiaBrabantdied1235B

[1844] fmg.ac/Projects/MedLands/CAPET.htm#Mariedied1238

[1845] fmg.ac/Projects/MedLands/BRABANT,%20LOUVAIN.htm#Elisabethdied1272

[1846] fmg.ac/Projects/MedLands/FRANCONIA%20(LOWER%20RHINE).htm#Dietrichdied1245

[1847] Jetté, René, Dulong, John P., Gagné, Roland-Yves, Moreau, Gail F. and Dubé, Joseph A. (2001) Table d'ascendance de Catherine Baillon: 12 générations (p 153). Montréal, Québec: Société Généalogique Canadienne Française.

[1848] https://en.wikipedia.org/wiki/Henry_I,_Duke_of_Brabant

☐ Mathilda de Clèves married Gerard de Luxembourg

☐ Marguerite de Luxembourg married Jean III de Ghistelles

■ Jean IV de Ghistelles married Marie de Haverskerke

■ Roger de Ghistelles married Élisabeth ~~Marguerite~~ de Dudzeele (see page 182 for updated explanation)

☐ Isabelle (Ysabeau) de Ghistelles married Arnould VI de Gavre

☐ Catherine de Gavre d'Escornaix married Guy I Le Bouteiller

■ Guy II Le Bouteillier married Isabeau Morhier

■ Jean Le Bouteillier married Marie de Venois

☐ Bénigne Le Bouteillier married Jacques Maillard

■ Miles Maillard married Marie Morant

☐ Renée Maillard married Adam de Baillon

■ Alphonse de Baillon married Louise de Marle

☐ Catherine de Baillon

Counts of Leuven

As denoted on Wikipedia [1849]

Near the end of the 10th century, the County of Leuven emerged when granted to Lambert I by the German Emperor. Originally limited by the rivers Demer, Dijle and Velp, more or less the region known today as Hageland, the County of Leuven rapidly increased in size and power.

After his marriage with Gerberga, the daughter of the Duke of Lower Lorraine, Lambert I incorporated the County of Brussels. In 1013, Lambert I annexed the Duchy of Bruningrode, located around Tongeren.

They acquired great influence in the Holy Roman Empire and acquired more titles over time. In 1183, they were created Dukes of Brabant.

The county of Leuven was absorbed into the Duchy of Brabant.

- Count Lambert I of Leuven married Gerberga of Lower Lorraine [1850] [1851]

- Count Lambert II of Leuven married Uda de Lotharingia [1852] [1853]

- Count Henry II of Leuven married Adelheid [1854] [1855]

[1849] https://en.wikipedia.org/wiki/Counts_of_Leuven
[1850] fmg.ac/Projects/MedLands/BRABANT,%20LOUVAIN.htm#LambertILouvaindied1015
[1851] fmg.ac/Projects/MedLands/LOTHARINGIA.htm#GerbergaMLambertILouvaindied1015
[1852] fmg.ac/Projects/MedLands/BRABANT,%20LOUVAIN.htm#LambertIILouvaindiedafterSep1062B
[1853] fmg.ac/Projects/MedLands/LOTHARINGIA.htm#UdaMLambertIILouvain

- Count Godfrey I of Leuven, Duke of Lower Lotharingia married Ida de Chiny [1856] [1857]

- Count Godfrey II of Leuven, Duke of Lower Lotharingia married Lutgardis von Sulzbach [1858] [1859]

- Count Godfrey III of Leuven, Duke of Lower Lotharingia married Margareta van Limburg [1860] [1861]

- Duke Henri I of Brabant married Princess Marie of France [1862] [1863]

- Élisabeth de Brabant marriedCount Dietrich (Thierry) de Clèves [1864] [1865]

[1854] fmg.ac/Projects/MedLands/BRABANT,%20LOUVAIN.htm#HenriIIILouvaindied1078
[1855] fmg.ac/Projects/MedLands/HOLLAND.htm#AdelheidMHenriIIILouvaindiedafter1086
[1856] fmg.ac/Projects/MedLands/BRABANT,%20LOUVAIN.htm#GodefroiILouvainVLowLothdied1139B
[1857] fmg.ac/Projects/MedLands/LOTHARINGIAN%20(UPPER)%20NOBILITY.htm#IdaChimaydiedbefore1125MGodefroiBrabant
[1858] fmg.ac/Projects/MedLands/BRABANT,%20LOUVAIN.htm#GodefroiVILowLothdied1142
[1859] fmg.ac/Projects/MedLands/BAVARIAN%20NOBILITY.htm#LutgardisSulzbachdiedafter1162
[1860] fmg.ac/Projects/MedLands/BRABANT,%20LOUVAIN.htm#GodefroiVIILowLothdied1190B
[1861] fmg.ac/Projects/MedLands/LIMBURG.htm#Margueritedied1172
[1862] fmg.ac/Projects/MedLands/BRABANT,%20LOUVAIN.htm#HenriILotharingiaBrabantdied1235B
[1863] fmg.ac/Projects/MedLands/CAPET.htm#Mariedied1238
[1864] fmg.ac/Projects/MedLands/BRABANT,%20LOUVAIN.htm#Elisabethdied1272
[1865] fmg.ac/Projects/MedLands/FRANCONIA%20(LOWER%20RHINE).htm#Dietrichdied1245

Élisabeth was also known as Ysabeau de Brabant; with regards to French records, the name Élisabeth is often used, interchangeably, with that of Isabelle. [1866] [1867]

☐ Mathilda deClèves married Gerard de Luxembourg

☐ Marguerite de Luxembourg married Jean III de Ghistelles

■ Jean IV de Ghistelles married Marie de Haverskerke

■ Roger de Ghistelles married Élisabeth ~~Marguerite~~ de Dudzeele (see page 182 for updated explanation)

☐ Isabelle (Ysabeau) de Ghistelles married Arnould VI de Gavre

☐ Catherine de Gavre d'Escornaix married Guy I Le Bouteiller

■ Guy II Le Bouteillier married Isabeau Morhier

■ Jean Le Bouteillier married Marie de Venois

☐ Bénigne Le Bouteillier married Jacques Maillard

■ Miles Maillard married Marie Morant

☐ Renée Maillard married Adam de Baillon

■ Alphonse de Baillon married Louise de Marle

☐ Catherine de Baillon

[1866] Jetté, René, Dulong, John P., Gagné, Roland-Yves, Moreau, Gail F. and Dubé, Joseph A. (2001) Table d'ascendance de Catherine Baillon: 12 générations (p 153). Montréal, Québec: Société Généalogique Canadienne Française.
[1867] https://en.wikipedia.org/wiki/Henry_I,_Duke_of_Brabant

Lambert and Gerberga of Lower Lorraine

Source: https://en.wikipedia.org/wiki/File:Lambert_Gerberga.jpg

Ardennes Verdun Dynasty

The Ardennes-Verdun dynasty is used as a label on the dynasty centered on Verdun who dominated Lotharingia in the 11th century.

The founder of the dynasty was Godfrey, known as the Captive. Godfrey was the brother of Adalbero, Archbishop of Reims. [1868]

Adalberon was also the chancellor of Kings Lothair and Louis V of France.

Upon the death of Louis V, in 987, Adalberon and Gerbert of Aurillac addressed the electoral assembly at Senlis in favour of Hugh Capet, to replace the Carolingian monarch. [1869]

It was Adalberon who pleaded ... *Crown the Duke. He is most illustrious by his exploits, his nobility*, his *forces. The throne is not acquired by hereditary right; no one should be raised to it unless distinguished not only for nobility of birth, but for the goodness of his soul.* Capet was elected and crowned at Noyon, on July 3, 987, by Adalberon. [1870]

The County of Verdun was given to Godfrey by Emperor Otto I between 944 and 951, and was held by several dynasty members over the following four generations. [1871] The Duchies of Upper and Lower Lorraine were the result of the division of the old kingdom, later duchy of Lotharingia in 959. [1872]

[1868] https://en.wikipedia.org/wiki/Godfrey_I,_Count_of_Verdun
[1869] https://en.wikipedia.org/wiki/Adalberon,_Archbishop_of_Reims
[1870] Ibid.
[1871] https://en.wikipedia.org/wiki/House_of_Ardennes-Verdun
[1872] Ibid.

Following the death of the childless Duke Otto in 1012, Godfrey the Childless was granted the Duchy of Lower Lorraine, after which Godfrey was succeeded in 1023 by his brother Gozelo, who also became Duke of Upper Lorraine in 1033. [1873]

Both duchies were in the control of the dynasty until 1046, when the rebellions of Godfrey the Beareded led to the loss of both titles. [1874] Godfrey was finally restored to Lower Lorraine in 1065, and passed this on to his son, Godfrey the Hunchback. [1875]

The *Crusader Godfrey of Bouillon* was a nephew of Godfrey the Hunchback, and the last of the dynasty to hold the Duchy. [1876]

The Castle of Bouillon is first mentioned in 988 in a letter to Godfrey the Captive from his brother Adalberon, Archbishop of Reims; it is believed that this castle, and the estate connected, was an original patrimony of the dynasty. [1877]

Bouillon was one of the central points of the dynasty's power, and was in their possession until it was sold by Godfey of Bouillon to cover expenses for the First Crusade. [1878]

■ Wigeric, Count Palatine of Lotharingia, married Cunigunde (granddaughter of King Louis II of France) [1879] [1880] [1881]

■ Count Gozelon of Bidgau and Methingau (brother of Adalbero, Bishop of Metz) married Uda of Metz [1882] [1883] [1884] [1885]

[1873] https://en.wikipedia.org/wiki/House_of_Ardennes-Verdun
[1874] Ibid.
[1875] Ibid.
[1876] Ibid.
[1877] Ibid.
[1878] Ibid.
[1879] www.stirnet.com/genie/data/continent/ll/lorraine02.php
[1880] https://en.wikipedia.org/wiki/Wigeric_of_Lotharingia
[1881] sites.rootsweb.com/~pmcbride/rfc/l525.htm

- Count Godrey I of Verdun married Mathilda of Saxony (Billung) [1886] [1887]

- Count Gozelon I, Duke of Upper Lotharingia married ---------- [1888]

□ Uda of Lotharingia (sometimes called Oda of Verdun) married Count Lambert II of Leuven [1889] [1890]

- Count Henry II of Leuven married Adelheid [1891] [1892]

- Count Godfrey I of Leuven, Duke of Lower Lotharingia married Ida de Chiny [1893] [1894]

- Count Godfrey II of Leuven, Duke of Lower Lotharingia married Lutgardis von Sulzbach [1895] [1896]

[1882] www.stirnet.com/genie/data/continent/ll/lorraine02.php
[1883] https://en.wikipedia.org/wiki/Wigeric_of_Lotharingia
[1884] sites.rootsweb.com/~pmcbride/rfc/l525.htm
[1885] https://en.wikipedia.org/wiki/Ardennes-Verdun_dynasty
[1886] fmg.ac/Projects/MedLands/LOTHARINGIAN%20(UPPER)%20NOBILITY.htm#Godefroidied995B
[1887] fmg.ac/Projects/MedLands/SAXONY.htm#Mechtilddied1008
[1888] fmg.ac/Projects/MedLands/LOTHARINGIA.htm#Gozelondied1044A
[1889] fmg.ac/Projects/MedLands/LOTHARINGIA.htm#UdaMLambertIILouvain
[1890] fmg.ac/Projects/MedLands/BRABANT,%20LOUVAIN.htm#LambertIIILouvaindiedafterSep1062B
[1891] fmg.ac/Projects/MedLands/BRABANT,%20LOUVAIN.htm#HenriIIILouvaindied1078
[1892] fmg.ac/Projects/MedLands/HOLLAND.htm#AdelheidMHenriIIILouvaindiedafter1086
[1893] fmg.ac/Projects/MedLands/BRABANT,%20LOUVAIN.htm#GodefroiILouvainVLowLothdied1139B
[1894] fmg.ac/Projects/MedLands/LOTHARINGIAN%20(UPPER)%20NOBILITY.htm#IdaChimaydiedbefore1125MGodefroiBrabant

- Count Godfrey III of Leuven, Duke of Lower Lotharingia married Margareta van Limburg [1897] [1898]

- Duke Henri I of Brabant married Princess Marie of France [1899] [1900]

- ☐ Élisabeth de Brabant marriedCount Dietrich (Thierry) de Clèves [1901] [1902]

Élisabeth was also known as Ysabeau de Brabant; with regards to French records, the name Élisabeth is often used, interchangeably, with that of Isabelle. [1903] [1904]

- ☐ Mathilda deClèves married Gerard de Luxembourg

- ☐ Marguerite de Luxembourg married Jean III de Ghistelles

- Jean IV de Ghistelles married Marie de Haverskerke

[1895] fmg.ac/Projects/MedLands/BRABANT,%20LOUVAIN.htm#GodefroiVILowLothdied1142

[1896] fmg.ac/Projects/MedLands/BAVARIAN%20NOBILITY.htm#LutgardisSulzbachdiedafter1162

[1897] fmg.ac/Projects/MedLands/BRABANT,%20LOUVAIN.htm#GodefroiVIILowLothdied1190B

[1898] fmg.ac/Projects/MedLands/LIMBURG.htm#Margueritedied1172

[1899] fmg.ac/Projects/MedLands/BRABANT,%20LOUVAIN.htm#HenriILotharingiaBrabantdied1235B

[1900] fmg.ac/Projects/MedLands/CAPET.htm#Mariedied1238

[1901] fmg.ac/Projects/MedLands/BRABANT,%20LOUVAIN.htm#Elisabethdied1272

[1902] fmg.ac/Projects/MedLands/FRANCONIA%20(LOWER%20RHINE).htm#Dietrichdied1245

[1903] Jetté, René, Dulong, John P., Gagné, Roland-Yves, Moreau, Gail F. and Dubé, Joseph A. (2001) Table d'ascendance de Catherine Baillon: 12 générations (p 153). Montréal, Québec: Société Généalogique Canadienne Française.

[1904] https://en.wikipedia.org/wiki/Henry_I,_Duke_of_Brabant

- Roger de Ghistelles married Élisabeth ~~Marguerite~~ de Dudzeele (see page 182 for updated explanation)

- ☐ Isabelle (Ysabeau) de Ghistelles married Arnould VI de Gavre

- ☐ Catherine de Gavre d'Escornaix married Guy I Le Bouteiller

- Guy II Le Bouteillier married Isabeau Morhier

- Jean Le Bouteillier married Marie de Venois

- ☐ BénigneLe Bouteillier married Jacques Maillard

- Miles Maillard married Marie Morant

- ☐ Renée Maillard married Adam de Baillon

- Alphonse de Baillon married Louise de Marle

- ☐ Catherine de Baillon

Counts of Boulogne

The County of Boulogne was a historical region in the Low Countries.

It consisted of a part of the present-day French département of the Pas-de-Calais (French Flanders), in parts of which there is still a Dutch-speaking minority; the city of Boulogne-sur-Mer became the centre of the county of Boulogne in the 9th century. [1905]

There is some uncertainly about the early counts. There are number of people called count but the first definite count does not appear until the 11th century.

Boulogne later became influential in the history of England when Eustace II of Boulogne accompanied *William the Conqueror* on his invasion of England (the Battle of Hastings) in 1066. [1906]

- Lideric married ---------- [1907] [1908] [1909]

- Enguerrand, 2nd Grand Forestier or High Ranger (an office that was hereditaty) married ---------- [1910] [1911] [1912]

- Odacre, Seigneur d'Harlebeek, Governor of Flanders, married ---------- [1913] [1914] [1915]

[1905] https://en.wikipedia.org/wiki/Counts_of_Boulogne
[1906] Ibid.
[1907] fmg.ac/Projects/MedLands/FLANDERS,%20HAINAUT.htm#_Toc413913464
[1908] www.stirnet.com/genie/data/continent/defg/flanders1.php#top
[1909] racineshistoire.free.fr/LGN/PDF/Flandres.pdf (page 2)
[1910] fmg.ac/Projects/MedLands/FLANDERS,%20HAINAUT.htm#_Toc413913464
[1911] www.stirnet.com/genie/data/continent/defg/flanders1.php#top
[1912] racineshistoire.free.fr/LGN/PDF/Flandres.pdf (page 2)
[1913] fmg.ac/Projects/MedLands/FLANDERS,%20HAINAUT.htm#_Toc413913464

- Baldwin I, Count of Flanders, married Judith, daughter of Emperor Charles II and Ermentrudis [1916] [1917] [1918] [1919]

- Baldwin II, Count of Flanders, married Ælfthryth of Wessex, daughter of King Alfred the Great [1920] [1921] [1922] [1923]

- Adalulf, the first Flemish Count of Boulogne married ---------- [1924] [1925] [1926]

- Arnulf II, Count of Boulogne married ----------

- Arnulf III, Count of Boulogne married ----------

- Baldwin II, Count of Boulogne, married Adelina of Holland [1927]

- Eustace I, Count of Boulogne, married Matilda of Leuven (d/o Lambert I, Count of Leuven and Gerberga of Lower Lorraine) [1928] [1929]

[1914] www.stirnet.com/genie/data/continent/defg/flanders1.php#top
[1915] racineshistoire.free.fr/LGN/PDF/Flandres.pdf (page 2)
[1916] fmg.ac/Projects/MedLands/FLANDERS,%20HAINAUT.htm#BaudouinIdied879B
[1917] fmg.ac/Projects/MedLands/CAROLINGIANS.htm#JudithM1AethelwulfM2AethelbaldM3Baudouin
[1918] www.stirnet.com/genie/data/continent/defg/flanders1.php#top
[1919] www.stirnet.com/genie/data/ancient/fh/franks3.php#link2
[1920] fmg.ac/Projects/MedLands/FLANDERS,%20HAINAUT.htm#BaudouinIIFlandersdied918
[1921] fmg.ac/Projects/MedLands/ENGLAND,%20AngloSaxon%20&%20Danish%20Kings.htm#Aelfthrythdied929MBaudouinIIFlanders
[1922] www.stirnet.com/genie/data/continent/defg/flanders1.php
[1923] racineshistoire.free.fr/LGN/PDF/Flandres.pdf (page 2)
[1924] fmg.ac/Projects/MedLands/NORTHERN%20FRANCE.htm#Adalolfdied933
[1925] fmg.ac/Projects/MedLands/NORTHERN%20FRANCE.htm#_Toc326733812
[1926] https://en.wikipedia.org/wiki/Adelolf,_Count_of_Boulogne
[1927] https://en.wikipedia.org/wiki/Baldwin_II,_Count_of_Boulogne

■ Count Lambert II of Lens (brother to Eustace II, Count of Boulogne, who accompanied William the Conqueror to England in 1066) married Adéläide of Normandy (sister to King William I (of England) de St. Clair (7th Duke of Normandy), known throughout history as *William the Conqueror*) [1930] [1931]

☐ Judith of Lens (first cousin to Eustace III, Count of Boulogne, as discussed in the opening) married Waltheof II, Earl of Northumbria [1932] [1933]

☐ Countess Maud de Huntingdon married married King David I of Scotland [1934] [1935] [1936] [1937]

■ Prince Henry of Scotland, 3rd Earl of Huntingdon, married Ada de Warenne [1938] [1939] [1940] [1941]

[1928] fmg.ac/Projects/MedLands/NORTHERN%20FRANCE.htm#EustacheIdied1049A
[1929] fmg.ac/Projects/MedLands/BRABANT,%20LOUVAIN.htm#MathildeLouvainMEustacheIBoulogne
[1930] fmg.ac/Projects/MedLands/NORTHERN%20FRANCE.htm#Lambertdied1054
[1931] fmg.ac/Projects/MedLands/NORMANDY.htm#Adelaisdied1081
[1932] fmg.ac/Projects/MedLands/NORTHERN%20FRANCE.htm#Judithdiedafter1086MWaltheof
[1933] fmg.ac/Projects/MedLands/ENGLISH%20NOBILITY%20MEDIEVAL.htm#Waltheofdied1076
[1934] fmg.ac/Projects/MedLands/ENGLISH%20NOBILITY%20MEDIEVAL.htm#Matildadied1131
[1935] fmg.ac/Projects/MedLands/SCOTLAND.htm#DavidIdied1153B
[1936] https://en.wikipedia.org/wiki/Maud,_Countess_of_Huntingdon
[1937] https://en.wikipedia.org/wiki/David_I_of_Scotland
[1938] fmg.ac/Projects/MedLands/SCOTLAND.htm#Henrydied1152
[1939] fmg.ac/Projects/MedLands/ENGLISH%20NOBILITY%20MEDIEVAL.htm#Adadied1078
[1940] https://en.wikipedia.org/wiki/Henry_of_Scotland
[1941] https://en.wikipedia.org/wiki/Ada_de_Warenne

☐ Ada of Huntingdon married Count Floris III of Holland [1942] [1943] [1944] [1945]

☐ Marguerite of Holland married Count Dietrich (Thierry) V de Clèves [1946] [1947]

■ Count Dietrich (Thierry) VI de Clèves married Mathilde de Dinslaken [1948]

■ Count Dietrich (Thierry) de Clèves married Élisabeth de Brabant (d/o Henri I, Duke of Brabant, and Princess Marie of France) [1949] [1950]

Élisabeth was also known as Ysabeau de Brabant; with regards to French records, the name Élisabeth is often used, interchangeably, with that of Isabelle. [1951] [1952]

☐ Mathilda deClèves married Gerard de Luxembourg

☐ Marguerite de Luxembourg married Jean III de Ghistelles

■ Jean IV de Ghistelles married Marie de Haverskerke

[1942] fmg.ac/Projects/MedLands/SCOTLAND.htm#Adadiedafter11Jan1205
[1943] fmg.ac/Projects/MedLands/HOLLAND.htm#FlorisIIIdied1190
[1944] https://en.wikipedia.org/wiki/Ada_of_Huntingdon
[1945] https://en.wikipedia.org/wiki/Floris_III,_Count_of_Holland
[1946] fmg.ac/Projects/MedLands/HOLLAND.htm#Margaretadiedafter1203
[1947] fmg.ac/Projects/MedLands/FRANCONIA%20(LOWER%20RHINE).htm#DietrichIIIdied12001203
[1948] fmg.ac/Projects/MedLands/FRANCONIA%20(LOWER%20RHINE).htm#DietrichIVdied1260
[1949] fmg.ac/Projects/MedLands/BRABANT,%20LOUVAIN.htm#Elisabethdied1272
[1950] fmg.ac/Projects/MedLands/FRANCONIA%20(LOWER%20RHINE).htm#Dietrichdied1245
[1951] Jetté, René, DuLong, John P., Gagné, Roland-Yves, Moreau, Gail F. and Dubé, Joseph A. (2001) Table d'ascendance de Catherine Baillon: 12 générations (p 153). Montréal, Québec: Société Généalogique Canadienne Française.
[1952] https://en.wikipedia.org/wiki/Henry_I,_Duke_of_Brabant

■ Roger de Ghistelles married Élisabeth ~~Marguerite~~ de Dudzeele (see page 182 for updated explanation)

☐ Isabelle (Ysabeau) de Ghistelles married Arnould VI de Gavre

☐ Catherine de Gavre d'Escornaix married Guy I Le Bouteiller

■ Guy II Le Bouteillier married Isabeau Morhier

■ Jean Le Bouteillier married Marie de Venois

☐ Bénigne Le Bouteillier married Jacques Maillard

■ Miles Maillard married Marie Morant

☐ Renée Maillard married Adam de Baillon

■ Alphonse de Baillon married Louise de Marle

☐ Catherine de Baillon

Meeting Byzantine emperor Alexius I Comnenus

Eustache III (white hair) with his brothers

Godfrey of Bouillon (Duke of Lower Lotharingia) and Baldwin of Boulogne

Source: https://en.wikipedia.org/wiki/File:Godefroy_de_Bouillon.jpg

House of Poitiers

As denoted on Wikipedia [1953]

The Ramnulfids, or the House of Poitiers, were a French dynasty ruling the County of Poitou and Duchy of Aquitaine in the ninth through twelfth centuries; their power base was Poitou. In the early tenth century, they contested the dominance of northern Aquitaine and the ducal title to the whole with the House of Auvergne. In 1032, they inherited the Duchy of Gascony, thus uniting it with Aquitaine. By the end of the eleventh century they were the dominant power in the southwestern third of France.

The founder of the family was Ranulf I, who became Count in 835. Ranulf's son, Ranilf II, claimed the title of King of Aquitaine in 888, but it did not survive him. Through his illegitimate son Ebalus he fathered the line of Dukes of Aquitaine that would rule continuously from 927 to 1204, from the succession of William III to the death of Eleanor, who brought the Ramnulfid inheritance first to Louis VII of France and then to Henry II of England.

Several daughters of this house achieved high status.

Adéläide married Hugues Capet and was thus the first Queen of France in the era of the Capetians.

Agnes married Henry III, Holy Roman Emperor, and ruled as regent for her son, the young Henry IV.

[1953] https://en.wikipedia.org/wiki/Ramnulfids

The most illustrious woman was certainly Aquitaine's ruler Eleanor, whose marriage crafted the Angevin Empire which was to cause so much discord between France and England.

The Ramnulfid house did much to encourage art, literature, and piety. It was under Duke William V, Duke William IX, and Duke William X, that Aquitaine became the centre for the art of poetry and song in the vernacular; the troubadour tradition was born and raised there. The Peace and Truce of God were fostered and the ideal of courtly love invented.

■ Count Ranulf I of Poitiers, Duke of Aquitaine, married Bilichild of Maine [1954]

■ Count Ranulf II of Poitiers, Duke of Aquitaine and unknown mistress [1955]

■ Duke Ebalus of Aquitaine (illegitimate issue) married Emillane [1956]

■ Duke William III of Aquitaine married Adela (Gerloc) of Normandy [1957] [1958]

☐ Adeläide of Aquitaine married King Hugues Capet of France (987 to 996) [1959] [1960]

■ King Robert II of France (996 to 1031) married Constance d'Arles [1961] [1962]

■ King Henri I of France (1031 to 1060) married Anne de Kiev [1963] [1964]

■ King Philippe I of France (1060 to 1108) married Berthe de Holland [1965] [1966]

[1954] fmg.ac/Projects/MedLands/AQUITAINE.htm#_Toc276227868
[1955] Ibid.
[1956] fmg.ac/Projects/MedLands/AQUITAINE.htm#_Toc276227869
[1957] fmg.ac/Projects/MedLands/AQUITAINE.htm#GuillaumeIPoitoudied963
[1958] fmg.ac/Projects/MedLands/NORMANDY.htm#Gerlocdiedafter969
[1959] fmg.ac/Projects/MedLands/AQUITAINE.htm#Adelaisdied1004
[1960] fmg.ac/Projects/MedLands/CAPET.htm#HuguesCapetdied996B
[1961] fmg.ac/Projects/MedLands/CAPET.htm#RobertIIdied1031B
[1962] fmg.ac/Projects/MedLands/PROVENCE.htm#ConstanceArlesMRobertIIFrancedied1031
[1963] fmg.ac/Projects/MedLands/CAPET.htm#HenriIdied1060B
[1964] fmg.ac/Projects/MedLands/RUSSIA,%20Rurik.htm#AnnaIaroslavnadied1075

- King Louis VI of France (1108 to 1137) married Adélaïde de Maurienne [1967] [1968]

- King Louis VII of France (1137 to 1180) married Adèle de Champagne [1969] [1970]

- King Philippe II Auguste of France (1180 to 1223) married <u>thirdly</u> Agnès d'Andechs de Méranie [1971] [1972]

  ☐ Princess Marie of France married Henri I, Duke of Brabant [1973] [1974]

  ☐ Élisabeth de Brabant married Count Dietrich (Thierry) de Clèves [1975] [1976]

  Élisabeth was also known as Ysabeau de Brabant; with regards to French records, the name Élisabeth is often used, interchangeably, with that of Isabelle. [1977] [1978]

  ☐ Mathilda de Clèves married Gerard de Luxembourg

  ☐ Marguerite de Luxembourg married Jean III de Ghistelles

[1965] fmg.ac/Projects/MedLands/CAPET.htm#PhilippeIdied1108B
[1966] fmg.ac/Projects/MedLands/HOLLAND.htm#Berthadied1093
[1967] fmg.ac/Projects/MedLands/CAPET.htm#LouisVIdied1137B
[1968] fmg.ac/Projects/MedLands/SAVOY.htm#Adélaïdedied1154
[1969] fmg.ac/Projects/MedLands/CAPET.htm#LouisVIIdied1180B
[1970] fmg.ac/Projects/MedLands/CENTRAL%20FRANCE.htm#AdeleBloisdied1206
[1971] fmg.ac/Projects/MedLands/CAPET.htm#PhilippeIIdied1223B
[1972] fmg.ac/Projects/MedLands/CARINTHIA.htm#AgnesMeranodied1201
[1973] fmg.ac/Projects/MedLands/CAPET.htm#Mariedied1238
[1974] fmg.ac/Projects/MedLands/BRABANT,%20LOUVAIN.htm#HenriILotharingiaBrabantdied1235B
[1975] fmg.ac/Projects/MedLands/BRABANT,%20LOUVAIN.htm#Elisabethdied1272
[1976] fmg.ac/Projects/MedLands/FRANCONIA%20(LOWER%20RHINE).htm#Dietrichdied1245
[1977] Jetté, René, DuLong, John P., Gagné, Roland-Yves, Moreau, Gail F. and Dubé, Joseph A. (2001) <u>Table d'ascendance de Catherine Baillon: 12 générations</u> (p 153). Montréal, Québec: Société Généalogique Canadienne Française.
[1978] https://en.wikipedia.org/wiki/Henry_I,_Duke_of_Brabant

- Jean IV de Ghistelles married Marie de Haverskerke

- Roger de Ghistelles married Élisabeth ~~Marguerite~~ de Dudzeele (see page 182 for updated explanation)

- ☐ Isabelle (Ysabeau) de Ghistelles married Arnould VI de Gavre

- ☐ Catherine de Gavre d'Escornaix married Guy I Le Bouteiller

- Guy II Le Bouteillier married Isabeau Morhier

- Jean Le Bouteillier married Marie de Venois

- ☐ Bénigne Le Bouteillier married Jacques Maillard

- Miles Maillard married Marie Morant

- ☐ Renée Maillard married Adam de Baillon

- Alphonse de Baillon married Louise de Marle

- ☐ Catherine de Baillon

Léonese Monarchs

In 910 AD, an independent Kingdom of Léon was founded when the King of Asturias divided his territory amongst his three sons. [1979]

- Peter, Duke of Cantabria [1980]

- Fruela (brother to King Alfonso I de Asturias) [1981]

- King Vermudo I de Asturias married Ozenda [1982]

- King Ramiro I de Asturias married ---------- [1983]

- King Ordoño I de Asturias married Muniadona (who is thought to be of Castilian origin) [1984]

- King Alfonso III de Asturias married Jimena Garcés of Pamplona [1985] [1986]

- King Ordoño II de Léon married Elvira Menéndez [1987] [1988]

[1979] https://en.wikipedia.org/wiki/Kingdom_of_Le%C3%B3n
[1980] fmg.ac/Projects/MedLands/ASTURIAS,%20LÉON.htm#_Toc111995033
[1981] Ibid.
[1982] fmg.ac/Projects/MedLands/ASTURIAS,%20LÉON.htm#VermudoIdied797A
[1983] Ibid.
[1984] fmg.ac/Projects/MedLands/ASTURIAS,%20LÉON.htm#OrdonoIdied866B
[1985] fmg.ac/Projects/MedLands/ASTURIAS,%20LÉON.htm#AlfonsoIIIdied910B
[1986] fmg.ac/Projects/MedLands/NAVARRE.htm#JimenaGarcesMAlfonsoIIIAsturias
[1987] fmg.ac/Projects/MedLands/ASTURIAS,%20LÉON.htm#OrdonoIIdied924B
[1988] fmg.ac/Projects/MedLands/SPANISH%20NOBILITY%20EARLY%20MEDIEVAL.htm#ElviraMenendezMOrdonoIILéon

- King Ramiro II de Léon married Adosinda Gutiérrez [1989] [1990]

- King Ordoño III de Léon and mistress Aragonta or Gontrada Peláez [1991] [1992]

- King Vermudo II de Léon (illegitimate issue) married Elvira Garcia de Castile [1993] [1994]

- King Alfonso V de Léon married Elvira Mendes [1995] [1996]

- Sancha de Léon married King Ferdinand I de Léon [1997] [1998]

- King Alfonso VI de Léon married Constance de Burgundy [1999] [2000]

- Queen Urraca de Léon and Castile married Raymond of Burgundy [2001] [2002] [2003] [2004]

[1989] fmg.ac/Projects/MedLands/ASTURIAS,%20LÉON.htm#RamiroIIdied951B
[1990] fmg.ac/Projects/MedLands/SPANISH%20NOBILITY%20EARLY%20MEDIEVAL.htm#AdosindaGutierrezMRamiroIILéon
[1991] fmg.ac/Projects/MedLands/ASTURIAS,%20LÉON.htm#OrdonoIVdied962
[1992] fmg.ac/Projects/MedLands/ASTURIAS,%20LÉON.htm#VermudoIIdied999A
[1993] fmg.ac/Projects/MedLands/ASTURIAS,%20LÉON.htm#VemudoIIdied999B
[1994] fmg.ac/Projects/MedLands/CASTILE.htm#Elviradied1017MVermudoIIILéon
[1995] fmg.ac/Projects/MedLands/ASTURIAS,%20LÉON.htm#AlfonsoVLéondied1028B
[1996] fmg.ac/Projects/MedLands/SPANISH%20NOBILITY%20EARLY%20MEDIEVAL.htm#ElviraMenendezdied1022
[1997] fmg.ac/Projects/MedLands/ASTURIAS,%20LÉON.htm#Sanchadied1067MFernandoICastile
[1998] fmg.ac/Projects/MedLands/CASTILE.htm#FernandoIdied1065B
[1999] fmg.ac/Projects/MedLands/CASTILE.htm#AlfonsoVIdied1109B
[2000] fmg.ac/Projects/MedLands/BURGUNDY.htm#ConstanceBourgognedied1093
[2001] fmg.ac/Projects/MedLands/CASTILE.htm#Urracadied1126B
[2002] fmg.ac/Projects/MedLands/BURGUNDY%20Kingdom.htm#RaimondAmousdied1107
[2003] https://en.wikipedia.org/wiki/Alfonso_VI_of_León_and_Castile
[2004] https://en.wikipedia.org/wiki/Constance_of_Burgundy

- King Alfonso VII de Léon and Castile married Berenguela (Berengaria) de Barcelona [2005] [2006] [2007]

☐ Constance de Castile married King Louis VII of France [2008] [2009]

☐ Princess Alys de France, Countess of the Vexin, married William II, Count of Ponthieu and Montreuil, on August 20, 1195 [2010] [2011]

☐ Marie, Countess of Ponthieu and Countess of Montreuil, married Simon de Dammartin before September 1208 [2012] [2013]

☐ Marie de Dammartin married Jean II Count de Roucy, Seigneur de Pierrepont [2014] [2015] [2016]

☐ Marie (Mathilde) de Roucy married Jean I de Garlande, Seigneur de Possesse [2017] [2018] [2019] [2020]

[2005] fmg.ac/Projects/MedLands/CASTILE.htm#_ALFONSO_VII_1112-1157,
[2006] fmg.ac/Projects/MedLands/CATALAN%20NOBILITY.htm#Berengueladied1149MAlfonsoVIICastile
[2007] michaelmarcotte.com/spanport.htm
[2008] fmg.ac/Projects/MedLands/CASTILE.htm#Constanzadied1160MLouisVIIFrance
[2009] fmg.ac/Projects/MedLands/CAPET.htm#LouisVIIdied1180B
[2010] fmg.ac/Projects/MedLands/CAPET.htm#Alixdiedafter1200MGuillaumeIIIPonthieu
[2011] fmg.ac/Projects/MedLands/NORTHERN%20FRANCE.htm#GuillaumeIIdied1221
[2012] fmg.ac/Projects/MedLands/NORTHERN%20FRANCE.htm#MariePonthieudied1250
[2013] fmg.ac/Projects/MedLands/NORTHERN%20FRANCE.htm#SimonDammartinAumalePonthieud1239B
[2014] fmg.ac/Projects/MedLands/NORTHERN%20FRANCE.htm#MarieDammartinMJeanIIRoucy
[2015] fmg.ac/Projects/MedLands/NORTHERN%20FRANCE.htm#JeanPierrepontRoucydied1251
[2016] DuLong, John. (2009) "Catherine de Baillon's de Roye Ancestry: Another Royal Gateway" (page 17). Michigan's Habitant Heritage: Journal of the French-Canadian Heritage Society of Michigan, Volume 30, Number 1, January 2009.

- Jean II de Garland, Seigneur de Possesse, married Agnès [2021] [2022]

  ☐ Alix de Garlande dit de Possesse married Dreux de Roye, Seigneur de Germigny [2023] [2024]

  ☐ Jeanne (Jacqueline) de Roye married Arnould V de Gavre [2025] [2026] [2027]

- Arnould VI de Gavre, Baron d'Escornaix married Isabelle (Ysabeau) de Ghistelles [2028] [2029]

  ☐ Catherine de Gavre d'Escornaix married Guy I Le Bouteiller [2030]

[2017] fmg.ac/Projects/MedLands/NORTHERN%20FRANCE.htm#dauJeanIIRoucyMJeanGarlande

[2018] fmg.ac/Projects/MedLands/PARIS%20REGION%20NOBILITY.htm#JeanGarlandePossessediedbefore1287

[2019] DuLong, John. (2009) "Catherine de Baillon's de Roye Ancestry: Another Royal Gateway" (page 17). Michigan's Habitant Heritage: Journal of the French-Canadian Heritage Society of Michigan, Volume 30, Number 1, January 2009.

[2020] racineshistoire.free.fr/LGN/PDF/Garlande.pdf (page 8)

[2021] Ibid.

[2022] DuLong, John. (2009) "Catherine de Baillon's de Roye Ancestry: Another Royal Gateway" (page 17). Michigan's Habitant Heritage: Journal of the French-Canadian Heritage Society of Michigan, Volume 30, Number 1, January 2009.

[2023] Ibid, pages 14 and 15.

[2024] racineshistoire.free.fr/LGN/PDF/Roye.pdf (page 6)

[2025] Jetté, René, DuLong, John P., Gagné, Roland-Yves, Moreau, Gail F. and Dubé, Joseph A. (2001) Table d'ascendance de Catherine Baillon: 12 générations (pages 124 and 125). Montréal, Québec: Société Généalogique Canadienne Française.

[2026] DuLong, John. (2009) "Catherine de Baillon's de Roye Ancestry: Another Royal Gateway" (page 13). Michigan's Habitant Heritage: Journal of the French-Canadian Heritage Society of Michigan, Volume 30, Number 1, January 2009.

[2027] racineshistoire.free.fr/LGN/PDF/Gavre.pdf (page 9)

[2028] Jetté, René, DuLong, John P., Gagné, Roland-Yves, Moreau, Gail F. and Dubé, Joseph A. (2001) Table d'ascendance de Catherine Baillon: 12 générations (page 112). Montréal, Québec: Société Généalogique Canadienne Française.

[2029] racineshistoire.free.fr/LGN/PDF/Gavre.pdf (page 9)

[2030] Ibid, page 10.

- Guy II Le Bouteillier married Isabeau Morhier [2031]

- Jean Le Bouteillier married Marie de Venois [2032]

- ☐ Bénigne Le Bouteillier married Jacques Maillard[2033]

- Miles Maillard married Marie Morant

- ☐ Renée Maillard married Adam de Baillon

- Alphonse de Baillon married Louise de Marle

- ☐ Catherine de Baillon

[2031] racineshistoire.free.fr/LGN/PDF/Gavre.pdf (page 10)
[2032] Ibid.
[2033] Ibid.

Counts of Castile

- Rodrigo, first Count of Castile [2034]

- Diego Rodríguez, Count of Castile [2035]

- ☐ GutinaDíaz married Fernando Núñez (s/o Munio Núñez and Argilo) [2036] [2037]

- Gonzalo Fernández, Count of Burgos and Castile, married Muniadomna de Castile (a member of the Asturian royal family; daughter of Ramiro de Asturias, titular King of León, and his wife Urraca) [2038] [2039]

- Fernando González, Count of Castile, married Sancha of Navarre [2040] [2041]

- Garcia Fernandez, Count of Castile, married Ava of Ribagorza [2042] [2043]

- ☐ Elvira Garcia de Castile married King Vermudo II de Léon [2044] [2045]

- King Alfonso V de Léon married Elvira Mendes [2046] [2047]

[2034] fmg.ac/Projects/MedLands/CASTILE.htm#_Toc342286366
[2035] Ibid.
[2036] fmg.ac/Projects/MedLands/CASTILE.htm#GutinaMFernandoNunezCasitlla
[2037] fmg.ac/Projects/MedLands/CASTILE.htm#FernandoNunezMGutinaA
[2038] fmg.ac/Projects/MedLands/CASTILE.htm#GonzaloFernandezCastilladied932
[2039] fmg.ac/Projects/MedLands/ASTURIAS,%20LÉON.htm#Muniadomnadied935
[2040] fmg.ac/Projects/MedLands/CASTILE.htm#GonzaloFernandezCastilladied932
[2041] fmg.ac/Projects/MedLands/NAVARRE.htm#SanchaSanchezdied959
[2042] fmg.ac/Projects/MedLands/CASTILE.htm#GarciaFernandezdied995B
[2043] fmg.ac/Projects/MedLands/ARAGONESE%20NOBILITY.htm#AbaMGarciaFernandezCastilla
[2044] fmg.ac/Projects/MedLands/CASTILE.htm#Elviradied1017MVermudoIILéon
[2045] fmg.ac/Projects/MedLands/ASTURIAS,%20LÉON.htm#VemudoIIdied999B

☐ Sancha de Léon married King Ferdinand I de Léon [2048] [2049]

■ King Alfonso VI de Léon married Constance de Burgundy [2050] [2051]

☐ Queen Urraca de Léon and Castile married Raymond of Burgundy [2052] [2053] [2054] [2055]

■ King Alfonso VII de Léon and Castile married Berenguela (Berengaria) de Barcelona [2056] [2057] [2058]

☐ Constance de Castile married King Louis VII of France [2059] [2060]

☐ Princess Alys de France, Countess of the Vexin, married William II, Count of Ponthieu and Montreuil, on August 20, 1195 [2061] [2062]

[2046] fmg.ac/Projects/MedLands/ASTURIAS,%20LÉON.htm#AlfonsoVLéondied1028B
[2047] fmg.ac/Projects/MedLands/SPANISH%20NOBILITY%20EARLY%20MEDIEVAL.htm#ElviraMenendezdied1022
[2048] fmg.ac/Projects/MedLands/ASTURIAS,%20LÉON.htm#Sanchadied1067MFernandoICastile
[2049] fmg.ac/Projects/MedLands/CASTILE.htm#FernandoIdied1065B
[2050] fmg.ac/Projects/MedLands/CASTILE.htm#AlfonsoVIdied1109B
[2051] fmg.ac/Projects/MedLands/BURGUNDY.htm#ConstanceBourgognedied1093
[2052] fmg.ac/Projects/MedLands/CASTILE.htm#Urracadied1126B
[2053] fmg.ac/Projects/MedLands/BURGUNDY%20Kingdom.htm#RaimondAmousdied1107
[2054] https://en.wikipedia.org/wiki/Alfonso_VI_of_León_and_Castile
[2055] https://en.wikipedia.org/wiki/Constance_of_Burgundy
[2056] fmg.ac/Projects/MedLands/CASTILE.htm#_ALFONSO_VII_1112-1157,
[2057] fmg.ac/Projects/MedLands/CATALAN%20NOBILITY.htm#Berengueladied1149MAlfonsoVIICastile
[2058] michaelmarcotte.com/spanport.htm
[2059] fmg.ac/Projects/MedLands/CASTILE.htm#Constanzadied1160MLouisVIIFrance
[2060] fmg.ac/Projects/MedLands/CAPET.htm#LouisVIIdied1180B
[2061] fmg.ac/Projects/MedLands/CAPET.htm#Alixdiedafter1200MGuillaumeIIIPonthieu

☐ Marie, Countess of Ponthieu and Countess of Montreuil, married Simon de Dammartin before September 1208 [2063] [2064]

☐ Marie de Dammartin married Jean II Count de Roucy, Seigneur de Pierrepont[2065] [2066] [2067]

☐ Marie (Mathilde) de Roucy married Jean I de Garlande, Seigneur de Possesse[2068] [2069] [2070] [2071]

■ Jean II de Garland, Seigneur de Possesse, married Agnès [2072] [2073]

[2062] fmg.ac/Projects/MedLands/NORTHERN%20FRANCE.htm#GuillaumeIIdied1221
[2063] fmg.ac/Projects/MedLands/NORTHERN%20FRANCE.htm#MariePonthieudied1250
[2064] fmg.ac/Projects/MedLands/NORTHERN%20FRANCE.htm#SimonDammartinAumalePonthieud1239B
[2065] fmg.ac/Projects/MedLands/NORTHERN%20FRANCE.htm#MarieDammartinMJeanIIRoucy
[2066] fmg.ac/Projects/MedLands/NORTHERN%20FRANCE.htm#JeanPierrepontRoucydied1251
[2067] DuLong, John. (2009) "Catherine de Baillon's de Roye Ancestry: Another Royal Gateway" (page 17). Michigan's Habitant Heritage: Journal of the French-Canadian Heritage Society of Michigan, Volume 30, Number 1, January 2009.
[2068] fmg.ac/Projects/MedLands/NORTHERN%20FRANCE.htm#dauJeanIIRoucyMJeanGarlande
[2069] fmg.ac/Projects/MedLands/PARIS%20REGION%20NOBILITY.htm#JeanGarlandePossessediedbefore1287
[2070] DuLong, John. (2009) "Catherine de Baillon's de Roye Ancestry: Another Royal Gateway" (page 17). Michigan's Habitant Heritage: Journal of the French-Canadian Heritage Society of Michigan, Volume 30, Number 1, January 2009.
[2071] racineshistoire.free.fr/LGN/PDF/Garlande.pdf (page 8)
[2072] Ibid.
[2073] DuLong, John. (2009) "Catherine de Baillon's de Roye Ancestry: Another Royal Gateway" (page 17). Michigan's Habitant Heritage: Journal of the French-Canadian Heritage Society of Michigan, Volume 30, Number 1, January 2009.

☐ Alix de Garlande dit de Possesse married Dreux de Roye, Seigneur de Germigny[2074][2075]

☐ Jeanne (Jacqueline) de Roye married Arnould V de Gavre[2076][2077][2078]

■ Arnould VI de Gavre, Baron d'Escornaix married Isabelle (Ysabeau) de Ghistelles [2079][2080]

☐ Catherine de Gavre d'Escornaix married Guy I Le Bouteiller [2081]

■ Guy II Le Bouteillier married Isabeau Morhier [2082]

■ Jean Le Bouteillier married Marie de Venois [2083]

☐ Bénigne Le Bouteillier married Jacques Maillard[2084]

■ Miles Maillard married Marie Morant

☐ Renée Maillard married Adam de Baillon

[2074] DuLong, John. (2009) "Catherine de Baillon's de Roye Ancestry: Another Royal Gateway" (pages 14 and 15). Michigan's Habitant Heritage: Journal of the French-Canadian Heritage Society of Michigan, Volume 30, Number 1, January 2009.
[2075] racineshistoire.free.fr/LGN/PDF/Roye.pdf (page 6)
[2076] Jetté, René, DuLong, John P., Gagné, Roland-Yves, Moreau, Gail F. and Dubé, Joseph A. (2001) Table d'ascendance de Catherine Baillon: 12 générations (pages 124 and 125). Montréal, Québec: Société Généalogique Canadienne Française.
[2077] DuLong, John. (2009) "Catherine de Baillon's de Roye Ancestry: Another Royal Gateway" (page 13). Michigan's Habitant Heritage: Journal of the French-Canadian Heritage Society of Michigan, Volume 30, Number 1, January 2009.
[2078] racineshistoire.free.fr/LGN/PDF/Gavre.pdf (page 9)
[2079] Jetté, René, DuLong, John P., Gagné, Roland-Yves, Moreau, Gail F. and Dubé, Joseph A. (2001) Table d'ascendance de Catherine Baillon: 12 générations (page 112). Montréal, Québec: Société Généalogique Canadienne Française.
[2080] racineshistoire.free.fr/LGN/PDF/Gavre.pdf (page 9)
[2081] Ibid, page 10.
[2082] Ibid.
[2083] Ibid.
[2084] Ibid.

■ Alphonse de Baillon married Louise de Marle

☐ Catherine de Baillon

House of Montdidier

The House of Montdidier was a medieval French noble house which ruled as Count of Montdidier, Dammartin and Roucy. [2085]

The area around Ponthieu, which extended approximately from the river Canche in the north to the river Somme in the south, was conquered by Arnoul I Count of Flanders in 940. [2086] It developed into a separate county in the early 11th century, based around territory which was granted by Hugues Capet, King of France, to Hugues, avocat de Saint-Riquier, who had married the king's daughter some time in the 980s. [2087]

The counts were vassals of the Capetian kings. The county was inherited by the Norman family of Bellême/Montgommery in the late 11th century, and by the family of the counts of Dammartin in the early 1220s. [2088]

Bellême was a fief held directly from the French crown. [2089] The Seigneurs de Bellême acquired the lordship of Alençon, located in the south of the duchy of Normandy close to the border with the county of Maine; the process whereby the lordship of Alençon evolved into the county of Alençon appears to have been accidental, occurring in the second half of the 12th century when the inheritance of Guillaume, Comte de Ponthieu was divided between his sons. [2090]

[2085] https://en.wikipedia.org/wiki/House_of_Montdidier
[2086] fmg.ac/Projects/MedLands/NORTHERN%20FRANCE.htm#_Toc336929884
[2087] Ibid.
[2088] Ibid.
[2089] Ibid.
[2090] Ibid.

- Helpuin, Comte de Arcis-Sur-Aube, married Hersinde [2091]

- Hildouin II, Comte de Montdidier [2092]

- Manassess, Comte de Dammartin and Dampmartin, married Princess Constance of France (d/o Robert II, King of France, and Constance of Arles) [2093] [2094]

- Hughes, Comte de Dammartin, married Countess Roaide of Bulles [2095]

- Aelis de Dammartin married Aubry de Mello (s/o Baron Gilbert de Mello) [2096]

- Alberic I, Comte de Dammartin, married Joan Bassett [2097]

- Alberic II, Comte de Dammartin, married Mathilde [Mabile] de Clermont-en-Beauvaisis [2098] [2099] [2100]

- Simon de Dammartin, Count de Aumâle, married Marie de Ponthieu [2101] [2102]

- Marie de Dammartin married Jean II Seigneur de Pierrepont, Count de Roucy [2103] [2104] [2105]

[2091] www.coltechpub.com/hartgen/htm/of-arcis-sur-aube.htm#name4394
[2092] Ibid.
[2093] Ibid.
[2094] https://en.wikipedia.org/wiki/Constance_of_Arles
[2095] www.coltechpub.com/hartgen/htm/of-arcis-sur-aube.htm#name4394
[2096] Ibid.
[2097] Ibid.
[2098] fmg.ac/Projects/MedLands/NORTHERN%20FRANCE.htm#SimonDammartinAumalePonthieud1239B
[2099] http://www.coltechpub.com/hartgen/htm/de-mello.htm
[2100] http://www.coltechpub.com/hartgen/htm/de-creil.htm#name5779
[2101] fmg.ac/Projects/MedLands/NORTHERN%20FRANCE.htm#SimonDammartinAumalePonthieud1239B
[2102] fmg.ac/Projects/MedLands/NORTHERN%20FRANCE.htm#MariePonthieudied1250

☐ Marie (Mathilde) de Roucy married Jean I de Garlande, Seigneur de Possesse [2106] [2107] [2108] [2109]

■ Jean II de Garland, Seigneur de Possesse, married Agnès [2110] [2111]

☐ Alix de Garlande dit de Possesse married Dreux de Roye, Seigneur de Germigny [2112] [2113]

☐ Jeanne (Jacqueline) de Roye married Arnould V de Gavre [2114] [2115] [2116]

[2103] fmg.ac/Projects/MedLands/NORTHERN%20FRANCE.htm#MarieDammartinMJeanIIRoucy

[2104] fmg.ac/Projects/MedLands/NORTHERN%20FRANCE.htm#JeanPierrepontRoucydied1251

[2105] DuLong, John. (2009) "Catherine de Baillon's de Roye Ancestry: Another Royal Gateway" (page 17). Michigan's Habitant Heritage: Journal of the French-Canadian Heritage Society of Michigan, Volume 30, Number 1, January 2009.

[2106] fmg.ac/Projects/MedLands/NORTHERN%20FRANCE.htm#dauJeanIIRoucyMJeanGarlande

[2107] fmg.ac/Projects/MedLands/PARIS%20REGION%20NOBILITY.htm#JeanGarlandePossessediedbefore1287

[2108] DuLong, John. (2009) "Catherine de Baillon's de Roye Ancestry: Another Royal Gateway" (page 17). Michigan's Habitant Heritage: Journal of the French-Canadian Heritage Society of Michigan, Volume 30, Number 1, January 2009.

[2109] racineshistoire.free.fr/LGN/PDF/Garlande.pdf (page 8)

[2110] Ibid.

[2111] DuLong, John. (2009) "Catherine de Baillon's de Roye Ancestry: Another Royal Gateway" (page 17). Michigan's Habitant Heritage: Journal of the French-Canadian Heritage Society of Michigan, Volume 30, Number 1, January 2009.

[2112] Ibid, pages 14 and 15.

[2113] racineshistoire.free.fr/LGN/PDF/Roye.pdf (page 6)

[2114] Jetté, René, DuLong, John P., Gagné, Roland-Yves, Moreau, Gail F. and Dubé, Joseph A. (2001) Table d'ascendance de Catherine Baillon: 12 générations (pages 124 and 125). Montréal, Québec: Société Généalogique Canadienne Française.

- Arnould VI de Gavre, Baron d'Escornaix married Isabelle (Ysabeau) de Ghistelles [2117] [2118]

- Catherine de Gavre d'Escornaix married Guy I Le Bouteiller [2119]

- Guy II Le Bouteillier married Isabeau Morhier [2120] [2121]

- Jean Le Bouteillier married Marie de Venois [2122]

- Bénigne Le Bouteillier married Jacques Maillard [2123]

- Miles Maillard married Marie Morant

- Renée Maillard married Adam de Baillon

- Alphonse de Baillon married Louise de Marle

- Catherine de Baillon

[2115] DuLong, John. (2009) "Catherine de Baillon's de Roye Ancestry: Another Royal Gateway" (page 13). Michigan's Habitant Heritage: Journal of the French-Canadian Heritage Society of Michigan, Volume 30, Number 1, January 2009.

[2116] racineshistoire.free.fr/LGN/PDF/Gavre.pdf (page 9)

[2117] Jetté, René, DuLong, John P., Gagné, Roland-Yves, Moreau, Gail F. and Dubé, Joseph A. (2001) Table d'ascendance de Catherine Baillon: 12 générations (page 112). Montréal, Québec: Société Généalogique Canadienne Française.

[2118] racineshistoire.free.fr/LGN/PDF/Gavre.pdf (page 9)

[2119] Ibid, page 10.

[2120] Ibid.

[2121] racineshistoire.free.fr/LGN/PDF/Morhier.pdf (page 4)

[2122] racineshistoire.free.fr/LGN/PDF/Gavre.pdf (page 9)

[2123] Ibid.

In keeping with the House of Montdidier, there exists a second line of descent.

- Helpuin, Comte de Arcis-Sur-Aube, married Hersinde [2124]

- Hildouin II, Comte de Montdidier [2125]

- Hildouin III, Comte de Montdidier [2126]

- Hildouin IV, Comte de Montdidier, married Alix de Roucy [2127] [2128]

- Hugh, Comte de Clermont, married Margaret de Montdidier [2129] [2130]

- Renaud II, Comte de Clermont-en-Beauvaisis, married Clémence de Bar-le-Duc [2131] [2132]

- ☐ Mathilde [Mabile] de Clermont-en-Beauvaisis married Alberic II, Comte de Dammartin [2133] [2134] [2135]

- Simon de Dammartin, Count de Aumâle, married Marie de Ponthieu [2136] [2137]

[2124] http://www.coltechpub.com/hartgen/htm/of-arcis-sur-aube.htm#name4394
[2125] Ibid.
[2126] Ibid.
[2127] Ibid.
[2128] http://www.coltechpub.com/hartgen/htm/de-roucy.htm#name4088
[2129] http://www.coltechpub.com/hartgen/htm/de-creil.htm#name4396
[2130] http://www.coltechpub.com/hartgen/htm/of-arcis-sur-aube.htm#name4394
[2131] http://www.coltechpub.com/hartgen/htm/de-creil.htm#name4396
[2132] http://www.coltechpub.com/hartgen/htm/de-mousson.htm#name4685
[2133] fmg.ac/Projects/MedLands/NORTHERN%20FRANCE.htm#SimonDammartinAumalePonthieud1239B
[2134] http://www.coltechpub.com/hartgen/htm/de-mello.htm
[2135] http://www.coltechpub.com/hartgen/htm/de-creil.htm#name5779
[2136] fmg.ac/Projects/MedLands/NORTHERN%20FRANCE.htm#SimonDammartinAumalePonthieud1239B

☐ Marie de Dammartin married Jean II Seigneur de Pierrepont, Count de Roucy [2138] [2139] [2140]

☐ Marie (Mathilde) de Roucy married Jean I de Garlande, Seigneur de Possesse [2141] [2142] [2143] [2144]

■ Jean II de Garland, Seigneur de Possesse, married Agnès [2145] [2146]

☐ Alix de Garlande dit dePossesse married Dreux de Roye, Seigneur de Germigny [2147] [2148]

☐ Jeanne (Jacqueline) de Roye married Arnould V de Gavre [2149] [2150] [2151]

[2137] fmg.ac/Projects/MedLands/NORTHERN%20FRANCE.htm#MariePonthieudied1250

[2138] fmg.ac/Projects/MedLands/NORTHERN%20FRANCE.htm#MarieDammartinMJeanIIRoucy

[2139] fmg.ac/Projects/MedLands/NORTHERN%20FRANCE.htm#JeanPierrepontRoucydied1251

[2140] DuLong, John. (2009) "Catherine de Baillon's de Roye Ancestry: Another Royal Gateway" (page 17). Michigan's Habitant Heritage: Journal of the French-Canadian Heritage Society of Michigan, Volume 30, Number 1, January 2009.

[2141] fmg.ac/Projects/MedLands/NORTHERN%20FRANCE.htm#dauJeanIIRoucyMJeanGarlande

[2142] fmg.ac/Projects/MedLands/PARIS%20REGION%20NOBILITY.htm#JeanGarlandePossessediedbefore1287

[2143] DuLong, John. (2009) "Catherine de Baillon's de Roye Ancestry: Another Royal Gateway" (page 17). Michigan's Habitant Heritage: Journal of the French-Canadian Heritage Society of Michigan, Volume 30, Number 1, January 2009.

[2144] racineshistoire.free.fr/LGN/PDF/Garlande.pdf (page 8)

[2145] Ibid.

[2146] DuLong, John. (2009) "Catherine de Baillon's de Roye Ancestry: Another Royal Gateway" (page 17). Michigan's Habitant Heritage: Journal of the French-Canadian Heritage Society of Michigan, Volume 30, Number 1, January 2009.

[2147] Ibid, pages 14 and 15.

[2148] racineshistoire.free.fr/LGN/PDF/Roye.pdf (page 6)

- Arnould VI de Gavre, Baron d'Escornaix married Isabelle (Ysabeau) de Ghistelles [2152] [2153]

- Catherine de Gavre d'Escornaix married Guy I Le Bouteiller [2154]

- Guy II Le Bouteillier married Isabeau Morhier [2155] [2156]

- Jean Le Bouteillier married Marie de Venois [2157]

- Bénigne Le Bouteillier married Jacques Maillard [2158]

- Miles Maillard married Marie Morant

- Renée Maillard married Adam de Baillon

- Alphonse de Baillon married Louise de Marle

- Catherine de Baillon

[2149] Jetté, René, DuLong, John P., Gagné, Roland-Yves, Moreau, Gail F. and Dubé, Joseph A. (2001) Table d'ascendance de Catherine Baillon: 12 générations (pages 124 and 125). Montréal, Québec: Société Généalogique Canadienne Française.

[2150] DuLong, John. (2009) "Catherine de Baillon's de Roye Ancestry: Another Royal Gateway" (page 13). Michigan's Habitant Heritage: Journal of the French-Canadian Heritage Society of Michigan, Volume 30, Number 1, January 2009.

[2151] racineshistoire.free.fr/LGN/PDF/Gavre.pdf (page 9)

[2152] Jetté, René, DuLong, John P., Gagné, Roland-Yves, Moreau, Gail F. and Dubé, Joseph A. (2001) Table d'ascendance de Catherine Baillon: 12 générations (page 112). Montréal, Québec: Société Généalogique Canadienne Française.

[2153] racineshistoire.free.fr/LGN/PDF/Gavre.pdf (page 9)

[2154] Ibid, page 10.

[2155] Ibid.

[2156] racineshistoire.free.fr/LGN/PDF/Morhier.pdf (page 4)

[2157] racineshistoire.free.fr/LGN/PDF/Gavre.pdf (page 9)

[2158] Ibid.

In keeping with the House of Montdidier, there exists a third line of descent.

- Fulcoin married Rothais [2159]

- Ives de Creil, Seigneur de Bellême, married Godehildis [2160] [2161]

- William I (Talvas) de Bellême, Seigneur de Bellême, Sire d'Alençon, married Mathilde, Dame de Condé-sur-Noireau [2162]

- William II (Talvas) de Bellême, Sire d'Alençon, married Hildeburge [2163]

- ☐ Mabile d'Alençon married Roger II de Montgommery [2164] [2165] [2166]

- Robert de Montgommery (de Bellême), Sire d'Alençon, Comte de Ponthieu, Earl of Shrewsbury, married Agnès de Ponthieu [2167] [2168] [2169]

- William I (Talvas), Comte de Ponthieu, married Hélie de Bourgogne [2170] [2171]

[2159] racineshistoire.free.fr/LGN/PDF/Gavre.pdf (page 9)
[2160] Ibid.
[2161] fmg.ac/Projects/MedLands/Tours.htm#GodehildisMIvesBelleme
[2162] fmg.ac/Projects/MedLands/NORMAN%20NOBILITY.htm#GuillaumeBellemedied10271035A
[2163] fmg.ac/Projects/MedLands/NORMAN%20NOBILITY.htm#GuillaumeBellemedied10271035A
[2164] fmg.ac/Projects/MedLands/NORMAN%20NOBILITY.htm#Mabiledied1079
[2165] fmg.ac/Projects/MedLands/NORMAN%20NOBILITY.htm#RogerMontgommeryShrewsburydied1094A
[2166] racineshistoire.free.fr/LGN/PDF/Montgomery.pdf (page 3)
[2167] fmg.ac/Projects/MedLands/NORMAN%20NOBILITY.htm#RobertMontgommeryBellemedied1131
[2168] fmg.ac/Projects/MedLands/NORTHERN%20FRANCE.htm#AgnesPonthieudied1100
[2169] racineshistoire.free.fr/LGN/PDF/Montgomery.pdf (pages 3 and 4)

- Guy II, Comte de Ponthieu, married Ida ---------- [2172]

- Jean I, Comte de Ponthieu, married Beatrix de Saint-Pol [2173] [2174]

- William II (Talvas), Comte de Ponthieu, married Princess Alys de France, Countess of the Vexin (d/o Louis VII, King of France, and his second wife, Constance de Castile) [2175] [2176]

☐ Marie de Ponthieu married Simon de Dammartin, Count de Aumâle [2177] [2178]

☐ Marie de Dammartin married Jean II Seigneur de Pierrepont, Count de Roucy [2179] [2180] [2181]

☐ Marie (Mathilde) de Roucy married Jean I de Garlande, Seigneur de Possesse [2182] [2183] [2184] [2185]

[2170] fmg.ac/Projects/MedLands/NORTHERN%20FRANCE.htm#GuillaumeIPonthieudied1171A
[2171] fmg.ac/Projects/MedLands/BURGUNDY.htm#HelieBourgognedied1141
[2172] fmg.ac/Projects/MedLands/NORTHERN%20FRANCE.htm#GuyIIPonthieudied1147
[2173] fmg.ac/Projects/MedLands/NORTHERN%20FRANCE.htm#GuyIIPonthieudied1147
[2174] fmg.ac/Projects/MedLands/NORTHERN%20FRANCE.htm#BeatrixSaintPolMJeanIPonthieu
[2175] fmg.ac/Projects/MedLands/NORTHERN%20FRANCE.htm#GuillaumeIIdied1221A
[2176] fmg.ac/Projects/MedLands/CAPET.htm#Alixdiedafter1200MGuillaumeIIIPonthieu
[2177] fmg.ac/Projects/MedLands/NORTHERN%20FRANCE.htm#MariePonthieudied1250
[2178] fmg.ac/Projects/MedLands/NORTHERN%20FRANCE.htm#SimonDammartinAumalePonthieud1239B
[2179] fmg.ac/Projects/MedLands/NORTHERN%20FRANCE.htm#MarieDammartinMJeanIIRoucy
[2180] fmg.ac/Projects/MedLands/NORTHERN%20FRANCE.htm#JeanPierrepontRoucydied1251
[2181] DuLong, John. (2009) "Catherine de Baillon's de Roye Ancestry: Another Royal Gateway" (page 17). <u>Michigan's Habitant Heritage: Journal of the French-Canadian Heritage Society of Michigan</u>, Volume 30, Number 1, January 2009.

- Jean II de Garland, Seigneur de Possesse, married Agnès [2186] [2187]

☐ Alix de Garlande dt de Possesse married Dreux de Roye, Seigneur de Germigny [2188] [2189]

☐ Jeanne (Jacqueline) de Roye married Arnould V de Gavre [2190] [2191] [2192]

- Arnould VI de Gavre, Baron d'Escornaix married Isabelle (Ysabeau) de Ghistelles [2193] [2194]

☐ Catherine de Gavre d'Escornaix married Guy I Le Bouteiller [2195]

[2182] fmg.ac/Projects/MedLands/NORTHERN%20FRANCE.htm#dauJeanIIRoucyMJeanGarlande

[2183] fmg.ac/Projects/MedLands/PARIS%20REGION%20NOBILITY.htm#JeanGarlandePossessediedbefore1287

[2184] DuLong, John. (2009) "Catherine de Baillon's de Roye Ancestry: Another Royal Gateway" (page 17). Michigan's Habitant Heritage: Journal of the French-Canadian Heritage Society of Michigan, Volume 30, Number 1, January 2009.

[2185] racineshistoire.free.fr/LGN/PDF/Garlande.pdf (page 8)

[2186] Ibid.

[2187] DuLong, John. (2009) "Catherine de Baillon's de Roye Ancestry: Another Royal Gateway" (page 17). Michigan's Habitant Heritage: Journal of the French-Canadian Heritage Society of Michigan, Volume 30, Number 1, January 2009.

[2188] Ibid, pages 14 and 15.

[2189] racineshistoire.free.fr/LGN/PDF/Roye.pdf (page 6)

[2190] Jetté, René, DuLong, John P., Gagné, Roland-Yves, Moreau, Gail F. and Dubé, Joseph A. (2001) Table d'ascendance de Catherine Baillon: 12 générations (pages 124 and 125). Montréal, Québec: Société Généalogique Canadienne Française.

[2191] DuLong, John. (2009) "Catherine de Baillon's de Roye Ancestry: Another Royal Gateway" (page 13). Michigan's Habitant Heritage: Journal of the French-Canadian Heritage Society of Michigan, Volume 30, Number 1, January 2009.

[2192] racineshistoire.free.fr/LGN/PDF/Gavre.pdf (page 9)

[2193] Jetté, René, DuLong, John P., Gagné, Roland-Yves, Moreau, Gail F. and Dubé, Joseph A. (2001) Table d'ascendance de Catherine Baillon: 12 générations (page 112). Montréal, Québec: Société Généalogique Canadienne Française.

[2194] racineshistoire.free.fr/LGN/PDF/Gavre.pdf (page 9)

[2195] Ibid, page 10.

- Guy II Le Bouteillier married Isabeau Morhier [2196] [2197]

- Jean Le Bouteillier married Marie de Venois [2198]

- Bénigne Le Bouteillier married Jacques Maillard [2199]

- Miles Maillard married Marie Morant

- Renée Maillard married Adam de Baillon

- Alphonse de Baillon married Louise de Marle

- Catherine de Baillon

[2196] racineshistoire.free.fr/LGN/PDF/Gavre.pdf (page 10)
[2197] racineshistoire.free.fr/LGN/PDF/Morhier.pdf (page 4)
[2198] racineshistoire.free.fr/LGN/PDF/Gavre.pdf (page 9)
[2199] Ibid.

In keeping with the House of Montdidier, there exists a fourth line of descent.

■ Roger I, Seigneur de Montgommery, Vicomte de l'Hiémois, married Josceline ---------- (daughter of ---------- and Sainsfrida, sister to Gunnora, mistress of Richard I (The Fearless) de St. Clair (3rd Duke of Normandy)) [2200] [2201]

■ Roger II de Montgommery married Mabile d'Alençon [2202] [2203] [2204]

■ Robert de Montgommery (de Bellême), Sire d'Alençon, Comte de Ponthieu, Earl of Shrewsbury, married Agnès de Ponthieu [2205] [2206] [2207]

■ William I (Talvas), Comte de Ponthieu, married Hélie de Bourgogne [2208] [2209]

■ Guy II, Comte de Ponthieu, married Ida ---------- [2210]

■ Jean I, Comte de Ponthieu, married Beatrix de Saint-Pol [2211] [2212]

[2200] fmg.ac/Projects/MedLands/NORMAN%20NOBILITY.htm#RogerIMontgommery
[2201] fmg.ac/Projects/MedLands/NORMAN%20NOBILITY.htm#JoscelineMRogerIMontgommery
[2202] fmg.ac/Projects/MedLands/NORMAN%20NOBILITY.htm#RogerMontgommeryShrewsburydied1094A
[2203] fmg.ac/Projects/MedLands/NORMAN%20NOBILITY.htm#Mabiledied1079
[2204] racineshistoire.free.fr/LGN/PDF/Montgomery.pdf (page 3)
[2205] fmg.ac/Projects/MedLands/NORMAN%20NOBILITY.htm#RobertMontgommeryBellemedied1131
[2206]
[2207] racineshistoire.free.fr/LGN/PDF/Montgomery.pdf (pages 3 and 4)
[2208] fmg.ac/Projects/MedLands/NORTHERN%20FRANCE.htm#GuillaumeIPonthieudied1171A
[2209] fmg.ac/Projects/MedLands/BURGUNDY.htm#HelieBourgognedied1141
[2210] fmg.ac/Projects/MedLands/NORTHERN%20FRANCE.htm#GuyIIPonthieudied1147

■ William II (Talvas), Comte de Ponthieu, married Princess Alys de France, Countess of the Vexin (d/o Louis VII, King of France, and his second wife, Constance de Castile) [2213] [2214]

☐ Marie de Ponthieu married Simon de Dammartin, Count de Aumâle [2215] [2216]

☐ Marie de Dammartin married Jean II Seigneur de Pierrepont, Count de Roucy [2217] [2218] [2219]

☐ Marie (Mathilde) de Roucy married Jean I de Garlande, Seigneur de Possesse [2220] [2221] [2222] [2223]

[2211] fmg.ac/Projects/MedLands/NORTHERN%20FRANCE.htm#GuyIIPonthieudied1147

[2212] fmg.ac/Projects/MedLands/NORTHERN%20FRANCE.htm#BeatrixSaintPolMJeanIPonthieu

[2213] fmg.ac/Projects/MedLands/NORTHERN%20FRANCE.htm#GuillaumeIIdied1221A

[2214] fmg.ac/Projects/MedLands/CAPET.htm#Alixdiedafter1200MGuillaumeIIIPonthieu

[2215] fmg.ac/Projects/MedLands/NORTHERN%20FRANCE.htm#MariePonthieudied1250

[2216] fmg.ac/Projects/MedLands/NORTHERN%20FRANCE.htm#SimonDammartinAumalePonthieud1239B

[2217] fmg.ac/Projects/MedLands/NORTHERN%20FRANCE.htm#MarieDammartinMJeanIIRoucy

[2218] fmg.ac/Projects/MedLands/NORTHERN%20FRANCE.htm#JeanPierrepontRoucydied1251

[2219] DuLong, John. (2009) "Catherine de Baillon's de Roye Ancestry: Another Royal Gateway" (page 17). Michigan's Habitant Heritage: Journal of the French-Canadian Heritage Society of Michigan, Volume 30, Number 1, January 2009.

[2220] fmg.ac/Projects/MedLands/NORTHERN%20FRANCE.htm#dauJeanIIRoucyMJeanGarlande

[2221] fmg.ac/Projects/MedLands/PARIS%20REGION%20NOBILITY.htm#JeanGarlandePossessediedbefore1287

[2222] DuLong, John. (2009) "Catherine de Baillon's de Roye Ancestry: Another Royal Gateway" (page 17). Michigan's Habitant Heritage: Journal of the French-Canadian Heritage Society of Michigan, Volume 30, Number 1, January 2009.

- Jean II de Garland, Seigneur de Possesse, married Agnès [2224] [2225]

- ☐ Alix de Garlande dit de Possesse married Dreux de Roye, Seigneur de Germigny [2226] [2227]

- ☐ Jeanne (Jacqueline) de Roye married Arnould V de Gavre [2228] [2229] [2230]

- Arnould VI de Gavre, Baron d'Escornaix married Isabelle (Ysabeau) de Ghistelles [2231] [2232]

- ☐ Catherine de Gavre d'Escornaix married Guy I Le Bouteiller [2233]

- Guy II Le Bouteillier married Isabeau Morhier [2234] [2235]

- Jean Le Bouteillier married Marie de Venois [2236]

- ☐ Bénigne Le Bouteillier married Jacques Maillard [2237]

[2223] racineshistoire.free.fr/LGN/PDF/Garlande.pdf (page 8)
[2224] Ibid.
[2225] DuLong, John. (2009) "Catherine de Baillon's de Roye Ancestry: Another Royal Gateway" (page 17). Michigan's Habitant Heritage: Journal of the French-Canadian Heritage Society of Michigan, Volume 30, Number 1, January 2009.
[2226] Ibid, pages 14 and 15.
[2227] racineshistoire.free.fr/LGN/PDF/Roye.pdf (page 6)
[2228] Jetté, René, DuLong, John P., Gagné, Roland-Yves, Moreau, Gail F. and Dubé, Joseph A. (2001) Table d'ascendance de Catherine Baillon: 12 générations (pages 124 and 125). Montréal, Québec: Société Généalogique Canadienne Française.
[2229] DuLong, John. (2009) "Catherine de Baillon's de Roye Ancestry: Another Royal Gateway" (page 13). Michigan's Habitant Heritage: Journal of the French-Canadian Heritage Society of Michigan, Volume 30, Number 1, January 2009.
[2230] racineshistoire.free.fr/LGN/PDF/Gavre.pdf (page 9)
[2231] Jetté, René, DuLong, John P., Gagné, Roland-Yves, Moreau, Gail F. and Dubé, Joseph A. (2001) Table d'ascendance de Catherine Baillon: 12 générations (page 112). Montréal, Québec: Société Généalogique Canadienne Française.
[2232] racineshistoire.free.fr/LGN/PDF/Gavre.pdf (page 9)
[2233] Ibid, page 10.
[2234] racineshistoire.free.fr/LGN/PDF/Gavre.pdf (page 10)
[2235] racineshistoire.free.fr/LGN/PDF/Morhier.pdf (page 4)
[2236] racineshistoire.free.fr/LGN/PDF/Gavre.pdf (page 9)

- Miles Maillard married Marie Morant

- ☐ Renée Maillard married Adam de Baillon

- Alphonse de Baillon married Louise de Marle

- ☐ Catherine de Baillon

[2237] racineshistoire.free.fr/LGN/PDF/Gavre.pdf (page 9)

Grimaldi of Beuil

The Grimaldis of Antibes, Beuil, and Monaco were originally from Genoa, Italy. [2238]

The Grimaldis played an important role in the history of Genoa. Grimaldo, whose given name would become the family surname, was appointed one of the consuls of Genoa in 1162, 1170, and 1184, as well as serving as an ambassador to Frederick Barbarossa, the Holy Roman emperor, to the King of Morocco, and to the court of the Byzantine emperor in Constantinople. [2239]

Grimaldo is my 22nd great grandfather.

The descendants of Catherine de Baillon are most fortunate that much of their Genoese ancestry can be found in the documents transcribed and published by the principality of Monaco.

- Oberto Canella, Commissioner of Genoa, married Carradina Spinola

- Grimaldo Grimaldi, Consul of Genoa

- Luchetto Grimaldi, Admiral of Genoa

- Barnabo Grimaldi married Tiburge ----------

- Andaro Grimaldi married Astruge de Beuil in June 1315

[2238] Dulong, John P. *Correction of Catherine Baillon's Grimaldi Ancestry* article located in the Journal of the French-Canadian Heritage Society of Michigan, Volume 28, Number, 2, April 2007, page 54.
[2239] Ibid, page 60.

☐ Tiburge Grimaldi de Beuil married Ludovic (Louis) Lascaris de Vintmille, Seigneur de la Briga et de Limone, in 1346.

■ Rainier Lascaris de Vintmille, Count de Vintmille, Co-seigneur de la Briga et de Limone, married Madeleine Grimaldi d'Antibes, between 1400 and 1403

■ Charles Lascaris de Vintmille, Co-seigneur de la Briga, married Jeannette Litti, dame de Bonson et de La Roquette du Var

☐ Baptistine de Lascaris de Vintmille married Pierre Chabaud, seigneur de Tourrettes, between 1470 and 1480

■ Jean Chabaud, seigneur de Tourrettes, married Louise de Berre in 1519

■ Antoine Chabot (Chabaud), sieur de La Fond en Provence, married Catherine Lombard on March 30, 1554 at Chappelain et Crucé, Paris

☐ Marguerite Chabot married Jean Bizet, seigneur de Paponville et de la Grandmaison, in 1580

☐ Anne Bizet married Mathurin de Marle, seigneur de Vaugien, about 1610 in the Chevreuse (Yvelines) region

☐ Louise de Marle married Alphonse de Baillon, seigneur de La Mascotterie, between 1630 and 1640 in the Chevreuse (Yvelines) region

☐ Catherine de Baillon

SOURCES

René Jetté, John Patrick DuLong, Roland-Yves Gagné, Gail F. Moreau, and Joseph A. Dubé. Table d'ascendance de Catherine Baillon (12 générations) (pages 26, 132, 147, 159). Montréal: Société Généalogique Canadienne-Française, 2001.

Dulong, John P. *Correction of Catherine Baillon's Grimaldi Ancestry* article located in the Journal of the French-Canadian Heritage Society of Michigan, Volume 28, Number, 2, April 2007, pages 53 to 63.

Grimaldi of Antibes

The Grimaldis of Antibes, Beuil, and Monaco were originally from Genoa, Italy.[2240]

The Grimaldis played an important role in the history of Genoa. Grimaldo, whose given name would become the family surname, was appointed one of the consuls of Genoa in 1162, 1170, and 1184, as well as serving as an ambassador to Frederick Barbarossa, the Holy Roman emperor, to the King of Morocco, and to the court of the Byzantine emperor in Constantinople.[2241]

Not only can the descendants of Catherine de Baillon claim Antoine Grimaldi d'Antibes, Admiral de Gênes, as their ancestor, but because his great-grandson, Lambert Grimaldi, married Claudine Grimaldi, the heiress of Monaco, the present Prince Albert II of Monaco is also his descendant.[2242]

The descendants of Catherine de Baillon are most fortunate that much of their Genoese ancestry can be found in the documents transcribed and published by the principality of Monaco.

- Oberto Canella, Commissioner of Genoa, married Carradina Spinola

- Ingon Grimaldi

- Luca Grimaldi, Podestà of Milan

[2240] Dulong, John P. *Correction of Catherine Baillon's Grimaldi Ancestry* article located in the Journal of the French-Canadian Heritage Society of Michigan, Volume 28, Number, 2, April 2007, page 54.
[2241] Ibid, page 60.
[2242] Ibid, page 62.

■ Gabriel Grimaldi married Catarina Zaccaria

■ Gaspard Grimaldi, Captain of the People of Genoa

■ Antoine Grimaldi d'Antibes, Admiral de Gênes, Co-seigneur de Monaco, Seigneur de Prats et de Lantosque, married Catherine Doria

■ Luc Grimaldi d'Antibes, Co-seigneur d'Antibes, de Cagnes, et de Menton, married Yolande ----------

It is important to denote here that the Princes of Monaco also descend from Luc Grimaldi d'Antibes through the marriage of his grandson, Lambert, with Claudia, the great great granddaughter of Charles I Grimaldi.

☐ Madeleine Grimaldi d'Antibes married Rainier Lascaris, Count de Vintmille, between 1400 and 1403

■ Charles Lascaris de Vintmille, Co-seigneur de la Briga, married Jeannette Litti, dame de Bonson et de La Roquette du Var

☐ Baptistine de Lascaris de Vintmille married Pierre Chabaud, seigneur de Tourrettes, between 1470 and 1480

■ Jean Chabaud, seigneur de Tourrettes, married Louise de Berre in 1519

■ Antoine Chabot (Chabaud), sieur de La Fond en Provence, married Catherine Lombard on March 30, 1554 at Chappelain et Crucé, Paris

☐ Marguerite Chabot married Jean Bizet, seigneur de Paponville et de la Grandmaison, in 1580

☐ Anne Bizet married Mathurin de Marle, seigneur de Vaugien, about 1610 in the Chevreuse (Yvelines) region

☐ Louise de Marle married Alphonse de Baillon, seigneur de La Mascotterie, between 1630 and 1640 in the Chevreuse (Yvelines) region

☐ Catherine de Baillon

SOURCES

René Jetté, John Patrick DuLong, Roland-Yves Gagné, Gail F. Moreau, and Joseph A. Dubé. Table d'ascendance de Catherine Baillon (12 générations) (pages 26, 119, 132, 147, 159). Montréal: Société Généalogique Canadienne-Française, 2001.

Dulong, John P. *Correction of Catherine Baillon's Grimaldi Ancestry* article located in the Journal of the French-Canadian Heritage Society of Michigan, Volume 28, Number, 2, April 2007, pages 53 to 63.

Jehanne d'Arc

While they claim that Joan of Arc was burned at the stake, in the Place du Vieux Marché, in Rouen, by the English on May 30, 1431, during the time of the Hundred Years War, according to an article written by Jean Pierre Bernard, [2243] this was *not* what happened.

In summation, it appears that Jehanne d'Arc was an illegitimate daughter of the Queen of France (Isabella of Bavaria, wife of Charles VI, the *mad King*) and Louis, Duke of Orléans (brother to the King), born November 10, 1407. This made her the aunt of King Henry VI of England, whose mother (Catherine of Valois) was also the daughter of Isabella. Jehanne was, of course, half-sister to Charles VII and his siblings. She was also a half-sister to both Jehan d'Orléans, Count Dunois (referred to as the bastard of Orléans, born to Mariette d'Enghien, whose father was the Duke Louis) and Charles d'Orléans, nobleman and poet (the son of Duke Louis and his wife, Valentina Visconti).

Being of royal blood, she was not burned.

A document, The Book of Poitiers, was discovered in the Vatican Library in 1935 by writer Edward Schneider (a friend of Pius XI and honorary citizen of the Vatican). Bishop Weaver, director of the library, immediately asked him not to publish his discovery, not wanting the legend of one who had become *Saint Joan of Arc* to be destroyed.

[2243] https://www.histoire-genealogie.com/Jehanne-d-Arc-n-a-pas-ete-brulee

Blason de la Pucelle.

Personal Coat of Arms for Jehanne d'Arc

www.zetetique.ldh.org/jeanne.html

The study of this coat of arms also confirms the fact that Jehanne d'Arc was of royal blood.

Jehanne married a knight of Lorraine, Sir Robert of Armoises, in Arlon. Sir Robert was the nephew of Alarde Chambly, wife of Robert de Beaudricourt, Captain of Vaucouleurs. They did not have any children. They lived in Castle Jaulny, near Metz.

Jehanne died in 1449 and was buried in the chapel of the church (Pulligny-sur-Madon, south of Toul) alongside her husband. On her headstone is found her coat of arms as well as her name: Joan, the Maid of France, wife of Sir Robert of Armoises.

Personal Coat of Arms for Jehanne d'Arc

https://www.jeanne-darc.info/biography/coat-of-arms/

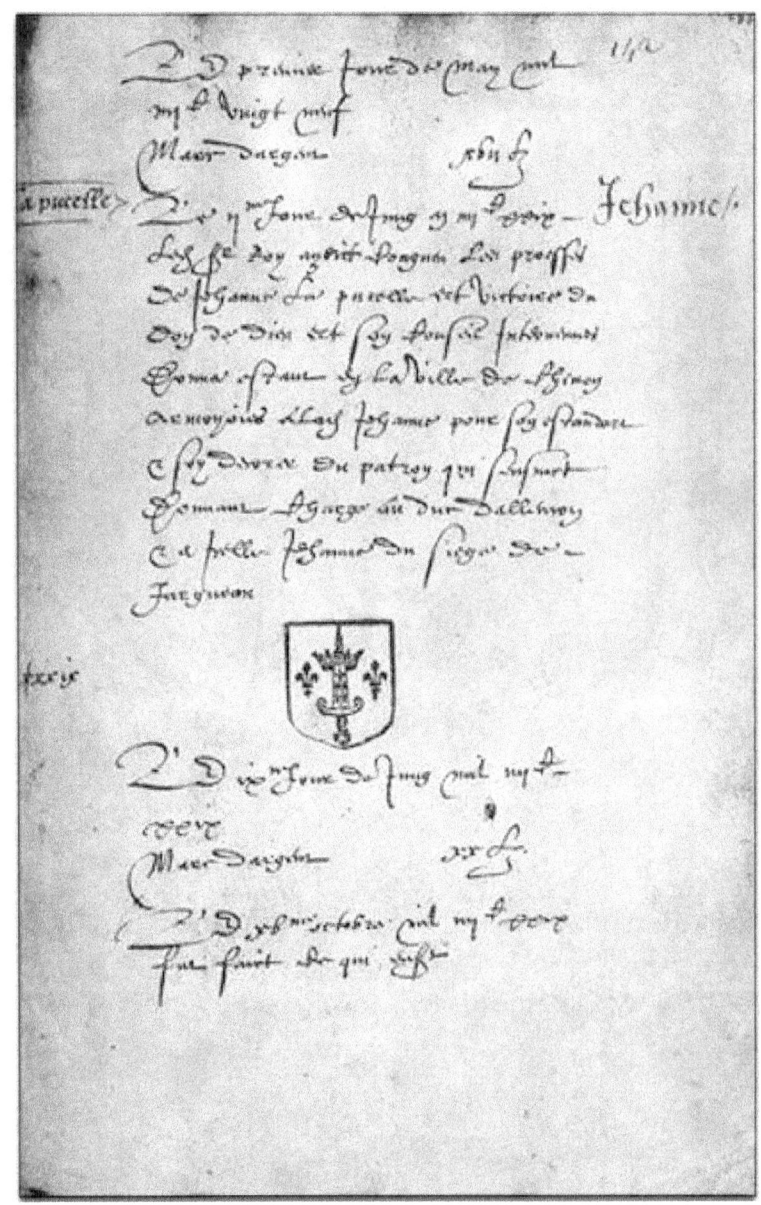

Patent Letters of Nobility (dated June 2, 1429) from Charles VII

https://www.jeanne-darc.info/biography/coat-of-arms/

Jehanne is granted a personal coat of arms, on the occasion of an authentic royal act, like a Princess of France; one that is hardly contestable.

Signature of Jeanne d'Arc

saint-joan-of-arc.com/signature.htm

https://en.wikipedia.org/wiki/File:Jehanne_signature.jpg

The Paternal Line of Jeanne d'Arc

- Charles I (dit *Charlemagne*), King of the Franks and Emperor of the West, married Hildegard ---------- in 771.

- Pépin I (originally born Carloman), King of Italy, married ---------- c. 795.

- Bernard (illegitimate issue), King of Italy, married Cunégonde of Laon ---------- c. 815.

- Pépin, Count de Vermandois and ----------

- Héribert I, Count de Vermandois and ----------

- ☐ Béatrice de Vermandois married Robert I, King of France, c. 895.

- Hugues *le Grand*, Duke of France, married <u>thirdly</u> Hedwige de Saxe between May 9 and September 14, 938 in either Mayence or Ingelheim.

- Hugues *Capet*, King of France, married Adélaïde ---------- in the summer of 968.

- Robert II, King of France, married Constance de Provence between 1003 and 1005.

- Henri I, King of France, married Anne de Russie on May 19, 1051 in Reims.

- Philippe I, King of France, married Berthe de Hollande between 1071 and 1073.

- Louis VI, King of France, married Adélaïde de Savoie in 1115.

- Louis VII, King of France, married Adèle de Blois et de Champagne on October 18, 1160.

- <u>King Philippe II Auguste of France</u> married <u>thirdly</u> Agnès d'Andechs de Méranie in June 1196.

This is the closest connection that I share with Jeanne d'Arc.

- King Louis VIII of France married Blanche of Castile

- King Louis IX of France married Margaret of Provence

- King Philippe III of France married Isabella of Aragon

- Prince Charles, Count of Valois, married Margaret, Countess of Anjou

- King Philippe VI of France married Joan of Burgundy

- King Jean II of France married Bonne of Luxembourg

- King Charles V of France married Joanna of Bourbon

- Louis, Duke of Orléans (brother to the King Charles VI) and an illegitimate tryst with Isabeau of Bavaria (wife of Charles VI, the *mad King*)

- Jehanne d'Arc

The Maternal Line of Jeanne d'Arc

- Otto I, Count of Scheyern [2244]

- Eckhard I, Count of Scheyern

- Otto IV, Count of Wittelsbach married Heilika of Pettendorf-Lengenfeld

- Otto I, Duke of Bavaria married Agnès of Loon

- Louis I, Duke of Bavaria married Ludmilla of Bohemia

- Otto II, Duke of Bavaria married Agnès of the Palatinate

- Louis II, Duke of Bavaria married Matilda of Habsburg

- Louis IV, Holy Roman Emperor married Béatrice of Silesia

- Stephen II, Duke of Bavaria married Elizabeth of Sicily

- Stephen III, Duke of Bavaria married Taddea Visconti

☐ Isabeau of Bavaria (wife of Charles VI, the *mad King*) and an illegitimate tryst with Louis, Duke of Orléans (brother to King Charles VI)

☐ Jehanne d'Arc

[2244] https://en.wikipedia.org/wiki/House_of_Wittelsbach

Further Descent from Antiquity

This proposal is based on an online document, *A 4,000 Year Old Descent from Antiquity: From the 12th Egyptian Dynasty to the Capetians and Beyond* [2245] in conjunction with Christian Settipani's 1991 publication, entitled <u>Nos Ancêtres de L'Antiquité: Etudes des possibilities de liens généalogiques entre les familles de l'Antiquité et celles du haut Moyen-Age européen</u> as published in Paris, France: Éditions Christian.

Christian Settipani, genealogist and historian (D.E.A. at the Sorbonne University), specializes in the genealogy and prosopography of elites in Europe and the Near East during the early Middle Ages and earlier; [2246] as such, he is a source for both historians in early mediæval and late antique Europe, as well as genealogists who work in the field of Descent from Antiquity (DFA).

I have done my best to enhance this work through the sourcing and cross-referencing of data and information gleaned from books as well as various websites. Further to this, any errors and/or omissions that result are, most assuredly, my own.

[2245] erwan.gil.free.fr/modules/freepages/pharaons/ramses_II.pdf
[2246] https://fr.wikipedia.org/wiki/Christian_Settipani

THE PARTHIAN EMPIRE, also known as the Arsacid Empire, was a major Iranian political and cultural power in ancient Persia. [2247]

GENERATION 1 (61G grandparents) [2248] [2249] [2250]

King Vonones II of Parthia married ---------- (a Greek concubine). [2251] [2252] [2253] [2254]

GENERATION 2 (60 G grandparents) [2255]

King Mithridates IV of Parthia [2256]

GENERATION 3 (59G grandparents) [2257]

King Sanatruces II of Parthia (Sanatruk) [2258]

[2247] https://en.wikipedia.org/wiki/Parthian_Empire
[2248] Settipani, Christian. (1991) <u>Nos Ancêtres de L'Antiquité: Etudes des possibilités de liens généalogiques entre les familles de l'Antiquité et celles du haut Moyen-Age européen</u> (page viii). Paris, France: Éditions Christian.
[2249] *A 4,000 Year Old Descent from Antiquity: From the 12th Egyptian Dynasty to the Capetians and Beyond* (page 12, entry 81). erwan.gil.free.fr/modules/freepages/pharaons/ramses_II.pdf
[2250] Starr, Brian. (2010) The Saints Tree (page 235). Bloomington, IN: Xlibris Corporation.
[2251] sites.rootsweb.com/~cousin/html/p265.htm#i5997
[2252] sites.rootsweb.com/~cousin/html/p265.htm#i5997
[2253] http://en.wikipedia.org/wiki/Vonones_II_of_Parthia
[2254] http://en.wikipedia.org/wiki/Vonones_II
[2255] Settipani, Christian. (1991) <u>Nos Ancêtres de L'Antiquité: Etudes des possibilités de liens généalogiques entre les familles de l'Antiquité et celles du haut Moyen-Age européen</u> (pages viii and 80). Paris, France: Éditions Christian.
[2256] https://en.wikipedia.org/wiki/Mithridates_IV_of_Parthia
[2257] Settipani, Christian. (1991) <u>Nos Ancêtres de L'Antiquité: Etudes des possibilités de liens généalogiques entre les familles de l'Antiquité et celles du haut Moyen-Age européen</u> (pages viii and 80). Paris, France: Éditions Christian.
[2258] https://en.wikipedia.org/wiki/Sanatruces_II_of_Parthia

GENERATION 4 (58G grandparents) [2259]

King Vologaeses I of Armenia (King Vologaeses III of Parthia) [2260]

THE ARSACID DYNASTY (a branch of the Iranian Parthian Arsacids) ruled the Kingdom of Armenia from 54 to 428. [2261]

The Arsacid Kings of Armenia reigned intermittently throughout the chaotic years following the fall of the Artaxiad Dynasty, until 62 when Tridates I secured Arsacid rule in Armenia. [2262]

An independent line of Kings was established by Volgaeses II of Armenia (also known as Vologaesus V of Parthia) in 180. [2263]

Two of the most notable events under Arsacid rule in Armenian history were the conversion of Armenia to Christianity by Gregory the Illuminator in 301 and the creation of the Armenian alphabet by Saint Mesrob c. 406. [2264]

[2259] Settipani, Christian. (1991) <u>Nos Ancêtres de L'Antiquité: Etudes des possibilities de liens généalogiques entre les familles de l'Antiquité et celles du haut Moyen-Age européen</u> (pages viii and 80). Paris, France: Éditions Christian.
[2260] https://en.wikipedia.org/wiki/Vologases_III_of_Parthia
[2261] https://en.wikipedia.org/wiki/Arsacid_dynasty_of_Armenia
[2262] Ibid.
[2263] https://en.wikipedia.org/wiki/Arsacid_dynasty_of_Armenia
[2264] Ibid.

GENERATION 5 (57G grandparents) [2265] [2266]

King Vologaesus II of Armenia and Vologaesus V of Parthia married a Princess of Iberia (d/o King Pharasmenes III). [2267] [2268] [2269] While was serving both as King of Parthia and Armenia, Vologaesus II abdicated his Armenian throne and gave the Armenian Kingship to Khosrov I, his son, who then served as Armenian King from 198 until 217. [2270] He was also denoted as King Vagharsh on the list of Armenia Arsacid Kings. [2271]

GENERATION 6 (56G grandparents) [2272] [2273]

King Khosrow I of Armenia married ---------- [2274] [2275]

[2265] Settipani, Christian. (1991) Nos Ancêtres de L'Antiquité: Etudes des possibilités de liens généalogiques entre les familles de l'Antiquité et celles du haut Moyen-Age européen (pages viii and 80). Paris, France: Éditions Christian.
[2266] *A 4,000 Year Old Descent from Antiquity: From the 12th Egyptian Dynasty to the Capetians and Beyond* (page 12, entry 86).
erwan.gil.free.fr/modules/freepages/pharaons/ramses_II.pdf
[2267] sites.rootsweb.com/~cousin/html/p285.htm#i24713
[2268] sites.rootsweb.com/~cousin/html/p51.htm#i5988
[2269] https://en.wikipedia.org/wiki/List_of_Parthian_kings (ruler 46)
[2270] Ibid.
[2271] www.armenianhighland.com/main.html
[2272] Settipani, Christian. (1991) Nos Ancêtres de L'Antiquité: Etudes des possibilités de liens généalogiques entre les familles de l'Antiquité et celles du haut Moyen-Age européen (page viii). Paris, France: Éditions Christian.
[2273] *A 4,000 Year Old Descent from Antiquity: From the 12th Egyptian Dynasty to the Capetians and Beyond* (page 13, entry 87).
erwan.gil.free.fr/modules/freepages/pharaons/ramses_II.pdf
[2274] sites.rootsweb.com/~cousin/html/p285.htm#i5985
[2275] https://en.wikipedia.org/wiki/Khosrov_I_of_Armenia

GENERATION 7 (55G grandparents) [2276] [2277]

King Tiridates II of Greater Armenia married ---------- [2278] [2279]

GENERATION 8 (54G grandparents) [2280] [2281]

King Khosrow II of West Armenia married ---------- [2282] [2283]

GENERATION 9 (53G grandparents) [2284] [2285]

King Tiridates III of Armenia married Ashkhen of the Alans. [2286] [2287] [2288] [2289] In 301, Tiridates proclaimed Christianity as the state religion of Armenia, making the Armenian kingdom the first state to embrace Christianity officially. [2290]

[2276] Settipani, Christian. (1991) <u>Nos Ancêtres de L'Antiquité: Etudes des possibilités de liens généalogiques entre les familles de l'Antiquité et celles du haut Moyen-Age européen</u> (page viii). Paris, France: Éditions Christian.
[2277] *A 4,000 Year Old Descent from Antiquity: From the 12th Egyptian Dynasty to the Capetians and Beyond* (page 13, entry 88). erwan.gil.free.fr/modules/freepages/pharaons/ramses_II.pdf
[2278] sites.rootsweb.com/~cousin/html/p285.htm#i5983
[2279] https://en.wikipedia.org/wiki/Tiridates_II_of_Armenia
[2280] Settipani, Christian. (1991) <u>Nos Ancêtres de L'Antiquité: Etudes des possibilités de liens généalogiques entre les familles de l'Antiquité et celles du haut Moyen-Age européen</u> (pages viii and 66). Paris, France: Éditions Christian.
[2281] *A 4,000 Year Old Descent from Antiquity: From the 12th Egyptian Dynasty to the Capetians and Beyond* (page 13, entry 89). erwan.gil.free.fr/modules/freepages/pharaons/ramses_II.pdf
[2282] sites.rootsweb.com/~cousin/html/p285.htm#i5981
[2283] https://en.wikipedia.org/wiki/Khosrov_II_of_Armenia
[2284] Settipani, Christian. (1991) <u>Nos Ancêtres de L'Antiquité: Etudes des possibilités de liens généalogiques entre les familles de l'Antiquité et celles du haut Moyen-Age européen</u> (pages viii and 66). Paris, France: Éditions Christian.
[2285] *A 4,000 Year Old Descent from Antiquity: From the 12th Egyptian Dynasty to the Capetians and Beyond* (page 13, entry 90). erwan.gil.free.fr/modules/freepages/pharaons/ramses_II.pdf
[2286] sites.rootsweb.com/~cousin/html/p286.htm#i5979
[2287] sites.rootsweb.com/~cousin/html/p51.htm#i5980

GENERATION 10 (52G grandparents) [2291] [2292]

King Khosrow III of Armenia married ---------- [2293] [2294]

GENERATION 11 (51G grandparents) [2295] [2296]

Arsacid Princess Bambishn of Armenia (sister of King Tigranes VII aka Tiran) married Athenagenes Souren-Pahlav (s/o Saint Husik I). [2297] [2298] [2299] [2300]

Saint Gregory the Illuminator (or Saint Gregory the Enlightener) is the patron saint and first official head of the Armenian Apostolic Church; he was a religious leader who is credited with converting Armenia from paganism to Christianity, Armenia thus being the first nation to adopt Christianity as its official religion in 301. [2301]

[2288] https://en.wikipedia.org/wiki/Tiridates_III_of_Armenia
[2289] https://en.wikipedia.org/wiki/Ashkhen
[2290] https://en.wikipedia.org/wiki/Tiridates_III_of_Armenia
[2291] Settipani, Christian. (1991) <u>Nos Ancêtres de L'Antiquité: Etudes des possibilities de liens généalogiques entre les familles de l'Antiquité et celles du haut Moyen-Age européen</u> (pages viii and 191). Paris, France: Éditions Christian.
[2292] *A 4,000 Year Old Descent from Antiquity: From the 12th Egyptian Dynasty to the Capetians and Beyond* (page 13, entry 91). erwan.gil.free.fr/modules/freepages/pharaons/ramses_II.pdf
[2293] http://sites.rootsweb.com/~cousin/html/p286.htm#i5977
[2294] https://en.wikipedia.org/wiki/Khosrov_III_the_Small
[2295] Settipani, Christian. (1991) <u>Nos Ancêtres de L'Antiquité: Etudes des possibilities de liens généalogiques entre les familles de l'Antiquité et celles du haut Moyen-Age européen</u> (pages viii, 55, 58 and 191). Paris, France: Éditions Christian.
[2296] *A 4,000 Year Old Descent from Antiquity: From the 12th Egyptian Dynasty to the Capetians and Beyond* (page 13, entry 92). erwan.gil.free.fr/modules/freepages/pharaons/ramses_II.pdf
[2297] sites.rootsweb.com/~cousin/html/p51.htm#i5972
[2298] sites.rootsweb.com/~cousin/html/p278.htm#i5971
[2299] https://en.wikipedia.org/wiki/Khosrov_III_the_Small
[2300] https://en.wikipedia.org/wiki/St._Husik_I
[2301] https://en.wikipedia.org/wiki/Gregory_the_illuminator

Gregory married a woman called Miriam, a devout Christian who was the daughter of a Christian Armenian Prince in Cappadocia; from their union, Miriam bore Gregory two children, their sons Vrtanes and Aristaces. [2302]

Vrtanes, also known Saint Vrtanes, succeeded immediately after Saint Gergory the Enlightener and Aristaces (his younger brother) as third in line to the hereditary Parthian line of Catholicoi. [2303] Vrtanes was the father of Saint Husik I, and Gregory, by an unnamed wife. [2304]

THE MAMIKONIANS OF ARMENIA were a noble family which dominated Armenian politics between the 4th and 8th centuries; they ruled the Armenian regions of Taron, Sasun, Bagrevand and others. [2305]

GENERATION 12 (50G grandparents) [2306] [2307]

Nerses Souren-Pahlav (aka Saint Nerses the Great) married Samdukht Mamikonian (daughter of Vardan I, Prince of the Mamikonians). [2308] [2309] [2310] [2311]

[2302] https://en.wikipedia.org/wiki/Gregory_the_illuminator
[2303] https://en.wikipedia.org/wiki/St._Vrtanes_I
[2304] Ibid.
[2305] https://en.wikipedia.org/wiki/Mamikonian
[2306] Settipani, Christian. (1991) <u>Nos Ancêtres de L'Antiquité: Etudes des possibilities de liens généalogiques entre les familles de l'Antiquité et celles du haut Moyen-Age européen</u> (pages viii, 55, 58 and 191). Paris, France: Éditions Christian.
[2307] *A 4,000 Year Old Descent from Antiquity: From the 12th Egyptian Dynasty to the Capetians and Beyond* (page 13, entry 93). erwan.gil.free.fr/modules/freepages/pharaons/ramses_II.pdf
[2308] sites.rootsweb.com/~cousin/html/p287.htm#i5967
[2309] sites.rootsweb.com/~cousin/html/p51.htm#i5968
[2310] https://en.wikipedia.org/wiki/St._Nerses_I
[2311] https://en.wikipedia.org/wiki/Mamikonian

A member of the Gregorid family (confirmed by contemporary evidence of high quality), his family line can be traced, without difficulty, to the Gregorid Armenian patriarch, St. Gregory I the Illuminator. [2312]

GENERATION 13 (49G grandparents) [2313] [2314]

Sahak Souren-Pahlav (aka Saint Isaac the Great of Armenia) was Patriarch of the Armenian Apostolic Church. [2315]

Through his father he was a Gregorid, descended from the family of St. Gregory I the Enlightener. [2316]

GENERATION 14 (48G grandparents) [2317] [2318]

Sahakanoys Souren-Pahlav married Prince Hamazasp I Mamikonian (s/o Manuel Mamikonian and grandson of Artashir Mamikonian), High Constable of Armenia [2319] [2320] [2321]

[2312] https://en.wikipedia.org/wiki/Gregorids
[2313] Settipani, Christian. (1991) <u>Nos Ancêtres de L'Antiquité: Etudes des possibilities de liens généalogiques entre les familles de l'Antiquité et celles du haut Moyen-Age européen</u> (pages viii, 55, 58 and 191). Paris, France: Éditions Christian.
[2314] *A 4,000 Year Old Descent from Antiquity: From the 12th Egyptian Dynasty to the Capetians and Beyond* (page 13, entry 94). erwan.gil.free.fr/modules/freepages/pharaons/ramses_II.pdf
[2315] sites.rootsweb.com/~cousin/html/p288.htm#i5965
[2316] https://en.wikipedia.org/wiki/Isaac_of_Armenia
[2317] Settipani, Christian. (1991) <u>Nos Ancêtres de L'Antiquité: Etudes des possibilities de liens généalogiques entre les familles de l'Antiquité et celles du haut Moyen-Age européen</u> (pages viii, 38, 66 and 191). Paris, France: Éditions Christian.
[2318] *A 4,000 Year Old Descent from Antiquity: From the 12th Egyptian Dynasty to the Capetians and Beyond* (page 13, entry 95). erwan.gil.free.fr/modules/freepages/pharaons/ramses_II.pdf
[2319] sites.rootsweb.com/~cousin/html/p51.htm#i5964

GENERATION 15 (47G grandparents) [2322] [2323]

General Hmayeak Mamikonian, the Ambassador of Armenia to the Eastern Empire, married Dzoyk (Dzovik), daughter of Vram, Prince of Artsrouni. [2324] [2325]

GENERATION 16 (46G grandparents) [2326] [2327]

Vard Mamikonian (Patriarch of Armenia) married ---------- [2328]

GENERATION 17 (45G grandparents) [2329] [2330]

Prince Hmayeak II Mamikonian married ---------- [2331]

[2320] sites.rootsweb.com/~cousin/html/p288.htm#i5963
[2321] https://en.wikipedia.org/wiki/Mamikonian
[2322] Settipani, Christian. (1991) Nos Ancêtres de L'Antiquité: Etudes des possibilités de liens généalogiques entre les familles de l'Antiquité et celles du haut Moyen-Age européen (pages viii, 38 and 191). Paris, France: Éditions Christian.
[2323] *A 4,000 Year Old Descent from Antiquity: From the 12th Egyptian Dynasty to the Capetians and Beyond* (page 13, entry 96).
erwan.gil.free.fr/modules/freepages/pharaons/ramses_II.pdf
[2324] sites.rootsweb.com/~cousin/html/p288.htm#i5961
[2325] sites.rootsweb.com/~cousin/html/p51.htm#i5962
[2326] Settipani, Christian. (1991) Nos Ancêtres de L'Antiquité: Etudes des possibilités de liens généalogiques entre les familles de l'Antiquité et celles du haut Moyen-Age européen (pages viii, 38 and 191). Paris, France: Éditions Christian.
[2327] *A 4,000 Year Old Descent from Antiquity: From the 12th Egyptian Dynasty to the Capetians and Beyond* (page 13, entry 97).
erwan.gil.free.fr/modules/freepages/pharaons/ramses_II.pdf
[2328] sites.rootsweb.com/~cousin/html/p290.htm#i5959
[2329] Settipani, Christian. (1991) Nos Ancêtres de L'Antiquité: Etudes des possibilités de liens généalogiques entre les familles de l'Antiquité et celles du haut Moyen-Age européen (pages viii, 38 and 191). Paris, France: Éditions Christian.
[2330] *A 4,000 Year Old Descent from Antiquity: From the 12th Egyptian Dynasty to the Capetians and Beyond* (page 13, entry 98).
erwan.gil.free.fr/modules/freepages/pharaons/ramses_II.pdf
[2331] sites.rootsweb.com/~cousin/html/p291.htm#i5957

GENERATION 18 (44G grandparents) [2332] [2333]

Governor Mušegh I Mamikonian married ---------- [2334]

GENERATION 19 (43G grandparents) [2335] [2336]

Vahan II Mamikonian (Prince of Taron) married ---------- [2337]

GENERATION 20 (42G grandparents) [2338] [2339]

Prince Dawith Mamikonian married ---------- [2340]

[2332] Settipani, Christian. (1991) Nos Ancêtres de L'Antiquité: Etudes des possibilities de liens généalogiques entre les familles de l'Antiquité et celles du haut Moyen-Age européen (pages viii, 35 and 191). Paris, France: Éditions Christian.
[2333] *A 4,000 Year Old Descent from Antiquity: From the 12th Egyptian Dynasty to the Capetians and Beyond* (page 13, entry 99). erwan.gil.free.fr/modules/freepages/pharaons/ramses_II.pdf
[2334] sites.rootsweb.com/~cousin/html/p294.htm#i5955
[2335] Settipani, Christian. (1991) Nos Ancêtres de L'Antiquité: Etudes des possibilities de liens généalogiques entre les familles de l'Antiquité et celles du haut Moyen-Age européen (pages viii, 38 and 191). Paris, France: Éditions Christian.
[2336] *A 4,000 Year Old Descent from Antiquity: From the 12th Egyptian Dynasty to the Capetians and Beyond* (page 13, entry 100). erwan.gil.free.fr/modules/freepages/pharaons/ramses_II.pdf
[2337] sites.rootsweb.com/~cousin/html/p295.htm#i5953
[2338] Settipani, Christian. (1991) Nos Ancêtres de L'Antiquité: Etudes des possibilities de liens généalogiques entre les familles de l'Antiquité et celles du haut Moyen-Age européen (pages viii, 38 and 191). Paris, France: Éditions Christian.
[2339] *A 4,000 Year Old Descent from Antiquity: From the 12th Egyptian Dynasty to the Capetians and Beyond* (page 13, entry 101). erwan.gil.free.fr/modules/freepages/pharaons/ramses_II.pdf
[2340] sites.rootsweb.com/~cousin/html/p51.htm#i5951

GENERATION 21 (41G grandparents) [2341] [2342]

Prince Hamazasp III Mamikonian married a daughter of Prince Théodore I, Rštouni. [2343] [2344] [2345]

GENERATION 22 (40G grandparents) [2346] [2347]

Artavazd Mamikonian (Nakharar of Taron) married ---------- [2348]

GENERATION 23 (39G grandparents) [2349] [2350]

Hmayeak Mamikonian (Patriarch of Armenia) married ---------- [2351]

[2341] Settipani, Christian. (1991) Nos Ancêtres de L'Antiquité: Etudes des possibilités de liens généalogiques entre les familles de l'Antiquité et celles du haut Moyen-Age européen (pages viii and 38). Paris, France: Éditions Christian.

[2342] *A 4,000 Year Old Descent from Antiquity: From the 12th Egyptian Dynasty to the Capetians and Beyond* (page 13, entry 102). erwan.gil.free.fr/modules/freepages/pharaons/ramses_II.pdf

[2343] Settipani, Christian. (1991) Nos Ancêtres de L'Antiquité: Etudes des possibilités de liens généalogiques entre les familles de l'Antiquité et celles du haut Moyen-Age européen (page 48). Paris, France: Éditions Christian.

[2344] sites.rootsweb.com/~cousin/html/p298.htm#i5947

[2345] sites.rootsweb.com/~cousin/html/p50.htm#i5948

[2346] Settipani, Christian. (1991) Nos Ancêtres de L'Antiquité: Etudes des possibilités de liens généalogiques entre les familles de l'Antiquité et celles du haut Moyen-Age européen (pages viii and 38). Paris, France: Éditions Christian.

[2347] *A 4,000 Year Old Descent from Antiquity: From the 12th Egyptian Dynasty to the Capetians and Beyond* (page 13, entry 103). erwan.gil.free.fr/modules/freepages/pharaons/ramses_II.pdf

[2348] sites.rootsweb.com/~cousin/html/p300.htm#i5945

[2349] Settipani, Christian. (1991) Nos Ancêtres de L'Antiquité: Etudes des possibilités de liens généalogiques entre les familles de l'Antiquité et celles du haut Moyen-Age européen (pages viii, 35 and 38). Paris, France: Éditions Christian.

[2350] *A 4,000 Year Old Descent from Antiquity: From the 12th Egyptian Dynasty to the Capetians and Beyond* (page 14, entry 104). erwan.gil.free.fr/modules/freepages/pharaons/ramses_II.pdf

GENERATION 24A (38G grandparents) [2352] [2353]

Artavazd Mamikonian (Nakharar and Byzantine strategist for Anatolia) married _____ [2354]

GENERATION 25A (37G grandparents) [2355]

Hmayeak Mamikonian married a daughter of Emperor Leo V [2356] [2357]

GENERATION 26A (36G grandparents) [2358]

Konstantinos Mamikonian married Pancalo Bagrationi [2359] [2360]

[2351] sites.rootsweb.com/~cousin/html/p301.htm#i5943
[2352] Settipani, Christian. (1991) <u>Nos Ancêtres de L'Antiquité: Etudes des possibilités de liens généalogiques entre les familles de l'Antiquité et celles du haut Moyen-Age européen</u> (pages viii, 35 and 38). Paris, France: Éditions Christian.
[2353] *A 4,000 Year Old Descent from Antiquity: From the 12th Egyptian Dynasty to the Capetians and Beyond* (page 14, entry 105). erwan.gil.free.fr/modules/freepages/pharaons/ramses_II.pdf
[2354] sites.rootsweb.com/~cousin/html/p304.htm#i5941
[2355] *A 4,000 Year Old Descent from Antiquity: From the 12th Egyptian Dynasty to the Capetians and Beyond* (page 14, entry 106). erwan.gil.free.fr/modules/freepages/pharaons/ramses_II.pdf
[2356] sites.rootsweb.com/~cousin/html/p304.htm#i5918
[2357] sites.rootsweb.com/~cousin/html/p50.htm#i5919
[2358] *A 4,000 Year Old Descent from Antiquity: From the 12th Egyptian Dynasty to the Capetians and Beyond* (page 14, entry 107). erwan.gil.free.fr/modules/freepages/pharaons/ramses_II.pdf
[2359] sites.rootsweb.com/~cousin/html/p50.htm#i5916
[2360] sites.rootsweb.com/~cousin/html/p50.htm#i5917

THE BYZANTINE EMPERORS

GENERATION 27A (35G grandparents) [2361]

Byzantine Emperor Basil I (The Macedonian) married Evdokia Ingerina [2362]

GENERATION 28A (34G grandparents) [2363] [2364]

Byzantine Emperor Leo VI (The Wise) married Zoë Tzautzina [2365] [2366] [2367] [2368]

THE LATE CAROLINGIANS

GENERATION 29A (33G grandparents) [2369] [2370]

Anna of Constantinople (Macedonia) married Holy Roman Emperor Louis III (The Blind) [2371] [2372] [2373]

[2361] *A 4,000 Year Old Descent from Antiquity: From the 12th Egyptian Dynasty to the Capetians and Beyond* (page 14, entry 108). erwan.gil.free.fr/modules/freepages/pharaons/ramses_II.pdf

[2362] fmg.ac/Projects/MedLands/BYZANTIUM.htm#_Toc204564496

[2363] Settipani, Christian. (1991) Nos Ancêtres de L'Antiquité: Etudes des possibilités de liens généalogiques entre les familles de l'Antiquité et celles du haut Moyen-Age européen (pages viii and 17). Paris, France: Éditions Christian.

[2364] *A 4,000 Year Old Descent from Antiquity: From the 12th Egyptian Dynasty to the Capetians and Beyond* (page 14, entry 109). erwan.gil.free.fr/modules/freepages/pharaons/ramses_II.pdf

[2365] sites.rootsweb.com/~cousin/html/p316.htm#i6437

[2366] sites.rootsweb.com/~cousin/html/p314.htm#i8224

[2367] https://en.wikipedia.org/wiki/Leo_VI_the_Wise

[2368] https://en.wikipedia.org/wiki/Zoe_Zaoutzaina

[2369] Settipani, Christian. (1991) Nos Ancêtres de L'Antiquité: Etudes des possibilités de liens généalogiques entre les familles de l'Antiquité et celles du haut Moyen-Age européen (pages viii and 9). Paris, France: Éditions Christian.

[2370] *A 4,000 Year Old Descent from Antiquity: From the 12th Egyptian Dynasty to the Capetians and Beyond* (page 14, entry 110). erwan.gil.free.fr/modules/freepages/pharaons/ramses_II.pdf

GENERATION 30A (32G grandparents) [2374] [2375]

Count Charles Constantine of Vienne married Tuetberga of Troyes [2376] [2377] [2378] [2379] [2380] [2381]

THE BOSONIDS

GENERATION 31A (31G grandparents) [2382] [2383]

Countess Constance of Vienne married Count Boson II of Provence [2384] [2385] [2386]

[2371] sites.rootsweb.com/~cousin/html/p315.htm#i8222
[2372] sites.rootsweb.com/~cousin/html/p318.htm#i8223
[2373] https://en.wikipedia.org/wiki/Louis_the_Blind
[2374] Settipani, Christian. (1991) <u>Nos Ancêtres de L'Antiquité: Etudes des possibilities de liens généalogiques entre les familles de l'Antiquité et celles du haut Moyen-Age européen</u> (pages viii and 9). Paris, France: Éditions Christian.
[2375] *A 4,000 Year Old Descent from Antiquity: From the 12th Egyptian Dynasty to the Capetians and Beyond* (page 14, entry 110). erwan.gil.free.fr/modules/freepages/pharaons/ramses_II.pdf
[2376] https://en.wikipedia.org/wiki/Charles_Constantine_of_Vienne
[2377] https://en.wikipedia.org/wiki/Zoe_Zaoutzaina
[2378] genealogie.quebec/testphp/info.php?no=39582
[2379] genealogie.quebec/testphp/info.php?no=39583
[2380] sites.rootsweb.com/~cousin/html/p324.htm#i8217
[2381] sites.rootsweb.com/~cousin/html/p323.htm#i8218
[2382] Settipani, Christian. (1991) <u>Nos Ancêtres de L'Antiquité: Etudes des possibilities de liens généalogiques entre les familles de l'Antiquité et celles du haut Moyen-Age européen</u> (pages viii and 6). Paris, France: Éditions Christian.
[2383] *A 4,000 Year Old Descent from Antiquity: From the 12th Egyptian Dynasty to the Capetians and Beyond* (page 15, entry 112). erwan.gil.free.fr/modules/freepages/pharaons/ramses_II.pdf
[2384] sites.rootsweb.com/~cousin/html/p324.htm#i8216
[2385] sites.rootsweb.com/~cousin/html/p325.htm#i8215
[2386] https://en.wikipedia.org/wiki/William_I_of_Provence

GENERATION 32A (30G grandparents) [2387] [2388]

Count William I of Provence married Countess Adélaïde Blanche of Anjou (d/o Count Fulk II of Anjou and Gerberga of Maine) [2389] [2390] [2391] [2392]

THE CAPETIANS

GENERATION 33A (29G grandparents) [2393] [2394]

Constance of Arles married King Robert II (of France) 996-1031 (s/o King Hugues Capet (first Capetian King of France) 987-996 and Adélaïde of Aquitaine) [2395] [2396] [2397] [2398]

[2387] Settipani, Christian. (1991) <u>Nos Ancêtres de L'Antiquité: Etudes des possibilities de liens généalogiques entre les familles de l'Antiquité et celles du haut Moyen-Age européen</u> (pages viii and 6). Paris, France: Éditions Christian.
[2388] *A 4,000 Year Old Descent from Antiquity: From the 12th Egyptian Dynasty to the Capetians and Beyond* (page 15, entry 113). erwan.gil.free.fr/modules/freepages/pharaons/ramses_II.pdf
[2389] sites.rootsweb.com/~cousin/html/p330.htm#i5098
[2390] sites.rootsweb.com/~cousin/html/p337.htm#i27786
[2391] https://en.wikipedia.org/wiki/William_I_of_Provence
[2392] https://en.wikipedia.org/wiki/Anne_of_Kiev
[2393] Settipani, Christian. (1991) <u>Nos Ancêtres de L'Antiquité: Etudes des possibilities de liens généalogiques entre les familles de l'Antiquité et celles du haut Moyen-Age européen</u> (pages viii and 6). Paris, France: Éditions Christian.
[2394] *A 4,000 Year Old Descent from Antiquity: From the 12th Egyptian Dynasty to the Capetians and Beyond* (page 15, entry 114). erwan.gil.free.fr/modules/freepages/pharaons/ramses_II.pdf
[2395] sites.rootsweb.com/~cousin/html/p338.htm#i5279
[2396] sites.rootsweb.com/~cousin/html/p338.htm#i5218
[2397] https://en.wikipedia.org/wiki/Constance_of_Arles
[2398] https://en.wikipedia.org/wiki/Robert_II_of_France

GENERATION 34A (28G grandparents) [2399] [2400]

King Henri I (of France) 1031-1060 married Anna of Kiev (d/o Grand Prince Yaroslav I (The Wise) of Kiev and Ingegerd of Sweden [2401] [2402] [2403] [2404]

Refer to **GENERATION 35** (page 476) for line continuation.

[2399] Settipani, Christian. (1991) Nos Ancêtres de L'Antiquité: Etudes des possibilities de liens généalogiques entre les familles de l'Antiquité et celles du haut Moyen-Age européen (page viii). Paris, France: Éditions Christian.
[2400] *A 4,000 Year Old Descent from Antiquity: From the 12th Egyptian Dynasty to the Capetians and Beyond* (page 15, entry 115). erwan.gil.free.fr/modules/freepages/pharaons/ramses_II.pdf
[2401] sites.rootsweb.com/~cousin/html/p345.htm#i5277
[2402] sites.rootsweb.com/~cousin/html/p349.htm#i5278
[2403] https://en.wikipedia.org/wiki/Henry_I_of_France
[2404] https://en.wikipedia.org/wiki/Anne_of_Kiev

Refer back to **GENERATION 23** (page 465).

THE MAMIKONIANS OF ARMENIA were a noble family which dominated Armenian politics between the 4th and 8th centuries; they ruled the Armenian regions of Taron, Sasun, Bagrevand and others. [2405]

GENERATION 24B (38G grandparents) [2406] [2407]

Artavazd Mamikonian (Nakharar and Byzantine strategist for Anatolia) married ---------- [2408]

GENERATION 25B (37G grandparents) [2409]

Marinos Mamikonian married Theoctista Phlorina of Paphlogonia [2410] [2411] [2412]

[2405] https://en.wikipedia.org/wiki/Mamikonian
[2406] Settipani, Christian. (1991) <u>Nos Ancêtres de L'Antiquité: Etudes des possibilities de liens généalogiques entre les familles de l'Antiquité et celles du haut Moyen-Age européen</u> (pages viii, 35 and 38). Paris, France: Éditions Christian.
[2407] *A 4,000 Year Old Descent from Antiquity: From the 12th Egyptian Dynasty to the Capetians and Beyond* (page 14, entry 105). erwan.gil.free.fr/modules/freepages/pharaons/ramses_II.pdf
[2408] sites.rootsweb.com/~cousin/html/p304.htm#i5941
[2409] Settipani, Christian. (1991) <u>Nos Ancêtres de L'Antiquité: Etudes des possibilities de liens généalogiques entre les familles de l'Antiquité et celles du haut Moyen-Age européen</u> (pages viii and 35). Paris, France: Éditions Christian.
[2410] sites.rootsweb.com/~cousin/html/p306.htm#i12320
[2411] sites.rootsweb.com/~cousin/html/p307.htm#i16263
[2412] https://en.wikipedia.org/wiki/Theodora,_wife_of_Theophilus

THE BYZANTINE EMPERORS

GENERATION 26B (36G grandparents) [2413]

Theodora Mamikonian married Byzantine Emperor Theophilos (the son of Byzantine Emperor Michael II and Thekla). [2414] [2415] [2416] [2417] [2418]

GENERATION 27B (35G grandparents) [2419]

Byzantine Emperor Michael III and his mistress Eudokia Ingerina [2420] [2421] [2422] [2423]

GENERATION 28B (34G grandparents) [2424] [2425]

Byzantine Emperor Leo VI (The Wise) married Zoë Tzautzina [2426] [2427] [2428] [2429]

[2413] Settipani, Christian. (1991) Nos Ancêtres de L'Antiquité: Etudes des possibilités de liens généalogiques entre les familles de l'Antiquité et celles du haut Moyen-Age européen (pages viii, 21 and 35). Paris, France: Éditions Christian.
[2414] Ibid, page 17.
[2415] https://en.wikipedia.org/wiki/Theodora,_wife_of_Theophilus
[2416] https://en.wikipedia.org/wiki/Theophilos_(emperor)
[2417] sites.rootsweb.com/~cousin/html/p311.htm#i12319
[2418] sites.rootsweb.com/~cousin/html/p308.htm#i12318
[2419] Settipani, Christian. (1991) Nos Ancêtres de L'Antiquité: Etudes des possibilités de liens généalogiques entre les familles de l'Antiquité et celles du haut Moyen-Age européen (pages viii, 17 and 35). Paris, France: Éditions Christian.
[2420] sites.rootsweb.com/~cousin/html/p310.htm#i8226
[2421] sites.rootsweb.com/~cousin/html/p312.htm#i8225
[2422] https://en.wikipedia.org/wiki/Michael_III
[2423] https://en.wikipedia.org/wiki/Eudokia_Ingerina
[2424] Settipani, Christian. (1991) Nos Ancêtres de L'Antiquité: Etudes des possibilités de liens généalogiques entre les familles de l'Antiquité et celles du haut Moyen-Age européen (pages viii and 17). Paris, France: Éditions Christian.
[2425] *A 4,000 Year Old Descent from Antiquity: From the 12th Egyptian Dynasty to the Capetians and Beyond* (page 14, entry 109). erwan.gil.free.fr/modules/freepages/pharaons/ramses_II.pdf
[2426] sites.rootsweb.com/~cousin/html/p316.htm#i6437

THE LATE CAROLINGIANS

GENERATION 29B (33G grandparents) [2430] [2431]

Anna of Constantinople (Macedonia) married Holy Roman Emperor Louis III (The Blind) [2432] [2433] [2434]

GENERATION 30B (32G grandparents) [2435] [2436]

Count Charles Constantine of Vienne married Tuetberga of Troyes [2437] [2438] [2439] [2440] [2441] [2442]

[2427] sites.rootsweb.com/~cousin/html/p314.htm#i8224
[2428] https://en.wikipedia.org/wiki/Leo_VI_the_Wise
[2429] https://en.wikipedia.org/wiki/Zoe_Zaoutzaina
[2430] Settipani, Christian. (1991) <u>Nos Ancêtres de L'Antiquité: Etudes des possibilities de liens généalogiques entre les familles de l'Antiquité et celles du haut Moyen-Age européen</u> (pages viii and 9). Paris, France: Éditions Christian.
[2431] *A 4,000 Year Old Descent from Antiquity: From the 12th Egyptian Dynasty to the Capetians and Beyond* (page 14, entry 110). erwan.gil.free.fr/modules/freepages/pharaons/ramses_II.pdf
[2432] sites.rootsweb.com/~cousin/html/p315.htm#i8222
[2433] sites.rootsweb.com/~cousin/html/p318.htm#i8223
[2434] https://en.wikipedia.org/wiki/Louis_the_Blind
[2435] Settipani, Christian. (1991) <u>Nos Ancêtres de L'Antiquité: Etudes des possibilities de liens généalogiques entre les familles de l'Antiquité et celles du haut Moyen-Age européen</u> (pages viii and 9). Paris, France: Éditions Christian.
[2436] *A 4,000 Year Old Descent from Antiquity: From the 12th Egyptian Dynasty to the Capetians and Beyond* (page 14, entry 110). erwan.gil.free.fr/modules/freepages/pharaons/ramses_II.pdf
[2437] https://en.wikipedia.org/wiki/Charles_Constantine_of_Vienne
[2438] https://en.wikipedia.org/wiki/Zoe_Zaoutzaina
[2439] genealogie.quebec/testphp/info.php?no=39582
[2440] genealogie.quebec/testphp/info.php?no=39583
[2441] sites.rootsweb.com/~cousin/html/p324.htm#i8217
[2442] sites.rootsweb.com/~cousin/html/p323.htm#i8218

THE BOSONIDS

GENERATION 31B (31G grandparents) [2443] [2444]

Countess Constance of Vienne married Count Boson II of Provence [2445] [2446] [2447]

GENERATION 32B (30G grandparents) [2448] [2449]

Count William I of Provence married Countess Adéläide Blanche of Anjou (d/o Count Fulk II of Anjou and Gerberga of Maine) [2450] [2451] [2452] [2453]

[2443] Settipani, Christian. (1991) <u>Nos Ancêtres de L'Antiquité: Etudes des possibilities de liens généalogiques entre les familles de l'Antiquité et celles du haut Moyen-Age européen</u> (pages viii and 6). Paris, France: Éditions Christian.
[2444] *A 4,000 Year Old Descent from Antiquity: From the 12th Egyptian Dynasty to the Capetians and Beyond* (page 15, entry 112). erwan.gil.free.fr/modules/freepages/pharaons/ramses_II.pdf
[2445] sites.rootsweb.com/~cousin/html/p324.htm#i8216
[2446] sites.rootsweb.com/~cousin/html/p325.htm#i8215
[2447] https://en.wikipedia.org/wiki/William_I_of_Provence
[2448] Settipani, Christian. (1991) <u>Nos Ancêtres de L'Antiquité: Etudes des possibilities de liens généalogiques entre les familles de l'Antiquité et celles du haut Moyen-Age européen</u> (pages viii and 6). Paris, France: Éditions Christian.
[2449] *A 4,000 Year Old Descent from Antiquity: From the 12th Egyptian Dynasty to the Capetians and Beyond* (page 15, entry 113). erwan.gil.free.fr/modules/freepages/pharaons/ramses_II.pdf
[2450] sites.rootsweb.com/~cousin/html/p330.htm#i5098
[2451] sites.rootsweb.com/~cousin/html/p337.htm#i27786
[2452] https://en.wikipedia.org/wiki/William_I_of_Provence
[2453] https://en.wikipedia.org/wiki/Anne_of_Kiev

THE CAPETIANS

GENERATION 33B (29G grandparents) [2454] [2455]

Constance of Arles married King Robert II (of France) 996-1031 (s/o King Hugues Capet (first Capetian King of France) 987-996 and Adéläide of Aquitaine) [2456] [2457] [2458] [2459]

GENERATION 34B (28G grandparents) [2460] [2461]

King Henri I (of France) 1031-1060 married Anna of Kiev (d/o Grand Prince Yaroslav I (The Wise) of Kiev and Ingegerd of Sweden [2462] [2463] [2464] [2465]

Refer to **GENERATION 35** (page 476) for line continuation.

[2454] Settipani, Christian. (1991) <u>Nos Ancêtres de L'Antiquité: Etudes des possibilities de liens généalogiques entre les familles de l'Antiquité et celles du haut Moyen-Age européen</u> (pages viii and 6). Paris, France: Éditions Christian.
[2455] *A 4,000 Year Old Descent from Antiquity: From the 12th Egyptian Dynasty to the Capetians and Beyond* (page 15, entry 114). erwan.gil.free.fr/modules/freepages/pharaons/ramses_II.pdf
[2456] sites.rootsweb.com/~cousin/html/p338.htm#i5279
[2457] sites.rootsweb.com/~cousin/html/p338.htm#i5218
[2458] https://en.wikipedia.org/wiki/Constance_of_Arles
[2459] https://en.wikipedia.org/wiki/Robert_II_of_France
[2460] Settipani, Christian. (1991) <u>Nos Ancêtres de L'Antiquité: Etudes des possibilities de liens généalogiques entre les familles de l'Antiquité et celles du haut Moyen-Age européen</u> (page viii). Paris, France: Éditions Christian.
[2461] *A 4,000 Year Old Descent from Antiquity: From the 12th Egyptian Dynasty to the Capetians and Beyond* (page 15, entry 115). erwan.gil.free.fr/modules/freepages/pharaons/ramses_II.pdf
[2462] sites.rootsweb.com/~cousin/html/p345.htm#i5277
[2463] sites.rootsweb.com/~cousin/html/p349.htm#i5278
[2464] https://en.wikipedia.org/wiki/Henry_I_of_France
[2465] https://en.wikipedia.org/wiki/Anne_of_Kiev

GENERATION 35 (27G grandparents) [2466]

King Philippe I (of France) 1060-1108 married Berthe of Holland (d/o Count Floris I of Holland and Gertrude of Saxony)

GENERATION 36 (26G grandparents) [2467]

King Louis VI (The Fat) (of France) 1108-1137 married Adélaide of Savoy (d/o Count Umberto (Humbert) II (The Fat) of Savoy and Gisela of Burgundy)

GENERATION 37 (25G grandparents) [2468]

King Louis VII (of France) 1137-1180 married Adèle (Alix) of Champagne (d/o Count Theobald III (The Great) of Champagne (Theobald IV of Blois) and Matilda of Carinthia)

GENERATION 38 (24G grandparents) [2469]

King Philippe II Auguste (of France) 1180-1223 married Agnès of Méranie (d/o Count Bertold IV of Andechs, Duke of Merania and Agnes von Rochlitz)

[2466] *A 4,000 Year Old Descent from Antiquity: From the 12th Egyptian Dynasty to the Capetians and Beyond* (page 15, entry 116). erwan.gil.free.fr/modules/freepages/pharaons/ramses_II.pdf
[2467] Ibid, page 15, entry 117.
[2468] Ibid, page 15, entry 118.
[2469] Ibid, page 15, entry 119.

The generations that follow have been added to the document entitled *A 4.000 Year Old Descent from Antiquity: From the 12th Egyptian Dynasty to the Capetians and Beyond*. As denoted throughout this book, they have already been authenticated.

GENERATION 39 (23G grandparents)

Princess Marie of France married Henri I, Duke of Brabant and Duke of Lower Lotharingia

GENERATION 40 (22G grandparents)

Élisabeth de Brabant married Count Dietrich (Thierry) VII de Clèves

GENERATION 41 (21G grandparents)

Mathilde de Clèves and Gérard de Luxembourg, seigneur de Durbury, were married in 1253.

GENERATION 42 (20G grandparents)

Marguerite de Luxembourg and Jean III, seigneur de Ghistelles, were married between 1284 and June 1289.

GENERATION 43 (19G grandparents)

Jean IV, seigneur de Ghistelles and Marie de Haverskerke, dame de Straten, were married after June 1337.

GENERATION 44 (18G grandparents)

Roger de Ghistelles, ~~Seigneur de Dudzeele et de Straten~~, married Élisabeth ~~Marguerite~~, Dame de Dudzeele, in, or shortly before, 1357 (see page 182 for updated explanation).

GENERATION 45 (17G grandparents)

Isabelle de Ghistelles and Arnould VI de Gavre, baron d'Escornaix, were married between 1380 and 1390.

GENERATION 46 (16G grandparents)

Catherine de Gavre d'Escornaix, dame de Vaux-sur-Orge et de La Boissière and Guy I Le Bouteiller, seigneur de La Bouteillerie et de La Roche-Guyon, were married sometime after April 1419 and before 1425.

GENERATION 47 (15G grandparents)

Guy II Le Bouteillier, seigneur de La Boiuteillerie et de La Roche-Guyon and Isabeau Morhier were married about 1450.

GENERATION 48 (14G grandparents)

Jean Le Bouteillier, seigneur de La Bouteillerie, de Roquemont, de Vaux-sur-Orge et de La Boissière and Marie de Venois were married between 1480 and 1490.

GENERATION 49 (13G grandparents)

Bénigne Le Bouteillier, dame de La Boissière and Jacques Maillard, seigneur de Champaigne, were married on April 16, 1516 at Montivilliers (Seine-Maritime).

GENERATION 50 (12G grandparents)

Miles Maillard, seigneur du Breuil et de La Boissière and Marie Morant were married on June 25, 1555.

GENERATION 51 (11G grandparents)

Renée Maillard and Adam Baillon, seigneur de Valence, were married about 1580.

GENERATION 52 (10G grandparents)

Alphonse Baillon, sieur de La Mascotterie, and Louise de Marle were married between 1630 and 1640 in the Chevreuse (Yvelines) region.

GENERATION 53 (9G grandparents)

Catherine Baillon and Jacques Miville dit Deschênes were married on November 12, 1669 at Notre-Dame de Québec, Québec.

GENERATION 54 (8G grandparents)

Charles Milville dit Deschênes and Marie Marthe Vallée were married on August 28, 1702 in Rivière Ouelle, Québec.

GENERATION 55 (7G grandparents)

Catherine Milville and Jean Baptiste Duval were married on February 6, 1736 in Ste-Anne-de-la-Pocatière, Québec.

GENERATION 56 (6G grandparents)

Marie Josette (Josèphe) Duval and Jean Baptiste LeClerc were married on February 8, 1757 in L'Islet, Québec.

GENERATION 57 (5G grandparents)

Jean Baptiste LeClerc and Madeleine Thébault were married on September 19, 1796 in Bathurst, New Brunswick.

GENERATION 58 (4G grandparents)

Madeleine LeClerc and Pascal Landry were married on February 9, 1824 in Pointe Sapin, New Brunswick.

GENERATION 59 (3G grandparents)

Alexis dit Alexandre Landry and Justine Lanteigne were married on May 1, 1854.

GENERATION 60 (2G grandparents)

Marie Landry and Louis Breau were married on June 14, 1880 in Pokemouche, New Brunswick.

GENERATION 61 (1G grandparents)

André Breau and Marie Philomène Mallet were married on October 17, 1906 in Chatham, New Brunswick.

GENERATION 62 (grandparents)

Mary Catherine (Kay) Breau and James Henry (Harry) Feeley were married on September 1, 1930 in Amherst, Nova Scotia.

GENERATION 63 (parents)

Anne Elizabeth Feeley and Albert Doucette were married on November 11, 1961 in Truro, Nova Scotia.

GENERATION 64

Michele Anne Doucette and Albert Joseph Stewart were married on August 24, 1985 in Truro, Nova Scotia.

Byzantium Empire 1

Byzantine Emperor Leo VI (The Wise), my 34th great grandfather, was very well-read; hence, the nickname by which he was known.

Born to the empress Evdokia Ingerina, Leo was either the illegitimate son of Emperor Michael III, or the second son of his successor, Basil the Macedonian, in that Evdokia was both Michael III's mistress as well as Basil's wife.

■ Byzantine Emperor Leo VI (The Wise) married Zoë Tzautzina [2470]

☐ Anna of Constantinople (Macedonia) married Holy Roman Emperor Louis III (The Blind) [2471] [2472]

■ Count Charles Constantine of Vienne married Tuetberga of Troyes [2473] [2474]

☐ Countess Constance of Vienne married Count Boson II of Provence [2475]

■ Count William I of Provence (The Liberator) married Countess Adélaïs Blanche of Anjou [2476] [2477]

[2470] fmg.ac/Projects/MedLands/BYZANTIUM.htm#_Toc204564497
[2471] fmg.ac/Projects/MedLands/BYZANTIUM.htm#Annadied914
[2472] fmg.ac/Projects/MedLands/PROVENCE.htm#LouisKingProvencedied928
[2473] fmg.ac/Projects/MedLands/PROVENCE.htm#CharlesConstantindied962
[2474] fmg.ac/Projects/MedLands/CHAMPAGNE%20NOBILITY.htm#TeutbergaTroyesdiedafter960
[2475] fmg.ac/Projects/MedLands/PROVENCE.htm#BosonIIArlesdied965B
[2476] fmg.ac/Projects/MedLands/PROVENCE.htm#GuillaumeIIArlesProvencedied993

☐ Constance of Provence married King Robert II of France (996 to 1031) [2478] [2479]

■ King Henri I of France (1031 to 1060) married Anne de Kiev [2480] [2481]

■ King Philippe I of France (1060 to 1108) married Berthe de Holland [2482] [2483]

■ King Louis VI of France (1108 to 1137) married Adélaïde de Maurienne [2484] [2485]

■ King Louis VII of France (1137 to 1180) married Adèle de Champagne [2486] [2487]

■ King Philippe II Auguste of France (1180 to 1223) married <u>thirdly</u> Agnès d'Andechs de Méranie [2488] [2489]

☐ Princess Marie of France married Henri I, Duke of Brabant [2490] [2491]

☐ Élisabeth de Brabant marriedCount Dietrich (Thierry) de Clèves [2492] [2493]

[2477] fmg.ac/Projects/MedLands/ANJOU,%20MAINE.htm#AdelaisM1M2LouisVFranksdied987M3M4
[2478] fmg.ac/Projects/MedLands/PROVENCE.htm#ConstanceArlesMRobertIIFrancedied1031
[2479] fmg.ac/Projects/MedLands/CAPET.htm#RobertIIdied1031B
[2480] fmg.ac/Projects/MedLands/CAPET.htm#HenriIdied1060B
[2481] fmg.ac/Projects/MedLands/RUSSIA,%20Rurik.htm#AnnaIaroslavnadied1075
[2482] fmg.ac/Projects/MedLands/CAPET.htm#PhilippeIdied1108B
[2483] fmg.ac/Projects/MedLands/HOLLAND.htm#Berthadied1093
[2484] fmg.ac/Projects/MedLands/CAPET.htm#LouisVIdied1137B
[2485] fmg.ac/Projects/MedLands/SAVOY.htm#Adélaïdedied1154
[2486] fmg.ac/Projects/MedLands/CAPET.htm#LouisVIIdied1180B
[2487] fmg.ac/Projects/MedLands/CENTRAL%20FRANCE.htm#AdeleBloisdied1206
[2488] fmg.ac/Projects/MedLands/CAPET.htm#PhilippeIIdied1223B
[2489] fmg.ac/Projects/MedLands/CARINTHIA.htm#AgnesMeranodied1201
[2490] fmg.ac/Projects/MedLands/CAPET.htm#Mariedied1238
[2491] fmg.ac/Projects/MedLands/BRABANT,%20LOUVAIN.htm#HenriILotharingiaBrabantdied1235B

Élisabeth was also known as Ysabeau de Brabant; with regards to French records, the name Élisabeth is often used, interchangeably, with that of Isabelle. [2494] [2495]

☐ Mathilda de Clèves married Gerard de Luxembourg

☐ Marguerite de Luxembourg married Jean III de Ghistelles

■ Jean IV de Ghistelles married Marie de Haverskerke

■ Roger de Ghistelles married Élisabeth ~~Marguerite~~ de Dudzeele (see page 182 for updated explanation)

☐ Isabelle (Ysabeau) de Ghistelles married Arnould VI de Gavre

☐ Catherine de Gavre d'Escornaix married Guy I Le Bouteiller

■ Guy II Le Bouteillier married Isabeau Morhier

■ Jean Le Bouteillier married Marie de Venois

☐ Bénigne Le Bouteillier married Jacques Maillard

■ Miles Maillard married Marie Morant

☐ Renée Maillard married Adam de Baillon

■ Alphonse de Baillon married Louise de Marle

[2492] fmg.ac/Projects/MedLands/BRABANT,%20LOUVAIN.htm#Elisabethdied1272

[2493] fmg.ac/Projects/MedLands/FRANCONIA%20(LOWER%20RHINE).htm#Dietrichdied1245

[2494] Jetté, René, DuLong, John P., Gagné, Roland-Yves, Moreau, Gail F. and Dubé, Joseph A. (2001) Table d'ascendance de Catherine Baillon: 12 générations (p 153). Montréal, Québec: Société Généalogique Canadienne Française.

[2495] https://en.wikipedia.org/wiki/Henry_I,_Duke_of_Brabant

☐ Catherine de Baillon

Christian Settipani discusses at length the legitimacy of Emperor Leo VI, concluding that he was the son of Emperor Michael III by Evdokia Ingerina who continued to be the Emperor's mistress until his death in 867, when his widow married co-Emperor Basil, mainly to preserve appearances. [2496]

Should this be correct, the lineage, in comparison, would appear thusly.

- <u>Byzantine Emperor</u> Michael II married Thekla [2497] [2498]

- <u>Byzantine Emperor</u> Theophilos married Theodora [2499] [2500] [2501] [2502] [2503]

- <u>Byzantine Emperor</u> Michael III married Evdokia Ingerina [2504]

- <u>Byzantine Emperor</u> Leo VI (The Wise) married Zoë Tzautzina [2505]

☐ Anna of Constantinople (Macedonia) married Holy Roman Emperor Louis III (The Blind) [2506] [2507]

- Count Charles Constantine of Vienne married Tuetberga of Troyes [2508] [2509]

[2496] fmg.ac/Projects/MedLands/BYZANTIUM.htm#_Toc204564497
[2497] fmg.ac/Projects/MedLands/BYZANTIUM.htm#_Toc204564492
[2498] Settipani, Christian. (1991) <u>Nos Ancêtres de L'Antiquité: Etudes des possibilities de liens généalogiques entre les familles de l'Antiquité et celles du haut Moyen-Age européen</u> (page 33). Paris, France: Éditions Christian.
[2499] fmg.ac/Projects/MedLands/BYZANTIUM.htm#Theophilosdied842B
[2500] fmg.ac/Projects/MedLands/BYZANTIUM.htm#Theodoradied867
[2501] Settipani, Christian. (1991) <u>Nos Ancêtres de L'Antiquité: Etudes des possibilities de liens généalogiques entre les familles de l'Antiquité et celles du haut Moyen-Age européen</u> (page 33). Paris, France: Éditions Christian.
[2502] https://en.wikipedia.org/wiki/Theodora,_wife_of_Theophilus
[2503] https://en.wikipedia.org/wiki/Mamikonian
[2504] fmg.ac/Projects/MedLands/BYZANTIUM.htm#_Toc204564493
[2505] fmg.ac/Projects/MedLands/BYZANTIUM.htm#_Toc204564497
[2506] fmg.ac/Projects/MedLands/BYZANTIUM.htm#Annadied914
[2507] fmg.ac/Projects/MedLands/PROVENCE.htm#LouisKingProvencedied928

☐ Countess Constance of Vienne married Count Boson II of Provence [2510]

■ Count William I of Provence (The Liberator) married Countess Adélaïs Blanche of Anjou [2511] [2512]

☐ Constance of Provence married King Robert II of France (996 to 1031) [2513] [2514]

■ King Henri I of France (1031 to 1060) married Anne de Kiev [2515] [2516]

■ King Philippe I of France (1060 to 1108) married Berthe de Holland [2517] [2518]

■ King Louis VI of France (1108 to 1137) married Adélaïde de Maurienne [2519] [2520]

■ King Louis VII of France (1137 to 1180) married Adèle de Champagne [2521] [2522]

■ King Philippe II Auguste of France (1180 to 1223) married thirdly Agnès d'Andechs de Méranie [2523] [2524]

[2508] fmg.ac/Projects/MedLands/PROVENCE.htm#CharlesConstantindied962
[2509] fmg.ac/Projects/MedLands/CHAMPAGNE%20NOBILITY.htm#TeutbergaTroyesdiedafter960
[2510] fmg.ac/Projects/MedLands/PROVENCE.htm#BosonIIArlesdied965B
[2511] fmg.ac/Projects/MedLands/PROVENCE.htm#GuillaumeIIArlesProvencedied993
[2512] fmg.ac/Projects/MedLands/ANJOU,%20MAINE.htm#AdelaisM1M2LouisVFranksdied987M3M4
[2513] fmg.ac/Projects/MedLands/PROVENCE.htm#ConstanceArlesMRobertIIFrancedied1031
[2514] fmg.ac/Projects/MedLands/CAPET.htm#RobertIIdied1031B
[2515] fmg.ac/Projects/MedLands/CAPET.htm#HenriIdied1060B
[2516] fmg.ac/Projects/MedLands/RUSSIA,%20Rurik.htm#AnnaIaroslavnadied1075
[2517] fmg.ac/Projects/MedLands/CAPET.htm#PhilippeIdied1108B
[2518] fmg.ac/Projects/MedLands/HOLLAND.htm#Berthadied1093
[2519] fmg.ac/Projects/MedLands/CAPET.htm#LouisVIdied1137B
[2520] fmg.ac/Projects/MedLands/SAVOY.htm#Adélaïdedied1154
[2521] fmg.ac/Projects/MedLands/CAPET.htm#LouisVIIdied1180B
[2522] fmg.ac/Projects/MedLands/CENTRAL%20FRANCE.htm#AdeleBloisdied1206

☐ Princess Marie of France married Henri I, Duke of Brabant[2525] [2526]

☐ Élisabeth de Brabant marriedCount Dietrich (Thierry) de Clèves [2527] [2528]

Élisabeth was also known as Ysabeau de Brabant; with regards to French records, the name Élisabeth is often used, interchangeably, with that of Isabelle. [2529] [2530]

☐ Mathilda de Clèves married Gerard de Luxembourg

☐ Marguerite de Luxembourg married Jean III de Ghistelles

■ Jean IV de Ghistelles married Marie de Haverskerke

■ Roger de Ghistelles married Élisabeth ~~Marguerite~~ de Dudzeele (see page 182 for updated explanation)

☐ Isabelle (Ysabeau) de Ghistelles married Arnould VI de Gavre

☐ Catherinede Gavre d'Escornaix married Guy I Le Bouteiller

■ Guy II Le Bouteillier married Isabeau Morhier

[2523] fmg.ac/Projects/MedLands/CAPET.htm#PhilippeIIdied1223B
[2524] fmg.ac/Projects/MedLands/CARINTHIA.htm#AgnesMeranodied1201
[2525] fmg.ac/Projects/MedLands/CAPET.htm#Mariedied1238
[2526] fmg.ac/Projects/MedLands/BRABANT,%20LOUVAIN.htm#HenriILotharingiaBrabantdied1235B
[2527] fmg.ac/Projects/MedLands/BRABANT,%20LOUVAIN.htm#Elisabethdied1272
[2528] fmg.ac/Projects/MedLands/FRANCONIA%20(LOWER%20RHINE).htm#Dietrichdied1245
[2529] Jetté, René, DuLong, John P., Gagné, Roland-Yves, Moreau, Gail F. and Dubé, Joseph A. (2001) <u>Table d'ascendance de Catherine Baillon: 12 générations</u> (p 153). Montréal, Québec: Société Généalogique Canadienne Française.
[2530] https://en.wikipedia.org/wiki/Henry_I,_Duke_of_Brabant

- Jean Le Bouteillier married Marie de Venois

- Bénigne Le Bouteillier married Jacques Maillard

- Miles Maillard married Marie Morant

- Renée Maillard married Adam de Baillon

- Alphonse de Baillon married Louise de Marle

- Catherine de Baillon

Byzantium Empire 2

Alexios I Komnenos, a Byzantine Emperor during the First Crusade, was my 28th great grandfather.

- Manuel Komenos married ---------- [2531]

- Ioannis Komnenos married Anna Dalassena, an important Byzantine noblewoman who played a significant role in the rise of the Komnenoi in the eleventh century. [2532] [2533] [2534] [2535] [2536]

- Byzantine Emperor Alexios I Komnenos (Komnenid dynasty) married Irene Doukaina in 1078 [2537] [2538] (see picture on page 407)

- Theodora Komnene married General Constantine Angelos, a senior Byzantine official [2539] [2540]

- General Andronicos Angelos (Asia Minor) married Euphrosyne Castamonitissa before 1155 [2541] [2542]

[2531] fmg.ac/Projects/MedLands/BYZANTIUM%2010571204.htm#IoannesKdied1067B
[2532] fmg.ac/Projects/MedLands/BYZANTIUM%2010571204.htm#_Toc264475974
[2533] fmg.ac/Projects/MedLands/BYZANTIUM%2010571204.htm#IoannesKdied1067B
[2534] fmg.ac/Projects/MedLands/BYZANTINE%20NOBILITY.htm#AnnaDalassenaMIoannesKomnenos
[2535] https://en.wikipedia.org/wiki/Anna_Dalassena
[2536] www.roman-emperors.org/annadal.htm
[2537] fmg.ac/Projects/MedLands/BYZANTIUM%2010571204.htm#_Toc264475974
[2538] fmg.ac/Projects/MedLands/BYZANTIUM%2010571204.htm#EireneDdied1123
[2539] fmg.ac/Projects/MedLands/BYZANTIUM%2010571204.htm#TheodoraKborn1096
[2540] fmg.ac/Projects/MedLands/BYZANTIUM%2010571204.htm#KonstantinosAdied1166

- <u>Byzantine Emperor</u> Alexios III Angelos (Angelid dynasty) married Euphrosyne Doukaina Kamatera [2543] [2544]

- ☐ Anna Angelos married <u>Emperor</u> Theodore I Lascaris of Nicea (Laskarid dynasty) in either February or March 1199 [2545] [2546]

- ☐ Irene Doukaina Komnene Lascaris married <u>Emperor</u> Jean III Doukas Vatazes of Nicea (Laskarid dynasty) about 1212 [2547] [2548]

- <u>Emperor</u> Theodore II Doukas Lascaris of Nicea (Laskarid dynasty) married Hélène of Bulgaria in the spring of 1235 [2549] [2550]

- ☐ Eudoxia Lascaris married Guillaume Pierre I, Count of Vintmille, in either 1262 or 1263, perhaps in Nicea [2551] [2552]

- Jean I de Lascaris de Vintmille, Count of Vintmille married ---------- [2553]

[2541] fmg.ac/Projects/MedLands/BYZANTIUM%2010571204.htm#AndronikosAdiedafter1185B

[2542] fmg.ac/Projects/MedLands/BYZANTINE%20NOBILITY.htm#EuphrosyneKastamonitissa

[2543] fmg.ac/Projects/MedLands/BYZANTIUM%2010571204.htm#AlexiosIIIdied1211

[2544] fmg.ac/Projects/MedLands/BYZANTINE%20NOBILITY.htm#EuphrosyneKamaterinadied1211

[2545] fmg.ac/Projects/MedLands/BYZANTIUM%2010571204.htm#AnnaAdied1212

[2546] fmg.ac/Projects/MedLands/NIKAIA.htm#TheodorosINikaiadied1222B

[2547] fmg.ac/Projects/MedLands/NIKAIA.htm#EireneLaskarinadied1239A

[2548] fmg.ac/Projects/MedLands/NIKAIA.htm#IoannesIIINikaiadied1254B

[2549] fmg.ac/Projects/MedLands/NIKAIA.htm#TheodorosIINikaiadied1258

[2550] fmg.ac/Projects/MedLands/BULGARIA.htm#ElenaDiedbefore1254

[2551] fmg.ac/Projects/MedLands/NIKAIA.htm#TheodorosIINikaiadied1258

[2552] jean.gallian.free.fr/vintimil/Images/p1b.pdf

■ Guillaume Pierre II de Lascaris de Vintmille, Count of Vintmille, married ---------- between 1310 and 1320 [2554]

■ Louis de Lascaris de Vintmille, Count of Vintmille and Co-seigneur of Briga, married Tiburge Grimaldi de Beuil in 1346 [2555]

■ Rainier de Lascaris de Vintmille, Count of Vintmille and Co-seigneur of Briga, married Madeleine Grimaldi d'Antibes between 1390 and 1400, but before 1403 [2556]

■ Charles de Lascaris de Vintmille, Co-seigneur of Briga, married Jeannette Litti, [2557] dame de Bonson et de La Roquette du Var, between 1420 and 1430 [2558]

☐ Baptistine de Lascaris de Vintmille married Pierre Chabaud, seigneur de Tourrettes, between 1460 and 1470 [2559]

■ Jean Chabaud, seigneur de Tourrettes, married Louise de Berre in 1519 (region de Nice) [2560]

■ Antoine Chabot (Chabaud), sieur de La Fond en Provence, married Catherine Lombard on March 30, 1554 at Chappelain et Crucé, Paris [2561]

[2553] Jetté, René, DuLong, John P., Gagné, Roland-Yves, Moreau, Gail F. and Dubé, Joseph A. (2001) Table d'ascendance de Catherine Baillon: 12 générations (p 158). Montréal, Québec: Société Généalogique Canadienne Française.
[2554] Ibid, page 146.
[2555] Ibid, pages 131 and 132.
[2556] Ibid, page 119.
[2557] Refer to article *Possible Jewish Ancestor for Catherine Baillon* located in Catherine de Baillon chapter (page 212).
[2558] Jetté, René, DuLong, John P., Gagné, Roland-Yves, Moreau, Gail F. and Dubé, Joseph A. (2001) Table d'ascendance de Catherine Baillon: 12 générations (page 103). Montréal, Québec: Société Généalogique Canadienne Française.
[2559] Ibid, pages 81 and 82.
[2560] Ibid, page 66.

☐ Marguerite Chabot married Jean Bizet, seigneur de Paponville et de la Grandmaison, in 1580 [2562]

☐ Anne Bizet married Mathurin de Marle, seigneur de Vaugien, about 1610 in the Chevreuse (Yvelines) region [2563]

☐ Louise de Marle married Alphonse de Baillon, seigneur de La Mascotterie, between 1630 and 1640 in the Chevreuse (Yvelines) region [2564]

☐ Catherine de Baillon

[2561] Jetté, René, DuLong, John P., Gagné, Roland-Yves, Moreau, Gail F. and Dubé, Joseph A. (2001) <u>Table d'ascendance de Catherine Baillon: 12 générations</u> (page 54). Montréal, Québec: Société Généalogique Canadienne Française.
[2562] Ibid, pages 45 and 46.
[2563] Ibid, page 40.
[2564] Ibid, page 31.

The Magyars

The Magyar tribes (from the region of the Ural Mountains) invaded the Carpathian Basin and established the Principality of Hungary. [2565] [2566] The evidence of their origins, through language, has been traced back to their ancestors, the Finno-Ugrian family of peoples who once lived between the Baltic Sea to the Ural Mountains. [2567]

- Ügyek married Emese (d/o Pr Önedbelia of Dentümoger) [2568] [2569] [2570]

- Álmos, Grand Prince of the Magyars [2571] [2572] [2573]

- Árpád, Grand Prince of the Magyars [2574] [2575] [2576]

- Prince Zaltas (Zoltán) of Hungary [2577] [2578] [2579]

- Taksony, Grand Prince of the Magyars [2580] [2581] [2582]

[2565] https://en.wikipedia.org/wiki/Magyar_tribes
[2566] fmg.ac/Projects/MedLands/HUNGARY.htm#_Toc396819731
[2567] www.thenagain.info/WebChron/EastEurope/Magyars.html
[2568] fmg.ac/Projects/MedLands/HUNGARY.htm#_Toc146273208
[2569] genealogy.euweb.cz/arpad/arpad1.html
[2570] https://en.wikipedia.org/wiki/Árpád_dynasty
[2571] fmg.ac/Projects/MedLands/HUNGARY.htm#_Toc146273208
[2572] genealogy.euweb.cz/arpad/arpad1.html
[2573] https://en.wikipedia.org/wiki/Álmos
[2574] fmg.ac/Projects/MedLands/HUNGARY.htm#_Toc146273208
[2575] genealogy.euweb.cz/arpad/arpad1.html
[2576] https://en.wikipedia.org/wiki/Árpád
[2577] fmg.ac/Projects/MedLands/HUNGARY.htm#_Toc146273208
[2578] genealogy.euweb.cz/arpad/arpad1.html
[2579] https://en.wikipedia.org/wiki/Zoltán_of_Hungary
[2580] fmg.ac/Projects/MedLands/HUNGARY.htm#_TAKSONY_955-970

- Duke Mihály (Michael) married Adelajda of Poland [2583] [2584] [2585] [2586]

- Duke Vazul married Katun Anastazya of Bulgaria [2587] [2588] [2589] [2590] [2591] [2592]

- King Béla I of Hungary married Ryska of Poland [2593] [2594] [2595]

- King Géza I of Hungary married ---------- Synadene [2596] [2597] [2598] [2599]

- Prince Álmos, Duke of Nitra (brother to King Coloman of Hungary) married Predslava of Kiev [2600] [2601] [2602]

[2581] https://en.wikipedia.org/wiki/Zoltán_of_Hungary
[2582] https://en.wikipedia.org/wiki/Taksony_of_Hungary
[2583] fmg.ac/Projects/MedLands/HUNGARY.htm#_TAKSONY_955-970
[2584] fmg.ac/Projects/MedLands/POLAND.htm#Adelajdadiedafter997
[2585] https://en.wikipedia.org/wiki/Vazul
[2586] https://en.wikipedia.org/wiki/Taksony_of_Hungary
[2587] fmg.ac/Projects/MedLands/HUNGARY.htm#_ANDRÁS_I_1047-1060
[2588] fmg.ac/Projects/MedLands/BULGARIA.htm#dauMVaszolyHungary
[2589] https://en.wikipedia.org/wiki/Vazul
[2590] https://en.wikipedia.org/wiki/Taksony_of_Hungary
[2591] https://en.wikipedia.org/wiki/Katun_Anastazya_of_Bulgaria
[2592] https://en.wikipedia.org/wiki/Samuil_of_Bulgaria
[2593] fmg.ac/Projects/MedLands/HUNGARY.htm#_BÉLA_I_1060-1063
[2594] fmg.ac/Projects/MedLands/POLAND.htm#Ryskadiedafter1059
[2595] https://en.wikipedia.org/wiki/Béla_I_of_Hungary
[2596] fmg.ac/Projects/MedLands/HUNGARY.htm#_GÉZA_I_1074-1077
[2597] fmg.ac/Projects/MedLands/BYZANTINE%20NOBILITY.htm#SynadeneMGezaIHungary
[2598] https://en.wikipedia.org/wiki/Géza_I_of_Hungary
[2599] https://en.wikipedia.org/wiki/Synadene
[2600] fmg.ac/Projects/MedLands/HUNGARY.htm#Almosdied1129
[2601] fmg.ac/Projects/MedLands/RUSSIA,%20Rurik.htm#PredslavaSviatopolkovnaMAlmosHungary
[2602] https://en.wikipedia.org/wiki/Prince_Álmos

- King Béla II of Hungary and Croatia married Helena of Rascia (d/o Duke Uroš of Rascia and Anna Diogene-Vukanović) [2603] [2604] [2605] [2606] [2607] [2608]

- King Géza II of Hungary and Croatia married Euphrosyne of Kiev (d/o Grand Prince Mstislav I of Kiev and Liubava Dmitrievna) [2609] [2610] [2611] [2612] [2613]

- King Béla III of Hungary and Croatia married Agnès of Antioch [2614] [2615] [2616] [2617] [2618] [2619] [2620]

- King Andrew II of Hungary married Gertrude d'Andechs of Méranie [2621] [2622] [2623] [2624]

[2603] fmg.ac/Projects/MedLands/HUNGARY.htm#_BÉLA_II_1131-1141
[2604] fmg.ac/Projects/MedLands/SERBIA.htm#Jelenadiedafter1146
[2605] https://en.wikipedia.org/wiki/Béla_II_of_Hungary
[2606] https://en.wikipedia.org/wiki/Helena_of_Serbia,_Queen_of_Hungary
[2607] https://en.wikipedia.org/wiki/Uroš_I,_Grand_Prince_of_Serbia
[2608] https://en.wikipedia.org/wiki/Anna_Diogene
[2609] fmg.ac/Projects/MedLands/HUNGARY.htm#_GÉZA_II_1141-1162
[2610] fmg.ac/Projects/MedLands/RUSSIA,%20Rurik.htm#IevfrosinaMstislavnadiedbefore1186
[2611] https://en.wikipedia.org/wiki/Géza_II_of_Hungary
[2612] https://en.wikipedia.org/wiki/Euphrosyne_of_Kiev
[2613] https://en.wikipedia.org/wiki/Mstislav_I_of_Kiev
[2614] fmg.ac/Projects/MedLands/HUNGARY.htm#_BÉLA_III_1172-1196
[2615] fmg.ac/Projects/MedLands/CENTRAL%20FRANCE.htm#AgnesAnnaChatillonMBelaIIIHungary
[2616] Gagné, Roland-Yves. (2001) "L'ascendance de Michel d'Aigneaux d'Ouville" (page 104). Mémoires de La Société Généalogique Canadienne Française, Volume 52, Number 2, Summer 2001.
[2617] https://en.wikipedia.org/wiki/Béla_III_of_Hungary
[2618] https://en.wikipedia.org/wiki/Agnes_of_Antioch
[2619] https://en.wikipedia.org/wiki/Raynald_of_Ch%C3%A2tillon
[2620] https://en.wikipedia.org/wiki/Constance_of_Antioch
[2621] fmg.ac/Projects/MedLands/HUNGARY.htm#_ANDRÁS_II_1205-1235
[2622] fmg.ac/Projects/MedLands/LATIN%20EMPERORS.htm#YolandeCourtenaydied1233

☐ Marie of Hungary married Asèn II, Tzar Ivan Asèn II of Bulgaria[2625 2626 2627 2628 2629]

☐ Hélène of Bulgaria married Emperor Theodore II Doukas Lascaris of Nicea (Laskarid dynasty) in the spring of 1235 [2630 2631 2632]

☐ Eudoxia Lascaris married Guillaume Pierre I, Count of Vintmille, in either 1262 or 1263, perhaps in Nicea [2633 2634 2635]

■ Jean I de Lascaris de Vintmille, Count of Vintmille married ---------- [2636 2637]

[2623] https://en.wikipedia.org/wiki/Andrew_II_of_Hungary
[2624] https://en.wikipedia.org/wiki/Yolanda_de_Courtenay
[2625] fmg.ac/Projects/MedLands/HUNGARY.htm#MariaMIvanAsenIIBulgaria
[2626] fmg.ac/Projects/MedLands/BULGARIA.htm#IvanAsenIIdied1241B
[2627] Gagné, Roland-Yves. (2001) "L'ascendance de Michel d'Aigneaux d'Ouville" (page 104). Mémoires de La Société Généalogique Canadienne Française, Volume 52, Number 2, Summer 2001.
[2628] https://en.wikipedia.org/wiki/Anna_Maria_of_Hungary
[2629] https://en.wikipedia.org/wiki/Ivan_Asen_II_of_Bulgaria
[2630] fmg.ac/Projects/MedLands/BULGARIA.htm#ElenaDiedbefore1254
[2631] fmg.ac/Projects/MedLands/NIKAIA.htm#TheodorosIINikaiadied1258
[2632] Gagné, Roland-Yves. (2001) "L'ascendance de Michel d'Aigneaux d'Ouville" (page 104). Mémoires de La Société Généalogique Canadienne Française, Volume 52, Number 2, Summer 2001.
[2633] fmg.ac/Projects/MedLands/NIKAIA.htm#TheodorosIINikaiadied1258
[2634] jean.gallian.free.fr/vintimil/Images/p1b.pdf
[2635] Gagné, Roland-Yves. (2001) "L'ascendance de Michel d'Aigneaux d'Ouville" (page 104). Mémoires de La Société Généalogique Canadienne Française, Volume 52, Number 2, Summer 2001.
[2636] Jetté, René, DuLong, John P., Gagné, Roland-Yves, Moreau, Gail F. and Dubé, Joseph A. (2001) Table d'ascendance de Catherine Baillon: 12 générations (p 158). Montréal, Québec: Société Généalogique Canadienne Française.
[2637] Gagné, Roland-Yves. (2001) "L'ascendance de Michel d'Aigneaux d'Ouville" (page 104). Mémoires de La Société Généalogique Canadienne Française, Volume 52, Number 2, Summer 2001.

■ Guillaume Pierre II de Lascaris de Vintmille, Count of Vintmille, married ---------- between 1310 and 1320 [2638]

■ Louis de Lascaris de Vintmille, Count of Vintmille and Co-seigneur of Briga, married Tiburge Grimaldi de Beuil in 1346 [2639]

■ Rainier de Lascaris de Vintmille, Count of Vintmille and Co-seigneur of Briga, married Madeleine Grimaldi d'Antibes between 1390 and 1400, but before 1403 [2640]

■ Charles de Lascaris de Vintmille, Co-seigneur of Briga, married Jeannette Litti, [2641] dame de Bonson et de La Roquette du Var, between 1420 and 1430 [2642]

☐ Baptistine de Lascaris de Vintmille married Pierre Chabaud, seigneur de Tourrettes, between 1460 and 1470 [2643]

■ Jean Chabaud, seigneur de Tourrettes, married Louise de Berre in 1519 (region de Nice) [2644]

■ Antoine Chabot (Chabaud), sieur de La Fond en Provence, married Catherine Lombard on March 30, 1554 at Chappelain et Crucé, Paris [2645]

[2638] Jetté, René, DuLong, John P., Gagné, Roland-Yves, Moreau, Gail F. and Dubé, Joseph A. (2001) Table d'ascendance de Catherine Baillon: 12 générations (page 146). Montréal, Québec: Société Généalogique Canadienne Française.
[2639] Ibid, pages 131 and 132.
[2640] Ibid, page 119.
[2641] Refer to article *Possible Jewish Ancestor for Catherine Baillon* located in Catherine de Baillon chapter (page 212).
[2642] Jetté, René, DuLong, John P., Gagné, Roland-Yves, Moreau, Gail F. and Dubé, Joseph A. (2001) Table d'ascendance de Catherine Baillon: 12 générations (page 103). Montréal, Québec: Société Généalogique Canadienne Française.
[2643] Ibid, pages 81 and 82.
[2644] Ibid, page 66.

☐ Marguerite Chabot married Jean Bizet, seigneur de Paponville et de la Grandmaison, in 1580 [2646]

☐ Anne Bizet married Mathurin de Marle, seigneur de Vaugien, about 1610 in the Chevreuse (Yvelines) region [2647]

☐ Louise de Marle married Alphonse de Baillon, seigneur de La Mascotterie, between 1630 and 1640 in the Chevreuse (Yvelines) region [2648]

☐ Catherine de Baillon

[2645] Jetté, René, DuLong, John P., Gagné, Roland-Yves, Moreau, Gail F. and Dubé, Joseph A. (2001) Table d'ascendance de Catherine Baillon: 12 générations (page 54). Montréal, Québec: Société Généalogique Canadienne Française.
[2646] Ibid, pages 45 and 46.
[2647] Ibid, page 40.
[2648] Ibid, page 31.

The First Crusade

At the time of the First Crusade, there was an Armenian kingdom situated in Cicilia [2649] (today called Cukurova, located in south-central Turkey), on the right bank of Ceyhan, ruled by both the Rupénides and the Héthoumides. [2650]

The Rubenids or Roupenids were an Armenian dynasty who dominated parts of Cilicia, and who established the Armenian Kingdom of Cilicia. [2651] The dynasty takes its name from its ancestor, the Armenian prince Ruben I.

The Rubenids were princes, later kings, of Cilicia from around AD 1080 until they were surpassed by the Hethumids in the mid-thirteenth century. [2652]

The new Armenian state established very close relations with European countries and played a very important role during the Crusades, providing the Christian armies with both a safe haven as well as provisions, including horses, on their way towards Jerusalem. [2653]

Intermarriage with European crusading families was common, and European religious, political, and cultural influence was strong. [2654]

[2649] https://en.wikipedia.org/wiki/Armenian_Kingdom_of_Cilicia
[2650] Gagné, Roland-Yves. (2001) "L'ascendance de Michel d'Aigneaux d'Ouville" (page 103). Mémoires de La Société Généalogique Canadienne Française, Volume 52, Number 2, Summer 2001.
[2651] https://en.wikipedia.org/wiki/Rubenid
[2652] Ibid.
[2653] Ibid.
[2654] Ibid.

The Hethumids (also spelled Hetoumids or Het'umids), also known as the House of Lampron (after Lampron castle), were the rulers of the Armenian Kingdom of Cilicia from 1226 to 1373. [2655]

William of Tyre described Gabriel de Mélitène as Greek by religion, and Armenian by race, language and custom. [2656] Byzantine seals bearing his name testify him as Gabriel, *protono belissimos and doux* of Mélitène. [2657]

When his daughter Morphia married Baldwin II of Jerusalem, it is said that Gabriel, who was reputedly very wealthy, gave 50,000 gold bezants as a dowry. [2658]

- Gabriel de Mélitène, Governor of Mélitène (today called Malatya in Turkey) married 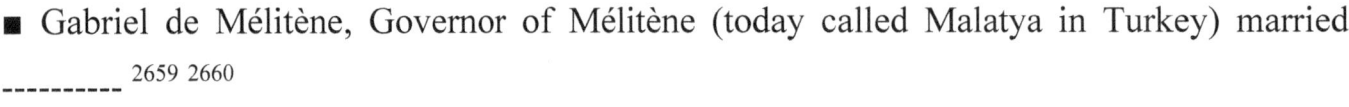 [2659] [2660]

  □ Morphia de Mélitène married King Baldwin II of Jerusalem [2661] [2662] [2663] [2664] [2665]

  □ Princess Alix de Jerusalem married Prince Bohémond II of Antioch [2666] [2667] [2668] [2669] [2670]

[2655] https://en.wikipedia.org/wiki/Hethumid
[2656] https://en.wikipedia.org/wiki/Gabriel_of_Melitene
[2657] Ibid.
[2658] https://en.wikipedia.org/wiki/Gabriel_of_Melitene
[2659] Gagné, Roland-Yves. (2001) "L'ascendance de Michel d'Aigneaux d'Ouville" (page 104). Mémoires de La Société Généalogique Canadienne Française, Volume 52, Number 2, Summer 2001.
[2660] https://en.wikipedia.org/wiki/Gabriel_of_Melitene
[2661] fmg.ac/Projects/MedLands/ARMENIA.htm#MorphiaMBaudouinIIJerusalem
[2662] fmg.ac/Projects/MedLands/JERUSALEM.htm#BaudouinIIB
[2663] Gagné, Roland-Yves. (2001) "L'ascendance de Michel d'Aigneaux d'Ouville" (page 104). Mémoires de La Société Généalogique Canadienne Française, Volume 52, Number 2, Summer 2001.
[2664] https://en.wikipedia.org/wiki/Morphia_of_Melitene
[2665] https://en.wikipedia.org/wiki/Baldwin_of_Bourcq
[2666] fmg.ac/Projects/MedLands/JERUSALEM.htm#AlixMBohemondIIAntioch

☐ Princess Constance of Antioch married Prince Raymond de Châtillon of Antioch [2671] [2672] [2673] [2674] [2675]

☐ Agnès of Antioch married King Béla III of Hungary and Croatia [2676] [2677] [2678] [2679] [2680]

■ King Andrew II of Hungary married Gertrude d'Andechs of Méranie [2681] [2682] [2683] [2684]

☐ Marie of Hungary married Asèn II, Tzar Ivan Asèn II of Bulgaria [2685] [2686] [2687] [2688] [2689]

[2667] fmg.ac/Projects/MedLands/ANTIOCH.htm#BohemondIIB

[2668] Gagné, Roland-Yves. (2001) "L'ascendance de Michel d'Aigneaux d'Ouville" (page 104). Mémoires de La Société Généalogique Canadienne Française, Volume 52, Number 2, Summer 2001.

[2669] https://en.wikipedia.org/wiki/Alice_of_Antioch

[2670] https://en.wikipedia.org/wiki/Bohemund_II_of_Antioch

[2671] fmg.ac/Projects/MedLands/ANTIOCH.htm#ConstanceAntiochdied1163B

[2672] fmg.ac/Projects/MedLands/CENTRAL%20FRANCE.htm#RenaudChatillondied1186

[2673] Gagné, Roland-Yves. (2001) "L'ascendance de Michel d'Aigneaux d'Ouville" (page 104). Mémoires de La Société Généalogique Canadienne Française, Volume 52, Number 2, Summer 2001.

[2674] https://en.wikipedia.org/wiki/Constance_of_Antioch

[2675] https://en.wikipedia.org/wiki/Raynald_of_Châtillon

[2676] fmg.ac/Projects/MedLands/CENTRAL%20FRANCE.htm#AgnesAnnaChatillonMBelaIIIHungary

[2677] fmg.ac/Projects/MedLands/HUNGARY.htm#_BÉLA_III_1172-1196,

[2678] Gagné, Roland-Yves. (2001) "L'ascendance de Michel d'Aigneaux d'Ouville" (page 104). Mémoires de La Société Généalogique Canadienne Française, Volume 52, Number 2, Summer 2001.

[2679] https://en.wikipedia.org/wiki/Agnes_of_Antioch

[2680] https://en.wikipedia.org/wiki/Béla_III_of_Hungary

[2681] fmg.ac/Projects/MedLands/HUNGARY.htm#_ANDRÁS_II_1205-1235,

[2682] fmg.ac/Projects/MedLands/LATIN%20EMPERORS.htm#YolandeCourtenaydied1233

[2683] https://en.wikipedia.org/wiki/Andrew_II_of_Hungary

[2684] https://en.wikipedia.org/wiki/Yolanda_de_Courtenay

[2685] fmg.ac/Projects/MedLands/HUNGARY.htm#MariaMIvanAsenIIBulgaria

[2686] fmg.ac/Projects/MedLands/BULGARIA.htm#IvanAsenIIdied1241B

☐ Hélène of Bulgaria married Emperor Theodore II Doukas Lascaris of Nicea (Laskarid dynasty) in the spring of 1235 [2690] [2691] [2692]

☐ Eudoxia Lascaris married Guillaume Pierre I, Count of Vintmille, in either 1262 or 1263, perhaps in Nicea [2693] [2694] [2695]

■ Jean I de Lascaris de Vintmille, Count of Vintmille married ---------- [2696] [2697]

■ Guillaume Pierre II de Lascaris de Vintmille, Count of Vintmille, married ---------- between 1310 and 1320 [2698]

[2687] Gagné, Roland-Yves. (2001) "L'ascendance de Michel d'Aigneaux d'Ouville" (page 104). Mémoires de La Société Généalogique Canadienne Française, Volume 52, Number 2, Summer 2001.
[2688] https://en.wikipedia.org/wiki/Anna_Maria_of_Hungary
[2689] https://en.wikipedia.org/wiki/Ivan_Asen_II_of_Bulgaria
[2690] fmg.ac/Projects/MedLands/BULGARIA.htm#ElenaDiedbefore1254
[2691] fmg.ac/Projects/MedLands/NIKAIA.htm#TheodorosIINikaiadied1258
[2692] Gagné, Roland-Yves. (2001) "L'ascendance de Michel d'Aigneaux d'Ouville" (page 104). Mémoires de La Société Généalogique Canadienne Française, Volume 52, Number 2, Summer 2001.
[2693] fmg.ac/Projects/MedLands/NIKAIA.htm#TheodorosIINikaiadied1258
[2694] jean.gallian.free.fr/vintimil/Images/p1b.pdf
[2695] Gagné, Roland-Yves. (2001) "L'ascendance de Michel d'Aigneaux d'Ouville" (page 104). Mémoires de La Société Généalogique Canadienne Française, Volume 52, Number 2, Summer 2001.
[2696] Jetté, René, DuLong, John P., Gagné, Roland-Yves, Moreau, Gail F. and Dubé, Joseph A. (2001) Table d'ascendance de Catherine Baillon: 12 générations (p 158). Montréal, Québec: Société Généalogique Canadienne Française.
[2697] Gagné, Roland-Yves. (2001) "L'ascendance de Michel d'Aigneaux d'Ouville" (page 104). Mémoires de La Société Généalogique Canadienne Française, Volume 52, Number 2, Summer 2001.
[2698] Jetté, René, DuLong, John P., Gagné, Roland-Yves, Moreau, Gail F. and Dubé, Joseph A. (2001) Table d'ascendance de Catherine Baillon: 12 générations (page 146). Montréal, Québec: Société Généalogique Canadienne Française.

■ Louis de Lascaris de Vintmille, Count of Vintmille and Co-seigneur of Briga, married Tiburge Grimaldi de Beuil in 1346 [2699]

■ Rainier de Lascaris de Vintmille, Count of Vintmille and Co-seigneur of Briga, married Madeleine Grimaldi d'Antibes between 1390 and 1400, but before 1403 [2700]

■ Charles de Lascaris de Vintmille, Co-seigneur of Briga, married Jeannette Litti, [2701] dame de Bonson et de La Roquette du Var, between 1420 and 1430 [2702]

☐ Baptistine de Lascaris de Vintmille married Pierre Chabaud, seigneur de Tourrettes, between 1460 and 1470 [2703]

■ Jean Chabaud, seigneur de Tourrettes, married Louise de Berre in 1519 (region de Nice) [2704]

■ Antoine Chabot (Chabaud), sieur de La Fond en Provence, married Catherine Lombard on March 30, 1554 at Chappelain et Crucé, Paris [2705]

☐ Marguerite Chabot married Jean Bizet, seigneur de Paponville et de la Grandmaison, in 1580 [2706]

[2699] Jetté, René, DuLong, John P., Gagné, Roland-Yves, Moreau, Gail F. and Dubé, Joseph A. (2001) <u>Table d'ascendance de Catherine Baillon: 12 générations</u> (pages 131 and 132). Montréal, Québec: Société Généalogique Canadienne Française.
[2700] Ibid, page 119.
[2701] Refer to article *Possible Jewish Ancestor for Catherine Baillon* located in Catherine de Baillon chapter (page 212).
[2702] Jetté, René, DuLong, John P., Gagné, Roland-Yves, Moreau, Gail F. and Dubé, Joseph A. (2001) <u>Table d'ascendance de Catherine Baillon: 12 générations</u> (page 103). Montréal, Québec: Société Généalogique Canadienne Française.
[2703] Ibid, pages 81 and 82.
[2704] Ibid, page 66.
[2705] Ibid, page 54.

☐ Anne Bizet married Mathurin de Marle, seigneur de Vaugien, about 1610 in the Chevreuse (Yvelines) region [2707]

☐ Louise de Marle married Alphonse de Baillon, seigneur de La Mascotterie, between 1630 and 1640 in the Chevreuse (Yvelines) region [2708]

☐ Catherine de Baillon

[2706] Jetté, René, DuLong, John P., Gagné, Roland-Yves, Moreau, Gail F. and Dubé, Joseph A. (2001) Table d'ascendance de Catherine Baillon: 12 générations (pages 45 and 46). Montréal, Québec: Société Généalogique Canadienne Française.
[2707] Ibid, page 40.
[2708] Ibid, page 31.

(Kings of Jerusalem) Counts of Rethel

- Manasses of Omont married Ordela de Castres [2709] [2710] [2711]

- Manasses II, Count of Rethel, married Dada [2712]

- Manasses III, Count of Rethel, married Judith of Roucy [2713] [2714] [2715]

- Hugh I, Count of Rethel, married Mélisende de Montlhéry (also known as Melisende of Crécy) [2716] [2717] [2718]

- King Baldwin II of Jerusalem married Morphia de Mélitène [2719] [2720] [2721] [2722] [2723]

[2709] fmg.ac/Projects/MedLands/CHAMPAGNE%20NOBILITY.htm#ManassesIRethelMOrdela
[2710] fmg.ac/Projects/MedLands/LOTHARINGIAN%20(UPPER)%20NOBILITY.htm#OrdelaMManassesIRethel
[2711] https://en.wikipedia.org/wiki/Manasses_II,_Count_of_Rethel
[2712] fmg.ac/Projects/MedLands/CHAMPAGNE%20NOBILITY.htm#ManassesIRethelMOrdela
[2713] fmg.ac/Projects/MedLands/CHAMPAGNE%20NOBILITY.htm#ManassesIIRetheldied1081B
[2714] fmg.ac/Projects/MedLands/NORTHERN%20FRANCE.htm#JudithRoucyMManassesIIRethel
[2715] https://en.wikipedia.org/wiki/Manasses_III,_Count_of_Rethel
[2716] fmg.ac/Projects/MedLands/JERUSALEM.htm#BaudouinIIB
[2717] fmg.ac/Projects/MedLands/PARIS%20REGION%20NOBILITY.htm#MelisendeMontlheryMHuguesIRethel
[2718] https://en.wikipedia.org/wiki/Hugh_I,_Count_of_Rethel
[2719] fmg.ac/Projects/MedLands/JERUSALEM.htm#BaudouinIIB

- Princess Alix de Jerusalem married Prince Bohémond II of Antioch [2724] [2725] [2726] [2727] [2728]

- Princess Constance of Antioch married Prince Raymond de Châtillon of Antioch [2729] [2730] [2731] [2732] [2733]

- Agnès of Antioch married King Béla III of Hungary and Croatia [2734] [2735] [2736] [2737] [2738]

- **King Andrew II of Hungary married Gertrude d'Andechs of Méranie** [2739] [2740] [2741] [2742]

[2720] fmg.ac/Projects/MedLands/ARMENIA.htm#MorphiaMBaudouinIIJerusalem
[2721] Gagné, Roland-Yves. (2001) "L'ascendance de Michel d'Aigneaux d'Ouville" (page 104). Mémoires de La Société Généalogique Canadienne Française, Volume 52, Number 2, Summer 2001.
[2722] https://en.wikipedia.org/wiki/Baldwin_of_Bourcq
[2723] https://en.wikipedia.org/wiki/Morphia_of_Melitene
[2724] fmg.ac/Projects/MedLands/JERUSALEM.htm#AlixMBohemondIIAntioch
[2725] fmg.ac/Projects/MedLands/ANTIOCH.htm#BohemondIIB
[2726] Gagné, Roland-Yves. (2001) "L'ascendance de Michel d'Aigneaux d'Ouville" (page 104). Mémoires de La Société Généalogique Canadienne Française, Volume 52, Number 2, Summer 2001.
[2727] https://en.wikipedia.org/wiki/Alice_of_Antioch
[2728] https://en.wikipedia.org/wiki/Bohemund_II_of_Antioch
[2729] fmg.ac/Projects/MedLands/ANTIOCH.htm#ConstanceAntiochdied1163B
[2730] fmg.ac/Projects/MedLands/CENTRAL%20FRANCE.htm#RenaudChatillondied1186
[2731] Gagné, Roland-Yves. (2001) "L'ascendance de Michel d'Aigneaux d'Ouville" (page 104). Mémoires de La Société Généalogique Canadienne Française, Volume 52, Number 2, Summer 2001.
[2732] https://en.wikipedia.org/wiki/Constance_of_Antioch
[2733] https://en.wikipedia.org/wiki/Raynald_of_Châtillon
[2734] fmg.ac/Projects/MedLands/CENTRAL%20FRANCE.htm#AgnesAnnaChatillonMBelaIIIHungary
[2735] fmg.ac/Projects/MedLands/HUNGARY.htm#_BÉLA_III_1172-1196,
[2736] Gagné, Roland-Yves. (2001) "L'ascendance de Michel d'Aigneaux d'Ouville" (page 104). Mémoires de La Société Généalogique Canadienne Française, Volume 52, Number 2, Summer 2001.
[2737] https://en.wikipedia.org/wiki/Agnes_of_Antioch
[2738] https://en.wikipedia.org/wiki/Béla_III_of_Hungary
[2739] fmg.ac/Projects/MedLands/HUNGARY.htm#_ANDRÁS_II_1205-1235,
[2740] fmg.ac/Projects/MedLands/LATIN%20EMPERORS.htm#YolandeCourtenaydied1233

- Marie of Hungary married Asèn II, Tzar Ivan Asèn II of Bulgaria[2743][2744][2745][2746][2747]

- Hélène of Bulgaria married Emperor Theodore II Doukas Lascaris of Nicea (Laskarid dynasty) in the spring of 1235 [2748][2749][2750]

- Eudoxia Lascaris married Guillaume Pierre I, Count of Vintmille, in either 1262 or 1263, perhaps in Nicea [2751][2752][2753]

- Jean I de Lascaris de Vintmille, Count of Vintmille married ---------- [2754][2755]

- Guillaume Pierre II de Lascaris de Vintmille, Count of Vintmille, married ---------- between 1310 and 1320 [2756]

[2741] https://en.wikipedia.org/wiki/Andrew_II_of_Hungary
[2742] https://en.wikipedia.org/wiki/Yolanda_de_Courtenay
[2743] fmg.ac/Projects/MedLands/HUNGARY.htm#MariaMIvanAsenIIBulgaria
[2744] fmg.ac/Projects/MedLands/BULGARIA.htm#IvanAsenIIdied1241B
[2745] Gagné, Roland-Yves. (2001) "L'ascendance de Michel d'Aigneaux d'Ouville" (page 104). Mémoires de La Société Généalogique Canadienne Française, Volume 52, Number 2, Summer 2001.
[2746] https://en.wikipedia.org/wiki/Anna_Maria_of_Hungary
[2747] https://en.wikipedia.org/wiki/Ivan_Asen_II_of_Bulgaria
[2748] fmg.ac/Projects/MedLands/BULGARIA.htm#ElenaDiedbefore1254
[2749] fmg.ac/Projects/MedLands/NIKAIA.htm#TheodorosIINikaiadied1258
[2750] Gagné, Roland-Yves. (2001) "L'ascendance de Michel d'Aigneaux d'Ouville" (page 104). Mémoires de La Société Généalogique Canadienne Française, Volume 52, Number 2, Summer 2001.
[2751] fmg.ac/Projects/MedLands/NIKAIA.htm#TheodorosIINikaiadied1258
[2752] jean.gallian.free.fr/vintimil/Images/p1b.pdf
[2753] Gagné, Roland-Yves. (2001) "L'ascendance de Michel d'Aigneaux d'Ouville" (page 104). Mémoires de La Société Généalogique Canadienne Française, Volume 52, Number 2, Summer 2001.
[2754] Jetté, René, DuLong, John P., Gagné, Roland-Yves, Moreau, Gail F. and Dubé, Joseph A. (2001) Table d'ascendance de Catherine Baillon: 12 générations (p 158). Montréal, Québec: Société Généalogique Canadienne Française.
[2755] Gagné, Roland-Yves. (2001) "L'ascendance de Michel d'Aigneaux d'Ouville" (page 104). Mémoires de La Société Généalogique Canadienne Française, Volume 52, Number 2, Summer 2001.

■ Louis de Lascaris de Vintmille, Count of Vintmille and Co-seigneur of Briga, married Tiburge Grimaldi de Beuil in 1346 [2757]

■ Rainier de Lascaris de Vintmille, Count of Vintmille and Co-seigneur of Briga, married Madeleine Grimaldi d'Antibes between 1390 and 1400, but before 1403 [2758]

■ Charles de Lascaris de Vintmille, Co-seigneur of Briga, married Jeannette Litti, [2759] dame de Bonson et de La Roquette du Var, between 1420 and 1430 [2760]

☐ Baptistine de Lascaris de Vintmille married Pierre Chabaud, seigneur de Tourrettes, between 1460 and 1470 [2761]

■ Jean Chabaud, seigneur de Tourrettes, married Louise de Berre in 1519 (region de Nice) [2762]

■ Antoine Chabot (Chabaud), sieur de La Fond en Provence, married Catherine Lombard on March 30, 1554 at Chappelain et Crucé, Paris [2763]

☐ Marguerite Chabot married Jean Bizet, seigneur de Paponville et de la Grandmaison, in 1580 [2764]

[2756] Jetté, René, DuLong, John P., Gagné, Roland-Yves, Moreau, Gail F. and Dubé, Joseph A. (2001) <u>Table d'ascendance de Catherine Baillon: 12 générations</u> (page 146). Montréal, Québec: Société Généalogique Canadienne Française.
[2757] Ibid, pages 131 and 132.
[2758] Ibid, page 119.
[2759] Refer to article *Possible Jewish Ancestor for Catherine Baillon* located in Catherine de Baillon chapter (page 212).
[2760] Jetté, René, DuLong, John P., Gagné, Roland-Yves, Moreau, Gail F. and Dubé, Joseph A. (2001) <u>Table d'ascendance de Catherine Baillon: 12 générations</u> (page 103). Montréal, Québec: Société Généalogique Canadienne Française.
[2761] Ibid, pages 81 and 82.
[2762] Ibid, page 66.
[2763] Ibid, page 54.

☐ Anne Bizet married Mathurin de Marle, seigneur de Vaugien, about 1610 in the Chevreuse (Yvelines) region [2765]

☐ Louise de Marle married Alphonse de Baillon, seigneur de La Mascotterie, between 1630 and 1640 in the Chevreuse (Yvelines) region [2766]

☐ Catherine de Baillon

[2764] Jetté, René, DuLong, John P., Gagné, Roland-Yves, Moreau, Gail F. and Dubé, Joseph A. (2001) Table d'ascendance de Catherine Baillon: 12 générations (pages 45 and 46). Montréal, Québec: Société Généalogique Canadienne Française.
[2765] Ibid, page 40.
[2766] Ibid, page 31.

Counts of Andechs

As denoted in Wikipedia [2767]

The House of Andechs was a feudal line of German princes in 12th and 13th century. The Counts of Dießen-Andechs (1100 to 1180) obtained territories in northern Dalmatia on the Adriatic seacoast, where they became Margraves of Istria and ultimately Dukes of a short-lived Imperial State named Merania from 1180 to 1248.

- Friedrich II von Diesson, married ---------- [2768]

- Friedrich III von Diesson, [2769] married Hadamut von Eppenstein [2770]

- Arnold, Count of Dießen, [2771] married Gisela of Schweinfurt [2772]

- Berthold II, Count of Dießen and Andechs in Bavarai, Count of Plassenburg and Kulmbach in Franconia, Vogt of Benediktbeuern Abbéy, married Sophia

- Berthold III, Count of Andechs (also known as Berthold I, Margrave of Istria), [2773] married Hedwig of Wittelsbach [2774]

[2767] https://en.wikipedia.org/wiki/House_of_Andechs
[2768] fmg.ac/Projects/MedLands/BAVARIAN%20NOBILITY.htm#_Toc413507698
[2769] fmg.ac/Projects/MedLands/BAVARIAN%20NOBILITY.htm#FriedrichIIIDiessendied1075B
[2770] fmg.ac/Projects/MedLands/CARINTHIA.htm#HadamutMFriedrichIIDiessen
[2771] fmg.ac/Projects/MedLands/BAVARIAN%20NOBILITY.htm#ArnoldDiessendiedafter1091
[2772] fmg.ac/Projects/MedLands/BAVARIAN%20NOBILITY.htm#GiselaSchweinfurtM1ArnoldDiessen

■ Berthold IV, Duke of Merania, [2775] married Agnes of Rochlitz (also known as Agnes of Wettin). [2776]

☐ Agnes d'Andechs of Méranie (a famous beauty) [2777] [2778] married King Philippe II Auguste, King of France, in June 1196. [2779]

☐ Princess Marie of France married Henri I, Duke of Brabant[2780] [2781]

☐ Élisabeth de Brabant marriedCount Dietrich (Thierry) de Clèves [2782] [2783]

Élisabeth was also known as Ysabeau de Brabant; with regards to French records, the name Élisabeth is often used, interchangeably, with that of Isabelle. [2784] [2785]

☐ Mathilda de Clèves married Gerard de Luxembourg

☐ Marguerite de Luxembourg married Jean III de Ghistelles

[2773] fmg.ac/Projects/MedLands/CARINTHIA.htm#BernhardIIAndechsdied1188B
[2774] fmg.ac/Projects/MedLands/BAVARIA.htm#Hedwigdied1174
[2775] fmg.ac/Projects/MedLands/CARINTHIA.htm#BertoldIIIAndechsMeranodied1204
[2776] fmg.ac/Projects/MedLands/MEISSEN.htm#Agnesdied1195
[2777] fmg.ac/Projects/MedLands/CARINTHIA.htm#AgnesMeranodied1201
[2778] https://en.wikipedia.org/wiki/Gertrude_of_Merania
[2779] fmg.ac/Projects/MedLands/CAPET.htm#PhilippeIIdied1223B
[2780] fmg.ac/Projects/MedLands/CAPET.htm#Mariedied1238
[2781] fmg.ac/Projects/MedLands/BRABANT,%20LOUVAIN.htm#HenriILotharingiaBrabantdied1235B
[2782] fmg.ac/Projects/MedLands/BRABANT,%20LOUVAIN.htm#Elisabethdied1272
[2783] fmg.ac/Projects/MedLands/FRANCONIA%20(LOWER%20RHINE).htm#Dietrichdied1245
[2784] Jetté, René, DuLong, John P., Gagné, Roland-Yves, Moreau, Gail F. and Dubé, Joseph A. (2001) Table d'ascendance de Catherine Baillon: 12 générations (p 153). Montréal, Québec: Société Généalogique Canadienne Française.
[2785] https://en.wikipedia.org/wiki/Henry_I,_Duke_of_Brabant

- Jean IV de Ghistelles married Marie de Haverskerke

- Roger de Ghistelles married Élisabeth ~~Marguerite~~ de Dudzeele (see page 182 for updated explanation)

- ☐ Isabelle (Ysabeau) de Ghistelles married Arnould VI de Gavre

- ☐ Catherine de Gavre d'Escornaix married Guy I Le Bouteiller

- Guy II Le Bouteillier married Isabeau Morhier

- Jean Le Bouteillier married Marie de Venois

- ☐ Bénigne Le Bouteillier married Jacques Maillard

- Miles Maillard married Marie Morant

- ☐ Renée Maillard married Adam de Baillon

- Alphonse de Baillon married Louise de Marle

- ☐ Catherine de Baillon

In keeping with the Counts of Andechs, there exists a second line of descent.

- Friedrich II von Diesson, married ---------- [2786]

- Friedrich III von Diesson, [2787] married Hadamut von Eppenstein [2788]

- Arnold, Count of Dießen, [2789] married Gisela of Schweinfurt [2790]

- Berthold II, Count of Dießen and Andechs in Bavarai, Count of Plassenburg and Kulmbach in Franconia, Vogt of Benediktbeuern Abbéy, married Sophia

- Berthold III, Count of Andechs (also known as Berthold I, Margrave of Istria), [2791] married Hedwig of Wittelsbach [2792]

- Berthold IV, Duke of Merania, [2793] married Agnes of Rochlitz (also known as Agnes of Wettin). [2794]

☐ Gertrude d'Andechs of Méranie married King Andrew II of Hungary [2795] [2796] [2797] [2798]

[2786] fmg.ac/Projects/MedLands/BAVARIAN%20NOBILITY.htm#_Toc413507698
[2787] fmg.ac/Projects/MedLands/BAVARIAN%20NOBILITY.htm#FriedrichIIIDiessendied1075B
[2788] fmg.ac/Projects/MedLands/CARINTHIA.htm#HadamutMFriedrichIIDiessen
[2789] fmg.ac/Projects/MedLands/BAVARIAN%20NOBILITY.htm#ArnoldDiessendiedafter1091
[2790] fmg.ac/Projects/MedLands/BAVARIAN%20NOBILITY.htm#GiselaSchweinfurtM1ArnoldDiessen
[2791] fmg.ac/Projects/MedLands/CARINTHIA.htm#BernhardIIAndechsdied1188B
[2792] fmg.ac/Projects/MedLands/BAVARIA.htm#Hedwigdied1174
[2793] fmg.ac/Projects/MedLands/CARINTHIA.htm#BertoldIIIAndechsMeranodied1204
[2794] fmg.ac/Projects/MedLands/MEISSEN.htm#Agnesdied1195
[2795] fmg.ac/Projects/MedLands/CARINTHIA.htm#GertrudMeranodied1213
[2796] fmg.ac/Projects/MedLands/HUNGARY.htm#_ANDRÁS_II_1205

☐ Marie of Hungary married Asèn II, Tzar Ivan Asèn II of Bulgaria[2799 2800 2801 2802 2803]

☐ Hélène of Bulgaria married Emperor Theodore II Doukas Lascaris of Nicea (Laskarid dynasty) in the spring of 1235 [2804 2805 2806]

☐ Eudoxia Lascaris married Guillaume Pierre I, Count of Vintmille, in either 1262 or 1263, perhaps in Nicea [2807 2808 2809]

■ Jean I de Lascaris de Vintmille, Count of Vintmille married ---------- [2810 2811]

[2797] https://en.wikipedia.org/wiki/Gertrude_of_Merania
[2798] https://en.wikipedia.org/wiki/Andrew_II_of_Hungary
[2799] fmg.ac/Projects/MedLands/HUNGARY.htm#MariaMIvanAsenIIBulgaria
[2800] fmg.ac/Projects/MedLands/BULGARIA.htm#IvanAsenIIdied1241B
[2801] Gagné, Roland-Yves. (2001) "L'ascendance de Michel d'Aigneaux d'Ouville" (page 104). Mémoires de La Société Généalogique Canadienne Française, Volume 52, Number 2, Summer 2001.
[2802] https://en.wikipedia.org/wiki/Anna_Maria_of_Hungary
[2803] httsp://en.wikipedia.org/wiki/Ivan_Asen_II_of_Bulgaria
[2804] fmg.ac/Projects/MedLands/BULGARIA.htm#ElenaDiedbefore1254
[2805] fmg.ac/Projects/MedLands/NIKAIA.htm#TheodorosIINikaiadied1258
[2806] Gagné, Roland-Yves. (2001) "L'ascendance de Michel d'Aigneaux d'Ouville" (page 104). Mémoires de La Société Généalogique Canadienne Française, Volume 52, Number 2, Summer 2001.
[2807] fmg.ac/Projects/MedLands/NIKAIA.htm#TheodorosIINikaiadied1258
[2808] jean.gallian.free.fr/vintimil/Images/p1b.pdf
[2809] Gagné, Roland-Yves. (2001) "L'ascendance de Michel d'Aigneaux d'Ouville" (page 104). Mémoires de La Société Généalogique Canadienne Française, Volume 52, Number 2, Summer 2001.
[2810] Jetté, René, DuLong, John P., Gagné, Roland-Yves, Moreau, Gail F. and Dubé, Joseph A. (2001) Table d'ascendance de Catherine Baillon: 12 générations (p 158). Montréal, Québec: Société Généalogique Canadienne Française.
[2811] Gagné, Roland-Yves. (2001) "L'ascendance de Michel d'Aigneaux d'Ouville" (page 104). Mémoires de La Société Généalogique Canadienne Française, Volume 52, Number 2, Summer 2001.

■ Guillaume Pierre II de Lascaris de Vintmille, Count of Vintmille, married ---------- between 1310 and 1320 [2812]

■ Louis de Lascaris de Vintmille, Count of Vintmille and Co-seigneur of Briga, married Tiburge Grimaldi de Beuil in 1346 [2813]

■ Rainier de Lascaris de Vintmille, Count of Vintmille and Co-seigneur of Briga, married Madeleine Grimaldi d'Antibes between 1390 and 1400, but before 1403 [2814]

■ Charles de Lascaris de Vintmille, Co-seigneur of Briga, married Jeannette Litti, [2815] dame de Bonson et de La Roquette du Var, between 1420 and 1430 [2816]

☐ Baptistine de Lascaris de Vintmille married Pierre Chabaud, seigneur de Tourrettes, between 1460 and 1470 [2817]

■ Jean Chabaud, seigneur de Tourrettes, married Louise de Berre in 1519 (region de Nice) [2818]

■ Antoine Chabot (Chabaud), sieur de La Fond en Provence, married Catherine Lombard on March 30, 1554 at Chappelain et Crucé, Paris [2819]

[2812] Jetté, René, DuLong, John P., Gagné, Roland-Yves, Moreau, Gail F. and Dubé, Joseph A. (2001) <u>Table d'ascendance de Catherine Baillon: 12 générations</u> (page 146). Montréal, Québec: Société Généalogique Canadienne Française.
[2813] Ibid, pages 131 and 132.
[2814] Ibid, page 119.
[2815] Refer to article *Possible Jewish Ancestor for Catherine Baillon* located in Catherine de Baillon chapter (page 212).
[2816] Jetté, René, DuLong, John P., Gagné, Roland-Yves, Moreau, Gail F. and Dubé, Joseph A. (2001) <u>Table d'ascendance de Catherine Baillon: 12 générations</u> (page 103). Montréal, Québec: Société Généalogique Canadienne Française.
[2817] Ibid, pages 81 and 82.
[2818] Ibid, page 66.

☐ Marguerite Chabot married Jean Bizet, seigneur de Paponville et de la Grandmaison, in 1580 [2820]

☐ Anne Bizet married Mathurin de Marle, seigneur de Vaugien, about 1610 in the Chevreuse (Yvelines) region [2821]

☐ Louise de Marle married Alphonse de Baillon, seigneur de La Mascotterie, between 1630 and 1640 in the Chevreuse (Yvelines) region [2822]

☐ Catherine de Baillon

[2819] Jetté, René, DuLong, John P., Gagné, Roland-Yves, Moreau, Gail F. and Dubé, Joseph A. (2001) <u>Table d'ascendance de Catherine Baillon: 12 générations</u> (page 54). Montréal, Québec: Société Généalogique Canadienne Française.
[2820] Ibid, pages 45 and 46.
[2821] Ibid, page 40.
[2822] Ibid, page 31.

Book Bibliography

MEROVINGIANS

Baird, Robert Bruce. (2008) *Merovingians: Past and Present Masters*.

Gardner, Laurence. (2003) *Realm of the Ring Lords: The Myth and Magic of the Grail Quest*.

Geary, Patrick J. (1994) *Before France and Germany: The Creation and Transformation of the Merovingian World*.

Murray, Alexander Callander. (2000) *From Roman to Merovingian Gaul: A Reader*.

Murray, Alexander Callander. (2005) *Gregory of Tours: The Merovingians*.

Wallace-Hadrill, J. M. (1982) *The Long-Haired Kings and Other Studies in Frankish History*.

Wood, I. (1995) *The Merovingian Kingdoms, 450-751*.

Feel free to add a twist to history upon the reading of books by Ahmed Osman; books that eusure the necessity for much lateral thinking. They are herein listed in proper chronological order, each building on the former title.

[1] <u>Moses and Ahkenaten: The Secret History of Egypt at the Time of the Exodus</u>

During his reign, the Pharaoh Akhenaten was able to abolish the complex pantheon of the ancient Egyptian religion and replace it with a single god, the Aten, who had no image or form. Seizing on the striking similarities between the religious vision of this *heretic* pharaoh and the teachings of Moses, Sigmund Freud was the first to argue that Moses was in fact an Egyptian. Now Ahmed Osman, using recent archaeological discoveries and historical documents, contends that Akhenaten and Moses were one and the same man.

In a stunning retelling of the Exodus story, Osman details the events of Moses/Akhenaten's life: how he was brought up by Israelite relatives, ruled Egypt for seventeen years, angered many of his subjects by replacing the traditional Egyptian pantheon with worship of the Aten, and was forced to abdicate the throne. Retreating to the Sinai with his Egyptian and Israelite supporters, he died out of the sight of his followers, presumably at the hands of Seti I, after an unsuccessful attempt to regain his throne.

Osman reveals the Egyptian components in the monotheism preached by Moses as well as his use of Egyptian royal ritual and Egyptian religious expression. He shows that even the Ten Commandments betray the direct influence of Spell 125 in the Egyptian Book of the Dead. *Moses and Akhenaten* provides a radical challenge to long-standing beliefs concerning the origin of Semitic religion and the puzzle of Akhenaten's deviation from ancient Egyptian tradition. In fact, if Osman's contentions are correct, many major Old Testament figures would have been of Egyptian origin.

[2] The Hebrew Pharaohs of Egypt: The Secret Lineage of The Patriarch Joseph

When Joseph revealed his identity to his kinsmen who had sold him into slavery, he told them that God had made him *a father to Pharaoh.* Throughout the long history of ancient Egypt, only one man is known to have been given the title a *father to Pharaoh* – Yuya, a vizier of the eighteenth dynasty king Tuthmosis IV. Yuya has long intrigued Egyptologists because he was buried in the Valley of Kings even though he was not a member of the Royal House. His extraordinarily well-preserved mummy has a strong Semitic appearance, which suggests he was not of Egyptian blood, and many aspects of his burial have been shown to be contrary to Egyptian custom.

As The Hebrew Pharohs of Egypt shows, the idea that Joseph and Yuya may be one and the same person sheds a whole new light on the sudden rise of monotheism in Egypt, spearheaded by Queen Tiye and her son Akhnaten. It would clearly explain the deliberate obliteration of references to the *heretic* king and his successors by the last eighteenth dynasty pharaoh, Horemheb, whom the author believes was the oppressor king in the Book of Exodus. The author also draws on a wealth of detailed evidence from Egyptian, biblical, and Koranic sources to place the time of the departure of the Hebrews from Egypt during the short reign of Ramses I, the first king of the nineteenth dynasty.

[3] Jesus in the House of the Pharaohs: The Essene Revelations on the Historical Jesus

Although it is commonly believed that Jesus lived during the first century C.E., there is no concrete evidence to support this fact from the Roman and Jewish historians who would have been his contemporaries. The Gospel writers themselves were of a later generation, and many accounts recorded in the Old Testament and Talmudic commentaries refer to the coming of the Messiah as an event that had already occurred.

Using the evidence available from archaeology, the Dead Sea Scrolls, the Koran, the Talmud, and biblical sources, Ahmed Osman provides a compelling case that both Jesus and Joshua were one and the same (a belief echoed by the early Church Fathers) and that this person was likewise the pharaoh Tutankhamun, who ruled Egypt between 1361 and 1352 B.C.E. and was regarded as the spiritual son of God. Osman contends that the Essene Christians (who followed Jesus' teachings in secret after his murder) only came into the open following the execution of their prophet John the Baptist by Herod, many centuries later. Yet it was also the Essenes who, following the death of Tutankhamun and his father Akhenaten (Moses), secretly kept the monotheistic religion of Egypt alive. The Essenes believed themselves to be the people of the New Covenant, established between their Lord and themselves, by the Teacher of Righteousness who was murdered by a wicked priest. The Dead Sea Scrolls support Osman's contention that this Teacher of Righteousness was in fact Jesus.

[4] Christianity: An Ancient Egyptian Religion

In Christianity: An Ancient Egyptian Religion author Ahmed Osman contends that the roots of Christian belief spring not from Judaea but from Egypt. He compares the chronology of the Old Testament and its factual content with ancient Egyptian records to show that the major characters of the Hebrew scriptures, including Solomon, David, Moses, and Joshua, are based on Egyptian historical figures. He further suggests that not only were these personalities and the stories associated with them cultivated on the banks of the Nile, but the major tenets of Christian belief – the One God, the Trinity, the hierarchy of heaven, life after death, and the virgin birth – are all Egyptian in origin. He likewise provides a convincing argument that Jesus himself came out of Egypt.

With the help of modern archaeological findings, Osman shows that Christianity survived as an Egyptian mystery cult until the fourth century AD, when the Romans embarked on a mission of suppression and persecution.

In AD 391 the Roman-appointed Bishop Theophilus led a mob into the Serapeum quarter of Alexandria and burned the Alexandrian library, destroying all records of the true Egyptian roots of Christianity. The Roman version of Christianity, manufactured to maintain political power, claimed that Christianity originated in Judaea. In Christianity: An Ancient Egyptian Religion Osman restores Egypt to its rightful place in the history of Christianity.

Robert Bauval, author of The Orion Mystery: Unlocking the Secrets of the Pyramids, has teamed up with Ahmed Osman in the writing of Breaking the Mirror of Heaven: The Conspiracy to Suppress the Voice of Ancient Egypt

Called the "Mirror of Heaven" by Hermes-Thoth and regarded as the birthplace of civilization, science, religion, and magic, Egypt has ignited the imagination of all who come in contact with it since ancient times, from Pythagoras and Plato to Alexander the Great and NapoLéon to modern Egyptologists the world over; yet, despite this preeminence in the collective mind, Egypt has suffered considerable destruction over the centuries.

Even before the burning of the Great Library at Alexandria, the land of the pharaohs was pillaged by its own people. With the arrival of foreign rulers, both Arabic and European, the destruction and thievery continued along with suppression of ancient knowledge as some rulers sought to cleanse Egypt of its "pagan" past.

Exploring the many cycles of destruction and suppression in Egypt, as well as moments of salvation, such as the first registered excavations by Auguste Mariette, Robert Bauval and Ahmed Osman investigate the many conquerors of Egypt through the millennia as well as what has happened to famous artifacts such as the Rosetta Stone.

They show how Napoléon, through his invasion, wanted to revive ancient Egyptian wisdom and art because of its many connections to Freemasonry.

They reveal how the degradation of monuments, theft of relics, and censorship of ancient teachings continue to this day.

Exposing recent cover-ups during the tenure of Antiquities Minister Zahi Hawass, they explain how new discoveries at Giza were closed to further research.

Clearing cultural and historical distortions, the authors reveal the long-hidden and persecuted voice of ancient Egypt and call for the return of Egypt to its rightful place as "the Mother of Nations" and "the Mirror of Heaven."

Website Bibliography

BALKANS AND EASTERN EUROPE

Albania [2823]

Bosnia and Hercegovina [2824]

Bulgaria [2825]

Byzantium (395 – 1057) [2826]

Byzantium (1057 – 1204) [2827]

Byzantium (1261 – 1463) [2828]

Byzantium Nobility [2829]

Constantinople, Latin Empire [2830]

Croatia [2831]

[2823] fmg.ac/Projects/MedLands/ALBANIA.htm
[2824] fmg.ac/Projects/MedLands/BOSNIA.htm
[2825] fmg.ac/Projects/MedLands/BULGARIA.htm
[2826] fmg.ac/Projects/MedLands/BYZANTIUM.htm
[2827] fmg.ac/Projects/MedLands/BYZANTIUM%2010571204.htm
[2828] fmg.ac/Projects/MedLands/BYZANTIUM%2012611453.htm
[2829] fmg.ac/Projects/MedLands/BYZANTINE%20NOBILITY.htm
[2830] fmg.ac/Projects/MedLands/LATIN%20EMPERORS.htm
[2831] fmg.ac/Projects/MedLands/CROATIA.htm

Ducs de Magyars [2832]

Empire Byzantin [2833]

Greece, Latin Lordships [2834]

Hungary Kings [2835]

Hungary Nobility [2836]

Montenegro [2837]

Serbia [2838]

Thessaloniki [2839]

BRITISH ISLES

A Synopsis of the Genealogical Descent of Her Most Gracious Majesty, Queen Victoria, from Rollo, the Founder of the Duchy of Normandy (online digitized edition) [2840]

Battle of Hastings Participants (October 14, 1066) [2841]

[2832] fjaunais.free.fr/h0magyars.htm
[2833] fjaunais.free.fr/h0byzance.htm
[2834] fmg.ac/Projects/MedLands/LATIN%20LORDSHIPS%20IN%20GREECE.htm
[2835] fmg.ac/Projects/MedLands/HUNGARY.htm
[2836] fmg.ac/Projects/MedLands/HUNGARIAN%20NOBILITY.htm
[2837] fmg.ac/Projects/MedLands/MONTENEGRO.htm
[2838] fmg.ac/Projects/MedLands/SERBIA.htm
[2839] fmg.ac/Projects/MedLands/THESSALONIKI.htm
[2840] https://books.google.ca/books?id=WFkEAAAAQAAJ&hl=fr&pg=PP5&redir_esc=y#v=onepage&q&f=false
[2841] genealogie.quebec/testphp/info.php?no=215024

Corrections to K S B Keats-Rohan's *Domesday* Series [2842]

England, Anglo-Saxon and Danish Kings [2843]

England, Anglo-Saxon Nobility [2844]

England, Earls (Created 1067 – 1122) [2845]

England, Earls (Created 1138 – 1143) [2846]

England, Earls (Created 1207 – 1466) [2847]

England, Kings (1066 – 1603) [2848]

Ireland, Kings and Nobility [2849]

Kings of England [2850]

Kings of Scotland [2851]

Royaume d'Angleterre [2852]

[2842] fmg.ac/Projects/Domesday/
[2843] fmg.ac/Projects/MedLands/ENGLAND,%20AngloSaxon%20&%20Danish%20Kings.htm
[2844] fmg.ac/Projects/MedLands/ENGLAND,%20AngloSaxon%20nobility.htm
[2845] fmg.ac/Projects/MedLands/ENGLISH%20NOBILITY%20MEDIEVAL.htm
[2846] fmg.ac/Projects/MedLands/ENGLISH%20NOBILITY%20MEDIEVAL1.htm
[2847] fmg.ac/Projects/MedLands/ENGLISH%20NOBILITY%20MEDIEVAL2.htm
[2848] fmg.ac/Projects/MedLands/ENGLAND,%20Kings%201066-1603.htm
[2849] fmg.ac/Projects/MedLands/IRELAND.htm
[2850] www.scotlandroyalty.org/kings.html
[2851] www.scotlandroyalty.org/scotland.html
[2852] fjaunais.free.fr/h0angleterre.htm

Royaume d'Écosse [2853]

Scotland, Kings [2854]

Scotland, Mormaers, Earls and Lords [2855]

Scotland, Earls (Created 1162 – 1398) [2856]

Scotland Untitled Nobility [2857]

Untitled English Nobility A – C [2858]

Untitled English Nobility D – K [2859]

Untitled English Nobility L – O [2860]

Untitled English Nobility P – S [2861]

Untitled English Nobility T – Z [2862]

Wales, Kings and Princes [2863]

[2853] fjaunais.free.fr/h0Écosse.htm
[2854] fmg.ac/Projects/MedLands/SCOTLAND.htm
[2855] fmg.ac/Projects/MedLands/SCOTTISH%20NOBILITY.htm
[2856] fmg.ac/Projects/MedLands/SCOTTISH%20NOBILITY%20LATER.htm
[2857] fmg.ac/Projects/MedLands/SCOTTISH%20NOBILITY%20UNTITLED.htm
[2858] fmg.ac/Projects/MedLands/ENGLISHNOBILITYMEDIEVAL3.htm
[2859] fmg.ac/Projects/MedLands/ENGLISHNOBILITYMEDIEVAL3D-K.htm
[2860] fmg.ac/Projects/MedLands/ENGLISHNOBILITYMEDIEVAL3L-O.htm
[2861] fmg.ac/Projects/MedLands/ENGLISHNOBILITYMEDIEVAL3P-S.htm
[2862] fmg.ac/Projects/MedLands/ENGLISHNOBILITYMEDIEVAL3T-Z.htm
[2863] fmg.ac/Projects/MedLands/WALES.htm

CHARLEMAGNE

Aachen Cathedral [2864]

Aachen Cathedral: UNESCO World Heritage Centre [2865]

Ahnentafel Study: William the Conqueror to Charlemagne [2866]

Charlemagne [2867] [2868]

Charlemagne Biography [2869]

Charlemagne Picture Gallery [2870]

Charter given by Charlemagne for St. Emmeram's Abbéy (showing Emperor's seal) [2871]

Dynastie des Carolingiens [2872]

Einhard – The Life of Charlemagne [2873]

[2864] www.sacred-destinations.com/germany/aachen-cathedral
[2865] whc.unesco.org/en/list/3
[2866] www.cynthiaswope.com/withinthevines/Normans/WmConqAhn/AT_TOC.HTM
[2867] https://en.wikipedia.org/wiki/Charlemagne
[2868] https://www.history.com/topics/charlemagne
[2869] sbaldw.home.mindspring.com/hproject/prov/charl000.htm
[2870] https://www.thoughtco.com/charlemagne-picture-gallery-4122735
[2871] lba.hist.uni-marburg.de/lba-cgi/kleioc/00101KlLBA/exec/apply2/width/%226109%22/height/%226109%22/url/%22http:%7B%7C%7D%7B%7C%7D137.248.186.134%7B%7C%7Dlba-cgi-local%7B%7C%7Dpic.sh%7B-%7Djpg%7B%7C%7DE306.jpg%22
[2872] fjaunais.free.fr/h0charlema.htm
[2873] https://sourcebooks.fordham.edu/basis/einhard.asp

EINHARDI VITA KAROLI MAGNI (in Latin) [2874]

Genealogy of Charlemagne [2875]

Les descendants de Charles 1er (Charlemagne) [2876]

Reconstructed Portrait of Charlemagne [2877]

The Annals of Fulda [2878]

The Sword of Charlemagne [2879]

EASTERN MEDITERRANEAN AND ASIA

Antioch [2880]

Armenia [2881]

Comtes d'Edesse [2882]

Comtes de Tripoli [2883]

Cyprus [2884]

[2874] www.thelatinlibrary.com/ein.html
[2875] ancestrees.com/pedigree/2379.htm
[2876] oratio.chez.com/Charles1er.html
[2877] https://www.reportret.info/gallery/charlemagne1.html
[2878] https://en.wikipedia.org/wiki/Annales_Fuldenses
[2879] myarmoury.com/feature_charlemagne.html
[2880] fmg.ac/Projects/MedLands/ANTIOCH.htm
[2881] fmg.ac/Projects/MedLands/ARMENIA.htm
[2882] racineshistoire.free.fr/LGN/PDF/Edesse.pdf
[2883] racineshistoire.free.fr/LGN/PDF/Tripoli.pdf
[2884] fmg.ac/Projects/MedLands/CYPRUS.htm

Edessa [2885]

Georgia [2886]

Jerusalem, Kings [2887]

Jerusalem, Nobility [2888]

Mongols [2889]

Nikaia [2890]

Princes d'Antioche (Poitiers) [2891]

Royaume d'Arménie [2892]

Seigneurs de Gibelet (Giblet, Jebail) Familles Embriaco, d'Hierges [2893]

The Periphery of Francia: Outremer [2894]

Trebizond [2895]

Tripoli [2896]

[2885] fmg.ac/Projects/MedLands/EDESSA.htm
[2886] fmg.ac/Projects/MedLands/GEORGIA.htm
[2887] fmg.ac/Projects/MedLands/JERUSALEM.htm
[2888] fmg.ac/Projects/MedLands/JERUSALEM%20NOBILITY.htm
[2889] fmg.ac/Projects/MedLands/MONGOLS.htm
[2890] fmg.ac/Projects/MedLands/NIKAIA.htm
[2891] racineshistoire.free.fr/LGN/PDF/Antioche.pdf
[2892] fjaunais.free.fr/h0armenie.htm
[2893] racineshistoire.free.fr/LGN/PDF/Gibelet-Embriaco.pdf
[2894] www.friesian.com/outremer.htm
[2895] fmg.ac/Projects/MedLands/TREBIZOND.htm
[2896] fmg.ac/Projects/MedLands/TRIPOLI.htm

West Asia and North Africa 1 [2897]

West Asia and North Africa 2 [2898]

EGYPT

A 4,000 year old Descent from Antiquity: From the 12th Egyptian Dynasty to the Capetians and Beyond [2899]

Dynastie d'Egypt [2900]

Egyptian Royal Genealogy [2901]

Journal of Royal and Noble Genealogy: Annotations to the Egyptian Descent in the Descents from Antiquities Charts [2902]

List of Ancient Egyptians [2903]

FAMILY NAMES

Famille d'Abos et d'Abos de Binanville [2904]

Famille Abra de Raconis [2905]

[2897] fmg.ac/Projects/MedLands/CALIPHATE.htm
[2898] fmg.ac/Projects/MedLands/TURKS.htm
[2899] erwan.gil.free.fr/modules/freepages/pharaons/ramses_II.pdf
[2900] fjaunais.free.fr/h0egypte.htm
[2901] www.tyndalehouse.com/Egypt/
[2902] humphrysfamilytree.com/Royal/Notes/bennett.annotations.pdf
[2903] https://en.wikipedia.org/wiki/List_of_ancient_Egyptians
[2904] racineshistoire.free.fr/LGN/PDF/Abos.pdf
[2905] racineshistoire.free.fr/LGN/PDF/Abra-de-Raconis.pdf

Famille d'Adhémar de Monteil alias d'Azémar [2906]

Famille Aguenin, Aguenin-Le-Duc [2907]

Famille d'Ailly [2908]

Famille d'Albert de Luynes [2909]

Familles Aleaume et Dolu (ou Dollu) [2910]

Famille Aleaume (alias Alleaume) [2911]

Famille d'Aligre (Haligre) [2912]

Famille Allegrain (alias Allegrin) [2913]

Famille d'Allenas (alias d'Allenois, d'Alnois, Aunoy) [2914]

Famille d'Allonville (branches Oysonville, Louville, Réclainville et Plessis-Saint-Bênoit) [2915]

Famille d'Aloigny [2916]

[2906] racineshistoire.free.fr/LGN/PDF/Adhemar-de-Monteil.pdf
[2907] racineshistoire.free.fr/LGN/PDF/Aguenin.pdf
[2908] racineshistoire.free.fr/LGN/PDF/Ailly.pdf
[2909] racineshistoire.free.fr/LGN/PDF/Albert_de_Luynes.pdf
[2910] racineshistoire.free.fr/LGN/PDF/Aleaume-Dolu.pdf
[2911] racineshistoire.free.fr/LGN/PDF/Aleaume.pdf
[2912] racineshistoire.free.fr/LGN/PDF/Aligre.pdf
[2913] racineshistoire.free.fr/LGN/PDF/Allegrain.pdf
[2914] racineshistoire.free.fr/LGN/PDF/Allenas.pdf
[2915] racineshistoire.free.fr/LGN/PDF/Allonville.pdf
[2916] racineshistoire.free.fr/LGN/PDF/Aloigny.pdf

Famille d'Amboise [2917]

Famille d'Angennes [2918]

Famille Anjorrant [2919]

Famille Arouet (alias Arrouet, Voltaire) [2920]

Famille Aubéry de Vatan (ou Vastan) [2921]

Famille Aubigne [2922]

Famille d'Aubigny (Albiny, d'Albini, de Albini, de Aubigne, d'Aubeney, Daubeney) [2923]

Familles d'Aulnay et Le Gal(l)ois d'Aulnay (alias Aunay, Aunoy) [2924]

Famille Babou de La Bourdaisière [2925]

Famille Baillet [2926]

Famille de Bailliencourt dit Courcol [2927]

[2917] https://fr.wikipedia.org/wiki/Famille_d'Amboise
[2918] racineshistoire.free.fr/LGN/PDF/Angennes.pdf
[2919] racineshistoire.free.fr/LGN/PDF/Anjorrant.pdf
[2920] racineshistoire.free.fr/LGN/PDF/Arouet-Voltaire.pdf
[2921] racineshistoire.free.fr/LGN/PDF/Aubery-de-Vatan.pdf
[2922] racineshistoire.free.fr/LGN/PDF/Aubigne.pdf
[2923] racineshistoire.free.fr/LGN/PDF/d_Aubigny.pdf
[2924] racineshistoire.free.fr/LGN/PDF/Aulnay.pdf
[2925] racineshistoire.free.fr/LGN/PDF/Babou_de_La_Bourdaisiere.pdf
[2926] racineshistoire.free.fr/LGN/PDF/Baillet.pdf
[2927] racineshistoire.free.fr/LGN/PDF/Bailliencourt.pdf

Famille de Baliol (Bailleul-en-Vimeu) [2928]

Famille de Baran [2929]

Famille des Barres [2930]

Famille de Barthomier (ou Berthomier) [2931]

Famille et Seigneurs de Baudricourt [2932]

Famille de Baussan [2933]

Famille de Bazanier (Bazannier, Basannier) [2934]

Famille de Beauharnais [2935]

Famille de Beaumont-en-Gâtinais [2936]

Famille de Beaune de Semblançay [2937]

Famille de Bellême, Seigneurs d'Alençon, et Château Gontier, et Château Renaud [2938]

[2928] racineshistoire.free.fr/LGN/PDF/Baliol.pdf
[2929] racineshistoire.free.fr/LGN/PDF/Baran.pdf
[2930] racineshistoire.free.fr/LGN/PDF/des_Barres.pdf
[2931] racineshistoire.free.fr/LGN/PDF/Barthomier.pdf
[2932] racineshistoire.free.fr/LGN/PDF/Baudricourt.pdf
[2933] racineshistoire.free.fr/LGN/PDF/Baussan.pdf
[2934] racineshistoire.free.fr/LGN/PDF/Bazanier.pdf
[2935] racineshistoire.free.fr/LGN/PDF/Beauharnais.pdf
[2936] racineshistoire.free.fr/LGN/PDF/Beaumont-en-Gâtinais.pdf
[2937] racineshistoire.free.fr/LGN/PDF/Beaune_Semblancay.pdf
[2938] racineshistoire.free.fr/LGN/PDF/Belleme.pdf

Famille de Bellièvre [2939]

Famille Bertran(d) de Bricquebec [2940]

Famille et Seigneurs de Béthune [2941]

Famille de Bignon [2942]

Famille Bleriot [2943]

Famille de Bohun [2944]

Famille de Boisse [2945]

Famille et Seigneurs de Boubers 1 [2946]

Famille et Seigneurs de Boubers 2 [2947]

Famille Boucher (d'Orsay) [2948]

Famille et Seigneurs de Boutigny (-sur-Opton) et Grandchamp [2949]

[2939] racineshistoire.free.fr/LGN/PDF/Bellievre.pdf
[2940] racineshistoire.free.fr/LGN/PDF/Bertran.pdf
[2941] racineshistoire.free.fr/LGN/PDF/Bethune.pdf
[2942] racineshistoire.free.fr/LGN/PDF/Bignon.pdf
[2943] racineshistoire.free.fr/LGN/PDF/Bleriot.pdf
[2944] racineshistoire.free.fr/LGN/PDF/Bohun.pdf
[2945] racineshistoire.free.fr/LGN/PDF/Boisse.pdf
[2946] racineshistoire.free.fr/LGN/PDF/Boubers1.pdf
[2947] racineshistoire.free.fr/LGN/PDF/Boubers2.pdf
[2948] racineshistoire.free.fr/LGN/PDF/Boucher_d-Orsay.pdf
[2949] racineshistoire.free.fr/LGN/PDF/Boutigny.pdf

Famille de Boves (de Boves ou des Bauves, voir de Voves) [2950]

Famille de Braose (Briouze, Breuse, Brewes) [2951]

Famille de Braque (alias Bracque) [2952]

Famille de Brézé [2953]

Famille de Brichanteau [2954]

Famille Briçonnet [2955]

Famille de Brinon [2956]

Famille Brossin de Méré [2957]

Famille de Brouilly [2958]

Famille Broun of Colstoun (Brown) [2959]

Famille de Brûlart et Sillery, Genlis [2960]

Famille Budé [2961]

_____

[2950] racineshistoire.free.fr/LGN/PDF/Boves.pdf
[2951] racineshistoire.free.fr/LGN/PDF/Braose.pdf
[2952] racineshistoire.free.fr/LGN/PDF/Braque.pdf
[2953] racineshistoire.free.fr/LGN/PDF/Breze.pdf
[2954] racineshistoire.free.fr/LGN/PDF/Brichanteau.pdf
[2955] racineshistoire.free.fr/LGN/PDF/Briconnet.pdf
[2956] racineshistoire.free.fr/LGN/PDF/Brinon.pdf
[2957] racineshistoire.free.fr/LGN/PDF/Brossin-de-Mere.pdf
[2958] racineshistoire.free.fr/LGN/PDF/Brouilly.pdf
[2959] racineshistoire.free.fr/LGN/PDF/Broun-Of-Colstoun.pdf
[2960] racineshistoire.free.fr/LGN/PDF/Brulart-de-Sillery.pdf
[2961] racineshistoire.free.fr/LGN/PDF/Bude.pdf

Famille de Bullion [2962]

Famille Bureau [2963]

Famille Carnot [2964]

Famille(s) de Caruel, de Boran, de Méré, de Saint-Martin [2965]

Famille Cassinel [2966]

Famille de Castile [2967]

Famille Cauchon [2968]

Seigneurs et Famille de Chabannes (ancient Cabanis, Chabanes) [2969]

Famille et Seigneurs de Chambly [2970]

Famille de Chanteprime [2971]

Famille Chartier [2972]

[2962] racineshistoire.free.fr/LGN/PDF/Bullion.pdf
[2963] racineshistoire.free.fr/LGN/PDF/Bureau.pdf
[2964] racineshistoire.free.fr/LGN/PDF/Carnot.pdf
[2965] racineshistoire.free.fr/LGN/PDF/Caruel.pdf
[2966] racineshistoire.free.fr/LGN/PDF/Cassinel.pdf
[2967] racineshistoire.free.fr/LGN/PDF/Castile.pdf
[2968] racineshistoire.free.fr/LGN/PDF/Cauchon.pdf
[2969] racineshistoire.free.fr/LGN/PDF/Chabannes.pdf
[2970] racineshistoire.free.fr/LGN/PDF/Chambly.pdf
[2971] racineshistoire.free.fr/LGN/PDF/Chanteprime.pdf
[2972] racineshistoire.free.fr/LGN/PDF/Chartier.pdf

Vidames de Chartres [2973]

Famille du Chastel [2974]

Famille de Châtillon (-sur-Marne) [2975]

Famille(s) Chevalier [2976]

Famille Clémont [2977]

Famille de Cochefilet [2978]

Famille Coeur [2979]

Famille des Cognets [2980]

Famille Colbert [2981]

Famille et Seigneurs de Coligny et Châtillon-Coligny [2982]

Familles de Combault et Martel [2983]

Famille de Conteville (Mortain, Bayeux) [2984]

[2973] racineshistoire.free.fr/LGN/PDF/Chartres-Vidames.pdf
[2974] racineshistoire.free.fr/LGN/PDF/du_Chastel.pdf
[2975] racineshistoire.free.fr/LGN/PDF/Chatillon.pdf
[2976] racineshistoire.free.fr/LGN/PDF/Chevalier.pdf
[2977] racineshistoire.free.fr/LGN/PDF/Clement.pdf
[2978] racineshistoire.free.fr/LGN/PDF/Cochefilet.pdf
[2979] racineshistoire.free.fr/LGN/PDF/Coeur.pdf
[2980] racineshistoire.free.fr/LGN/PDF/des_Cognets.pdf
[2981] racineshistoire.free.fr/LGN/PDF/Colbert.pdf
[2982] racineshistoire.free.fr/LGN/PDF/Chatillon-Coligny.pdf
[2983] racineshistoire.free.fr/LGN/PDF/Combault&Martel.pdf
[2984] racineshistoire.free.fr/LGN/PDF/Conteville.pdf

Famille de Contremoret [2985]

Famille de Cossé-Brissac [2986]

Famille Courtin [2987]

Famille de Cou(s)tes [2988]

Famille de Creil [2989]

Famille de Crépon [2990]

Famille de Cuisy [2991]

Famille Culdoë (aussi Cudoë, Cul-d'Oue) [2992]

Famille de Jeanne d'Arc (alias Darc et du Lis) [2993]

Famille de Daillon et Seigneurs du Lude [2994]

Famille de Dampierre [2995]

Famille de Dauvet [2996]

[2985] racineshistoire.free.fr/LGN/PDF/Contremoret.pdf
[2986] racineshistoire.free.fr/LGN/PDF/Cosse-Brissac.pdf
[2987] racineshistoire.free.fr/LGN/PDF/Courtin.pdf
[2988] racineshistoire.free.fr/LGN/PDF/de_Coustes.pdf
[2989] racineshistoire.free.fr/LGN/PDF/Creil.pdf
[2990] racineshistoire.free.fr/LGN/PDF/Crepon.pdf
[2991] racineshistoire.free.fr/LGN/PDF/Cuisy.pdf
[2992] racineshistoire.free.fr/LGN/PDF/Culdoe.pdf
[2993] racineshistoire.free.fr/LGN/PDF/D-Arc_du-Lis.pdf
[2994] racineshistoire.free.fr/LGN/PDF/Daillon.pdf
[2995] racineshistoire.free.fr/LGN/PDF/Dampierre.pdf
[2996] racineshistoire.free.fr/LGN/PDF/Dauvet.pdf

Familles de La Grange et de La Grange-Trianon [2997]

Famille Degroote et Familles Tully, Delbauffe, Fournier et Wiklund [2998]

Famille Desmazis (alias Desmazzis, des Maz(z)is) [2999]

Famille Diane de Poitiers, Poitiers-Valentinois, Poitiers-Saint-Vallier [3000]

Famille de Dion et Wandonne [3001]

Famille Dolu (ou Dollu) [3002]

Famille de Dormans [3003]

Famille du Drac [3004]

Famille Dreux d'Aubray et Gobelin de Brinvilliers, d'Offémont [3005]

Famille d'Elbée [3006]

Famille d' Escorchevel (alias Ecorchevel) [3007]

[2997] racineshistoire.free.fr/LGN/PDF/De-La-Grange.pdf
[2998] racineshistoire.free.fr/LGN/PDF/Degroote.pdf
[2999] racineshistoire.free.fr/LGN/PDF/Desmazis.pdf
[3000] racineshistoire.free.fr/LGN/PDF/Diane-de-Poitiers.pdf
[3001] racineshistoire.free.fr/LGN/PDF/de_Dion-Wandonne.pdf
[3002] racineshistoire.free.fr/LGN/PDF/Dolu.pdf
[3003] racineshistoire.free.fr/LGN/PDF/Dormans.pdf
[3004] racineshistoire.free.fr/LGN/PDF/du_Drac.pdf
[3005] racineshistoire.free.fr/LGN/PDF/Dreux_d_Aubray_&_Gobelin_de_Brinvilliers.pdf
[3006] racineshistoire.free.fr/LGN/PDF/Elbee.pdf
[3007] racineshistoire.free.fr/LGN/PDF/Escorchevel.pdf

Famille d'Escrones [3008]

Familles des Essarts [3009]

Famille d'Estouteville [3010]

Famille d'Estrées [3011]

Familles de Fenoÿl-Thurey, Gayardon de Grézolles ey Gayardon de Fenoÿl [3012]

Famille de Ferrers (Ferrières) [3013]

Famille de Flésselles (alias Flécelles, Flexelles) [3014]

Famille de Flot(t)e, Flote de Revel (alias Flotte) [3015]

Seigneurs et Famille des Fossés (alias des Fossez) [3016]

Famille de Forbin [3017]

Famille de Foucault [3018]

[3008] racineshistoire.free.fr/LGN/PDF/Escrones.pdf
[3009] racineshistoire.free.fr/LGN/PDF/des_Essarts.pdf
[3010] racineshistoire.free.fr/LGN/PDF/Estouteville.pdf
[3011] racineshistoire.free.fr/LGN/PDF/Estrees.pdf
[3012] racineshistoire.free.fr/LGN/PDF/Fenoyl-Gayardon.pdf
[3013] racineshistoire.free.fr/LGN/PDF/Ferrers.pdf
[3014] racineshistoire.free.fr/LGN/PDF/Flesselles.pdf
[3015] racineshistoire.free.fr/LGN/PDF/Flote.pdf
[3016] racineshistoire.free.fr/LGN/PDF/des_Fosses.pdf
[3017] racineshistoire.free.fr/LGN/PDF/Forbin.pdf
[3018] racineshistoire.free.fr/LGN/PDF/Foucault.pdf

Famille Fouquet (alias Foucquet) Fouquet de Belle-Isle [3019]

Famille Fournier [3020]

Famille de Frédet [3021]

Famille de La Taille et Fief de Fresnay (Garancières) [3022]

Les Fulcherides (Haut-Vendômois) [3023]

Famille Gaillard de Longjumeau [3024]

Famille de Gamaches [3025]

Famille de Garencières [3026]

Famille de Garlande [3027]

Famille Garrault (Garraut, Garro) [3028]

Famille Gentien ou Gencien (d'Erigné) [3029]

Famille de Ghistelles [3030]

[3019] racineshistoire.free.fr/LGN/PDF/Fouquet.pdf
[3020] racineshistoire.free.fr/LGN/PDF/Fournier.pdf
[3021] racineshistoire.free.fr/LGN/PDF/Fredet.pdf
[3022] racineshistoire.free.fr/LGN/PDF/Fresnay_de-La-Taille.pdf
[3023] racineshistoire.free.fr/LGN/PDF/Fulcherides.pdf
[3024] racineshistoire.free.fr/LGN/PDF/Gaillard-de-Longjumeau.pdf
[3025] racineshistoire.free.fr/LGN/PDF/Gamaches.pdf
[3026] racineshistoire.free.fr/LGN/PDF/Garencieres.pdf
[3027] racineshistoire.free.fr/LGN/PDF/Garlande.pdf
[3028] racineshistoire.free.fr/LGN/PDF/Garrault.pdf
[3029] racineshistoire.free.fr/LGN/PDF/Gentien.pdf
[3030] racineshistoire.free.fr/LGN/PDF/Ghistelles.pdf

Famille Giffard (alias Giffart) [3031]

Famille Gilbert et Voisins [3032]

Famille Giroie, Seigneurs d'Echauffour et de Montreuil [3033]

Famille de Gondi [3034]

Famille et Seigneurs de Gontaut, Gontaut-Biron et Badefols [3035]

Famille de Goth (Gotz, Gout) [3036]

Famille Gouffier [3037]

Famille Grenier (alias Garnier, Granier, d'Agrain) [3038]

Famille de Grentemesnil (alias Grandmesnil, Grantmesnil, Grantemesnil) [3039]

Famille du Guesclin (alias Waglip, Gayclip, Guarclip, Guerplic, Glerquin, Claquin, Glaquin, Glayequin) [3040]

Famille de Guincheux [3041]

[3031] racineshistoire.free.fr/LGN/PDF/Giffard.pdf
[3032] racineshistoire.free.fr/LGN/PDF/Gilbert-de-Voisins.pdf
[3033] racineshistoire.free.fr/LGN/PDF/Giroie-Echauffour.pdf
[3034] racineshistoire.free.fr/LGN/PDF/Gondi.pdf
[3035] racineshistoire.free.fr/LGN/PDF/Gontaut-Biron.pdf
[3036] racineshistoire.free.fr/LGN/PDF/Goth.pdf
[3037] racineshistoire.free.fr/LGN/PDF/Gouffier.pdf
[3038] racineshistoire.free.fr/LGN/PDF/Grenier.pdf
[3039] racineshistoire.free.fr/LGN/PDF/Grantmesnil.pdf
[3040] racineshistoire.free.fr/LGN/PDF/du_Guesclin.pdf
[3041] racineshistoire.free.fr/LGN/PDF/Guincheux.pdf

Famille Habert de Montmort [3042]

Famille de Hacqueville [3043]

Famille de Hallot [3044]

Famille de Halewi(j)n (Halewyn, Halluin) [3045]

Famille d'Harcourt [3046]

Famille et Seigneurs d'Hargeville [3047]

Famille de Harlay [3048]

Famille de Hauteville [3049]

Famille de Hélin (alias Hellin) [3050]

Famille Hennequin [3051]

Famille Hérault, de Fénilly, de Séchelles [3052]

[3042] racineshistoire.free.fr/LGN/PDF/Habert-de-Montmort.pdf
[3043] racineshistoire.free.fr/LGN/PDF/Hacqueville.pdf
[3044] racineshistoire.free.fr/LGN/PDF/Hallot.pdf
[3045] racineshistoire.free.fr/LGN/PDF/Halluin.pdf
[3046] racineshistoire.free.fr/LGN/PDF/Harcourt.pdf
[3047] racineshistoire.free.fr/LGN/PDF/Hargeville.pdf
[3048] racineshistoire.free.fr/LGN/PDF/Harlay.pdf
[3049] racineshistoire.free.fr/LGN/PDF/Hauteville.pdf
[3050] racineshistoire.free.fr/LGN/PDF/Helin.pdf
[3051] racineshistoire.free.fr/LGN/PDF/Hennequin.pdf
[3052] racineshistoire.free.fr/LGN/PDF/Herault_de_Sechelles.pdf

Famille Hermant [3053]

Famille Hotman [3054]

Famille Hurault (Saint-Denis, Cheverny, Le Marais, Boistaillé, Bellebat, Auneux, Vignay) [3055]

Famille de Ibelin [3056]

Famille et Seigneurs de Jaucourt et de Dinteville [3057]

Famille Jayer et alliances (Brulart, Buyer, Chartier, Le Ferron, Montholon) [3058]

Famille de Johanne(s) (alias Joanne(s), Jouanne(s)) [3059]

Famille Jouvenal (ou Juvenel, Juvenal) (des Ursins) [3060]

Famille de L'Arbaleste (Arbalete, Larbaleste) [3061]

Famille de La Balue [3062]

Famille de Labriffe (alias de La Briffe) Gambais et Neuville [3063]

[3053] racineshistoire.free.fr/LGN/PDF/Hermant.pdf
[3054] racineshistoire.free.fr/LGN/PDF/Hotman.pdf
[3055] racineshistoire.free.fr/LGN/PDF/Hurault.pdf
[3056] racineshistoire.free.fr/LGN/PDF/Ibelin.pdf
[3057] racineshistoire.free.fr/LGN/PDF/Jaucourt-Dinteville.pdf
[3058] racineshistoire.free.fr/LGN/PDF/Jayer.pdf
[3059] racineshistoire.free.fr/LGN/PDF/Johannes.pdf
[3060] racineshistoire.free.fr/LGN/PDF/Jouvenel-des-Ursins.pdf
[3061] racineshistoire.free.fr/LGN/PDF/L-Arbaleste.pdf
[3062] racineshistoire.free.fr/LGN/PDF/La-Balue.pdf
[3063] racineshistoire.free.fr/LGN/PDF/Labriffe.pdf

Famille de La Chaussée [3064]

Famille L'Estendart (Lestendart) [3065]

Famille Lallemant de Macqueline [3066]

Famille de La Loëre [3067]

Famille De La Marck [3068]

Familles de Lamoignon [3069]

Famille et Seigneurs de Landas et Mortagne et Warlaing, Cysoing, Esnes, Bailliencourt, Warenghien et de Le Cambe [3070]

Famille des Landes [3071]

Famille de Landouillette de Logivière [3072]

Famille et Seigneurs de Lannoy [3073]

Famille L'Orfèvre (d'Orfeuil) [3074]

[3064] racineshistoire.free.fr/LGN/PDF/La-Chaussee.pdf
[3065] racineshistoire.free.fr/LGN/PDF/L-Estendart.pdf
[3066] racineshistoire.free.fr/LGN/PDF/Lallemant-de-Macqueline.pdf
[3067] racineshistoire.free.fr/LGN/PDF/La-Loere.pdf
[3068] racineshistoire.free.fr/LGN/PDF/La-Marck.pdf
[3069] racineshistoire.free.fr/LGN/PDF/Lamoignon.pdf
[3070] racineshistoire.free.fr/LGN/PDF/Landas.pdf
[3071] racineshistoire.free.fr/LGN/PDF/des_Landes.pdf
[3072] racineshistoire.free.fr/LGN/PDF/Landouillette-de-Logiviere.pdf
[3073] racineshistoire.free.fr/LGN/PDF/Lannoy.pdf
[3074] racineshistoire.free.fr/LGN/PDF/L-Orfevre-d-Orfeuil.pdf

Famille de La Panouse [3075]

Famille de La Rochefoucauld [3076]

Famille de La Trémoïlle [3077]

Famille de La Rivière [3078]

Guillaume de La Vieuville et autres familles de La Vieuville, La Viefville [3079]

Famille Le Baveux [3080]

Famille Le Boistel [3081]

Famille Le Clerc de Fleurigny [3082]

Famille Le Clerc de Lesseville [3083]

Famille Le Coigneux [3084]

Famille Le Coq ou Le Cocq [3085]

[3075] racineshistoire.free.fr/LGN/PDF/La-Panouse.pdf
[3076] racineshistoire.free.fr/LGN/PDF/La-Rochefoucauld.pdf
[3077] racineshistoire.free.fr/LGN/PDF/La-Tremoille.pdf
[3078] racineshistoire.free.fr/LGN/PDF/La_Riviere.pdf
[3079] racineshistoire.free.fr/LGN/PDF/La-Vieuville.pdf
[3080] racineshistoire.free.fr/LGN/PDF/Le-Baveux.pdf
[3081] racineshistoire.free.fr/LGN/PDF/Le-Boistel.pdf
[3082] racineshistoire.free.fr/LGN/PDF/Le_Clerc_de_Fleurigny.pdf
[3083] racineshistoire.free.fr/LGN/PDF/Le_Clerc_de_Lesseville.pdf
[3084] racineshistoire.free.fr/LGN/PDF/Le-Coigneux.pdf
[3085] racineshistoire.free.fr/LGN/PDF/Le-Coq.pdf

Famille Le Febvre (Lefebvre, Lefèvre) de Plinval [3086]

Famille Le Féron [3087]

Famille Lefèvre d' Ormesson [3088]

Famille Le Picart (alias Picard) [3089]

Famille Le Riche d'aprés Depoin (Cartulaire Saint-Martin de Pontoise) [3090]

Famille Lescalopier puis de L'Escalopier [3091]

Famille Le Tonnelier de Breteuil [3092]

Famille Le Tremblay: Mignon, Le Clerc du Tremblay [3093]

Famille Le Veneur (de Tillières) [3094]

Famille de Lévis [3095]

Famille(s) de Lhospital (alias L'Hôpital) [3096]

[3086] racineshistoire.free.fr/LGN/PDF/Le-Febvre-de-Plinval.pdf
[3087] racineshistoire.free.fr/LGN/PDF/Le-Feron.pdf
[3088] racineshistoire.free.fr/LGN/PDF/Ormesson.pdf
[3089] racineshistoire.free.fr/LGN/PDF/Le-Picart.pdf
[3090] racineshistoire.free.fr/LGN/PDF/Le_Riche_Depoin.pdf
[3091] racineshistoire.free.fr/LGN/PDF/Lescalopier.pdf
[3092] racineshistoire.free.fr/LGN/PDF/Le-Tonnelier-de-Breteuil.pdf
[3093] racineshistoire.free.fr/LGN/PDF/Le-Tremblay-&-Le_Clerc.pdf
[3094] racineshistoire.free.fr/LGN/PDF/Le-Veneur.pdf
[3095] racineshistoire.free.fr/LGN/PDF/Levis.pdf
[3096] racineshistoire.free.fr/LGN/PDF/Lhospital.pdf

Famille de Longueil [3097]

Famille de Longuejoüe [3098]

Famille de Loré [3099]

Famille Luillier (ou Lhuillier) [3100]

Famille de Lusignan [3101]

Famille de Luxembourg-Saint-Pol [3102]

Famille de Machault [3103]

Famille(s) Maillard (ou Maillart) [3104]

Familles Malet de Graville (alias Mallet) et Malet de Coupigny (Artois) [3105]

Famille Mantes et Meulan, Origines et Alliances [3106]

Famille Marcel [3107]

[3097] racineshistoire.free.fr/LGN/PDF/Longueil.pdf
[3098] racineshistoire.free.fr/LGN/PDF/Longuejoue.pdf
[3099] racineshistoire.free.fr/LGN/PDF/Lore.pdf
[3100] racineshistoire.free.fr/LGN/PDF/Luillier.pdf
[3101] racineshistoire.free.fr/LGN/PDF/Lusignan.pdf
[3102] racineshistoire.free.fr/LGN/PDF/Luxembourg-Saint-Pol.pdf
[3103] racineshistoire.free.fr/LGN/PDF/Machault.pdf
[3104] racineshistoire.free.fr/LGN/PDF/Maillard.pdf
[3105] racineshistoire.free.fr/LGN/PDF/Malet-de-Graville.pdf
[3106] racineshistoire.free.fr/LGN/PDF/Mantes-Meulan.pdf
[3107] racineshistoire.free.fr/LGN/PDF/Marcel.pdf

Famille(s) de Marcilly [3108]

Famille(s) de Marescot [3109]

Famille de Marigny [3110]

Familles de Marle [3111]

Les Maule Anglo-Saxons [3112]

Famille de Maupeou [3113]

Famille et Seigneurs de Mauquenchy de Blainville [3114]

Famille Mauvoisin [3115]

Famille de Mazancourt et Merlin-Mazancourt [3116]

Familles Mazarin et Mancini [3117]

Famille de Meaux [3118]

[3108] racineshistoire.free.fr/LGN/PDF/Marcilly.pdf
[3109] racineshistoire.free.fr/LGN/PDF/Marescot.pdf
[3110] racineshistoire.free.fr/LGN/PDF/Marigny.pdf
[3111] racineshistoire.free.fr/LGN/PDF/Marle.pdf
[3112] racineshistoire.free.fr/LGN/PDF/Maule-GB&USA.pdf
[3113] racineshistoire.free.fr/LGN/PDF/Maupeou.pdf
[3114] racineshistoire.free.fr/LGN/PDF/Mauquenchy-de-Blainville.pdf
[3115] racineshistoire.free.fr/LGN/PDF/Mauvoisin.pdf
[3116] racineshistoire.free.fr/LGN/PDF/Mazancourt.pdf
[3117] racineshistoire.free.fr/LGN/PDF/Mazarin-&-Mancini.pdf
[3118] racineshistoire.free.fr/LGN/PDF/Meaux.pdf

Famille et Vicomtes de Melun [3119]

Famille de Mérault [3120]

Famille Meschin (Meschines) de Chester [3121]

Famille de Mesmes [3122]

Famille et Seigneurs du Mesnil-Simon [3123]

Famille Mignon [3124]

Famille Milon [3125]

Famille Miron [3126]

Famille Molé [3127]

Famille de Monchy [3128]

Famille de(s) Monstiers-Mérinville (alias Montier(s)) [3129]

[3119] racineshistoire.free.fr/LGN/PDF/Melun.pdf
[3120] racineshistoire.free.fr/LGN/PDF/Merault.pdf
[3121] racineshistoire.free.fr/LGN/PDF/Merault.pdf
[3122] racineshistoire.free.fr/LGN/PDF/de-Mesmes.pdf
[3123] racineshistoire.free.fr/LGN/PDF/Mesnil-Simon.pdf
[3124] racineshistoire.free.fr/LGN/PDF/Mignon.pdf
[3125] racineshistoire.free.fr/LGN/PDF/Milon.pdf
[3126] racineshistoire.free.fr/LGN/PDF/Miron.pdf
[3127] racineshistoire.free.fr/LGN/PDF/Mole.pdf
[3128] racineshistoire.free.fr/LGN/PDF/Monchy.pdf
[3129] racineshistoire.free.fr/LGN/PDF/Monstiers-Merinville.pdf

Famille de Montagu (alias Montaigu) [3130]

Famille de Montenay [3131]

Famille de Montgomery [3132]

Famille de Montholon [3133]

Famille de Montmorency [3134]

Famille de Morainvillier [3135]

Famille Morant (alias Morand) [3136]

Famille Moreau (Grosbois, Auteuil et Thoiry) [3137]

Famille Morhier (alias Le Morhier) [3138]

Famille de Mornay [3139]

Familles de Mortemer et Mortimer [3140]

[3130] racineshistoire.free.fr/LGN/PDF/Montagu.pdf
[3131] racineshistoire.free.fr/LGN/PDF/Montenay.pdf
[3132] racineshistoire.free.fr/LGN/PDF/Montgomery.pdf
[3133] racineshistoire.free.fr/LGN/PDF/Montholon.pdf
[3134] racineshistoire.free.fr/LGN/PDF/Montmorency.pdf
[3135] racineshistoire.free.fr/LGN/PDF/Morainvillier.pdf
[3136] racineshistoire.free.fr/LGN/PDF/Morant.pdf
[3137] racineshistoire.free.fr/LGN/PDF/Moreau.pdf
[3138] racineshistoire.free.fr/LGN/PDF/Morhier.pdf
[3139] racineshistoire.free.fr/LGN/PDF/Mornay.pdf
[3140] racineshistoire.free.fr/LGN/PDF/Mortemer.pdf

Familles de Morvilliers [3141]

Famille de Mussegros (Muscegros, Mucelgros, Musgrave) [3142]

Famille de Neufville-Villeroy [3143]

Famille de Nicolaÿ (ou Nicolaï) [3144]

Famille de Nogaret de La Valette [3145]

Famille de Noyers [3146]

Famille d'O [3147]

Famille d'Orgemont [3148]

Famille de Paillard (alias Paillart) [3149]

Famille Paynel [3150]

Famille Percheron [3151]

[3141] racineshistoire.free.fr/LGN/PDF/Morvilliers.pdf
[3142] racineshistoire.free.fr/LGN/PDF/Mussegros.pdf
[3143] racineshistoire.free.fr/LGN/PDF/Neufville-de-Villeroy.pdf
[3144] racineshistoire.free.fr/LGN/PDF/Nicolay.pdf
[3145] racineshistoire.free.fr/LGN/PDF/Nogaret-de-La-Valette.pdf
[3146] racineshistoire.free.fr/LGN/PDF/Noyers.pdf
[3147] racineshistoire.free.fr/LGN/PDF/d_O.pdf
[3148] racineshistoire.free.fr/LGN/PDF/Orgemont.pdf
[3149] racineshistoire.free.fr/LGN/PDF/Paillard.pdf
[3150] racineshistoire.free.fr/LGN/PDF/Paynel.pdf
[3151] racineshistoire.free.fr/LGN/PDF/Percheron.pdf

Famille de Phélypeaux [3152]

Famille(s) de Philippe(s) de Lenrouillé, des Vignettes et Phélippes de La Marnierre [3153]

Famille de Piédefer [3154]

Plantagenêts (d'Angleterre) et Lancaster et Tudor [3155]

Famille du Plessis-Richelieu [3156]

Famille Poignant [3157]

Famille de Poilloüe [3158]

Famille de Pomereu (alias Pommereuil, Pommereu) [3159]

Famille Poncher [3160]

Famille Pot [3161]

Famille Potier [3162]

[3152] racineshistoire.free.fr/LGN/PDF/Phelypeaux.pdf
[3153] racineshistoire.free.fr/LGN/PDF/Philippes.pdf
[3154] racineshistoire.free.fr/LGN/PDF/Piedefer.pdf
[3155] racineshistoire.free.fr/LGN/PDF/Plantagenets.pdf
[3156] racineshistoire.free.fr/LGN/PDF/du_Plessis-Richelieu.pdf
[3157] racineshistoire.free.fr/LGN/PDF/Poignant.pdf
[3158] racineshistoire.free.fr/LGN/PDF/Poilloue.pdf
[3159] racineshistoire.free.fr/LGN/PDF/Pomereu.pdf
[3160] racineshistoire.free.fr/LGN/PDF/Poncher.pdf
[3161] racineshistoire.free.fr/LGN/PDF/Pot.pdf
[3162] racineshistoire.free.fr/LGN/PDF/Potier.pdf

Famille de Prunelé (alias Prunelay) [3163]

Famille Quiéret (alias Kiéret) [3164]

Famille de Quincy (Cuinchy, Quinchy, Quincey) [3165]

Famille Raguier [3166]

Famille et Seigneurs de Rambures [3167]

Famille de Rancher [3168]

Famille de Refuge (alias Reffuge) [3169]

Famille de Renouard de Villayers [3170]

Famille de Rigoley d'Ogny [3171]

Famille Robertet [3172]

Famille Robespierre (alias de Robespierre, Derobespierre) [3173]

Famille de Rochechouart Mortemart et Vicomtes de Rochechouart [3174]

[3163] racineshistoire.free.fr/LGN/PDF/Prunele.pdf
[3164] racineshistoire.free.fr/LGN/PDF/Quieret.pdf
[3165] racineshistoire.free.fr/LGN/PDF/Quincy.pdf
[3166] racineshistoire.free.fr/LGN/PDF/Raguier.pdf
[3167] racineshistoire.free.fr/LGN/PDF/Rambures.pdf
[3168] racineshistoire.free.fr/LGN/PDF/Rancher.pdf
[3169] racineshistoire.free.fr/LGN/PDF/de-Refuge.pdf
[3170] racineshistoire.free.fr/LGN/PDF/Renouard-de-Villayers.pdf
[3171] racineshistoire.free.fr/LGN/PDF/Rigoley_d-Ogny.pdf
[3172] racineshistoire.free.fr/LGN/PDF/Robertet.pdf
[3173] racineshistoire.free.fr/LGN/PDF/Robespierre.pdf
[3174] racineshistoire.free.fr/LGN/PDF/Rochechouart-Mortemart.pdf

Famille Rollin (alias Rolin) [3175]

Famille de Rougé [3176]

Familles de Rouillé (branches du Coudray, de Meslay et d'Orfeuil) [3177]

Famille de Rouvroy de Saint-Simon [3178]

Famille de Rubentel [3179]

Famille Ruzé [3180]

Famille Sabrevois [3181]

Famille de Sacquenville [3182]

Famille(s) de Saint-Léger et Seigneurie de Saint-Léger [3183]

Famille de Saint-Martin [3184]

Familles Sanguin, de Livry et de Meudon [3185]

Famille de Sans-Avoir [3186]

[3175] racineshistoire.free.fr/LGN/PDF/Rollin.pdf
[3176] racineshistoire.free.fr/LGN/PDF/Rouge.pdf
[3177] racineshistoire.free.fr/LGN/PDF/Rouille.pdf
[3178] racineshistoire.free.fr/LGN/PDF/Rouvroy-de-Saint-Simon.pdf
[3179] racineshistoire.free.fr/LGN/PDF/Rubentel.pdf
[3180] racineshistoire.free.fr/LGN/PDF/Ruze.pdf
[3181] racineshistoire.free.fr/LGN/PDF/Sabrevois.pdf
[3182] racineshistoire.free.fr/LGN/PDF/Sacquenville.pdf
[3183] racineshistoire.free.fr/LGN/PDF/Saint-Leger.pdf
[3184] racineshistoire.free.fr/LGN/PDF/Saint-Martin.pdf
[3185] racineshistoire.free.fr/LGN/PDF/Sanguin.pdf
[3186] racineshistoire.free.fr/LGN/PDF/Sans-Avoir.pdf

Famille Séguier [3187]

Famille(s) de Sève et de Sève de Rochechouart [3188]

Famille de Silly [3189]

Famille Spifame [3190]

Famille Talon [3191]

Famille Tesson (Taisson) [3192]

Famille Teste [3193]

Famille Testu de Balincourt [3194]

Famille de Thou [3195]

Famille Thourotte (alias Thorotte) [3196]

Famille de Thumery [3197]

Famille du Tillet [3198]

[3187] racineshistoire.free.fr/LGN/PDF/Seguier.pdf
[3188] racineshistoire.free.fr/LGN/PDF/de_Seve.pdf
[3189] racineshistoire.free.fr/LGN/PDF/Silly.pdf
[3190] racineshistoire.free.fr/LGN/PDF/Spifame.pdf
[3191] racineshistoire.free.fr/LGN/PDF/Talon.pdf
[3192] racineshistoire.free.fr/LGN/PDF/Tesson.pdf
[3193] racineshistoire.free.fr/LGN/PDF/Teste.pdf
[3194] racineshistoire.free.fr/LGN/PDF/Testu-de-Balincourt.pdf
[3195] racineshistoire.free.fr/LGN/PDF/de-Thou.pdf
[3196] racineshistoire.free.fr/LGN/PDF/Thourotte.pdf
[3197] racineshistoire.free.fr/LGN/PDF/Thumery.pdf
[3198] racineshistoire.free.fr/LGN/PDF/du_Tillet.pdf

Famille et Seigneurs de Tosny [3199]

Famille et Seigneurs de Triest [3200]

Famille Turpin de Crissé [3201]

Famille(s) du Val (alias Duval) [3202]

Famille de Valognes (Valoignes, Valoines, Valoins, Valons, Valeynes, Valeignes, Valens, Valence, Valance, Valange) [3203]

Famille de Vaudétar [3204]

Famille de Vaultier [3205]

Famille de Vaux [3206]

Famille Vialart (Vialar, Vialard) [3207]

Famille de Vic [3208]

Famille de Vieuxpont [3209]

[3199] racineshistoire.free.fr/LGN/PDF/Tosny.pdf
[3200] racineshistoire.free.fr/LGN/PDF/Triest.pdf
[3201] racineshistoire.free.fr/LGN/PDF/Turpin-de-Crisse.pdf
[3202] racineshistoire.free.fr/LGN/PDF/du_Val.pdf
[3203] racineshistoire.free.fr/LGN/PDF/Valognes.pdf
[3204] racineshistoire.free.fr/LGN/PDF/Vaudetar.pdf
[3205] racineshistoire.free.fr/LGN/PDF/Vaultier.pdf
[3206] racineshistoire.free.fr/LGN/PDF/Vaux.pdf
[3207] racineshistoire.free.fr/LGN/PDF/Vialart.pdf
[3208] racineshistoire.free.fr/LGN/PDF/Vic.pdf
[3209] racineshistoire.free.fr/LGN/PDF/Vieuxpont.pdf

Famille Autier de Villemontée et Chazeron [3210]

Famille de La Villeneuve [3211]

Familles de L'Isle (-Adam), de Villiers, et de Villiers de L'Isle-Adam [3212]

Famille de Viole [3213]

Famille de Vion [3214]

Famille Vipart [3215]

Famille de Vitry [3216]

Famille de Vogüé [3217]

Famille de Voisins [3218]

Famille de Voyer, d'Argenson et de Paulmy [3219]

FRANCE, KINGS AND EARLY NOBILITY

Capetian Dynasty [3220]

[3210] racineshistoire.free.fr/LGN/PDF/Villemontee.pdf
[3211] racineshistoire.free.fr/LGN/PDF/Villeneuve.pdf
[3212] racineshistoire.free.fr/LGN/PDF/Villiers-de-L-Isle-Adam.pdf
[3213] racineshistoire.free.fr/LGN/PDF/Viole.pdf
[3214] racineshistoire.free.fr/LGN/PDF/Vion.pdf
[3215] racineshistoire.free.fr/LGN/PDF/Vipart.pdf
[3216] racineshistoire.free.fr/LGN/PDF/Vitry.pdf
[3217] racineshistoire.free.fr/LGN/PDF/Vogue.pdf
[3218] racineshistoire.free.fr/LGN/PDF/Voisins.pdf
[3219] racineshistoire.free.fr/LGN/PDF/Voyer-d-Argenson.pdf
[3220] https://en.wikipedia.org/wiki/Capetian_dynasty

Comtes d'Artois puis Seigneurs de Conches (Capétiens) [3221]

Comtes puis Ducs d'Alençon (Capétiens et Valois) [3222]

Descent from Antiquity from Hugh Capet [3223]

Dynastie des Mérovingiens [3224]

Dynastie des Capétiens et Origines (Robertiens) [3225]

Franks, Merovingian Kings [3226]

Franks, Merovingian Nobility [3227]

Franks, Carolingian Kings [3228]

Franks, Carolingian Nobility [3229]

France, Capetian Kings [3230]

Hughes Capet [3231]

[3221] racineshistoire.free.fr/LGN/PDF/Artois.pdf
[3222] racineshistoire.free.fr/LGN/PDF/Alencon_duche.pdf
[3223] www.mikesclark.com/genealogy/descent%20from%20antiquity.html
[3224] fjaunais.free.fr/h0merovin.htm
[3225] fjaunais.free.fr/h0capet.htm
[3226] fmg.ac/Projects/MedLands/MEROVINGIANS.htm
[3227] fmg.ac/Projects/MedLands/FRANKSMaiordomi.htm
[3228] fmg.ac/Projects/MedLands/CAROLINGIANS.htm
[3229] fmg.ac/Projects/MedLands/FRANKISH%20NOBILITY.htm
[3230] fmg.ac/Projects/MedLands/CAPET.htm
[3231] https://fr.wikipedia.org/wiki/Hugues_Capet

Hughes le Grand [3232]

La Maison Capétienne d'Artois [3233]

La Maison Capétienne de Dreux [3234]

Les Le Riche: ascension d'une famille à travers ses alliances sous les premiers Capétiens (Filiations directs) [3235]

Les Le Riche: ascension d'une famille à travers ses alliances sous les premiers Capétiens (Alliances et Agenda) [3236]

Les Mérovingiens (420 – 639) [3237]

La Dynastie des Carolingiens (751 – 987) [3238]

La Dynastie des Capétiens Direct (987 – 1328) [3239]

Royaume de Cologne [3240]

Simplified Family Tree (Carolingiens, Ottoniens, Robertiens) [3241]

[3232] https://fr.wikipedia.org/wiki/Hugues_le_Grand_(Robertien)
[3233] https://fr.wikipedia.org/wiki/Maison_capétienne_d'Artois
[3234] https://fr.wikipedia.org/wiki/Maison_capétienne_de_Dreux
[3235] racineshistoire.free.fr/LGN/PDF/Le-Riche-1.pdf
[3236] racineshistoire.free.fr/LGN/PDF/Le-Riche-2.pdf
[3237] www.ballade-medievale.fr/z_index_mero.htm
[3238] www.ballade-medievale.fr/carolingiens/index.htm
[3239] www.ballade-medievale.fr/capetiens/index.htm
[3240] fjaunais.free.fr/h0cologne.htm
[3241] http://fr.wikipedia.org/wiki/Fichier:Généalogie_Hugues_Capet.svg

FRANCE, BURGUNDY/FRANCHE-COMTE

Bosonids [3242]

Burgundy Duchy, Dukes [3243]

Burgundy Duchy, Nobility [3244]

Burgundy Kingdom, Kings [3245]

Burgundy Kingdom, Nobility [3246]

Comtes d'Altenburg, d'Habsburg et de Montbéliard [3247]

Comtes de Genève [3248]

Comtes de Nevers [3249]

Comtes de Poitiers-Valentinois et seigneurs de Saint-Vallier [3250]

Comtes de Tonnerre [3251]

Ducs de Bourgogne [3252]

[3242] https://en.wikipedia.org/wiki/Bosonids
[3243] fmg.ac/Projects/MedLands/BURGUNDY.htm
[3244] fmg.ac/Projects/MedLands/BURGUNDIAN%20NOBILITY.htm
[3245] fmg.ac/Projects/MedLands/BURGUNDY%20KINGS.htm
[3246] fmg.ac/Projects/MedLands/BURGUNDY%20Kingdom.htm
[3247] fjaunais.free.fr/h0mtbeliard.htm
[3248] fjaunais.free.fr/h0Genève.htm
[3249] fjaunais.free.fr/h0nevers.htm
[3250] racineshistoire.free.fr/LGN/PDF/Poitiers-Valentinois.pdf
[3251] fjaunais.free.fr/h0tonnerre.htm
[3252] fjaunais.free.fr/h0bourgogne.htm

Ducs Valois de Bourgogne [3253]

Dynastie Bosonide [3254]

Dynastie de Provence [3255]

Dynastie de Savoie [3256]

Le Comté de Bourgogne [3257]

Le Duché de Bourgogne [3258]

Maison d'Anjou en Provence [3259] [3260]

Maison de Savoie [3261]

Maison Capétienne de Valois-Alençon [3262]

Provence Kings, Comtes and Nobility [3263]

Royaume de Bourgogne [3264]

[3253] racineshistoire.free.fr/LGN/PDF/Bourgogne-Valois.pdf
[3254] fjaunais.free.fr/h0bosonide.htm
[3255] fjaunais.free.fr/h0provence.htm
[3256] fjaunais.free.fr/h0savoie.htm
[3257] https://fr.wikipedia.org/wiki/Comté_de_Bourgogne
[3258] https://fr.wikipedia.org/wiki/Duché_de_Bourgogne
[3259] https://fr.wikipedia.org/wiki/Maisons_d'Anjou
[3260] https://www.provence7.com/portails/histoire-portails/personnalites-de-lhistoire-en-provence/maison-danjou/
[3261] https://fr.wikipedia.org/wiki/Maison_de_Savoie
[3262] https://fr.wikipedia.org/wiki/Maison_capétienne_de_Valois
[3263] fmg.ac/Projects/MedLands/PROVENCE.htm
[3264] https://fr.wikipedia.org/wiki/Royaume_de_Bourgogne

Royaume de Burgondie [3265]

Royaume des Burgondes [3266]

Savoy [3267]

Seigneurs de Baudément [3268]

Seigneurs de Donzy et de Vergy [3269]

Seigneurs de Mailly [3270]

Seigneurs de Mont-Saint-Jean et de Charny [3271]

Seigneurs de Saint-Vérain [3272]

Seigneurs de Thury [3273]

The Paternal Origins of the Counts of Geneva [3274]

FRANCE, NORTHERN

Bâtards de Flandres (Vlaanderen) [3275]

[3265] fjaunais.free.fr/h0burgondie.htm
[3266] https://fr.wikipedia.org/wiki/Royaume_des_Burgondes
[3267] fmg.ac/Projects/MedLands/SAVOY.htm
[3268] racineshistoire.free.fr/LGN/PDF/Baudement.pdf
[3269] racineshistoire.free.fr/LGN/PDF/Donzy-Vergy.pdf
[3270] racineshistoire.free.fr/LGN/PDF/Mailly.pdf
[3271] racineshistoire.free.fr/LGN/PDF/Mont-Saint-Jean.pdf
[3272] racineshistoire.free.fr/LGN/PDF/Saint-Verain.pdf
[3273] racineshistoire.free.fr/LGN/PDF/Thury.pdf
[3274] gilles.maillet.free.fr/histoire/pdf/Geneva.pdf
[3275] racineshistoire.free.fr/LGN/PDF/Flandres-Batards.pdf

Champagne, Nobility [3276]

Châtelains de Douai [3277]

Châtelains de Gand (Burggrafen van Gent), Seigneur d'Aalst (Alost) et Famille Vilain de Gand [3278]

Châtelains de Lille et Seigneurs de Fresnes-sur-Escaut [3279]

Châtelains de Saint-Omer et Morbecque, Fauquembergues [3280]

Comtes de Boulogne [3281]

Comtes de Boulogne et Saint Pol [3282]

Comtes de Brienne [3283]

Comtes de Flandres [3284]

Comtes de Flandres (Vlaanderen) [3285]

Comtes de Guines [3286] [3287]

[3276] fmg.ac/Projects/MedLands/CHAMPAGNE%20NOBILITY.htm
[3277] racineshistoire.free.fr/LGN/PDF/Douai.pdf
[3278] racineshistoire.free.fr/LGN/PDF/Gand.pdf
[3279] racineshistoire.free.fr/LGN/PDF/Lille-Fresnes-sur-Escaut.pdf
[3280] racineshistoire.free.fr/LGN/PDF/Saint-Omer.pdf
[3281] racineshistoire.free.fr/LGN/PDF/Boulogne.pdf
[3282] fjaunais.free.fr/h0stpol.htm
[3283] fjaunais.free.fr/h0brienne.htm
[3284] fjaunais.free.fr/h0flandre.htm
[3285] racineshistoire.free.fr/LGN/PDF/Flandres.pdf
[3286] racineshistoire.free.fr/LGN/PDF/Guines.pdf
[3287] fjaunais.free.fr/h0guines.htm

Comtes de Laon [3288]

Comtes de Montdidier, Comtes de Dammartin et Seigneurs de Ramerupt [3289]

Comtes de Ponthieu et de Clermont [3290]

Comtes de Réthel [3291]

Comtes de Roucy et de Reims [3292]

Comtes de Sancerre [3293]

Comtes de Sens et du Mâcon [3294]

Comtes de Vermandois [3295]

Counts of Flanders [3296]

Famille de Châtillon (-sur-Marne) [3297]

Flanders, Counts [3298]

_____

[3288] fjaunais.free.fr/h0laon.htm
[3289] racineshistoire.free.fr/LGN/PDF/Montdidier-Dammartin-Ramerupt.pdf
[3290] fjaunais.free.fr/h0ponthieu.htm
[3291] racineshistoire.free.fr/LGN/PDF/Rethel.pdf
[3292] fjaunais.free.fr/h0roucy.htm
[3293] racineshistoire.free.fr/LGN/PDF/Sancerre.pdf
[3294] fjaunais.free.fr/h0sens.htm
[3295] fjaunais.free.fr/h0vermandois.htm
[3296] fmg.ac/Projects/MedLands/FLANDERS,%20HAINAUT.htm
[3297] racineshistoire.free.fr/LGN/PDF/Chatillon.pdf
[3298] fmg.ac/Projects/MedLands/FLANDERS,%20HAINAUT.htm

Flanders, Nobility [3299]

La Dynastie Châtillon-sur-Marne [3300]

La Maison de Brienne [3301] [3302] [3303]

La Maison de Coucy [3304]

La Maison de Dampierre [3305]

La Maison de Flandre [3306]

La Maison de Saint-Pol Campdavène (1067-1240) Comtes de Saint-Pol [3307]

La Maison de Traînel (alias Trainel, Traynel) [3308]

La Maison de Vermandois [3309]

La Maison de Wavrin [3310]

[3299] fmg.ac/Projects/MedLands/FLEMISH%20NOBILITY.htm
[3300] https://en.wikipedia.org/wiki/House_of_Ch%C3%A2tillon
[3301] racineshistoire.free.fr/LGN/PDF/Brienne.pdf
[3302] https://fr.wikipedia.org/wiki/Maison_de_Brienne
[3303] www.monarchie-noblesse.net/noblesse/france/brienne/brienne.htm
[3304] https://fr.wikipedia.org/wiki/Maison_de_Coucy
[3305] https://fr.wikipedia.org/wiki/Maisons_de_Dampierre
[3306] https://fr.wikipedia.org/wiki/Maison_de_Flandre
[3307] racineshistoire.free.fr/LGN/PDF/Saint-Pol-Campdavene.pdf
[3308] racineshistoire.free.fr/LGN/PDF/Trainel.pdf
[3309] https://fr.wikipedia.org/wiki/Herbertiens
[3310] racineshistoire.free.fr/LGN/PDF/Wavrin.pdf

Northern France, Nobility [3311]

Premiers Comtes et Châtelains d'Amiens [3312]

Premiers Comtes et Châtelains et Evêques d'Arras [3313]

Premiers Comtes et Vicomtes de Sens [3314]

Premiers Comtes de Troyes [3315]

Seigneurs d'Ache, de Boves puis Comtes de Dreux [3316]

Seigneurs d'Aigremont [3317]

Seigneurs d'Ardres et Marquise, Cayeu, Courteville et Hodicq [3318]

Seigneurs d'Ath, de Roeulx et de Montdidier [3319]

Seigneurs d'Auneau [3320]

Seigneurs de Beaufort et Noyelles-Vion [3321]

Seigneurs de Beaumetz (alias Beaumez) [3322]

[3311] fmg.ac/Projects/MedLands/NORTHERN%20FRANCE.htm
[3312] racineshistoire.free.fr/LGN/PDF/Amiens.pdf
[3313] racineshistoire.free.fr/LGN/PDF/Arras.pdf
[3314] racineshistoire.free.fr/LGN/PDF/Sens.pdf
[3315] racineshistoire.free.fr/LGN/PDF/Troyes.pdf
[3316] fjaunais.free.fr/h0dreux.htm
[3317] racineshistoire.free.fr/LGN/PDF/Aigremont.pdf
[3318] racineshistoire.free.fr/LGN/PDF/Ardres.pdf
[3319] fjaunais.free.fr/h0roeulx.htm
[3320] racineshistoire.free.fr/LGN/PDF/Auneau.pdf
[3321] racineshistoire.free.fr/LGN/PDF/Beauffort_Noyelles-Vion.pdf
[3322] racineshistoire.free.fr/LGN/PDF/Beaumetz.pdf

Famille et Seigneurs de Béthune [3323]

Seigneurs de Biencourt [3324]

Seigneurs de Bouville [3325]

Seigneurs de Broyes et Châteauvillain [3326]

Seigneurs de Chérisy, Quierzy et Pierrefonds [3327]

Famille et Seigneurs de Coligny et Châtillon-Coligny [3328]

Seigneurs de Conflans (-Sainte-Honorine) [3329]

Seigneurs de Coucy, Boves et Vervins, Montmirel et Chimay [3330]

Seigneurs de Créquy [3331]

Famille et Seigneurs de Croÿ [3332]

Seigneurs de Dampierre [3333]

Seigneurs de Fiennes [3334] [3335]

[3323] racineshistoire.free.fr/LGN/PDF/Bethune.pdf
[3324] racineshistoire.free.fr/LGN/PDF/Biencourt.pdf
[3325] racineshistoire.free.fr/LGN/PDF/Bouville.pdf
[3326] racineshistoire.free.fr/LGN/PDF/Broyes-Chateauvillain.pdf
[3327] racineshistoire.free.fr/LGN/PDF/Cherisy-Quierzy-Pierrefonds.pdf
[3328] racineshistoire.free.fr/LGN/PDF/Chatillon-Coligny.pdf
[3329] racineshistoire.free.fr/LGN/PDF/Conflans.pdf
[3330] racineshistoire.free.fr/LGN/PDF/Coucy.pdf
[3331] racineshistoire.free.fr/LGN/PDF/Crequy.pdf
[3332] racineshistoire.free.fr/LGN/PDF/Croy.pdf
[3333] fjaunais.free.fr/h0dampierre.htm
[3334] racineshistoire.free.fr/LGN/PDF/Fiennes.pdf

Seigneurs de Gaucourt [3336]

Seigneurs de Gavre (van Gavere) [3337]

Seigneurs de Guise [3338]

Famille et Seigneurs de Jaucourt et de Dinteville [3339]

Seigneurs de Joinville [3340] [3341]

Famille et Seigneurs de Landas et Mortagne et Warlaing, Cysoing, Esnes, Bailliencourt, Warenghien et de Le Cambe [3342]

Famille et Seigneurs de Lannoy [3343]

Seigneurs de Mailly-Couronnel [3344]

Seigneurs de Moreuil (Soissons) [3345]

Seigneurs de Mouchy-Le-Châtel [3346]

Seigneurs de Nesle et Falvy (alias Flavy) [3347]

[3335] fjaunais.free.fr/h0fiennes.htm
[3336] racineshistoire.free.fr/LGN/PDF/Gaucourt.pdf
[3337] racineshistoire.free.fr/LGN/PDF/Gavre.pdf
[3338] racineshistoire.free.fr/LGN/PDF/Guise.pdf
[3339] racineshistoire.free.fr/LGN/PDF/Jaucourt-Dinteville.pdf
[3340] racineshistoire.free.fr/LGN/PDF/Joinville.pdf
[3341] fjaunais.free.fr/h0joinville.htm
[3342] racineshistoire.free.fr/LGN/PDF/Landas.pdf
[3343] racineshistoire.free.fr/LGN/PDF/Lannoy.pdf
[3344] racineshistoire.free.fr/LGN/PDF/Mailly-Couronnel.pdf
[3345] racineshistoire.free.fr/LGN/PDF/Moreuil-Soissons.pdf
[3346] racineshistoire.free.fr/LGN/PDF/Mouchy.pdf
[3347] racineshistoire.free.fr/LGN/PDF/Nesle-Falvy.pdf

Seigneurs de Picquigny [3348]

Comtes de Ponthieu, Montreuil et Saint-Pol [3349]

Seigneurs de Raineval [3350]

Famille et Seigneurs de Rambures [3351]

Seigneurs de Roubaix [3352]

Seigneurs de Roucy et Comtes de Reims [3353]

Seigneurs de Roye [3354]

Seigneurs de Tournai et de Mortagne, Famille Van Peteg(h)em [3355]

Seigneurs de Trie [3356]

Famille et Seigneurs de Triest [3357]

Seigneurs de Wignacourt (alias Vignacourt) [3358]

Vermandois, Valois et Vexin [3359]

[3348] racineshistoire.free.fr/LGN/PDF/Picquigny.pdf
[3349] racineshistoire.free.fr/LGN/PDF/Ponthieu.pdf
[3350] racineshistoire.free.fr/LGN/PDF/Raineval.pdf
[3351] racineshistoire.free.fr/LGN/PDF/Rambures.pdf
[3352] racineshistoire.free.fr/LGN/PDF/Roubaix.pdf
[3353] racineshistoire.free.fr/LGN/PDF/Roucy.pdf
[3354] racineshistoire.free.fr/LGN/PDF/Roye.pdf
[3355] racineshistoire.free.fr/LGN/PDF/van-Peteghem-Tournai.pdf
[3356] racineshistoire.free.fr/LGN/PDF/Trie.pdf
[3357] racineshistoire.free.fr/LGN/PDF/Triest.pdf
[3358] racineshistoire.free.fr/LGN/PDF/Wignacourt.pdf
[3359] racineshistoire.free.fr/LGN/PDF/Vermandois-Valois-Vexin.pdf

Vicomtes de Chaumont-en-Vexin, Seigneurs de Quitry (ou Guitry) [3360]

FRANCE, NORTHWEST AND CENTRAL

Anjou, Counts and Nobility [3361]

Brittany, Dukes and Nobility [3362]

Central France, Nobility [3363]

Château de Blois [3364]

Comtes d'Anjou [3365] [3366]

Comtes d'Anjou et Gâtinais (et Plantagenêts) [3367]

Comtes d'Avranches puis du Perche [3368]

Comtes de Blois et de Champagne [3369]

Comtes de Blois et Chartres (Blois-Champagne) [3370]

[3360] racineshistoire.free.fr/LGN/PDF/Chaumont-en-Vexin&Quitry.pdf
[3361] fmg.ac/Projects/MedLands/ANJOU,%20MAINE.htm
[3362] fmg.ac/Projects/MedLands/BRITTANY.htm
[3363] fmg.ac/Projects/MedLands/CENTRAL%20FRANCE.htm
[3364] http://en.wikipedia.org/wiki/Château_de_Blois
[3365] fjaunais.free.fr/h0anjou.htm
[3366] https://fr.wikipedia.org/wiki/Comté_d'Anjou
[3367] racineshistoire.free.fr/LGN/PDF/Anjou-Gâtinais.pdf
[3368] fjaunais.free.fr/h0perche.htm
[3369] fjaunais.free.fr/h0champagne.htm
[3370] racineshistoire.free.fr/LGN/PDF/Blois-Champagne.pdf

Comtes de Brionne et de Dammartin [3371]

Comté et Vicomté de Corbeil [3372]

Comtes de Dreux [3373]

Comtes d'Eu [3374]

Comtes d'Eu et de Soissons [3375]

Comtes d'Evreux et Famille Devereux [3376]

Comtes du Maine [3377]

Comtes et Vicomtes du Maine [3378]

Comtes de Meulan, Seigneurs de Beaumont (-Le-Roger) et Earls of Leicester [3379]

Comtes de Montdidier, Comtes de Dammartin et Seigneurs de Ramerupt [3380]

Comtes de Montfort [3381]

[3371] fjaunais.free.fr/h0dammartin.htm
[3372] racineshistoire.free.fr/LGN/PDF/Corbeil.pdf
[3373] racineshistoire.free.fr/LGN/PDF/Dreux.pdf
[3374] racineshistoire.free.fr/LGN/PDF/Eu.pdf
[3375] fjaunais.free.fr/h0soissons.htm
[3376] racineshistoire.free.fr/LGN/PDF/Evreux.pdf
[3377] fjaunais.free.fr/h0maine.htm
[3378] racineshistoire.free.fr/LGN/PDF/Maine.pdf
[3379] racineshistoire.free.fr/LGN/PDF/Meulan-Beaumont.pdf
[3380] racineshistoire.free.fr/LGN/PDF/Montdidier-Dammartin-Ramerupt.pdf
[3381] fjaunais.free.fr/h0montfort.htm

Comtes de Nantes [3382]

Comtes du Perche et Comtes de Mortagne [3383]

Comtes de Soissons [3384]

Comtes de Vintzgau, d'Orléans et Gâtinais [3385]

Comtes et Vicomtes de Bayeux, Seigneurs d'Ivry [3386]

Ducs de Brétagne [3387]

Ducs de Normandie [3388]

Ducs d' Orléans, Angoulême et Longueville [3389]

Dynastie de Blois-Champagne [3390] [3391]

Dynastie des Bourbons (Branche de La Marche) [3392]

Dynastie des Bourbons (Branche Vendôme) [3393]

[3382] fjaunais.free.fr/h0nantes.htm
[3383] racineshistoire.free.fr/LGN/PDF/Perche.pdf
[3384] racineshistoire.free.fr/LGN/PDF/Soissons.pdf
[3385] fjaunais.free.fr/h0vintzgau.htm
[3386] racineshistoire.free.fr/LGN/PDF/Bayeux-Ivry.pdf
[3387] fjaunais.free.fr/h0bretagne.htm
[3388] racineshistoire.free.fr/LGN/PDF/Normandie.pdf
[3389] racineshistoire.free.fr/LGN/PDF/Orleans.pdf
[3390] https://en.wikipedia.org/wiki/House_of_Blois
[3391] https://fr.wikipedia.org/wiki/Maison_de_Blois
[3392] https://fr.wikipedia.org/wiki/Maison_de_Bourbon-La_Marche
[3393] https://fr.wikipedia.org/wiki/Maison_de_Bourbon-Vendôme

Dynastie de Normandie [3394]

Famille d'Amboise [3395]

Famille de Brézé [3396]

La Maison de Montmorency [3397]

La Maison de Clermont [3398] [3399]

La Maison de Courtenay [3400]

La Maison de La Tour Landry [3401]

La Maison de L'Aubespine [3402]

La Maison de Maillé [3403]

La Maison de Montreuil-Bellay (ancien Montreuil-Berlai) [3404]

La Maison de Rohan [3405] [3406]

[3394] fjaunais.free.fr/h0normandie.htm
[3395] https://fr.wikipedia.org/wiki/Famille_d'Amboise
[3396] racineshistoire.free.fr/LGN/PDF/Breze.pdf
[3397] https://fr.wikipedia.org/wiki/Maison_de_Montmorency
[3398] https://fr.wikipedia.org/wiki/Maison_de_Clermont-Tonnerre
[3399] https://fr.wikipedia.org/wiki/Maison_de_Clermont-en-Beauvaisis
[3400] racineshistoire.free.fr/LGN/PDF/Courtenay.pdf
[3401] https://fr.wikipedia.org/wiki/Famille_de_La_Tour-Landry
[3402] racineshistoire.free.fr/LGN/PDF/L_Aubespine.pdf
[3403] https://fr.wikipedia.org/wiki/Maison_de_Maill%C3%A9
[3404] racineshistoire.free.fr/LGN/PDF/Montreuil-Bellay.pdf
[3405] https://en.wikipedia.org/wiki/House_of_Rohan
[3406] https://fr.wikipedia.org/wiki/Maison_de_Rohan

La Première Dynastie de Brétagne [3407] [3408] [3409]

Les Fulcherides (Haut-Vendômois) [3410]

Les premiers Seigneurs de Boury [3411]

Les Comtes de Blois [3412] [3413]

Les Comtes de Vendôme [3414]

Les Ducs de Normandie [3415] [3416]

Les Seigneurs de Laval [3417] [3418]

Maine and Vendôme [3419]

Noblesse d'Andelu (familles Vassal, Gobinard de La Mare et Guibourg) [3420]

[3407] www.sahpl.asso.fr/site_sahpl/le_mouel_guy_généalogie_des_très_anciens_roys_de_bretagne.pdf
[3408] https://fr.wikipedia.org/wiki/Liste_des_rois_puis_ducs_de_Bretagne
[3409] ablogjeanfloch.over-blog.com/article-30269050.html
[3410] racineshistoire.free.fr/LGN/PDF/Fulcherides.pdf
[3411] racineshistoire.free.fr/LGN/PDF/Boury.pdf
[3412] https://en.wikipedia.org/wiki/Counts_of_Blois
[3413] https://fr.wikipedia.org/wiki/Liste_des_comtes_de_Blois
[3414] racineshistoire.free.fr/LGN/PDF/Vendome.pdf
[3415] jpm14.pagesperso-orange.fr/genealogie/ducs_de_normandie.htm
[3416] https://fr.wikipedia.org/wiki/Liste_des_ducs_de_Normandie
[3417] https://fr.wikipedia.org/wiki/Liste_des_seigneurs_de_Laval
[3418] https://fr.wikipedia.org/wiki/Maison_de_Laval
[3419] fmg.ac/Projects/MedLands/MAINE.htm
[3420] racineshistoire.free.fr/LGN/PDF/Andelu.pdf

Normandy, Dukes [3421]

Normandy, Nobility [3422]

Norman Hierarchy [3423]

Paris Region, Nobility [3424]

Seigneurs d'Alluyes [3425]

Seigneurs d'Amboise et Clermont d'Amboise [3426]

Seigneurs puis Comtes d'Aumale [3427]

Seigneurs de Banthelu [3428]

Seigneurs de Beaugency (ancient Boisgency) [3429]

Seigneurs de Beaumont-sur-Oise [3430]

Famille de Bellême, Seigneurs d'Alençon, et Château Gontier, et Château Renaud [3431]

Seigneurs de Beynes [3432]

[3421] fmg.ac/Projects/MedLands/NORMANDY.htm
[3422] fmg.ac/Projects/MedLands/NORMAN%20NOBILITY.htm
[3423] www.scotlandroyalty.org/royal.html
[3424] fmg.ac/Projects/MedLands/PARIS%20REGION%20NOBILITY.htm
[3425] racineshistoire.free.fr/LGN/PDF/Alluyes.pdf
[3426] racineshistoire.free.fr/LGN/PDF/Amboise.pdf
[3427] racineshistoire.free.fr/LGN/PDF/Aumale.pdf
[3428] racineshistoire.free.fr/LGN/PDF/Banthelu.pdf
[3429] racineshistoire.free.fr/LGN/PDF/Beaugency.pdf
[3430] racineshistoire.free.fr/LGN/PDF/Beaumont-sur-Oise.pdf
[3431] racineshistoire.free.fr/LGN/PDF/Belleme.pdf
[3432] racineshistoire.free.fr/LGN/PDF/Beynes.pdf

Seigneurs de Blaison et d'Ile-Bouchard [3433]

Seigneurs de Boubers Tuncq et Bernâtre [3434]

Famille et Seigneurs de Boubers 1 [3435]

Famille et Seigneurs de Boubers 2 [3436]

Famille et Seigneurs de Boutigny (-sur-Opton) et Grandchamp [3437]

Seigneurs de Briollay, Beauvau et Jarzé [3438]

Seigneurs de Breteuil, Vicomtes de Chartres [3439]

Seigneurs de Bricqueville [3440]

Seigneurs de Bruyères-Le-Châtel [3441]

Seigneurs et Famille de Bueil [3442] [3443]

[3433] fjaunais.free.fr/h0isle.htm
[3434] racineshistoire.free.fr/LGN/PDF/Boubers-Abbéville-Tuncq.pdf
[3435] racineshistoire.free.fr/LGN/PDF/Boubers1.pdf
[3436] racineshistoire.free.fr/LGN/PDF/Boubers2.pdf
[3437] racineshistoire.free.fr/LGN/PDF/Boutigny.pdf
[3438] fjaunais.free.fr/h0briollay.htm
[3439] racineshistoire.free.fr/LGN/PDF/Breteuil.pdf
[3440] racineshistoire.free.fr/LGN/PDF/Bricqueville.pdf
[3441] racineshistoire.free.fr/LGN/PDF/Bruyeres-Le-Chatel.pdf
[3442] racineshistoire.free.fr/LGN/PDF/Bueil.pdf
[3443]
https://books.google.ca/books?id=rbzozw0wGVoC&pg=PA291&lpg=PA291&dq=Seigneurs+and+Family+de+Bueil&source=bl&ots=KCKdlGZvmU&sig=LZIyZ2odj2sfLZ9HaqvHDcxlrPU&hl=en&sa=X&ei=MhQpUIeoD_S86QHdm4H4Cw&ved=0CEIQ6AEwCDgK#v=onepage&q=Seigneurs%20and%20Family%20de%20Bueil&f=false

Famille et Seigneurs de Chambly [3444]

Seigneurs de Château-Landon, Vicomtes de Fessard [3445]

Seigneurs de Chevreuse, Maincourt, Choisel et Dampierre [3446]

Seigneurs de Clermont-en-Beauvaisis et de Clermont-Nesle [3447]

Seigneurs de Clisson [3448]

Seigneurs de Coëtivy [3449]

Seigneurs de Craon [3450]

Seigneurs de Craon, Bazougers et d'Anthenaise [3451]

Seigneurs du Bec-Crespin [3452]

Seigneurs de Creully [3453]

Famille de Daillon et Seigneurs du Lude [3454]

Seigneurs de Dreux-Bû (ancien Beu) et Seigneurs de Beausart et Châteaudun [3455]

[3444] racineshistoire.free.fr/LGN/PDF/Chambly.pdf
[3445] racineshistoire.free.fr/LGN/PDF/Chateau-Landon.pdf
[3446] racineshistoire.free.fr/LGN/PDF/Chevreuse.pdf
[3447] racineshistoire.free.fr/LGN/PDF/Clermont-Beauvaisis-Nesle.pdf
[3448] racineshistoire.free.fr/LGN/PDF/Clisson.pdf
[3449] racineshistoire.free.fr/LGN/PDF/Coetivy.pdf
[3450] racineshistoire.free.fr/LGN/PDF/Craon.pdf
[3451] fjaunais.free.fr/h0craon.htm
[3452] racineshistoire.free.fr/LGN/PDF/Crespin.pdf
[3453] racineshistoire.free.fr/LGN/PDF/Creully.pdf
[3454] racineshistoire.free.fr/LGN/PDF/Daillon.pdf
[3455] racineshistoire.free.fr/LGN/PDF/Dreux-Bu.pdf

Seigneurs d' Epernon [3456]

Seigneurs d' Etampes [3457]

Seigneurs et Famille des Fossés (alias des Fossez) [3458]

Seigneurs de Fréteval [3459] [3460]

Famille Giroie, Seigneurs d' Echauffour et de Montreuil [3461]

Seigneurs de Gisors [3462]

Premiers Seigneurs de Gometz [3463]

Seigneurs de Goupillières [3464]

Seigneurs de Gournay [3465]

Seigneurs de Guiry [3466]

Seigneurs d'Harcourt et de Montgommery [3467]

[3456] racineshistoire.free.fr/LGN/PDF/Epernon.pdf
[3457] racineshistoire.free.fr/LGN/PDF/Etampes.pdf
[3458] racineshistoire.free.fr/LGN/PDF/des_Fosses.pdf
[3459] racineshistoire.free.fr/LGN/PDF/Freteval.pdf
[3460] fjaunais.free.fr/h0freteval.htm
[3461] racineshistoire.free.fr/LGN/PDF/Giroie-Echauffour.pdf
[3462] racineshistoire.free.fr/LGN/PDF/Gisors.pdf
[3463] racineshistoire.free.fr/LGN/PDF/Gometz.pdf
[3464] racineshistoire.free.fr/LGN/PDF/Goupillieres.pdf
[3465] racineshistoire.free.fr/LGN/PDF/Gournay.pdf
[3466] racineshistoire.free.fr/LGN/PDF/Guiry.pdf
[3467] fjaunais.free.fr/h0montgom.htm

Famille et Seigneurs d'Hargeville [3468]

La Baume-Le Blanc, Ducs de La Vallière [3469]

Seigneurs de La Ferté [3470]

Seigneurs de La Ferté-Fresnel et Chambray [3471]

Seigneurs de Laigle [3472]

Famille et Seigneurs de Languedoüe [3473]

Seigneurs de La Queue [3474]

Seigneurs de La Roche-Guyon [3475]

Seigneurs de Lèves et de Gallardon [3476]

Seigneurs de Loudun, de Faye la Vineuse, et de Montsoreau [3477]

Seigneurs de Maintenon [3478]

[3468] racineshistoire.free.fr/LGN/PDF/Hargeville.pdf
[3469] racineshistoire.free.fr/LGN/PDF/La-Baume-Le-Blanc.pdf
[3470] racineshistoire.free.fr/LGN/PDF/La-Ferte.pdf
[3471] racineshistoire.free.fr/LGN/PDF/La-Ferte-Fresnel_Chambray.pdf
[3472] racineshistoire.free.fr/LGN/PDF/Laigle.pdf
[3473] racineshistoire.free.fr/LGN/PDF/Languedoue.pdf
[3474] racineshistoire.free.fr/LGN/PDF/La-Queue.pdf
[3475] racineshistoire.free.fr/LGN/PDF/La-Roche-Guyon.pdf
[3476] racineshistoire.free.fr/LGN/PDF/Leves-Gallardon.pdf
[3477] fjaunais.free.fr/h0faye.htm
[3478] racineshistoire.free.fr/LGN/PDF/Maintenon.pdf

Seigneurs de Maizelan (alias Mézelan, Mésalant, Méselant) [3479]

Seigneurs de Maule [3480]

Famille et Seigneurs de Mauquenchy de Blainville [3481]

Seigneurs de Mayenne [3482]

Seigneurs de Mello [3483]

Famille et Vicomtes de Melun [3484]

Famille et Seigneurs du Mesnil-Simon [3485]

Seigneurs de Milly [3486]

Seigneurs de Montfort (-L'Amaury) [3487]

Seigneurs de Montfort-sur-Risle [3488]

Seigneurs de Montlhéry (Bray-sur-Seine, La Ferté-Milon) [3489]

Seigneurs de Montmirail (Gouët) [3490]

[3479] racineshistoire.free.fr/LGN/PDF/Maizelan.pdf
[3480] racineshistoire.free.fr/LGN/PDF/Maule.pdf
[3481] racineshistoire.free.fr/LGN/PDF/Mauquenchy-de-Blainville.pdf
[3482] fjaunais.free.fr/h0mayenne.htm
[3483] racineshistoire.free.fr/LGN/PDF/Mello.pdf
[3484] racineshistoire.free.fr/LGN/PDF/Melun.pdf
[3485] racineshistoire.free.fr/LGN/PDF/Mesnil-Simon.pdf
[3486] racineshistoire.free.fr/LGN/PDF/Milly.pdf
[3487] racineshistoire.free.fr/LGN/PDF/Montfort.pdf
[3488] racineshistoire.free.fr/LGN/PDF/Montfort-sur-Risle.pdf
[3489] racineshistoire.free.fr/LGN/PDF/Montlhery.pdf
[3490] racineshistoire.free.fr/LGN/PDF/Montmirail-Gouet.pdf

Seigneurs de Nanteuil-Le-Haudouin [3491]

Seigneurs de Neauphle (-Le-Château) [3492]

Seigneurs de Nemours [3493]

Seigneurs de Nézel [3494]

Seigneurs de Palaiseau [3495]

Seigneurs de Poissy [3496]

Seigneurs de Pontchartrain [3497]

Seigneurs et Barons de Preuilly et Vendôme [3498]

Seigneurs du Puiset [3499]

Seigneurs de Reviers (Rivers) et de Vernon [3500]

Seigneurs de Richebourg et Familles de Richebourg et Tranchelion [3501]

Seigneurs de Rochefort (-en-Yvelines) [3502]

[3491] racineshistoire.free.fr/LGN/PDF/Nanteuil-Le-Haudouin.pdf
[3492] racineshistoire.free.fr/LGN/PDF/Neauphle.pdf
[3493] racineshistoire.free.fr/LGN/PDF/Nemours.pdf
[3494] racineshistoire.free.fr/LGN/PDF/Nezel.pdf
[3495] racineshistoire.free.fr/LGN/PDF/Palaiseau.pdf
[3496] racineshistoire.free.fr/LGN/PDF/Poissy.pdf
[3497] racineshistoire.free.fr/LGN/PDF/Pontchartrain.pdf
[3498] fjaunais.free.fr/h0preuilly.htm
[3499] racineshistoire.free.fr/LGN/PDF/Le-Puiset.pdf
[3500] racineshistoire.free.fr/LGN/PDF/Reviers.pdf
[3501] racineshistoire.free.fr/LGN/PDF/Richebourg.pdf
[3502] racineshistoire.free.fr/LGN/PDF/Rochefort.pdf

Seigneurs de Sablé [3503]

Seigneurs de Saint-Valéry, Auffay et Neufmarché (Newmarch) [3504]

Seigneurs de Sully [3505]

Seigneurs et Vidames de Senlis, Bouteiller de Senlis, Saint-Liz, St.Liz (Angleterre, Écosse) [3506]

Seigneurs deThoiry [3507]

Seigneurs de Tilly [3508]

Famille et Seigneurs de Tosny [3509]

Seigneurs de Trèves [3510] [3511]

Seigneurs de Tyrel de Poix [3512]

Seigneurs, Comtes, Vicomtes et Familles de Vendôme et Vendômois [3513]

Seigneurs de Villemomble et Villebéon (Villebon) [3514]

[3503] fjaunais.free.fr/h0sable.htm
[3504] racineshistoire.free.fr/LGN/PDF/Saint-Valery-Auffay-Neufmarche.pdf
[3505] racineshistoire.free.fr/LGN/PDF/Sully.pdf
[3506] racineshistoire.free.fr/LGN/PDF/Senlis.pdf
[3507] racineshistoire.free.fr/LGN/PDF/Thoiry.pdf
[3508] racineshistoire.free.fr/LGN/PDF/Tilly.pdf
[3509] racineshistoire.free.fr/LGN/PDF/Tosny.pdf
[3510] fjaunais.free.fr/h0treves.htm
[3511] https://en.wikipedia.org/wiki/Robert_le_Maçon
[3512] racineshistoire.free.fr/LGN/PDF/Tyrel-de-Poix.pdf
[3513] racineshistoire.free.fr/LGN/PDF/Vendome.pdf
[3514] racineshistoire.free.fr/LGN/PDF/Villemomble-Villebeon.pdf

Seigneurs de Villepreux [3515]

Seigneurs de Wideville [3516]

The Chevalier de La Tour Landry [3517]

Vicomtes d'Avranches [3518]

Vicomtes de Blois [3519]

Vicomtes de Châteaudun [3520] [3521]

Vicomtes d'Orléans [3522]

FRANCE, SOUTHWEST

Angoulême, La Marche, Perigord [3523]

Aquitaine, Dukes [3524]

Auvergne [3525]

[3515] racineshistoire.free.fr/LGN/PDF/Villepreux.pdf
[3516] racineshistoire.free.fr/LGN/PDF/Wideville.pdf
[3517] https://circle.ubc.ca/bitstream/handle/2429/37224/UBC_1966_A8%20R8.pdf?sequence=1
[3518] racineshistoire.free.fr/LGN/PDF/Avranches.pdf
[3519] racineshistoire.free.fr/LGN/PDF/Blois_Vicomtes.pdf
[3520] racineshistoire.free.fr/LGN/PDF/Chateaudun-Vicomtes.pdf
[3521] fjaunais.free.fr/h0chateaudun.htm
[3522] racineshistoire.free.fr/LGN/PDF/Orleans_Vicomtes.pdf
[3523] fmg.ac/Projects/MedLands/ANGOULEME.htm
[3524] fmg.ac/Projects/MedLands/AQUITAINE.htm
[3525] fmg.ac/Projects/MedLands/AUVERGNE.htm

Bourbon [3526]

Bourbon Condé et Conti [3527]

Bourbon Deux-Siciles [3528]

Bourbon d'Espagne [3529]

Comtes d'Angoulême [3530]

Comtes d'Autun et d'Auvergne [3531]

Comtes de Bigorre et Rois de Pampelune [3532]

Comtes de Carcassonne, Comminges et Razès

Comtes de Foix [3533]

Comtes puis Ducs de Gascogne et Fézensac, Armagnac, Astarac (origines) [3534]

Comtes de Gévaudan [3535]

Comtes de La Marche et du Perigord [3536]

[3526] fmg.ac/Projects/MedLands/BOURBON.htm
[3527] racineshistoire.free.fr/LGN/PDF/Bourbon-Conde-Conti.pdf
[3528] racineshistoire.free.fr/LGN/PDF/Bourbon-Deux-Siciles.pdf
[3529] racineshistoire.free.fr/LGN/PDF/Bourbon-Espagne.pdf
[3530] racineshistoire.free.fr/LGN/PDF/Angouleme.pdf
[3531] fjaunais.free.fr/h0auvergne.htm
[3532] fjaunais.free.fr/h0bigorre.htm
[3533] racineshistoire.free.fr/LGN/PDF/Foix.pdf
[3534] racineshistoire.free.fr/LGN/PDF/Gascogne.pdf
[3535] fjaunais.free.fr/h0gevaudan.htm
[3536] fjaunais.free.fr/h0marche.htm

Comtes de La Marche et de Périgord etTalleyrand-Périgord [3537]

Comtes de Rouergue et de Rodez [3538]

Comtes de Toulouse [3539]

Comtes de Toulouse et de Rouergue [3540]

Ducs d'Aquitaine et Comtes de Poitou [3541]

Ducs d' Orléans, Angoulême et Longueville [3542]

Ducs de Gascogne et Comtes d'Astarac [3543]

Dynastie des Bourbons-Orléans [3544]

Dynastie des Bourbons (Branche Orléans-Galliera) [3545]

Dynastie des Bourbons (Branche Orléans-Longueville) [3546]

Famille et Seigneurs de Gontaut, Gontaut-Biron et Badefols [3547]

[3537] racineshistoire.free.fr/LGN/PDF/La_Marche-Perigord.pdf
[3538] racineshistoire.free.fr/LGN/PDF/Rouergue-Rodez.pdf
[3539] racineshistoire.free.fr/LGN/PDF/Toulouse.pdf
[3540] fjaunais.free.fr/h0toulouse.htm
[3541] racineshistoire.free.fr/LGN/PDF/Aquitaine-Poitou.pdf
[3542] racineshistoire.free.fr/LGN/PDF/Orleans.pdf
[3543] fjaunais.free.fr/h0gascogne.htm
[3544] https://fr.wikipedia.org/wiki/Quatrième_maison_d'Orléans
[3545] https://en.wikipedia.org/wiki/House_of_Orléans#House_of_Orléans-Galliera
[3546] https://fr.wikipedia.org/wiki/Famille_d%27Orl%C3%A9ans-Longueville
[3547] racineshistoire.free.fr/LGN/PDF/Gontaut-Biron.pdf

Famille de Rochechouart Mortemart et Vicomtes de Rochechouart [3548]

Gascony, Dukes and Nobility [3549]

La Maison d'Albret [3550]

La Maison d'Armagnac [3551]

La Maison de Bourbon-Busset [3552]

La Maison Royale de Bourbon [3553]

La Maison de Bourbon [3554]

La Maison de La Tour d'Auvergne [3555]

La Maison de Lorraine et Mercœur [3556]

La Maison de Toulouse [3557]

La Première Dynastie de Bourbon [3558]

Les Bourbons [3559]

[3548] racineshistoire.free.fr/LGN/PDF/Rochechouart-Mortemart.pdf
[3549] fmg.ac/Projects/MedLands/GASCONY.htm
[3550] https://fr.wikipedia.org/wiki/Maison_d'Albret
[3551] https://fr.wikipedia.org/wiki/Maison_d'Armagnac
[3552] racineshistoire.free.fr/LGN/PDF/Bourbon-Busset.pdf
[3553] racineshistoire.free.fr/LGN/PDF/Bourbon-Dynastie-Royale.pdf
[3554] racineshistoire.free.fr/LGN/PDF/Bourbon-duche.pdf
[3555] https://fr.wikipedia.org/wiki/Maison_de_La_Tour_d'Auvergne
[3556] https://fr.wikipedia.org/wiki/Maison_de_Lorraine
[3557] https://fr.wikipedia.org/wiki/Maison_de_Toulouse
[3558] https://fr.wikipedia.org/wiki/Première_maison_de_Bourbon
[3559] https://fr.wikipedia.org/wiki/G%C3%A9n%C3%A9alogie_des_Bourbons

Les Comtes d'Auvergne et de Poitou, Les Ducs d'Aquitaine [3560]

Limousin [3561]

Poitou [3562]

Première Maison de Bourbon (Bourbon ancien) [3563]

Royaume des Wisigoths [3564]

Seigneurs de Bourdeilles (ou Bourdeille) [3565]

Seigneurs de Bourbon-Dampierre [3566]

Seigneurs de Caumont-La Force [3567]

Seigneurs et Famille de Chabannes (ancient Cabanis, Chabanes) [3568]

Seigneurs de Châteauneuf-en-Thymerais [3569]

Seigneurs et Famille de Comarque (alias Commarque) [3570]

Seigneurs de Grailly et Captals de Buch [3571]

[3560] racineshistoire.free.fr/LGN/PDF/Aquitaine-Poitou.pdf
[3561] fmg.ac/Projects/MedLands/LIMOUSIN.htm
[3562] fmg.ac/Projects/MedLands/AQUITAINE%20NOBILITY.htm
[3563] racineshistoire.free.fr/LGN/PDF/Bourbon-ancien.pdf
[3564] fjaunais.free.fr/h0wisigoth.htm
[3565] racineshistoire.free.fr/LGN/PDF/Bourdeilles.pdf
[3566] fjaunais.free.fr/h0bourbonarch.htm
[3567] racineshistoire.free.fr/LGN/PDF/Caumont-La-Force.pdf
[3568] racineshistoire.free.fr/LGN/PDF/Chabannes.pdf
[3569] racineshistoire.free.fr/LGN/PDF/Chateauneuf-en-Thymerais.pdf
[3570] racineshistoire.free.fr/LGN/PDF/Comarque.pdf
[3571] racineshistoire.free.fr/LGN/PDF/Grailly_captals-de-Buch.pdf

Seigneurs de L'Isle-Bouchard [3572]

Saint-Lary, Seigneurs de Bellegarde [3573]

Seigneurs et Vicomtes de Thouars [3574]

Toulouse, Kings, Dukes and Counts [3575]

Toulouse, Nobility [3576]

Vicomtes de Carlat et Millau [3577]

Vicomtes de Châtellerault [3578]

Vicomtes de Narbonne [3579]

FRANCE, SOUTHEAST

Comtes d'Albon [3580]

GERMANY, BAVARIA

Austrasie [3581]

[3572] racineshistoire.free.fr/LGN/PDF/L-Isle-Bouchard.pdf
[3573] racineshistoire.free.fr/LGN/PDF/Saint-Lary_Bellegarde.pdf
[3574] racineshistoire.free.fr/LGN/PDF/Thouars.pdf
[3575] fmg.ac/Projects/MedLands/TOULOUSE.htm
[3576] fmg.ac/Projects/MedLands/TOULOUSE%20NOBILITY.htm
[3577] fjaunais.free.fr/h0carlat.htm
[3578] fjaunais.free.fr/h0chatellera.htm
[3579] fjaunais.free.fr/h0narbonne.htm
[3580] fjaunais.free.fr/h0albon.htm
[3581] fjaunais.free.fr/h0austrasie.htm

Austria [3582]

Bavaria, Dukes [3583]

Bavaria, Nobility [3584]

Carinthia, Dukes and Nobility [3585]

Ducs de Bavière [3586]

Dynastie de Carinthie [3587]

GERMANY, EASTERN MARCHES

Bohemia [3588]

Brandenburg [3589]

Mecklenburg [3590]

Meissen [3591]

Moravia [3592]

[3582] fmg.ac/Projects/MedLands/AUSTRIA.htm
[3583] fmg.ac/Projects/MedLands/BAVARIA.htm
[3584] fmg.ac/Projects/MedLands/BAVARIAN%20NOBILITY.htm
[3585] fmg.ac/Projects/MedLands/CARINTHIA.htm
[3586] fjaunais.free.fr/h0Bavière.htm
[3587] fjaunais.free.fr/h0carinthie.htm
[3588] fmg.ac/Projects/MedLands/BOHEMIA.htm
[3589] fmg.ac/Projects/MedLands/BRANDENBURG,%20PRUSSIA.htm
[3590] fmg.ac/Projects/MedLands/MECKLENBURG.htm
[3591] fmg.ac/Projects/MedLands/MEISSEN.htm
[3592] fmg.ac/Projects/MedLands/MORAVIA.htm

Silesia [3593]

GERMANY, FRANCONIA

Comtes de Laurenbourg [3594]

Franconia, Nobility [3595]

Hessen [3596]

Lower Rhine, Nobility [3597]

Nassau [3598]

Palatinate [3599]

Thuringia [3600]

Thuringia, Nobility [3601]

Kôln Archbishopric [3602]

Mainz Archbishopric [3603]

[3593] fmg.ac/Projects/MedLands/SILESIA.htm
[3594] fjaunais.free.fr/h0laurenbourg.htm
[3595] fmg.ac/Projects/MedLands/FRANCONIA.htm
[3596] fmg.ac/Projects/MedLands/HESSEN.htm
[3597] fmg.ac/Projects/MedLands/FRANCONIA%20(LOWER%20RHINE).htm
[3598] fmg.ac/Projects/MedLands/NASSAU.htm
[3599] fmg.ac/Projects/MedLands/PALATINATE.htm
[3600] fmg.ac/Projects/MedLands/THURINGIA.htm
[3601] fmg.ac/Projects/MedLands/THURINGIAN%20NOBILITY.htm
[3602] fmg.ac/Projects/MedLands/Koeln.htm
[3603] fmg.ac/Projects/MedLands/Mainz.htm

GERMANY, KINGS (EMPERORS)

Germany, Kings [3604]

Germany, Early Nobility [3605]

La Dynastie de Palatinate [3606]

Royaume d'Alémanie [3607]

GERMANY, LOTHARINGIA

Lotharingia, Kings and Dukes, Pfalzgrafen [3608]

Lower Lotharingia, Nobility [3609]

Upper Lotharingia, Nobility [3610]

Bar [3611]

Brabant and Louvain [3612]

Burgraves de Tournai [3613]

[3604] fmg.ac/Projects/MedLands/GERMANY,%20Kings.htm
[3605] fmg.ac/Projects/MedLands/GERMAN%20NOBILITY.htm
[3606] https://en.wikipedia.org/wiki/House_of_Palatinate-Zweibrücken
[3607] fjaunais.free.fr/h0aleman.htm
[3608] fmg.ac/Projects/MedLands/LOTHARINGIA.htm
[3609] fmg.ac/Projects/MedLands/LOTHARINGIAN%20(LOWER)%20NOBILITY.htm
[3610] fmg.ac/Projects/MedLands/LOTHARINGIAN%20(UPPER)%20NOBILITY.htm
[3611] fmg.ac/Projects/MedLands/BAR.htm
[3612] fmg.ac/Projects/MedLands/BRABANT,%20LOUVAIN.htm
[3613] fjaunais.free.fr/h0tournai.htm

Comtes de Bar [3614] [3615]

Comtes de Betuwe et de Maasgau [3616]

Comtes de Calw et Sarrebrück [3617]

Comtes de Grandpré [3618]

Comtes de Gueldre, de Clèves, et de Wassenberg [3619]

Comtes de Hainaut [3620]

Comtes de Hainaut (Hennegau) [3621]

Comtes de Montaigu [3622]

Comtes de Namur [3623] [3624]

Comtes de Paris et de Woevre [3625]

Comtes et Châtelains de Cambrai [3626]

_____

[3614] racineshistoire.free.fr/LGN/PDF/Bar.pdf
[3615] https://fr.wikipedia.org/wiki/Liste_des_comtes_puis_ducs_de_Bar
[3616] fjaunais.free.fr/h0betuwe.htm
[3617] fjaunais.free.fr/h0sarrebruck.htm
[3618] racineshistoire.free.fr/LGN/PDF/Grandpre.pdf
[3619] fjaunais.free.fr/h0gueldre.htm
[3620] fjaunais.free.fr/h0hainaut.htm
[3621] racineshistoire.free.fr/LGN/PDF/Hainaut.pdf
[3622] racineshistoire.free.fr/LGN/PDF/Montaigu.pdf
[3623] racineshistoire.free.fr/LGN/PDF/Namur.pdf
[3624] fjaunais.free.fr/h0namur.htm
[3625] fjaunais.free.fr/h0woevre.htm
[3626] racineshistoire.free.fr/LGN/PDF/Cambrai.pdf

Ducs de Brabant [3627] [3628]

Ducs de Clèves [3629]

Ducs de de Gueldre [3630]

Ducs de Lorraine [3631]

Dutch Nobility [3632]

Dynastie de Hollande [3633]

Dynastie de Limbourg [3634]

Dynastie de Lotharingie [3635]

Famille et Seigneurs de Baudricourt [3636]

Hainaut [3637]

Holland and Frisia [3638]

[3627] racineshistoire.free.fr/LGN/PDF/Brabant.pdf
[3628] https://fr.wikipedia.org/wiki/Liste_des_ducs_et_duchesses_de_Brabant
[3629] https://fr.wikipedia.org/wiki/Liste_des_comtes_et_ducs_de_Clèves
[3630] https://fr.wikipedia.org/wiki/Liste_des_comtes_et_ducs_de_Gueldre
[3631] fjaunais.free.fr/h0lorraine.htm
[3632] fmg.ac/Projects/MedLands/DUTCH%20NOBILITY.htm
[3633] fjaunais.free.fr/h0hollande.htm
[3634] fjaunais.free.fr/h0limbourg.htm
[3635] fjaunais.free.fr/h0lotharingie.htm
[3636] racineshistoire.free.fr/LGN/PDF/Baudricourt.pdf
[3637] fmg.ac/Projects/MedLands/HAINAUT.htm
[3638] fmg.ac/Projects/MedLands/HOLLAND.htm

La Maison de Barbençon [3639]

La Maison d'Avesnes [3640]

La Maison de Lorraine-Bavière [3641]

La Maison de Lorraine-Guise [3642]

La Maison de Luxembourg [3643]

La Première Dynastie Luxembourgeoise [3644]

Les Comtes de Hollande [3645]

Limburg [3646]

Lorraine [3647]

Luxembourg [3648]

Namur [3649]

Première Dynastie de Bar et de Mousson [3650]

[3639] racineshistoire.free.fr/LGN/PDF/Barbencon.pdf
[3640] https://fr.wikipedia.org/wiki/Maison_d'Avesnes
[3641] https://fr.wikipedia.org/wiki/Maison_de_Lorraine
[3642] racineshistoire.free.fr/LGN/PDF/Lorraine-Guise.pdf
[3643] https://fr.wikipedia.org/wiki/Maison_de_Luxembourg
[3644] www.persee.fr/doc/rbph_0035-0818_1946_num_25_3_1764
[3645] https://fr.wikipedia.org/wiki/Liste_des_comtes_de_Hollande
[3646] fmg.ac/Projects/MedLands/LIMBURG.htm
[3647] fmg.ac/Projects/MedLands/LORRAINE.htm
[3648] fmg.ac/Projects/MedLands/LUXEMBOURG.htm
[3649] fmg.ac/Projects/MedLands/NAMUR.htm
[3650] fjaunais.free.fr/h0bar.htm

Première Dynastie de Luxembourg [3651]

Pre-Roman Frisia (present day Netherlands) [3652]

Robert dit Baudricourt, Captain of Vaucouleurs [3653] [3654]

Seigneurs d'Antoing [3655]

Seigneurs d'Avesnes [3656]

Seigneurs d' Enghien [3657]

Seigneurs de Florennes et Rumigny [3658]

Seigneurs d'Ham-sur-Heure [3659]

Famille et Seigneurs de Lalaing [3660]

Seigneurs et Châtelains de Lens Herchies, Annequin (Hainaut et Artois) et Famille de Recourt (Lens, 62) [3661]

Seigneurs de Mons, de Conde et de Morialmes [3662]

[3651] fjaunais.free.fr/h0luxembourg.htm
[3652] www.historyfiles.co.uk/KingListsEurope/FranceHolland.htm
[3653] https://en.wikipedia.org/wiki/Robert_de_Baudricourt
[3654] www.maidofheaven.com/joanofarc_long_biography.asp#vaucouleurs
[3655] racineshistoire.free.fr/LGN/PDF/Antoing.pdf
[3656] racineshistoire.free.fr/LGN/PDF/Avesnes.pdf
[3657] racineshistoire.free.fr/LGN/PDF/Enghien.pdf
[3658] racineshistoire.free.fr/LGN/PDF/Florennes-Rumigny.pdf
[3659] fjaunais.free.fr/h0ham.htm
[3660] racineshistoire.free.fr/LGN/PDF/Lalaing.pdf
[3661] racineshistoire.free.fr/LGN/PDF/Lens.pdf
[3662] fjaunais.free.fr/h0conde.htm

Seigneurs de Mouscron et La Maison de La Barre [3663]

Seigneurs du Roeulx [3664]

Seigneurs de Rumigny [3665]

Seigneurs de Trazegnies [3666]

Seigneurs de Werchin [3667]

Trier Archbishopric [3668]

GERMANY, SAXONY

Saxony, Dukes and Electors [3669]

Saxony, Nobility [3670]

Anhalt [3671]

Brunswick [3672]

Dynastie de Saxe [3673]

[3663] racineshistoire.free.fr/LGN/PDF/Mouscron.pdf
[3664] racineshistoire.free.fr/LGN/PDF/Roeulx.pdf
[3665] fjaunais.free.fr/h0rumigny.htm
[3666] racineshistoire.free.fr/LGN/PDF/Trazegnies.pdf
[3667] racineshistoire.free.fr/LGN/PDF/Werchin.pdf
[3668] fmg.ac/Projects/MedLands/Trier.htm
[3669] fmg.ac/Projects/MedLands/SAXONY.htm
[3670] fmg.ac/Projects/MedLands/SAXON%20NOBILITY.htm
[3671] fmg.ac/Projects/MedLands/ANHALT.htm
[3672] fmg.ac/Projects/MedLands/BRUNSWICK.htm
[3673] fjaunais.free.fr/h0saxe.htm

Les Comtes d'Oldenbourg [3674]

Oldenburg [3675]

Schleswig-Holstein [3676]

GERMANY, SWABIA

Swabia, Dukes [3677]

Swabia, Nobility [3678]

Alsace [3679]

Baden [3680]

Comtes de Metz, Nordgau et Dagsbourg [3681]

Dynastie de Souabe [3682]

La Maison d'Alsace Hénin-Liétard [3683]

La Maison de Lorraine et Guise [3684]

[3674] https://fr.wikipedia.org/wiki/Liste_des_souverains_d'Oldenbourg
[3675] fmg.ac/Projects/MedLands/OLDENBURG.htm
[3676] fmg.ac/Projects/MedLands/SCHLESWIG-HOLSTEIN.htm
[3677] fmg.ac/Projects/MedLands/SWABIA.htm
[3678] fmg.ac/Projects/MedLands/SWABIAN%20NOBILITY.htm
[3679] fmg.ac/Projects/MedLands/ALSACE.htm
[3680] fmg.ac/Projects/MedLands/BADEN.htm
[3681] fjaunais.free.fr/h0metz.htm
[3682] fjaunais.free.fr/h0souabe.htm
[3683] racineshistoire.free.fr/LGN/PDF/Alsace_Henin-Lietard.pdf
[3684] https://fr.wikipedia.org/wiki/Maison_de_Guise

Württemberg [3685]

IBERIA

Aragon, Kings [3686]

Aragon, Nobility [3687]

Asturias and Léon, Kings [3688]

Asturias, Galicia, Léon, Nobility [3689]

Castile and Léon, Counts and Kings [3690]

Castile and Léon, Nobility 1 [3691]

Castile and Léon, Nobility 2 [3692]

Catalonia, Nobility [3693]

Comtes de Barcelone [3694]

[3685] fmg.ac/Projects/MedLands/WURTTEMBERG.htm
[3686] fmg.ac/Projects/MedLands/ARAGON%20&%20CATALONIA.htm
[3687] fmg.ac/Projects/MedLands/ARAGONESE%20NOBILITY.htm
[3688] fmg.ac/Projects/MedLands/ASTURIAS,%20LÉON.htm
[3689] fmg.ac/Projects/MedLands/SPANISH%20NOBILITY%20EARLY%20MEDIEVAL.htm
[3690] fmg.ac/Projects/MedLands/CASTILE.htm
[3691] fmg.ac/Projects/MedLands/SPANISH%20NOBILITY%20LATER%20MEDIEVAL.htm
[3692] fmg.ac/Projects/MedLands/SPANISH%20NOBILITY%20LATER%20MEDIEVAL%202.htm
[3693] fmg.ac/Projects/MedLands/CATALAN%20NOBILITY.htm
[3694] fjaunais.free.fr/h0barcelone.htm

Comtes du Portugal [3695]

La Maison Capétianne d'Evreux-Navarre [3696]

Les Conquistadores, conquérants du Nouveau-Monde [3697]

Moorish Spain [3698]

Navarre, Kings [3699]

Navarre, Nobility [3700]

Portugal, Kings [3701]

Portugal, Nobility [3702]

Royaume d'Aragon [3703]

Royaume de Castile [3704]

Royaume d'Espagne [3705]

Royaume d'Ibérie [3706]

[3695] fjaunais.free.fr/h0portugal2.htm
[3696] https://fr.wikipedia.org/wiki/Maison_capétienne_d'Évreux-Navarre
[3697] racineshistoire.free.fr/LGN/PDF/Conquistadores.pdf
[3698] fmg.ac/Projects/MedLands/MOORISH%20SPAIN.htm
[3699] fmg.ac/Projects/MedLands/NAVARRE.htm
[3700] fmg.ac/Projects/MedLands/NAVARRE%20NOBILITY.htm
[3701] fmg.ac/Projects/MedLands/PORTUGAL.htm
[3702] fmg.ac/Projects/MedLands/PORTUGUESE%20NOBILITY%20MEDIEVAL.htm
[3703] fjaunais.free.fr/h0aragon.htm
[3704] fjaunais.free.fr/h0Castile.htm
[3705] https://fr.wikipedia.org/wiki/Espagne
[3706] fjaunais.free.fr/h0iberie.htm

Royaume de Léon et des Asturies [3707]

Royaume de Navarre [3708]

Royaume de Portugal [3709]

Royaume des Wisigoths [3710]

Seigneurs de Castrogeriz et de Bivar [3711]

Spain: Vandals, Suevi and Visigoths [3712]

Vizcaya [3713]

ITALY

Ducs de Milan Visconti, Sforza [3714]

Dynastie d'Este [3715]

Dynasties des Guelfes [3716]

Dynastie des Unrochides [3717]

[3707] fjaunais.free.fr/h0Léon.htm
[3708] fjaunais.free.fr/h0navarre.htm
[3709] fjaunais.free.fr/h0portugal.htm
[3710] fjaunais.free.fr/h0wisigoth.htm
[3711] fjaunais.free.fr/h0bivar.htm
[3712] fmg.ac/Projects/MedLands/VANDALS,%20SUEVI,%20VISIGOTHS.htm
[3713] fmg.ac/Projects/MedLands/VIZCAYA.htm
[3714] racineshistoire.free.fr/LGN/PDF/Milan.pdf
[3715] fjaunais.free.fr/h0este.htm
[3716] fjaunais.free.fr/h0guelfes.htm
[3717] fjaunais.free.fr/h0frioul.htm

House of Este [3718]

Italy, Emperors and Kings [3719]

Central Italy [3720]

Northern Italy 1 [3721]

Northern Italy 2 [3722]

Northern Italy 3 [3723]

Southern Italy 1 [3724]

Southern Italy 2 [3725]

Dynastie des Bourbons (Branche de Deux-Siciles) [3726]

Dynastie des Bourbons (Branche Montpensier) [3727] [3728]

Dynastie des Bourbons (Branche Parme) [3729]

[3718] https://en.wikipedia.org/wiki/House_of_Este
[3719] fmg.ac/Projects/MedLands/ITALY,%20Kings%20to%20962.htm
[3720] fmg.ac/Projects/MedLands/CENTRAL%20ITALY.htm
[3721] fmg.ac/Projects/MedLands/NORTHERN%20ITALY%20900-1100.htm
[3722] fmg.ac/Projects/MedLands/NORTHERN%20ITALY%201100-1400.htm
[3723] fmg.ac/Projects/MedLands/NORTHERN%20ITALY%20after%201400.htm
[3724] fmg.ac/Projects/MedLands/SOUTHERN%20ITALY,%20PRE-NORMAN.htm
[3725] fmg.ac/Projects/MedLands/NEAPOLITAN%20NOBILITY.htm
[3726] https://fr.wikipedia.org/wiki/Maison_de_Bourbon-Siciles
[3727] https://fr.wikipedia.org/wiki/Première_maison_de_Bourbon-Montpensier
[3728] https://fr.wikipedia.org/wiki/Seconde_maison_de_Bourbon-Montpensier
[3729] https://fr.wikipedia.org/wiki/Maison_de_Bourbon-Parme

La Maison de Savoie Carignan [3730]

La Maison d'Este et Modène [3731]

Milan [3732]

Modena, Ferrara [3733]

Monferrato, Saluzzo [3734]

Princes da Capoue et de Bénévent [3735]

Princes de Salerne et Ducs de Spolète [3736]

Royaume de Naples et Sicily [3737]

Royaume des Lombards [3738]

Royaume des Ostrogoths [3739]

Seigneurs de Montferrat (Aleramici, Monteferrato) [3740]

Sicily / Naples, Counts and Kings [3741]

[3730] https://fr.wikipedia.org/wiki/Savoie-Carignan
[3731] https://fr.wikipedia.org/wiki/Maison_d%27Este
[3732] fmg.ac/Projects/MedLands/MILAN.htm
[3733] fmg.ac/Projects/MedLands/MODENA,%20FERRARA.htm
[3734] fmg.ac/Projects/MedLands/MONFERRATO,%20SALUZZO,%20SAVONA.htm
[3735] fjaunais.free.fr/h0capoue.htm
[3736] fjaunais.free.fr/h0salerne.htm
[3737] http://www.de-bric-et-de-broc.com/France/ar_sicile.html
[3738] fjaunais.free.fr/h0lombard.htm
[3739] fjaunais.free.fr/h0ostrogoth.htm
[3740] racineshistoire.free.fr/LGN/PDF/Montferrat.pdf
[3741] fmg.ac/Projects/MedLands/SICILY.htm

Venice [3742]

JEHANNE D'ARC

Claude, the Second Face of Joan of Arc [3743]

Famille de Jeanne d'Arc (alias Darc et du Lis) [3744]

Jeanne d'Arc: Princesse de sang royal? [3745]

Les secrets de Jeanne [3746]

La bannière d'Orléans (The Banner of Orléans) [3747]

La descendance de Jeanne (The Offspring of Joan) [3748]

Le souterrain de Rouen (The Underground Rouen) [3749]

Le château de Rouen en 1431 (The Castle of Rouen in 1431) [3750]

La dame des Armoises (The Lady of Armoises) [3751]

Pulligny: Le tombeau de Jeanne (Pulligny: The tomb of Jeanne) [3752]

[3742] fmg.ac/Projects/MedLands/VENICE.htm
[3743] www.monio.info/2012/04/27/claude-the-second-face-of-joan-of-arc/
[3744] racineshistoire.free.fr/LGN/PDF/D-Arc_du-Lis.pdf
[3745] www.zetetique.ldh.org/jeanne.html
[3746] www.jeannedomremy.fr/
[3747] www.jeannedomremy.fr/S_RouenClery/banniere.htm
[3748] www.jeannedomremy.fr/S_ChinonRouen/descendance.htm
[3749] www.jeannedomremy.fr/S_RouenClery/souterrain.htm
[3750] www.jeannedomremy.fr/S_RouenClery/chateau_rouen.htm
[3751] www.jeannedomremy.fr/S_RouenClery/armoises.htm
[3752] www.jeannedomremy.fr/S_RouenClery/pulligny.htm

Le vrai visage de Jeanne (The True Face of Jeanne) [3753]

L'origine des d'Arc (The Origin of Arc: The Family of the Knights of the Lily) [3754]

La noblesse des d'Arc (The Nobility of Arc) [3755]

Généalogie d'Isabelle Romée (Genealogy of Isabelle Romée) de Vouthon [3756]

De la naissance de Jeanne (The Birth of Jeanne) [3757]

The + Jhesus + Maria + Ring: Saint Joan of Arc Center [3758]

A Thesis Regarding Specific Testimony in Jeanne d'Arcs Trial of Condemnation [3759]

Relics of Joan of Arc [3760]

Saint Joan of Arc Center (Albuquerque, New Mexico) [3761]

Saint Catherine's Hill, Rouen [3762]

MEDIEVAL GENEALOGY

Agnès Sorel (alias Soreau), Mistress of King Charles VII of France [3763] [3764]

[3753] www.jeannedomremy.fr/S_Questions/visagedejeanne.htm
[3754] www.jeannedomremy.fr/S_Questions/origine.htm
[3755] www.jeannedomremy.fr/S_Questions/noblesse.htm
[3756] www.jeannedomremy.fr/S_Questions/isabelle_romee.htm
[3757] www.jeannedomremy.fr/S_Questions/naissance.htm
[3758] www.stjoan-center.com/GoldRing/Announcement.htm
[3759] www.stjoan-center.com/Thesis/Thesis.htm
[3760] www.stjoan-center.com/2012-frohlick/c_ap04_relics/apen04.htm
[3761] www.stjoan-center.com/
[3762] www.stjoan-center.com/hill/catherine.html
[3763] racineshistoire.free.fr/LGN/PDF/Agnes_Sorel.pdf

Ahnentafel Study: William the Conqueror to Charlemagne [3765]

Ancestry Charts of the current British Royal Family [3766]

Ancient Familes from Israel to Europe [3767]

Foundation for Medieval Genealogy [3768]

Foundation for Medieval Genealogy: Links [3769]

Foundation for Medieval Genealogy: Scanned Sources [3770]

Graphical Index to the Ancestry of Charles II of England [3771]

Kings of France [3772]

Les Mérovingiens (420 – 639) [3773]

La Dynastie des Carolingiens (751 – 987) [3774]

La Dynastie des Capétiens Direct (987 – 1328) [3775]

[3764] https://en.wikipedia.org/wiki/Agnès_Sorel
[3765] www.cynthiaswope.com/withinthevines/Normans/WmConqAhn/AT_TOC.HTM
[3766] https://en.wikipedia.org/wiki/Ancestry_Charts_of_the_Current_British_Royal_Family
[3767] www.scotlandroyalty.org/royal-genealogy.html
[3768] fmg.ac/
[3769] fmg.ac/FMG/Links.htm
[3770] fmg.ac/FMG/Scanned_Sources.htm
[3771] fmg.ac/Projects/CharlesII/
[3772] www.scotlandroyalty.org/france.html
[3773] www.ballade-medievale.fr/z_index_mero.htm
[3774] www.ballade-medievale.fr/carolingiens/index.htm
[3775] www.ballade-medievale.fr/capetiens/index.htm

Les Valois Directs (1328 – 1498) [3776]

Les Valois Orléans (1498 – 1515) [3777]

Les Valois Angoulême (1515 – 1589) [3778]

Les Bourbons [3779]

Les Orléans [3780]

Liste de Maisons (Généalogie) [3781]

Master Index to Royal Genealogical Data (maintained by Brian Tompsett) [3782] [3783]

Monarchie et Noblesse [3784]

Monarchs of Britain [3785]

My Lines (meticulous website of Robert Brian Stewart) [3786]

Regions of France [3787]

[3776] chrisagde.free.fr/valdirects/valdirects.htm
[3777] cercle-genealogique-goelo.over-blog.com/article-des-valois-indirects-aux-orleans-37870501.html
[3778] cassius.e-monsite.com/pages/les-dynasties/les-valois-1/les-valois.html
[3779] his.nicolas.free.fr/Personnes/PageDynastie.php?mnemo=RoisBourbons
[3780] www.sport-histoire.fr/Histoire/Maison_Orleans.php
[3781] https://fr.wikipedia.org/wiki/Liste_de_maisons_(généalogie)
[3782] http://www.hull.ac.uk/php/cssbct/genealogy/royal/gedFx.html
[3783] https://rockdoveblog.wordpress.com/2017/12/21/in-appreciation-of-dr-brian-tompsetts-royal-genealogical-data-website-now-quashed-by-university-of-hull-management/
[3784] www.monarchie-noblesse.net/index.htm
[3785] www.britannia.com/history/h6f.html
[3786] sites.rootsweb.com/~cousin/html/index.htm
[3787] readramble.typepad.com/.a/6a014e8985672c970d0168e768332e970c-pi

Royal Genealogies [3788] [3789]

The Peerage (Master Index) [3790]

The French Royal Family: Bastard and Illegitimate Lines [3791]

The Royal Family: A Genealogy [3792]

MISCELLANEOUS

FORVM Ancient Coins [3793]

Haplogroups of European Kings and Queens [3794]

NEW FRANCE (QUÉBEC) RESEARCH RELATED

Archives des notaries du Québec des origins à 1931 [3795]

Beauport (La-Nativité-de-Notre-Dame) Parish Records (Drouin Collection) 1673 to 1699 [3796]

Bibliothèque et Archives nationals Québec [3797]

[3788] www.edstephan.org/Rulers/
[3789] www.royaltymonarchy.com/genealogy.html
[3790] www.thepeerage.com/master_index.htm
[3791] www.heraldica.org/topics/france/roygenea.htm#bastards
[3792] www.heraldica.org/topics/france/roygenea.htm
[3793] www.forumancientcoins.com/catalog/roman-and-greek-coins.asp?vpar=18&pos=0
[3794] https://www.eupedia.com/forum/showthread.php?25236-Haplogroups-of-European-kings-and-queens
[3795] bibnum2.banq.qc.ca/bna/notaires/index.html
[3796] https://www.ancestry.ca/interactive/1091/d13p_16411094
[3797] pistard.banq.qc.ca/unite_chercheurs/recherche_simple

Carignan-Salières Regiment Officers and Soldiers (who settled in Canada) [3798]

Dictionnaire généalogique de nos origines (Denis Beauregard) [3799]

Dictionnaire Généalogique des Familles Canadiennes (Cyprien Tanguay) [3800]

Dictionnaire généalogique et héraldique de la noblesse canadienne-françaises du XVlle au XIXe siècle (Yves Drolet) [3801]

Fichier Origine [3802]

France: Ancient Provinces [3803]

France: Current Departments [3804]

FrancoGene (stupendous website belonging to Denis Beauregard) [3805]

Genealogical Tables of the Québec Noblesse (Yves Drolet) [3806]

Genealogie Québec (wonderful website belonging François Marchi) [3807]

Histoire du Régiment de Carignan-Salière des origines à 1671 [3808]

[3798] https://fillesduroi.org/cpage.php?pt=19
[3799] www.francogene.com/dgo/dgo.php
[3800] bibnum2.banq.qc.ca/bna/dicoGenealogie/
[3801] www.shrt.qc.ca/PDF/DGHNCF-Juin%202010.pdf
[3802] www.fichierorigine.com
[3803] genealogy.happyones.com/ancient-france.html
[3804] genealogy.happyones.com/modern-france.html
[3805] www.francogene.com/genealogy/
[3806] www.shrt.qc.ca/PDF/20070317.pdf
[3807] genealogie.quebec
[3808] www.migrations.fr/histoireduregiment.htm

Kamouraska (St-Louis parish) RC Records 1727 to 1763 [3809]

Notre-Dame des Victoires Church in Québec City [3810]

PRDH (Programme de recherche en démographie historique) [3811]

Québec Genealogy Records Online [3812]

Québec (Notre-Dame) Parish Records 1667 to 1679 [3813]

Québec Resources for Genealogy [3814]

Québec Royal Descendants [3815]

Québec Vital and Church Records (Drouin Collection) 1621 to 1967 [3816]

The Pioneers [3817]

PALEOGRAPHY

Introduction to Paleography [3818]

[3809] www.kamouraska.ca/histoire/notre-genealogie/
[3810] https://photosbykenn.wordpress.com/2009/03/22/leglise-notre-dame-des-victoires-place-royale-lower-town-quebec-city/
[3811] https://www.prdh-igd.com/fr/LePrdh
[3812] www.genealogysearch.org/canada/quebec.html
[3813] https://www.ancestry.ca/interactive/1091/d13p_31410727
[3814] www.francogene.com/qc-res/index.php
[3815] www.francogene.com/gfna/gfna/998/qrd30.htm
[3816] https://search.ancestry.ca/search/db.aspx?dbid=1091
[3817] https://www.prdh-igd.com/en/LesPionniers
[3818] www.francogene.com/search-fr/paleo.php

Paleography [3819]

Paleography: A Practical Online Tutorial [3820]

Reading Old Handwriting (Online Document Examples and Tutorials) [3821]

What is Paleography? [3822]

PARTHIAN (PERSIAN) EMPIRE

Royaume de Perse [3823]

Royaume de Pont-Euxin [3824]

Royaume des Parthes [3825]

POLAND AND BALTIC STATES

Baltic States [3826]

Lithuania [3827]

Poland [3828]

[3819] https://en.wikipedia.org/wiki/Palaeography
[3820] www.nationalarchives.gov.uk/palaeography/
[3821] https://www.thoughtco.com/reading-old-handwriting-1422260
[3822] medievalwriting.50megs.com/whatis.htm
[3823] fjaunais.free.fr/h0perse.htm
[3824] fjaunais.free.fr/h0pont.htm
[3825] fjaunais.free.fr/h0parthes.htm
[3826] fmg.ac/Projects/MedLands/BALTIC%20STATES.htm
[3827] fmg.ac/Projects/MedLands/LITHUANIA.htm
[3828] fmg.ac/Projects/MedLands/POLAND.htm

Pomerania [3829]

Royaume de Pologne [3830]

RESOURCES: PÈRE ANSELME

Père Anselme was a French historian, genealogist and heraldic. His most important work was <u>Histoire généalogique de la maison royale de la France et des grands officiers de la couronne</u> (which is a genealogy of the French royal family and its principle officers), of which two volumes were published in 1674.

Volume 1 [3831]

Volume 2 [3832]

<u>Histoire généalogique et chronologique de la maison royale de France, des pairs, grands officiers de la Couronne, de la Maison du Roy et des anciens barons du royaume</u>

Volume 1 [3833]

Volume 2 [3834]

Volume 3 [3835]

Volume 4 [3836]

[3829] fmg.ac/Projects/MedLands/POMERANIA.htm
[3830] https://fr.wikipedia.org/wiki/Royaume_de_Pologne
[3831] https://gallica.bnf.fr/ark:/12148/bpt6k573088/f2
[3832] https://gallica.bnf.fr/ark:/12148/bpt6k57309m/f2
[3833] https://gallica.bnf.fr/ark:/12148/bpt6k76026j
[3834] https://gallica.bnf.fr/ark:/12148/bpt6k76027w
[3835] https://gallica.bnf.fr/ark:/12148/bpt6k76035h
[3836] https://gallica.bnf.fr/ark:/12148/bpt6k760763

Volume 5 [3837]

Volume 6 [3838]

Volume 7 [3839]

Volume 8 [3840]

Volume 9 [3841]

RESOURCES: FRANÇOIS ALEXANDRE AUBERT DE LA CHENAYE-DESBOIS ET JACQUES BADIER

<u>Dictionnaire de la noblesse, contenant les généalogies, l'histoire et la chronologie des familles nobles de France</u> (1863 to 1876)

Volume 1 [3842]

Volume 2 [3843]

Volume 3 (appears to be unavailable)

Volume 4 [3844]

Volume 5 [3845]

[3837] https://gallica.bnf.fr/ark:/12148/bpt6k76078s
[3838] https://gallica.bnf.fr/ark:/12148/bpt6k76080b
[3839] https://gallica.bnf.fr/ark:/12148/bpt6k76083c
[3840] https://gallica.bnf.fr/ark:/12148/bpt6k76084q
[3841] https://gallica.bnf.fr/ark:/12148/bpt6k760852
[3842] https://gallica.bnf.fr/ark:/12148/bpt6k54249211
[3843] https://gallica.bnf.fr/ark:/12148/bpt6k61523704
[3844] https://gallica.bnf.fr/ark:/12148/bpt6k54249441

Volume 6 (appears to be unavailable)

Volume 7 [3846]

Volume 8 [3847]

Volume 9 [3848]

Volume 10 [3849]

Volume 11 [3850]

RESOURCES: J. ORTON BUCK AND TIMOTHY FIELD BEARD

Pedigrees of Some of the Emperor Charlemagne's Descendants, Volume 1 [3851]

Pedigrees of Some of the Emperor Charlemagne's Descendants, Volume 2 [3852]

Pedigrees of Some of the Emperor Charlemagne's Descendants, Volume 3 [3853]

[3845] https://gallica.bnf.fr/ark:/12148/bpt6k54249107
[3846] https://gallica.bnf.fr/ark:/12148/bpt6k5424928x
[3847] https://gallica.bnf.fr/ark:/12148/bpt6k5424931d
[3848] https://gallica.bnf.fr/ark:/12148/bpt6k54249174
[3849] https://gallica.bnf.fr/ark:/12148/bpt6k61523259
[3850] https://gallica.bnf.fr/ark:/12148/bpt6k5424948p
[3851] https://search.ancestry.ca/search/db.aspx?dbid=48068
[3852] https://search.ancestry.ca/search/db.aspx?dbid=48069
[3853] https://search.ancestry.ca/search/db.aspx?dbid=48070

RESOURCES: EUGÈNE VIOLLET-LE-DUC

<u>Dictionnaire raisonné de l'architecture française du XIe au XVIe siècle</u> [3854]

This online resource, originally published in 1856, is a guide to French architecture; one that has many fine line drawings of castles, cathedrals, monasteries, etc.

ROMAN EMPIRE

Empire Romain [3855]

RUSSIA

Dynastie de Kiev [3856]

Russia, Rurikid [3857]

SCANDINAVIA

Denmark, Kings [3858]

Denmark, Nobility [3859]

Dynastie de Norvège [3860]

[3854] https://fr.wikisource.org/wiki/Dictionnaire_raisonné_de_l'architecture_française_du_XIe_au_XVIe_siècle
[3855] fjaunais.free.fr/h0rome.htm
[3856] fjaunais.free.fr/h0kiev.htm
[3857] fmg.ac/Projects/MedLands/RUSSIA,%20Rurik.htm
[3858] fmg.ac/Projects/MedLands/DENMARK.htm
[3859] fmg.ac/Projects/MedLands/DANISH%20NOBILITY.htm
[3860] fjaunais.free.fr/h0Norvège.htm

Norway, Kings [3861]

Norway, Nobility [3862]

Royaume de Danemark [3863]

Royaume de Norvège [3864]

Royaume de Suède [3865]

Sweden, Kings [3866]

Sweden, Nobility [3867]

SHIPS THAT BROUGHT CARIGNAN-SALIÈRE REGIMENT TO QUÉBEC

Le Brézé (1664) [3868]

Le Vieux Siméon de Dunkerdam (1665) [3869]

Le Cat de Hollande (1665) [3870]

L'Aigle d'Or de Brouage (1665) [3871]

[3861] fmg.ac/Projects/MedLands/NORWAY.htm
[3862] fmg.ac/Projects/MedLands/NORWEGIAN%20NOBILITY.htm
[3863] fjaunais.free.fr/h0frise.htm
[3864] https://fr.wikipedia.org/wiki/Royaume_de_Norvège_(872-1397)
[3865] https://fr.wikipedia.org/wiki/Liste_des_monarques_de_Suède
[3866] fmg.ac/Projects/MedLands/SWEDEN.htm
[3867] fmg.ac/Projects/MedLands/SWEDISH%20NOBILITY.htm
[3868] www.migrations.fr/le_breze_1664.htm
[3869] www.migrations.fr/le_vieux_s_de_dunker_1665.htm
[3870] www.migrations.fr/le_cat_de_hollande_1665.htm
[3871] www.migrations.fr/l_or_de_brouage.htm

La Paix (1665) [3872]

Le Saint-Sébastien (1665) [3873]

La Justice (1665) [3874]

SHIPS THAT BROUGHT FILLES DU ROI TO QUÉBEC

Le Phoénix de Flessingue (1663) [3875]

Le Saint-Jean Baptiste de Dieppe (1664) [3876]

Le Saint-Jean Baptiste de Dieppe (1665) [3877]

Le Saint-Jean Baptiste de Dieppe (1666) [3878]

La Constance de Cadix (1667) [3879]

Le Saint-Louis de Dieppe (1667) [3880]

La Nouvelle France (1668) [3881]

Le Saint-Jean Baptiste (1669) [3882]

[3872] www.migrations.fr/La%20Paix%201665.htm
[3873] www.migrations.fr/le_st_sebastien_1665.htm
[3874] www.migrations.fr/la_justice_1665.htm
[3875] www.migrations.fr/NAVIRES_LAROCHELLE/phoenixflessingue.htm
[3876] www.migrations.fr/lestjbdedieppe1665.htm
[3877] www.migrations.fr/lestjeanbaptistededieppe1665.htm
[3878] www.migrations.fr/NAVIRES_DIEPPE/stjeanbaptistedieppe_1666.htm
[3879] www.migrations.fr/NAVIRES_LAROCHELLE/laconstancedecadix.htm
[3880] www.migrations.fr/NAVIRES_DIEPPE/stlouis_dieppe1667.htm
[3881] www.migrations.fr/NAVIRES_LAROCHELLE/lanouvellefrance1668.htm
[3882] www.migrations.fr/NAVIRES_LAROCHELLE/lestjeanbaptiste1669.htm

La Nouvelle France (1670) [3883]

Le Prince Maurice (1671) [3884]

Le Saint-Jean Baptiste (1671) [3885]

La Nativité (1672) [3886]

SYRIAN EMPIRE

Royaume de Syrie [3887]

TRANSLATOR ASSISTANCE

Google Translator (for translating text as well as documents and webpages) [3888]

[3883] www.migrations.fr/NAVIRES_LAROCHELLE/lanouvellefrance1670.htm
[3884] www.migrations.fr/princemaurice1671.htm
[3885] www.migrations.fr/NAVIRES_LAROCHELLE/stjeanbaptiste_1671.htm
[3886] www.migrations.fr/NAVIRES_LEHAVRE/lanativite_1672.htm
[3887] fjaunais.free.fr/h0syrie.htm
[3888] https://translate.google.com

About the Author

Michele Doucette holds a Master's Degree in Literacy Education from Mount Saint Vincent University (Halifax, NS). A native of Truro, NS, she has been living on the west coast of Newfoundland since 1985 where she is employed as a Special Education teacher.

She is the author of many spiritual (metaphysical) works; namely, [1] *The Ultimate Enlightenment For 2012: All We Need Is Ourselves*, a book that was nominated for the Allbooks Review Best Inspirational Book for 2011, [2] *Turn Off The TV: Turn On Your Mind*, [3] *Veracity At Its Best*, [4] *The Collective: Essays on Reality* (a composition of essays in relation to the Matrix), [5] *Sleepers Awaken: The Time Is Now To Consciously Create Your Own Reality*, [6] *Healing the Planet and Ourselves: How To Raise Your Vibration*, [7] *You Are Everything: Everything Is You*, [8] *The Awakening of Humanity: A Foremost Necessity*, [9] *The Cosmos of the Soul: A Spiritual Biography*, [10] *Getting Out Of Our Own Way: Love Is The Only Answer*, [11] *Living The Jedi Way* and [12] *Vicarius Christi: The Vicar of Christ*, all of which have been published through St. Clair Publications. In addition, she has written a volume that deals with crystals, aptly entitled *The Wisdom of Crystals*.

She is also the author of *A Travel in Time to Grand Pré*, a visionary metaphysical novel that historically ties the descendants of Yeshua (Jesus) to modern day Nova Scotia. As shared by a reviewer, *Veracity At Its Best* "constructs the context for the spiritual message" parted in *A Travel in Time to Grand Pré*.

Against the backdrop of 1754 Acadie, it was the blending of French Acadian history with current DNA testing that contributed to the weaving of this alchemical tale of time travel, romance and intrigue.

From Henry I Sinclair to the Merovingians, from the Cathari treasure at Montségur to the Knights Templar, this novel, together with the words of Yeshua as spoken at the height of his ministry, has the potential to inspire others; for it is herein that we learn how individuals can find their way, their truth(s), in order to live their lives to the fullest.

Several years in the making, she was also driven to write *Back Home With Evangeline*, the sequel to *A Travel in Time to Grand Pré*. It is here that Madeleine and Michel find themselves back in the twentieth century with a message that must be shared with the world. So, too, and even more importantly, must the message be lived, and experienced, by one and all.

So, too, is she the author of *Time Will Tell*, a uniquely moving tale that begins in the present day before weaving its way backward through time to connect a glowing thread of historic discoveries. Courtesy of past-life regression, Michaela (Dr. Mike) Callaghan, a brilliant metaphysical scientist, in the twenty-first century, discovers that she lived as a young, noble, Cathari herbalist healer, in the Languedoc area of France, during a time when political change was in the air.

When not working as a Special Education teacher, she continues to read, research and write, exploring her personal genealogies, all of which constitute her passion.

In the words of the Dalai Lama … *In order to be happy, one must first possess inner contentment; and inner contentment cannot come from having all we want; rather it comes from having and appreciating all we have.*